NAVIGATE 2
eBOOK

MW01092045

Management
Skills

FOR THE NEW
HEALTH CARE
SUPERVISOR

EIGHTH EDITION

Rachel Ellison, PhD

Associate Professor, University of Louisiana at Lafayette
College of Nursing and Allied Health Professions

JONES & BARTLETT
LEARNING

World Headquarters
Jones & Bartlett Learning
25 Mall Road
Burlington, MA 01803
978-443-5000
info@jblearning.com
www.jblearning.com

Jones & Bartlett Learning books and products are available through most bookstores and online booksellers. To contact Jones & Bartlett Learning directly, call 800-832-0034, fax 978-443-8000, or visit our website, www.jblearning.com.

Substantial discounts on bulk quantities of Jones & Bartlett Learning publications are available to corporations, professional associations, and other qualified organizations. For details and specific discount information, contact the special sales department at Jones & Bartlett Learning via the above contact information or send an email to specialsales@jblearning.com.

Copyright © 2025 by Jones & Bartlett Learning, LLC, an Ascend Learning Company

All rights reserved. No part of the material protected by this copyright may be reproduced or utilized in any form, electronic or mechanical, including photocopying, recording, or by any information storage and retrieval system, without written permission from the copyright owner.

The content, statements, views, and opinions herein are the sole expression of the respective authors and not that of Jones & Bartlett Learning, LLC. Reference herein to any specific commercial product, process, or service by trade name, trademark, manufacturer, or otherwise does not constitute or imply its endorsement or recommendation by Jones & Bartlett Learning, LLC and such reference shall not be used for advertising or product endorsement purposes. All trademarks displayed are the trademarks of the parties noted herein. *Umiker's Management Skills for the New Health Care Supervisor, Eighth Edition* is an independent publication and has not been authorized, sponsored, or otherwise approved by the owners of the trademarks or service marks referenced in this product.

There may be images in this book that feature models; these models do not necessarily endorse, represent, or participate in the activities represented in the images. Any screenshots in this product are for educational and instructive purposes only. Any individuals and scenarios featured in the case studies throughout this product may be real or fictitious but are used for instructional purposes only.

This publication is designed to provide accurate and authoritative information in regard to the Subject Matter covered. It is sold with the understanding that the publisher is not engaged in rendering legal, accounting, or other professional service. If legal advice or other expert assistance is required, the service of a competent professional person should be sought.

26527-9

Production Credits
Vice President, Product Management: Marisa R. Urbano
Vice President, Content Strategy and Implementation:
    Christine Emerton
Director, Content Management: Donna Gridley
Manager, Content Strategy: Orsolya Gall
Director, Product Management: Matt Kane
Product Manager: Sophie Fleck Teague
Content Strategist: Tess Sackmann
Director, Project Management and Content Services:
    Karen Scott
Manager, Project Management: Jackie Reynen
Project Manager: Eliza Lewis
Senior Digital Project Specialist: Angela Dooley

Senior Marketing Manager: Susanne Walker
Content Services Manager: Colleen Lamy
Rights and Permissions Manager: John Rusk
Rights Specialist: Maria Leon Maimone
Media Development Editor: Faith Brosnan
Cover and Text Design: Michael O'Donnell
Procurement Manager : Wendy Kilborn
Cover Image (Title Page, Part Opener, Chapter Opener):
    © antishock/Shutterstock
Printing and Binding: The P.A. Hutchison Company
Cover Printing: The P.A. Hutchison Company
Composition: Straive
Project Management: Straive

Library of Congress Cataloging-in-Publication Data
Names: Ellison, Rachel, PhD, author. | McConnell, Charles R. Umiker's
    management skills for the new health care supervisor.
Title: Umiker's management skills for the new health care supervisor /
    Rachel Ellison.
Other titles: Management skills for the new health care supervisor
Description: Eighth edition. | Burlington, Massachusetts : Jones &
    Bartlett Learning, [2025] | Preceded by Umiker's management skills for
    the new health care supervisor / Charles R. McConnell. Seventh edition.
    [2018] | Includes bibliographical references and index.
Identifiers: LCCN 2023020715 | ISBN 9781284265231 (paperback)
Subjects: MESH: Health Facility Administrators | Health Facility
    Administration--methods | Personnel Management--methods | BISAC: LAW /
    Health
Classification: LCC RA971.35 | NLM WX 155 | DDC
    362.1068/3--dc23/eng/20230706
LC record available at https://lccn.loc.gov/2023020715

6048

Printed in the United States of America
28 27 26 25 24   10 9 8 7 6 5 4 3 2 1

Contents

Preface xiii

About the Author xv

New to the Eight Edition xvii

PART 1 Fundamentals for the Supervisor 1

CHAPTER 1 Do You Really Want to Be a Supervisor? 3

Entering the Arena Untrained? 4

Definitions and Essentials 5

Essential Management Functions of Supervisors 6

Essential Supervisory Skills 6

Transition to Supervision 7

Relationships with Other Supervisors 9

Relationship with Your Manager 9

Adjusting to the New Routine 10

Pitfalls 10

Launching a Successful Supervisory Career 10

References 12

CHAPTER 2 Customer Service 13

Who Are Our Customers, and What Do They Want? 14

Influence of Managed Care 14

Three Essentials of Customer Service 15

Techniques for Improving Customer Service 16

Designing a Customer Satisfaction System . . 17

Customer Service Concepts 18

References 20

CHAPTER 3 Basic Management Functions 21

Interrelated Concepts 22

Planning 22

Organizing 27

The Informal Organization 30

Coordinating 30

Controlling 31

Just Four? 32

Reviewing Joan's Busy Day 32

References 35

CHAPTER 4 Reengineering, Mergers, and the Supervisor 37

Reengineering 37

Mergers and Affiliations 41

References 48

CHAPTER 5 Position Descriptions and Performance Standards 49

Position Descriptions 50

Performance Standards 54

References 62

CHAPTER 6 Policies and Policy Making 63

Introducing Policies 63

Uses of Policies 64

Policies Formulated by Supervisors 65

Potential Problems with Policies 66

Special Case: Americans with
   Disabilities Act 67

References 69

CHAPTER 7 **The Supervisor's Legal Environment** **71**

The Legal Environment 71

Pre-1964: Minimal Regulation 72

The Relevant Laws 72

For the Organization: Greater
   Responsibility, Increased Cost 81

A Cumulative Effect 82

References 83

CHAPTER 8 **Employee Recruitment** **85**

Finding Employees 85

Essentials of the Selection Process 86

Desirable Candidates 86

Legal Constraints to Hiring 87

Recruiting in the Twenty-First Century . . . 89

How Supervisors Can Help in
   the Recruiting Process 91

Employee Selection Methods 91

References 94

CHAPTER 9 **Interviewing and Employee Selection** **95**

Who Should Conduct the Interview? 96

Preparing for the Interview 96

Two Initial Interview Steps 97

Questions to Ask of Applicants 97

Questions to Avoid 98

Recommended Questions 100

Candidates with No Previous Employment . . 101

Addressing Sensitive Issues 102

Clues to Untruthfulness 102

Questions from Candidates 103

Evaluation of Candidates 103

Getting Candidates to Accept Job Offers . . 103

Closing the Interview 104

Post-Interview Activities 104

Obtaining References 105

References 108

CHAPTER 10 **Orientation and Training of New Employees** **109**

Orientation Timing 109

Objectives of an Orientation Program . . . 110

Ten Important Assumptions 111

General Orientation Programs 111

Preparations for the Arrival of
   New Orientees 113

First Day: Welcome Wagon 113

"Nuts and Bolts" Talks 113

Major Departmental Values 114

Show and Tell 114

Meeting Colleagues 114

Get Help from Your Specialists 115

Training the New Employee 115

References 118

CHAPTER 11 **Team Leadership** **119**

A Growing Need for Teams 119

Kinds of Teams 120

Benefits of Teams 121

Disadvantages of Teams 121

Characteristics of Effective Teams 121

Why Teams Fail 122

Team Dynamics 122

Rituals and Status Symbols 123

Team Leadership 124

The Self-Perpetuating Team 125

Revisiting the Biweekly Team Meeting . . . 125

Leadership Style 126

Taking On the Inherited Team 126

Rewarding Team Performance 127

References 128

CHAPTER 12 **Safety and Workplace Violence** **129**

Violence in Health care 129

Causes of Violence. 130

Effects of Violence on Victims. 131

Laws and Standards Relating to
Workplace Violence 132

Responsibilities of Management 132

Essentials of a Violence-Control
Program 132

Supervisory Principles for Reducing
Workplace Violence 134

Bomb Threats. 136

Breaking Up Fights 136

References 137

PART 2 Leading People 139

CHAPTER 13 Leaders and Managers 141

What Is It?. 142

Organizational Culture. 142

Leading Versus Managing. 142

Basic Leadership Styles 144

Leadership Approaches: Special
Variations 146

Contemporary Leadership Activities 146

Foundation of Leadership 147

Characteristics of Effective Leaders. 147

Common Supervisory Mistakes 149

References 151

CHAPTER 14 Coaching and Counseling 153

Coaching. 153

Characteristics of Effective Coaches 154

Role of the Coach in Improving
Performance. 154

Management by Wandering Around
(MBWA) 155

Enhancing Employee Self-Sufficiency . . . 155

Defending, Facilitating, Empowering,
and Supporting. 156

Coaching Feedback 156

Coaching Pitfalls 159

Counseling: Preventing Bigger Problems. . 160

Most Common Reasons for Employee
Counseling 160

Preparing for the Counseling Interview . . 161

Conducting a Counseling Interview 162

Common Defensive Responses by
Employees. 164

Follow-Up. 165

Common Barriers to Successful
Counseling 166

References 168

CHAPTER 15 Motivation, Reward, and Recognition 169

Morale and Health Care 169

Morale Versus Motivation 170

Major Factors Affecting Morale 170

Signs of a Morale Problem 171

Methods of Obtaining Information
About Morale 172

How Employers Improve Morale. 172

How Supervisors Influence Morale. 173

Motivation. 173

Reward and Recognition 177

An Effective Reward System 177

Compensation: Rewards Bearing
Price Tags 178

Nonfinancial Rewards. 180

Implementing a Reward System. 180

Recognition. 181

References 184

CHAPTER 16 Performance Feedback 185

The Need for Feedback 185

Day-to-Day Feedback 186

Formal Performance Evaluations. 186

Preparation for Performance
Evaluations of Individuals 189

Four Phases of the Evaluation Interview. . 191

Performance Evaluation of Work Teams . . 193

Common Pitfalls of Performance
  Evaluation 193

References 197

**CHAPTER 17 Disciplining:
Correction of Behavior 199**

Scenario: "Why Should I?" 199

Counseling Versus Disciplining 200

Reward-to-Risk Ratio 201

Progressive Discipline 201

Termination Meeting 204

Employee Reactions to Being
  Disciplined 204

Behavior Versus Performance 205

Returning to "Why Should I?" 205

Eight Sound Disciplinary Practices 206

Disciplinary Principles for the Supervisor . . 206

Getting Rid of "Deadweight" 207

Reference 209

**CHAPTER 18 Cultural Diversity:
Managing the Changing
Workforce 211**

A Diverse and Changing Workforce 211

Cultural Core Values 212

Corporate Values 212

Personal Core Values 213

Diversity Management Programs 214

Supervisor Responsibilities 215

Generational Diversity 216

The Aging Workforce 217

Advancement for Women 217

References 220

**CHAPTER 19 Conflict and
Confrontation 221**

Conflict and the Healthcare
  Organization 221

Dangers of Escalating or Suppressing
  Conflict 222

Fundamental Strategies for Coping
  with Conflict 223

Confrontation and the Supervisor 224

References 228

**CHAPTER 20 Employees
with Problems 229**

The Marginal Performer 229

The Absent Employee 231

Employees with Personal Problems
  Affecting Performance 233

A True Supervisory Challenge 235

When Employees Fail to Get Along 236

Reference 238

**CHAPTER 21 Ethics in the
Workplace 239**

Ethical Behavior 239

Unethical Behavior 240

Organizational Climate 240

Ethical Principles 241

Ethics Programs 241

Supervisory Enforcement of Ethical
  Behavior 242

References 244

**CHAPTER 22 Managing Difficult
Employees 245**

A Matter of Attitude 245

Coaching and Counseling for Behavioral
  Change 246

Chronically Critical Employees 247

When You Are the Focus of a Negative
  Attitude 247

Negative Employees 247

Know-It-All Employees 248

The Uncooperative Silent Ones 248

Super-Sensitive Employees 250

Moody People 250

Jealous Coworkers 250

Gossips 250

Incessant Talkers and Socializers 251
Employees of Questionable
  Appearance 251
Caution Is in Order 253
References 255

**CHAPTER 23 Complaints,
Grievances, and Appeals 257**
Complaints 257
Role of the Supervisor 258
Supervisor "On the Spot" 259
Appeals and Grievances 261
Sexual Harassment 261
References 266

**CHAPTER 24 Employee
Retention 267**
Focus on Retention 267
Loyalty and Employee Retention 268
Why Employees Seek Greener Pastures . . 270
Analyzing a Retention Problem 270
Retention Incentives 271
Recruitment and Selection for Retention . . 271
Further Implications for Retention 272
Identifying and Measuring Turnover 272
References 275

**CHAPTER 25 Privacy and
Confidentiality: Employees
and Customers 277**
Privacy and Changing Times 278
Health Insurance Portability and
  Accountability Act 281
References 288

PART 3 Healthcare Cost Control 289

CHAPTER 26 Managed Care 291
The Arrival of Managed Care 292
Features of Managed Care Plans 292

Significant Challenges 293
Strategies of Care Providers 295
Strategies of Managed Care Agencies . . . 295
Outcomes Management 296
Education 296
Provider Reactions to Managed Care 297
Employment Opportunities in
  the Managed Care Industry 297
Here to Stay 298
References 300

**CHAPTER 27 Budgets and Cost
Control 303**
A Key Supervisory Activity 303
Budgets and Their Functions 303
Controlling Process 305
Continuing Control of Overtime 306
Cutting Costs 308
Benchmarking 310
References 312

PART 4 Developing Employees 313

CHAPTER 28 Staff Development . . 315
Education and Experience 315
Benefits of a Career Development
  Program 316
Educational Planning 316
Accountability for Career
  Development 316
Educational Needs Assessment 317
Development Program 318
Mentoring 319
Creativity in Employee Development 320
Reference 324

**CHAPTER 29 Change as
a Way of Life 325**
A New Broom Does What? 326

Essentials of Change 326

Barriers to Change 327

Employee Concerns 327

Preparing for Change 327

Carrying Out the Plans 329

Helping People Through
the Stressful Phase 330

Employee Responses to Change 331

How to Overcome Resistance 332

Job Fit 334

Quality of Work Life 334

Job Redesign 334

Special Considerations 335

References 339

**CHAPTER 30 Delegation and
Empowerment 341**

Why Does It Not Always Work? 342

Assigning Versus Delegating 342

Why Some Supervisors Are Reluctant
to Delegate 342

Willingness of Employees to Accept
Delegated Activities 342

Dumping 343

How to Delegate 343

The Supervisor's Two Kinds of Tasks 344

References 350

PART 5 Special Supervisory Skills   351

**CHAPTER 31 Spoken
Communication 353**

The Most Important Managerial Skill 353

The Informal Communication System . . . 354

Sending More Powerful Messages 354

Barriers to Verbal Communication 355

Listening Skills 356

Basic Forms of Negotiation 360

Preparing for Negotiation 360

Major Steps in Negotiation 361

Barriers to Successful Negotiation 362

Negotiating with Your Boss 362

References 365

**CHAPTER 32 Written
Communication 367**

A Widespread Need 367

Selecting an Appropriate
Communication Channel 368

Steps in Preparing a Document 368

Editing an Employee's Writing 369

Email 370

Instant Messaging/Text Messaging 371

Grant Writing 371

Reference 373

**CHAPTER 33 Holding Effective
Meetings 375**

Getting Together to Solve a Problem 375

A Necessity 376

Major Purposes of Meetings 376

Components of a Meeting 376

Advance Preparations by
the Chairperson 377

The Meeting 378

Tips for Meeting Attendees 379

Problem Attendees 380

Committee Meetings 381

Telephone Conference Calls 381

Reference 383

**CHAPTER 34 Decision-Making
and Problem-Solving 385**

Problems Are a Given 385

Decision-Making Today 385

Decision-Making and Leadership 386

The Logical Process: Key Steps in
Solving Large Problems 388

Useful Tools for Problem-Solving. 388

Your Intuitive Process: Key to Creative
　Problem-Solving. 392

Group Problem-Solving. 393

Creative Problem-Solving Groups. 394

References 396

CHAPTER 35 Time Management. . 397

Ten Minutes to Spare?. 397

Time and the Supervisor. 398

Time Wasters and What to
　Do About Them. 400

Tips for Saving Time 402

Time Theft by Others 402

What About Those 10 Minutes?. 402

Reference 404

PART 6 The Supervisor's Continuing Development 405

**CHAPTER 36 Coping with Stress
and Burnout. 407**

More Prominent Today Than Ever. 407

External Causes of Stress. 408

Internal Factors Aggravating Stress. 408

Management Style and
　the Responsibilities of Supervisors. . . . 408

How to Reduce Stress in Your
　Department. 409

Departmental Stress Programs 410

Burnout. 410

Managing Your Personal Stress 411

References 413

**CHAPTER 37 The Supervisor's
Future 415**

Criteria for Success. 415

Characteristics of Achievers. 416

Steps to Success 418

Beware the Career Killers. 418

Negotiating for More Compensation 418

Succession Planning 419

Workplace Politics 421

Networking. 422

Relating to the Person to Whom
　You Report 424

Doing Today's Job While Preparing for
　Tomorrow 427

Dedication and the Balancing Act. 428

The Supervisor's Obligations 428

Some Unchanging Fundamentals 429

The Supervisor's Future 429

Reference 431

Index 433

Preface

As the new author of the eighth edition of *Umiker's Management Skills for the New Health Care Supervisor*, I was insistent on preserving Dr. William Umiker's style and organization from the earliest editions of this text. Mr. McConnell, the author of many of the editions after Dr. Umiker, consistently added relevant information for future healthcare supervisors, providing me a working text with a confident tone to inform and educate its readers.

The primary strengths of the earlier editions were found in the simplicity of presentation, making the book an extremely usable text for all level of students. A number of chapters have been updated and a good amount of new material has been provided, continuing, I hope, to enhance the book's value for the classroom and the health care profession.

All material carried over to this *Eighth Edition* has been "tuned up" to include the ever-evolving healthcare environment and to include the impact of the COVID-19 pandemic on the healthcare environment and, particularly, healthcare supervisors. Throughout the book, the case studies, exercises, and questions were updated and improved where possible. Also, the references were updated to include recent literature.

In addressing the *Eighth Edition*, it has been my goal to preserve the ambience of the earlier editions. Among the more significant improvements is the addition of the new Chapter 21, "Ethics in the Workplace," recognizing the importance of ethical practices and unethical behaviors and identifying them. Ethical practice is a topic that is becoming more prevalent and relative in today's healthcare environment. Also new is the addition of COVID-19 pandemic information throughout the entire text. The pandemic has changed the core of health care in many ways. Supervisors are now tasked with managing workers who work remotely, attending meetings via Zoom, and helping employees who suffer from stress and burnout.

Dr. Umiker and Mr. McConnell always used a straightforward way of presenting information and guidance in concise terms. I believe this approach to the material is well suited for students seeking careers in the healthcare industry and the aspiring, new, or even experienced supervisors who wish to do their very best in what has become a position of increasing responsibility, importance, and challenge.

The advice and guidance provided by this book can help enable you in the following ways:

- Enhance your supervisory and management skills to secure a job and build a career in the healthcare industry
- Endure the transition from professional or technical employee to supervisor
- Improve customer satisfaction
- Plan, organize, and delegate work to achieve greater productivity
- Improve policies, position descriptions, and work standards
- Recruit, select, orient, and train new employees more skillfully
- Implement organizational changes to build high-performing teams
- Improve safety and manage violence in the workplace
- Boost your leadership, coaching, counseling, and disciplinary skills
- Cultivate your communication, meeting, and negotiating expertise
- Provide your employees with helpful performance feedback

- Cope with cultural diversity, conflict, and problem employees
- Adjust to changes, the requirements of managed care, and the demands of cost control
- Encourage creativity, solve problems, and delegate more
- Stimulate staff development and train a potential successor
- Improve your time management skills and reduce time lost from external influences
- Reduce workplace stress and prevent burnout
- Increase your marketability and career development
- Develop an efficient personal and professional network
- Sharpen your workplace political skills
- Improve your skills to budgeting and cost control skills
- Withstand the consistent changes of the healthcare environment

About the Author

Rachel Ellison, PhD, is an associate professor and program director of the Health Services Administration program at the University of Louisiana at Lafayette. She has been teaching in higher education for more than 10 years. Before her career in education, she worked in healthcare organizations, mainly in finance, where she supervised many employees. As an author, coauthor, and professor, she has published a number of books and articles in various publications. She is a lifelong learner and has found a passion in teaching and inspiring her students.

New to the Eight Edition

The *Eighth Edition* maintains the overall organizational scheme of the previous edition, continuing to present the material in several "Parts" by general topic but with some changes within chapters.

A number of changes, improvements, and additions were made in response to helpful comments by readers and users. All chapters were re-edited for the purpose of clarifying some material, correcting a few minor errors, improving language and clarity, and updating material in a number of places. One chapter was completely removed, and a new chapter was added, maintaining the book at 37 chapters.

The case studies, exercises, and questions that appear throughout the text were improved where possible. Additional cases and examples have been provided, most of them embedded within chapters in the form of real-world scenarios. Several references were updated in most every chapter.

The more significant changes from the *Seventh Edition* to the *Eighth Edition* are encapsulated as follows:

- Chapter 2, "Customer Service," has been expanded to discuss customer service concepts including theories on customer service satisfaction.
- Chapter 8, "Employee Recruitment," expands recruitment sources to include social media and new technology that has simplified the recruitment process.
- Chapter 11, "Team Leadership," provides expanded content on team meetings and holding them on Zoom for work-from-home employees.

- Chapter 18, "Cultural Diversity: Managing the Changing Workforce," provides essential updates concerning the aging workforce in regard to the COVID-19 pandemic as well as new information on the advancement of women in executive healthcare positions.
- Chapter 20, "Employees with Problems," has been edited to focus on identifying problems and assisting the supervisor with addressing them. The ethical content that was originally in this chapter now has its own chapter.
- Chapter 21, "Ethics in the Workplace," is a new chapter for this edition. The importance of ethics in the workplace deserved its own chapter to discuss ethical principles and identifying unethical behaviors.
- Chapter 23, "Complaints, Grievances, and Appeals," has had information added to include increasing sexual harassment events in health care and the "Me Too" movement and its direct relation to women working in the healthcare field.
- Chapter 26, "Managed Care," has a section addressing the Patient Protection and Affordable Care Act of 2010 and the updated legislation since the last edition was published.
- Chapter 29, "Change as a Way of Life," has added information in the telecommuting section with information to include how the pandemic and changing environments have evolved to allow telecommuting and work-from-home to be more prominent in the workforce.
- Chapter 32, "Written Communication," provides additional information on the importance and correct ways of using email. Also,

text messaging is introduced as another way of written communication.

- Chapter 33, "Holding Effective Meetings," discusses Zoom meetings and work-from-home employees utilizing different ways to attend meetings and contribute to the organization.
- Chapter 36, "Coping with Stress and Burnout," has replaced the Seventh Edition's

"Supervising in a Union Environment" chapter. Coverage of supervising unions and the legal backdrop of a union can be found throughout the textbook. The new Chapter 36 includes updated statistics regarding stress and burnout of healthcare professionals during and after the COVID-19 pandemic.

PART 1

Fundamentals for the Supervisor

CHAPTER 1

Do You Really Want to Be a Supervisor?

CHAPTER OBJECTIVES

- Encourage the reader or student to carefully examine his or her reasons for aspiring to supervision and to assess the willingness of the individual to accept the responsibilities of supervision along with its perceived advantages.
- Provide simple, practical definitions of management and supervision, and establish the importance of the supervisory role in the organization.
- Convey an understanding of the basic functions of supervision and place the performance of these in perspective with their applicability at other levels of management.
- Outline the skills and capabilities essential for success in supervision.
- Review some of the significant changes the individual may experience in making the transition from member of a work group to leader of a group.
- Highlight the elements of a new supervisor's relationships with subordinates, peers, and superiors.
- Identify potential pitfalls that can interfere with the growth and development of the supervisor.
- Offer some practical advice for achieving success in a supervisory career.

KEY TERMS

Supervisor; First-Line Supervisor; First-Line Manager: In the use of these terms throughout this text, these three labels ordinarily refer to the same position at the bottom of the management hierarchy—the person who oversees the labors of those who do the hands-on work.

Management: Management is getting things done through people. It may of course involve a great deal of activity, but it all comes down to directing the application of resources, both human and material, to accomplish a goal.

Manager: A generic term describing anyone overseeing the labor of others from the newest first-line supervisor to the chief executive officer, and second, a position-specific title that may appear at any organizational level.

Middle Manager: Management position residing in a hierarchical layer between first-line supervisors and higher management, such as a department or division head or executive, depending on organization size. Middle managers generally supervise the first-line supervisors.

Entering the Arena Untrained?

Unfortunately, not all healthcare organizations provide supervisory training to the technical or professional employees who are promoted to supervisory positions, and few if any provide supervisory orientation for unskilled or semi-skilled entry-level workers who are elevated to group-leader or supervisory positions. Realistically, most organizations do not provide adequate orientation to supervision. This failure compounds the problems caused by the tendency to promote technically skilled employees who frequently show no particular leadership skills or who sometimes even have little interest in becoming supervisors but accept because of the title and pay.

Many workers do indeed accept promotion to supervision because of the increased salary and accompanying benefits or because they feel obligated to accept what is offered to them; it is a fairly common feeling among many employees that refusing a promotion is a career-limiting move in the eyes of one's organizational superiors. However, insightful employers and employees know that "doing" skills do not convert easily to "leading" skills; that is, the good worker does not necessarily make a good supervisor. If a good worker is to become a good supervisor, the organization needs to make it happen. Unless the promoted employee happens to be a "natural leader" (there are a few of these around, though not too many), those who do the promoting have to do more than just confer a title and pile on some responsibilities.

However, in far too many instances a promotion to supervision mirrors the experience of the relatively new groundskeeper who was placed in charge of a grounds crew of five employees. He lamented: "My total orientation to supervision consisted of my manager saying, 'Here's how to approve time cards; now you're the boss.'" His first week found him having to address the following: Rescheduling a day's work and scrambling to cover because one person failed to show up; quickly learning how to obtain parts for a mower that broke down; intervening in a heated dispute between two of his employees; and deciding whether a particular employee's behavior warranted disciplinary action. He referred to his first week on the job as "orientation by sink or swim."

If you have never been in a position of leadership, promotion to supervisor represents a major vocational change. You must usually give up some tasks you enjoy and take on others you either dislike or feel uncomfortable doing. It is highly likely that you were promoted because of your professional knowledge, technical skills, or seniority, or some combination of these, with little or no attention to your inexperience as a leader.

Certainly, to be offered a supervisory job is flattering. You can use the extra pay, and your family will be proud of you. But accepting the position could be a decision you regret for several reasons. Your relationship with former teammates will never be the same. You are now part of "them" and no longer "us." Your daily routine, your interpersonal relationships, and your self-concept all must change. Your loyalties will be divided; although you must remain loyal to those who are now your employees, some elements of the organization will expect your primary loyalty to lie with management. And even in these days of a relatively enlightened workforce, there are always a few non-management employees who regard management as "the enemy."

In some ways assuming a supervisory position separates you from your coworkers. Occasionally, you will feel alone. Your decisions and your efforts to enforce policies and rules will not always be popular. Your decisions and actions may create adversaries for you. New peers (mostly other supervisors and managers) may be reluctant to accept you, especially if you continue to identify closely with your old group, a clear danger if you become the supervisor of a group of which you were formerly a member.

If you have not thought about or prepared for the necessary role change, proceed with care. Weigh the advantages and disadvantages of the change. Think through all that seems to be involved, and consider the following questions:

- Do I truly want to become a supervisor, or am I considering doing so because I desire the increased income or other benefits or because I believe I really have no choice?
- Do I honestly want the opportunity to get things done the way I believe they should be done?
- Am I prepared to take the risk and let go of old patterns of behavior?
- Will I enjoy instructing people and evaluating their performance?
- How will I react to the necessity of enforcing policies and counseling and disciplining employees when needed?
- Am I willing to engage in budget preparation and other forms of planning activity?
- Can I accept the inevitability of participating in workplace politics?
- Do I stand ready and willing to adopt an attitude of continuous learning about supervision?

As you wrestle with questions such as these, seek the advice of your present supervisor, mentors, if any, and experienced employees whose judgment you trust. Also, think hard about the apparent advantages and disadvantages of the supervisory role. There may be much you find appealing about being a supervisor, and thus part of management, but you need to take care to prevent that which is appealing from obscuring your view of possible drawbacks.

Definitions and Essentials

Management is getting things done through people. The term "manager" is used in both a generic and a titular sense. In the generic sense, it refers to any member of the management team, from newest first-line supervisor to chief executive officer. As a position title, it describes someone who is ordinarily at an organizational level below executive but above first-line supervisor. We generally use "manager" to describe those above the rank of supervisor and "executive" to describe members of top management. However, considerable care must be taken in using various labels and titles; what means one thing in one organization or department may mean something entirely different in another setting. For example, "supervisor," as used in this text, refers to the lowest level of management, but in some nursing service structures "supervisor" has long been used to describe someone in charge of a wing or collection of units having authority over several head nurses who, in that capacity, are the first-line supervisors.

A distinguishing characteristic of supervisors, as the term is used in this text, is that they oversee the activities of the people who perform the hands-on work; that is, the people who report to them do not oversee the work of others. In this text the terms "supervisor," "first-line supervisor," and "first-line manager" are synonymous.

For a frequently cited legal definition, in the Taft-Hartley Act of 1947 (the proper name of this legislation is the Labor-Management Relations Act of 1947) a supervisor is "any individual having the authority to hire, transfer, suspend, recall, or discipline other employees; or responsibility to direct them, or to adjust their grievances."[1]

The supervisor is often depicted as the person in the middle, beset by the opposing forces of higher management and the workers. Higher management wants quality work, productivity, and low costs. Workers want higher pay, more benefits, and greater job satisfaction. Although the primary loyalty of the supervisor—for that matter, the primary loyalty of any employee at any level—should be to the organization and its customers, clients, or patients, subordinates nevertheless expect their supervisors to represent their needs and to be their spokespersons.

Supervisors spend much of their time meeting goals, implementing plans, and enforcing policies. At the next higher level, often referred to as "middle management," managers spend much of their time setting goals, planning, and establishing policies. Supervisors are more likely than middle managers to be able to fill in for absent workers. In small departments, supervisors often spend much of their time performing technical or professional work alongside the people who report to them.

Anyone who aspires to a successful career in supervision, perhaps leading to middle management or higher, would do well to always remain aware of two essential characteristics of supervision. First, supervisors need subordinates more than subordinates need supervisors. A group can function without a supervisor, perhaps not very well but still it can function. However, a supervisor alone, with no one to supervise, cannot accomplish all of the work. Second, supervisors do not get paid primarily for what they know or what they do. Rather, they are paid for what their subordinates do, and—especially—they are paid for bearing the responsibility for ensuring that the work gets done and gets done correctly.

In the past, a great many supervisors were primarily "bosses" who gave orders and generally managed autocratically. However, given today's generally enlightened workforce, today's supervisors must be leaders. They are the primary source of answers, instructions, assistance, and guidance for the employees who report to them. Their primary function is to help their employees get the daily work done. Many employees believe that their supervisors have forgotten this, but as a supervisor you must accept full responsibility for the success or failure of your staff.

Essential Management Functions of Supervisors

In addition to the professional and technical duties from which a supervisor never completely separates, a supervisor has management responsibility related to the following essential functions:

1. *Planning:* for example, budgets, new methods and procedures, goals and objectives, and continuing education programs
2. *Organizing:* for example, position descriptions, locations of equipment, and arrangement of workstations and storage areas

3. *Directing:* including selection and orientation of new employees, scheduling, making assignments, training, coaching, and resolution of employee grievances
4. *Controlling:* applying policies and rules, enforcing standards of performance, conducting performance appraisals, and addressing issues of quality, safety, cost, inventory control, counseling, discipline, and such
5. *Coordinating:* cooperation with other sections of the department, other departments, and various staff activities and services

Time is precious for supervisors and managers. Typically, 54% of their time is spent on their own administrative work, 30% is spent on problem-solving and collaborating, 10% on strategy innovation, and 7% on developing stakeholders.[2]

Essential Supervisory Skills

First, a supervisor must be technically and professionally competent. Most supervisors regularly help with some technical tasks, and in larger units some supervisors serve as pinch-hitters. In either case, supervisors need professional competency for making decisions and solving problems.

Your influence as a leader must not be limited to the authority granted by your employer. Your knowledge and experience give you much more power. Most healthcare workers promoted to supervisory roles have specific professional or technical competencies. This does not mean they must know more about everything or be technically more proficient than their subordinates, but rather that their expertise must be sufficient to earn the respect of subordinates.

Basic Skills for Every Supervisor

Successful supervisors need leadership skills in the following areas:

- Communication
- Employee motivation
- Problem-solving and decision-making

- Delegation
- Time management
- Career development

The importance of these vital leadership skills comes through loud and clear in the experiences related by some healthcare supervisors. Some healthcare supervisors found the following activities to pose the most difficulties for them:

- Preparing written communication
- Interviewing, whether for employee selection, discipline, or performance evaluation
- Setting goals for themselves and subordinates
- Offering suggestions for improving work processes
- Delegating authority
- Developing data for budgets
- Developing job descriptions
- Resolving conflicts among subordinates[3]

Traits Exhibited by Effective Supervisors

Certain traits are exhibited by supervisors of proven effectiveness:

- *Self-confidence.* Good supervisors do not become defensive when criticized. They accept responsibility for their own actions and the actions of their subordinates.
- *Respect for others.* Good supervisors welcome input from all sources and are effective listeners. They praise more often than they criticize.
- *Good humor.* Competent supervisors display a sense of humor and can laugh at themselves. They seldom lose their temper.
- *Ability to make decisions.* Effective supervisors make decisions promptly but not before careful consideration. They do not pass the buck.
- *Flexibility and resilience.* Good supervisors adjust rapidly to changing situations, conditions, and demands. They overcome setbacks without becoming bitter.
- *Energy and enthusiasm.* Good supervisors possess a strong work ethic. They are optimistic and cheerful, even when under stress.
- *Creativity.* Good supervisors are always thinking about better ways of doing things. They encourage others to be innovative.
- *Customer awareness.* Good supervisors know their external and internal customers and strive to exceed the expectations of these customers.
- *Quality orientation.* Good supervisors insist on things being done right the first time. They support all quality improvement measures.
- *Empowering.* Good supervisors practice participative management and are effective team builders.
- *Risk-taking.* Good supervisors are willing to express opinions, encourage creativity, and accept responsibility.

Supervisors as Seen by Their Employees

Following are statements that workers have been heard to make about the supervisors they respect:

- "He discusses problems with me and listens to what I have to say."
- "She shares credit, telling the big boss when we do a good job."
- "She lets me know how she feels about my work, whether good or bad."
- "I can trust him to go to bat for me."
- "He means it when he pays me a compliment, and I know exactly what I did that he liked."
- "He always has time to listen to me."
- "She tries to help me do a better job."

Transition to Supervision

Moving into a supervisory position in the department in which you have been working has both advantages and disadvantages. On the plus side, you know the people, and you know the department and its activities. On the other hand, you must establish new relationships with former peers and friends and must henceforth identify with management without completely losing your identification with the work group. The transition is easiest if the following have already occurred:

- You have already been accepted as an informal leader within the department.
- You have previously served in leadership roles, such as committee chair, trainer, or substitute supervisor.
- You have had experience performing administrative tasks.
- You have prepared for this eventuality through formal educational programs or self-study.

Leading Versus Doing

Your new role requires you to spend more time getting the group's work done through others and less time doing the work yourself. Many new supervisors find it nearly impossible to stop doing what they did before they were promoted. This is so partly because they performed their former tasks well and partly because they were not trained to be supervisors. Since they know one side of the role very well (the working side) but do not know the other side (the supervisory side) nearly as well, they tend to favor the side with which they are most comfortable. Some supervisors become frustrated when they realize they no longer can do everything better than their subordinates; however, although a supervisor must understand the work, he or she does not need to be able to perform every task in a superior manner. Trying to serve as both a full-time leader and a full-time worker simultaneously ends in burnout or failure.

Supervisors must maintain enough technical or professional expertise to answer questions and serve as a resource. They must often pitch in and help with the daily work. Some positions, especially in smaller units or on evening, night, or weekend shifts, legitimately call for hybrid leadership–worker roles.

Relationships with Subordinates

As a supervisor you naturally want to be liked by the people you supervise, but you cannot continue to be part of the old gang. Strive for the respect of the employees rather than looking for their affection. Be firm, fair, and consistent. Make up your mind to develop your managerial skills while maintaining your professional knowledge.

If you previously earned the respect of your teammates, you are off to a good start. On the other hand, if they resent your promotion, believe someone else was more deserving, or believe you were selected because of favoritism, you may experience some rough going.

Honeymoon Phase

Immediately after the promotion, you and most of your subordinates will most likely make a special effort to cooperate. Your former pals may have mixed feelings toward you; this is referred to as the phenomenon of ambivalence. They want to like and trust you, but they resent your control over them. Certainly they congratulate you and say they are happy to have you as their new leader, and you reciprocate with equal enthusiasm. You tell them that nothing has changed and that with their help you will correct all the problems and annoyances that have long bothered the group. During this phase, those at organizational levels both above and below you will watch you carefully and will judge your competence.

After the Honeymoon

The honeymoon phase, during which just about everyone cooperates, acts friendly, and conceals problems, lasts about as long as a typical marital honeymoon. It may give way abruptly to a phase of discomfort when a sensitive problem, such as the need for a reduction in staff, arises. More often, however, the honeymoon ends gradually as the new supervisor turns down requests or exhibits ineffectiveness. In their desire to be liked, new supervisors often go too far with the friendship approach. This ultimately hampers their ability to provide direction, criticize work performance, or make unpleasant decisions. It is necessary to risk friendship to gain respect. Like it or not, you must finally realize that you are now viewed as one of "them" and no longer as one of "us."

Some subordinates take advantage of the goodwill of the supervisor; the rest take a wait-and-see attitude. The chronic complainers, cynics, passive-aggressives, and negativists cannot stay silent for long. They soon begin to talk about all the weaknesses of the new boss, compare this boss unfavorably with predecessors, and point out how things have been getting worse instead of better.

In most instances, work should be the primary topic of conversation. This does not rule out casual conversation, but your main job is to ensure that the group's work is completed. You must enforce orders from your superiors, even when these orders do not seem sensible or fair to you or to your subordinates. You may well feel an urge to dissociate yourself from these orders, but if you yield to that temptation, you will lose the respect of your subordinates. You gain nothing by claiming that "I don't like this any better than you do; *they* made me do it." Instead, discuss such orders with your manager and see what can be done about changing them or somehow making them more acceptable. You should at least explain to your people the reasons for such directives. Above all, do not discredit higher management by siding with the unhappy employees.

If you let your authority go to your head and lower the boom on your employees, they will unite against you. It is essential to meld humility with firmness. Micromanaging largely involves one-way communication: no listening and a great deal of ordering. This may occur either because a new supervisor wants to do a good job or perhaps because he or she enjoys the feeling of authority.

Because of your new supervisory responsibilities, you should spend less time with former teammates and more with fellow supervisors. Ideally, this should extend to time spent in social activities. Others are more likely to charge you with favoritism if you retain close social ties with your old buddies; you may not be guilty of favoritism at all, but the mere perception of favoritism can be extremely damaging. You are also more likely to reveal confidential information while socializing with your former coworkers. As a supervisor, you must remember that your words carry a certain weight they did not have before you were promoted. Comments you make about others are more often repeated and can get you into hot water.

On the other hand, do not destroy old relationships. The temptation to please higher management may reduce your sensitivity to your employees. You should take time to continue personal, positive contacts with each person, chiefly during brief encounters on the job or during breaks. Do not be afraid to ask questions or solicit help from them.

Relationships with Other Supervisors

Your new peers, your fellow supervisors, will not accept you unless you start meeting with them and acting as though you are one of them. These contacts are important for other reasons. Sharing problems and ideas with other supervisors enhances your growth as a supervisor. The health-care industry has almost always had an excessive emphasis on professional growth; thus, we tend to identify with fellow professionals rather than with fellow managers, and each occupation or profession tends to become a "club" of sorts.

Another reason for moving closer to fellow supervisors is the increasing need for coordinating the flow of work. Sharing equipment and overlapping services requires close cooperation between and among departments and other units.

Relationship with Your Manager

If you have been promoted from the ranks, you already know something about the person who is now your immediate boss. You know whether he or she prefers to communicate verbally or in writing. You have learned how to interpret the boss's body language, when to stay out of the way, and what pleases or displeases this manager. If you are new to the department, you need to learn these things as soon as you can.

Good supervisors help their managers control their time by handling trifles themselves. They give the managers all necessary information, even when the news is bad. They don't run to their managers with problems asking for help; they do their homework and offer recommended solutions. They admit their mistakes and do not make the same mistake twice.

Adjusting to the New Routine

The transitional phase consists of preparing for your behavioral changes. This involves enhancing your communication processes, learning how to best get the work completed effectively and efficiently, and applying the right skills at the right time. This is called "situational leadership."

Endeavor to balance a task-oriented style with people-oriented needs. Model the behavior you want to encourage in others. Never overlook the potential effects of a strong, visible, positive role model, and remain aware of the damaging effects of the negative role model projected by the supervisor whose attitude toward employees is "do as I say, not as I do."

Pitfalls

Supervisors should do their best to be aware of and to avoid the potential problems that can sometimes encroach upon supervisory behavior:

- Lacking flexibility in dealing with attitudes, biases, perceptions, emotions, and feelings. Previous nonsupervisory experience depended largely on objective measurement and on circumstances one could objectively control and measure, but now the ambiance is murky and decisions are more frequently based on subjective factors.
- Lacking assertiveness. Introverts often struggle with leadership roles.
- Unwilling to pay the price of loneliness, with fewer peers and more stress.
- Striving to be liked rather than respected.

- Unwilling to determine specifically what superiors expect.
- Failing to maintain technical and management competence and thus not remaining marketable.
- Withholding important information from peers, subordinates, or superiors.
- Becoming a bottleneck rather than a supporter and expediter.

Refer to the chapter "Leaders and Managers" for more information about leadership.

Launching a Successful Supervisory Career

Provide yourself with the best possible chance of succeeding as a supervisor by observing the following:

- Know what is expected of you. Be thoroughly familiar with all aspects of your job description.
- Hold regular one-to-one meetings with each employee. Group meetings, although necessary, are not enough; each employee deserves your undivided attention from time to time—and not just when criticism is necessary.
- Work to build relationships and establish a personal network.
- Learn to trust your intuition more than you ever had to before you became a supervisor.
- Remain available to help others; become a great listener.
- Be sensitive to the feelings, needs, and desires of the people who report to you.
- Keep your people as fully informed as possible.
- Maintain high ethical and moral standards; be a model of integrity.
- Be willing to ask for help when needed and to ask questions.
- Join professional organizations serving your field and attend their meetings.
- Maintain an active self-education program, recognizing that the supervisor who does not continue to learn will steadily fall behind.

- Insist on good performance, and acknowledge and reward it.
- Remain calm under stress; avoid shouting and pouting.
- Display self-confidence at all times.
- Remain fair; always keep your conduct free from favoritism or discrimination.

- Defend your employees from hostile people and tormentors.
- Display the courage to make unpopular decisions and see them through.

WRAP-UP

Think About It

Entering supervision is not a matter of simply accepting a promotion and performing tasks different from what you had been doing.

Entering supervision is literally the adoption of a second career.

Questions for Review and Discussion

1. Why should the first-line supervisor be proficient in both doing and leading? Explain.
2. Do you believe it is better to rise to supervision from within the group or to move into the position from outside? Why?
3. What do you believe are the fundamental differences between a traditional "boss" and a true leader?
4. Why is it necessary for the first-line supervisor to be technically or professionally competent as well as a capable leader?
5. Why is delegation a critically important supervisory skill?
6. Concerning the section "Supervisors as Seen by Their Employees," write one additional statement that you would like to hear said of you as a supervisor. Explain why you wrote this particular statement.
7. Why is it of particular importance for the supervisor to identify primarily with management?
8. As a first-line supervisor, how would you attempt to relate honestly with your immediate superior if that manager's attitude strongly suggests that "bad news" is never welcome?
9. As a newly hired or recently appointed supervisor, how would you go about trying to determine what expectations you will be called on to meet?
10. What would you do if you found yourself in strong disagreement with a mandate your immediate superior expects you to implement through your employees?

Case: Sarah's Promotion

After spending several years as a staff nurse in the same medical–surgical unit, Sarah was promoted to the position of head nurse of that unit. Immediately after the staff meeting at which her promotion was announced, Sarah was surrounded by several of her coworkers, members of her lunchtime "coffee club," offering congratulations.

"Great news," said Jane, "but does this blow the carpool? I don't think your hours will be the same as ours anymore."

Emily said, "There goes the coffee club. Management commitments, don't you know." Sarah felt she detected a sarcastic edge to Emily's mention of management.

Debbie said, "Well, maybe now we can get someone to listen to us. Don't forget, Sarah, you used to complain just like the rest of us."

Helen said, "Complaining has been a way of life around here. I personally don't think that our recently departed supervisor ever passed any of our concerns up the line." Her tone turned sharp as she added, "Now that Sarah's going to be in a position to do something, let's hope she doesn't forget who her friends are."

Following a brief, awkward silence, the group broke up and the nurses went their separate ways.

Questions

1. Describe the advantages Sarah may enjoy in taking over as supervisor for this group of which she has long been a member.
2. What principal disadvantages might Sarah face?
3. Put yourself in Sarah's position and describe the approach you would take in attempting to alter her relationships with her small group of friends.

References

1. Taft-Hartley Act of 1947 (Labor-Management Relations Act of 1947), Section 101, Subsection 2(11).
2. Ryba K. Making time and space for performance management. Employee Success Software. https://www.quantumworkplace.com/future-of-work/how-much-time-should-a-manager-spend-developing-employees. Published July 13, 2022. Accessed March 14, 2023.
3. Wilder R. How one lab gauges job satisfaction. *Medical Laboratory Observer.* 1981;13:35–39.

CHAPTER 2

Customer Service

CHAPTER OBJECTIVES

- Develop an understanding of what the various customers served by the healthcare organization and its employees need from their relationship with healthcare provider organizations.
- Briefly describe the impact of managed care on the delivery of services to the customers of the organization.
- Identify the essential elements of customer service.
- Address techniques that can be applied in providing and sustaining superior customer service.
- Identify the elements of an effective customer satisfaction system.
- Develop an understanding of theories and concepts that drive customer service.

KEY TERMS

Managed Care: An approach to the delivery of care intended to address the problems of providing reasonable access to quality care at affordable cost, including economic incentives for providers and patients. The most common form is the health maintenance organization (HMO), made possible by the Health Maintenance Organization Act of 1973.

Customers, External: External customers are those from outside of the organization with whom you may have working contact, including patients or clients, families, visitors, vendors, contractors, and others.

Customers, Internal: Internal customers are all those persons internal to the organization with whom you may have working contact, foremost among them your employees, employees of other departments, physicians and other professionals, and others.

Expectancy-Disconfirmation Model: The model says that satisfaction or dissatisfaction results from a customer's comparison of performance (of a product or service) with predetermined standards of the performance. The predetermined standards are the customer's predictive expectations.

Expectancy-Value Theory: Customers often make some judgment about a service, its benefits, and the likely outcomes of using the service. People will learn to perform a behavior that they expect will lead to positive outcomes. There remains a need to provide a direct link between satisfaction and the service.

Who Are Our Customers, and What Do They Want?

The foregoing question is fundamental to the operation of any activity that provides goods or services. And "customers" include more than just those who purchase the goods or services. Any activity in any business has both external and internal customers. Customers external to healthcare organizations include patients, patients' families and visitors, referring physicians, doctors' offices, blood donors, and third-party payers. Internal customers include nurses, staff physicians and other professionals, students, trainees, employees, departments, and committees.

There is a distinct difference between a person's wants and that individual's genuine needs. As the widow in the retirement home said, "I need a husband; I want Tom Selleck." Patients are ordinarily aware of their wants. By and large they want quiet, clean rooms with all the conveniences of a first-rate hotel. They want tasty food served hot and on time. They want painless procedures and no waiting on gurneys or in ready rooms. They want courteous, attentive, skillful, and professional-looking staff. Most of all, they want to leave the institution alive and feeling better than when they arrived. On the other hand, few patients are completely aware of their needs for diagnostic tests or therapeutic modalities.

Physicians are not always cognizant of what they should order for their patients until they learn about some new diagnostic or therapeutic procedure. Then they demand it. They invariably want fast and courteous service and all the latest technology.

Insightful care providers take steps to determine what their customers must have (their needs), what they want, and what they do not want. To stimulate or modify the needs and wants of their customers, healthcare providers make their customers aware of new services or products as they become available. What they often forget to do is find out what new services or products their external customers want or need;

in others words, some providers readily advise customers of what they are able to offer but fail to ask those customers what they would really like to have available.

In this twenty-first century, the importance of customer service is continually increasing. At one time patients and even physicians had very few choices as far as points of care delivery were concerned; the acute care hospital was essentially the center of the healthcare system. Now, however, with organizational fragmentation resulting in a wide range of independent and often free-standing entities and control of resources largely in the hands of primary physicians, there are choices. And the provider organizations that develop a strong reputation for positive customer service are the ones that will fare best in what has lately become a far more competitive environment than it was in the past.

The final few words of the preceding paragraph—what has lately become a far more competitive environment—are extremely important. Before the beginning of the managed care era, competition in the provision of health care was not a significant factor. Now, however, the environment is decidedly competitive and in some areas is becoming even more so. Today many consumers of health care have choices; often multiple alternatives are available to them. A great many consumers who have such choices and elect to exercise them find that providers are competing for their business. And chances are these consumers will elect to go to where service is most convenient for them and where they feel they receive the best treatment both medically and as individuals. As it has long been in many other areas in which service is provided to people, the medical providers who offer the best in care and overall treatment will attract the most business.

Influence of Managed Care

The shift to managed care has had considerable impact on customer service. In terms of their effects on customers, managed care organizations—such as health maintenance organizations and preferred provider organizations—have placed certain restrictions on access to care and yet they compete with each other for patients. Government and insurers have forced providers to find ways of operating on less money than they might have received in the absence of managed care. Provider organizations have had to adjust to the financial limitations imposed on them. As a result the healthcare industry has experienced numerous mergers and affiliations and other forms of restructuring, making it necessary to tighten staffing overall at precisely the same time managed care is forcing an increase in customer service communication with an increasing number of internal and external customers.

Under managed care, for the first time in the history of American health care, significant restrictions have been placed on the use of healthcare services. Customers have been introduced to the use of the primary care physician as the "gatekeeper" to control access to specialists and other services. Under the gatekeeper concept, visits to specialists and certain others are covered only if the patient is referred by his or her primary care physician. Before the arrival of managed care one could safely say that the acute care hospital was the center of the healthcare system. Now, however, in the role of gatekeeper it is the primary care physician who functions as the practical center of the healthcare system.

As managed care continues to mature and individuals gain more experience in dealing with it, enrollees are becoming more sophisticated in their knowledge of what is promised and what is delivered. Many people are increasingly critical of how they are handled, especially concerning real and perceived barriers to their access to medical specialists and expensive procedures. Customer inquiries and complaints are on average becoming more complex and articulate and thus more difficult to address.

Although all agencies claim that quality care and patient satisfaction remain important, the emphasis on cost control and limitation of services is unmistakable. Managed care has been directly or indirectly responsible for staff reductions and for the replacement of numerous highly trained staff with employees who have been educated to a lesser level and thus are paid less.

The impact of managed care is not likely to diminish in the foreseeable future. Many people depend on managed care plans. Present membership may represent the overwhelming majority of people suitable for managed care. In-and-out participation of some groups, such as the younger aging and Medicaid patients, is expected, but the bulk of people on whom managed care plans can best make their money are already enrolled.

Three Essentials of Customer Service

The essentials of customer service in any activity in which employees deal directly with customers are systems, strategies, and employees.

Systems

Systems include policies, protocols, procedures, arrangement and accessibility of the physical facilities, staffing, operations, workflow, and performance monitoring. Policy statements and procedure manuals provide behavior guidelines, rules, and regulations. For effective and customer-friendly policies, several things must be done:

1. Eliminate policies that adversely affect client satisfaction (for example, unnecessarily strict visiting hours).
2. Annually review all policies affecting customer service.
3. Establish a committee of supervisors and knowledgeable employees to address policy matters.
4. Introduce new policies designed to improve client service (for example, a special parking area for blood donors, more convenient locations and times for specimen collections).

For each new service that is introduced, consider a policy specific to that service.

Discussions elsewhere in this text address policies relating to recruitment, orientation and training, reward systems, communication, empowering people, and building teams.

Strategies

Strategy in customer service consists of developing a customer-oriented culture. A customer-oriented culture is achieved when every employee understands that good service is expected, that exceptional service is rewarded, and that unsatisfactory service is not tolerated. Such strategy is embodied in statements of vision, values, mission, goals, objectives, and action plans.

Customer feedback is essential to strategy. We obtain feedback from a number of sources, including complaints, suggestions, incident reports, surveys, interdepartmental meetings, cross-functional work groups, task forces, and focus groups.

Employees

We can never forget our internal customers. Employees in all capacities are our best customers in that we must satisfy them before we can please other customers. A well-satisfied employee is one who is capable of extending the best in customer service to others. Concerning employee satisfaction, the principal responsibilities of supervisors are to do the following:

1. Determine and respond to the legitimate needs and wants of their employees.
2. Field the best possible team of employees.
3. Empower employees to solve problems (can each of your employees say "I rarely need anyone else to help me handle customer problems or questions"?).
4. Teach by example.
5. Insist on excellent customer service and constantly monitor the delivery of this service.

Techniques for Improving Customer Service

Position Descriptions

In the summary statement of every position description, the word "customer" should appear, with an indication of how the customer is to be regarded. (For example, "The goal of this position is to meet or exceed customers' expectations and needs. Our external and internal customers include ….")

Modify performance standards to include items addressing quality and customer service. Here are some examples:

- Exercises discretion with patient information
- Accepts night and weekend assignments willingly
- Displays tact in personal interactions with customers and staff
- Frequently reports customer comments and suggestions

Recruiting Process

Your goal should be to hire employees who are competent, caring, and resistant to turnover. Assist in the recruiting process by providing the employment section of your human resources department with concise, up-to-date position descriptions. Be sure the attractive aspects of each job are prominent in those descriptions, but be honest concerning job duties that may not appear quite so attractive. Help the recruiters by recommending the most effective means for identifying potential job candidates. Answer inquiries about jobs enthusiastically, and interview candidates promptly.

Selection Process

The ability to sell jobs to candidates is important. The stronger the candidates appear to be, the more likely it is that other organizations will be trying to hire them. You can learn a great deal about a candidate's attitude toward customer service by asking the following questions: What does superior service mean to you? What gives you the strongest feeling of satisfaction about your workday? Provide an example of how you made an extra effort to serve a client.

Orientation and Training System

Make certain new employees know who their external and internal customers are. Orient them toward exceptional customer service. Infuse them with the latest ideas in quality improvement. Emphasize the importance of a "can do" attitude and how this can affect performance ratings. Review workflow and carefully address each point at which the providers and recipients of service come into direct contact. Alert new employees to questions that customers frequently ask, and let them know where the answers can be found. Describe what you regard as proper telephone and electronic communication etiquette. Introduce them to the department's major customers.

Performance Review and Reward Systems

Refocus performance objectives and performance appraisals to strongly address customer satisfaction. Discuss customer service when reviewing past performance and when formulating objectives for future activities. Encourage employees to set objectives such as attending seminars on communication skills or customer service, visiting internal customers, or learning to speak customers' languages.

Tie your recognition and reward strategy to customer service. Unfortunately, the healthcare workers who have the most client contact are among the lowest paid, receive the least training, and have the least opportunity for promotion, yet these are the employees who need to know of the vital importance of outstanding customer service and who need to receive strong positive feedback for their efforts in providing good service.

In-service Educational Programs

In-service education topics for all employees should include customer identification, recognition of customer expectations, customer problem-solving, presenting new services, and communication skills, telephone courtesy in particular. Topics for employees responsible for contact with customers should also include empathic interactions, listening skills, dealing with complaints, assertiveness, and how to cope with angry people.

Employee Retention

Turnover of employees present a major impediment to customer service. Unfortunately, the employees who provide the most hands-on service, experience the highest turnover rates. (These topics are addressed in greater detail elsewhere in this text.)

Designing a Customer Satisfaction System

Principles of effective customer service for supervisors and employees include the following:

- Always treat customers as you would like to be treated; this should be a cardinal rule.
- Anticipate your customers' needs and wants.
- Hire employees who have a caring attitude, and retrain, reassign, or remove those who do not.
- Include customer satisfaction in your orientation and training programs.
- Make yourself a model of good customer service.
- Make customer satisfaction a condition of satisfactory performance.
- Monitor the behavior of your service providers, and coach those who demonstrate any deficiencies.
- Obtain frequent feedback from internal and external customers.
- Under-promise and over-deliver; whenever possible giving customers more than they expect.
- Recognize and reward those who make special efforts to please customers.
- Give your employees the authority to resolve customer complaints.

Address Complaints

Patients are most likely to complain about noise, food, their rooms, waiting, and lack of courtesy. Customers are displeased when the following occur:

- They do not receive what is expected or promised.
- They have to wait for what they consider excessive amounts of time.

- Someone who represents the organization is rude, patronizing, or indifferent.
- They believe they are getting the brush-off or the runaround.
- Someone expresses a "We can't do it" attitude or hits them with the rule book (for example, "It's our policy").

Always regard complaints as suggestions for improving service. Some complaints are not legitimate, but a great many are. Legitimate or otherwise, an employee's initial response to any complaint should be careful listening. Complaints are the least costly source of customer feedback. Invite additional comments and ask for specific suggestions for improvement. Encourage your staff to report complaints and make suggestions for eliminating them, and record these suggestions. Express your appreciation of these suggestions at performance reviews as well as at the time they are offered.

Ask for customer comments and suggestions at every staff meeting. Suggestions need not be elaborate or complicated. In one large hospital, for example, soothing music was piped into the waiting room for visitors, most of whom were waiting for patients undergoing surgery. The results of a study of this practice indicated that self-reported stress levels of visitors were reduced.[1]

Maintain a comment log. Empower your front-line staff to solve customer problems. Most customers are understanding if they believe that providers care about them, so give your employees the authority they need.

When faced with a complaint, acknowledge its validity and offer an apology as appropriate. Accept responsibility without blaming others. Empathize with the complainers and ask them what they would like done. If you receive no response, make an offer. Thank the person for bringing the matter to your attention. Promise to do what you agreed to do, then do it promptly.

Customer Service Concepts

Understanding what drives customer behavior can help achieve the best customer satisfaction. Two concepts and/or theories that lead the research on customer service are expectancy-disconfirmation model and expectancy-value theory. Each of these are important concepts to understanding customer behaviors and how to respond to them.

Expectancy-Disconfirmation Model

The expectancy-disconfirmation model says that satisfaction or dissatisfaction results from a customer's comparison of performance (of a product or service) with predetermined standards of the performance. The customer or patient has predetermined ideas from previous experiences or from hearing the experiences from friends or family members.[2] The predetermined standards are the customer's predictive expectations. These are positive or negative and can set the tone for the patient and his or her behavior.

Expectancy-Value Theory

Expectancy-value theory is when customers make some judgment about a service, its benefits, and the likely outcome of using the service. People will learn to perform a behavior that they expect will lead to positive outcomes. For example, motivating healthcare employees can increase customer and patient satisfaction.[3] Supervisors influence their employees with tools from an effective customer service system.

Customers have specific needs and wants when it comes to their care and the care of their loved ones. Providing the highest level of customer service is the goal. Understanding how customer behavior is driven through concepts and models is one way to increase customer satisfaction.

WRAP-UP

Think About It

A satisfied customer is your best advertisement. The customer who believes he or she received good service may or may not tell others about the experience, but you can be certain that the customer who received poor service will tell others, perhaps many.

Questions for Review and Discussion

1. Why is it necessary to concern ourselves with internal customers?
2. Why are employees our best customers?
3. How would you respond to customer demands that were clearly unreasonable?
4. Why do you think hospital patients are more likely to complain about food, cleanliness, and staff treatment rather than about the quality of care they receive?
5. Do you believe managed care has made customer service more difficult? Why or why not?
6. How are the quality of health care and excellence in customer service related to each other?
7. How do customer service concepts play a role in customer satisfaction?
8. Is employee turnover ever a significant barrier to good customer service? Why or why not?
9. What do you believe has the greatest influence on an employee's willingness to deliver excellent customer service?
10. Relative to customer service, why is it suggested that we "under-promise" and "over-deliver"?

Exercise: Identifying Customers and Their Needs

Designate a specific healthcare organization function or department (for example, nursing service, physical therapy, housekeeping, or food service).

Create two blocks of space on a sheet of paper (same if being done on a word document); label one "Internal Customers" and the other "External Customers" (with "internal" and "external" referring to the organization, not just the department—in other words, employees of another department remain your "internal" customers). In each space list as many internal and external customers as you can for your designated department. Next, for each customer designation write a one-sentence description of the services you provide to that customer.

If this exercise is done in a classroom setting, compare your lists with others and attempt to reconcile any differences that arise.

Case: The Crabby Receptionist

"I don't know what I'm going to do about Louise," said supervisor Missy Clare to her friend and fellow supervisor, Janet Stevens. "She was a good worker for the longest time, but now I'm getting complaints."

"What kinds of complaints?" Janet asked.

"That she's abrupt to the point of rudeness when she answers the phone and that she snaps at other employees when they just ask simple questions. I've had at least three doctors tell me I'd better get someone more pleasant out front, and obviously someone complained to Carson—you know, my boss—because he asked me about the crabby receptionist in my section he was hearing about."

"Has she been experiencing any kind of problem that you know of? Something personal that's bothering her?"

"I don't know," Missy answered, "and it's a cinch she doesn't want to talk about it, even if there is a problem. I've given her every opportunity to talk but she's not having any of it."

Janet said, "Well, to be completely honest with you, I've heard a few things about Louise."

"Like what?"

"Like how some of your outpatients are afraid to approach her because they don't know if they're going to be snapped at, glared at, or ignored."

Missy said, "Louise is such a long-time employee. I hate to just lower the boom on her."

"Well," said Janet, "you'd better lower something before Carson and his higher-ups get any more complaints."

Questions

1. Which customers are likely to cause Missy the most grief over Louise's behavior? Why?
2. Recommend an approach for Missy to consider in addressing the problem with Louise.
3. Should Missy and Janet be discussing Louise's behavior? Is this acceptable?

References

1. Routhieaux RL, Tansik DA. The benefits of music in hospital waiting rooms. *Health Care Supervisor.* 1997;16:31–39.
2. Oliver, RL. *Satisfaction: A Behavioral Perspective on the Consumer.* Routledge; 2010.
3. De Simone, S. Expectancy value theory: motivating healthcare workers. *American International Journal of Contemporary Research.* 2015;5(3):19–23.

CHAPTER 3

Basic Management Functions

CHAPTER OBJECTIVES

- Establish the benefits of planning and address the implications of the failure to plan.
- Describe the types of plans used in business activity and identify the key elements of planning.
- Establish the role of planning in an organization's vision and mission.
- Establish the significance of goals and objectives in planning.
- Define action plans and examine the elements of a typical action plan.
- Define organizing and describe its place among the basic management functions.
- Convey the importance of values in organizational life.
- Explain the concept of authority and describe how authority is apportioned to those responsible for its application.
- Define the concepts of "unity of command" and "span of control" as they apply to the role of the first-line supervisor.
- Define the informal organization and describe its potential impact on organizational functioning.
- Define coordinating and controlling, and describe their relationship to the other management functions.

KEY TERMS

Planning: The projection of actions or desired results in a period that has not yet arrived, whether minutes or years into the future.

Organizing: The establishment of the structure within which work gets accomplished.

Unity of Command: For each task that must be done, the employee who performs it is directly accountable to someone for its completion.

Span of Control: The number of employees who report to a single leader or who can be effectively supervised by a single leader.

Coordinating: The process of synchronizing activities and participants so that they function smoothly with each other.

Controlling: Follow-up and correction, as necessary.

Interrelated Concepts

Before getting into detailed discussions of the individual management functions, it may be helpful to first establish the interrelated nature of the functions; that is, although we can examine them separately, it is necessary to appreciate that these are not freestanding concepts but rather interrelated to a considerable extent. Although planning can perhaps be examined as separate from the others, a plan itself is nothing without application of other functions to convert it to reality. Consider the following example:

Joan's Busy Day

Joan, a registered nurse of considerable experience, was assistant director of nursing service at Suburban Hospital. As a result of a merger with the remnants of an underutilized facility not far away, Suburban is undergoing an expansion that will add 70 beds as the other facility is phased out. As assistant director, Joan was expected to determine the staffing requirements for the new beds.

Joan developed a staffing plan based on allowing each unit a core staff set at 90% of the staff required at average expected census. To compensate for instances of understaffing, she created a float pool to augment staff as needed.

One morning the hospital received word that a severe storm was imminent and the emergency department should be prepared for flood-related activity. About the same time, Joan learned that one of her key people, the manager of the largest medical–surgical unit, had fallen seriously ill during the night.

From the float pool, partially depleted by vacations and illness, Joan was able to pull one licensed practical nurse with emergency department experience. She then located two staff nurses with similar experience and told them they might be called upon; if this happened, they could expect to have to stay after their regular

shift. She then made arrangements to cover their normal positions with float nurses should the move be necessary.

As for the unit without its regular manager, Joan was tempted to step into the role herself. However, she had no idea how long this coverage would be necessary, and she did not want to spread herself too thin because she might be needed elsewhere.

After brief consideration she decided to place the unit under the temporary direction of a young staff nurse whom she already had been considering for promotion.

Floodwaters rose, driven by heavy rain that also triggered a rash of traffic accidents. Emergency department activity stepped up considerably, and it became necessary to make Joan's planned changes.

That day, in a 7-hour period, the emergency department handled as many visits as it normally would in a peak 24-hour day, and it did so with patient waiting time no longer than usual. When she was later asked whether the hospital's disaster plan showed any weaknesses, Joan was able to suggest some constructive changes.

Keep Joan's hectic day in mind while going through the chapter, and decide which basic management functions describe her behavior.

Planning

Planning is the most fundamental of the management functions, and as such it logically precedes all other functions. Planning is the projection of actions intended to reach specific goals. In other words, a plan is a blueprint for the future; it is the expression of what we wish to accomplish or the best prediction of what might occur in the future. Planning begins with the questions of *what* and *why*, then focuses on the *how, when, who,* and *where.*

Benefits of Planning

Planning ensures that we work effectively and efficiently, or at the very least, it improves our chances of doing so. Planning reduces procrastination, ensures continuity, and provides for more intelligent use of resources. Planning improves our chances of doing things right the first time, reducing the chances of false starts, and results in the satisfaction of having everything under control at present and knowing what to do next.

Planning is proactive. It decreases the need to manage from crisis to crisis. It is a prerequisite for practically all necessary managerial activities, including teaching or mentoring, preparing for and running committee and staff meetings, conducting performance appraisal discussions or employment interviews, preparing budgets, and numerous other activities. Planning is essential for coping with crises such as fires, natural disasters, strikes, bomb threats, hostage incidents, and all other forms of emergencies.

Because plans work out exactly as anticipated only once in a while, why bother? Is not planning just wasted effort, consuming time that could be better spent acting and doing? Perhaps those whose thinking runs along such lines feel uneasy because they can see the amount of time spent in planning but are uneasily aware that nothing concrete is happening during that time to advance the completion of the work. However, those who discount the value of planning often discover that, without planning, their efforts are wasted on false starts and misdirection such that valuable time is consumed in setting things right.

If things often do not happen exactly as we planned for them to happen, what have we gained by planning? We have been able to apply our efforts more effectively than without a plan, and even though we might not have hit the target precisely, we nevertheless have acquired some important information. As a result we know by how much the target was missed, and we can proceed to determine whether (1) we need to readjust our direction to attain the target or (2) conditions have changed such that the target should be adjusted. In any case, the effort expended in planning is never wasted.

We have all undoubtedly heard the expression, "If we fail to plan, we plan to fail." This is largely true. Without planning, even that which does get done suffers to an extent because it has consumed more time and effort than necessary, and without the direction established through planning, the pursuit of any particular result can be an expensive journey into chaos.

Classifications of Plans

Strategic plans are made for achieving long-range goals and living up to the expectations expressed in statements of mission and values. Without strategic planning, few visions are realized.

Tactical plans translate broad strategies into specific objectives and actions.

Organizational plans begin with a table of organization. They include position descriptions, staffing, and channels of communication.

Physical plans concern topography (for example, the site of a building, the layout of an office, or the location of diagnostic and therapeutic equipment).

Functional plans are concerned with the workings of major functional units such as a nursing service, clinical laboratory, human resources department, financial or clinical services, and others.

Operational plans address systems, work processes, procedures, quality control, safety, and other supportive activities.

Financial plans address the inflow and outflow of money, profit and loss, budgets, cost and profit centers, charges, and salaries.

Career planning, time management, and daily work planning are also vital forms of planning. Daily work planning, the simplest, most elementary form of planning in the working world, frequently proves to be the form of planning most immediately beneficial to the individual supervisor.

Key Elements of Planning

The essential elements of planning are vision, mission, goals, objectives, strategy, and action.

Vision statements and mission statements deal with purpose and alignment at an organizational level. Without these, the energy of an organization can become scattered rather than focused. Leaders create a vision around which people rally, and managers marshal the resources to pursue that vision. Vision provides a premise that leaders commit to and dramatize to others. A vision statement should not read like a financial report or a concise statement of purpose. Rather, an effective vision statement must tap peoples' emotions; it must conjure up a compelling positive vision that fires people up. Dr. Martin Luther King, Jr., provided perhaps the best and simplest example of a vision statement with his "I have a dream" speech.

An organization's vision statement should be clear, exciting, and should leave broad latitude for the pursuit of new opportunities. The vision of top management must be broad enough that the vision of the lower echelons of the organization fits within it.[1]

One segment of an organization's vision can be aimed at the consumer (for example, "Our vision is to have a fully staffed, high-quality, committed workforce that is efficient and effective in providing the highest quality service in our community"). Another portion can be directed at employees:

We envision an organization staffed by dedicated, enthusiastic, customer-oriented people who act as partners. Our people readily adapt to change, seek continuous technical improvements, and exhibit a caring attitude. Our organization is preferred by most patients and admitting physicians. It is the darling of third-party payers and is a local preferred employer.

An organization's vision must be sustained through action consistent with the elements of the vision. Next, a vision is translated into an organizational mission that is then expressed in a mission statement. Goals are enunciated, strategy is developed, and action plans are constructed.

Mission

Mission statements proclaim the purpose of an organization or department, literally stating why this entity exists. Like visions, mission statements should serve to define the organization and inspire its employees. Too many supposed mission statements are vague, platitudinous, and quickly forgotten; most of them cannot pass the "snicker test" (the informal test that ought to be well understood by anyone who has ever reacted to a vague or hollow statement or motto as "corny" or "silly"). Too many organizations work hard to develop vision and mission statements, then let them become just framed pieces of paper decorating a wall.

An effective mission statement must be expressed clearly in a single, brief paragraph and in language that everyone can understand. When workers participate actively in the formulation of mission statements, they understand why the organization exists and what their work is all about. This understanding greatly increases the chances that they will do their best to make the virtual visions come to life.

Some mission statements include the vision plus goals and strategy. They answer the key questions of why ("Why does this organization or department exist?"), what ("What is our goal?"), and how ("How will we achieve our goal?"). Following is a departmental mission statement appropriate for a small hospital unit. Note that it begins with a goal, adds objectives, and concludes with a strategy:

We seek a service that surpasses the expectations of our clinician customers. We will improve the quality of reported results, shorten turnaround time, reduce costs, and promote a spirit of cooperation between our staff, our customers, vendors, and associates in other departments. To accomplish this, we will meet weekly to analyze service needs, investigate complaints and suggestions, and explore new methods or equipment. We will make recommendations to management, monitor progress, and evaluate results.

Before accepting a mission statement, those responsible for managing the department or unit must ensure that it answers four critical questions:

1. Do you know where you want to be 5 years from now?
2. Is the mission clearly and definitively expressed in a single paragraph?
3. Is the statement expressed in language that a 10th grader can understand?
4. Will the mission be believable to everyone in the organization?

Goals and Objectives

Leaders share their visions and involve their associates in setting goals and objectives. Goals are characterized by specific ends or conclusions, whereas mission statements are generally open-ended. Many employees prefer activities leading to specific conclusions; for example, they usually prefer to work on projects rather than perform routine work because projects have clear destinations. All riders on a train know when they have arrived at the station. A significant number of retirees die shortly after retiring because mentally their goal—the end of employment—has been reached and they have never developed a clear mission for dealing with the future.

Targets become more specific when goals are subdivided into objectives. Objectives are milestones to be passed on the journey toward reaching a goal. Objectives should be realistic, understandable, measurable, behavioral, achievable, and specific. An objective such as "reduce inventory costs" is not sufficiently specific. Instead, use "reduce inventory costs by 10% within 12 months"; any appropriate objective should relate to *what* is to be done (reduce inventory costs), *how much* is to be done (by 10%), and by *when* it should be done (within 12 months).

Assign priorities to objectives and set target dates. Objectives should always be expressed in writing to provide a permanent record and to keep them foremost in the minds of employees. Although there should always be some degree of challenge—employees are motivated by achieving difficult but not impossible tasks—objectives must be attainable. If a plan holds little chance of success, it will frustrate rather than motivate. Here are some examples of over-inflated objectives:

Within 12 months, a repeat survey of employee morale will show an increase in the average employee satisfaction rating from the current level 3 to level 2.

By the end of the next quarter, we will provide point-of-care testing for all patients in the north wing.

Following are examples of objectives for a more comprehensive goal relating to customer satisfaction. Note that although these are open-ended, all are valid as ongoing objectives for this hypothetical organizational unit:

- Hire employees who are client oriented, technically or professionally competent, and likely to remain onboard.
- Provide an orientation and training program that stresses client satisfaction.
- Anticipate changes in customers' needs or expectations, and continually monitor customer satisfaction.
- Provide an intensive continuing education program that stresses client satisfaction.

Strategy

Successful organizations build on their existing strengths and eliminate their weaknesses or render them irrelevant. They constantly search for innovative ways to please their customers. The moves they make to please their customers, to position themselves relative to their markets, to adapt to the changing environment, and to address their relationships to their competition are all reflections of their strategy. Keys to success in the pursuit of an organizational strategy include the following:

- Vision, mission, goals, objectives, and action plans
- Committed and visible support of top management
- Effective and efficient systems, processes, and procedures
- Quality tools and techniques
- Sufficient time to carry out plans
- Empowered, caring, competent employees

Action Plans

Action plans are typically composed of five steps:

Step 1. Identify the Problem or Need. To identify and understand the problem or need, answer the following questions:

- Why is there a need for change? What is wrong with the present service or system?
- What are our strengths and weaknesses and those of our competitors?
- What are the potential gains, losses, or risks of a change?
- Who will be affected?
- What will it cost?
- What is likely to happen if no action is taken?

Step 2. Obtain and Analyze Data. Select a method of collecting information and build a databank. Be thorough in collecting information. Become familiar with statistical analysis and the use of charts, electronic data interchange, electronic mail, and workflow automation. Document current deficiencies and opportunities for improvement.

Step 3. Determine the Best Action. Appropriate action plans should answer the following questions:

- What is to be done?
- Why must it be done?
- When should it be started and when should it be completed?
- Who is to do it?
- Where is the action to take place?
- How should it be done?

Step 4. Carry Out the Plan. It is essential that a plan be doable, understandable, comprehensive, cost-effective, approved, and periodically reviewed. Complex plans should always include an executive summary describing how the proposal affects the mission statement and service quality and operating costs. Also to be added is your assessment of how you believe clients and employees will react to the changes brought by the plan. The implementation process includes the following:

- Identifying resources (for example, people, supplies, equipment, facilities, time, and funds)
- Preparing checklists of important tasks to be performed
- Assigning tasks, authority, and responsibility
- Preparing work schedules
- Providing necessary training
- As necessary, formulating new policies, systems, and procedures

Sequencing and Scheduling of Tasks. Use Gantt charts, flowcharts, and flow diagrams or other logic diagrams to document tasks and analyze the times required for the work processes. On a chart, chronologically list the tasks to be done on one side opposite the appropriate calendar periods.

Preparing a Budget. Estimate all costs associated with each task. Build in some slack for inflation or other unanticipated costs. Prepare a cost spreadsheet with tasks listed vertically and cost factors (for example, labor, supplies) listed horizontally and totaled at the right of each line.

Establishing Priorities. Priorities are a vital part of any plan. To avoid frustration, be flexible; that is, remain prepared to modify your priority list as circumstances change. Unexpected interruptions are the rule rather than the exception.

Step 5. Monitor the Process, Report Progress, and Make Adjustments. Formal control is planned control consisting of data gathering, analysis, and documentation. Informal control consists of day-by-day observations and impromptu meetings with other participants. Informal controls are more proactive than formal controls; that is, they provide information that is valuable in heading off difficulties or identifying problems while they are small and manageable. Periodic status reports should be required for large projects.

Monitoring progress usually necessitates tying up some loose ends. These may involve changes in plans, reassignment of tasks, removal of barriers, or requests for additional resources. In all instances, the earlier a problem can be identified, the easier it is to correct.

Organizing

Organizing is the process of preparing to implement decisions that result from the planning process; in other words, it is the establishment of the structure in which the work gets done. Organizing involves delineating tasks and establishing a framework of authority and responsibility for the people who will perform these tasks; that is, building the aforementioned structure. It further involves analyzing the workload, distributing it among employees, and coordinating the activities so that work proceeds smoothly.

Supervisors perform organizing functions using the authority of their positions in the organizational hierarchy, or "table of organization" or "organizational chart" as it is sometimes described. Essential organizing tools include policies, procedures, work rules, position descriptions, and the all-important activities of assigning and delegating.

Values

Corporate Values

In value statements, most employers express what they regard as evidence of loyalty, expected behavior, or ethical practice. Organizational cultures encompass and reflect the values that guide that organization in its daily activities; that is, the sum total of all the ways people are expected to act in pursuing the goals and objectives of the organization. As work moves across departmental boundaries—for example, the flow of patients moving from admitting to a nursing unit, to radiology and back—inevitable differences in values affect what is done and how and when things are done.

When corporations overall or individual supervisors or other members of management violate their own values, employees become cynical.

They remember what they have been told, and they talk of past promises that have been broken. They use descriptors such as "unfair" or "double-talk," accusing management of "talking the talk" but not "walking the walk."

Personal Values

What we as individuals consider ethical or unethical depends on our personal value systems, those fundamental concepts and motives in which we believe. Personal values concern what is important regarding work, for example challenges, tasks, recognition, creativity, and authority. These values encompass relationships, personal finances, living and recreational activities, hobbies, and entertainment. Other values may include ambition and the desire for fame or the wish to have one's own enterprise. Attitudes continually reflect the core beliefs and values of individuals. Attitudes can change when beliefs and values change, but that happens neither easily nor often.

Authority

Authority possessed by an individual in the organizational hierarchy is formal power that is delegated; that is, it is passed on down the hierarchy to the point at which it is to be applied. Supervisors require authority to fulfill their responsibilities. It is obvious that people should not be given responsibilities without sufficient authority to completely fulfill those responsibilities and thus get the job done. Although authority is the power that makes a management job a reality, it can be relatively weak in its application. To be effectively applied, authority must be supplemented by other conditions or characteristics as follows:

- Expertise; for example, licensure, certification, knowledge, skill, or experience
- Credibility, as in being trusted and respected
- Leadership skill, whether natural or acquired
- Persuasiveness or charisma
- Influence, sometimes as determined by whom one knows or is connected with

Ideally, the extent of a supervisor's authority is expressed in the position description. Some of the more important activities over which supervisors possess variable amounts of authority fall into three categories: employee administration, fiscal administration, and procedures. Employee administration includes the following:

- Selecting, orienting, and training new employees
- Assigning or delegating to subordinates
- Scheduling and approving overtime (although in some settings, overtime approval may reside with the supervisor's manager)
- Coaching, counseling, and disciplining employees

Fiscal administration includes the following tasks:

- Selecting supplies or equipment or approving such purchases
- Selecting vendors and establishing inventory levels
- Participating at some level in budget preparation

The third category, procedures, involves the following:

- Selecting or modifying methods or processes
- Formulating departmental policies and rules and enforcing them
- Participating in administrative activities (for example, quality management, safety, and education)

Unity of Command

The principle of unity of command originally meant that each employee reported to one and only one superior. However, matrix management arrangements, split-reporting relationships, and other complex organizational patterns have altered that concept. Presently, unity of command simply means that for each task that must be done, the employee who performs it is directly accountable to someone. From the first-line supervisor's viewpoint, unity of command ordinarily represents a normal working arrangement under which every task that must be done is assigned to someone, and each person responsible for performing a specific task is accountable to the supervisor. This means that never, at any time, should there be cause for the department's employees to wonder: whose job is this?

Span of Control

In simplest terms, span of control, at times described as span of management, refers to the number of employees who report to a single leader. In practical terms, it is a reckoning of how many employees a single supervisor can effectively manage, how many the supervisor can keep track of and still provide the necessary supervisory attention.

Factors such as computers and autonomous work teams have led top management to expand spans of control and strip away layers of management. Organizational flattening, which often accompanies reengineering, reorganizing, or other restructuring efforts, can also reduce management layers and force more responsibility down to lower management levels. The result is that many supervisors are increasingly likely to find themselves directing greater numbers of people. Staff reductions, which have sometimes had the effect of replacing highly qualified staff with workers of lesser overall qualifications, have placed additional burdens on overworked supervisors. This condition is compounded by the fact that most of today's supervisors are left with fewer fellow supervisors from whom to solicit advice and support.

A supervisor's effective span of control depends on numerous factors, including the skill level of the employees, employee mobility, and the variability of the department's work, so it is not possible to supply a magic number representing an ideal span of control. However, when the number of people who report to a supervisor is too low, the supervisor, having too little to do at times, often micromanages, much to the discomfort of the employees. When the number of people reporting to a supervisor is too great, there is the danger of problems and needs going unaddressed and the likelihood that some employees will not receive the supervisory attention they require.

Staffing

The staffing process starts with human resource planning, recruitment, employee selection, and orientation of new employees. It continues with training, career development, control, and the appraisal of performance. It sometimes leads to promotion, transfer, demotion, or separation.

It is essential to avoid staffing with people who are clearly over-qualified; these people will not remain long; costs and turnover can be excessive. Under-qualified job candidates may or may not represent good investments; some may make it, and some may fail. The key factor is whether they can be trained without excessive cost or loss of time. These individuals, when trained, are less likely to be bored with routine tasks, and their turnover rate is generally lower than that of over-qualified people.

Availability and morale are enhanced when you can adjust work hours to suit your employees. More than half of all healthcare workers are female, and many prefer work hours that allow them to meet family responsibilities. Part-time employment, flextime, and job-sharing opportunities can be powerful incentives. The use of these staffing strategies also helps provide the needed flexibility for jobs that experience peaks and lows of activity.

Assigning

The terms "assigning" and "delegating" do not have the same meaning, although they are sometimes assumed to be synonymous. However, assigning and delegating have one thing in common: If they are not done, the supervisor is left to do all the work, a clearly unrealistic situation. Assigned tasks are those described in position descriptions. These are activities ordinarily performed by employees in each particular job classification, and the employees have limited choice in their specific assignments. A delegated task, on the other hand, involves transfer of authority, with accompanying responsibility, from supervisor to employee. It is often voluntary. Delegation is addressed in depth elsewhere in this text.

A composite list of the qualifications of all your department's employees is like all the pieces in a set of Tinkertoys® in that all the pieces (qualifications) are not always used; in fact, some pieces may be missing. Your task is to match the expertise and available work hours to the requirements of the department.

Supervisors who maintain an inventory chart of the skills of their employees find such charts helpful in assigning backup services. They also use this information when designing educational and cross-training programs.

Supervisors make the specific assignments and ensure that these assignments are carried out. To do this effectively, supervisors must know the following:

- What must be done
- What equipment and supplies are needed
- What authority the supervisor has
- What quality and productivity requirements must be met
- What the cost constraints are
- Where each task is to be performed
- Where supplies and service supports are found
- Where to obtain help
- Who does what
- When the work must be done (deadlines, turnaround time, etc.)
- When changes must be made
- How the work is to be performed (method or procedure)
- How well, how quickly, and how economically the work must be done
- Why the work must be done (how an employee's work fits into the big picture)

It is also necessary for the supervisor to make an honest effort to match each assignment with an individual's ability. The supervisor must do the following:

- Ensure that the employee to be assigned has time available in which to accomplish the work. Overloading an employee, even inadvertently, is unfair to the individual, and it creates the risk that the employee will fail to do justice to the task.
- Provide all necessary training. It is never appropriate to hand a task to an individual and let that person learn by trial and error.
- Explain each assignment without overloading the explanation with trivial details. Ask the employee to repeat the instructions or perform the work under observation to ensure he or she understands.
- Provide complicated orders in writing, perhaps in procedural form.

- Alert the employee to potential pitfalls, barriers, or constraints, and let the person know how, when, and where to report problems or ask for help.
- Whenever possible, make holistic assignments; that is, assign a complete task to an individual rather than breaking it up. For example, many nurses prefer being responsible for all the nursing care of an individual patient rather than providing only part of that care, such as passing medications.

The Informal Organization

Every organization has beneath its visible surface a network that constitutes another arrangement of interrelationships not represented on any organizational chart. This is the informal organization, which at times is perhaps even more powerful simply because of its lack of visibility. This informal organization even has its own communication system; we refer to it as "the grapevine."

Of course, labor unions are certainly visible and have their share of power and influence partially inside but also outside of the formal organization. In addition, the informal organization includes persons or groups that have no formal power but are able to intimidate or ostracize workers and, at times, even unofficially negotiate with management. Within formal work groups there are cliques in which people gravitate toward informal leaders based on expertise, personality, persuasiveness, charisma, or physical power. Sometimes informal leaders and union leaders possess more power than the organization's formal leaders. When members of these informal groups are frustrated or are led to feel disloyal, they may sabotage equipment, block workflow, start malicious rumors, or even inflict physical harm.

Supervisors must be aware of informal networks. An astute supervisor can often tap into the grapevine and use it to advantage. The grapevine can carry correct information when formal means cannot be trusted or when formal means are not fast enough to squelch rumors by circulating the truth. The supervisor who is well tuned to the grapevine is often in a position to learn what is really going on at the employee level. For all of the frustration it can create, the grapevine nevertheless has two extremely helpful attributes: speed and depth of penetration. It often carries information faster than most official means, and it reaches people who would never bother to read a memo or a newsletter or bulletin board notice.

The astute supervisor also identifies the informal leaders and makes a special effort to get along with them. These informal leaders sometimes turn out to be strong candidates for promotion to supervisory positions and likely employees to handle important delegated tasks.

Coordinating

Coordinating is the process of synchronizing activities and participants so that they function smoothly with each other. When coordination fails, conflict and confusion run rampant. Proactive coordinating involves activities intended to anticipate and prevent problems. Reactive coordinating consists of regulatory activities aimed at the maintenance of existing structural and functional arrangements and corrective activities that rectify errors after they have occurred.

The more steps and the more gatekeepers involved in a workflow process, the greater the need for coordination. Joint projects and services that require interdepartmental cooperation also demand active coordination. Breakdowns in coordination are largely a result of faulty communication, personality conflicts, turf battles, and job design problems. Other causes include training deficiencies, flawed physical arrangements, conflicts of authority, and lack of appropriate policies or procedures.

Workflow coordination is easier when every employee interaction is regarded as a customer service engagement with a provider and a service user (client or customer). Recipients are encouraged to provide positive or negative feedback to the providers and make suggestions for improving such interactions.

Coordinating Requires Persuasive Ability

The definition of management can be expanded to include not only getting things done through people but also getting things done *with* people. "With people" signifies the importance of influencing persons who are neither bosses nor subordinates. These relationships are lateral, or collegial, rather than hierarchical. As organizations grow more complex and more highly specialized, supervisors are likely to spend less time with superiors and subordinates and more time with their peers. Peer groups include internal and external customers, vendors, and other outside providers, as well as employees who precede or follow them in workflows.

Most managers and supervisors are involved in both intradepartmental and interdepartmental coordination. The inability to function effectively and efficiently as a coordinator in such relationships can impair careers.

Tools of Coordination
Committees

A major purpose of committees is to increase coordination of the task, but many committees are costly, time consuming, and often ineffective. The strength of a committee comes from the people and environment where the facilitated action is being implemented.[2] Committees can have a large impact on a department and healthcare organization.

Coordinators

As interdepartmental coordination becomes more important, new coordinating and facilitating roles may be established. Coordinators play an important role in quality management, employee safety, risk management, customer service, staff training, and cost containment.

Improved Interdepartmental Coordination

To achieve improved interdepartmental coordination, and with it improvements in communication

and cooperation, keep in mind the following points:

- Make all service requests clear and direct. Whenever possible, make the requests directly to the person or persons who provide the service.
- Anticipate negative responses to requests and problems, and be ready to respond positively.
- When a request is initially made, secure agreement on the date or time by which the necessary action will be taken.
- Always follow up a verbal request with the same in written form; a verbal request can be forgotten or ignored, but any request is less likely to fall by the wayside if documented.
- Listen to the problems of employees and do your best to empathize.
- Seek collaborative (win–win) solutions whenever possible, but be prepared to compromise when necessary.
- Treat others as partners or collaborators; let them know this is "ours" rather than "mine."
- Always place teamwork above competition.
- Be patient and reasonable, never demanding or critical.
- Avoid becoming upset and avoid upsetting the other person; anger only hinders the cooperative process.
- Eliminate all kidding and sarcasm from your repertoire. You never know when innocent kidding could be taken to heart. Also, sarcasm is never found among the legitimate tools of communication.
- Always strive to know your staff and your colleagues better and to improve your understanding of their work.
- Always express sincere appreciation for the efforts of others. Honest appreciation of work well done is one of the surest ways of ensuring that future work is well done.

Controlling

The simplest and perhaps the most appropriate definition of controlling is follow-up and correction. Controlling is an essential activity because the environment in which all supervisors work is in a constant state of change. What applies today may well not be valid tomorrow; the conditions that prevail when a project is started or a decision is made do not necessarily remain static. For an undertaking that is planned to extend over several weeks, for example, we can rest assured that a number of changes potentially having some effect on the project's outcome will occur and that some of these, if not addressed, could conceivably derail the undertaking.

We must keep in mind that planning is by its very nature an uncertain process. Whether a chief executive officer planning on what the organization will be doing 5 years from now or a first-line supervisor planning what to do tomorrow morning, planning remains a person's best estimate of what the future will hold. Because we never know the future for sure until it becomes the present, we can never know for certain whether our plans will be realized exactly as planned. Thus controlling and monitoring what occurs as a plan unfolds or monitoring the implementation of a decision and making new decisions or adjustments as needed is always necessary for remaining on track toward the desired results.

Follow-up on implementation has traditionally been the weakest part of the decision-making process, and it is likely also the weakest part of the implementation of any plan. Lack of follow-up is often the primary reason for errors large or small occurring during implementation of any decision. Because the environment is in a constant state of change, it is usually necessary to make adjustments to any decision or plan to ensure success.

It will seem at times—and rightly so—that the supervisor works much of the time in a continuing cycle of deciding, coordinating, and controlling. These actions constitute the essence of getting things done.

Just Four?

The preceding paragraphs introduced and discussed four processes identified as "basic management functions." You need not look far in management literature to discover lists of five, six, or even seven "basic" management functions. Why the differences?

The differences in how supposed basic management activities are identified are essentially artificial, mere conveniences to assist our recognition and understanding of the things that managers do. Thus, we find the often-cited breakdown "planning, organizing, *directing*, coordinating, and controlling" and the sometimes cited "planning, organizing, *leading*, coordinating, and controlling." Some approaches include *staffing* as a separately designated function, while some breakdowns—including the one presented in this chapter—include *staffing* activities as part of organizing. As to the absence of *directing* or *leading* in the present breakdown, it is suggested that directing and leading are largely overlapping terms that can either or both refer to the application of all of the other basic management activities; that is, one cannot plan, organize, coordinate, or control without directing or leading. Thus, directing or leading is essentially by definition part of everything a manager does.

Reviewing Joan's Busy Day

A number of observations can be made about Joan's hectic day as far as the basic management functions are concerned.

In preparing for bringing new beds into service, Joan was actively involved in both planning and organizing, in determining what needed to be done for the expansion, and in establishing projected staff levels. Her master-staffing-plan activity was primarily organizing, but this role included planning in that she determined how staff shortages might be compensated for with a float pool.

When Joan pulls from her float pool and locates additional nurses with emergency department experience, she is engaged in both controlling—literally, follow-up and correction—and coordinating. By not personally stepping into the vacancy created by the absence of the large unit's head nurse, she avoided a working trap of sorts and kept herself available for continued coordinating and controlling, which were highly likely to be necessary given the day's circumstances.

More controlling occurred in placing the young staff nurse in the acting head nurse role. And controlling was again in the forefront when Joan implemented the emergency staffing alternative she had planned for earlier. Joan also engaged in a form of controlling and also in providing input for future planning when she suggested strengthening the hospital's disaster plan. What was learned from one disaster situation could then enhance the hospital's ability to better cope with future disasters.

Controlling—follow-up and correction—ordinarily leads to more planning and sometimes to more organizing and coordinating. This illustrates the frequently cyclical nature of the management functions; it also suggests that usually two or more basic functions are experienced together. Only sometimes, as in long-range strategic planning, for example, do any of the basic management functions occur in isolation from the others.

WRAP-UP

Think About It

Conditions change, circumstances change, the environment is forever in a state of flux, so oftentimes plans are themselves not particularly useful. However, the planning *process* is invaluable. And since plans are rarely realized exactly as planned, to a considerable extent the typical supervisory job is a nearly constant exercise in coordinating and controlling.

Questions for Review and Discussion

1. If we believe that planning is so important, why, knowing this, do we so often rush directly into doing without pausing to plan?
2. What do we stand to gain from applying planning principles to supposedly routine activities?
3. What are two significant reasons why a particular objective or target may not be attained as planned?
4. What are the principal characteristics of planning that apparently cause many to bypass it altogether?
5. What kinds of plans are of most concern to the working supervisor? Why?
6. What are the primary differences between mission and vision?
7. What are the three essential components of an appropriate objective?
8. Describe fully the relationship between planning and organizing.
9. As a supervisor, what would be your response when seriously incorrect information reaches you by way of the grapevine?
10. How would you handle a situation in which the supervisor of another department approaches you with a strong complaint about one of your employees?

Essay Question: Authority and Responsibility

In essay form, describe in detail the appropriate relationship between authority and responsibility in assigning and delegating. Concerning authority and responsibility, explain why only one of these can actually be fully assigned or delegated.

Case: And Here We Go Once More

The position of business manager at Smalltown Hospital has been a hot seat, with incumbents changing frequently. When the position was vacated last May, the four senior employees in the department were interviewed. All were told that because they were at the top of grade and the compensation structure for new supervisors had not yet caught up with that of other positions; the position would involve just a miniscule increase in pay, an increment one could readily consider insultingly small. All four refused the position, and all were given the impression that they were not really considered qualified just yet but that they might be considered for supervision again at a later date.

That same month a new business manager was hired from the outside, and the four senior employees were instructed to show their new boss in detail how things worked in the department. Over the following several months, the business manager's boss, the finance director, told all four senior employees that they had "come along very well" and would be considered for the manager's position should it again become vacant.

In October of that same year the new manager resigned. However, none of the four senior employees got the job; the process was repeated, and again a new manager was hired from outside.

Instructions

1. Viewing the department and its needs from the perspective of the finance director, describe a better plan for hiring a business manager.
2. Also, summarize what you believe to be the inappropriate consequences of the finance director's failure to plan.

Case: Looking for the Limits of Authority

When you accepted the position as supervisor of a housekeeping team, your manager, June Arnold, the assistant director of building services, told you that you would not find a great deal of decision-making guidance written out in policy and procedure form. As June put it, "Common sense is the overriding policy." However, June cautioned you about the need to see her concerning matters involving employee discipline because the organization was presently sensitive to union organizing overtures in the service areas.

Early in your third week on the job there was an occurrence that seemed to call for routine disciplinary action. Remembering June's precaution, you tried to see her several times over a period of 3 days. Being unable to get to her and getting no response to the messages you left, you went ahead and took action rather than risk credibility through procrastination. When you were finally able to see June and explain what you had done, she said, "No big deal. Common sense, like I said."

Some weeks later a similar situation arose. Again you could not get to June, and again you took what you believed to be appropriate action, but this time the problem involved an employee you later learned was a strong informal leader within a contingent of generally dissatisfied employees. The disciplinary action blew up in your face and provided the active union organizers with an issue they immediately inflated for their purposes. June was furious with you. She accused you of intentionally overstepping your authority by failing to bring such problems to her attention as instructed.

Instructions

1. Explain how you would go about trying to establish the true limits of your decision-making authority.
2. Because the limits of your authority are ultimately those limits set by your manager, develop a possible approach to getting June to help you define the limits of your authority.

References

1. Fisher K. *Leading Self-directed Work Teams: A Guide to Developing New Team Leadership*. McGraw-Hill; 1993:136.
2. Mulumba M, London L, Nantaba J, Ngwena C. Using health committees to promote community participation as a social determinant of the right to health: lessons from Uganda and South Africa. *Health Hum Rights*. 2018 Dec;20(2):11–17. PMID: 30568398; PMCID: PMC6293345.

CHAPTER 4

Reengineering, Mergers, and the Supervisor

CHAPTER OBJECTIVES

- Define reengineering and identify the classic errors that have frequently undermined potential reengineering benefits.
- Define the impact of the present-day trend toward organizational mergers and affiliations on organizational structuring and address the important implications of this trend for the role of the supervisor.

KEY TERMS

Reengineering: The redesign of processes and the systems, policies, or structures that support them.

Merger: As used throughout this chapter, merger is intended to mean combination of two or more corporate entities into one new corporation; the original corporations cease to exist, replaced in their entirety by the new corporation.

Affiliation: A term covering a broad range of possible arrangements from a legal merger to a contractual arrangement between organizations to a simple formal agreement to provide or share some specific service. All forms of affiliation are agreements to engage in some activity together.

Outsourcing: The practice of going to outside suppliers for services formerly performed inside or for services for which the organization lacks the capacity to provide economically.

Organizational Flattening: The effect on an organization's structure when layers of management, most particularly those referred to as "middle management," are eliminated, reducing the number of levels of management.

Reengineering

What It Is, What It Is Not

Reengineering is a potentially powerful approach to improving operations. Elapatha and Jehan[1] defined business process re-engineering (BPR), also simply known as reengineering, "the fundamental rethinking and radical redesign of business process to achieve dramatic improvements in critical, contemporary measures on performance." It means, quite literally, to engineer again, to go back to square one and start over as though there was nothing already in place. The ultimate goal may be increased productivity, reduced costs, improved quality, enhanced competitiveness, improved profitability, greater customer satisfaction, or some combination of these. Sometimes the ultimate goal, simply described but dramatically critical, is organizational survival.

Reengineering done properly ordinarily involves the entire organization. This is so because few if any departments, especially departments of a healthcare organization, operate in such isolation as to be self-contained. That is, virtually all departments and activities receive inputs from and send outputs to other departments and changing the manner in which a department's outputs are structured affects the ways in which other departments do their work. Most departments are effectively open systems; that is, inputs and outputs freely cross system boundaries. It is of course possible to apply reengineering processes within a single department, but if that department is an open system, the effort may improve the internal workings of the reengineered department, but it is also likely to create problems elsewhere in the organization. The ideal limits of a reengineering effort are those of a closed or semi-closed system, a system for which the only inputs and outputs crossing its boundaries are the clients who enter and the clients who leave. Within the system is a network of sometimes complex interrelationships among departments and services, and that which is done within one is likely to affect what is done in others.

Reengineering includes abandoning obsolete systems, involving departments in cross-functional teams, amalgamating jobs, discarding old rules and assumptions, introducing new technologies, and creating new principles for task organization. Reengineering invariably proves to be far more difficult than it first appears; many people find it extremely difficult to take their thinking back to square one and begin anew without being unduly influenced by the manner in which activities are pursued at present.

Reengineering as a term achieved buzzword status roughly three decades ago, and it is still used lightly—and incorrectly—to describe routine methods improvement: chart and study an activity, identify wasted time and effort, and create a more streamlined process. Concentration on present methods with a view to making them more efficient is not reengineering; it is methods improvement (or work simplification, to name an even earlier iteration). The critical focus of any reengineering activity is not on the existing process but solely on *the desired result*. The essential question is this: Starting from zero, what do I have to do to best achieve this result?

Reengineering is not the same as any of the other processes thought to be synonymous with reengineering: downsizing, rightsizing, reorganizing, restructuring, and so on. The use of these terms and others interchangeably is unfortunate because to an organization's employees all these terms have come to mean *some of us are going to lose our jobs*.

It is a fact that layoffs often occur as a result of reengineering; when reengineering fosters operating efficiencies, it is often the case that fewer employees are required to perform the same amount of work. So, reengineering can indeed lead to downsizing, although downsizing is not the primary purpose of reengineering. Reengineering can also lead to centralization or decentralization of activities, structural changes in the organization, the formation of strategic alliances, and merger or other affiliation.

Reengineering and Leadership

Successful reengineering requires a leadership style that relies heavily on participative management, delegation, employee empowerment, and the use of self-directed teams. It also requires a great deal of sensitive employee relations; as noted, to a great many employees in today's healthcare organizations the mere mention of "reengineering" is suspect because it conjures up visions of layoffs. And employees who fear for their jobs are surely not best positioned to provide the enthusiastic participation that is so important in a reengineering effort. To be successful in a reengineering effort, management must tap the expertise of the rank-and-file employees, recognizing that few understand a desired result better than the person who pursues it every day.

Fully committed top management is absolutely essential for successful reengineering. Many a loudly heralded reengineering effort has suffered the same fate as numerous total quality management (TQM) undertakings when top management, having begun with visible and apparently enthusiastic commitment, backed away and relegated leadership to a lower level of management after the first few weeks.

Interdepartmental Collaboration

How well departments work together is fully as important as the performance of individual departments. This is regularly illustrated in the treatment of patients in the emergency department. In this critical unit, collaboration of physicians and nurses with the laboratory, blood bank, respiratory therapy, radiology, and electrocardiographic services is essential. And it falls to the individual supervisor or manager to avoid territorialism, the tendency to protect one's own turf, and enter into collaborative efforts for the good of the total system.

Successful reengineering eliminates much monitoring, checking, waiting, tracking, and other unproductive work, leaving more time for doing productive work. In one hospital, a cross-functional team cut patient admission waiting time by 17%. Another team at that facility reduced the paperwork process of hiring from an average of 9.5 days to 4.5 days.[2]

Many healthcare processes are complex and nonlinear and cannot be simplified into strings of quick sequential tasks. The desired result often requires a high degree of collaboration among individuals and functions. Processes are often more efficient if they consist of multiple operational channels. For example, a large emergency department may be more efficient if one section cares for major trauma cases, another handles minor injuries, and a third treats nonsurgical patients.

Signs of the Need for Reengineering

A current process may appear dysfunctional in that parts of it just do not seem to be working as they should. There may be chronic problems, frequent breakdowns, excessive losses of time or money (for example, too much waiting in the admissions office, slow turnaround time for laboratory or radiology work), difficulties obtaining physician discharge notes, excessive inventory, or a breakdown in quality.

Another factor in identifying weaknesses that suggest the need for reengineering is the importance of any given process, such as an assessment of how seriously customer service, employee morale, or profitability is affected. Feasibility also enters into the equation. It is necessary to ask whether we have the wherewithal—the time, the skills, the material resources—to accomplish significant change. Is the desired change cost-effective?

Hospital processes that will receive increasing attention are those that cut across departmental lines. Interdepartmental systems involve multiple compartmentalized functions, many different employees, and diverse priorities. Because of their complexity and the need for cooperation, these systems are the most difficult to modify, but they promise the greatest dividends in terms of time and money saved. Such processes may be as complicated as the handling of a trauma patient from the time of admission to the time of discharge, or it may be as simple as getting a blood transfusion for an outpatient.

Getting Ready

Rather than jumping directly into a reengineering effort, it is always helpful to see how other organizations have addressed the kinds of services and improvements that your organization will be dealing with. Visits to facilities that have reputations for outstanding service can prove valuable in that you can learn how others have approached desired results similar to yours. Also, this learning process can help you avoid certain obstacles others have encountered and avoid making critical errors other might have made.

Consultants and Reengineering

Consultants of various kinds are overused or misused in many organizations, but reengineering is one broad area of need in which external consultants can often be used to considerable effect. The operative word is "external"; consultants can be useful in reengineering precisely because they are outsiders. The outsider's perspective is likely to be broader than that of the insider, and the consultant can be more open to input because the person from outside does not have the emotional or intellectual stake in present processes that the insider is likely to have. The external perspective can often clearly identify that to which the internal perspective is blind, and—of extreme importance—the outsider is usually more capable of focusing on desired results without being distracted by present methods.

Another important reason for the outsider's involvement in reengineering is found in a reasonably unbiased view of organizational changes that may appear to be needed. Employees guiding a reengineering effort can hardly be expected to recommend themselves out of their jobs should such drastic changes be indicated. The insider whose position or territory might be affected is ill-prepared to participate constructively in reengineering.

Classic Reengineering Errors

One classic reengineering error that has already been alluded to is attempting to apply reengineering within a specific department or organizational unit or attempting to reengineer, as more than one organization has tried, a single department as a "model" or pursue an inappropriate decision to reengineer "one department at a time." Rarely is any single unit or department responsible for a whole process; reengineering must address an entire process, and in fact, identifying the organization's primary business processes is a critical part of reengineering.

Another classic error is inaction, proclaiming a reengineering effort without actually doing it. If there is no more than a token bit of methods improvement activity and top management has done little more than talk, no true reengineering will occur, and employees will come to see "reengineering" in a negative light.

An additional common mistake is being overly conservative, even timid, in redesigning systems. Successful reengineering requires imaginative, even daring, thinking. Breakthrough ideas do not come about when caution and conservatism rule the process. Reengineering requires radical approaches to process redesign; employees must be encouraged to reach for lofty goals, and leadership must be open to considering any new idea no matter how far out it may seem initially.

Another commonly encountered error is allowing the reengineering effort to drag on for too long. Successful reengineering requires a great deal of work in a relatively short time; if the effort limps along for a year or longer, it will grind to a halt on its own. If months pass with nothing substantial to show for the activity, top management may lose faith and begin diverting resources to other competing needs.

It is also a mistake to restrict the scope of the reengineering effort by declaring some departments or functions off limits. Most process changes ripple through the organization, and it is not possible to do justice to reengineering's improved processes by deliberately shying away from making certain organizational changes.

Finally, and saving the potentially biggest mistake for last, a classic error is to underestimate the needs and concerns of employees. The people who are expected to cooperate with the reengineering effort, essentially everyone whether rank-and-file, first-line supervisor, or middle-manager, will understandably feel threatened by what is seen as possibly significant change that can affect them and their future. Reengineering may have to be sold to them every step of the way; the improved process must offer some benefit to most people who are expected to embrace enormous change. The classic reengineering errors are summarized in **Exhibit 4.1**.

Mergers and Affiliations

Continuing Change

Reengineering and other changes affecting the manner in which the healthcare industry is organized for the delivery of care are driving changes in the role of the healthcare supervisor. Not many people are especially eager to make what are sometimes dramatic changes in the way they do their work, but usually the circumstances inducing change lie well beyond the control of the individual.

The more management structures and organizational patterns change, however, the more the supervisor's essential task of *getting things done through people* stands out unchanged. But *how* the supervisor's essential task is approached is changing at a sometimes bewildering pace, and a considerable amount of change in the fulfillment of the supervisor's role is being forced by changes in the healthcare organizational environment. A great deal of the environmental change has been driven by the movement to managed care as organizations have reacted to the pressure to deliver care more economically. Much of the change that has affected the day-to-day fulfillment of the healthcare supervisor's role has come about as healthcare organizations have combined and grown through merger and acquisition.

With but a few notable exceptions, a few decades ago the healthcare "system" was an informal network of providers who were loosely related by a common purpose. The acute care hospital was perceived by most as the center of the system, the focal point for the concentration of the more complex activities involved in preserving life and restoring health. Today, however, if one can even say at all that the healthcare system has a center, we could identify that center as the primary care physician.

It is well known that over the years, pressure has steadily mounted to contain healthcare costs. Much of this cost-containment pressure has been aimed at improving the access to care while increasing the quality of service.[3]

In most instances the first step on the road to the creation of merged organizations was the sharing of services. Initially, administrative services were the most frequently shared, led by purchasing, electronic data processing, education and training, laundry, insurance programs, credit and collections, and management engineering. The most commonly shared clinical services included blood banking, laboratory services, and diagnostic radiology. Sharing continued to expand, with the rate of growth for sharing administrative services exceeding that of clinical services.[4]

Overall, the general progression was from shared services to groups engaged in various cooperative ventures, then in some instances to management contracts and eventually leases that entailed full management without ownership, then to decentralized ownership as represented by hospital "chains," and ultimately centralized ownership as represented by merger or acquisition.

Hospitals existed for years as autonomous, free-standing entities that were in control of their own destinies. Many hospitals entered into mergers with others or joined healthcare systems, while at the same time there remained a tendency for hospitals that were stable financially and in terms of market served to remain separate and independent. Now some of these stable institutions are becoming the nuclei of healthcare systems as they gather in smaller providers. However, healthcare cost reform is making inroads into institutions' and systems' financial stability and forcing "reform" in the ongoing delivery of care. The resulting financial problems have driven some previously independent institutions to seek some form of affiliation and forced healthcare systems to increase in size, often in search of improved operating efficiency. The growth and development of multi-institutional arrangements represents an attempt, through organizational integration and consolidation, to restructure the industry from within to effectively meet the challenges being faced.[5] In addition to combining or affiliating to form larger organizations, healthcare organizations are seeking more flexibility in work arrangements by substituting contracted services and employee leasing for permanent employees. Also, outsourcing, the practice of going to outside suppliers for services formerly performed inside, has been increasing steadily, primarily as a means of saving money.

Obvious advantages are to be gained through merger or affiliation. One of the first to be accessed is increased buying power whether for physical products, services, or employee benefits such as insurance. Another advantage lies in the creation of a single board of directors and management structure where multiples previously existed. Still another plus of combining organizations is the elimination of the duplication of resources and functions.

In some instances, hospital mergers have been resisted for years on issues of community pride. Often, logic and common sense has dictated that two communities could best respond to the pressures mounting on the hospital system by combining their resources into a merged entity more efficient than either alone. However, their competitive postures regarding each other, a condition not uncommon between hospitals in the same town or in adjoining communities, have precluded agreement to come together as one or both refuses to surrender any part of their individual identity. Some organizations that should logically have been merged with others have held out for so long that they failed financially or were forced to close for other reasons. Occasionally, some boards of directors have resisted merger for so long that, when they finally agreed to do so, there was hardly anything remaining that was worth acquiring.

Most transactions such as those just described may legally be mergers, but they will likely be seen as acquisitions by some managers and employees. Usually, the larger organization is perceived as acquiring—even swallowing up—the smaller. However, people in the smaller organization may conscientiously refer to the process as a merger and vocally reject the notion of being absorbed by the larger organization, often doing so out of fear of the impending loss of their individual organizational identity.

Essentially, all benefits sought through various organizational combinations are financial. Some are clearly economic, such as the scale economies of a larger organization and perhaps the increased borrowing power of a larger corporation. Some relate to staffing issues or the sharing of services, ultimately affecting direct costs. Other benefits, like access to larger markets, increased referral base, and expanded political clout, all have at their core financial reasons driving them.

Dark Times Ahead?

Most of the time reduced staffing is one of the results of a merger. Also, even if reduced staff is not a merger goal some amount of reduction ordinarily results from the establishment of scale economies. Therefore, it should come as no surprise that talk of a potential merger immediately gives rise to fears of potential job loss, and the closer to actuality the merger progresses, the more intense this fear becomes.

Because an overwhelming number of mergers do indeed result in layoffs of both managers and non-managerial staff, many employees have good reason to feel uneasy when a merger is in the offing. To many employees at most organizational levels, an impending merger appears as doom on the horizon—even if the merger does not do away with their positions, at the very least it will change, perhaps drastically, the way they perform their jobs. But few organizations can realistically offer a no-layoff guarantee in advance of a merger, nor will any realistically oriented top managements attempt to do so.

Cultural Effects

Economic factors loom large in considering merger or affiliation, but often the issues of whether organizational cultures mesh or not are overlooked. Financial and operational issues are usually prominent in considering merger or affiliation, but similar to the manner in which reengineering is sometimes approached, often there is insufficient consideration of people issues. Decision-makers are ordinarily using so-called hard data in assessing the worth of a merger situation, and whether consciously or unconsciously, they do not want to risk clouding the situation with people issues that are invariably seen as "soft" and are thus arguable.

Corporate culture issues must be examined in advance of a merger or affiliation because they can sometimes indicate whether a particular deal will or will not work. However, most mergers are usually undertaken with little or no consideration of cultures. It then becomes necessary to attempt to structure a hybrid culture incorporating the elements of the cultures of both parties even though most employees invariably perceive one culture or the other as dominant. It is more frequently suggested that healthcare collectives are so focused on increased size that they are no longer attuned to people concerns.

Cultural change is always difficult, usually painful, and invariably much more involved and time-consuming than anyone expects. After a merger it is necessary to create a blended culture and doing so requires plenty of time. Even when one organization is so small as to be perceived as totally absorbed by the other, it nevertheless takes time for the remnants of the old culture of the smaller organization to assimilate. Different approaches can be used to blend the culture immediately after the merger, which then leads for a more successful transition. A supervisor can do a few things to help ease the process:

1. Plan ahead. Have conversations with other supervisors and managers before the merger is complete to determine what is the best way to blend cultures.
2. Consider hiring professionals who have experience in integrating cultures.
3. Involve the employees. Create teams from both organizations. This will give them ownership of their ideas and solutions as well as bring them together as one unit.
4. Be transparent and communicate openly about the process. Retain the best practices, policies, and procedures while engaging employees about the decisions being made.
5. Make the most of your time together with both parties. Seminars, meetings, group functions—it is important to keep everyone talking about the blended culture.
6. Give it some time. Just like the merger took time, blending the cultures will take time. Continue to communicate and monitor progress throughout the process.

Effects on the Supervisor's Role

When a merger or affiliation is happening, in spite of how well executive management and the corporate directors believe communication is occurring, at the non-managerial staff level most people will feel largely in the dark. Because people feel left out, a significant proportion of them will automatically resist the changes that are occurring. And it is true in many supposedly stable organizations, and especially true in organizations undergoing merger, that the people in upper management have very little understanding of what is actually on the minds of the workers at the bottom of the organizational structure.

Most people feel the need to be in control of their circumstances or to at least feel as though they have some measure of control, but employees become aware—often painfully so—that a corporate merger is totally beyond their control. So people resist that which they fear and that which they cannot control, often with all the determination they can command. It may well be that resistance is no more or no less than people's need to protect themselves from harm. And human resistance can be an extremely potent force. In the past 10 years, the number of hospitals has declined but the number of health systems has increased.[5]

Mergers and affiliations usually result in lay-offs, and layoffs can affect supervisors and managers as well as rank-and-file staff. In many merger situations, management salaries are a source of considerable savings due to the elimination of duplicate management. Consider, for example, the merger of Hospital A with Hospital B. Both were small acute care facilities serving a semi-rural population. After the merger took place, where once there were two human resource managers, there was one, and where once there were two physical therapy managers, there was one. Two of each of several other department managers became one. Within a few weeks, nearly half of the two hospitals' combined management was eliminated, leaving the surviving managers with responsibility for larger departments split between two locations. The few related costs that had to be reckoned with as additions, primarily travel between facilities and a few other considerations, were inconsequential compared with the cost of the duplicate management positions that were eliminated.

Except at the highest organizational levels, an individual in management is both a worker and a supervisor of other workers, so the first-line supervisor is both management generalist and functional specialist. However, when a supervisor's territory is expanded, the supervisor will find it necessary to become *more* manager and *less* worker. Under these circumstances something has to give.

Among the first things to give are some concepts upon which many of today's managers were educated, specifically *unity of command, span of control*, and *visibility and availability*.

The previously inviolate concept of *unity of command* has given way in many instances to split-reporting relationships. Such relationships, in which one person reports to two or more superiors, are now common in merged organizations and multi-facility systems. *Span of control*, referring to the breadth of responsibility and the number of employees that a supervisor can effectively handle, is continually tested as supervisors find themselves with dramatically expanded "territory" over which they must exercise control.

Consider a situation in which unity of command no longer exists because of a split-reporting arrangement: You are the surviving business office supervisor following a merger, so you move between two facilities. In each facility you report to a finance manager, so you have two bosses. One day while you are at Facility A, Boss A directs you to cover an important outside meeting for the remainder of the day, but Boss B calls from Facility B and gives you an assignment that will require several hours' work and must be on his desk first thing the next morning. What do you do?

If your two bosses are reasonable people and you can talk with both and get them to speak with each other, there may be no problem because one will give and you will not have to choose. If you cannot readily talk with them, for example if one or both are authoritarian or intimidating, then you might cover the meeting for A and work all evening to complete the assignment for B.

The point to make about such split-reporting arrangements: They work smoothly only if all parties are in constant communication with each other, if neither manager insists on always being the first served, and if the employee works conscientiously to serve each equally and avoids all temptation to play off one boss against the other.

It has long been considered important for the supervisor of a group to maintain a significant level of *visibility and availability*. To a considerable extent, many employees take some level of comfort from the supervisor's regular presence; that person is seen as reachable when needed and usable as a resource. For many supervisors, visibility and availability presented no problems when supervising and working with a specific group in a single location. After merger and reorganization, however, the supervisor may be forced by expanded responsibilities to be less visible on a regular basis and thus less available to the staff.

Another common feature of reorganizing as it occurs in today's environment, whether happening via merger or affiliation or within the context of "reengineering," is *flattening* of the management structure. Flattening refers to the effects on an organization chart when layers of management, most particularly those referred to as "middle management," are eliminated. On occasion when flattening accompanies the reorganizing that is part of the fallout of a merger, there is some vertical integration of responsibilities as well as the horizontal integration of duties that happens when two comparable management positions become one. This creates additional pressure for the person in the supervisory position to become more of a manager and thus less of a worker.

Overall, the increased scope of the supervisor in the merger situation brings a number of changes in how the supervisor functions. This expanded scope necessitates the following:

- More time spent managing and thus less time spent doing non-managerial work
- More planning and organizing on an ongoing basis
- Greatly increased need to practice proper delegation
- Increased attention to the priorities among a greater number of responsibilities
- Improvements in one's ability to use time effectively
- Constant attention to personal organizing for effectiveness
- More people to oversee and all that goes with this (meaning more performance appraisals, more disciplinary actions, more people problems in general)

The Supervisor Adapts

The easier parts of organizational change usually involve processes, methods, procedures, tools, structures, and such. The more difficult parts of change involve human reactions: attitude, commitment, or lack thereof, and resistance.

It is relatively easy for the supervisor in the merger situation to become spread too thin, to be forced into trying to do too many things at once. When this occurs, it is frequently the supervisor's newly expanded staff that suffers for lack of attention. It is necessary to remember that for a significant proportion of the staff, specifically those people who used to report to the other supervisor, *you* may be one of the most significant causes of resistance: You are the unknown quantity. A change in department leadership is virtually guaranteed to be accompanied by uneasiness that shows up as resistance, especially if the incoming supervisor is a stranger to the surviving staff.

As one's staff increases so do the potential people problems increase and so do the number of staff-related duties increase. With more people to supervise comes the need to establish and maintain the all-important one-to-one relationship with more employees. This relationship with each employee is a critical aspect of maintaining employees as effective producers, yet the supervisor in the merger situation is likely to be affected by an increase in non-people concerns as well. In short, in this new situation the supervisor will likely have more people to be concerned with and less time to devote to people concerns.

From an individual supervisor's perspective, three major enemies of productivity are personal disorganization, inadequate planning, and procrastination. Productivity depends on attention to *priorities*; no matter how much work there is to do, at any given time one can do no better than focusing on the single most important task in the pile. Because the job will appear as an endless series of demands, one can only ensure that the demands left unaddressed are of lowest priority.

In many instances the supervisor of a merged function will be split between two staffs in two locations. This alone makes proper delegation absolutely essential. With more and more to do, it becomes increasingly obvious that the supervisor cannot do everything, so it is necessary to take the time to educate and properly delegate and get the most effective performance from those employees who are capable of expanding their scope. Employee development takes on new importance and may include the development of some capability for backing up the supervisor at each site.

Also, moving between sites makes travel part of some of the supervisor's days. With time consumed in travel, the supervisor may feel the pressure to either become more efficient or to compensate by allowing the workday to lengthen. Also, the supervisor who moves between sites should expect to experience a few occasions when the item or document needed at the moment is at the other location.

More than ever, the supervisor in the merger situation needs to be proactive and exercise control of the job each and every day. The supervisor who assumes a reactive posture in these expanded circumstances quickly becomes spread out and used up. In other words, in the merged organization it is necessary for the manager to get organized and stay that way.

When the Dust Settles

It was stated earlier that mergers are driven largely by financial issues and other "hard" data and that all too often the human issues—the "soft" side of the merger—are overlooked or afforded too little attention. Too often the focus on organizational growth is accompanied by the failure to encourage the development of the needed culture of operational excellence. There is, however, a strong need for a culture of continuous quality improvement. Without such, as organizations grow and their activities expand, quality problems also expand as a function of size.

Too often a great many of the problems and issues to be faced in making one organization out of two or more are rarely evident to the executives and trustees who decide to merge. Because the executives and trustees operate at a macro level, their view is ordinarily one of being outside looking in, but to the first-line supervisors, middle managers, and rank-and-file employees who must do the organization's work, the view is entirely different. Those inside see what the external decision-makers do not see.

Consider again the merger of Hospital A with Hospital B, two small acute care facilities just a few miles apart, both providing the same services to the people in overlapping service areas. Several physicians were on staff at both, and a few employees of A worked part-time or per diem at B and vice versa. Externally, it looked like a simple merger of two similar organizations. Internally, however, there appeared to be vast differences of two kinds. First were the differences encountered in the *details of task performance*, necessitating the application of extensive, unanticipated effort in merging methods, procedures, policies, practices, and such. This entailed resolving many conflicts based on "our way" versus "their way." Then there were the *cultural differences*. Hospital B, the larger of the two, had experienced several years of severe financial difficulty and had undergone three significant staff reductions in 4 years. The culture of B reflected pessimism, insecurity, and defeat. Hospital A, the smaller, had been fiscally sound right up to the point of the merger and had never experienced a staff reduction in its history. The culture of A, having long reflected optimism, suddenly gave rise to resentment at being "absorbed" by the larger or being "used to save B from bankruptcy." There was considerable clash of attitudes when the staffs were merged.

In the last analysis, whether it is the merger of two small provider organizations into one or the creation of a major healthcare system from a dozen formerly separate organizations, human values must rank high among the governing concerns. If human values are not prominent in forging the merged organization or system, it follows that these values are not likely to be prominent in either the regard for employees or the delivery of service. It remains for the supervisor who is caught up in a merger situation to be ever mindful of human values in the provision of service to people (patients) through people (employees).

WRAP-UP

Think About It

An impending reengineering effort or merger of two or more organizations invariably causes unrest and uncertainty among a work group's employees. It is up to the supervisor, who may privately share the employees' concerns, to put an optimistic face forward, emphasize whatever positives there may be, and provide the leadership needed to navigate difficult times.

Questions for Review and Discussion

1. Explain how you would respond to an employee who says to you, "Don't hand me this reengineering stuff. That's just a fancy way of saying you're going to cut staff."

2. What is vertical integration of responsibilities? Horizontal integration of responsibilities?

3. Why is the prospect of a major reengineering effort or a merger of organizations stressful to non-management employees and supervisors alike?

4. Organizations undergoing significant reengineering efforts often engage the services of an outside consultant. Why do you believe this is done?

5. Why should a supervisor make regular use of reasonable deadlines for employee assignments, and why is follow-up on such deadlines crucial?

6. When two departments are combined under a single supervisor, how does the supervisor adapt to this change without automatically working significantly longer hours?

7. Why is reengineering often more difficult than expected? Explain, using an example.

8. The environment within which an individual supervisor must work is often subject to significant change, so how can we legitimately say that the supervisor's essential task remains constant?

9. Explain what is meant by "the soft side of management" and further explain why attention to it is of extreme importance.

10. Why does a supervisor's visibility and availability remain important even at times when the staff are experiencing no problems and raising no questions?

Essay Question: What to Tell Your Staff?

You have just returned to your department after a meeting of the hospital's entire management: you and your fellow first-line supervisors, all middle managers and clinical service directors, the chief executive officer, and administrative staff. At this meeting you learned the board of directors recently voted to merge the hospital organization with the only other hospital in your county, a facility roughly twice the size of yours. You were further told that without this merger your hospital would descend into bankruptcy within 1 year. You have been directed to hold a department meeting to advise your staff of the merger.

You are well aware that a sense of rivalry, at times reflected in antagonism and dislike, has existed between your hospital and the other institution for many years. Also, because no merger agreement is concluded overnight, you are seriously wondering why events leading up to the merger had apparently been kept secret. Before convening your department meeting, you take some quiet time to think about the points to cover with staff and how to present them.

Write out the core of your announcement to your employees, including questions you can anticipate from them and how you will respond.

Case: "I Think They Hate Me"

The county's two hospitals, about 10 miles apart, were long-standing rivals with overlapping services areas. To the dismay of many employees at both facilities, these hospitals were merged into a single organization. For several years, you had been the supervisor of the business office at the smaller of the two hospitals, but after completion of the merger, you became supervisor of the combined department. Because the other facility had a larger business office, your total staff number nearly tripled. It was decided that you needed to move between locations on a daily basis, spending the morning at one place and the afternoon at the other, and that once things had "settled down," you would become involved in determining the feasibility of centralizing some of the department's function.

The business office supervisor who was displaced at the larger facility was relatively new at the job but reasonably well liked; however, you received the combined supervisory job after a series of interviews with higher management. On each of your first several afternoon visits to the other facility's business office, you were greeted with extreme resentment, rudeness, and unwilling cooperation. No one extended themselves to help you become acclimated, and questions you asked were answered roughly or not at all.

As you conveyed to a friend at your home facility, "I don't know how I can get anywhere with that bunch at the other place. They resent me like crazy. At times I even think they hate me."

Instructions

Outline the approach you believe you might follow in attempting to win over the staff of the larger business office or at least get them to constructively cooperate. At what stage, if at all, would you consider involving your immediate superior, the merged organization's finance director, who appears to be having his own problems with combined employee groups?

References

1. Elapatha VW, Jehan SN. An analysis of the implementation of business process re-engineering in public services. *Journal of Open Innovation Technology Market and Complexity.* 2020;6:114.

2. McKenzie L. Cross-functional teams in health care organizations. *Health Care Supervisor.* 1994;12(3):1–10.

3. Shrank WH, DeParle N-A, Gottlieb S, Jain SH, Orszag P, Powers BW, Wilensky GR. Health costs and financing: challenges and strategies for a new administration. *Journal of Health Affairs.* 2021;40(2). https://www.healthaffairs.org/doi/10.1377/hlthaff.2020.01560

4. D'Aunno T, Alexander JA, Laughlin C. Business as usual? Changes in health care's workforce and organization of work. *Hospital and Health Services Administration.* 1996;41(1):4.

5. Brown, TC Jr., Werling KA, Walker BC, Burgdorfer RJ, Shields JJ. Current trends in hospital mergers and acquisitions: Healthcare reform will result in more consolidation and integration among hospitals, reversing a recent trend in which hospitals tended to stay away from such transactions. *Healthcare Financial Management.* 2012;66(3):114+. https://go.gale.com/ps/i.do?id=GALE%7CA286114649&sid=googleScholar&v=2.1&it=r&linkaccess=abs&issn=07350732&p=AONE&sw=w&userGroupName=anon%7E628d37bc

CHAPTER 5

Position Descriptions and Performance Standards

CHAPTER OBJECTIVES

- Introduce the position description (also referred to as job description interchangeably in this chapter) and develop an understanding of its importance.
- Review the essential elements of the position description, identifying what must be included in this instrument and setting forth the reasons for inclusion.
- Highlight those legitimate uses of the position description of special significance to the first-line supervisor.
- Explain the effects of the Americans with Disabilities Act on present-day position descriptions.
- Define the different kinds of performance standards and review the purposes for which they are commonly used.
- Identify the characteristics of an appropriate standard.
- Provide advice applicable in formulating standards for departmental use and identify pitfalls that can hamper the establishment of readily usable standards.

KEY TERMS

Position Description (Job Description): A multi-purpose document conveying basic information about a specific position, including job title and classification, summary of duties, reporting relationships, qualifications, principal duties, and other pertinent information.

Fair Labor Standards Act (FLSA): Originally passed in 1938, the FLSA, regularly amended and updated, remains the country's principal legislation governing wages and hours and various other aspects of employment.

Exempt Employee: An employee who is exempt from the overtime requirements of the FLSA; a "salaried" employee; one who is not required to receive overtime pay under the law.

Nonexempt Employee: An employee who is not exempt from the overtime requirements of the FLSA; essentially an "hourly" employee; one who must be paid overtime as specified in the wage and hour law.

Americans with Disabilities Act (ADA): Legislation passed in 1990 for the purpose of ensuring equal employment opportunity for individuals with disabilities and strengthening some of the anti-discrimination features of the Civil Rights Act of 1964 with respect to disabled individuals.

Position Descriptions

The standards of the Joint Commission (TJC, formerly the Joint Commission on Accreditation of Healthcare Organizations, or JCAHO) include specific guidelines for creating and applying job descriptions and performance appraisals.[1] The Americans with Disabilities Act (ADA) of 1990 also focuses on these two functions, with the intent of preventing discrimination against persons having physical or mental conditions that may be considered disabilities.[2]

Job descriptions should be regarded as contracts between employers and employees. In addition to spelling out the manner in which employees are expected to perform, they establish a rational link with performance appraisals. They are versatile documents that are regularly put to a variety of uses (more concerning uses in section titled "Uses of Job Descriptions").

A position description actually defines requirements for a particular job as it was done in the past, that is, at a particular point in time. As such, it is a snapshot that is at risk of growing outdated as soon as it is committed to paper. Because job responsibilities often change rapidly, many job descriptions are out of date a significant part of the time. To avoid rapid obsolescence and to provide greater flexibility, many managers are becoming less specific about assigned tasks and are making use of more general terminology, broadly defining core tasks so that their descriptions are not rendered obsolete by alteration of a detail or two.

Far too many employees simply do not fully know what is expected of them; this is a significant cause of both unsatisfactory performance and employee discontent. Professional athletes seldom have written position descriptions, but they know precisely what they must do and how well those things must be done because this is drilled into them via repetition. Work organizations and other institutions use position descriptions and work standards to designate what must be done and how well it must be done.

Title and Classification

Job titles are important not only for the convenience of the organization in identifying and classifying jobs, but also for employee prestige and self-esteem. Sometimes a title change is accompanied by a pay raise, but even without pay increases most employees appreciate more prestigious titles. For example, many a "secretary" would rather be referred to as an "administrative assistant," someone who was known as a "housekeeper" might prefer the title of "building service worker," and even the top person in the organization is likely to prefer "chief executive officer" over "administrator." Such changes have in fact been regularly occurring in health care; the title of "administrator" is a vanishing label.

Positions are classified as salaried or hourly and as part time or full time. Salaried positions are referred to as "exempt" positions, meaning they are exempted from the overtime provisions of the Fair Labor Standards Act (FLSA, the basic federal wage and hour law). Hourly positions are "nonexempt," meaning that workers in these positions are eligible for overtime pay according to the provisions of the FLSA. The classification of a job includes designation of a job grade and wage range. The position classification may also note that an employee is permanently assigned to a particular shift or is required to rotate shifts. If the employee must occasionally work after normal hours, take weekend assignments, or be subject to recalls, those requirements should be stated up front to avoid future disagreements. Promises made orally before hiring have been known to be notoriously inaccurate.

Summary Statement

The summary statement that leads off a position description, also referred to as a position summary, umbrella statement, position purpose or goal, mission statement, or function statement, condenses the responsibilities of the position. It may include the goals, reporting channel, and other features of the job. The following is an example of such a statement:

The incumbent plans, directs, and controls the hematology section of the laboratory. The major goal of this position is to meet or exceed customer expectations. Our customers include patients, patient's families and visitors, clinicians and other care providers, third-party payers, teammates, students and trainees, and hospital departments or committees served by the department. The incumbent is also responsible for teaching students and new employees. The incumbent performs a wide range of hematological procedures. The incumbent reports to the administrative director of the laboratory.

Required Competencies

Competencies or qualifications describe the requirements of the job, not the qualifications of the person holding the job. These competencies include those that the incumbents must have and sometimes additional skills you would like them to have. For some positions, the basic qualifications can be eliminated because they are detailed in the credentialing process. For example, in the position description for a radiologist, the competency requirement may simply be that applicants must be board certified and hold a state license. This eliminates the need for a long list of tasks that radiologists perform.

In addition to educational and experience requirements, special skills may be required. For example, a medical transcriptionist is required to be familiar with medical terminology, and the position description reflects this requirement.

Temperament, traits, and personality are important, as are characteristics such as flexibility, ability to adjust to change, and willingness to learn new skills. However, these are highly subjective, so justification for including them should be provided in the descriptions of duties and responsibilities.

It is always desirable to go beyond technical or professional skills and look for people who are willing to walk the extra mile for customers. To assist in the candidate selection process, carefully describe requirements of special importance or sensitivity. Express these in behavioral terms; for example, "is discrete with patient information," "shows composure under stress," "accepts night and weekend assignments," "recognizes or anticipates needs of customers," or "uses tact in personal interactions with customers and staff." Including "soft skill" items is especially helpful when orienting and training new employees because they express in clear terms the kind of behavior expected of them.

Reporting and Coordinating Relationships

The reporting-relationships section of the job description identifies, by position title, an incumbent's immediate superior and others to whom he or she may be directly accountable. Many employees must work closely with colleagues in other sections of their departments, in other departments, and with outside agencies. Radiology and laboratory supervisors must cooperate with staff in the surgical suite, the emergency department, and critical care units. Following is an example:

The radiology supervisor must establish and maintain close working relationships with admissions, the surgical suite, the emergency department, special care units, and the quality assurance coordinator. He or she advises the technical director of the school for radiology technicians and frequently consults with the director of hospital information systems.

Scope of Authority

Delineating specific levels of authority avoids misunderstanding and embarrassment, especially when supervisors undertake disciplinary actions or incur major expenses. Three levels are recommended for each major responsibility.

Level 1, the highest designation, includes unlimited power to make decisions and to take action without consulting superiors. Level 2 authority has some limitations; for example, a supervisor may be authorized to assign overtime but must inform his or her manager of the action on the next day. At level 3, a supervisor must obtain approval before taking action. A global statement may suffice in some situations. For example, "The supervisor has the authority to discharge all the responsibilities of the job within the constraints of the law, organizational and departmental policy, and the labor contract. He or she has signing authority for up to $1,000 for instrument repair."

Degrees of Independence

Degrees of independence are important in descriptions of nonsupervisory positions. Pertinent questions concerning relative independence include the following:

- Are detailed written instructions always available or available only for new or difficult tasks? These instructions may include policy or safety manuals and specific aids' such as procedure manuals.
- Does the employee organize his or her daily work and rearrange or modify it when appropriate, or does the supervisor do this?
- Does the incumbent perform any supervisory or administrative functions? If so, to what extent?

One such classification follows:

- Level 1: No responsibility for directing others.
- Level 2: Performs same kind of work as other members of the work group but spends about 10% of time serving as trainer, instructor, or resource person.
- Level 3: Rotates as five-person team leader with five other technical employees, with minimal direction from supervisor.
- Level 4: Permanent team leader. Functions include directing, controlling, assigning, and scheduling. Reports to supervisor. No authority to discipline without approval of supervisor.

Special Demands and the Working Environment

Working conditions include physical space, temperature variations, ambient noise, and exposure to infectious agents, chemicals, radiation, and other hazards. The position description document may describe the types of safety equipment and attire that must be used.

Physical demands have assumed new significance with the passage of the ADA, and as expressed in a position description, these must be based on the current requirements of actual incumbents. Most professional and technical positions make special demands. Such demands include absolute integrity and accuracy in reporting observations, discretion with patient information, willingness to alter work schedules, and the ability to work under stress.

Responsibilities, Duties, and Tasks

Match each responsibility with a statement that describes the type of behavior or outcome that identifies successful job performance. These descriptors serve as performance criteria. Content validity is thus established because these criteria are based on observable work behavior or results rather than on traits of individuals.

Responsibilities describe activities in their broadest sense; tasks describe them in the most specific terms. An example of a responsibility is "teach radiology students." An example of a duty would be "provide instruction for 20 three-hour sessions." Examples of tasks are "prepare agenda, demonstrate method, grade students." List responsibilities in order of importance or according to the percentage of time needed for each.

The subdivision of duties requires more effort and lengthier documents. However, the effort may be worthwhile when detailed instructions are necessary, for example, for jobs filled by individuals who have limited cognitive skills or who lack previous experience.

Select the best descriptive terminology, using action verbs when possible. Consider the clarification of the duty, the self-esteem of the employee, and the effect of the terminology on the salary classification. Use language carefully. "Makes visitors feel welcome" is better than "greets people," "evaluates clinical results" is better than "checks records," and "establishes controls that prevent release of erroneous information" is better than "sets quality controls."

The following list contains verbs useful for position descriptions:

Apply (current knowledge)
Arrange (meeting room)
Calibrate (instruments)
Design (new workflow)
Determine (suitable methods)
Establish (procedures for)
Evaluate (new techniques)
Instruct (orientees)
Maintain (document systems)
Monitor (work of new employees)
Perform (tests)
Practice (ethical standards)
Process (specimens)
Promote (public relations)
Recognize (errors)
Record (complaints)
Report (violations)
Select (new employees)

Effects of the ADA on Position Descriptions

The ADA protects individuals with physical or mental disabilities that limit major life activities. Included among those protected by it are persons with AIDS, rehabilitated drug and alcohol abusers, obese persons, and those with cosmetic disfigurement. The law prohibits employers from discriminating against people who have any such limitation when hiring or firing. Generally, the law is also relevant to issues of salary, training, promotion, and other conditions of employment for individuals who are considered disabled under its provisions. This legislation has had a major impact on hiring and promotion. People who can otherwise qualify for a job now may not be disqualified because they cannot perform tasks that bear only a marginal relationship to a particular job.

The ADA forces employers to make changes in the work environment to accommodate persons with disabilities. The law specifies that "reasonable accommodations" be provided for physically or mentally challenged employees. Accommodations may be physical, such as installing ramps, repositioning workstations, widening doors, and installing grab bars in toilet stalls.

Accommodations may also involve deletion of certain nonessential tasks from position descriptions. An accommodation may entail deletion of a task performed only occasionally and assigning that task to another employee. For example, if a job calls for occasional driving of an automobile, that responsibility may be assigned to a coworker or a driver may be assigned to transport the person with the disability. Duties must therefore be designated as essential or nonessential. The essential functions of a job are those that, in the judgment of the employer, constitute business necessity. If a person cannot carry out essential responsibilities, that person is not qualified for the job. Employers are not obligated to lower qualification standards related to the essential functions of a job.

The ADA is concerned with factual determinations of essential functions, such as the percentage of time spent on the function and the consequences of not requiring the incumbent to perform the function. The physical requirements portion of the position description is critically important in terms of ADA compliance. It must delineate the actual level of physical demands. Information includes kinds and amounts of lifting, types of work surfaces, and any auxiliary devices used, such as ladders. Management must indicate whether the physical demand is occasional, frequent, or constant.

Unfortunately, the determination of whether a particular condition constitutes a valid disability under the ADA can sometimes be difficult. A significant number of conditions and circumstances have been claimed as disabilities; many of these are legally challenged and have caused the courts to decide what is or is not a disability. It is possible to compile a lengthy list of conditions that have become "disabilities" under ADA, and thus the ADA is regularly amended by what is referred to as "case law" resulting from court decisions.

Uses of Job Descriptions

When using job descriptions, it is likely what first comes to mind are interviewing prospective employees, training and orienting employees, and functions related to performance evaluation such as developing standards of performance and conducting evaluation interviews. However, job descriptions are also useful in a number of other ways:

- Preparation of recruitment advertising, to convey the essentials of a job for employment seekers
- Job evaluation, the determination of an appropriate classification and pay grade for a new or altered position
- Employee counseling, including criticism or disciplinary action related to task performance
- Determination of a job's legal status; that is, whether the job is to be considered exempt or nonexempt
- Evaluating a position's compliance with legal, regulatory, contractual, and accrediting requirements
- Providing a record of a job's content as of a certain date
- Determination of whether a given position should or should not be included under a collective bargaining agreement (union contract)
- Providing information pertinent to the evaluation of workers' compensation claims
- Providing information pertinent to the resolution of employment-related complaints such as human rights complaints, complaints from the Equal Employment Opportunity Commission, and other charges of disparate or discriminatory treatment

Performance Standards

As far as the work itself is concerned, a basic job description states only the required tasks and responsibilities and the qualifications needed to perform them. In addition, performance standards are required. Performance standards have

two cardinal purposes: first, to inform employees how well they must do their work and often how much they must do and, second, to simplify performance evaluations, especially if a pay-for-performance strategy is in place. Without performance standards, employee evaluations are necessarily highly subjective and can lead to charges of discrimination or favoritism.

All employees like to know the following about themselves and their work, even if they do not articulate these as specific requests:

- "Exactly what is it that you want me to do?"
- "How well and how fast must I perform these tasks?"
- "Show me how to do what I'm presently unable to do."
- "Let me know how I'm doing."

Position descriptions and performance standards directly address the first two of these queries and lay the foundation for responding to the others.

Uses of Performance Standards

Performance standards are used for a variety of purposes:

- Providing guidelines for orienting and training new employees
- Enabling employees to assess their own performance
- Providing a solid basis for performance appraisals, counseling, and disciplinary actions
- Supporting pay-for-performance and promotion selection strategies
- Identifying training and development needs
- Satisfying the requirements of accrediting and licensing agencies
- Avoiding charges of discrimination and protecting against grievance actions

Levels of Performance

A few organizations use only two levels of performance: "meets standard" and "fails to meet standard." Significantly more organizations use three levels: (1) does not meet expectations (fails), (2) meets expectations (passes), and

(3) exceeds expectations (excels). Two-level systems (pass–fail) seldom aid motivation, except for new employees whose immediate interest is often whether they do or do not shed probationary status and become regular employees. Adding an "exceeds expectations" or "superior" level introduces challenge and motivation.

Standards for two-level and three-level systems are easiest to administer, but five-level systems are also popular. These systems sometimes include a category designated on the order of "meets expectations, but needs improvement." The fifth class is derived by splitting the "exceeds expectations" group into "superior" and "outstanding." A supervisor faced with an indignant overachiever who wants to know why he or she is rated as only "superior" instead of "outstanding" appreciates the difficulty inherent in using a five-level system and highlights the fact that these terms need to be defined as specifically as possible (not an easy task for the majority of positions).

Importance of Setting Appropriate Levels

A minimum-level standard provides a pass–fail situation. Performance below that level is unacceptable, signaling a need for remedial or administrative action. If this level is set too low, it leads to the acceptance of poor performance and the accumulation of "dead wood." On the other hand, if the level is too high, there may be frustration and loss of self-esteem when standards are not met. Any standard that employees are expected to meet must be realistically attainable.

Compliance Standards

Compliance standards concern compliance with policies and procedures. They relate to attendance, punctuality, appearance, and so forth. These standards need not be duplicated in every position description. They are best disposed of with a global statement such as "complies with the conditions of employment described in our Employee Policy and Procedures Manual." Although you need not duplicate these criteria, variations from

what are prescribed in employment manuals may be necessary. For example, the dress code for patient care technicians or phlebotomists may be more stringent than that for employees who have no patient contact.

Temperament and Interrelationship Standards

Temperament and interrelationship standards pertain to work habits, initiative, creativity, self-development, reliability, and communication skills. These standards rely on "soft data" because they are highly subjective. Most of them cannot be tied directly to specific tasks and therefore are presented in a special segment of the position description. Although these traits are often omitted from position descriptions, they frequently show up in performance evaluation systems, especially older systems that rely far too heavily on subjective assessments, and in counseling sessions and other interviews.

Task Standards

Task standards are based on outcomes and results. They use "hard data" because most of them are objective. Examples are turnaround time, infection rates, and compliance with budget. Task standards address several important dimensions of task performance, notably:

- Quality (errors, accuracy)
- Productivity (completing daily tasks)
- Timeliness (meeting deadlines)
- Cost effectiveness (meeting budgets, controlling inventory)
- Manner of performance (courtesy, cooperation)

Characteristics of an Appropriate Standard

An appropriate performance standard has a number of essential characteristics:

- It identifies a level below which performance is not acceptable.
- It provides a challenge but is attainable by most incumbents.

- It is results-based and quantifiable whenever possible.
- It is specific, objective, and measurable.
- It deals with performance over which the employee has control.
- It excludes imprecise words such as professional, suitable, timely, attitude, and ethical, unless these words are accompanied by specific descriptors.
- It limits the use of absolute terms such as never, always, or 100% to actions that are life threatening or serious in other ways (for example, issuing compatible blood for transfusions).
- It is understood and agreed to by both employee and supervisor.
- It does not discriminate against any member of a group protected by the Equal Employment Opportunity Commission.
- It directly or indirectly benefits customers.

Practical Approach for Preparing Standards

The simplest approach to preparing performance standards is to list the major task standards and then add appropriate descriptors that represent one or more of the five dimensions listed previously. An example follows:

Task: Answer the telephone.

Standards:

- Provides information sought by callers and ensures that transfers are completed. (Quality)
- Keeps lines open and avoids personal calls. (Quantity)
- Answers calls within three rings. (Timeliness)
- Identifies department and self. Asks "How can I help?" (Manner)
- Uses caller's name frequently. (Manner)
- Closes by thanking caller. (Manner)

Do not be discouraged when you must settle for descriptors that are not as precise as you would like. Periodic modifications dictated by experience are a key to success.

General Customer-Oriented Performance Standards

Performance standards that apply to an employee's interactions with customers frequently include the following:

- Uses tact in personal interactions.
- Communicates in an honest, straightforward manner.
- Reports employee concerns to department management.
- Reacts constructively to criticism and to changes.
- Maintains high team spirit and morale.
- Interacts in a positive manner.
- Rarely receives complaints from customers or staff.
- Maintains confidentiality of customer information.

Examples of Performance Standards for a Specific Position

With few if any exceptions, performance standards for the position of phlebotomist or patient care technician can be expected to appear as follows:

- Maintains appearance, dress, and decorum that conform to special lab code.
- Greets patients courteously by introducing self and calling patient by name.
- Explains procedure about to be performed.
- Complies with institutional policies and procedures with special attention to isolation procedures.

Quantification When Applicable and Possible

The introduction of numbers or percentages to standards adds objectivity and gives employees a more accurate description of what is required of them. For example, "answer within three rings" is precise; "answer courteously" is not.

Percentages indicate the amount of tolerance or the number of errors permitted. This can be important. Consider "answer within three rings 90% of the time" and "correctly cross-match blood 90% of the time." This would be appropriate for the telephone rings but would be completely unacceptable for compatibility testing the blood. Often, it is not possible or advantageous to apply percentages; objections to their use have been voiced because one would have to record each episode before percentages could be calculated, converting supervisors into "bean counters."

There is no interpretive problem with terms like "always," "never," or "without exception," but there is a problem of achievement. Even the best employees slip occasionally. Therefore, terms like "with rare exception" are often more appropriate than absolute terms. The adverbs "generally," "ordinarily," and "usually" mean more than 50% of the time; "sometimes," "seldom," and "infrequently" denote occurrences less than 50%.

Tips for Formulating Standards

In developing standards for a particular job, start by updating the position description, particularly the segment that delineates responsibilities; this section is the skeleton for the standards. If you have a long list of duties, arrange these into groups of related topics. Call these key results areas, significant job segments, or some similar title. For example, for an administrative assistant, all activities that relate to preparing for a meeting can be grouped under "meeting preparations." For a nursing unit supervisor, these groups could consist of the following:

- Employee functions
- Financial functions
- Operational functions
- Patient care functions
- Professional growth and development[3]

In health care, new technologies, services, and responsibilities translate into frequent changes in position descriptions. Spending too much time developing comprehensive standards leads to spending far too much time

back at the drawing board. Most authorities believe that only six or seven major responsibilities of professional or technical specialists need descriptors.

Solicit the help of current employees when deciding what should and should not be included. Current employees are also helpful when selecting the degree of difficulty for standards. Contrary to what we may expect, employees consistently peg their expectations higher than their supervisors do.

When working on minimum standards, be sure you know what level of performance is acceptable and what is not. If descriptors are too soft, that is, if standards are too easily met, you may accumulate dead wood you cannot get rid of. To use the old quality assurance cliché, "Do it right the first time." If you subsequently raise those standards, you should negotiate the changes with all the members of the group. Do not forget to raise the same standards for all other employees who hold the same position.

It is helpful to recall what kinds of problems your borderline performers have had or are having. Perhaps they tend to forget a step in a complicated procedure or have difficulty dealing with certain customers. Composing standards based on such practical knowledge can produce great standards. When pondering descriptors for superior levels, watch one of your best employees at work. What does this person do that makes the difference? These observations give you clues to good indicators.

Pitfalls

Some pitfalls are commonly encountered in standards formulation:

- The list of duties and responsibilities is either incomplete or excessively detailed.
- An average performance level is used rather than a properly established standard. Contrary to much common usage, "average" and "standard" are not identical; average is the actual average performance of a group, and standard is the target for minimum

acceptable performance, so someone who is performing at the average level of the group is performing above the standard; that is, above the required minimum level of performance, assuming, of course, that the majority of the group is performing above the standard.

- All designated responsibilities are not under the complete control of the employee.
- A standard is based on invalid or unreliable data.
- The expectations established are either too low or too high.
- Too few of the standards are based on outcomes or results.
- The supervisor or the employee is unwilling to renegotiate the level of a standard that appears inadequate.
- There is little or no commitment on the part of the employee.
- There is no input into standard formulation by the employee.
- There is inadequate monitoring of subsequent performance.

For examples of performance standards, see **Exhibits 5.1**, **5.2**, **5.3**, and **5.4**.

Standards: Where Do They Come From?

Consider Exhibit 5–4; the very first standard listed indicates that processing 28–32 bills per shift is the standard for "Meeting Expectations." How was it decided that 28–32 bills was a fair requirement for acceptable performance? In this instance, the source of the standard was probably a combination of history and judgment. If history was limited or nonexistent, then observation and judgment may have been combined to set the initial standard. Many "objective" standards are set this way; some history, some experience, some observation, and judgment. Such standards may be refined through experience or adjusted as methods change, and as long as they are generally accepted by both worker and manager, they usually suffice.

The most accurate standards available—and thus the costliest to set—are established via stopwatch time study. Many iterations of a repetitive task are studied in detail and a performance standard is built from the data. This process can be applied in any work setting, but it is economical only in instances of very high volume of repetitive tasks so it is ordinarily applied in mass-production-manufacturing settings.

Exhibit 5.1 Sample Duties and Performance Standards for a Payroll Clerk

---

- Collect source documents (time sheets and time cards) from department secretaries within *1 business day following the end of the bi-weekly payroll period.*
- Review and verify all source documents *on the day collected*; follow-up with departments on missing source documents and apparent reporting errors.
- Submit all completed source documents to the payroll manager *within two hours following the start of business of the second day of the new period.*
- Update payroll records by recording approved changes in pay rates, insurance coverage, loan payments, garnishments, and other changes *within 1 business day of receipt.*
- Process new hires, terminations, transfers, and promotions *within 1 business day of receipt* from human resources.
- Print and distribute departmental payroll reports *within 2 business days* following bi-weekly payroll distribution.
- Investigate payroll discrepancies, errors, and employee complaints as reported and recommend resolution to the payroll manager.
- Distribute paychecks and direct-deposit receipts to department managers *no later than 1:00 p.m. on the assigned payday.*
- Serve as payroll department liaison between the department managers and the payroll manager.

Note: The standards, in this instance largely deadlines or time requirements, appear in italics.

Exhibit 5.2 **Sample Format for Coupling of Duties and Performance Standards**

Duty: Orient New Employees

Standards:

- Submit schedule and agenda to office 1 week before arrival of new hire.
- Notify trainers at least 1 week before arrival of new employees.
- Complete orientation within 5 workdays.
- Return check-off list to office within 1 week of completion.
- Receive favorable evaluations from new employees more than 90% of the time.

Exhibit 5.3 **Performance Standards for Phlebotomists**

Duty: Draws blood from patient and returns tubes and requests to clinical laboratory.

Standards:

- Greets patient by introducing self and calling patient by formal name.
- Verifies correct patient by checking name on requisition form against name on patient's wrist band. Explains procedure to patient.
- Follows infection prevention instructions in phlebotomist's procedure manual.
- Performs phlebotomy. No more than three unsuccessful attempts are permitted. Calls supervisor if help is needed.
- Labels blood tubes immediately after blood is obtained by following procedure in manual.
- Disposes used needles in accordance with procedure in manual.
- Returns tubes and requisitions to the blood collection station within the time allowed by supervisor.

Exhibit 5.4 **Sample of Behaviorally Anchored Performance Standards: Business Office Biller**

Productivity

Meets Expectations
Processes 28 to 32 bills per shift, normal mix of Blue Cross/Blue Shield, Medicare, Medicaid, Workers' Compensation, commercial carrier, and self-pay. Includes notification to supervisor of apparent problems or inconsistencies in billing information received.

Exceeds Expectations
Consistently processes more than 32 bills per shift, including notification to supervisor of apparent problems or inconsistencies in billing information received.

Fails to Meet Expectations
Consistently averages processing fewer than 28 bills per shift.

Quality

Meets Expectations
Consistently generates an error rate of less than 3% (no more than three errors in 100 bills processed).

Exceeds Expectations
Consistently generates an error rate of less than 1% (fewer than one error per 100 bills).

Fails to Meet Expectations
Consistently generates an error rate greater than 3% (more than three errors per 100 bills).

(continues)

Exhibit 5.4 Sample of Behaviorally Anchored Performance Standards: Business Office Biller

(Continued)

Note: There may also be standards associated with **cost** and separate standards associated with **time**. Although timely processing is implied in the **productivity** standard, there can be other specific turnaround-time requirements related to the position of business office biller. In addition, standards may be associated with adherence to policy; for example, one common such standard relates to attendance and addresses numbers of absences in some period (usually 1 year).

Next down the scale of cost is the use of predetermined motion times. These are small bits of time associated with reasonably small movements that can be combined in "building up" the allowable amount of time for performing a task. Entire systems of such building blocks of time have been developed for many healthcare tasks, but their application is generally time-consuming and thus uneconomical unless the tasks involved are somewhat high volume or the process is being used to set, for example, a staffing standard that can be applied over and over again.

There is also work sampling, a technique by which many observations are made on a random basis of an activity and a standard developed from the information obtained. This is time-consuming but less costly than the processes described previously; it can be applied in many instances when the others are impractical, but it is not as accurate as stop-watch study and predetermined motion times.

The process heavily relied on today is known as benchmarking. Benchmarking consists simply of comparing one's own operation with others,

examining how other organizations approach the activity you are interested in. For example, if you wish to set a standard for the discharge cleaning of a patient room you may check with other similar organizations to determine how long it takes to do this at their facilities; visit other facilities to observe their processes for yourself; research those organizations identified with so-called "best practices"; and also research published sources of benchmarking information.

The simplified view of benchmarking is comparing what your organization does with the way others have approached the same activity.

The major precaution to observe in benchmarking involves *methods*. If you are satisfied with the method used at your institution, when you compare times with others make sure you are comparing similar methods. Also, in doing so you may sometimes learn that another's method is more efficient than yours, so the process may involve altering your own method. Regardless, benchmarking is a more effective process for establishing a standard than relying on your own observations and judgment.

WRAP-UP

Think About It

To repeat an extremely important point made earlier: Whether in the expression of performance standards or in the evaluation of employee performance, "average" and "standard" are not equivalent. Standard is minimum acceptable performance; average is the actual average of a group's

performance. Because normal processes should weed out substandard performers or improve their performance, the lowest level of performance in the group will be at "standard," and the "average" performance of the group will tend to be higher than "standard."

Questions for Review and Discussion

1. In preparing to write or update a position description, why should the supervisor solicit the participation of the employee or employees presently doing that job?

2. In addition to their important application in assessing employee work performance, how can performance standards be helpful in other ways?

3. What are competencies? Explain and provide two or three examples.

4. Select a job with which you are reasonably familiar and write a summary statement for the position description.

5. Why is it suggested that a title such as "administrative assistant" is generally preferred over one such as "secretary"?

6. Should a proper job description cover absolutely everything the employee could ever be expected to do? Why or why not?

7. What is a "reasonable accommodation" under the ADA? Provide an example.

8. Describe in detail at least three important uses of the job description.

9. How would you develop and express a reasonable performance standard when there is no objective means available for measuring task performance?

10. Select a specific task with which you are familiar and develop a brief set of performance standards for that task.

Exercise: Writing a Job Description

Select a nonsupervisory job with which you are familiar and develop a job description for that job. Follow the early sections of the text in creating the position description, and keep in mind the various uses that your finished description might possibly have to serve.

Case: If It Isn't in the Job Description...

Harry Jones, maintenance supervisor, was troubled about mechanic Dan Wilson. Harry considered Dan a good mechanic based on Dan's consistently good work in completing his preventive maintenance tasks and his success with tough repair jobs. The problem was Dan's apparent lack of motivation to do more or better; he did exactly as told, then waited to be told what to do next. If he had no specific assignment to go to next when he finished a job, he took a prolonged break until Harry found him and gave him a new assignment.

Harry's frustration got the better of him one day when a small plumbing problem got out of hand and became a larger problem. He knew Dan must have seen the leak because it was right next to his most recent assignment, but when Harry asked why he had done nothing about the leak, Dan answered, "Plumbing's not part of my job."

Harry said, "You could at least have reported it."

Dan said, "There's nothing in my job description about reporting anything. I stick to my job description."

"Dan, you're a good mechanic, but you never extend yourself, never reach out to help without being told."

"I'm not paid to extend myself. You're the boss, and I do what you tell me."

Harry responded, "I know, and you always do it right. But I know you're capable of doing more. For some reason or other you're not working up to your capabilities."

Dan shrugged. "I do what I'm told, and if it isn't in the job description, I don't have to do it."

Instructions

Put yourself in Harry's position and consider some possible ways of dealing with Dan. Identify a few steps that you might recommend to Harry in an effort to get Dan to perform more in line with his capabilities.

References

1. Joint Commission on Accreditation of Healthcare Organizations. *Accreditation Manual for Hospitals.* Vol. 2. JCAHO;2023. 2022.
2. Americans with Disabilities Act, US Code 42 (1990), § 12101.
3. Berte L. *Developing Performance Standards for Hospital Personnel.* ASCP Press; 1989:61.

CHAPTER 6

Policies and Policy Making

CHAPTER OBJECTIVES

- Define policies and describe their overall purpose and function.
- Establish the necessity for comprehensive policies addressing all aspects of the organization's operations.
- Describe the significant uses of policies that establish the necessity for policy observance at all organizational levels.
- Differentiate between organizational policies and department policies, and establish the supervisor's relationship to the latter.
- Identify potential problems concerning policies.

KEY TERMS

Policy: A policy is a guide that spells out required, prohibited, or suggested courses of action and defines boundaries or limitations on action; a policy pre-decides an issue and limits actions such that repetitive situations are handled in a consistent manner; for example, a sexual harassment policy defines sexual harassment and prohibits its practice and enumerates the consequences of violations.

Procedure: A procedure is a guide that spells out the steps necessary for the active implementation of a policy; for example, a sexual harassment procedure provides the guidelines for reporting allegations of harassment and for investigating such allegations.

Introducing Policies

Policies are guidelines established for pursuing goals and shaping behavior. They reflect the mission and values of organizations and are made more specific by procedures, rules, and regulations. They are of increasing importance to the modern healthcare organization because of the growing propensity for litigation of various kinds. Legal, moral, and ethical problems; sexual harassment; all forms of discrimination; and patients' rights regularly necessitate reevaluation of existing policies.

Unnecessary or vague policies create red tape and pointless rules that frustrate employees and supervisors. Poorly worded policies lead to confusion. Inappropriate, ill-conceived, unfair, or illogical policies are barriers to effective performance, and worse, they necessitate many exceptions.

The absence of policies results in management by crisis and leads to inconsistencies as the same issues are dealt with differently at different times. Without policy guidance, managers waste time making the same decisions and answering the same questions repeatedly. Confusion, uncertainty, and conflict become prevalent.

When practices stray from policies and the procedures that implement them or when practices turn into unwritten policies, problems arise. Lax and inconsistent adherence to policies can readily cause legal problems and endanger staff morale.

Although legal risks are always involved in documenting policies, it is always more hazardous to operate without an employee handbook or policy manual than to have a comprehensive set of policies in place. The employee handbook should be understood by all employees and should cover important policies, rules, and regulations. Management must update policies constantly because of changes in laws, revisions of services, and ever-changing employee needs. Several areas of policy regularly—and deservedly—receive considerable attention:

- Salary and benefits programs, as employee needs change and new laws regulating benefits are passed
- Alternative staffing and scheduling practices, such as job sharing, flexible scheduling, and remote work-at-home arrangements
- Smoking and drugs
- Exposure to hazardous agents; "Right to Know" laws
- Precautions regarding the care of patients with AIDS
- Sexual harassment
- Individual privacy rights (HIPAA)
- Cultural diversity in both the workforce and customer base
- Discrimination because of age or disability
- Employment of persons with disabilities
- Requirements of accreditation and regulatory agencies

Policy regarding the use and abuse of email provides an impressive example of why policy manuals are in a constant state of flux. When employers fail to develop appropriate email policies and procedures, they run the risk of legal problems. Significant email problems frequently involve sexual harassment and interference with the privacy rights of employees. Also, policies governing email must be clear concerning what should not be communicated via email (for example, proprietary information) and any prohibitions related to the personal use of email while at work.

Many states have laws that require written policies be distributed to all employees. Therefore, it should be considered mandatory that every organization provide its employees with knowledge of the organization's policies. This is ordinarily accomplished by providing a detailed policy and procedure manual that is available to all for reference and by supplying each employee with a handbook that summarizes all pertinent policies. To reduce exposure to legal liability, properly written employee handbooks include disclaimer language throughout, advising employees that various provisions are subject to change at the discretion of the employer. Also, it is common practice to require each new employee to sign and submit a confirmation indicating that he or she has received and reviewed the employee handbook. On numerous occasions, an employer has successfully turned back an employee's plea of ignorance of a particular requirement by producing a confirmation of the employee handbook.

Uses of Policies

Properly formulated policies have a number of important uses. They promote understanding, clarity, and consistency of behavior. Employees who know what is expected of them feel more confident, and they police themselves by following policy. Policies eliminate repetitive decision-making, standardize responses, and save time by providing a standard, repeatable way of addressing issues. Good policies also help in the orientation of newly hired employees. Finally, they provide documented controls as required by licensing and accrediting agencies.

To be effective, policies must be explicit, publicized as well as published, and enforced without favoritism. The first-line supervisor is the chief activator or enforcer of policies. Supervisors must know, interpret, promulgate, and enforce policies. Often, supervisors must carry out policies that they have had no hand in developing. They might not comprehend the rationale behind, or agree with, some of these policies, but they still must enforce them. Simply handing out employee handbooks is not enough.

Supervisors must understand the purpose of each policy and know how much freedom they have in modifying policies or originating policies independently.

For example, Supervisor Sue says to one of her employees: "Sally, you don't look well. Take the rest of the day off. It won't count as sick time." This is a good-faith action and is legal, but what is the policy of the organization regarding such an action? Supervisor Sue, as well intentioned as she is, needs to know whether the policies of the organization sanction her action. If her actions are not sanctioned by policy, she is in effect creating policy; because she took this action for Sally on this particular occasion, she might then be expected to do the same for anyone else who is similarly situated.

Insecure managers attempt to divorce themselves from unpopular policies by saying things such as, "Don't blame me for that stupid policy" or "Management expects you to...." Even worse, they may ignore the policy or depend on others to enforce it. The result is a loss of respect for both the organization and the supervisor who takes this approach. When supervisors believe a policy is inappropriate or causing problems, they should discuss the problem with their superiors. Usually, there is a rational explanation for it. If you find that a policy is hurting morale more than helping a situation, discuss the problem with your manager. Perhaps you have a suggestion on how the policy could be modified. In any event, keep your employees posted on your efforts to change the situation.

There are times when supervisors must bend or even ignore a policy. This is a matter of risk taking. For example, Hospital A has a strict policy that prohibits employees from bringing young children into the clinical laboratory. A blood bank technologist receives an urgent call late one night to return to the hospital because of an emergency. Having no one to care for her 6-year-old daughter, she brings her daughter with her to the laboratory. Should this technologist be reprimanded or thanked for this behavior?

Policies Formulated by Supervisors

Common Situations Indicating the Need for a New Policy or a Policy Change

The following situations may require the creation of a policy or the modification of an existing policy:

- The introduction of a new service or substantial change in an existing service
- Frequent violations of procedures or rules
- Problems of productivity, quality, schedules, or time
- Frequent complaints from customers or employees
- Legal, ethical, or moral problems
- Behavioral inconsistencies
- Repetitive questions being asked about particular procedures or rules

Departmental policies must harmonize with those put in place for the organization overall. These policies must not exceed your supervisory authority. Use plain language; avoid using legalistic phraseology or jargon to impress people or to make the policy sound more authoritative. (See **Exhibit 6.1** for more information on how to formulate a policy.)

Once a departmental policy is created, publish it and make certain that every employee receives a copy and signs a log acknowledging they received it. Enforce the policy fairly, firmly, and uniformly. Policies that are not enforced become meaningless. Supervisors often overlook transgressions by their more valued employees, but unfairness of this nature often translates to the filing of grievances or complaints of discrimination. Furthermore,

---

Exhibit 6.1 **Procedure for Formulating a Policy**

---

1. State the need for and describe the purpose of a new policy or a revision of an existing policy.
2. Decide whether the need is great enough to warrant a new policy or a policy change.
3. Consider alternate solutions (for example, a notice on the bulletin board or a memo).
4. Gather data and input from others, especially the people affected by the policy.
5. Check the rough draft of the policy for the following:
   - Compliance with institutional philosophy, mission, values, ethics, and established policies, rules, and regulations
   - Completeness, clarity, and understandability
   - Answers to questions of what, when, where, who, how, and why
   - Anticipated acceptance by persons who are affected
   - Enforcement problems that may occur
6. Circulate the rough draft and discuss it with others. Get the approval of superiors. Have a legal expert check to determine whether there are liability aspects.
7. Make necessary modifications. Ask whether the policy meets the following criteria:
   - It is needed.
   - It will be understood.
   - It is achievable (workable).
   - It is flexible and fair.
   - It will be acceptable.
   - It can be enforced.

---

supervisors must make certain that they themselves comply with the letter of the policies. Supervisors must always serve as models for their staffs. "Do as I say, not as I do" does not work for the supervisor or, for that matter, for any manager at any level.

Heavy handedness in policy enforcement can be counterproductive. Most employees are more skillful in avoiding compliance than managers are in enforcing policies. Sometimes the violation of rules becomes a game, especially when the supervisor is unpopular or autocratic. Be willing to admit when one of your policies turns out to be a dud. Modify or eliminate such policies when appropriate. Never regard any policy as written in stone, forever unchanging. Every policy manual needs an annual checkup.

Potential Problems with Policies

Selection of Job Candidates

Usually, the human resources department screens candidates, but the actual employee selection is left to supervisors. This is as it should be; the person who will be a new hire's immediate supervisor is the person who should make the final hiring decision. Hazards for inexperienced interviewers—and there are plenty—include numerous questions that cannot be asked legally and the absence of legitimate basis for excluding certain candidates. Also, when job descriptions or performance standards are inadequate or obsolete, even experienced interviewers can be led to select the wrong candidates. Employee selection policies must support the supervisor in acquiring staff and at the same time provide guidelines for keeping the interviewing and selection process legal.

Orientation of New Hires

Human resource departments may be responsible for new employee orientation and some training, but part of these tasks, especially departmental orientation, is left to supervisors. However, most supervisors are not sufficiently knowledgeable to address detailed questions about payroll deductions and benefits programs, so they should not attempt to address such matters.

Faulty orientation or negligent implementation of guidelines results in poor work performance and the overrating of poor performers at the completion of their probationary periods.

Schedules

Vague or unwritten policies concerning schedules can destroy morale and lead to the filing of grievances, especially in unionized organizations. Hazards include discrimination in assigning work, vacation, overtime, or call-back schedules.

Safety and Health

Given the steadily increasing volume of workers' compensation claims, supervisors must be emphatic about reporting, correcting, and following up on suspected safety or health hazards. Failure to follow established policy, including the careful documentation and the prompt handling of injuries, can be costly to the organization and can also damage the careers of supervisors who have failed in this responsibility.

A specific situation is presented by the presence of AIDS in the workforce. First, there is consideration for the employee who has the disease or is known to be HIV-positive, and then there is consideration for the coworkers who are concerned about the chances of becoming infected. This is a particularly sensitive issue in health care, where there is an increased risk of workers contracting AIDS from patients and where problems of confidentiality are involved.

Supervisors should be prepared to cope with workers who object to working with an employee who has a limiting disability. Training programs for managers and workers are essential. The inadvertent mishandling of an employee with a disease or disability that is protected by the Americans with Disabilities Act (ADA) can leave an organization vulnerable to charges of discrimination, invasion of privacy, or unauthorized disclosure.

Handling Problems or Special Employees

Grievances are often filed to protest disciplinary measures that have been taken. Poor leadership leads to poor "followership," which leads to reprimands or other disciplinary actions. This then leads to grievances.

Mishandled severance procedures can be costly in terms of both dollars and feelings. Supervisory mishandling of charges of sexual harassment or discrimination can be embarrassing and expensive for employers.

Effective resolutions of employee problems begin with sound policies and end with skillful enforcement of these policies. Concerning sexual harassment, the blanket grievance or complaint procedure usually calls for the immediate supervisor to be the first person contacted. However, when allegations of sexual harassment are made, the immediate supervisor may often be the perpetrator. Therefore, a separate policy for reporting allegations of sexual harassment and for confidentially investigating such charges is mandatory.

Also, employment policy must spell out the limits to be observed with employee drug testing. Is it routine or random testing? Who is to be tested, and how will the potential invasion of privacy issues be addressed?

Special Case: Americans with Disabilities Act

It is necessary to have policies that address the complex federal regulations regarding hiring, assigning, promoting, and accommodating people who have physical or mental disabilities, as specified by the ADA. This translates into making changes in position descriptions and performance standards and in the recruiting, testing, and interviewing of candidates.

A particularly sensitive area of concern to supervisors is the occasional need to accommodate a disabled individual. "Reasonable accommodation" under the ADA can include making existing facilities accessible to individuals with disabilities, job restructuring, or job reassignment. Managers may sometimes offer part-time employment or modified work schedules or may grant unpaid leave. Often, it is necessary to acquire or modify equipment, provide readers or interpreters, and modify examinations, training materials, or policies.[1]

Reasonable accommodation also frequently requires employers to modify examinations, training materials, and policies. Jobs must be restructured so that marginal or nonessential duties that exclude people with disabilities are eliminated when possible. For example, a data entry position requiring 7.5 hours at the keyboard and 30 minutes walking around delivering reports might be modified such that someone else does the report delivery. The data entry activities would be the job's "essential function"; the report delivery would not be considered an essential function of a data entry position. (Report delivery surely would be an essential function of the position of an interdepartmental messenger.)

Sometimes reasonable accommodation requires physical changes in layout, equipment, furnishings, and such. Recognizing potential expenses of renovations, the ADA gives the organization something of an out by saying that such changes need not be made if they impose "undue hardship" (as in potentially spending large sums for renovations). However, there is no workable definition of undue hardship, giving rise to occasional conflicts over what is or is not reasonable.

Employers must be able to justify exclusionary qualifications or capabilities. Candidates cannot be tested for functions and knowledge that are not essential to the job under consideration. Supervisors should be aware, however, that they will not be required to displace another employee from a position for the sake of hiring a disabled job candidate.

To further complicate matters, the rules for addressing needs that arise relative to compliance with the ADA are not carved in stone. In addressing complaints of disability discrimination, the U.S. Supreme Court and numerous state courts continue to create case law that affects interpretation and implementation of the basic ADA legislation. Thus, it becomes necessary to periodically revisit ADA-related policies to keep them up to date.

WRAP-UP

Think About It

The operative word concerning the observance of policies and the application of the procedures that implement them is "consistency." Policies provide a common direction for everyone in the organization to follow.

Questions for Review and Discussion

1. It was stated above that a policy should be publicized as well as published. What is the difference between these terms, and why would this be said about policies?
2. As a supervisor, what should you do about a policy that is unpopular with your employees or that appears to you to be potentially harmful?
3. Cite an example of one realistic occurrence that could suggest the need for a policy change. Why might the change be necessary?
4. Why be concerned with modeling behavior for employees? The supervisor is the boss—why not simply tell them what to do?
5. What problems might the supervisor create through inconsistent treatment of employees?
6. Explain fully why each employee is asked to sign and submit a confirmation that they received and reviewed the employee handbook?
7. Explain the essential difference between a policy and a procedure.
8. As a department supervisor, what would you consider to be the primary

benefit of having complete, up-to-date organizational policies?

9. Describe a situation in which inconsistent policy adherence could potentially cause legal problems.

10. Provide one fairly detailed example of a reasonable accommodation under the ADA.

Exercise: Writing a Policy

Assume you are supervisor of a large group of employees, both male and female, who work in an office setting. You are to draft a policy governing the use of email in the department, keeping in mind that your draft is also to be submitted as a possible model for a policy for the entire organization.

Case: Bending the Break

Assume you are supervisor of a hospital admitting department and also responsible for the reception area and information center (switchboard and main lobby desk). Like other employees, your people are entitled to 15-minute breaks in both morning and afternoon. Most of your employees have some flexibility as to when they can take breaks, but the person who works the switchboard and the one who works the main lobby desk have breaks scheduled for specific times because you have to provide relief for them. You often have no one to spare, so much of the time you yourself provide their relief.

This was a horrible week. Two key people were absent most of the week, admitting activity was up, and a few other problems popped up. You personally had to relieve Alice, the switchboard operator, for morning breaks the entire week. On Monday and Tuesday, Alice stayed on break about 20 minutes. Wednesday she was gone 25 minutes, and both Thursday and Friday she stretched her morning breaks to a half hour. With all the work you had to do, you felt you could not tolerate such lengthy breaks, so on Friday you spoke with Alice about her practice of taking longer than the allowed time.

Alice's response was, "I can't help it. The coffee shop is all jammed up most of the morning. Two days last week I didn't get coffee at all, and another day I got it but didn't have time to drink it all so I could get back here in 15 minutes. I know I'm supposed to have only 15 minutes, but the way things are in that coffee shop I can't get served, enjoy my coffee, and get back in time."

You also checked with the employee at the reception desk who echoed Alice's complaint about the coffee shop and added, "What we'd really like is to have our own coffee supply nearby, but you know as well as I do that the big boss forbids coffee pots and cups in office and public areas. Except, of course," she added with a skyward glance, "for the coffeemaker in his own office."

You checked with a number of your admitting employees and learned that most of them who did not have specific break times had learned how to take advantage of fluctuations in the morning crowd at the coffee shop. However, as far as you were able to determine, the morning coffee break appeared on average to consume 5 or 6 minutes longer than the allotted 15 minutes because of waiting time.

Instructions

How might you go about solving the problem of having coffee available to your employees and still accomplish the morning break within the allowed time? What other possibilities might you explore?

Reference

1. EEOC Regulation Pertaining to ADA under Title I Employment (Title VII, Civil Rights Act of 1964). *Federal Register.* July 26, 1991;35:736.

CHAPTER 7

The Supervisor's Legal Environment

CHAPTER OBJECTIVES

- Outline the development of the regulated environment within which the healthcare supervisor must function.
- Identify historical years affecting employment legislation and the onset of shifting social responsibility to employers.
- Present a chronology of legislation affecting employment and thus affecting the supervisory role.
- Describe the cumulative effects of employment legislation to date.

KEY TERMS

Employment Legislation: Within the context of this chapter, employment legislation consists primarily of federal laws that have a bearing on the employer–employee relationship and in some manner influence the role of the supervisor.

The Legal Environment

This text provides an overview of the laws affecting various aspects of the employment relationship. Each law is described in nonlegal terminology, focusing on its stated or apparent intent and noting the effect it might conceivably have on the functioning of the supervisor. Some of the effects of the more significant laws are considered, and in a few instances, some apparently unintended effects are described.

This text is intended to provide sufficient background and information of employment legislation so the first-line supervisor can develop an understanding of the effect of employment law on the supervisory role. Nothing in this text constitutes legal advice, and no such advice should be inferred from its contents. The manager with a question about the applicability of any particular point of law should take it to the appropriate people in the organization: human resources, administration, risk management, and, in some instances, in-house legal counsel. Answers to legal questions must come from those qualified to address such questions.

Human resources began to change dramatically in 1964, when sweeping civil rights legislation came into being. Title VII of the Civil Rights Act of 1964 marked the beginning of significant changes in relations between government and business, as well as a change in philosophy that would result in a completely new direction for government in its concern for its citizens.

Pre-1964: Minimal Regulation

Before 1964, businesses were free to deal with employees essentially as they chose, except for the requirements of wage and hour laws and labor relations laws. Prior to 1964, the only laws that had a noticeable impact on the employment relationship were the Fair Labor Standards Act (FLSA) and related state laws, and the National Labor Relations Act (NLRA).

The FLSA governed—and to this day, as regularly amended, continues to govern—wage payment and certain other conditions of employment. This and similar laws in some states are commonly referred to as wage and hour laws.

The NLRA (and similar laws in some states), governing relationships between work organizations and labor unions, was relevant only to organizations in which employees were unionized or where there was active union organizing.

One early landmark piece of legislation that forever affected employers and employees alike was the Social Security Act, passed by the 74th Congress during President Roosevelt's first term and effective as of August 14, 1935. This was social welfare legislation that created, among other things, the Social Security system. It instituted a payroll tax paid half by the employee via payroll deduction and half by the employer.

Thus, before 1964 there were few legal restrictions on how employers could operate and how supervisors could manage. Most business organizations complied with the wage and hour laws as a matter of operating routine, and those organizations having a union presence, either actively organizing or in place, generally complied with applicable labor laws.

The turning point of 1964 represented a change in philosophy concerning government's relationship with business. For years the governing philosophy had largely been one of "hands off" to the maximum practical extent; employers needed to concern themselves only with wage and hour requirements and labor relations restrictions and remit their Social Security taxes. But 1964 marked a significant change in the direction government would be taking from then forward on behalf of its citizens. Since 1964, government has been addressing many of the perceived needs of employees by involving employers in meeting those needs.

The Relevant Laws

Norris–LaGuardia Act (1932)

The first legislation to significantly address the growing organized labor movement was the Norris–LaGuardia Act of 1932. This Act marked a significant shift in public policy concerning labor unions, from a posture of legal repression of unions and their activities to one of encouragement of union activity. Although the Act essentially legalized union organizing and affirmed workers' rights to organize for collective bargaining purposes, it did little to directly restrain employers in their conduct toward labor organizations.

National Labor Relations Act (NLRA) (1935)

The National Labor Relations Act, also known as the Wagner Act, established rules for the behavior of both unions and employers in labor organizing and collective bargaining situations. Although the NLRA seemed to favor unions and encourage their presence, it also set some boundaries on what unions could do in their organizing activities. In addition to affirming employees' right to organize, the NLRA made it illegal for an employer to simply refuse to deal with a union provided the union had conducted a legal organizing campaign and had won a proper representation election.

The NLRA created the National Labor Relations Board (NLRB), the body charged with administering the Act by conducting representation elections to determine whether employees in particular groupings ("bargaining units") wished to have union representation.

The Act specified that a union chosen by the majority of the employees in an appropriate unit would be the exclusive representative of all the employees in that unit. The NLRA was later modified by the Taft-Hartley Act and the Landrum-Griffin Act.

Social Security Act (1935)

The Social Security Act established a basic system of contributory social insurance and a supplemental program for the low-income elderly.

The system was expanded in 1939 to provide benefits to survivors of covered workers and dependents of retirees. Subsequently it was further expanded to cover workers who had become permanently disabled, and it was again expanded in 1965 to provide Medicare health insurance coverage for the elderly.

Fair Labor Standards Act (FLSA) (1938)

One dimension of the congressional intent of the Fair Labor Standards Act was to reduce the high unemployment rate that typified the years of the Great Depression by reducing workweek hours to a uniform standard, thus spreading available work over a greater number of workers. In addition to defining a "normal" workweek, the FLSA set minimum pay rates, established rules and standards for the payment of overtime, and regulated the employment of minors. The FLSA remains the country's basic wage and hour law and generally the model for the wage and hour laws of the individual states.

Labor Management Relations Act (1947)

This Act, popularly referred to as the Taft-Hartley Act, was an amendment to the NLRA, which clearly favored unions over employers; the principal effect of Taft-Hartley was to level the playing field to some extent by more appropriately balancing

the responsibilities and advantages of union and employer. Taft-Hartley also listed specific unfair labor practices. Although still viewed by many as a law favoring labor unions, Taft-Hartley was clearly a swing in the direction of management's rights. When we presently see or hear mention of the NLRA, the reference is actually to the NLRA as amended by Taft-Hartley. This law was itself amended in 1975 to address not-for-profit hospitals by removing the exemption that had been in place under Taft-Hartley since its passage in 1947.

Labor-Management Reporting and Disclosure Act (1959)

Commonly known as the Landrum-Griffin Act, this was another amendment to the NLRA. Among its numerous provisions, this Act required employers, including not-for-profit hospitals and other nonprofit healthcare facilities, to report in detail to the U.S. Secretary of Labor any financial arrangements or transactions intended to improve or retard the process of unionization. Various reporting and disclosure requirements were also placed on unions.

Equal Pay Act (1963)

The Equal Pay Act was actually an amendment to the FLSA. It prohibited the payment of unequal wages for men and women who worked for the same employer in the same establishment for equal work on jobs requiring equal skill, effort, responsibility, and performed under similar working conditions. Simply put, people doing the same work in the same place in the same way had to be paid equally regardless of gender. Although this law was in place before 1964, it had no noticeable impact on the first-line supervisor's role.

Title VII of the Civil Rights Act of 1964

With the enactment of this pivotal legislation, business in general began to experience steadily increasing regulation of the employment relationship. Title VII provided the legal basis for all people to pursue the work of their choosing and to advance in their chosen occupations subject to the limitations of only their individual qualifications, talents, and energies. This legislation defined unlawful employment discrimination as follows:

- The failure or refusal to hire an individual, or to discharge an individual, or to discriminate against any individual with respect to compensation or other terms, conditions, or privileges of employment because of that individual's race, color, religion, sex, or national origin.
- Limiting, segregating, or classifying employees or applicants for employment in any way that would deprive them of employment opportunities or otherwise adversely affect their status as employees because of race, color, religion, sex, or national origin.

The Civil Rights Act of 1964 also established the Equal Employment Opportunity Commission (EEOC) to enforce the anti-discrimination requirements of Title VII. The Act was amended in later years to compensate for perceived erosion of its strength and effectiveness owing to a number of U.S. Supreme Court decisions.

Age Discrimination in Employment Act (ADEA) (1967)

The Age Discrimination in Employment Act legally established the basic right of individuals to be treated in employment on the basis of their ability to perform the job rather than on the basis of age-related stereotypes or artificial age limitations. The ADEA prohibits discrimination in employment on the basis of age in hiring, job retention, compensation, and all other terms, conditions, and privileges of employment. The threshold for defining age discrimination is 40; workers age 40 and older are a "protected class" for EEOC purposes. The ADEA applies to employers of 20 or more persons, as opposed to Title VII, which applies to employers of 15 or more persons.

The ADEA has had a direct effect on retirement. Before the ADEA, employers were free to mandate retirement at a specific age, most commonly 65. The ADEA raised the limit such that employers could no longer mandate retirement at any age younger than 70. When the ADEA was amended in 1986, the age 70 limitation was removed. Retirement can no longer be mandated by any specific age, and the sole legal criterion for continuing in one's employment is one's continued ability to do the job. There are some exceptions under which retirement by a certain age can be mandated. This occurs when age is designated as a *bona fide occupational qualification (BFOQ),* such as for police officers, firefighters, airline pilots, surgeons, and certain policy-making executives. In many instances, the ADEA has enabled people who wished to keep working to do so and, thus, has ensured the continuing employment of some workers who might otherwise have to depend on government assistance.

The ADEA was again amended in 1991 by the Older Workers Benefits Protection Act.

Occupational Safety and Health Act (OSHA) (1970)

Passed in 1970 and effective in 1971, the Occupational Safety and Health Act represents highly influential legislation concerning employee safety in the workplace. Before passage of this law, efforts to ensure health and safety in the workplace were minimal. The intent of Congress in establishing OSHA was to provide all employees with a workplace free from recognized hazards that are causing or can cause death or serious physical harm to employees. This legislation created the Occupational Safety and Health Administration (OSHA), the federal agency authorized to promulgate legally enforceable workplace safety standards, respond to employee complaints, and make on-site inspections as necessary to follow up on employee safety complaints or on lost-workday injury rates that are considered excessive. (Both the agency and the legislation are referred to by the same acronym, OSHA).

On May 25, 1986, OSHA began enforcing the second phase of an elaborate set of rules known formally as "Hazard Communication."[1] These rules provide workers the right to know what they are dealing with on the job in the way of hazardous substances. According to OSHA's hazard communication rules, health facilities are required to do the following:

- Create programs for informing and training employees about hazardous substances in their workplace
- Ensure that warning labels on all incoming containers are intact and clearly readable
- Maintain copies of material safety data sheets (MSDS) for all hazardous substances in the workplace
- Supply copies of MSDS to employees upon request
- Maintain MSDS in a current state, accessible to employees on all work shifts
- Inform and train employees in the nature and appropriate handling of hazardous substances at the time of initial assignment.

More than 1,000 substances are listed as hazardous under OSHA regulations. In addition, a number of states now have "right to know" laws with similar requirements.

Generally, under federal and state standards for the handling of hazardous substances, employers must disseminate MSDS, make certain that warning labels are always in evidence on workplace containers, and at all times be able to produce a written employee orientation program. It ordinarily falls to the supervisor to ensure that these requirements are fully satisfied within the department.

Rehabilitation Act (1973)

Although disabled persons were mentioned in the Civil Rights Act of 1964, they were addressed separately for the first time in the Rehabilitation Act of 1973. This Act formally recognized that the handicapped were subject to cultural myths and prejudices similar to biases against women and ethnic minorities.[1] However, this law applied only to employees of the federal government and

employers doing a certain amount of business with the government. The Rehabilitation Act is most significant as a precursor to the Americans with Disabilities Act (1990).

Employee Retirement Income Security Act (ERISA) (1974)

Prior to enactment of ERISA, a great many corporations with pension plans made all payments to retirees out of current income. As the business climate changed and some troubled organizations, especially in heavy manufacturing, such as steel, went out of business, retirees lost out. The idea driving ERISA was the preservation of retirement benefits so they could not be affected by dramatic changes in the fortunes of a corporation. It called for organizations with retirement plans to fund such plans annually under certain rules.

ERISA established four basic requirements governing employee retirement plans:

1. Employees must become eligible for retirement benefits after a reasonable length of service (vesting rules).
2. Adequate funds must be reserved to provide the benefits promised under the plan (and these funds could not be accessed for any other purpose).
3. The persons who administer the plan and manage its funds must meet certain standards of conduct.
4. Sufficient information must be made available on a regular basis, so it may be determined whether the ERISA requirements are being met.

This Act was later reinforced by legislation included in the Retirement Equity Act of 1984, which greatly increased the complexity of ERISA and added multiple layers of Internal Revenue Service (IRS) regulations.

Pregnancy Discrimination Act (1978)

The Pregnancy Discrimination Act defined discrimination on the basis of pregnancy, childbirth, or related medical conditions as unlawful sex discrimination under Title VII of the Civil Rights Act of 1964. From this point forward, pregnancy has been considered a medical disability and is treated accordingly as a disability of 6–8 weeks' duration (length depending on whether federal or certain states' guidelines are applied).

Consolidated Omnibus Budget Reconciliation Act (COBRA) (1986)

This complex piece of legislation addressed many concerns; most pertinent to employment is that COBRA allowed for the extension of group insurance coverage to employees and their dependents on a self-pay basis for set periods (ranging up to 36 months maximum, depending on the "qualifying event," i.e., the reason for accessing COBRA), for those who would otherwise lose group health or dental coverage because of loss of employment, change in employment status, or certain other defined events. By making it possible for these employees and dependents to remain on the group contracts under which they had been covered, COBRA shifted to employers some of the cost of health coverage for many individuals who would otherwise be uninsurable except under government programs. As far as health insurance is concerned, COBRA is simply stopgap coverage; those who continue coverage under COBRA must secure other coverage after the eligibility period expires. Coverage can be continued up to 18 months for laid-off employees, 29 months for the disabled, and 36 months for dependents following separation, divorce, or the death of the employee. However, should the employer go out of business or for some other reason terminate its health insurance plan, rights under COBRA cease immediately.

Immigration Reform and Control Act (IRCA) (1986)

This Act required employers to review and as necessary modify their hiring practices, instituting procedures to verify that job applicants are either U.S. citizens or are otherwise legally authorized to work in the United States. This law established civil and criminal penalties for knowingly hiring, recruiting, referring, or retaining in employment persons designated as unauthorized aliens if so identified on or after November 6, 1986. The Act also prohibited employers from discriminating against job applicants on the basis of citizenship status or national origin.

Most employment legislation specifies the minimum size organization to which it applies; for example, the Family and Medical Leave Act (FMLA) applies only to employers of 50 or more employees. The Immigration Reform and Control Act pointedly applies to all employers of *one or more employees*, based on the premise that a significant number of undocumented aliens find work as domestic help.

This legislation created work in the form of a verification document known as the "I-9 Form," which is ordinarily completed in human resources as part of the hiring process. The new employee or employee-to-be must furnish certain proofs of identity and, in the instance of legal aliens, proof of authorization to work in the United States. After examining (and usually copying) the appropriate documents, a representative of the employer signs the I-9 to attest to having seen those documents. Completed I-9 Forms are retained in employment files, where they are subject to inspection and audit by Immigration and Customs Enforcement (ICE) and certain other agencies. Financial penalties are imposed for missing or incomplete I-9s. Also, there can be significant legal repercussions should illegal aliens be discovered in the workforce.

Pension Protection Act (1987)

This Act requires organizations with underfunded pension plans to make additional payments to the Pension Benefit Guarantee Corporation (PBGC), an agency established to guarantee benefit payments to participants of legally qualified defined-benefit pension plans. In addition to increasing employers' payments to the PBGC, this legislation reduces or eliminates the deduction of contributions by employers for better-funded plans.

The Drug-Free Workplace Act (1988)

The Drug-Free Workplace Act requires organizations having $25,000 or more in federal contracts or grants to make good-faith efforts to maintain a drug-free workplace and to establish drug education and awareness programs for employees. As a precondition to receiving a contract or grant, the law requires the organization to certify that it will provide and maintain a drug-free workplace. A number of requirements must be fulfilled by the manager of any department involved in any portion of a federal contract or grant.

All healthcare institutions have an interest in keeping the work environment free from the dangers to patients, visitors, and employees created by the use of illegal drugs or controlled substances. For a number of years the drug abuse problem in the workplace has made it necessary for employers to develop and implement various means of addressing this growing problem. Although the requirements of the Drug-Free Workplace Act apply only to employees engaged in federal contracts and grants, conscientious management suggests that a comprehensive policy and drug-free awareness program be implemented for all employees. Surely conscientious departmental management will have a strong interest in maintaining a drug-free work environment whether or not there are external requirements for doing so.

Employee Polygraph Protection Act (EPPA) (1988)

This legislation prevents most private-sector employers from requiring job applicants or current employees to take polygraph (lie detector) tests. Under EPPA, routine use of polygraph tests is permitted only in organizations that produce and distribute controlled substances and those involved in nuclear power, transportation, currency, commodities, or proprietary information.

In most organizations, an employee may be asked to submit to a polygraph when "other evidence" gives management reason to suspect an individual employee; we may hear this referred to as "reasonable suspicion" or, somewhat inaccurately, as "reasonable cause." However, an employee may not be disciplined or discharged based solely on the results of a polygraph test. Under EPPA the employer may not do the following:

- Ask an employee or applicant to submit to a polygraph test (other than in instances covered by legal exceptions)
- Take adverse action against an individual for refusing to take a polygraph test
- Initiate any adverse action based on a polygraph test an individual may have submitted to for a different reason (in other words, the results of a polygraph test a person has submitted to for one specific reason cannot be used for a different purpose)

Worker Adjustment and Retraining Notification Act (WARN) (1988)

This law requires employers with 100 or more employees at any individual site to provide advance notification of major reductions in force. The employer must provide 60 days' notice of an impending layoff of 50 or more employees and must also notify local government and the state dislocated worker unit that provides employment and training services.

Americans with Disabilities Act (ADA) (1990)

This Act provides individuals with disabilities with the same protections afforded minorities and other protected classes under the Civil Rights Act of 1964, calling for access equal to that available to others in regard to employment; services and facilities available to the public, whether under private or public auspices; transportation; and telecommunications. Modeled after portions of the Civil Rights Act of 1964, the

ADA is essentially an equal opportunity law for people with disabilities.

Disabilities are broadly defined under the Act and include hearing and visual impairments, paraplegia, epilepsy, HIV or AIDS, and literally dozens if not hundreds of other conditions. The list of recognized disabilities is long, and it continues to expand as legal wrangling continues over what is or is not a disability. There have been and continue to be many court cases concerned with defining disabilities, and unfortunately the courts of various states have rendered conflicting decisions.

The ADA prohibits employers from asking about a job applicant's medical conditions, if any, and imposing major limitations on pre-employment physical examinations. In actuality, a physical examination cannot be conducted until after a job offer has been extended. If a physical examination reveals a medical condition that does not affect the person's ability to perform the major functions of the job, the employer may be expected to make a "reasonable accommodation." The key to applicability of the ADA lies in an individual's ability to satisfactorily perform the "major functions" of a job; thus, an individual cannot be denied a job because an impairment prevents performance of a minor or nonessential activity. Thus, the employer may find it necessary to make a reasonable accommodation for the condition, provided that such accommodation does not cause unreasonable expense or hardship.

From time to time, the supervisor may have reason to become familiar with some aspects of the law concerning disabilities. Involvement surely will come the supervisor's way should there have to be a "reasonable accommodation" for one or more employees in the department. However, it is not always possible to tell on sight whether an individual is disabled. Unlike race or gender, a disability may not be readily identifiable.

The supervisor need not be concerned unless he or she knows factually that a disability exists. To obtain the protection available under anti-discrimination laws, an employee must identify himself or herself as disabled; if a disability is neither apparent nor declared, the employee in question should be treated the same as any other employee.

If as a manager you suspect the presence of a disability, but if one has not been declared, do not ask the employee. Moreover, do not give an employee unsolicited advice about some possible but undeclared problem; to do so is considered "disparate treatment."

The ADA has been in the news many times over the past 30 years since its inception. Fully 10 years after its passage, it was argued before the U.S. Supreme Court that the ADA went too far in allowing disabled public employees to sue state and local governments in federal court.[2] States and localities generally have immunity against such lawsuits unless Congress has documented sufficient discrimination to deny them that immunity and to invoke its power under the 14th Amendment to ensure that people have equal protection under the law.

In a decision rendered in January 2002, the Supreme Court unanimously narrowed the number of people covered by the ADA. The opinion held that "[m]erely having an impairment does not make one disabled for purposes of the ADA"; that a person's ailment must extend beyond the workplace and affect everyday life; and that the ability to perform tasks that are of central importance to most people's daily lives must be "substantially limited" before an individual can qualify for coverage under the 1990 law.[3] In other words, the Court ruled that an individual who could function normally in daily living could not claim disability status because of physical problems that limited his or her ability to perform certain manual tasks on the job.

In another opinion that was viewed by some as a defeat for disabled workers, the U.S. Supreme Court ruled that disabled workers are not always entitled to premium assignments intended for more senior workers.[4] The practical implication of this ruling is that in the majority of instances seniority can take precedence over disability. Continuing its series of clarifications and rulings limiting rights under the ADA, in early June 2002 the Court ruled that disabled workers cannot demand jobs that would threaten their lives or health. This arose from a case in which a worker with a particular medical condition wanted to return to his original position although it was considered medically risky for him to do so. The ADA's requirement for "reasonable accommodation" has always made exception for those who might be a threat to the health or safety of others on the job, but this most recent decision interpreted the exception as also applying to workers who may present a risk only to themselves.

In September 2008, Congress passed the ADA Amendments Act (ADAAA), intended to provide broader protections for disabled workers and reverse a number of court decisions that Congress considered too restrictive. Today, in 2022, a number of cases are still pending, and it is likely that the ADA will continue to be refined through Supreme Court decisions for several years to come.

Older Workers Benefit Protection Act (OWBPA) (1990)

This Act, amending the ADEA, clarified the authority of the ADEA relative to employee benefits. Although it required equal benefits for all workers, following a number of legal decisions the ADEA allowed reductions in benefits for older workers in instances where added costs were involved. The OWBPA removed the option for the employer to justify lower benefits for older workers and required that any waivers or releases of age discrimination must be voluntary, part of an understandable written agreement between employer and employee. In effect, this law says that an employer cannot unilaterally provide a reduced benefit to an employee on the basis of age.

Civil Rights Act of 1991

Amending the Civil Rights Act of 1964, the Civil Rights Act of 1991 allows employees to receive compensatory and punitive damages for violations committed with malice or reckless disregard for an individual's protected rights and also allows women and disabled workers to sue for compensatory and punitive damages (a right they previously did not have). This Act also provides for jury trials in such discrimination cases; previously

these were handled through nonjury processes. For employers the overall impact of this Act has been to increase the likelihood of longer and costlier legal processes and to increase potential penalties. The effect of this Act was to add "teeth" to portions of the Civil Rights Act of 1964, expand certain other parts, and generally make possible more and larger damage awards.

Family and Medical Leave Act (FMLA) (1993)

Applying to employers of 50 or more employees, FMLA permits eligible employees (those having been employed for at least 1 year and having worked at least 1,250 hours during the previous 12 months) to take up to 12 weeks of unpaid leave during any 12-month period when unable to work because of a serious health condition; to care for a child upon birth, adoption, or foster care; or to care for a spouse, parent, or child with a serious health condition. Under certain circumstances, leave may be taken intermittently or on some reduced leave schedule, potentially stretching any given leave over a period longer than 12 calendar weeks. Employees who are entitled to a certain amount of paid time off are ordinarily required to use that time as part of their 12 weeks, which most employees on leave ordinarily do rather than experiencing the entire leave without pay.

While on approved leave, employees must continue to receive healthcare benefits but are not entitled to accrue vacation, sick time, or seniority. The employer must guarantee that upon returning from leave an employee will be reinstated to the previous position held or placed in a fully equivalent position with no loss of benefits.

In many instances the FMLA has made life considerably more difficult for supervisors. When an employee in an essential position takes leave, that position must be covered; some positions cannot be left vacant for a few days, let alone for a 12-week period. Filling the position and later returning the employee to "an equivalent position" is not often readily accomplished; "equivalent" has repeatedly been interpreted by courts and other external agencies as essentially the same in all ways—pay, benefits, tasks, responsibilities, often even hours and shift. The strict interpretation of "equivalent" often makes the safest course of action the preservation of one's original position, so the manager is left to juggle coverage—perhaps with temporary employees, overtime, reassignments, and other means—until the employee returns from leave. The FMLA has thus made staffing and scheduling more difficult and time-consuming for some managers.

It is likely that the FMLA, along with the ADA, will be affected by periodic adjustments and clarifications for some time to come.

Retirement Protection Act (1994)

The Retirement Protection Act strengthens and accelerates funding of underfunded pension plans and increases Pension Benefit Guarantee Corporation (PBGC) premiums for plans that pose the greatest risk, improves the flow of pension-related information for workers, and increases PBGC's authority to enforce compliance with pension obligations.

Small Business Job Protection Act (1996)

Despite the name of this Act, its provisions are not applicable to small businesses only. This legislation included the 1996 increase in the minimum wage. It also increased pension protection and made it easier for workers to roll over their retirement savings upon changing employers. It also somewhat simplified pension administration and reduced the vesting period for certain multi-employer plans from 10 years to 5 years. It also made it possible for certain smaller employers to establish simplified 401(k) plans.

Health Insurance Portability and Accountability Act (HIPAA) (1996)

When it came upon the scene in 1996, as far as most persons working in health care were concerned, HIPAA had little effect. At the time the most visible portion of HIPAA addressed "portability and accountability" in reference to employee health insurance. The intent was to enable workers to change jobs without losing coverage. This let workers move from one employer's plan to another's without gaps or waiting periods and without restrictions based on pre-existing conditions. A worker could move from plan to plan without interruption of coverage.

Not many managers in health care concerned themselves with HIPAA in 1996. Human resource (HR) managers were the ones who became most aware of this new legislation because it affected their benefit plans. However, even many HR managers had little involvement with HIPAA; in most instances the required notifications were handled by the employers' health insurance carriers, so there was little for HR to do other than answering employee questions. At that time nothing about HIPPA affected the role of the individual non-HR manager. In the minds of many who did not look beyond the simple implications of the law's title, the organization had little more to do than ensuring the portability of health insurance. However, the real impact of HIPAA was yet to come, and its arrival was a surprise to many.

Today, the HIPAA Privacy Rule provides the first national standards for protecting the privacy of health information. The Privacy Rule regulates how certain entities (covered entities) use and disclose certain individually identifiable health information, called protected health information (PHI).[5] PHI is individually identifiable health information that is transmitted or maintained in any form or medium such as oral, electronic, or paper.

The Privacy Rule gives patients more control over their health information, sets boundaries on the use and release of health records, empowers patients to make informed choices on how their health information should be used and the right to limit what is shared with any covered entity.

The HIPAA Privacy Rule will affect health-care supervisors and managers. The evolving technology advancements in health care will make it increasingly important to follow the law and policies put into place. Supervisors will need to be well informed and continuously train their employees on the best practices of patient privacy.

The Patient Protection and Affordable Care Act of 2010 (PPACA)

The PPACA was signed into law on March 23, 2010, and was immediately amended by the Health Care and Education Act of 2010, which became law on March 30, 2010. The PPACA (commonly referred to today as the ACA or the Affordable Care Act) is the debated "health care reform" undertaking of the Obama administration. The law included provisions intended to take effect over several years, including expanding Medicaid to cover more lower income people, subsidizing insurance premiums for persons of a certain income level, providing incentives for businesses to provide healthcare benefits, prohibiting denial of claims or coverage because of pre-existing conditions, and other fixes aimed at expanding coverage to include greater numbers of people, controlling costs, and reducing the deficit.

As of this writing (mid-2022), there have been changes in government administration, Congress, and failed attempts of a repeal. The ACA has many layers and is discussed in-depth in another chapter within this text.

The PPACA is likely to affect most healthcare supervisors in two ways. First, the supervisor may be affected as a participant in the employer's health insurance plan. Depending on the nature of the plan and its features there could be changes that affect coverage for all employees, including the manager. Second, the individual supervisor is likely to be asked questions by employees who want to know how the plan's changes will affect them and what will happen to their present coverage. The supervisor will need to be knowledgeable enough to respond to general questions and to know where in human resources to go for more complete answers. For the most part, the interpretation of the features and effects of plan reform on the organization's health insurance plan will reside with the benefits-management function in the HR department.

For the Organization: Greater Responsibility, Increased Cost

The foregoing chronology is not complete. There are numerous state laws to contend with, as well as other federal laws that sometimes have employment implications. The closing decades of the twentieth century saw government spreading its influence over an increasing number of aspects of the employment relationship. Fortunately, the proliferation of employment legislation has slowed since the turn of the twenty-first century; most of the more recent activity has involved court decisions creating case law. In addition to creating added work for human resources, many of the laws affecting employment, in designating what cannot be done or what must be done, have prescribed boundaries within which management must manage.

Overall, the effect of employment legislation has been to make employers more socially responsible for their employees. This is especially evident in significant legislation such as the ADA and the FMLA. These laws affecting social responsibility, and most of the other pertinent laws, have added work and supporting systems to the organization and increased the cost of doing business—and thus increased costs to the ultimate consumers of all goods and services.

Some new laws have required only minor changes in procedures or modest alterations in recordkeeping practices. However, most have clearly increased the cost of doing business because the provider organization, and eventually its customers, are the only ones available to pay. Legislators well know that it usually costs something to implement a new law in the workplace (although the legislators and the organizations that must comply with the law are often far from agreement about how much it will actually cost). When legislators create a new program, they undoubtedly know there are but three ways available to pay for its implementation: (1) they can discontinue an existing program to free up some funds, but rarely does this happen because it is always a politically unpopular move; (2) they can raise taxes to pay for it, but suggesting to do so is even more politically unpopular; or (3) they can find someone else to pay for it. The "someone else" who has been paying to implement these laws affecting the employment relationship is business and, eventually, the consumer.

A Cumulative Effect

Exhibit 7.1 lists the laws discussed by decade of passage. It is not difficult to see the shift from the pre-1964 concern with collective bargaining and wage and hour issues to the growing post-1964 concern with social responsibility.

A simple comparison of the pre-1964 years with the present day should serve to demonstrate how significantly the employment environment has changed. Although a few of the laws replaced features of earlier legislation, most of the laws passed since 1964 have exerted new and different influences on how employers treat employees and how managers can manage their departments. The accumulation of more than four decades of legislation affecting the employment relationship has placed upon the average supervisor countless "rules" for managing employees.

A new law can come into being in a relatively brief period, yet the changes in human behavior required by that law can be a long time happening. A strong case in point is Title VII of the Civil Rights Act of 1964. Employment discrimination has now been prohibited by law for nearly five decades, but problems of discrimination continue in many organizations. Nevertheless, the workforce in the United States is becoming increasingly diverse, and only the organizations that eliminate discrimination will be able to properly value and manage this diversity.

Exhibit 7.1 Employment-Related Legislation by Decade

1930s
Norris–LaGuardia Act (1932)
National Labor Relations Act (1935)
Social Security Act (1935)
Fair Labor Standards Act (1938)

1940s
Labor-Management Relations Act (Taft-Hartley) (1947)

1950s
Labor-Management Reporting and Disclosure Act (1959)

1960s
Equal Pay Act (1963)
Title VII of the Civil Rights Act (1964)
Age Discrimination in Employment Act (1967)

1970s
Occupational Safety and Health Administration (OSHA) (1970)
Rehabilitation Act (1973)
Pregnancy Discrimination Act (1978)

1980s
Consolidated Omnibus Budget Reconciliation Act (COBRA) (1986)
Immigration Reform and Control Act (IRCA) (1986)
Pension Protection Act (1987)
Drug-Free Workplace Act (1988)
Employee Polygraph Protection Act (1988)
Worker Adjustment and Retraining Notification Act (1988)

1990s
Americans with Disabilities Act (ADA) (1990)
Older Workers Benefit Protection Act (OWBPA) (1990)
Civil Rights Act of 1991
Family and Medical Leave Act (FMLA) (1993)
Retirement Protection Act (1994)
Small Business Job Protection Act (1996)
Health Insurance Portability and Accountability Act (HIPAA) (1996)

2000s
The Patient Protection and Affordable Care Act (PPACA) (2010)

WRAP-UP

Think About It

For the greater part of 2020 and 2021 the COVID-19 pandemic changed the world. It also changed the employment environment, health care, individual rights, and many others. We can expect the interest in individual rights to continue, even intensify from time to time. The employment environment has changed and will continue changing; those who manage within this environment must either change with it or be left behind.

Questions for Review and Discussion

1. Explain why 1964 and the passage of Title VII of the Civil Rights Act of 1964 are referred to as the turning point in the evolution of human resources. Other than 1964 representing the beginning of a steady flow of regulations, what is it that truly constituted a change of direction? Why?

2. Define and describe a "bargaining unit" as pertinent to present-day applicability of the National Labor Relations Act.

3. Review when and how the EEOC was established and what its purpose is.

4. Define a bona fide occupational qualification (BFOQ) and provide at least two specific examples.

5. Explain what the "right to know" laws primarily address and what they are intended to accomplish.

6. Well before the passage of the ADA, certain employers were required in some instances to provide "reasonable accommodation" of the limitations of an employee or applicant. Specify when this occurred and enumerate the conditions under which this requirement applied.

7. Identify the primary intended purpose of the ERISA. Explain why this legislation was likely seen as necessary.

8. Discuss the principal business effects of the IRCA.

9. Pose two hypothetical examples of situations in which a healthcare employer might legally require a polygraph (lie detector) test as a condition of either initial employment or continued employment.

10. Consider the FMLA from the perspective of a working department manager and describe the ways in which this legislation has affected the manager's ability to manage.

References

1. Fox S. Employment provisions of the Rehabilitation Act. *Personnel Journal*. October 1987;66(10):132.

2. Hearst News Service. High court scrutinizes Disabilities Act. *Rochester Democrat & Chronicle*. October 12, 2000.

3. Newsday. High court limits Disability Law. *Rochester Democrat & Chronicle*. January 9, 2002.

4. The Associated Press. Seniority outweighs disability, court says. *Rochester Democrat & Chronicle*. April 30, 2002.

5. Thacker S. HIPAA Privacy Rule and Public Health. *MMWR*. https://www.cdc.gov/mmwr/preview/mmwrhtml/m2e411a1.htm

CHAPTER 8

Employee Recruitment

CHAPTER OBJECTIVES

- Convey the importance of the employee selection process in building a stable and motivated workforce.
- Describe the kinds of job candidates the supervisor should ordinarily seek to interview.
- Review the significant legal constraints affecting the recruitment and employment process, including designation of the kinds of information that may not legally be requested on an employment application.
- Review the various sources customarily used for locating appropriate job candidates.
- Briefly introduce the concept of the aging workforce, highlight its effects on employment recruiting, and explore the potential use of the "mature" worker in meeting vital staffing needs.
- Review several ways in which healthcare organizations might stimulate recruiting during periods of staff shortage.
- Review the role of the department supervisor in the recruitment process.

KEY TERMS

Affirmative Action: A federal requirement for employers to identify areas of minority and female underutilization and set specific numerical hiring and promotion goals and other actions to increase minority and female employment where they are underutilized. (For the most part, presently no longer a significant concern.)

Equal Employment Opportunity Commission (EEOC): The federal agency charged with enforcement of the anti-discrimination requirements of Title VII of the Civil Rights Act of 1964.

Division of Human Rights (DHR): A state counterpart to the EEOC, usually working in concert with EEOC concerning charges of discrimination.

Finding Employees

Finding the right employees in today's fast-changing healthcare environment is becoming an increasingly important—and increasingly difficult—activity for supervisors. Of all their responsibilities, the selection of new employees ranks near the top in importance. Motivational problems, disciplinary issues, employee turnover, and susceptibility to union organizing can all be reduced or controlled by hiring the right people.

Improved selection of new employees is an integral part of improved customer service, team building, successful quality management, and cost control. Poor recruitment and selection are expensive. The eventual cost of a single bad hire may amount to several times that employee's annual salary. The supervisor who hires in haste in the belief that "If this one doesn't work out, I can always hire another" is making a potentially costly mistake. The expenses associated with a poor hiring choice can include the following:

- Cost of recruiting and training a replacement
- Cost of repeat advertising
- Time and productivity lost while a position is vacant
- Cost of overtime to cover essential tasks
- Reduced productivity while a replacement is learning
- Possible unemployment compensation expense
- Potential loss of customers
- Potential legal problems arising from dismissal

Essentials of the Selection Process

Institutions known for excellent customer service are careful to hire people who have displayed positive customer service attitudes in their previous work and social conduct. Once a person has been hired, it is considerably easier to reinforce good attitudes than it is to change bad habits. Obtaining the kind of employees we should desire is governed by three imperatives:

1. A recruiting program that provides a broad choice of good candidates
2. A selection process that can choose the best candidate with a high degree of confidence
3. The ability to persuade the most desirable candidates to accept our offers

If the number of job competencies sought in applicants can be reduced without ill effects, there will be a greater number of candidates to choose from. Concerning competencies, it is necessary to separate the must-haves from the nice-to-haves. For example, does the person really need a college degree and 3 years of experience, or will 1 or 2 years of experience suffice? Be careful in

specifying mandatory qualifications; if your standard is challenged by a candidate from a legally protected group, would you be able to justify the requirement in court? This risk can be reduced by stating that a particular competency is highly desirable, not mandatory.

Desirable Candidates

Healthcare institutions are looking for more people who can contribute to the continuous improvement of customer service, productivity, and creativity. Finding candidates with the technical or professional skills needed is easier than finding people who exhibit the types of behaviors that fit into the culture of your organization.

In addition to job expertise, other factors also make for success in dealing with customers. These factors include social skills, that is, the ability to be articulate and the ability to say and do what is necessary to establish and maintain understanding with customers. Other positive attributes include a sense of teamwork, cooperation, and collaboration. However, it seems that the questions most frequently asked of job candidates, and the principal influences on selecting new employees, relate primarily to work experience and professional or technical skill. The most desirable candidates for most positions are those who exhibit the following traits:

- Have a broad technical or professional background
- Are effective communicators and rapid learners
- Can deal effectively with people
- Are flexible (for example, can readily move among different competencies as needed)

When we hire only highly specialized individuals, we run the risk of falling into the talent obsolescence trap. Because of rapid changes in technologies and services offered by organizations, the qualifications needed by those we seek to hire also change rapidly. Job descriptions that are too finely tuned can result in hiring employees who are qualified for today's job but who become obsolete when tomorrow's needs arrive.

Legal Constraints to Hiring

The primary thrust of federal and state employment legislation is to ensure that hiring, retention, and promotion decisions are made only on the basis of the ability of an employee to do the job. Thus, the focus must now be on what the job applicant knows and can do, to the complete exclusion of all of the applicant's personal characteristics.

Affirmative Action

The Civil Rights Act of 1964 and Executive Order 11246 (amended by Executive Order 11375) required employers to identify areas of minority and female underutilization and called for specific numerical hiring and promotion goals and other actions to increase minority and female employment in job classifications where they are currently underutilized. However, most healthcare supervisors do not need to be concerned with formal affirmative action plans. Executive Order 11246 required written affirmative action plans of federal contractors having 50 or more employees and government contracts amounting to $50,000 or more. However, although many healthcare organizations employ more than 50 people, very few are ever involved with government contracts.

Nevertheless, supervisors must be aware of the legal requirements of Equal Employment Opportunity Commission (EEOC) regulations and of their own organization's policies and practices as they relate to EEOC and the Americans with Disabilities Act (ADA). They must recognize and eliminate stereotyping and preconceptions and provide clear and achievable expectations for all their employees.

Unlawful Inquiries

Each state also has its own requirements regarding Title VII of the Civil Rights Act of 1964, and most states have some agency, going perhaps by the name of the Division of Human Rights or something similar, that parallels the EEOC at the state level. Generally, however, when both state and federal governments address the same issues via regulation and those regulations happen to differ to some extent, the more stringent of the two is assumed to apply.

Under Title VII and various state laws, it is forbidden to ask a job applicant for certain information, whether on an employment application or in a personal interview. If in doubt concerning questions that may be asked, consult your human resources department. Following is a partial list of the kinds of information that cannot legally be solicited from a job applicant:

- Any inquiries that could reveal the applicant's age, nationality, or marital status.
- The applicant's spouse's occupation or place of employment (or even if there is a spouse).
- Whether one is pregnant or has plans for pregnancy.
- Childcare or baby-sitting arrangements (without asking specifically about children, an application could ask the applicant about availability to work various shifts and the ability to accommodate call-ins, call-backs, etc.).
- Character of military discharge or service record, except as military experience might relate to job qualifications.
- Arrest record. (For some time, applications have been able to ask whether the person has been *convicted* of a crime but even this is now open to question. See the following chapter.)
- Membership in organizations other than those related to one's work or occupation (but not labor unions; no candidate may be asked about union membership or related activities).
- Religious affiliation.
- Nature, severity, or existence of physical or mental impairments. Avoid inquiries about the use of sick leave or whether the individual was ever out on disability or workers' compensation. (You may ask how much work time the individual missed as long as the question is not limited to absences resulting from illness or injury.)
- Questions that would be asked only of members of a protected group. For example, if you want to ask women whether they can lift a 50-pound child, you must also ask male candidates that same question.

Recognize that this list could be expanded to encompass many more specific inquiries that cannot be made on an employment application (and that cannot be asked in an interview, to be addressed in more detail in the chapter "Interviewing and Employee Selection"). Title VII of the Civil Rights Act of 1964, along with subsequent legislation, forever altered the employment application by strictly limiting the kinds of information that can be requested. Legal refinements still occur, occasionally based on case law and new legislation; it is fairly safe to say that any employment application that has not been revised in the past 4 or 5 years or so is most likely illegal.

Of course, some information that cannot legally be requested on an application or in an interview can and must be obtained after the person has accepted an offer of employment. Certain personal information is required for human resources, payroll, and benefits purposes.

Age Discrimination in Employment Act of 1967

As amended in 1986, the Age Discrimination in Employment Act prohibits employers from placing an age limit on candidates for employment and from making retirement mandatory at some designated age. For most hiring purposes, there is only one age-related question that can legally be asked: Are you at least 18 years of age? This lower age barrier exists because of the application of child labor laws below the age of 18. Concerning mandatory retirement, there are exceptions for a few occupations for which age is a *bona fide occupational qualification* (BFOQ) (for example, police officer, firefighter, and airline pilot).

Rehabilitation Act of 1973 and the Americans with Disabilities Act of 1992

The major thrusts of the Rehabilitation Act of 1973 and the ADA of 1992 are provisions (1) dealing with hiring and promotion practices and (2) that require reasonable accommodation. Again, the cardinal rule is that any question asked of candidates should relate to the job in some way. You can ask whether an applicant can perform all job-related functions and meet attendance requirements; you may not inquire about an applicant's current or past medical or health conditions. If an applicant reveals that he or she cannot perform an essential function, do not probe into the individual's medical history.

Instead, attempt to identify how the disability renders the applicant unable to perform the essential functions of the job, and find out what accommodations, if any, would enable the applicant to do the job.

Reasonable accommodation refers to measures that an employer may take to enable a person to perform essential functions. These could be physical changes such as wider doors or magnified displays, or they could be the elimination of some nonessential or infrequently performed tasks. For example, if a job requires occasional typing and the candidate lacks the mechanical ability to type, that activity could be assigned to other employees.

When the ADA became law, the task of screening job applicants became more hazardous. Following are five questions that are now illegal:

1. Have you ever filed a workers' compensation claim?
2. Do you have any physical problems or injuries?
3. How many days were you sick last year?
4. Are you currently taking any medications?
5. Have you ever been treated for drug abuse?

Under revised guidelines, the EEOC permits employers to inquire about accommodations at the initial interview stage in a few specific situations. For example, the employer reasonably believes an applicant will need accommodations because of an obvious disability (say the applicant uses a wheelchair or has severe visual impairment) or the applicant voluntarily reveals the need for accommodation during the interview (for example, the person discloses a hidden disability such as diabetes or states the need for breaks to take medication). Except for these circumstances, the law concerning inquiries remains unchanged. All other disability-related inquiries must wait until after a job offer has been made.

Recruitment Sources

- Employee referrals
- Social media
- Recruitment firms
- Employment agencies
- College recruitment
- Internship programs
- Job fairs
- Professional organizations
- Unsolicited résumés

One of the most effective recruitment methods is employee referral. Your workers have friends and acquaintances who are either working for other employers in your area or are actively seeking employment. Employees have their own networks and may encourage their friends to fill out applications. A number of organizations have discovered that a satisfied workforce is a strong force in recruiting.

The internet is actively used as a tool in recruiting. The popularity of social media has increased over the past few years. It is used in different ways, and one of those ways is recruitment. Social media can connect people from all over the world, which is very helpful when recruiting for employment. All organizations have their own recruitment websites. Today, it is very uncommon to go to a physical location and apply for a job in person; everything is done on the company website or another website linking the application to the hiring company.

If your organization has a reputation as a great place to work, the best people will find you.

Recruiting in the Twenty-First Century

The Aging Workforce

The term "old" is outdated and no longer used to address the aging population in the workforce.

This text will use the term "mature" to address people of a certain age in the workforce. It is no secret to those who spend large amounts of time trying to keep a healthcare organization staffed with the right kinds of talent that the workforce is, on the average, getting older. The oldest of the "baby boomers," the 76 million Americans born between 1946 and 1964, are now 75, and the population of persons older than 50 continues to grow. At the same time, the number of younger people entering the workforce have been declining. Important healthcare occupations such as nursing are experiencing shortages of new entrants while the average age of those presently working continues to advance.

Overall, the pool of younger people available for employment is not growing nearly as rapidly as organizations' needs are growing. Also, for a variety of reasons, many of them economic, many workers who are able to do so are remaining employed beyond what was formerly considered retirement age. The amended Age Discrimination in Employment Act eliminated so-called mandatory retirement for most people, so many continue to work past the age at which they might have been made to retire—some still working because they want to, some because they feel that doing so is necessary economically.

Whereas the supply of younger workers grows slower than the demand for their services, the supply of available mature workers, augmented by the displacements caused by staffing cutbacks, mergers, acquisitions, closures, and the needs of some to continue working out of economic necessity, continues to grow. Yet in spite of age discrimination legislation and a readily available supply of mature workers, most present-day recruiting is focused on attracting younger employees. In today's job market, it is the younger workers who enjoy greater employability.

Recruiting Mature Workers

A significant contradiction is frequently encountered in the working world today. Many organizations that are hurting for help are constantly recruiting for experienced and reliable workers.

At the same time, significant numbers of willing and able workers are available who cannot readily find employment. These experienced and capable workers face difficulty in securing employment for one reason: They are considered "too old."

We know that age discrimination in employment is illegal and that age is not legitimately a consideration for employment except in a very limited number of instances. Legal protection against age discrimination officially kicks in at age 40, but for all practical purposes the group facing the hardest times on the employment market are those aged 50 and older. In their reluctance to seriously consider this age group as a potential source of talent, some employers are behaving as though they believe someone older than 50 will not be able to do the same job as a younger person. This age bias is often subtle, sometimes as elementary as supervisors' unwillingness to take on workers older than themselves.

The pool of available workers older than 50 constitutes a rapidly growing source of talent and ability. And Americans 65 and older will double in number in the coming years to become about 20% of the population by the year 2030. This means a growing supply of mature workers.

The employment of mature workers makes good business sense in several ways. Many mature workers offer a lifetime of experience that can substantially benefit employers. Workers older than 50 have repeatedly been shown to be more productive and more dependable than their younger counterparts, and studies have shown that on average mature workers are more punctual and take less time off. The facts stand in direct contradiction to the beliefs of many employers that hiring mature workers is to buy in to excessive sick time and undesirable effects on health insurance costs.

Some mature workers do not need or desire full-time work, so this labor pool is a good source of knowledgeable and capable part-time help, especially in health care where part-time needs are abundant.

The fear of the possibility of charges of age discrimination seems to rank low among the reasons for not employing mature workers. Although age discrimination is illegal, it is one of the more difficult instances of discrimination to successfully pursue within the legal system. Rather, it is the capabilities that many readily available mature workers bring to the job that signify the wisdom inherent in taking advantage of their available knowledge and experience. Simply, age should not be a factor in hiring. Rather, the principal criterion for employment in most positions should forever remain one's ability to do the job. Whether a particular job applicant is 20 years old or 50 years old should make no difference whatsoever as long as the individual can do the job.

Recruiting During Periods of Shortage

The COVID-19 pandemic increased the workforce shortage specifically in the healthcare industry. By the end of 2020, the healthcare industry lost close to 2 million workers.[1] The turbulent time in the world was difficult for healthcare workers. For recruiters, it was difficult to retain employees and even harder to hire new ones. It was an "all hands-on deck" situation. Nurses, doctors, and healthcare professionals from all walks of life and those who were retired came back to work. Today, there is still a shortage of healthcare workers.

On the other side of workforce shortage, recruiting becomes more difficult during periods of low unemployment and when certain needed skills are in short supply on the labor market. When people having certain skills become difficult to find, the specialists in the occupations in demand have their choice of employers. In the face of this "seller's market," a number of special approaches may be considered for attracting new employees.

Internship programs can be effective for recruiting scarce professionals. For example, a hospital that provides an internship experience for a pharmacy student may find the student willing to return as an employee after graduation. A person who has had a pleasant internship experience is more likely to become an employee than is a candidate to whom the organization is new and strange.

Moving expenses may be paid or partial moving allowances offered to professional and managerial employees recruited from out-of-town. This has long been a standard practice when recruiting top management employees. As particular professionals become more scarce and in greater demand, organizations are more likely to offer such enticements.

Signing bonuses have been used as incentives during periods of employee shortage. Currently, one can find numerous advertisements for nursing staff offering signing bonuses to new employees. A common industry practice is to pay one-half of the bonus when the person is hired and pay the second half when the individual has been successfully employed for a stated period.

During shortage periods, a finder's fee or bounty may be offered to current employees who refer candidates for specific positions. The fee is paid to the person making the referral when a new candidate is then hired to fill a vacancy in a shortage occupation. This process is often described as an employee referral program. The finder's fee is ordinarily paid out in the same manner as a signing bonus: one-half of the bonus when the new person is hired and the second half when the new individual has been successfully employed for a stated period.

In spite of the visible costs involved, an employee referral program can save money when compared with the costs of advertising. In many instances, a signing bonus and finder's fee together add up to less than the cost of a modest size display ad placed in an area newspaper. An employee referral program can often be shown to generate new employees at the lowest cost per hire of all recruiting practices.

Finally, extremely specialized arrangements may be made with individuals who are needed to fill critical positions. It is common to employ physicians, for example, using individual or personal-service contracts. Another occasionally used practice involves an arrangement to pay off an individual's outstanding student loans in exchange for a contractual agreement to remain with an organization for a specific amount of time.

How Supervisors Can Help in the Recruiting Process

As an individual supervisor, quite likely one of many, you may believe that you have no influence on the recruiting practices of your organization. However, you can play an important role in the recruiting process. Do not overlook the possibility of finding good job candidates internal to the organization; be on the lookout for potential candidates in other departments. That young lady in the housekeeping department who always greets you with a smile might do a great job as a receptionist or perhaps could be trained as a phlebotomist or patient-care technician. Encourage your staff to serve as unofficial recruiters.

Provide your recruiters with condensed versions of position descriptions that also highlight the attractive features of the job. Recommend what you believe to be the most appropriate publications or websites in which to place advertisements. Obtain a list of technical or professional schools where potential candidates train and share this list with the employment recruiters. Participate actively in career programs and job fairs.

Employee Selection Methods

Applications and Résumés

Résumés are the public relations handouts of job candidates. As candidates' "balance sheets" they stress—and at times, unfortunately, greatly overstress—individuals' assets without mentioning liabilities. We can realistically expect that no job applicants will say anything unfavorable about themselves on their résumés. Unfortunately, we can also expect that a good half or more of the résumés we see are going to contain exaggerations if not outright untruths. As Dorch[2] states, "Some of the best fiction writing in the world is in the form of résumés."

Study each résumé carefully, and do not be shy about questioning claims that seem to you to be out of line. When reviewing applications and résumés, be especially alert for indications of customer service experience (for example, volunteer work and membership in social organizations), teamwork, and responsibilities that exceeded job requirements.

Frequent job changes call for close questioning of candidates. When moves are at best lateral or to jobs that pay less, involve less responsibility, or require less competency, watch out. Equally significant are job changes attributed to "personal reasons" or covered by explanations like "My boss and I had different chemistries." Other red flags are unexplained time gaps in employment, inconsistencies in salary history, incomplete contact information about previous employers, and vague reasons for leaving previous jobs.

A candidate's outside interests could indicate the presence of certain desirable capabilities, although there could be a risk that some of these activities might interfere with attendance or performance. However, the supervisor must proceed with care in questioning a candidate about outside activities; what people do on their own time is their own business. Avoid the oft-cited halo effect. The success an individual enjoyed in one kind of employment does not ensure his or her success in a different kind of job. Pay attention to the grammar, spelling, and clarity of expression in the résumé and in any correspondence with the applicant, especially if you seek a meticulous worker.

Credentialing

Confirm all licenses, certifications, and registrations. In most organizations new hires are required to furnish copies of current licenses. And given the current times with many unemployed people competing for a relatively small number of attractive positions, it is sometimes wise to take steps to verify educational qualifications. One of the more common areas of résumé "puff" involves claiming nonexistent

college degrees or writing up one's educational experience in a manner that can lead the casual reader to assume graduation when in fact it did not occur.

Pre-Employment Testing

Pre-employment tests can be very revealing, but in general they are underutilized. Employment managers are frequently hesitant to administer certain kinds of tests for fear of violating anti-discrimination laws; employers can be called on to prove that the tests they use possess validity and reliability. However, as long as a test is based on a required skill or on knowledge as documented in the job description, such fears are without foundation. Examples of such tests are as follows:

- Phlebotomist or patient-care technician candidates can be tested on making preparations for collecting a blood specimen.
- Clerk-receptionist candidates can take some incoming phone calls.
- Candidates applying for jobs having teaching responsibilities can be asked to deliver a short lecture or perform a demonstration.
- Certain candidates can sometimes be tried in temporary jobs before being hired on a regular basis.
- In one of the most common kinds of pre-employment tests, individuals applying for jobs involving keyboarding are often tested on typing skills.

An alternative to these action tests is to ask candidates to tell you in as much detail as possible how they performed certain tasks. Only people who have actually done what they claim can tell you in detail how the work is done.

Questionnaires

Some commercial job-applicant questionnaires intend to measure honesty, loyalty, and positive attitudes, but the jury is still out on the validity of these tools. Many of these instruments are of the kind that can give rise to charges of discrimination.

WRAP-UP

Think About It

Recruiting is all about finding the right employees to carry out the department's mission and properly serve its customers. The trouble is, there is no completely foolproof recruiting process; we never know for sure who the "right" employees are until they have spent some time on the job. But careful recruiting can greatly reduce the chances of making inappropriate placement decisions.

Questions for Review and Discussion

1. What could be wrong with an employment application question asking whether the applicant has been arrested? Is not the employer entitled to know whether one who might be hired has been in trouble with the law?

2. If age alone is no longer a reason to avoid hiring someone or for forcing one to retire, what then is the principal criterion for getting hired or remaining employed?

3. A recruiter in human resources is going to find five job candidates for you to interview. In addition to being sure they possess the stated job qualifications, what would you advise the recruiter to look for in these candidates? Why?

4. On an employment application, can you ask if the applicant rents or owns a home? Why or why not?

5. Write one brief statement that summarizes everything you are not allowed to request on an employment application.

6. Is it of any particular importance to sometimes seek new employees for your department from within the organization? Why or why not?

7. It has often been said that the most effective means of filling available jobs is personal networking and referral. Why might this be so?

8. Do you believe that the process of checking applicants' credentials for appropriate licenses should also include verifying educational qualifications? Why or why not?

9. Explain how the COVID-19 pandemic changed the recruitment process.

10. When recruiting during times of staff shortages, it is the practice of some employers to lure help away from other local organizations by offering more money. What do you believe are the principal results of this practice?

Case: The Employee Who Didn't Fit

Bob Long was hired by County Hospital as supervisor of engineering and maintenance. Although well experienced in his field, this was his first management job. Soon after Bob's arrival, a maintenance helper job came open. This was an important job because of a number of preventive maintenance activities that had to be performed, and Bob recognized the need to fill this job as soon as possible. Bob asked human resources to find some candidates for him to interview.

Bob's manager, General Services Director Jack Parsons, chose to sit in on the interviews, giving as his reason Bob's newness to management. Jack indicated that because Bob had never recruited before, he should be assisted in the process.

Bob and Jack agreed that given the entry-level nature of the job, they need not look for experience but instead should look for apparent willingness to learn. Together they interviewed five candidates. Of the five, two seemed reasonable choices. One of these, a young man named Simon, was already employed by the hospital as a kitchen helper in food service. The other, a young man named Kelsey, had not worked recently but had had several months' experience in the custodial department of a school.

Bob expressed his desire to take on Simon from food service because he appeared to have the aptitude and ability and showed a strong desire to better himself, but Jack disagreed. He told Bob he could do the hiring the next time a job opened and made the decision to hire Kelsey.

As the probation period progressed, it became increasingly clear to Bob that Kelsey was not shaping up as a satisfactory employee. Even extending every benefit of the doubt, which he did because Kelsey was the boss's choice, he could conclude only that Kelsey was not going to work out in the long run.

Just before the end of Kelsey's probationary period, Bob went to see Jack. He had kept Jack advised all along, so it was no surprise to Jack when Bob said they should cut Kelsey loose and start over.

"Okay," Jack agreed, "let Kelsey go."

Bob hesitated, wondering briefly if he should say anything, then finally said to Jack, "I don't believe I should let him go. I didn't hire him."

"He's your employee," Jack said. "Get rid of him."

Questions

1. Did Jack dodge his responsibilities by ordering Bob to get rid of the unsatisfactory employee? Why or why not?
2. What are two other ways in which this situation could have been handled more equitably?
3. What effect might this incident have on the future relationship between Bob Long and Jack Parsons?

Case: Recruiting Inside Versus Outside—Bungled

With adequate notice and with the knowledge of his staff, the manager of information systems left the hospital to take a position elsewhere. Within the department, it was assumed that Mr. Smith—"Smitty" to everyone— would move up from his senior position and become manager, but even with the passage of a full week, no appointment had been made.

One week became several weeks. The vice president to whom the information systems group normally reported began to make administrative decisions for information systems. Smitty was left the growing task of overseeing the functions of the group in addition to performing his regular work.

The employees in the department became aware that the hospital was advertising for an information systems manager and that interviews were being conducted at a fairly high level. However, nobody was hired. Finally, after the group had been 6 months without a manager, Smitty was elevated to manager and was immediately authorized to hire a replacement for his old position.

Questions

1. In a scenario such as that just described, what are the likely effects of leaving a supposedly important position open for so long?
2. What do you believe would be the effects on the information systems employees discovering that apparently "secret" recruiting was taking place?
3. Provide two or three possible reasons why the choice for manager reverted to Mr. Smith, even though external recruiting had been pursued.

References

1. Gupta N, Balcom SA, Gulliver A, Witherspoon RL. Health workforce surge capacity during the COVID19 pandemic and other global respiratory disease outbreaks: A systematic review of health system requirements and responses. *Int J Health Plann Manage.* 2021;36(Suppl 1):26–41. doi:10.1002/hpm.3137
2. Dortch CT. Job-person match. *Personnel Journal.* 1989;68:46.

CHAPTER 9

Interviewing and Employee Selection

CHAPTER OBJECTIVES

- Establish the department supervisor as the individual primarily responsible for interviewing and employee selection.
- Review the essential preparations that should precede every interview.
- Spell out the supervisor's approach to the selection interview, including review of kinds of questions that can legally be asked and the questions that must be avoided.
- Provide guidance for the evaluation of job candidates.
- Address the essential follow-up activities necessary to complete the interview process.
- Describe the supervisor's relationship to and involvement in the process of checking employment references.
- Provide advice on how to deal with unsuccessful job candidates.

KEY TERMS

Legally Valid Interview: An interview conducted in accordance with questioning guidelines based on Title VII of the Civil Rights Act of 1964 and other pertinent antidiscrimination legislation.

Placement Interview, or Employee Selection Interview: Interview of a job applicant conducted by the manager who will be the immediate supervisor of the person hired.

Prohibited Question: Any interview question intended, either directly or indirectly, to elicit information that may not legally be used in making an employment decision.

Defamation: A charge that one's name or reputation has been damaged by comments made by a present or past employer (in reference to comments offered in response to a reference request).

Negligent Hiring: A charge made against an organization alleging failure to make a good-faith effort to check references in the hiring of an employee with a past record of wrongdoing who subsequently causes harm in a new employment situation.

To a considerable extent, most approaches to employment selection interviewing are based on the premise that job candidates who have already displayed certain competencies are likely to continue to display those competencies. But in addition to seeking individuals who have done well in the past, we should also be seeking those who appear to have the potential for doing well in the future.

Who Should Conduct the Interview?

The primary interviewer should be the supervisor to whom this candidate will report if hired. It is fundamental that the individual supervisor be the person who interviews and chooses his or her own employees. However, a selection interview is so important that the interviewing supervisor must be well trained in this essential skill.

In the past it was a practice of some organizations to have a central activity—say an "employment office"—hire people and hand them off to the supervisors. Today this process is most likely valid only when hiring "day labor" for unskilled work of a temporary nature. No interviewer can assess an applicant for both technical competence and "fit" as an individual better than the supervisor of the position in question. To hire people centrally and simply hand them off to the supervisors is to invite problems, not the least of which is the likelihood of increased turnover. An appropriate hiring process will likely have the employment section of the human resources department doing screening interviews and supplying the supervisor with several candidates who meet the stated qualifications of the job; interviewing and selection then fall to the supervisor.

Experienced interviewers can sometimes hold unstructured interviews in which no prepared questions are asked and still conduct fair and legally valid interviews, but this is possible only because of familiarity gained through many interviews. Inexperienced interviewers must prepare questions in advance and, to ensure fairness and validity, use the same questions for each candidate who interviews for the same position. Skilled interviewers ask the right questions and then observe and listen. Experienced interviewers show enthusiasm about their organization, their staff, and the job under consideration.

When a team approach to interviewing is used, one or more of the candidate's potential future peers should serve on the interview team. Employees have a decided self-interest in seeing who will become their new associates, and they

can often spot people they would like to have or not like to have working with them. However, the team approach should be applied with caution; some applicants are intimidated by the presence of multiple interviewers. The team approach to interviewing is most applicable in filling technical, professional, and managerial positions.

Computer-Assisted Interviews

Computer-assisted interviews have seen only limited use; however, corporations that use expert computer systems report improvement in the quality of new employees and claim beneficial effects on turnover, absenteeism, theft, and productivity. Surprisingly, some candidates seem more willing to feed information into computers than provide it orally to interviewers. A typical interview program consists of about 100 multiple-choice questions and takes about 20 minutes to complete.

Preparing for the Interview

Following are guidelines to assist you, the supervisor, in ensuring effective interviews:

- Familiarize yourself with the position description such that you can discuss the position confidently without having to refer to a document. Make certain the position description is up to date. Concentrate on the duties and required qualifications.
- Study applications and résumés, making sure that everyone applying possesses at least the minimum qualifications. Human resources should have supplied only candidates who possess the proper qualifications, but a brief recheck is sometimes helpful.
- Draft a list of questions for the candidates, staying away from all questions that might raise questions of legality.
- List the positive features of the job, those aspects most likely to appeal to the greatest number of applicants.

- Familiarize yourself with the salary range and benefits for the position but be prepared to advise applicants that salary and benefits details will be addressed by human resources.
- Visualize the tour of your facilities that you will provide for applicants and alert the people you want the candidates to meet.
- Schedule a time and place that ensure privacy and freedom from interruptions.

Two Initial Interview Steps

Breaking the Ice

A nonthreatening introduction can make candidates feel comfortable and relaxed. Be enthusiastic and persuasive but be honest and sincere. You get only one chance to make a good first impression, so start right. People wish to make good first impressions in recruitment and interviewing situations.[1] Also, your first impression of each candidate is important; what you see is what future customers will see when they first meet this person.

Be on time and greet job applicants by name. When you introduce yourself, include your title. Thank them for coming. Offer a rest stop or coffee before you get down to talking.

Do not interview from behind a desk. Seat an applicant next to your desk rather than across from you. Do not remain standing and do not perch on the edge of your desk.

Make brief small talk as necessary to get interviewees into a talking mode and, just as important, to get you into the all-important listening mode. However, even in supposedly off-the-record small talk, take care to avoid questions that could violate Equal Employment Opportunity Commission antidiscrimination restrictions. Instead, ask how the candidates learned about the job, what their understanding of the job is, whether they had a parking problem on arrival, and about any outside interests mentioned in the résumé.

Review the interview agenda, assuring interviewees that they will have the opportunity to ask all the questions they wish to ask. Ask whether the allotted time poses any problem; they may be scheduled elsewhere after your interview. Then briefly describe the job being offered.

Chronological Review

One potentially productive way to begin is to have the candidate supply a brief chronological review starting with formal education. Inquire about academic standing, jobs held, social activities, and leadership roles.

Move on to the work history, for example, "For each job you've held, I'd like to know things like duties and job responsibilities, how you handled setbacks, the most and least enjoyable aspects of your job, reason for leaving, and what your supervisor was like." Some interviewers like to ask candidates to describe a typical workday.

Ask probing questions using the list you prepared. Finally, market the job, the department, and the organization, but in doing so resist the temptation to speak at length. Finally, respond to the questions or concerns of the candidate; a candidate's questions are important in that they provide clues to the strength of the individual's interest in the available position.

Questions to Ask of Applicants

Kinds of Questions

Whenever possible avoid short-answer or closed-ended questions, those that can be answered with just a word or two, for example, "Did you like working there?" (Response: "Yes"; this surely tells you very little about the applicant.) Use closed-ended questions only to obtain basic data but not to elicit detailed information. You will learn little by asking a question like "Did you like your last supervisor?"

Open-ended questions cannot be answered with only a few words and are better for getting detailed information. Change the previous closed-ended question to "Tell me about your last supervisor," and you will learn much more (and may obtain some information that reveals weaknesses, if the candidate is highly critical of a past employer; it is extremely poor form to "bad-mouth" a present or past employer during an interview). Be careful, however, to avoid questions that are too open-ended, giving the applicant no clue as to how much to say or when to stop. The best questions are those that require perhaps two or three sentences for response.

Probing questions address the five "Ws": why, what, who, when, and where, plus how. These are excellent, but if overused, they may create a dialogue that sounds like interrogation. Here are a few examples of probing questions:

- How did that situation arise?
- Why do you believe that was allowed to happen?
- In retrospect, what would you have done differently?

Hypothetical questions include questions such as, "What would you do if…?" These situational queries can be very informative when discussing technical or personal skills.

Illegal questions are those prohibited by federal and state statutes. Forbidden areas of questioning are reviewed in the following section. If you do not have a comprehensive list of questions to avoid, get one from your human resources department before you interview your next candidate.

Avoid leading questions, those that reveal to the applicant the answer you want, for example, "You're willing to serve on committees, aren't you?" Most applicants hearing a leading question know instantly the answer you want to hear.

Questions about general responsibilities can be formulated based on the position description and job qualifications. These questions cover education, training, experience, knowledge, and skill. Questions used to evaluate service attitudes and interactive skills are also useful. Novice interviewers ask questions that deal more with technical skills and experience rather than people skills. The best questions are those that help you evaluate competence ("can do") and motivation ("will do").

Questions to Avoid

This list is partially duplicative of information about job application inquiries covered in the previous chapter. Generally, the legal prohibitions against soliciting certain kinds of information apply equally to questions asked in writing, as on an application, and questions asked orally, as in a personal interview. Appreciate, however, that the personal interview permits variations of questioning that are not possible on a fill-in-the-blank application.

- You may not ask questions that require an applicant to reveal age, date of birth, race, religion, or national origin. Direct questions like "What's your date of birth?" are easy to avoid, but there are hazards in indirect questions that can be interpreted as fishing for personal information, for example, "That's a great school—when were you there?" Also stay away from questions related to an applicant's long-term intentions, such as "How long would you plan on working before thinking about retirement?" Because of the age-related inferences that might be drawn, there is no safe question you can ask about age except to inquire whether an apparently young person is of legal age to enter full-time employment.
- Similar to concerns about age, there are few if any safe questions you can ask about disability, whether an applicant's disability is evident or not. You can ask only whether the applicant believes there are any conditions or circumstances that could interfere with performance of the essential functions of the job.
- You may not ask whether the applicant has a recommendation from a present employer. This can be taken as discriminatory because it may be difficult for the person to secure such a recommendation for reasons other than job performance, for example, race, religion, and so on.
- You may not ask the identity of the person's nearest relative or "next of kin" because this can be taken as probing into the existence of

spouse or family. Asking about the person to be notified in case of emergency must wait until the applicant is actually employed.

- It is generally permissible to ask if an applicant is a U.S. citizen or legally eligible for employment. But this will not be an active concern for the interviewing supervisor if human resources have screened the applicant.
- In asking about the applicant's military service, you may inquire only into training and experience. You may not ask the character of the person's discharge or separation; whether a discharge was honorable, general, or otherwise remains privileged information that the applicant may offer voluntarily but that you may not request.
- You may not ask the marital status of the applicant at the time of the interview. Many women have been able to claim they were denied employment because of marital status. Employers often acted on the assumption that young women recently engaged often quit soon after they get married, that some recently married women may leave soon to begin families, and that single women with small children will have poorer attendance records than other workers.
- You may not ask if the applicant owns a home or a car. This can be interpreted as seeking to test affluence, which may be taken as discriminatory against certain minorities. You may, however, ask if the applicant has a driver's license if driving is a requirement of the job.
- You may not ask if the applicant's wages were ever attached or garnished or if the person has outstanding loans or other financial obligations. Credit information is privileged information covered under privacy laws as well as under Title VII.
- You may not directly ask an applicant's height or weight. Neither of these factors should have a bearing on the applicant's suitability for the job unless there is a specific job-related requirement that applies to all applicants.
- There are also problems sometimes encountered in asking an applicant's educational

level. The employer may require specific educational levels when these are directly related to job performance. For example, you can require a nurse to possess a diploma or degree and a state license because these are essential to the performance of the job. However, you cannot require a housekeeper or kitchen worker to have a high school diploma because it is possible to demonstrate that people in these entry-level jobs may perform equally well with or without a diploma.

- You cannot ask whether the applicant has ever been arrested because an arrest is simply a charge, not a conviction. It has even become risky to ask if a person has ever been convicted of a crime; in many parts of the United States, the box on applications that asks this is being removed, the reason being that most kinds of convictions have no bearing a person's suitability for a job. However, if the job in question involves exposure to drugs or is clearly related to safeguarding money or security, it is permissible to ask about *related* convictions; for example, an individual with a drug conviction can be denied a position requiring access to pharmaceuticals.
- You may not ask whether an applicant is or has been a member of a union or has been involved in organizing or other union activities.
- You may not ask obviously mature applicants if they are receiving Social Security benefits. Some employers have been known to discriminate in favor of applicants for part-time jobs who are receiving Social Security payments in the belief that a person receiving a combined income may be more likely to remain on the job longer.

Consider all of the foregoing prohibited areas of questioning for what they have in common. In one way or another they all relate to what the applicant *is*: single or married, of a certain age, responsible for dependents or not, of a specific ethnic or religious group, educated to a certain level or not, a homeowner or renter, a financially stable individual or not, and on and on, all of which are descriptive of what the person is. And all of what the person is has little or no bearing on the individual's ability to do the job in question. Rather, the kinds of questions that can and should be asked, the essential information legally solicited in an interview relates to what the individual *knows, has done, can do*, and *would like to do*. In interviewing, you are seeking to know the future employee, not the private individual.

A Brief Example: Blindsided by an Applicant

You are the supervisor of a pool of secretaries at a large hospital. You have an opening for a key position. Human resources provided you with five candidates, all of whom look good relative to the stated requirements of the job.

Over a period of 6 or 7 workdays you scheduled and held interviews with all five candidates. All of them, including the fifth, appeared good on paper, and they all interviewed well. You conducted all interviews strictly "by the book" and never touched upon any forbidden areas of questioning.

However, at the end of the fifth interview, the young female candidate (who had been personable and appropriately responsive throughout the interview) looked you straight in the eye just before leaving and said, "I'm pregnant, and if I don't get this job, I'm going to claim discrimination."

As you go through the next few sections, think about how you might best react to this out-of-the-blue threat that has taken you completely by surprise.

Recommended Questions

Questions for Determining Professional or Technical Competency

These questions should be criteria-referenced; that is, they should be related to duties and responsibilities as documented in the job descriptions. Use hypothetical situations or pose questions along these lines:

- How would you...?
- Describe the technique for....
- If you encountered..., what would you do?
- Tell me about your experience with....
- Explain your role in....
- What aspect of this job would you find most difficult?
- What strengths would you bring to this position?
- What competency would your former boss recommend that you strengthen?

Questions for Assessing Motivation

In every department there are clock watchers and other people who could do better if they cared to apply themselves. Answers to these questions may help you spot the potential goof-offs:

- What have you done at work that shows strong initiative?
- What did you do to become more effective in your previous position?
- Tell me about a time when you went the extra mile.

Questions for Evaluating Teamwork Potential

Teamwork demands communication skills, congenial relationships, cooperation, the ability to compromise, and much exchange of ideas. The following questions can help evaluate one's ability to work as part of a team:

- Do you prefer responsibility for your own work, or do you like to share responsibility with others?
- What kinds of people do you get along with best? What kinds of people do you find difficult? How do you deal with them?

- What other departments did you have dealings with, and what difficulties did you encounter with any of these?

Questions for Evaluating Followership Skill and Attitude

Although you are not looking for a clone of yourself and you want people who complement your strong points, neither do you want problem followers. Award bonus points to candidates who speak well of previous employers. Even if an individual's previous employment experience was less than satisfactory, there are diplomatic ways that he or she can relate this without being openly critical of someone. As suggested earlier, beware of the applicant who bad-mouths a present or previous employer in an interview. The following inquiries may help you select a congenial teammate:

- Describe the style of the best boss you ever had. Describe the style of your worst boss. (Watch the applicant's body language while responding to these.)
- What are some issues you and your previous supervisor disagreed about?
- Provide an example of how you handled criticism that you do not believe you deserved.

Questions for Evaluating Resistance to Stress

All people have different stress thresholds; what one person might be able to take in stride might send another person scrambling up the walls. Also, different jobs generate different amounts of stress. If you believe the position under consideration to be potentially stressful, include questions such as the following:

- When was the last time you got really angry at work? What caused it, and how did you react?
- What was the most difficult situation you faced at work? What feelings did this situation produce, and how did you react to them?
- What are some of your pet peeves concerning work?

Questions for Assessing Retention Potential

Because one important objective of employee selection is to improve employee retention, the following questions may be helpful:

- What do you want to be doing 5 years from now?
- What do you believe you will be doing 5 years from now?
- How much do you believe you will be earning 5 years from now?
- Let's briefly review your career goals and plans.

Questions for Assessing Customer Service Orientation

- What does superior service mean to you?
- Who do you consider to be our external and internal customers?
- Provide an example of how you made an extra effort to serve a client/patient.
- How do you handle the situation when a caller becomes insulting or abusive on the phone?
- How could your previous employer have provided better service?
- Did you ever provide care for a chronically ill individual? Tell me about it.
- Did you ever work in a nursing home? What was it like?
- Did you ever work in the customer service industry (babysit or work in a restaurant)? Describe the experience.

Candidates with No Previous Employment

Most college graduates have held part-time or summer jobs or were employed before attending college. Inquiries into such employment can be worthwhile. The following questions assume greater importance when an applicant's employment history is skimpy or nonexistent:

- Describe a teacher with whom you had problems. How did you handle that situation?
- What were some problems or situations you faced at school or at home? If you had it to do all over, what would you do differently?
- What have you done that shows initiative and willingness to work?
- What are your long-range goals and expectations? How do you plan to fulfill these?

Addressing Sensitive Issues

Be tactful when you probe into what might appear to be individuals' soft or sensitive spots. Start by saying that one way you evaluate maturity is by the ability of people to recognize performance that could be improved. Point out that such people have already taken the first step toward career improvement.

Avoid strong terms such as "weakness" and "deficiency." Substitute phrases such as "area of concern," "need for more experience," and "need to enhance full potential." Use the questions "Is it possible that...?" or "How did you happen to...?"

Clues to Untruthfulness

Not every candidate will be 100% truthful with you (some experienced interviewers may consider this a dramatic understatement). After all, the individual is seeking employment and in doing so will try to present himself or herself in the best possible light. It is fairly common practice for interviewees to "forget" the unfavorable aspects of past employment and dwell only on that which is favorable. At times they may also exaggerate the favorable and even invent experience and qualifications they believe will make them look good.

One early clue resides in résumés and comments on applications that appear too good to be true. As the old saying goes, "If it seems too good to be true, it probably is." That is, if it's perfect, something has likely been invented, masked, or omitted. Always remain aware that a high percentage of résumés contain exaggerations or outright falsehoods, and even more—one might say expectedly so—are favorably slanted.

Watch out for wording that tends to imply more than it actually means. This frequently emerges concerning educational background. For example, some applicants may say "attended" State University and let the casual reader who skims the page infer "graduated" when that is not the case. Saying even less, the individual who writes something like "State University, Business Administration, 2008" is hoping the less-than-careful reader will assume graduation when the person may have had only a semester or so. There are dozens of similar reasons why the interviewing supervisor must read résumés and applications very carefully. Educational achievements are frequently exaggerated or falsified, perhaps because only some employers make an effort to verify the educational records of all job applicants.

You may also be interviewing in the presence of untruthfulness if an applicant's answers to normally challenging questions lack substance. Consider it a red flag if the answers to questions bearing on the person's supposed field of interest come across as thin and unconvincing.

Watch also for what an applicant's body language may be telling you. Provide a little slack for applicants who are obviously nervous, especially those who are young and new to interviewing. The ones to be most aware of are those who have apparently been around for a while, have presented themselves in glowing terms on paper, but show signs of discomfort or restlessness when closely questioned. Some avoid eye contact; some blush or perspire noticeably; some experience a change in vocal tone, pitch, volume, or rate of speech; some squirm, fidget, or blink excessively.

Be aware also of inconsistencies between what applicants say in interviews and what their written résumés claim. The more padding or untruth in the résumé, the more difficulty the individual may have remembering everything when questioned.

Finally, when reference checking is done—usually not until a tentative offer of employment has been extended—watch for inconsistencies between what you receive from previous employers and what the applicant has claimed.

Questions from Candidates

Some candidates ask only selfish questions, such as those that deal with salary, benefits, vacation policies, and overtime. Others ask only superficial questions, such as how many employees are on board. Then there are those who do not ask any questions at all. This tips you off that they may not be particularly sharp or have little interest in this particular job.

Questions from candidates reveal insights about their values and goals as well as their professional or technical knowledge. This is especially true of the questions they pose and the interest they show when given a tour of your department. Superior candidates are those who not only ask technical questions but also ask questions such as, "How would you describe the personality of your organization?" or "How long have you worked here, and what attracted you to this organization?" Another great question coming from an applicant is, "Please describe your mentoring and training programs."

Evaluation of Candidates

Interviewers usually have a gut reaction to candidates. Some react impulsively and make poor decisions, whereas others do their best to ignore these instinctive responses. Skilled interviewers pay attention to these feelings and decide whether these intangible factors are truly job related.

Additional Tips for Evaluating Candidates

Finally, also consider the following points when evaluating a candidate:

- Give negatives somewhat more weight than positives. One or two significant negatives can render a candidate unsuitable.
- Evaluate the candidate's flexibility and ability to adjust to change.

- Watch for strong feelings and beliefs. These often suggest rigidity and intolerance.
- Note the candidate's emphasis. Customer-oriented people talk about service and interpersonal relationships; task-oriented individuals focus on duties. Burned-out workers frequently use the word "stress," and they tend to sigh a lot.
- Avoid leaping to conclusions during the initial phase of an interview.

Getting Candidates to Accept Job Offers

Remember that the higher the quality of the candidates, the more competition there is for them. When you interview outstanding candidates, you may find they are interviewing you and your organization. They know you want them, but for the most part, they have yet to decide whether they want you. Here are some practical tips that can help sell the job:

- Send a map and directions for getting to the interview site. Include a copy of the position description. These touches display a caring attitude and a serious interest on your part.
- Provide a tour of your facilities. Show off the pleasant environment, efficient arrangements, modern equipment, and access to other departments and facilities.
- Introduce the candidate to one or two key people (but do not overdo this).
- Create a positive vision in the mind of the candidate by matching what the job offers with what you have learned the candidate wants. Focus on any special features that are attractive to the person.
- If the person has shown a special interest (for example, in research or teaching), discuss what you have to offer. Create a positive picture of the daily routine.
- Do not forget spouses, especially when recruiting from out of town. Frequently, spouses cast the deciding vote. It is often wise to have the spouse sit in on part of the interview. How does the spouse feel about the

community and the job opportunity? Is this person also looking for new employment? If so, what can you offer or suggest?

- Answer questions completely and honestly. Do not conceal negative aspects of the job but rather refer to these aspects as challenges. On the other hand, do not dwell on the undesirable features or say that it has been difficult to keep people in that position.
- Avoid salary negotiations until you're ready to make an offer, then do so only through human resources (wage and salary administration). If the person expects more than you are authorized to offer, keep the door open. Say that you will look into it and report back.
- If you have a mentoring program, mention that to candidates. The availability of such programs is an attractive feature to some candidates.

Special Incentives

In addition to cash bonuses, under certain circumstances there may be noncash hiring incentives, including relocation packages, tuition reimbursement, paid employee training, flextime, and transportation reimbursement.

Closing the Interview

At the end of the interview ask for the candidate's level of interest; for example, "Although neither of us can make a decision at this point, do you think you're interested in the job?" Explore doubts or reservations. If the person is noncommittal but appears to be a good candidate, set a deadline for an answer.

State when the selection decision will be made and how you will notify the applicant. Make certain you have the person's current phone number and email address. Escort the candidate to the next interviewer, to another on-site destination, or back to the employment section of the human resources department, and always remember to thank the candidate for coming.

Post-Interview Activities

Writing and Organizing Your Report

Eyeballing rough notes is not the preferred approach. Match your findings with a written list of criteria you have established. Review information from other sources such as the application form, résumé, and reference reports. If you believe you must use subjective terminology (especially negative terms such as "cocky," "pompous," "immature," and such), describe what was said or done that caused you to form those impressions. However, use subjective terminology as little as possible; should a legal challenge arise from failure to hire a particular applicant, subjective reasons for rejecting the person for employment are not easily defended.

Prepare a brief summary of the strengths and weaknesses of the candidate. You may want to use a numerical weighting system to evaluate the major assets and liabilities. If multiple interviewers participated, compare notes with them. Second interviews with the more promising candidates are often desirable.

Notification and Medical Testing

Do not wait too long before offering the job (24 hours is usually too short and a month is too long). For jobs for which there are few candidates but many competitors, you must make a decision quickly. Have your top choice notified first and wait for that person's response before moving on to others.

The job offer can be extended in many ways, usually it is an email, phone call, or a formal letter from your human resources department. The candidate should be told how much time he or she has to respond. Once the employer has made a conditional job offer, the organization is free to ask the applicant to undergo a pre-employment physical examination.

Responding to Questions of "Why Not Me?"

Except in the rare instances when there is but a single applicant who is interviewed and hired, there will be unsuccessful candidates. These unsuccessful candidates will vary considerably in their reaction to not being chosen; some of them will try to find out why they were not hired.

It is usually the job of the recruiter or employment representative in human resources to close the loop with unsuccessful candidates and let them know they were not selected. Naturally, most people wish to know why they did not get the job. Human resources will consider it essential to follow up with unsuccessful candidates and will do so via a telephone call that may be followed with a brief, polite letter thanking them for their interest.

Unsuccessful candidates will ordinarily be told only that "a more appropriate candidate was selected," "an individual with more experience was chosen," or something similarly nonspecific. Sometimes, a candidate will bypass human resources and contact you directly, wanting to know why he or she did not get the job. Such an individual's perspective is not that another person was chosen but that "I was rejected," and the person will wish to know why. For your part, your response, politely and diplomatically delivered, should be no more or less than the human resources response: A more appropriate candidate was selected.

Do not allow yourself to be drawn into an argument with an unsuccessful candidate. In demanding to know why he or she was not chosen, one may suggest discriminatory treatment based on protected status; another will want to know the character of references received from former employers, and so on. However, you do not have to justify your selection to the unsuccessful candidates, and you do not have to address their probing questions or respond to their accusations. When the occasional unsuccessful applicant reaches you directly, simply refer the individual back to the human resources recruiter.

Returning to the "Blindsider"

What will you do about the threat? Give in? Use the threat to reject her? (Remember, you cannot use personal information in making a decision to either hire or reject, no matter how you acquired this information.)

What you will have to do in this instance is carefully document the results of all five interviews, comparing the qualifications of all relative to every requirement of the position—then make your choice. If the "blindsider" turns out to be the best on paper overall, you probably should offer her the position. But in a little one-on-one conversation, she will have to be told that her threat was out of line and the only reason she is getting the job is that she is the best qualified of the five. If she is not the best qualified overall, you need to go with your best choice and wait to see whether the "blindsider" goes through with her threat. In preparation for the legal issue that might arise, you must be able to demonstrate through complete, honest, and largely objective documentation that another candidate was the best fit for the position.

Obtaining References

An employee may fail in one position but perform as a standout in another, so if at all possible, references should be obtained from more than one source. Obviously, the job that most resembles the one being offered is the most important to check.

Offers of employment are ordinarily extended as tentative offers, contingent on passing the appropriate pre-employment physical examination and on the receipt of satisfactory references. At one time, previous immediate supervisors were considered the best sources of reference information, but it has become legally hazardous to deal supervisor to supervisor without involving the human resources departments.

The whole topic of employment references is a messy situation of potential legal traps for both the supervisor and the human resources department. Ideally, human resources should have secured the applicant's signed permission to check references as part of the screening interview, usually asking for a specific signed release for each former employer. For good reasons, many applicants indicate that their present employers not be approached for reference information, but they ordinarily grant permission to check with most previous employers. No reference checks should be performed by anyone in the absence of an applicant's signed authorization to do so. Even if a signed release is presented, reference checking should be left to the human resources department. Under no circumstances should an interviewing supervisor check an applicant's references personally.

In these controversial times, many unsuccessful applicants are quick to charge that they were not hired because of defamatory information acquired from previous employers. It is therefore important for all references to be checked by persons who do so regularly enough to be sensitive to the potential legal pitfalls. For example, an applicant might claim to have been defamed in being labeled in a reference check as "uncooperative and unreliable"—and can succeed in pursuing such a claim if there is insufficient information in the individual's past employment record to reasonably verify such contentions. Reference information used in making a decision not to hire needs to be substantiated in the past employment record. For example, to stand up as valid if challenged, a reference of "poor attendance" should be backed up in the employment file maintained by the employer supplying the reference with attendance records or with records of disciplinary actions dealing with attendance.

Because of the possibility of legal problems, many organizations have backed away from supplying much pertinent reference information, limiting themselves, by policy, to verifying job title and dates of employment and giving out nothing else. In recent years, however, an increasing number of organizations have been subject to charges of negligent hiring because of harm done by employees who were hired with little, or no effort expended to check their employment histories. Although many prior employers may respond with dates and titles only, or with no information at all, your human resources department should make certain it is able to demonstrate that the organization made a good-faith effort to check references.

Regardless, the details and actual performance of reference checking should remain with human resources. Should you be in a position to use personal contacts, such as colleagues in other organizations, to check on potential new employees, never actively use information so obtained in justifying a decision not to hire a particular person. You may perhaps feel that a private, unofficial conversation with your counterpart across town is safe, but this too can be problematic. Say an applicant who is denied a position states that you received an unfavorable reference from your counterpart. Say also that this complaint goes on to become a legal proceeding and you are asked—under oath—whether you spoke with the other supervisor about this applicant. What are you going to say, and what will your counterpart say? Better to avoid all such possible difficulties by letting human resources do all of the reference checking.

All reference information used in making employment decisions should be objective (always fact-based, never opinion-based) and verifiable in the records of the organization providing the information.

Reference checking has become almost something of a game between organizations, with each organization trying to give out as little information as possible while trying to get as much as they can from other organizations.

Those on one side of the reference issue argue that it is only former supervisors who know best what kind of worker a person was. This may be so, but it is almost impossible to convey such information to others without being subjective, and it is subjectivity—"poor attitude," "uncooperative," "unmotivated," "crabby," and so on—that causes the trouble. The only information that can safely be exchanged in reference checking is that which can be verified in the record, the record being the individual's employment file. Thus, a human resources employee is in the preferred person to address reference checking safely.

WRAP-UP

Think About It

It has long been believed that the employment interview is not a particularly effective means of determining who will or will not turn out to be a good employee. However, no one has yet managed to come up with a more reliable alternative. Asking the "right" questions can offer some insight to hiring a good employee.

Questions for Review and Discussion

1. A "nonquestion" question often used to begin an interview is "Tell me all about yourself." Is this a reasonable request? Why or why not?

2. Would it be a good idea to have job applicants submit a photograph with the application or résumé? Why or why not?"

3. In some instances, it has been claimed that even requesting an applicant's address on an application should be considered inappropriate. Why might this be so?

4. How would you proceed to assess the ability of a candidate to fit in with your work group?

5. When interviewing, why is it important to try to fill in the gaps in a candidate's employment history?

6. How would you react if an individual you were interviewing voluntarily revealed forbidden information? What would you do with this information?

7. What can be implied from the dates of education and employment on an application or résumé?

8. You should ordinarily be supplied a candidate's application or résumé in advance of the interview. What will you do if an unexpected applicant is sent to you with application or résumé in hand?

9. We know it is permissible to ask an applicant for a driver's license for a job that requires driving, but do you believe we can also probe into the person's driving record with the motor vehicle bureau? Why or why not?

10. What, if anything, do you believe is wrong with interviewing from behind a desk? Is some other arrangement likely to be more effective? Why?

Essay Question: Learning About Interviewing

Imagine you are applying for a supervisory position in a local healthcare organization. You know that interviewing will be an important part of the supervisory job, but you have never interviewed anyone and you yourself have been interviewed only a couple of times early in your working life and you did not remember much about those occasions. Therefore, you made up your mind to pay close attention to the interview you were about to experience to see what you could learn about interviewing.

You were scheduled to interview with the middle manager to whom you would report should you be hired. Hitting just certain high spots of the experience, your interview proceeded as follows:

- You showed up at the manager's office at the appointed time. The manager was not there. A phone call by the secretary revealed that he had forgotten the appointment. You were rescheduled for the following morning at 9:00 a.m.

- The next morning you waited from 8:55 a.m. until 9:35 a.m. for the manager to see you. No reason for the delay was offered.
- The manager, facing you across a broad expanse of conference table, spent several minutes looking for your application, then asked what position it was you were applying for.
- The manager then said, "Well, tell me all about yourself."
- Over the following three-quarters of an hour, the manager took two incoming telephone calls; made one call, having "just remembered" it was important; rang the secretary to ask for a copy of the job description of the position for which you were interviewing; and consumed 30 of the 45 minutes talking about himself and the value and importance of the department.

Instructions

In essay form, identify what you believe was right or wrong about the interview situation, and describe in detail what you believe you learned about the interviewing process.

Case: Too Much Information?

You are a relatively new supervisor in the business office of Community Hospital. Thus far you have interviewed prospective employees only a few times. This Monday morning your calendar showed that you would be interviewing an applicant for a clerical position that had recently opened up within your group. The applicant, Ms. Arthur, arrived at the appointed time. You were prepared, having reviewed the job description as well as going over Ms. Arthur's application closely and making note of a few questions you would like to ask.

Upon entering the private office, you had borrowed for the interview, Ms. Arthur, well dressed and neat appearing, first said, "Thanks for seeing me. I hope you like me because I really need this job."

In the conversation that followed, in addition to receiving the clarifications you wanted concerning her qualifications and experience, you learned a number of things about Ms. Arthur. All from statements she made voluntarily, you learned that Ms. Arthur had been married but was divorced, was a single mother with two children to care for, had been out of work for some time because of a work-related injury, believed she had lost her last job because she filed a workers' compensation claim, was facing financial hardship, and spoke of a chronic health condition that "might be considered a disability."

Questions

1. What information has Ms. Arthur given you that you would not be legally entitled to request?
2. Keeping in mind that all the personal information you received was provided voluntarily, what can you do with this information?
3. In response to the comment about the condition that "might be a disability," can you ask the nature of that condition? Why or why not?
4. Might you and the hospital be vulnerable to any legal problems if Ms. Arthur is not hired? Explain.

Reference

1. Woolley K, Fishbach A. Underestimating the importance of expressing intrinsic motivation in job interviews. *Organ Behav Hum Decis Process.* 2018;148:1–11. https://doi .org/10.1016/j.obhdp.2018.06.004

Orientation and Training of New Employees

CHAPTER OBJECTIVES

- Establish the primary objectives of an employee orientation program, both organization-wide and department specific.
- Highlight the general contents of the organizational orientation common to all new employees.
- Establish the means of determining the needs of a department-specific orientation program.
- Convey the importance of providing each new employee a strong, knowledgeable start on the job.
- Specify the departmental values that must be communicated to all employees early in their employment.
- Review the primary sources of information and assistance used to round out a new employee's introduction to the department.
- Provide a means of evaluating the departmental orientation program to maintain its quality and completeness.

KEY TERMS

General Orientation: Orientation to the overall organization, ordinarily provided by human resources but sometimes by a separate education department, to expose new employees to information of importance concerning the organization and its operations.

Departmental Orientation: Department-specific orientation conducted to reinforce general orientation knowledge, introduce new employees to the department and coworkers, address departmental policies, and get new employees properly started in their jobs.

Orientation Timing

It should go without saying that every new employee should be brought into the organization and department in a manner that ensures each person's comfort in what for most will be a new and perhaps potentially bewildering environment. But when should this introduction occur, or at least when should it begin? The obvious answer is "day one." Yet in many instances a significant part of each new employee's orientation is delayed.

In a healthcare organization of any appreciable size such as a hospital, there will ordinarily be two important orientations: general orientation, the introduction to the total organization, and departmental orientation, the introduction to the new employee's assigned work group and job.

A small organization, for example a rural hospital of a relatively few number of beds, may not offer a general orientation but rather rely on new-employee intake in human resources or departmental orientation to cover everything. In a small organization, weeks may pass with only an occasional new hire. A mid-size or large institution will likely offer a formal, general orientation, but this will not occur at the ideal time; that is, it will not happen on every new employee's first day of work. Full, general orientation may be presented but once each month, or perhaps every week or two in a large institution. The only control that an individual supervisor has concerning general orientation is to ensure that his or her new employees attend when they are scheduled to do so. But the individual supervisor has total control over departmental orientation and can ensure that this begins on day one—and ensure that certain information that will be provided in detail later in general orientation is summarized during the departmental orientation to the extent that the employee may need this information.

It is often a great temptation for a supervisor to allow or even encourage a new employee to skip general orientation; it is not uncommon for the supervisor to feeling pressure from a work backlog owing to a position that has been vacant for some time. Do not give in to this temptation; the general orientation might sometimes seem like an expenditure of time that could be put to better use, but there will always be some important aspects of general orientation that do not come up in departmental orientation.

At no other time is there a better opportunity to establish open lines of communication with new hires than at new employee orientation. New employees are free from the distortions of peer groups. They have not yet formed strong opinions about the job, the organization, or the boss, and they are eager to please.[1]

Three important considerations govern the design of an orientation program. The first is the need to nudge new employees toward the delivery of superior customer service. The second is to regard the orientees as our clients because we, as their supervisors, provide them with training services. The third is the need to infuse within the new employee the latest concepts of quality improvement and cost containment. This chapter concentrates on the first two of these objectives. Our mission is to help trainees see their jobs as direct contributions to the total impact of the organization on the customer and start them in their pursuit of successful employment.

Objectives of an Orientation Program

On the first day make newcomers feel like honored guests. By the second week you should be making them feel like part of the team and included in all aspects.

We want to get new employees off on the right foot, and these people are most impressionable when they first come onboard. In planning for their orientation, you should endeavor to accomplish a number of things:

- Create and reinforce a favorable impression of the organization, of the department, and of you, the supervisor.
- Establish responsibilities and accountabilities. Your expectations of their performance must be crystal clear.
- Ensure that they learn everything they need to perform their work.
- Provide clear information about pay scales, benefits programs, the working environment, and conditions of employment, including opportunities for training and advancement. If you don't have all the information (e.g., healthcare benefits), refer them to the correct department such as human resources.
- Describe policies, rules, and regulations in detail.

- Emphasize the importance of teamwork, flexibility, innovativeness, and the ability to adapt to change.
- Facilitate their need to be accepted by coworkers and to establish rapport through collegial communication.
- Provide initial experiences that result in early successes. This creates a sense of self-value, instills confidence, and promotes a positive attitude.
- Identify the kinds of customers to be dealt with and emphasize the importance of satisfying them.
- Initiate the newcomers into the rituals and practices of your work group and your quality improvement program. These rituals and practices may include activities such as team project completion celebrations, customer attendance at staff meetings, group "brag sessions," and ceremonies for such occasions as special achievements, perfect attendance, and promotions or role changes.
- Provide a checklist to ensure that all topics in the orientation process are covered.
- Encourage employee feedback on the effectiveness of the orientation program.

Ten Important Assumptions

Human resources professionals have experienced the positive and negative outcomes of orientation. Following are 10 important assumptions of a new employee orientation:[2]

1. Early impressions last.
2. Include realistic information.
3. Prepare and be organized.
4. Day one is crucial.
5. Provide general support and reassurance.
6. Teaching the basics comes first.
7. New employees should understand the organization's culture.
8. 8 Information is timed to employees' needs.
9. Informational overload must be avoided to reduce stress.
10. Orientation doesn't work unless the employee's supervisor is involved.

General Orientation Programs

New employees are usually enrolled in a general orientation program conducted by the human resources department or a separate education department, if such exists. Traditionally, these programs start with the history, mission, and core values of the organization. Other important topics include information about fire safety, safety in general, infection control, and other policies and procedures.

However, new employees mostly prefer to receive information that helps them adjust to their new roles. Such information includes when they get paid, where they park their cars, when the snack bar is open, and how they go about requesting educational support and accessing other benefits.

General orientation for a typical hospital is likely to include most of the following topics:

- The organization's mission, vision, and values
- The organization's history and structure
- Overview of the compensation and benefits structure
- Blood-borne pathogens, tuberculosis control
- Confidentiality of patient information
- Cultural proficiency and diversity awareness
- Electrical safety, the Safe Medical Device Act
- Emergency preparedness, disaster plan
- Fire safety
- Hazardous communications, the Right-to-Know Law
- Improving organizational performance
- Risk management
- Incident reporting
- Infection control
- No-smoking policy
- Patients' rights
- Professional misconduct
- Security management
- General age-specific competencies
- Use of the organization's property and systems
- Internet, email, and social media use
- Overview of employee policy manual
- Employee identification badge

- Confidentiality statement
- Employee handbook review

As previously suggested, it will likely be the rare employee for whom general orientation occurs on the first day of work. Therefore, it will be necessary for the departmental orientation to cover, at least briefly, a number of general orientation items that the new employee needs to know when they first begin work.

The final item on the previous list, the employee handbook review, is extremely important. This should ideally be addressed on an employee's first day, usually in human resources where the employee, before being turned over to the department supervisor, is given the opportunity to review the handbook and sign and submit the handbook confirmation. This confirmation becomes an important part of the employee's human resource file, verifying that this handbook of policies and rules has been received.

The conceptualization of a departmental program starts with an analysis of what is needed by new employees joining the department. Such assessment considers both current and future requirements. The planning and the implementation phases are often slighted because at the time new employees are coming on board, the department is likely to be understaffed, and pressures are understandably on getting the newcomers into a productive mode as soon as possible.

Most new employees arrive loaded with questions. Whether or not they are consciously aware of doing so, they are looking for someone to help them reach a level of comfort and familiarity with their new environment. Orientation planning is greatly improved by addressing the following questions before they are actually asked by the new hires:

- Where is my workstation? And where are the cafeteria, restrooms, and parking areas?
- What are my duties and responsibilities?
- How do I answer the telephone, obtain supplies, and operate the computer and other office equipment?
- How will I know if I am doing satisfactory work?

- Why do I have to do the things that have been assigned to me?
- Why must we do things this particular way?
- What are my starting and quitting times, when do we get breaks and how long are they, when is payday, and when does my probationary period end?
- To whom do I report? Who will answer my questions, evaluate my work, or be my friend?

Preparations for the Arrival of New Orientees

There are many ways to prepare for the arrival of new employees:

- Send letters of welcome. Include verification of date, time, and place of reporting, and provide the first day's agenda and any special instructions or suggestions, such as what they should bring or wear.
- Arrange your schedule so you can devote most of the first day to the newcomer(s).
- Review the orientation and training check-off lists.
- Prepare an agenda covering the first week.
- Prepare an orientation packet that includes the following:
  1. A statement of departmental vision, mission, values, and goals
  2. A department organizational chart
  3. A position description and work standards of the job
  4. The employee handbook
  5. Orientation and training schedules
  6. Checklists and program evaluation forms
  7. Performance appraisal forms
  8. Probationary evaluation form (if different from appraisal form)
  9. Safety, infection control, and quality assurance policies, procedures, and rules
  10. Names, titles, and locations of trainers
  11. Key telephone numbers or a condensed telephone directory

First Day: Welcome Wagon

New employees usually report first to the human resources department. Get off to a good start by meeting your new people there. Greet them as you would visiting friends. Have a few well-prepared remarks and deliver them with enthusiasm.

For example,

> One reason we selected each of you is that you've shown the kind of attitude we always look for. As you know, the major goal of your position is to meet or exceed our customers' expectations. Our customers include patients, the patient's families and visitors, clinicians and other care-providers, third-party payers, teammates, students and trainees, and departments we serve. I know you understand the importance of customer service, and you'll soon learn how we want you to deliver that service. You're obviously not allergic to work or to change, and in your past jobs you showed the flexibility and innovativeness we like.

Finally, review the agenda of the orientation program and give the new employees their orientation packets.

"Nuts and Bolts" Talks

On the second day, ask the new employees how their first day went. Then establish a dialogue based on the following:

- The mission, corporate values, and goals of the organization (which they may not have been tuned in to during the organization-wide orientation or which they might not yet have heard). Explain how the functions of the department focus on supporting the corporate mission, values, and goals.
- Each employee's position description and performance standards. Refer to these documents as contracts that must be honored.

Describe the behavior that is rewarded and that which is unacceptable.
- Survival information: work hours, overtime rules, compensatory time, vacation and sick leave policies, assignment of lockers, and completion of human resources data.
- How performance is evaluated and reported.
- Current managerial initiatives. These may include reengineering, new quality improvement or cost-cutting strategies, employee empowerment, or self-directed team building.
- Current educational or marketing programs relating to customer service. For example, telephone courtesy, point-of-care testing, cost cutting, or improvements in quality or turnaround time.
- Other information you want them to have. This could include your personal likes and dislikes, your preferences for behavior, and whatever else you believe they should know about you and your management of the department. Obviously, they will not find such information in the formal documentation. It is better to let them know these things up front rather than having to correct them after the fact. You may want to cover the following:
  1. How you prefer to be addressed (formally or on a first name basis)
  2. That you expect innovativeness of everyone
  3. That you welcome suggestions and insist on hearing about any complaints or other comments from customers (Say, "In this department we don't kill messengers who bring bad tidings; we applaud them.")
  4. Things that annoy you (for example, tardiness, abuse of sick leave, chronic lateness for meetings, untidy clothes, or expressions, such as "That's not in my job description," "I only work here," or comments suggesting that customers get in the way, such as "I wish those relatives would stop making all those nuisance calls")
- How each job has a chain-reaction effect on other staffers' ability to do their jobs, which therefore eventually affects customers.

- The list of internal and external customers and the critical importance of customer satisfaction. Remind them how hard your unit has worked to attract customers and how important it is to keep them. Explain how poor service creates stress for all parties and how they'll gain benefits when they treat customers properly. If true, state, "Your pay and advancement will depend on how well our customers are served."
- Your interest in the development of their (the employees') potential rather than in their immediate output.

Major Departmental Values

Essential values should be shared with all new employees. Honesty is not concealing mistakes or blaming others and not calling in sick when you healthy. Integrity means always doing what you promise to do. Demonstrate pride in your appearance and performance, maintaining a tidy workstation. Show loyalty by putting in an honest day's work and by not bad-mouthing management. Courtesy means knocking on a patient's door before entering, addressing people by their formal names (not calling them "honey" or "dearie"). Demonstrate your work ethic by reporting for work on time, not abusing breaks, or—again—not calling in sick when you are well. Finally, customer service involves going the extra mile, listening patiently, and exhibiting a can-do attitude.

Show and Tell

Avoid informational overload. Do not try to cover everything during a single tour of the premises; this tends to be confusing. Do not stop repeatedly to introduce all of the staff; this can happen later when people are less busy. Show them where the supplies are kept, reports are filed, and paper copies are made.

On a subsequent tour, follow the sequences of various workflows. For example, trace a test request from its point of origin to the physician's receipt of the results. Instruct the orientees to diagram these workflows. Show how customer service is affected by glitches in any step of these workflows.

Devote one session to a discussion of budgets, charges, and costs. As necessary, show orientees how charges appear on patients' bills and how employees can respond to customers' questions about them.

Direct attention to the communication systems and demonstrate their use. Stress the importance of proper telephone etiquette. Include the intercom, bulletin boards, mailboxes, and message centers. Point out where schedules for work, off-duty assignments, and vacations are posted. Show them how the different shifts communicate with each other. Demonstrate how photocopying and filing are done. Later, discuss the location and use of safety equipment.

Meeting Colleagues

It is recommended that you limit the number of introductions during tours of the department. Some employees do not like to be interrupted in the middle of their tasks, and their reaction or lack thereof may be misinterpreted by the orientees as signs of unfriendliness. Also, the new folks can become confused by all the faces, names, and titles when these are encountered in rapid succession. Make the introductions during break times when people are relaxed and more inclined to be amiable. Also, present newcomers at a staff meeting. Encourage them to talk about their educational and recreational interests at that time.

When you introduce someone, explain how that employee's responsibilities or interests relate to those of the newcomer. An introduction might go like this: "Joyce, I'd like you to meet Sue Smith. Sue is in charge of our main storeroom. If you can't find something there, see Sue." The new employee should meet with each senior member of the staff, preferably in each member's office.

Get Help from Your Specialists

In medium to large departments, certain staff members have special expertise or responsibilities that make them better qualified to cover certain topics. In the absence of these specialists, you are responsible for this training.

Trainer or Educational Coordinator

If you delegate training, have the new employee meet the trainer early in the orientation process. Pick trainers with care. Prerequisites include teaching ability, professional or technical expertise, sufficient time to be thorough, willingness, and loads of enthusiasm. Trainers should be aware of the qualifications and experience of the new employees so they can tailor the training to the particular needs of each individual.

Give trainees folders in which to keep their continuing education records. Most departments have requirements for the number of educational hours required for each job category. Show the trainees how to keep these records, and remind them that it is their responsibility to do so.

Safety Coordinator

Some departments have a safety coordinator who shows new hires the location and proper use of safety equipment and reviews safety policies and regulations. New people often have questions about the dangers of hepatitis, AIDS, and other infectious diseases. The safety expert can allay these fears while explaining the best way to minimize the dangers. When discussing AIDS, the expert must also warn against disclosure of confidential information.

Quality Assurance or Quality Improvement Coordinator

This person may be the chair or the recorder for the quality assurance committee. The coordinator may limit the discussion to the global aspects of the program, leaving specific quality control details for the new employee's immediate supervisor to cover.

Mentors and Buddies

Mentors are experienced employees who willingly share their wisdom or political clout with their protégés. They are unofficial advisors, supporters, and confidants. Encourage new employees to find and to establish alliances with those individuals who go out of their way to please customers. In some departments the buddy system is used; each new arrival is assigned to an experienced employee in the same work section.

Training the New Employee

The triple approach to success in customer satisfaction is train, train, train. It is no accident that much of this text is devoted to that subject. Training is especially important during and immediately after new employee orientation because new hires are most open to learning at these times. Encourage good work habits, behavior, ethics, and attitudes before bad ones develop. Assign your best people to do your training. This is a long-term investment that pays off early and continues to pay.

Training during the orientation phase must be tailored to each orientee's needs, and those needs depend on his or her previous education and experience. At this juncture, list all the skills necessary to handle the job, and prepare check-off lists of tasks to be learned. Divide the individual tasks or responsibilities into those that can be learned on the job, those that must be taught formally, and those that can be self-taught. Prepare a rough timetable for achieving the training goals.

At the completion of the formal orientation or training program, solicit feedback from each participant on the value of the program. See **Exhibit 10.1** for an example of an orientation checklist. Get written or verbal comments from each person who helped with the training.

Exhibit 10.1 Checklist for Evaluating the Orientation Program

Check all of the items with which you agree:

- On the first day I was welcomed with enthusiasm.
- By the end of the first week, I knew I had been accepted by the team.
- My immediate supervisor spent enough time with me.
- The entire orientation was well organized.
- Everyone was patient and encouraging.
- I quickly learned what was expected of me and how to do my job.
- The new employee handbook (packet of information) was very helpful.
- They made it easy and relatively painless to learn about important policies and rules.
- My fears of infection and other safety factors were alleviated quickly.
- I was made to feel important.
- I received much more praise than criticism. When my work had to be corrected, they always explained why.
- During the first few days I met not only my colleagues but also important people in other departments.
- I now understand how my job fits into the big picture of what our organization is all about.
- I know how the communications systems work and how to make full use of them.
- I had plenty of opportunities to ask questions and express my opinions.
- I am familiar with the salary and benefits package and how performance is evaluated.
- I understand my role in the quality improvement program.

WRAP-UP

Think About It

One of the surest ways to stimulate unwanted turnover is to turn new employees loose with little or no departmental orientation or personal guidance in finding their places in the group. Even a skilled professional can feel abandoned, left to survive alone and unaided in a new and possibly strange environment. Many of those who feel lost or in over their heads early in their employment simply bail out of what they see as a disappointing situation.

Questions for Review and Discussion

1. Describe how you might try to avoid information overload during a new employee's first few days.

2. Much of the material in the chapter conveys the need to fill the new employee with a sense of the mission, vision, and values of the organization. Why is this important?

3. Why do we need to offer a relatively formal orientation, complete with checklists of items to cover?

4. Why do we need to bother with individual orientation for a new employee who is a trained specialist hired to perform exactly the same tasks performed at a previous job?

5. Why should we be more interested in developing employee potential than in obtaining immediate output?

6. What do you see as the primary advantages of a strong new-employee orientation? Why?

7. Explain why the chapter states that new-employee orientation begins before the new employees arrive.
8. What are the primary advantages of a mentoring relationship as part of a new employee's orientation?
9. What, if anything, is wrong with the apparently time-honored practice of letting new employees learn by trial and error and by watching others?
10. Why not simply have the department supervisors provide all of a new employee's orientation rather than have a separate organization-wide orientation as well?

Case: No Departmental Orientation?

Assume you have just been hired from outside of the organization to serve as a first-line supervisor in one of the clinical support areas (laboratory, radiology, pharmacy, etc.). Staffing in the department has been lean, with some staff positions being open for weeks, but as luck would have it, you were able to fill both open positions during your first 2 weeks on the job.

Being new to supervision and new to this organizational environment, the Friday before the two new employees were scheduled to start work, you asked a more experienced supervisor, "Is there anything special I'm supposed to do with these new employees when human resources turns them over to me on Monday?" The response was simply "Nothing other than your standard departmental orientation."

You asked each of your employees in turn about their departmental orientation. Their answers were consistent: There was no departmental orientation. They were simply shown their workstations and told where the cafeteria and restrooms were located.

Instructions

In written form, describe what you intend to do about (1) the two new employees who start work on Monday and (2) other new employees who join your department in the future.

Case: The Inherited Employee

Soon after she became a supervisor in the building services department, Donna Paine decided that a housekeeping aide named Sally Clark was emerging as a problem employee. An employee of about 4 months, and thus a month past the end of the probationary period, Sally was frequently idle. She seemed always to do exactly what she was supposed to do, if only at a minimally acceptable level, and then do nothing until specifically assigned to another task. Donna grew especially sensitive to the situation when she began to hear complaints from other employees about Sally not doing her share of the work.

Donna pulled the file the previous supervisor had started concerning Sally. There was very little in the file. She set up an appointment with Sally. In opening the discussion, Donna said, "I am unable to find your 3-month probationary review. Do you still have your copy?"

The reply was "What review? I never had one."

Donna then asked, "What about your orientation checklist from when you started in the department? Still have your copy?"

"Never got one. I don't think I had any orientation."

"How did you first learn about your duties and about the department?" asked Donna.

"I watched someone else—Janie, I think her name was—for a couple of hours. But Janie left that week."

At this point, Donna dropped her tentative plans to address what she considered Sally's substandard performance. Instead, she thought she had best look into the apparent absence of a probationary review and attempt to determine why Sally had never received an orientation to the department.

Questions

1. What should Donna do about the departmental orientation that Sally had apparently never received?
2. Sally has apparently gone beyond the end of the standard probationary period without receiving a probationary evaluation. What can Donna do about this, and how might this affect Sally's status?

References

1. Werther WB Jr. *Dear Boss*. Meadowbrook; 1989:189.
2. Wanous JP, Reichers AE. New employee orientation programs. *Human Resource Management Review.* 2000;10(4):435–451. https://doi.org/10.1016/s1053-4822 (00)00035-8

Team Leadership

CHAPTER OBJECTIVES

- Define the kinds of teams to be found within the organization.
- Document both the benefits and the disadvantages of the use of special-purpose teams and examine their potential legal pitfalls.
- Establish the characteristics of an effective team.
- Examine the more common reasons for team failure.
- Describe the interactive forces involved in the formation, assembly, growth, and functioning of most teams, including team rituals and the relative strength of group norms and their role in a team's success or failure.
- Discuss the responsibilities of team leadership and explore the implications of leadership styles.
- Suggest how the manager who inherits a team formed under a previous leader can constructively approach the new assignment.
- Briefly consider various means of evaluating and rewarding team performance.

KEY TERMS

Team: A group of people assembled for and committed to achieving common objectives.
Special-Purpose Team: *Ad hoc*, assembled for a one-time purpose and disbanded when that purpose has been served.
Special-Purpose Standing Team: Ongoing with permanent or rotating membership and handling a certain kind of business or problem on a regular basis (example: Safety Committee).
Departmental Team: A group of employees and the single supervisor to whom they report.
"The Healthcare Team": Essentially all those involved in designing and delivering and paying for health care; this is the greater team.

A Growing Need for Teams

As business enterprises of all kinds become more complex, they depend more on the effectiveness of group efforts and cross-functional activities. In health care, no longer do many individuals work as solo practitioners. For example, in the old days an emergency department was usually staffed by a physician and a few nurses and aides. Now an emergency department can feature dozens of different professionals and technicians with diverse skills and experience who work as a team to save lives.

Various healthcare institutions are establishing satellite facilities, developing new services, implementing changes to comply with legal and other mandated requirements, and establishing comprehensive quality improvement programs. In the new healthcare paradigm, cross-functional teams regularly span departmental boundaries, and the third-party payers become senior partners on a healthcare team.

A team is a group of people who are committed to achieving common objectives. An effective team has members who work well together and enjoy doing so and who produce high-quality outcomes. Teams have become the utility vehicles of today's organizations.

The term "team" is actually representative of several different kinds of collectives, and it is necessary to know at most times the kind of team to which you may be referring. We regularly encounter special-purpose teams, departmental teams, and the greater team.

Kinds of Teams

Two types of special-purpose teams are encountered in the workforce. One is characterized by the group that is assembled for a specific purpose, often including people from different departments or disciplines. This kind of team may be ad hoc, assembled for a one-time purpose and disbanded when that purpose has been served, or it may be ongoing with permanent or rotating membership, handling a certain kind of business or problem on a regular basis. These are the teams of team-oriented problem-solving or quality circles, such as your organization's safety committee or product evaluation committee.

The departmental team is a group of employees and the single supervisor to whom they report. Team composition is simple; most people understand that everyone in the group has a job to do and together they accomplish the work of the group. Such a group can operate as a number of individuals doing their jobs, but when these people are united into a true team, the potential of the group is expanded dramatically. Much that

is said about team building is applicable to forging and maintaining a strong departmental team, a collection of like-minded people who report to the same manager and cooperatively serve the common purpose of the department.

Frequent reference may be made to the healthcare team, essentially all those involved in designing and delivering and paying for health care; this is the greater team. At times, the employing organization and all those it encompasses may be appropriately described as a team. Regardless of its kind, composition, reason for being, or degree of permanence, however, there is one significant factor that unites the members of any team: common purpose.

The Project or Employee Team

The organization of a project or employee team can be relatively simple: A decision is made to assemble a number of people with the appropriate knowledge, skills, or experience to undertake some specific tasks as a group. Most of these kinds of teams include both managers and nonmanagerial staff, and because often nonsupervisory employees are the majority of team members, there are potential legal difficulties depending on the kinds of problems or issues addressed.

Just as important as leadership and cooperation are to the success of any team is sensitivity to potential legal pitfalls. Out of a desire to solicit employee participation, some organizations have discovered that a team can easily stray into questionable territory. There are areas of employee involvement in which teams are seen as intruding on the territory of labor unions, so there is a constant risk that a given employee team could be considered an illegal labor organization under the National Labor Relations Act, infringing on the rights of collective bargaining organizations.

An employee team or committee could be considered an employer-dominated illegal labor organization if the group gets involved in addressing any terms and conditions of employment such as wages, hours, benefits, grievances, or such. A team might also be seen as an illegal labor organization if its recommendations result in management decisions but the group itself has no power to make the decisions.

Any team consisting of a majority of non-managerial workers should have its activities strictly limited so that the group never addresses terms and conditions of employment in any form. This essentially limits these kinds of teams to dealing with issues of quality and productivity.

Benefits of Teams

Healthcare organizations regularly use teams to handle a wide variety of tasks and problems, taking advantage of the following benefits of teams:

- *Greater total expertise.* Although team formation is not a panacea, it does serve to expand its collective ability to solve problems. Teams are especially useful in addressing procedures, relationships, quality, productivity, and problem-solving.
- *Synergy.* The total achievements of teams are invariably greater than what can be achieved by members acting independently.
- *Improved morale.* The motivational needs of affiliation, achievement, and control are often satisfied in the team setting.
- *Improved employee retention.* Employees are less prone to leave when they are members of teams, especially teams recognized for their successes.
- *Increased flexibility.* Team efforts reduce dependence on individuals. Services do not suffer when one member of a team is missing.

Disadvantages of Teams

Teams, however, have their downside. Healthcare managers must also be aware of the occasionally encountered disadvantages of team activity.

- *Teams are not always needed.* Many situations can be handled as well or better by individuals. Specialists handle specific situations more rapidly and without having to consult others or obtain the approval of other members of a work group. Attempts to introduce work teams in departments where there are no interdependencies are largely a waste of time and effort. However, in most healthcare departments, people do depend on one another.
- *Team building requires start-up time.* There is always that period early in the life of a team when effort must be invested in team formation but little if anything specific is being accomplished.
- *Teams may become bureaucratic.* A once-enthusiastic task force can become a self-perpetuating standing committee, and its business often becomes repetitive and boring.
- *Teams are not appropriate for all situations.* When fast action is required, someone—an individual—must take charge and get things rolling.

Characteristics of Effective Teams

An effective team can be described as follows:

- It is not always limited to a departmental work group or even an interdepartmental collection of members. As necessary, its members may include vendors, customers, people from other departments, and key support staff.
- It possesses all the necessary knowledge, skill, and experience required to fulfill its charge and get the job done.
- As a body, its members search for excellence in quality, productivity, and customer service. The team removes factors that inhibit quality performance.
- It welcomes innovation, new services, and improved processes and techniques.
- It is democratic. There is an absence of rank or formal authority. It has a leader who refers to his or her coworkers as associates, colleagues, or teammates, not as subordinates.
- It demonstrates effective multidirectional communication and as a group displays openness and candor.

- It remains inspired by a vision of what it is trying to accomplish. Its charge is clear, its goals are clear, and all members are unified in their pursuit.
- It actively constructs formal and informal networks that include people who aid in its mission.
- It possesses power not based on formal authority, but on the credibility the team has earned through performance.
- Its members trust each other and are sensitive to each other's needs. They understand their roles, responsibilities, and degrees of authority.
- It addresses and eliminates conflict with other teams or nonteam employees through collaboration, coordination, and cooperation.
- It adheres to strict ethical and moral considerations.
- It conveys optimism, and its members enjoy serving and contributing.

Why Teams Fail

Teams fail for many reasons. Unrealistic mandates from higher management and a lack of purpose and direction are major factors. However, poor leadership is the most common problem leading to team failure. This may be the fault of the person to whom the team reports or the unwillingness of any individual team member to assume a leadership role. Reviews of failed teams almost always reveal a serious breakdown in communication.

Other factors also contribute to team failure:

- Domination of the team by players possessing higher status or greater knowledge or who are more aggressive. Other problem members include the pessimists, negativists, obstructionists, prima donnas, and goof-offs.
- Lack of organizational support; for example, insufficient resources or time, understaffing, or unpleasant work environment.
- Internal politics, hidden agendas, conformity pressures, favoritism, and excessive paperwork.
- The development within the team of cliques that have the effect of isolating the group from the rest of the organization.

- Destructive competition among team individuals for promotions, merit raises, recognition, and access to superiors.
- Unrealistic expectations, resulting in discouragement in the face of setbacks.
- Disapproval by upper management of a team's output or lack of action on the team's suggestions or recommendations. Also, failure of a team to respond to the ideas of its individual members can quickly quench enthusiasm.
- Lack of progress, failure to meet deadlines, setbacks, and bad results, any of which may be disheartening.

Some teams are weakened, though not necessarily to the point of failure, by attendance issues and uneven participation by members. Imagine yourself in the position of the team leader in the following scenario.

The Biweekly Team Meeting

Fourteen people from several departments comprise the long-standing methods improvement team you were assigned to take over as leader 3 months ago. It has been the practice to hold a meeting at 3:00 p.m. every second Wednesday, or perhaps we should say you attempt to hold it at 3:00 p.m. because about half of the team members are more than 5 minutes late, and two or three are usually late by 15 minutes or longer.

You have made repeated announcements about being there on time, but to no avail. Come the next meeting at 3:00 p.m., you usually find yourself and the same few punctual members present and waiting for the latecomers.

Think about different ways to hold this meeting and what you might be able to do to encourage punctuality at the team meetings.

Team Dynamics

Team dynamics refers to the interactive forces brought to bear by individuals singly or collectively in a group activity. The success of group dynamics depends largely on how willing team leaders are to share authority, responsibility, information, and resources. Sharing is a large part of what participative management is all about.

Stages in Team Formation and Development

Stage 1: Confusion

This initial stage represents the transition from a group of individuals to a team. Participation is tentative or hesitant as members wonder what is expected of them. Team members may show suspicion, fear, and anxiety, and productivity may suffer.

Stage 2: Dissatisfaction

Some members may display negativity, hostility, bickering, or outright resistance. Infighting, defensiveness, and competition are common at this stage because a number of participants have not yet clearly seen themselves as members of the group. Low productivity may persist.

Stage 3: Resolution

If the team is to be successful, group norms and roles emerge once the dissatisfaction is on the way to resolution. Dissatisfaction and conflict diminish, and a sense of cohesiveness starts to develop. Dependence on strong formal leaders decreases. Cohesion is achieved when individual members feel responsible for the success of the team. Productivity attains moderate levels.

Stage 4: Maturation

Productivity is high and performance is smooth. Members have developed insight into personal and collective processes. Team members have learned how to resolve their differences and provide each other with constructive feedback. All of this requires time, and progress is not steady but up and down, in fits and starts. Mature teams usually experience some turnover in membership, mostly planned or expected. Moreover, priorities change, and a host of other variables constantly affect the nature and makeup of mature teams.

Group Norms

Group norms may be functional or dysfunctional. A functional form is evident when team members defend their team and their organization. A dysfunctional form develops when members believe their organization is taking advantage of them and they perhaps believe that teams are being assembled only to squeeze more work out of the participants.

In some dysfunctional forms, members struggle so hard to avoid conflict that team decisions suffer. Some conflict is essential to effective problem-solving. Cohesion does not mean the complete absence of differences of opinion, arguments, or disagreements. Members of great teams can frequently be heard debating heatedly among themselves.

Instructors at Marine Corps Boot Camp teach key lessons and model behavior they want. Their group norms are consistently very high because of the lessons they are taught:

- Tell the truth.
- Do your best, no matter how trivial the task.
- Choose the difficult right over the easy wrong.
- Look out for the group before you look out for yourself.
- Don't whine or make excuses.
- Judge others by their actions, not their race.
- Don't use "I" or "me."[1]

Rituals and Status Symbols

Certain rituals are important to team success. The truly important positive rituals are mainly expressions of appreciation, such as trophies, awards, parties, picnics, and special dinners. A negative ritual, largely undesirable but nevertheless a ritual of sorts, is the hazing or taunting of new employees. However, even some positive rituals may change their polarity; for example, the employee of the month award may be regarded with scorn when undeserving candidates are selected or deserving employees are overlooked.

Team status symbols can also be important. Take uniforms for instance. For years the long, white hospital coat was worn only by attending physicians and senior house staff members. This is no longer the case; in many units, the green scrub suit, complete with stethoscope, has become a uniform of choice of caregivers at all levels. The time-honored nurse's cap has all but disappeared.

Team Leadership

Many healthcare managers are unwilling or unable to adopt the concept of the self-directed team or even to take measures that encourage team efforts. Healthcare leaders must develop dual professional and supervisory skills. Team players must be given opportunities to develop their professional or technical skills (task skills) and skills that pull teams together. The five major responsibilities of team leaders are presented in detail as follows.

First, the team leader must plan. Team leaders must know how to make their teams effective and efficient, encouraging them to work smart. This cannot be accomplished without planning. Managers, in concert with their team members, should be able to answer these questions:

- What do our customers want or need?
- What additional information do we need?
- What past successes have we had in meeting the wants and needs of our customers?
- What are our strengths, and what needs to be improved?
- What new objectives and strategies do we need?
- How can we provide superior customer service faster or at less cost?
- What barriers do we face, and how can they be eliminated?
- Should we learn how others are doing what we are doing?

It is a team leader's job to develop people. Members of a work team, like members of an athletic team, have certain competencies, plus the ability to develop additional competencies. After structuring position descriptions and performance standards, a team leader selects the best people for the team and then orients, educates, trains, coaches, and motivates them. When a team is just getting started, ask all members to share a one-word characteristic each wants to see in a teammate and relate a scenario in which someone either possessed or lacked that trait. The story rounds out the understanding of the desired characteristic. If all members share a trait they value, the group will develop common ground on which to function.

Building a team is like converting a group of musicians into an orchestra. The leader must build the team. Team building involves developing relationships, communicating, holding meetings, and interacting on a daily basis. Leaders must -create an atmosphere that supports and rewards creativity, openness, fairness, trust, mutual respect, and a commitment to safety and health. There must also be opportunities for career growth. Evaluate your team-building ability by taking the quiz in **Exhibit 11.1**.

The leader must truly lead the team. With the help of the other team members, team leaders prepare mission statements, set goals, develop strategies and plans, design or improve work processes, facilitate, coordinate, and troubleshoot. Leaders must satisfy the affiliation needs of each team member. All employees want to be accepted by their colleagues. Leaders also encourage team members to train and coach each other.

The following is an example of a simple departmental mission statement:

> *Our department is committed to providing quality care at low cost to inpatients and outpatients. Staff members maintain their expertise through continuing education and development.*

The leader must coordinate team activities. The team or its individual members often participate in cross-functional activities. Team leaders must coordinate these activities with other departments and services. Leaders must also be ready to serve as followers in some interdepartmental task forces, committees, and focus groups. Typical topics relate to new services, safety, quality management, customer satisfaction, and employee morale.

Exhibit 11.1 Rate Yourself as a Team Builder

Check all of the following that you honestly believe describe you as a team leader:

- My teammates help each other and share advice.
- My team functions well when I am not present.
- I hire people who may be able to perform some tasks better than I can.
- I try to avoid hiring people who are just like me.
- Each member of my team learns at least one new skill every year.
- Each member of my team makes at least one suggestion every month.
- I encourage both differences of opinion and suggestions for improvement.
- We resolve rather than avoid conflict and problems.
- Every member of my team can name all our external and internal customers.
- Every member of my team can state the mission of our organization.
- Every member of my team knows how our quality program affects our service.
- Every member of my team follows safety procedures.
- We prefer team collaboration over individual competition.
- Every member of my team feels valued and accepted.
- Our team has a can-do attitude. We strive to produce more than we promise.
- Our team has a reputation for cooperating with other teams and individuals.
- Our team attitude is one of optimism and enthusiasm. Negativism is rare.

The Self-Perpetuating Team

Once in a while a team established for a specific purpose fails to go away after its original mission has been accomplished. This sort of a "team" revolves around a few members of the original team who enjoy their regular gatherings and seem able to come up with enough "new business" to keep them getting together on a regular basis for what has become a welcome break from daily activities. This self-perpetuating team may even produce some useful output at times but generally not enough to justify tying up its members for a time.

Wise management may of course recognize when an ad hoc team has fully served its purpose and must be dissolved. However, the managers who create such teams sometimes pay little attention once they are up and running.

The self-perpetuation is a micro reflection of a tendency found in some successful corporations and nearly all sizeable arms of government involving an important fact of organizational life: It is relatively easy to create a new department, division, bureau, or whatever, but once any such entity has served its primary purpose it is extremely difficult to dissolve. Jobs and sometimes even careers are at stake, so the entity's management fights to remain in place and searches for a new purpose for its existence.

Revisiting the Biweekly Team Meeting

You have fallen into a difficult situation in taking on leadership of this team. Some steps you might consider:

- Host the meetings virtually. Zoom Meeting's is the most used web-conferencing platform in the world.[2] Since the COVID-19 pandemic, the number of meetings that have been held virtually (online) has skyrocketed. Virtual meetings could increase attendance of meetings.
- Acknowledge the six or seven people who are consistently punctual. If minutes are generated, list the punctual attendees followed by "late arrivals."

- If hosting meetings virtually on Zoom Meetings, use the function of the "waiting room." This function allows people to be manually entered by the host. If a team member is late to the meeting, they can be denied entry.
- Examine the necessity of a biweekly meeting. Is this really necessary, or has it become an automatic gathering? Would a monthly meeting make more sense? If change is in order, settle on the apparently most sensible meeting frequency and announce it to the group.

Virtual meeting platforms such as Zoom Meetings, Microsoft Teams, and Go To Meeting among many other web-based platforms have changed the way organizations conduct meetings on a regular basis. The COVID-19 pandemic limited face-to-face communication; web-based meeting platforms took over the majority of team meetings on a daily basis. Currently, in many healthcare organizations, web-based meetings are the chosen form of meeting do to the convenience of attending.

Leadership Style

The ideal leadership style for team building is based on the perception that personal power is having and exercising power *with* people, not *over* people. Situational leadership fits that perception. When new employees join a team, the leader uses a directive or paternalistic style; he or she tells the employees what to do, shows them how to do it, explains why the work is important, and relates how it fits into the big picture. Knowing that workers at this stage are frightened, insecure, and stressed, team leaders are patient and highly supportive at this time.

As employees develop confidence in their ability, the leader backs off, giving them more latitude and encouraging them to solve their own problems. Some supervisors fail to move on from the initial show-and-tell stage to one that demonstrates confidence in their employees. The result is that employees remain dependent on their leaders or become annoyed with the continual spoon-feeding. Parents encounter the same difficulty

when they continue to treat adolescents as though they were still small children. Most employees can advance to a comfortable level of self-confidence or even to a consultative stage in which they participate actively in planning, decision-making, and problem-solving.

The delegating style, in which team members assume some or many supervisory responsibilities, is appropriate for some team members. In this participative paradigm, the team leader serves as a facilitator and moderator rather than as a manager. Autonomous or self-directed teams feature a democratic system in which there are no supervisors or first-line managers. The team members select a group leader or leadership is rotated.

Taking On the Inherited Team

It is possible that you may be assigned to lead a new team, be promoted to a leadership role, or come into such a position as an outsider. If you have been a member of the team, you must make adjustments, such as those discussed in Chapter 1, "Do You Really Want to Be a Supervisor?" If you worked previously with the group in a cross-functional activity, put aside old prejudices and stereotypes. Overlook previous areas of friction or irritation.

If you are new to the organization, get as much information as you can about the history, reputation, culture, and rituals of your new employer. Look into the leadership style of the previous group leader. How did the group members respond? How effective was that style? You can learn about this from the person to whom you report and from present team members. Hold group meetings to discuss mission, strategy, values, plans, your leadership style, and your previous experience.

Study the position descriptions for every job and the performance reviews of each employee and hold individual meetings with team members. Find out as much as you can about their aspirations, complaints, and suggestions and about how you can make better use of their services. Prepare an inventory chart of the team's skills.

Rewarding Team Performance

An increasing focus on teams necessitates changing the way organizations reward people. Traditional reward and recognition systems encourage individual achievement. When traditional merit pay systems are used, team cooperation often suffers. Individual rewards may cause competing employees to withhold information, undermine peers, and hamper cooperation. On the other hand, in the absence of individual rewards, some resentment among the high performers is bound to occur, and the slackers have no incentive to improve. This dilemma is resolved by providing for both team and individual rewards. The group recognition builds camaraderie and cooperation. Also, when employees know their performance ratings are affected by the extent to which they display teamwork, the adverse effects of individual rewards are mitigated.

It is recommended that some of the following be included in your team reward strategy:

- Reward employees who participate in group functions, such as serving on committees or working with problem-solving groups or task forces.
- Recognize the entire team when goals are met.
- Arrange for a team to present its special projects to other departments or to higher management.
- Bring in a snack or refreshment for the team.
- Organize a car-wash day when managers wash employees' cars.
- Thank the team at a special luncheon or coffee hour.
- Attend some of the team's committee meetings or problem-solving meetings. Comment favorably and encourage them to maintain their excellent performance.
- Display photos of the group in action.
- Broadcast congratulatory news about completed projects, new services, favorable customer comments, or successful cost cutting.
- Spruce up the lounge and provide new amenities, such as a coffeemaker or microwave oven.
- Take practical measures to improve communication systems and make more information available.
- Eliminate unnecessary meetings and use technology to streamline necessary meetings to reduce wasted time.
- Delegate greater authority to the team.

WRAP-UP

Think About It

Although teams and committees have received some derogatory comments, few if any forces in business are as potentially creative and productive as a team. Fully participating individuals who are united in pursuit of a common objective form teams with purpose and passion to get the "job" done.

Questions for Review and Discussion

1. What do you believe should be done concerning a team member who monopolizes every meeting? What if the person who monopolizes is the team leader?
2. Why is shared authority important to proper team functioning?
3. Fully explain why some conflict is essential to effective team problem solving.

4. What has the COVID-19 pandemic changed about team meetings?

5. What do you believe is the primary hazard or significant drawback of a permanent team?

6. What is the "situational leadership" mentioned in the discussion of leadership style? Explain.

7. If you have just inherited a team and must take over today as its leader, how would you go about quickly getting an understanding of the style of the previous leader?

8. How would you suggest that a generally well-functioning team handle a single nonproductive member?

9. What are two significant disadvantages of team action? How can these disadvantages be overcome?

10. What do you believe is meant by the claim that team power is based on credibility? How does a team and its leader go about acquiring this power?

Case: The Quiet Bunch

You learned during your first week on the job as the newly hired admitting supervisor that each departmental supervisor was expected to lead one of the hospital's numerous quality improvement teams. It came as no surprise that the team to which you were assigned was the team your predecessor, the former admitting supervisor, had served as leader. Your team, you soon learned, consisted of several of your department's people plus employees from a scattering of other departments.

As you held individual meetings to become acquainted with both your employees (in the admitting department) and other members of your team, you were quickly inundated with complaints and other indications of discontent from both your employees and other team members. Complaints were vocal about the way the department had been run and the "useless quality improvement team." From a couple of your employees who served on the quality team, you received complaints about "those who shall remain nameless" who regularly "carry tales to administration."

You listened to all the complaints. You detected some common themes in what you were hearing, leading you to believe that perhaps some misunderstandings could be cleared up if some of the issues could be aired openly with each concerned group. You scheduled two meetings, one for your admitting staff and one for the quality improvement team. You felt encouraged because a number of individuals had told you they would be happy to speak up at such a meeting.

Your first meeting, held with your admitting staff, was brief; nobody spoke up, even when urged to do so in the most nonthreatening way possible. Your subsequent meeting with the quality team was no better. You got zero discussion going with either group, although before and between the meetings you had been bombarded by complaints from individuals. This left you extremely frustrated because most of the complaints you heard were group issues, not individual problems.

Questions

1. What can you do to get either or both groups to open up in a group setting about what is bothering them?

2. Can you suggest what might lie in the immediate past that could have rendered these employees unwilling to speak up?

3. Because you have two groups (with overlapping membership) to be concerned with, where would you initially concentrate your efforts?

References

1. Ricks TE. What we can learn from them: Lessons from Parris Island. *Parade Magazine*. November 1997;9:4–6.

2. Mansoor I. Zoom revenue and usage statistics (2023). Business of Apps Web site. https://www.businessofapps.com/data/zoom-statistics. Accessed March 23, 2023.

CHAPTER 12

Safety and Workplace Violence

CHAPTER OBJECTIVES

- Convey an understanding of the apparent principal causes of violence in the healthcare workplace.
- Review the effects of workplace violence on victims.
- Review the laws and standards pertinent to violence in the workplace and describe the responsibilities of management concerning the maintenance of a safe workplace.
- Outline the essential steps involved in instituting a violence-control program.
- Describe a number of actions the individual supervisor can take to reduce workplace violence.
- Provide guidance concerning the handling of certain violent or potentially violent incidents.

KEY TERMS

Violence-Prone Individual: Usually a person experiencing low self-esteem, paranoia, possibly a loner who resents authority and likely to blame others for any problem that arises

Violence in Health Care

Violence in healthcare institutions is escalating, and it is not limited to emergency departments and psychiatric units. A federal study found that workers in hospitals and other healthcare facilities are at higher risk of becoming victims of workplace violence than employees in most other job settings. Workplace violence is a serious concern for millions of healthcare workers, with psychiatric aides, nursing assistants, nurses, and patient care technicians among those experiencing the highest rates of violence. The

Government Accountability Office reported that patients are the primary perpetrators of nonfatal violence in health care, followed by patients' relatives and visitors.

The incidence rate of nonfatal workplace violence to healthcare workers has increased significantly between 2013 and 2018. In 2013, the percentage was 7.8; in 2018, it jumped to 10.4%. These statistics validate health care as one of the most violent industries in the country outside of law enforcement. Emergency department physicians nationwide report being the target of workplace violence yearly; psychiatrists report physical assault; and home healthcare workers report violence annually. But all of the statistics that can readily be cited might not reflect the full extent of the problem; most studies have relied on retrospective surveys, which are not always reliable. Much more research is needed to fully understand the scope of workplace violence in health care.

Much of the material presented in earlier versions of this chapter addressed, either directly or by implication, violence by employees against employees and others. The signs and guidelines provided suggest that, while addressing violence by employees, "outsiders" may at times create safety concerns for employees. And these signs of potential violence and the advice presented for dealing with them suggest a focus on exceptional and significant acts and potential acts of a serious nature. This focus is not sufficiently inclusive of the various sources from which violence in health care arises.

It was stated previously that the primary perpetrators of workplace violence in healthcare settings are patients, patients' relatives, and visitors. The kinds of incidents are often spontaneous occurrences, such as when a nurse is slapped or shoved or a frustrated visitor elbows an aide aside. There are numerous such incidents, and it would surely be impractical to dwell on possible means of recognizing in advance the potential of some persons for this sort of violence. Most of the guidelines that follow represent an attempt to more or less "profile" potential perpetrators of serious violent incidents.

Employers and managers share responsibility for providing a work environment that minimizes the danger of injury. This cannot be stressed too strongly. Medical costs and litigation expenses absorbed by medical institutions because of injuries to or caused by patients and others are considerable. Expenditures for security, workers' compensation, and legal services continue to escalate. It must be a goal of management to decrease the number of assaults and disruptive incidents that occur and to provide protection for all who work within, are served by, or visit the institution.

Causes of Violence

In our multiracial, multiethnic society, we face many situations from which violence may emerge. A list of common predisposing factors is provided in **Exhibit 12.1**. **Exhibit 12.2** enumerates some

---

Exhibit 12.1 Factors Predisposing to Violence

Societal factors

- Easy availability of weapons
- High crime rate in the community
- Catastrophic life events (e.g., illness, accident, or death of loved ones)
- Distraught or vengeful spouses or other family members

Workplace situations

- Layoffs, job outplacements, mergers, reengineering, affiliations, and alliances
- Series of threats of violence or aggressive incidents
- Jobs that involve handling money, drugs, or valuable property
- Employees working alone, especially late at night
- Assignments in emergency departments or psychiatric units
- Frequent harassment by coworkers or superiors
- Weapons brought to the work site
- Interpersonal conflicts in the workplace
- Chronic labor–management problems or disputes
- Frequent grievances or stress-related workers' compensation claims filed by employees
- Poorly lighted and monitored parking areas

Management deficiencies

- Inept handling of work problems
- Inconsistent, inequitable, or insensitive supervision
- Failure to recognize and intervene early in the cycle of violence
- Lack of responsiveness to the warning signs of a potentially violent situation
- Authoritarian management
- Lack of staff training in violence prevention

Exhibit 12.2 Characteristics of Violence-Prone Individuals

- Reputation as a loner
- History of drug or alcohol abuse
- Obsession with weapons
- Involvement with racist hate groups
- Tendency to frequently claim unjust treatment; files many grievances
- Lack of tolerance for criticism
- Low or nonexistent tolerance for frustration
- Dramatic change in personality, behavior, or performance
- History of violence toward animals, women, and others
- Pattern of verbal or physical aggression (threats, intimidation, verbal abuse)
- "Hair-trigger" temper: kicking vending machine, punching wall, throwing chairs, etc.
- Frequent disputes with superiors over policy violations
- Object of criticism or harassment from coworkers, whether real or perceived
- Mentally disturbed, especially paranoid individual who perceives injustice
- Tendency to project responsibility for problems onto others
- Has made statements suggesting feelings of despair about personal or job-related matters
- Is experiencing heightened stress at work or at home
- Obsessive behavior toward coworkers (e.g., holding a grudge or having a romantic obsession)

possible characteristics of violence-prone individuals; however, keep in mind that there is likely no completely accurate profile of a violence-prone individual available.

Violent incidents sometimes involve disgruntled or vengeful employees or former employees. These incidents are often the result of real or perceived maltreatment or inept management of conflicts arising in the workplace. The addition of just one more problem, even an apparently minor concern, may push a person over the edge into a violent reaction.

Investigations following violent incidents usually reveal clearly visible warning signs that should have raised concern. Awareness of such signals is a key to violence prevention initiatives.

Overt threats of violence may be absent, but warning signs are usually present. Violence-prone individuals often express bizarre thoughts and sometimes have a fixation with weapons, experience a romantic obsession, or suffer from depression or chemical dependence. Offenders may be involved in bitter, repetitive arguments, and they often cease to associate with coworkers and even old friends.

There is no thoroughly reliable profile of a violence-prone employee. It can be said, however, that the individual who is led to commit a violent act often suffers from low self-esteem, paranoia, or depression and may be seen as a loner who resents authority. This person is likely to blame coworkers, management, or someone else for any problem that arises. There is sometimes a history of drug or alcohol abuse or a record of criminal assault. The likelihood of such a person becoming violent accelerates if there is unresolved conflict and frustration at home or at work.

Several common events can predispose some individuals to violence. The person may have recently undergone counseling or been subject to disciplinary action. He or she may have been passed over for promotion or have become overly concerned about job security. Perhaps the individual encountered a series of stressful events or a single but significant emotional shock. There may be extreme frustration or an assault on self-esteem; for example, an employee's request for time off is abruptly denied or a customer is treated poorly. One may have been on the receiving end of harsh criticism, a verbal attack, or a threat of physical harm.

Effects of Violence on Victims

Employers and managers must be continually sensitive to the effects of violence and the potential danger to their employees. Potential victims include internal customers (for example, caregivers and students) and external customers (for example, patients, physicians, and visitors), to name but a few.

After a violent event, victims and their associates are generally less productive; some may become severely depressed and seek treatment for conditions such as anxiety, insomnia, or panic attacks. Family relationships may suffer, and some individuals may turn to alcohol or drugs. Victims may often express rage at employers or managers for failing to protect them. Injured employees may seek to recover lost wages and medical expenses through workers' compensation rather than by suing, although employees are protected by law from being discharged for suing their employers.[1]

Laws and Standards Relating to Workplace Violence

The Occupational Safety and Health Administration (OSHA) has long held that well-informed workers are less at risk than those who are unaware of the potential dangers. Unfortunately, training is often the most overlooked part of compliance with OSHA standards. The general duty clause of the newer OSHA regulations includes many guidelines.[2]

When an employee injures another person, his or her employer may be liable under the doctrine of *respondeat superior*. State and federal courts charge employers with the responsibility for ensuring a safe, nonviolent work environment. Simultaneously, employers must not violate the individual rights of employees.

In 1995, the Joint Commission on Accreditation of Healthcare Organizations (JCAHO, now known simply as The Joint Commission [TJC]) added the requirement that all hospitals conduct security assessments and provide personnel with training in the management of workplace violence.[3]

Responsibilities of Management

Employers must make every effort to avoid hiring individuals who pose risks to employees and customers. When an employer becomes aware of a dangerous employee, that employer has a duty to investigate, and sometimes remove, the employee. Although the expense of security measures can be considerable, the lack of such precautions can be much more costly. In addition to financial costs, violent episodes can have many other consequences, including a negative impact on employee attendance, morale, employee retention, and recruitment. Employees should be told whom to contact—preferably through a hotline—and be provided with a step-by-step protocol to follow in the event of real or perceived violent behavior or threats.

Essentials of a Violence-Control Program

Significant Policies

Employer responsibility requires policies, procedures, and protocols that foster workplace harmony and minimize the potential for violence. There must be vigorous implementation of these measures.

An effective initiative begins with a statement of zero tolerance for violence and harassment. This statement includes descriptions of prohibited behavior, for example banning the use of controlled substances on the job and carrying weapons on the premises. The delineation of possible scenarios of workplace violence is highly recommended so that employees are familiar to some extent with how a violent situation might unfold.

Supervisors must understand the reasons behind any policies relating to violence control and respond effectively to situations that require intervention. Policies should cover the following essentials:

- Employee conduct as part of a formal performance evaluation
- Regulations concerning the use of alcohol and drugs
- When and how workplace searches for drugs or weapons are conducted

- Comprehensive procedures for disciplinary action up to and including termination of employment
- Accommodations for employees with mental impairments and other kinds of disabilities
- Proper means of restraining violent patients and others who may become violent

Improved Screening of Job Candidates

To help eliminate candidates who have histories of workplace violence or whose past behavior suggests the capacity for violence, the screening process may include pre-employment psychological testing, background investigations, reference checks, and drug testing.

Pre-employment psychological testing may be used at times and under certain circumstances or for candidates for jobs considered sensitive or highly responsible. However, there are various laws regulating this kind of testing, and the organization that uses such tests must be prepared to prove their tests are statistically validated as nondiscriminatory.

Through reference checks, a previous employer has an obligation to inform a prospective employer of documented violent tendencies of the employee in question if there is a probability of recurrence. Should an employee cause harm to others, and there is a history of violence or other major misconduct in the employee's past, the hiring employer could face a negligent hiring charge. To guard against such charges, the employer should be in a position to demonstrate that the organization made a good-faith effort to check the references of every employee before hiring. This essentially means that a complete record of reference checks should be retained for every employee, including—and we might even say especially including—records indicating which previous employers failed to respond to reference requests. For fear of legal entanglements, some previous employers will withhold even information concerning severe misconduct; however, they need not fear repercussions if the inappropriate conduct is verifiable with accurate documentation.

Finally, pre-employment drug testing has become a relatively common practice in the recruitment process for all levels of staff.

Education and Training of Supervisors and Workers

Supervisors and employees should become thoroughly familiar with the safety rules and procedures of the organization. The employer must do the following:

- Train interviewers to recognize potential troublemakers during employment interviews.
- Teach communication skills that help prevent aggression.
- Teach managers and supervisors how to recognize the victims of domestic violence.
- Describe how the organization's employee assistance program (EAP) or alternative employee support program's function, including when and how to refer employees and how to handle employees during and after treatment.
- Provide periodic staff training and retraining in the following:
  - Prevention and control of violence
  - How to recognize early warning signs of potential violence
  - Conflict resolution and de-escalation techniques
  - Behavior modification
  - Self-preservation techniques and how to protect bystanders
  - Use of specific telephone number or an alternative system to trace phone calls from harassers or callers who report bomb threats

During their education and orientation many caregivers receive advice concerning ways of responding to patients and others who come across as distressed, belligerent, aggressive, agitated, or fearful. For the most part the people who deliver the hands-on care are advised to be calm in the face of such behavior, to do what is necessary for the safety of the patient, and to call for the facility's security service if there seems to be a possibility of physical harm to anyone.

More formal programs exist in some specific settings, for example psychiatric facilities and facilities devoted to the care of individuals with developmental disabilities. In the latter, many employees are required to complete "SCIP Training" (Strategies for Crisis Intervention and Prevention) (or whatever label this sort of activity may have in any particular state). The focus of such training is to teach caregivers how to deal with agitated or assaultive clients and defuse potentially violent behavior while minimizing the risk of harm to the clients and themselves.

In addressing the potential for violence emanating from everyday situations, caregivers' best responses are those born of patience, understanding, and knowledge of how to react to such situations when they arise.

Improved Communication

Management is expected to do the following:

- Determine the need for or effectiveness of safety improvement by gathering accurate baseline data, setting precise goals, providing ongoing feedback, and rewarding success.
- Establish a hotline or a confidential procedure for reporting threats, intimidation, belligerence, and other inappropriate workplace behavior. The hotline can also be used to allow disgruntled people to complain.
- Devise special forms and reporting mechanisms for violent incidents.
- Improve collaboration between the institution's security staff and community law enforcement agencies, similar to working arrangements with fire departments.
- Hold crisis-aftermath sessions.

Modifying Environmental Factors Affecting Susceptibility to Violence

To enhance safety, management can take a number of positive steps:

- Install bulletproof glass, metal detectors, alarm systems, surveillance cameras, and escape doors in high-risk areas, such as the emergency department and cashiers' stations.

- Improve lighting in parking areas and provide security escorts for departing employees. Security can also be provided for threatened individuals, especially for victims of domestic violence.
- Provide easy-to-read identification badges and enforce their use.
- Identify potentially violent or suicidal patients; flagging their charts is encouraged.
- Provide law enforcement officials with a telephone system for their use in receiving reports of bomb threats and other crises.

Also, improving the availability of EAPs or counseling referral procedures and the formation of violence-response teams to intervene in cases of violence or threats of violence can be extremely helpful. In instances involving battered female employees, employers can provide photographs of the violent individuals to security officers, install panic buttons at employee workstations, and provide personal escorts between transportation or parking facilities and the workplace. EAPs should include therapists specially trained in the treatment of domestic violence victims.

Supervisory Principles for Reducing Workplace Violence

The following rules can help supervisors reduce workplace violence:

- *Avoid hiring problem people*. Before interviewing job applicants, prepare a list of questions that elicit or can help reveal a tendency toward violence:
  - What kinds of people do you find difficult to get along with? How do you manage to get along with these people?
  - When was the last time you became angry at work? What caused it, and how did you react?
  - What was the most difficult situation you faced at work? What feelings did you have, and how did you react to them?
  - What kinds of behavior did your boss or fellow workers exhibit that you disliked?

- *Treat employees with dignity and respect.* From supervisors to the chief executive officer, the management of a healthcare institution should model behavior that encourages trust, helps open communication, and promotes loyalty.

- *Maintain open communication.* Encourage people to say what is on their minds by using open-ended questions, such as "Jess, what is it that's troubling you?" Listen and respond with empathy and sensitivity to employee concerns and grievances. Take the initiative and point out potential problems to superiors and recommend specific additional security measures. Participate in risk management programs, labor–management discussions, and safety committee meetings.

- *Educate your staff.* Train people to recognize symptoms of potential violence and encourage them to report threats or acts of violence. Assure them that their names will be kept confidential to prevent reprisals. Articulate your expectations of self-control on the job, and make certain that employees know what behavior you expect and what you will not tolerate.

- *Be alert for potential situational and behavioral problems.* Effective staff control requires cognizance of violence-prone profiles and alertness for internal or external factors that may be propelling an employee in the direction of inappropriate behavior. Be on the lookout for conflict over equipment, space, or services. Associates are usually the first to recognize that something is wrong, but they often find that management does not respond appropriately or promptly to these concerns. When this occurs, workers can become frightened and anxious.

- *Enforce policies that address violence and its control.* Violent outbursts can often be prevented when aggressive behavior elicits a quick and appropriate response at the time that behavior first emerges. When aggressive individuals note a lack of workplace controls or consequences for their erratic behavior, the potential for unacceptable behavior escalates. Lack of controls or consequences include management denying that a problem exists, lack of investigation or follow-up of violent or potentially violent situations, failure to tell aggressive or threatening employees that they will be held responsible for any inappropriate behavior, and performance appraisals that do not reflect erratic behavior.

- *Sharpen counseling and disciplinary skills.* Be consistent and fair in your disciplinary actions. Document counseling sessions and follow up on them. Never meet alone with suspected dangerous employees. Do not try to psychoanalyze employees, but do use common sense, reason, and logic. Persuade people that it is to their benefit to try to resolve conflicts. Do not argue or get caught up in ping-pong repartee, such as "You will do as I say," "No, I won't," "Yes, you will," "No, I won't." Choose your words carefully during counseling sessions. Keep your comments and behavior neutral and nonjudgmental. Be sure the employee knows exactly what behavior you want changed. Avoid referring to yourself (as in, for example, "I think you should … " or "I'm going to recommend … "). This can trigger an explosion of pent-up rage, especially if you do not get along very well with the person. Instead, quote rules or standards (for example, "Hospital protocol is that you contact our EAP"). If the employee begins to lose control, terminate the meeting. If he or she refuses to leave your office, you can leave. Even better, hold such meetings somewhere other than in your office, say in the employee health area or in a readily accessible conference room.

- *Have the courage to get rid of troublemakers.* If termination of employment is required, do it with empathy and compassion, but do it matter-of-factly, properly applying the appropriate policies. Do it in private unless violence is likely. If you feel violence is a real possibility, have someone from the security service nearby or at least on alert. This kind of termination must be done with the greatest of care. Follow mandated procedures to the letter, and thoroughly document each incident leading to the dismissal. Consult with your superiors or your human resources department at all stages. Firings often require legal advice, especially where possible violations of union contracts or antidiscrimination laws are concerned. Because a person whose employment has been terminated may exhibit aggressive behavior, security, or in severe instances perhaps local law enforcement officers, should escort the employee off the premises.

Bomb Threats

Bomb threats are a serious concern in today's society. The Department of Homeland Security offers the following concerning telephoned bomb threats:[4]

- Take every such threat seriously.
- Keep the caller on the line as long as possible. Ask questions numerous times if possible.
- Collect as much information as possible. Ask where the bomb is, when it will explode, what it looks like, who and where the caller is, and why the bomb was planted.
- Take notes and ask a coworker to pick-up the extension.
- Have a coworker call the Federal Protective Services, local law enforcement, or security officer.

- Don't allow the phone line to be used again so that law enforcement can trace the call.

Breaking Up Fights

Fights usually arise out of attempts to save face, to defend property or territory, or simply because of the tendency of some individuals to fight in response to disagreements. Several organizations such as the World Health Organization and OSHA have thoughts on how to mitigate workplace violence:[5]

- Be familiar with the policies and procedures of your organization.
- Know your responsibilities and the extent of your authority.
- Consider the safety of everyone near the altercation.
- Be consistent in setting limits.
- Be alert for warning signs.
- Report the incident, providing thorough documentation.
- Use effective communication.

WRAP-UP

Think About It

The supervisor's primary defense against violence that comes from outside of the work group—whether from patients, visitors, or others—is vigilance and clear procedures for addressing violence when it occurs. However, the supervisor's strongest means of preventing violence within the work group is fair, humane, compassionate leadership.

Questions for Review and Discussion

1. Share your thoughts on the increase of workplace violence over the past 8–10 years. What statistics have surprised you?
2. Why is it important to hold crisis-aftermath sessions? What do we want to accomplish with such sessions?
3. What sort of answers or comments might you hear in an employment interview that might suggest the tendency of an applicant toward violence?
4. What do most of the potential causes of violent behavior have in common? Explain fully.

5. What is obvious in the rules and regulations addressing workplace violence in healthcare organizations that reflects a perceived trend toward increased violence?
6. How much do you believe you may legally ask a job candidate about arrests and convictions?
7. Why might you encounter injunctions against the use of pre-employment psychological testing?
8. Why do you believe a significant proportion of potential perpetrators of workplace violence have low self-esteem?
9. In many organizations carrying weapons or fighting are infractions that result in immediate dismissal. Why do you believe this is so?
10. Why has it become a practice following certain instances of violence to make counselors available even to people who were not directly involved in the violence?

Case: The Employee in the Corner

You are a supervisor in the housekeeping section of the facilities and maintenance department of County Hospital. Your daily activities include a walking tour of all the sections of the facility within the responsibility of your team.

Early afternoon found you walking along a short third-floor corridor that connected the hospital's surgical wing with one of the larger medical-surgical patient units. It was at a time when about half of the staff assigned to the two areas was still at lunch, and the angled corridor was empty. Or at least it appeared empty until you rounded the bend at the middle of the corridor. You then saw two people at the very end of the corridor in a corner beside the closed double doors that led into the surgical wing.

You stopped in place when you saw the two people. They did not seem to be aware of your presence. At the distance you were from them, you could tell that one was a woman. Although you did not recognize her, you could tell she was wearing a hospital uniform. She appeared to be pinned tightly into the corner by the other party, apparently male, whom you could see only from behind. He did not appear to be wearing hospital clothing.

As you hesitated before proceeding, you saw the man place his right forearm across the woman's throat. The woman struggled against the arm; you heard her curse and say, "No, leave me alone!" The man said something that you could not hear, but his words apparently made the woman struggle harder.

Instructions

Describe in detail what you would do in this situation. For each decision or action you mention, explain why you are taking this particular step. (It is acceptable for you to make a few reasonable assumptions about you and your circumstances, as long as you explain these.)

References

1. McCormick K, Stewart JD. Employers confront violence in the workplace of the '90s. *Medical Laboratory Observer.* 1996;28:34–38.
2. Daugherty DA. *The New OSHA: Blueprints for Effective Training and Written Programs.* American Management Association; 1996:9–12.
3. Joint Commission on Accreditation of Healthcare Organizations. *Quality Improvement Standards.* JCAHO; 1995.
4. Ensuring building security. U.S. Department of Homeland Security Web site. https://www.dhs.gov /ensuring-building-security.
5. Kumari A, Kaur T, Ranjan P, Chopra S, Sarkar S, Baitha U. Workplace violence against doctors: Characteristics, risk factors, and mitigation strategies. *J Postgrad Med.* 2020 Jul-Sep;66(3):149–154. doi: 10.4103/jpgm.JPGM_96_20. PMID: 32675451; PMCID: PMC7542052

Leading People

CHAPTER 13

Leaders and Managers

CHAPTER OBJECTIVES

- Explore the relationship between leadership and the culture of the organization in terms of how one has an influence in shaping the other.
- Describe the perceived differences between the popular conceptions of "leading" and "managing."
- Identify the principal characteristics defining the various styles of leadership.
- Identify several special leadership approaches that some leaders have incorporated into their approaches to managing people.
- Discuss some of the primary activities of leadership at the department level that are pursued in the process of getting things done through people.
- Examine in detail the characteristics of effective leaders.
- Identify a number of common mistakes made by supervisors in attempting to fulfill their leadership responsibilities.

KEY TERMS

Authoritarian Leadership: A dictatorial leadership style; the boss is the boss, and what the boss says goes, no questions; can be and often is harsh and exploitative.

Paternalistic Leadership: Still authoritarian, but kindly; a sort of "father-knows-best" rule.

Micromanagement: A form of authoritarian leadership in which employees are treated as incapable of making decisions or doing the job correctly without the leader's constant intrusion and involvement.

Participative Leadership: The participative leader is people-oriented and believes that, if treated properly, people can be trusted and will put forth their best efforts.

Consultative Leadership: A style in which the leader invites employee input but reserves the right to make all of the decisions.

Bureaucratic Leadership: An impersonal leadership style typified by rules-oriented, by-the-book management.

Situational Leadership: A flexible style in which the leader adapts his or her approach to specific situations and to the particular needs of different members of the team.

Laissez-Faire Leadership: This is essentially hands-off or absentee leadership, appropriate only if sufficient prior leadership has been involved in building the team to a position of independence and self-reliance. This is often the refuge of the lazy or incompetent manager.

Organizational Culture: A pattern of basic assumptions that has worked well enough to be considered valid and to be taught to new members as the correct way to perceive, think, and feel in relation to coping with problems.

What Is It?

Leadership is not a process learned in seminars by remembering and following a specific number of steps or behaving according to some formula. Rather, leadership is either intuitive or gained through experience. The best leaders strive to develop the leadership skills of their teammates so that the success of the team does not depend on a single person. Many organizations have failed because charismatic leaders did not develop new leaders, and when they were no longer around, their backups were unable to step up and perform as required.

True leaders often influence people over whom they have no formal authority. This is often referred to as "horizontal management" and its practitioners as "informal leaders." To meet today's interdepartmental needs for coordination and cooperation, healthcare managers must possess leadership ability.

The best leaders understand how their own prejudices influence the way they lead. Because they can confront their own prejudices and shortcomings, they can deal with those of others. They censure intolerance and ensure equality of opportunity. They pay special attention to people outside of the mainstream work culture, knowing that these people can easily come to feel isolated. They learn about the values and cultural heritage of others and become aware of the differences in communication styles and interpersonal relationships.[1]

If you are a full-time manager, you are rewarded for what your employees do and for the responsibilities you fulfill, not for the tasks you perform personally.

Organizational Culture

Management Provides

- Mission statements (why we do what we do)
- Visions (what it will look like when we get where we want to go)
- Goals (so we know we have arrived)
- Strategies (the journey taken in getting there)
- Values (how we behave on the journey)

Leaders shape the culture of their organization, and to a considerable extent the culture shapes the leaders. Organizational culture can be defined as follows: a "pattern of basic assumptions that has worked well enough to be considered valid and to be taught to new members as the correct way to perceive, think, and feel in relation to coping with problems."[2] In addition, "a culture in which the leadership style of the manager features coercion and other direct power processes is less effective than a culture characterized by collaboration and participation."[3] In other words, organizational culture is simply the broad-based perception of the way things are done at work.

The healthcare culture of today demands pervasive and honest communication: openness and authentic interaction in all operations. This translates into the sharing of knowledge, skills, news, experiences, problems, and setbacks. The result is learning at all levels.

To foster a service-oriented culture, supervisors express values that are spin-offs from the mission statement. They put values into action by treating employees as they want customers to be treated. They get personally involved in service activities, and they use periodic meetings of their work groups to inspire people and solve problems.

Leading Versus Managing

To address differences between leading and managing it is necessary to get beyond dictionary definitions and examine popular perceptions. The definitions in any good dictionary tell us that leading and managing are essentially the same, often to the point of defining one in terms of the other. And almost any thesaurus we open lists "leader" and "manager" as synonyms for each other. In terms of word meanings on paper, leader and manager are one. When we speak of differentiating between leader and manager, however, we are dealing not with word definitions but with human perceptions. A great many people perceive a difference between the two words, and in the perceiver's mind, perception is reality.

Decide for yourself how much difference, if any, exists between the two terms. When you hear about leadership, do you equate this with management? Or do you perceive a difference between the two, with leadership somehow the more acceptable, indeed the more desirable, of the two? Popular perception generally holds that leadership is on a somewhat higher level than management, and it is this perceived difference on which most of what is said here about leadership is based. This popularly perceived difference between management and leadership may be owing at least in part to the overuse of "management" in describing not only the acts of managing but also as a noun heavily used in describing a group of people who run an organization. We can, however, come closer to clarifying the perceived differences by using some common adjectives; surely there can be "good" management or "poor" management as well as "good" or "poor" leadership. Chances are that what we might call leadership is close in meaning to good management.

The foregoing enables us to say that in a practical sense we have among us many good managers but that we often experience a shortage of good leaders. Business schools develop managers, not leaders, although, unfortunately, some schools readily attach the label of leader to their graduates, again because "leader" is perceived as the "better" word. Perception, plus observation of such individuals in action, suggests the following practical differences between leading and managing:

- People obey managers because they must, or they expect to; people follow leaders because they want to.
- Leaders envision (for example, Dr. Martin Luther King, Jr.'s "I Have a Dream" speech); managers marshal resources to achieve the visions of others.
- Leaders often rely on their intuition. Although some managers are intuitive, managers by and

large rely more on analysis, objectivity, and rationality.

- Leaders generally demonstrate more self-confidence and are willing to take more and greater risks than managers.
- Leaders emphasize creativity; managers are more likely to emphasize conformity.
- Managers project power *over* people; leaders project power *with* people.
- Managers strive to satisfy the needs and wants of their customers; leaders endeavor to astonish customers by exceeding their wants and needs.
- The goals of managers usually arise from necessity; the goals of leaders are more likely to arise from desire.
- Managers are more like scientists (methodical, organized); leaders are more like artists (spontaneous, creative).
- Managers say, "I will support you"; leaders say, "Follow me."
- Managers are more concerned with the how; leaders are more concerned with the what.
- Managers seek obedience; leaders seek commitment.
- Managers control; leaders empower.
- Managers correct problems; leaders prevent problems.
- Managers learn how successful people do things and emulate them; leaders explore new paths.
- Managers may place primary emphasis on system, structure, and process; leaders are more likely to emphasize team building and employee development.

There have been long-standing discussions concerning whether management is an art or a science; the conclusions drawn usually suggest that it is both art and science. We might further suggest that if indeed there is a real fundamental difference between management and leadership, it is that management is more science than art, whereas leadership is more art than science.

Certainly, managers can be leaders as well. It is most likely that the very best managers are also excellent leaders.

Basic Leadership Styles

Clusters of particular leadership characteristics and behaviors have been described as leadership styles. Like clothing styles, leadership styles come and go; some even return for a while, and others prevail for a time and vanish, never to return.

Authoritarian Leadership

Leaders who use this style are often described as task-oriented, paternalistic, or autocratic. They "run a tight ship," and they order or direct their employees. This style is also referred to as top-down or "I" (the leader comes first) management (also referred to as Theory X, from the classic article *The Human Side of Enterprise,* by Douglas McGregor).

Authoritarian leaders believe that people must be controlled closely and provided with external motivation (for example, pay, benefits, and good working conditions). They are task-oriented rather than people-oriented. They tell employees what they want but do not necessarily tell them why. They do not invite input from their people and may in fact even discourage it. Autocratic leaders encourage dependency. Employees of authoritarian leaders often exhibit apathy or hostility.

A subset of the pure authoritarian style is the paternalistic approach. Paternalistic leaders exhibit either the features of a kind, nurturing parent—call this the benevolent dictator—or those of a critical and oppressive parent or, if you will, a tyrant. A paternalistic approach is appropriate when one is dealing with emergencies in which one must instantly obey without questioning (for example, fire or disaster) and may, at times, be the best way to deal with inexperienced or insecure employees or hostile people who challenge authority.

"Micromanagement" is a form of authoritarian leadership. Despite nearly universal condemnation of the practice, many supervisors micromanage because they believe their employees are unable to function without them. They believe they must stay on top of things at all times to prevent mistakes or to make sure the work gets done. They are certain their staffers are incapable of making decisions. Some simply believe this is what managers are supposed to do. To be successful in the long run, however, these managers must learn to delegate authority and trust their employees.

Participative Leadership

Leaders who behave according to this style are often referred to as people-oriented. They run a "happy ship." This style is also described as bottom-up or "we" (all of us together) management (Theory Y, again from *The Human Side of Enterprise*, by Douglas McGregor).

Participative leaders believe that people want to work and are willing to assume responsibility. They believe that, if treated properly, people can be trusted and will put forth their best efforts. Participative leaders motivate by means of internal factors (for example, task satisfaction, self-esteem, recognition, and praise). They explain why things must be done, listen to what employees have to say, and respect their opinions. They delegate wisely and effectively.

There are several subsets of this style. When in a consultative mode, leaders seek input from their followers before making important decisions. When in a delegative mode, leaders share responsibility with their colleagues.

One simple way to learn whether participative management is in place is to keep track of the number of suggestions each employee makes annually. In many Japanese companies, where participative management flourishes, each employee submits dozens of ideas each year. Equally important is the percentage of suggestions actually acted on by management.

Participative managers can be counted on to articulate two magic phrases: "What do you think?" and "I need your help."

Consultative Leadership

Generally, the majority of leaders who engage in consultative leadership seem to believe they are actually exhibiting a participative style. After all, they bring employees into consideration of the problem or a decision situation, they put the employees to work developing solutions and alternatives, and they may even ask them to identify a course of action and describe the manner of its implementation. Up to this point we are speaking of participative leadership, but then it all goes out the window when the leader sorts through the employees' contributions and makes the final decision based solely on what he or she wants (and may have already decided on). The consultative leader is never able to completely turn loose of the decision-making authority of the management position and trust the employees to make the right decision.

Bureaucratic Leadership

Terms descriptive of this style include rules-oriented, by-the-book management, and "they" management (essentially impersonal). Bureaucratic managers act as monitors or police. They enforce policies, rules, procedures, and orders from upper management. They tend to be buck-passers who take little or no responsibility for directives and who often experience near-paralysis of thought and action when encountering a situation for which no rule exists.

For the most part, bureaucrats do not see themselves as bureaucrats. The very term bureaucrat carries a negative connotation, and few if any people will consciously label themselves that way. Nevertheless, bureaucrats exist in some places in large numbers, and they often play negative, self-serving political games. They advance in stable or static organizations by not making mistakes, reducing risk-taking, and blaming others. Government agencies and military services tend to house many bureaucrats, as do other organizations occasionally, such as major not-for-profits in which employees have found the maximum likelihood of continued employment and minimum likelihood of significant change.

True leadership is incompatible with the stifling character of bureaucracy. However, a bureaucratic style may sometimes be suitable for operations in which tasks must always be performed in the same way (for example, sorting mail or typing reports).

Situational Leadership

Terms used to describe this style include contingency-based, flexible, adaptive, and "different strokes for different folks" leadership. As the name suggests, flexible leaders adapt their approach to specific situations and to the particular needs of different members of the team. As employees gain experience and confidence, the leadership style changes from highly directive to supportive (from task-related to people-related). For example, two new employees may start work on the same date. If one has had previous experience and the other has had none, different directive styles are needed. A show-and-tell approach is required by the novice, but the same may not be appropriate for the experienced person.

A practical guideline is to consider a consultative or delegative style in reference to areas of expertise and to provide specific direction in areas of weakness. Some managers, in an effort to always be participative, fail to be directive when direction is needed.

Laissez-Faire Leadership

This kind of leadership is described as hands-off, fence-straddling, absentee, Catch-22, and "not me" management. Laissez-faire managers avoid giving orders, solving problems, or making decisions. They are physically evasive and are sometimes nowhere to be found when needed. Verbally, they are often masters of double-talk.

A positive form of laissez-faire leadership is the democratic style that features self-directed (autonomous) teams in which leadership is delegated to highly trained work groups. The members of these teams know more about the organization and are better trained, more motivated, and more productive than their counterparts in traditional settings. They solve problems, redesign work processes, set standards and goals, select and monitor new employees, and evaluate team and individual performance.

Clearly, this hands-off style of leadership can work extremely well if sufficient leadership has been involved in building the teams and seeing that they are properly charged and appropriately oriented. However, this can also be the refuge of the lazy or incompetent manager who is self-deluded into believing that he or she is backed by strong self-directed teams when this is nowhere near the case.

Leadership Approaches: Special Variations

Manipulation

Unfortunately, organizational management includes its share of manipulators. Manipulative managers get people to do their bidding by using the following tactics:

- Intimidating them, in effect making them fearful of the consequences of not complying
- Engaging in emotionalism: using anger, tears, yelling, or playing to seek sympathy
- Making people feel guilty if they do not immediately do what is wanted of them
- Implying the employees owe the manager something for past favors
- Name dropping; for example, "The Director will be very unhappy if this isn't resolved right away" (more or less intimidation-by-proxy)

Management by Crisis

Management by crisis is also referred to as "fire-fighting management," and it is always easy to recognize the people who use this approach. They are surrounded by noise, confusion, and emotional upheaval. Every day is characterized by a series of crises for them. They complain that they cannot get things done because they are too busy putting out fires. They react rather than anticipate; they solve problems instead of preventing them. Their behavior suggests that planning is a concept completely foreign to them. Everything they do is reactive; they are never proactive.

Management by Exception

Managers who have adopted the practice of managing by exception act as facilitators, supporters, and resource people. Their message is "I do not interfere as long as your actions and results remain within broad limits of acceptable performance. Come to me with problems you can't solve or when you need something I can get you." Management by exception is appropriate when leading certain categories of professionals or specialists.

Management by Objectives

Management by objectives is considered by many to have been one of the management "flavor of the month" ideas that enjoy immense popularity for a while and then fade away. Still used in places, this particular approach has remained popular longer than most other special management approaches. For example, when you are reviewing the performance of an employee, one helpful way to focus on the future is to do so in terms of future performance objectives.

Management by Wandering Around

This particular informal practice, discussed in greater detail in the chapter entitled "Coaching and Counseling," involves little more than its name implies. At its heart, however, is something of great importance to managers at all levels: visibility. A manager who is "out there" to see and be seen accomplishes much more than the manager who never leaves the office.

Contemporary Leadership Activities

Leadership has evolved over the ages, and at different periods the emphasis has been on different leadership activities. The needs of the times influence the activities in which the leaders of any era are engaged. For example, given the state of health care today, today's leaders are more likely to be concerned with matters of productivity and cost containment than were the leaders of 40 or 50 years ago. For the most part, contemporary leaders are deeply involved in the following activities:

- Team building and group problem-solving
- Cross-training for efficiency and flexibility
- Employee empowerment
- Improved quality and customer service
- Cost cutting
- Managing change (new services, products, or facilities)
- Staff reductions or other staff rearrangements
- Decentralizing activities or establishing satellite activities
- Worker safety and health programs
- Environmental preservation
- Patient home care
- Point-of-care services (for example, expanded bedside services)

Foundation of Leadership

One prominent feature of a well-led workforce is the absence of cynicism. Cynicism disappears when employees respect their leaders. They respect their leaders because they perceive them as competent, caring, truthful, and ethical. Those leaders "walk the talk." Their behavior matches their words, and it features integrity and trust. Trust has two parts: being trusting (that is, displaying the ability to believe in others) and being trustworthy (that is, fully deserving others' belief in them). Leadership in its strongest form is leadership by example. Leading is not only walking the talk, but also talking the walk. Talking the walk is explaining to your employees why you are taking or rejecting certain actions. Your employees must respect what you do and understand why you are doing it. If you achieve that with your employees, you will succeed as a leader. For more on effective leadership, see **Exhibit 13.1**.

Exhibit 13.1 The 12 Commandments of Leadership

1. Know what you want.
2. Take control of your career.
3. Believe in yourself.
4. Go for the goal.
5. Enjoy the game.
6. Be capable.
7. Let your expertise show.
8. Rely on others.
9. Look for opportunities.
10. Learn the ropes.
11. Never stop networking.
12. Get a mentor.

Characteristics of Effective Leaders

Leaders must be walking mission statements who make their visions come alive by talking about them with enthusiasm and conviction. They must express themselves in attitudes and actions more than in words. Enthusiasm is almost magical; it is a positive and optimistic mindset that generates energy, enhances creativity, builds networks, and attracts other winners. It is especially necessary for the supervisory functions of motivation, communication, delegation, and problem-solving.

No matter how you feel, start the day with a burst of enthusiasm. Throughout the day, feed positive thoughts into your subconscious mind by saying positive things about your performance. Surround yourself with other optimistic doers. Shun the complaining observers. Use success imagery; that is, visualize good outcomes in whatever you do. Recharge your energy by relaxing or meditating, especially after setbacks.

Good team leaders use both the helicopter approach and the management-by-wandering-around approach. Like helicopters, they hover over the work area where they can view the total operation. When they spot trouble, they descend for a closer look or to get involved. In the proactive management-by-wandering-around process, leaders do not wait for people to bring problems into their offices. Instead, they make frequent visits to each workstation. Here they spot potential problems and ask for suggestions. They also seek ideas from vendors and customers. Good team leaders do not micromanage.

As evident from the following lists, a number of factors figure into the characteristics of an effective leader. It should perhaps be conceded at the outset that only rarely will a particular leader possess every last one of the following characteristics. It is, in fact, possible to point to any number of apparently successful leaders who are clearly lacking several of what we might consider essential characteristics. However, every leader who has succeeded in the job has enjoyed one significant advantage: the followers accepted that person's leadership.

Important Characteristics of Effective Team Leaders

- *Effective team leaders are competent.*
  - They possess both technical and team leadership skills, recognizing that the leader must be proficient in both areas.
  - People look up to them and respect their expertise.
  - Their opinions and advice are sought after by associates both inside and outside their departments.
  - They are asked to serve on important committees.
  - They work to constantly improve their professional and leadership capabilities.
  - They can answer most questions, and when they cannot, they know where to get the answers.
  - They cooperate fully with their counterparts in other departments.
- *Effective team leaders are emotionally stable.*
  - They exhibit a relaxed leadership style.
  - They remain cool and calm under trying circumstances.
  - They handle stress well.

- When they get upset with people, they focus on behavior, not on personalities or individual traits.
- *Effective team leaders get the job done.*
  - They provide a sense of direction and set high expectations and standards.
  - They expect and demand good performance.
  - They are well organized and always prepared.
  - They are proactive; they anticipate and prepare for change.
  - They focus on important matters; they do not nitpick.
  - They place the right people in the right jobs.
  - They do not waste their time or that of their followers.
  - They stimulate innovativeness and invite ideas.
  - They provide all the resources their teams need.
  - They do not tolerate deadwood.
- *Effective team leaders are effective communicators.*
  - They use memos, meetings, and other communication channels effectively.
  - They provide clear instructions and request feedback to make sure that their directions are understood.
  - They are articulate and persuasive, but they do not manipulate people.
  - They are excellent listeners and are easy to talk with.
  - They share information but do not repeat gossip.
  - They do not withhold bad news, but they deliver it with consideration.
  - They are effective teachers.
  - They provide feedback, both positive and negative, as needed.
  - They criticize behavior, not people or personalities.
  - They are quick to praise and to give credit. They praise in public and criticize in private.
  - They acknowledge their own mistakes and make sure they learn from them.

- They always seem to know what's going on.
- *Effective team leaders are unafraid.*
  - They thrive on responsibility.
  - They take risks, and they bend rules when doing so makes sense.
  - They are innovative and flexible.
  - They chalk up failures to experience.
  - They keep their fears to themselves.
  - They encourage creativity and risk-taking.
  - They accept responsibility for failures.
- *Effective team leaders are credible.*
  - They are dedicated to telling the truth.
  - They keep their promises and fulfill their commitments.
  - They admit their mistakes.
  - They do not take credit for the ideas of others.
  - They do not play favorites, and their credibility is above reproach.
- *Effective team leaders develop committed followers.*
  - They care about their followers, and they show it.
  - They are willing to roll up their sleeves and help out when necessary.
  - They go to bat for their people.
  - They empower employees and encourage autonomy and self-reliance.
  - They provide their people with whatever they need to get their work done.
  - They allow people freedom in how the work is done, but they insist on getting the results they expect.
  - They do not play favorites.
  - They are as fully attentive to people below them as to those above them in the organization, perhaps even more so.
  - They invite and respect the opinions and suggestions of all their employees.
  - They provide opportunities for employees to use newly learned skills or previously untapped skills.
  - They encourage and support suggestions, comments, and proposals from all management levels.
  - They articulate what they value and back this up with their everyday behavior.

- They reward cooperation as highly as they reward individual achievement.
- They are helpful and anticipate the needs and problems of their team members.
- They defend their people from outside harassment.
- *Effective team leaders exhibit charisma.*
  - They maintain a childlike fascination with things and people.
  - They make it a point to catch people doing something right and tell them so.
  - They hold a warm handshake and smile for a few seconds longer than the other person.
  - They use the other person's name often during conversation.
  - They project energy and enthusiasm.
  - They are good role models.

Common Supervisory Mistakes

Everyone makes mistakes; to do so is human nature. But when someone in a leadership capacity makes a mistake, the effect is frequently multiplied through the leader's area of responsibility. A mistake by a supervisor is often visible throughout the immediate work group and beyond. Supervisory errors diminish the effectiveness of the supervisor and, even more so, often negatively affect the effectiveness of the group. Here are some of the more common mistakes made by supervisors:

- They try to avoid accepting responsibility, which is directly contrary to what is expected of a supervisor.
- They fail to delegate properly and empower their employees, leaving themselves open to overwork, criticism, and burnout while the employees go unchallenged.
- They take the narrow view of customer service and ignore their internal customers.
- They pay inadequate attention to budgetary concerns and fail to control costs.
- They associate with losers, mindless of the effect on their credibility.

- They use a cookie-cutter approach to managing, as though every problem was solvable by formula.
- They seek to be liked by all instead of seeking respect.
- They tolerate incompetence and fail to set performance standards.

- They neglect their own training and career development as well as the training and development of their employees.
- They recognize and reward only their top performers.

WRAP-UP

Think About It

Being a good leader can be thought of as an art form. The skill can be gained through experience, or it is intuitive. Managing people and leading them are different roles, but both play a vital part in the supervisor's job and success of the organization.

Questions for Review and Discussion

1. Explain what is meant by the following statement: "Leadership cannot be taught, but it can be learned."
2. How is it that true leaders can often influence people over whom they have no formal authority?
3. How does a successful, well-functioning, self-directed leaderless team get to be that way? Does it ever need a leader once it achieves that state?
4. A portion of this chapter addressed perceived differences between the terms "manager" and "leader." What, if any, do you believe are the differences between "manager" and "boss"?
5. Under what kind of leadership would an organization be least likely to change? Why do you believe this is so?

6. An effective leader has many characteristics. Choose one from Exhibit 13.1 and explain your experience with this type of leader.
7. Why is failure to delegate thoroughly and properly of particular importance to a group's leader? Provide several possible reasons.
8. As a supervisor, what do you believe you would have to do to become comfortable with managing by exception?
9. Why do you believe teams and team building have enjoyed such increasing popularity in recent years?
10. Why do we claim that leading by example is extremely important? What are some of the problems that can arise when we fail to do so?

Essay: Examining the Micromanager

Surely most, if not all, readers of this text are familiar with the term "micromanagement." Perhaps some have found themselves in circumstances in which they have been micromanaged and thus have gained some firsthand understanding of it. Micromanagers often give employees the distinct impression that they do not trust them or think them capable of correctly fulfilling their responsibilities on their own.

In essay form, explain in detail why you believe micromanagers behave as they do and why supervisors who attempt to lead by micromanaging employees are destined for failure in the long run.

Case: That's Her Responsibility, Not Mine

Susan Wilson is the administrative supervisor of Diagnostic Imaging at Central Hospital. Supervising in an expanding department and coping with steadily increasing outpatient activity, she found her workload increasing to the extent that she believed help was required with some of her duties. Taking a hard look at tasks she could legitimately delegate, that is, tasks that did not require supervisory authority, she settled on her monthly statistical report. The report itself was fairly easy to create, but gathering the necessary data consumed a fair amount of time.

She selected employee George Peters to do the report and provided him with all necessary instructions, even to the point of creating a detailed written procedure. She believed George was capable of doing a thorough job; he had sufficient time available to incorporate the report into his workload, and she further thought that George might appreciate some variety in his work. George expressed no feelings for or against doing the report.

A few days after assigning the report, Susan discovered that the current report had not yet been started and that if it were not completed at once it would be late. Susan reminded George; his reply was that other necessary work was delaying the data collection. Susan emphasized the need to get the report done on time, but George seemed in no particular hurry to get on with the task.

The following day Susan accidentally overheard a portion of a conversation between George and another employee to whom George was saying: "...her lousy statistics. I think she should keep doing it herself. After all, that report's her responsibility, not mine."

Instructions

1. Identify and describe any actions Susan might have taken incorrectly in delegating the statistical report to George.

2. Decide what, if anything, Susan can do to try to correct the attitude revealed by George in his comments to the other employee.

References

1. Rosen RH. *Leading People*. Viking Press; 1996:207, 213.
2. Schein E. Organizational culture. *American Psychologist.* 1990;45:109–119.
3. Young JA, Smith B. Organizational change and the HR professional. *Personnel*. 1988;65:44.

CHAPTER 14

Coaching and Counseling

CHAPTER OBJECTIVES

- Explore the important role of the supervisor as coach and examine the characteristics of an effective coach.
- Specify the principal reasons behind poor employee performance, and describe the role that coaching plays in improving performance.
- Expand on the concept of "management by wandering around."
- Describe the role of the supervisor in enhancing employee self-sufficiency through effective coaching.
- Address the supervisor's follow-up in the aftermath of coaching with particular emphasis on dispensing praise and delivering constructive criticism and, in general, providing constructive feedback to employees.
- Identify the pitfalls occasionally encountered by the supervisor as coach.
- Define the purpose of employee counseling, and identify the principal circumstances under which counseling should be used.
- Provide the supervisor with detailed guidelines for the conduct of an employee-counseling interview.
- Establish the necessity for systematic follow-up to every counseling session.
- Identify the common barriers to effective counseling.

KEY TERMS

Coaching: The ongoing process of helping employees fulfill their responsibilities and achieve results.

Completed Staff Work: When an employee comes to a supervisor with a problem, the employee also brings potential solutions and a recommendation.

Counseling: Either remedial or preventive in nature, counseling involves addressing employee performance or behavior that appears to be straying from established norms or standards.

Coaching

Coaching is the ongoing process of helping employees fulfill their responsibilities and achieve results. It is an integral part of face-to-face leadership. Zemke, a keen observer and prolific author, crystallizes coaching wisdom as follows: "Select the right players, inspire them to win, and show them you care. Tell them where they stand, how much they are improving, and what they could do to improve more."[1]

Coaching goes beyond the activities of instruction. Coaches deal not only with task outcomes, but also with attitudes, morale, discipline, ethics, and career development. The effective coach is instructor, cheerleader, counselor, disciplinarian, evaluator, resource person, and troubleshooter.

Coaches are expected to clarify management's expectations of employee performance, modify inappropriate attitudes, instill self-sufficiency, and enhance competencies. Coaches shape values, remove obstacles, build on employees' strengths, stretch worker skills, and build interpersonal relationships.

Characteristics of Effective Coaches

Effective coaches are dedicated, enthusiastic leaders who are technically or professionally competent. They push or pull people to the level of their capability but never to a level of discouragement.

The organizational goal of every coach is to get work completed on schedule, ensure quality of service outcomes, and satisfy customers. This is the opposite of the human resources department; coaches' goals are to get substandard performers up to speed and help the other employees achieve self-fulfillment. Skilled coaches do the following:

- Exhibit the leadership traits enumerated in the chapter entitled "Leaders and Managers"
- Keep workers informed, letting them know what is going on
- Show workers how to get the job done
- Help workers who have problems
- Listen—really listen—to the employees
- Direct their negative feedback at performance and results, not people
- Are quick to praise and do so in public whenever possible
- Set a good example, always modeling appropriate behavior
- Provide psychological support
- Pitch in and help with routine work during emergencies and when there is a shortage of staff
- Are technically or professionally competent in their primary fields of expertise

Role of the Coach in Improving Performance

A number of reasons are commonly behind poor employee performance. Some of the more prominent reasons, and the response of the coach to them, are briefly described here.

First, and most likely foremost, many employees do not fully understand what is expected of them. Everyone working at every level must know the results expected of them and perform capably; coaches tell them, coaches remind them, and coaches clarify management's expectations of them.

Some employees do not fully understand how to do what is expected of them. Coaches show them how and help them learn.

At times, some employees do not know that their performance is substandard. When such is the case, coaches inform them of this and show them how to achieve standard performance. Also, in some instances employees could do better if they tried harder. Coaches motivate them, encourage them, and cheer them on.

When employees face obstacles that hinder performance, coaches remove the obstacles and show them how to clear the barriers that arise in their path. When employees get discouraged, coaches support and encourage them.

Sometimes, employees believe their work goes unnoticed or unappreciated. Coaches are the first to praise, and coaches ensure that others are made aware of work well done.

Coaching is an integral part of the daily activity of every supervisor. Coaching begins when a new employee reports to the department for the first time. It begins with orientation and training. From this beginning forward, supervisors coach when someone asks for advice or help, needs assistance, or steps out of line. The more time coaches spend listening to their people and observing what those people are doing, the more opportunities they find to coach. These remarks provide a natural transition into a discussion of the concept of management by wandering around.

Management by Wandering Around (MBWA)

One of Tom Peters' appealing contributions is his concept of MBWA. The wandering he advocates includes frequent contact with people outside of one's own department, for example customers and suppliers, but we limit this discussion to departmental worksite wandering. Following are the principal features of MBWA offered by Peters and Austin:[2]

- MBWA is meeting people in their offices or work areas rather than in yours; it's getting out and visiting.
- MBWA is listening much more than talking.
- MBWA is asking whether employees are having any problems and, if so, offering to help.
- MBWA is asking employees and others for advice and opinions.
- MBWA is catching people doing something right and saying so, not catching them doing something wrong.
- MBWA is carrying a little black book to write down employees' suggestions for improving customer service and to note meritorious performance.
- MBWA is spotting activities, facilities, and problems that need fixing.
- MBWA is calling employees by their names and asking about their families or special interests.
- MBWA, when successful, reduces the number of needed memos and eliminates unnecessary meetings.
- As with any particular management strategy, MBWA must be practiced properly to be effective. There are potential problems:
- MBWA can backfire if the "wanderers" are perceived by their staffs as spies, inspectors, critics, or interrupters.
- MBWA is not rambling around smiling and waving or saying, "How are you doing?"
- MBWA does not consist of nitpicking, intruding on peoples' work time for no apparent valid reason, or spreading gossip.

When you supervise people who require a great deal of support, make your visits at the same time each day so they know when to expect you. If some of your people are often not where they should be, vary the times at which you make your rounds.

Enhancing Employee Self-Sufficiency

Do not overdo the helping-hand character of coaching by allowing employees to take advantage of your assistance. For example, consider a nurse who is having a problem hooking up an orthopedic traction setup. Say the nurse calls for help, but instead of staying to watch how the specialist arranges all the ropes and pulleys, the nurse slips off for coffee. The specialist, usually the supervisor, should see that the employee stays at hand and uses the set-up process as a training demonstration.

Do not let employees transfer all their problems to you. New supervisors must learn when not to solve other people's problems for them. You do not want to be a "Teflon manager" from whom all the cries for help slide off. Neither do you want to be a "Velcro manager" and let all the problems of other people stick to you.

Insist on completed staff work. This term simply means that when employees come to a supervisor with a problem, they must also bring ideas for solving the problem. Once people become aware of this expectation, they will bring you fewer problems, and when they do bring in the problems and their proposed solutions, you may find their ideas are better than yours.

Do not overdo the dispensing of advice. Try asking first. When someone wants an opinion, respond with "What do you think?" instead of an immediate "Here's what you should do." Finding a solution may take longer this way, but doing so pays off in the long haul.

Encourage people to take small career risks. When they make bad decisions, as we all do from time to time, or fail to pick the best solution, do not punish them for their mistakes. Regard their errors as learning experiences. However, do not tolerate repetition of the same mistakes.

Insist that employees do what they say they will do. Ask for definite commitments. Set deadlines, and, when appropriate, get them in writing.

Defending, Facilitating, Empowering, and Supporting

Employees of effective leaders see their coaches as defenders who protect them from outside harassment. A major source of frustration for employees is being attacked by people against whom they are powerless. Coaches are the defenders against such hostility.

Coaches are facilitators who get their teams the employees, time, and other resources needed to function effectively. At times, supervisors must go to the mat with suppliers or people in other departments to demand that some action be taken.

Coaches empower their staff and strip away red tape to enable the workers to make decisions and solve customer or operational problems. Simply being authorized to answer customer questions is appreciated by employees.

Coaches should not be afraid of rolling up their sleeves and pitching in to help occasionally. Support also involves providing user-friendly policies, instruments, and procedures and showing respect, fairness, and trust. It is giving a great deal as well as expecting much. It is being available and visible. It is ensuring employee safety and wellness and fighting for employees' rights, benefits, and rewards.

Coaching Feedback

According to the contingency theory of reinforcement, behavior reinforced by positive consequences improves. Behavior that begets negative consequences or that is ignored diminishes. We violate this every time we overload our reliable performers and reduce the workload of our goof-offs. We neglect this theory of reinforcement when we fail to provide both positive and negative feedback.

Why Praise?

The topic of praise came up during a management development class when the group was discussing feedback and its essential place in communication between supervisors and employees. The question was asked: "Why praise people for doing what they're expected to do? Even if they do a little better than expected, isn't it all just part of the job?" Opinions went back and forth for a few minutes until one long-tenured supervisor said, sternly and over crossed arms suggesting a defensive posture, "My people know that coming from *me*, silence is praise!"

Think about it. Can silence really be praise? You have just completed a task, and you offer the results to the supervisor. Your results are accepted without comment. How did you do? You of course know that if your work is not acceptable you will hear about it. But when your work is accepted without comment, can you determine how well you did? The fact of the matter is that the absence of feedback means you might have performed at any level from superior down to marginally acceptable; you simply do not know how well you did.

Failure to deliver praise when it is deserved is to overlook one of the most powerful motivators. A simple comment such as "I knew you could do a bang-up job on that important project" makes even an experienced veteran happy and proud. But delivering undeserved praise consistently reduces the power of positive feedback and makes recipients believe they are being manipulated.

What to Praise

Always praise performance that goes above and beyond the call of duty, performing helpful actions that are not always expected or not usually part of one's regular job. Praise is deserved by the person who does the following:

- Willingly puts in extra time when needed
- Substitutes for an absent colleague

- Submits a report ahead of schedule or gets a rush report done on time
- Reports a problem and suggests several good solutions
- Handles a delicate situation diplomatically
- Earns accolades for his or her work unit
- Receives special awards, achieves an outstanding educational record, or earns an advanced degree

Praise is also appropriate for performance that may not be outstanding but is consistently acceptable. Praise the person who does the following:

- Can always be relied on
- Has a good attendance record and is rarely tardy
- Is flexible and willing to adjust to changes
- Consistently meets job standards and work objectives

Also deserving of praise is someone whose substandard performance is improving, even though it may not yet be up to your expectations.

Given all that is known about the power of praise, it is surprising to frequently encounter supervisors who say they seldom dispense praise because their people are doing only what they are supposed to do. It would not be surprising, however, to discover that these are the supervisors whose departments experience the highest turnover rates and the poorest productivity.

When Not to Praise

- Do not hand out praise when it is clearly insincere or represents only flattery. Not only is it bad form from a supervisory point of view, employees can usually see through hollow praise in an instant.
- Do not praise when it is not earned. To do so is to diminish the value of all earned praise that you might dispense.
- Do not praise when doing so might embarrass you, the recipient, or others.
- Do not dispense praise before you are certain who has really earned it.

Praise Should Not Be Delayed

Praise, much like criticism, is time sensitive. The longer it is delayed after the behavior has occurred, the weaker and less relevant it becomes. If you delay praise, you might forget to deliver it altogether.

If praise is delayed, the recipient is more likely to believe that what he or she did is not particularly important or, even worse, might believe you were ignoring praiseworthy performance. Also, when praise is delayed, the recipient may be confused about what behavior is being acknowledged.

Why Praise Should Be Specific

Recipients of praise are entitled to know exactly what it was they did that was appreciated. Misunderstandings are prevented, and the behavior in question is reinforced.

Praise is more believable when it is clearly related to a specific occurrence or result. Also, it is important to avoid conveying the impression that you like absolutely everything the person has been doing. When your praise is specific, employees know that you know what is going on. Nonspecific praise dilutes the impact of the positive behavior, whereas specific praise reinforces that particular behavior. It is inappropriately nonspecific to say, for example, "You did a great job last night." But there is strength in specific praise such as "You did a great job getting that emotional parent calmed down last night."

How to Praise

We have already mentioned that praise should be delivered as soon as possible after the deed, that it should be specific, and that the right person or persons should receive it. The famous 1-minute praisings of Blanchard and Johnson[3] enhance praise by including comments about how the praiseworthy event made you, the coach, feel. These authors also recommend that you pause for a moment after delivering the praise to emphasize its importance. Then shake hands or touch the person to show your support. Phraseology, such as "great job" or "wow," is important, but the accompanying vocal tone, facial expression, and body language are even more important.

There are sometimes exceptions to the old rule "praise in public." Some people are embarrassed when praised in front of their peers. They may be subjected to harassment from some coworkers, and you may be deemed guilty of showing favoritism. Praise these people privately or in writing. Some supervisors write brief thank-you notes on sticky notes and put them on the outside of people's doors or at their workstations. Do not be surprised when the recipients of these notes leave them in place for several days.

A thank-you note or memo with a copy to the human resources department, where it will likely be entered into the staff file, or to upper management amplifies the effects of a verbal compliment. In selected instances of outstanding accomplishment, get your boss to send a congratulatory note to the person or make a special visit to your unit to thank the employee personally.

Consider submitting a report to the editor of your organization's newsletter or a local newspaper. Put a notice on the bulletin board.

There are very few exceptions to the second part of that old rule: "criticize in private." Under rare circumstances, it can be appropriate to air criticism of an employee with others. Say, for example, a glib chronic offender leaves your office after being reprimanded but boasts to coworkers that he was in your office helping you out of a jam. Next time, arrange for the presence of a representative witness or two from the group; the offender's behavior will change quickly.

There are other times when witnesses are required. If you are being subjected to sexual harassment, for example, voicing your objections in public is the intelligent thing to do so that you will not stand alone when the allegations are investigated.

How People React to Negative Feedback

Nobody is fond of receiving criticism because even if true and deserved, it nevertheless attacks self-esteem. Although many say they welcome constructive criticism, this is not strictly true for most people; criticism, even constructive, still has something of a sting to it. How we react to criticism depends largely on a number of conditions:

- Who is delivering the criticism
- How legitimate we believe the criticism to be
- Who else hears it
- How fragile our sense of self-worth is
- How high our stress level is at that moment

People may react defensively, counterattack, flee, or become emotional. They may respond by looking for shortcomings in the critic or weaknesses in the criticism itself, or they may reluctantly accept the reprimand and promise to improve. But they may instead try to blame others or strive to change the subject.

How to Criticize While Preserving Self-Esteem

When supervisors encounter employee mistakes, they usually respond in one of four ways:

1. They ignore the situation and hope someone else will correct it or that the employee will somehow realize it is wrong and correct it without being told.
2. They point out the mistake and ask the person to correct it.
3. They use an indirect approach by asking how things are going, hoping the employee will admit to making the error. If not, they then call attention to it.
4. They use the enhancing-value technique. This technique starts with saying something nice about what the person does and then making specific suggestions for improvement. The basis for this approach is to make the person believe you are there to help, not to judge or demean. A good example follows: "Ruth, your report is always on

time and I appreciate that. Now, let's try to eliminate those typos, okay?" If you follow the foregoing statement with another positive statement, such as "I know that I can rely on you to take care of this" or "You're too good an employee to make mistakes like this," you have just used the "sandwich technique." The sandwich technique consists of two slices of praise with a reprimand in between.

Providing Appropriate Constructive Feedback

- Remember always that your goal is to alter behavior, not to criticize.
- Maintain a high ratio of praise to criticism. Aim for about a 4-to-1 ratio; it ordinarily takes at least four positive strokes to neutralize one negative stroke.
- Criticize behavior, never personality or character traits. For example, instead of saying "You're too careless," describe what the person is specifically doing or not doing that provoked your criticism.
- Provide feedback as soon as possible after the act but not before you have all the necessary information.
- Avoid critical comments when either you or the employee is emotionally upset. A good rule to remember is never criticize in anger.
- Use "I," not "you," language. For example, instead of saying "You have a bad habit of …," say "I get upset when people …." This is less of a blow to one's ego and is less likely to evoke defensiveness.
- Avoid subjective terms such as "attitude," "work ethic," and "professionalism." If you believe you must use such words, make certain you qualify them with specific behavioral descriptions or examples.
- Avoid absolute terms such as "always" or "never" (for example, "You're always late for my meetings"). "Always" and "never" can be two of the most damaging terms in interpersonal dealings in that they are absolutes, rarely if ever true.

- Do not try to diagnose or read minds. When you say, "The trouble with you is …," you are diagnosing. When you say, "You think what you did is clever," you are trying to get into their heads.
- Don't ask "why" when you don't expect an answer. For example, instead of "Why did you do such a stupid thing?" say, "That wasn't a very smart thing to do."
- Know when to be tentative. This is usually when you are not sure what happened or who the guilty party is. For example: "I've been told that someone in our unit has been making very critical remarks in the dining room about upper management. Can you shed some light on this?" Other helpful phraseology includes, "What concerns me …," "I'm worried about …," or "Perhaps we have a problem with …."
- Always give the person a chance to respond without interruption.
- Avoid being too critical or coming down too hard on your people. If you do, they may react by devising ways to keep their mistakes hidden from you rather than trying to avoid making the mistakes.

Coaching Pitfalls

Supervisors may encounter several shortcomings from time to time in coaching:

- Using a cookie-cutter approach to coaching all employees, assuming that the same approach fits everyone. Inexperienced or insecure employees often require greater care and more of your time and support. Situational leadership is flexible and more appropriate.
- Believing you have all the right answers.
- Neglecting the coaching process because you do not believe you have the time to provide this attention to each employee.
- Labeling employees as above or below average or, for that matter, fitting employees with any label that constitutes a stereotype or implies substandard status.

- Addressing attitude, personality, or character rather than outcomes or behavior.
- Failing to allow some leeway in how things get done.
- Overusing criticism or undeserved praise.
- Offering excessive amounts of unsolicited advice.

Counseling: Preventing Bigger Problems

The two kinds of counseling a supervisor may encounter from time to time are career counseling, which involves functioning as an advisor or mentor, and preventive or remedial counseling, which addresses employee performance or behavior that appears to be straying from established norms. This chapter focuses on the latter, and from this point through the remainder of the chapter the term "counseling" is used to mean preventive or remedial counseling.

The goal of counseling is to correct poor performance or behavior or prevent its occurrence while preserving the self-esteem of the individual employee. A counseling session provides the employee with an opportunity to examine his or her behavior and decide whether to change. The objective should never be to release anger or frustration or to punish. Unsuccessful counseling, that is, counseling that fails to correct or prevent the poor performance or behavior, usually culminates in the application of disciplinary measures.

Most Common Reasons for Employee Counseling

The principal reasons for employee counseling include the following:

- Unsatisfactory productivity or diminishing quality of work
- Poor or apparently deteriorating work habits
- Violations of policies, rules, procedures, or ethics or behavior that indicates tendencies in that direction

- Inability to get along with others
- Chronic complaining
- Complaints from customers (whether external or internal)

Deciding If the Need for Counseling Exists

When performance or behavior is borderline or was once acceptable and is noticeably deteriorating, it is necessary to decide whether action is needed and, if so, what that action should be. In marginal instances in which you are initially unsure if you should proceed with counseling, ask yourself, "What would happen if everyone did that?" or "If I do nothing, what, if any, adverse results are likely to occur?"

If you have a team of overachievers, you may regard the performance of marginal performers as unsatisfactory because it compares unfavorably with that of the overachievers. This sort of trap can be avoided if you measure performance with established standards and do not make comparisons with other employees.

Counseling is not the remedy for all staff problems. As often as not, it is preventive medicine. It can solve small problems before they become big ones that require formal disciplinary action. **Figure 14.1** offers a flowchart that can be used for this purpose. Note that counseling is usually not the most appropriate remedy.

Why Employees Violate Rules

Employees are likely to break rules, violate policies, or ignore procedural requirements for the following reasons:

- They never learned—or they forgot—what was required of them.
- They see rules and regulations as meaningless, restrictive, or unfair.
- They are aware that rules are rarely enforced.
- They are influenced by other workers.
- They consider the rewards of misbehavior to be greater than the risks or the penalties.

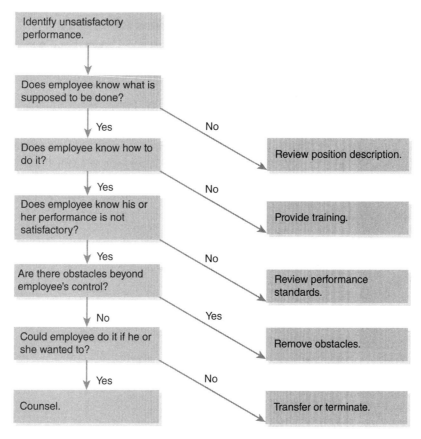

Figure 14.1 Analysis of and Responses to Unsatisfactory Performance.

Where Supervisors Often Go Wrong

Supervisors often fail to counsel or apply other remedies for a number of reasons. First, they may not be aware of the problem. Second, they may simply ignore the problem and project the attitude "If I'm very quiet, maybe it will go away." Third, they postpone action for a "more convenient time," such as an employee's next performance evaluation. Finally, a supervisor may readily ascribe a particular employee's behavior to a "poor attitude" and decide that little can be done.

A supervisor who has conscientiously applied counseling can go very wrong by failing to follow up; that is, failing to monitor and respond to post-counseling behavior, as necessary. A supervisor who fails to escalate from counseling to disciplining when no improvement occurs or frequent relapses are evident is not doing his or her job.

Preparing for the Counseling Interview

The supervisor's initial step in preparing for a counseling interview is accumulation of the facts. As a supervisor you should proceed to assemble the following information:

- What have you or others observed concerning the situation?
- What have you documented?
- Does this situation represent a relapse? If so, what was decided at previous meetings?

- What does a review of the employee's record reveal in the way of written reprimands or customer complaints?
- What does the person's most recent formal performance evaluation reveal?
- What rule or regulation or policy is involved? Study the document carefully.
- What patterns of behavior are evident? For example, concerning absenteeism, some individuals may call in sick only on Mondays, Fridays, or on days when scheduled for unpleasant assignments.

Explore the perceived benefit-to-risk ratio of the behavior from the point of view of the employee. For example, when an employee goes shopping on sick days or takes long breaks and is never called on it, the benefit-to-risk ratio is high; that is, the employee has no incentive to reform.

Do not procrastinate. Think about the damage that could be taking place while you hesitate. Also, the more you delay, the harder it will be to convince the person that the matter is important.

If you are inexperienced in these matters and the apparent problem appears to be serious, consult with your manager or with the human resources department. Schedule a place, date, and time for a counseling interview. The location should be one where there will be no interruptions. Your office might not be the best location if it ordinarily attracts a lot of traffic, so you may need to use an available conference room or an empty office. Hold the meeting in the morning so that you will then have the rest of the day to show by words and behavior that you do not bear a grudge toward the individual, that it is the behavior and not the person that has attracted your criticism. Smile and chat just as you would if you had not held a counseling session.

Mentally rehearse the most important or sensitive aspects of the upcoming meeting, specifically as follows:

- Your exact opening remarks
- Statements intended to boost the employee's confidence
- The solution you hope to reach
- How you will respond to rebuttals, defensive reactions, anger, tears, or threats

Conducting a Counseling Interview

This is a review of your counseling interview with hypothetical employee Joyce, who has exhibited a behavioral problem.

Step 1. The theme of the initial session should be one of helpfulness and caring. Greet Joyce with a smile. You intend to help her, not punish her. Thank her for coming. Do not apologize for calling the meeting; you weaken your position when you start with something such as "Joyce, I hate to bring this up, but …." Equally inappropriate is socking her with an intimidating statement, such as "Joyce, we've got to talk about your poor performance." Assume she wants to do a good job, and say so. Affirm that assumption by articulating some specific attribute (for example, "Joyce, I receive many compliments from our medical staff about your gentleness toward patients"). Continue with, "Joyce, I have a problem that I need your help with." (This is true; it really is your problem!)

Step 2. Find out whether Joyce is aware of the problem, especially if a policy or rule is being violated. Describe the situation in specific, non-judgmental terms. Be tentative if there is some question as to the validity of the charge. Use the words you selected carefully in your preparation. Attack the behavior, not Joyce. Your hope is that Joyce joins you in that attack. The more able you are to move into a problem-solving mode, the more successful the outcome will be.

Step 3. Explain how the behavior affects your department and other people. To convince her that this is important, emphasize how the behavior affects you (for example, "When I see [this happen], I become upset"). Avoid absolute terms such as "always" and "never." These words are usually inaccurate and invite contradiction. Avoid sarcasm, kidding, or other put-downs. These elicit resentment and serve no useful purpose. Do not quote from policy manuals unless the employee challenges the authenticity of your charge. Taking refuge in a handbook can make you appear weak. For the same reason, do not say, "Management expects ...." Do say, "I expect ...."

Step 4. Give Joyce time to respond. Listen until her initial reaction runs its course. Do not interrupt, even if she utters untruths or makes countercharges. Do not become defensive or lose your cool. Respond appropriately. Instead of judgmental responses ("You don't try hard enough") or defensive responses ("That's not true and you know it"), use empathetic responses ("I can understand why you . . . ") and probing responses (when, where, who, why, and how). Paraphrase ("What I hear you saying is . . .") and summarize ("Then we agree that . . . "). Jot down key points Joyce makes; you may need to refer to these later.

Step 5. Get Joyce to admit that there is a problem and that she is part of it. This is often difficult, especially if the behavior has been tolerated for an extended period. She may respond sarcastically with "big deal" or some similar remark. Ask her what she believes the effects of this continued behavior could be on her employment or relationships (for example, the impact on her next performance appraisal). This can force her to reflect on the consequences that are not in her best interest. Empathize with any aired frustration ("You say that you feel like a victim of the system. I can appreciate that").

Step 6. Emphasize that the problem must be solved and that it is up to her to solve it. Add that you are always there to

help. Reiterate the point that she should solve her own problem. You should avoid prescribing solutions:

- A quick solution on your part can make the other person feel inadequate.
- When your solution fails to work, you appear inadequate.
- The employee may feel obliged to take your advice, even when he or she knows a better solution is available.
- An employee who owns the solution tries harder to make it work.
- An employee can become dependent on you for all solutions.

If you cannot accept Joyce's first offering, keep asking for alternatives until she comes up with one you can live with. Discuss the pros and cons of each suggestion. Avoid directive phrases, such as "If I were you . . . " or "Here's what you should do." Compliment her for coming up with solutions. If the discussion stalls, ask some leading questions to guide her to more options. Do not impose your solution unless absolutely necessary. Offer to help, for example, "Joyce, it's up to you to take care of this. However, I will cooperate. When I notice [such-and-such happening], I'll remind you."

Step 7. Summarize what is agreed on. Repeat your expectations clearly, and insist on her commitment to the solution. Include a deadline for the problem to be solved. End on a positive note and with an affirmation. Thank her for cooperating, and express confidence in her ability to solve the problem. For example, "Joyce, I appreciate your cooperation. I knew I could depend on you to take care of this. This past performance is way below what I know you are capable of." If it is obvious that despite your best efforts you're not getting near a solution, do not make it a matter of wills. Simply state your position and what you expect, then end the meeting. It is sometimes a good idea to set a date for a follow-up meeting.

Step 8. Document the agreement and the intended follow-up. A common and serious deficiency is the lack of documentation. All too often counseling is not successful and must be repeated or ratcheted up to the level of disciplinary action. In either instance, you will be grateful for having the record. The record should include the following:

- The date of the discussion
- A description of the problem
- The employee's comments (exact words are best)
- The agreed-on resolution
- Any warning you delivered
- The deadline for resolution of the problem

Do not submit this documentation for inclusion in the employee's file in human resources. If you do so, it can appear to be a written reprimand. Simply put this documentation away in your own files, being sure to first supply the employee with a copy. You may have to become a disciplinarian at some later date, but at this stage you are a counselor, and what you have done to this point is informal.

Maintain confidentiality. Keep your personal files locked away, secure from prying eyes. Do not discuss the meeting with anyone other than your immediate superior as may be necessary.

Also, be careful about what you say in the documentation you keep in your personal file. Do not name-call (for example, label the person "a real slacker" or "a big mouth") or use other unfavorable subjective terminology. Chances are your personal files will always remain personal, but remain aware that any and all documentation about a specific employee—including what is in your personal files—may have to be produced in the event of a legal proceeding involving that employee. It is best to imagine how you would feel to see your comments go public and write accordingly.

Common Defensive Responses by Employees

Keep in mind that any behavior displayed or comments made by employees during counseling interviews represent behavior that they have probably found effective at some time in the past.

- They may say they do not want to discuss the matter at the present time.
- They may deny everything you say.
- They may refuse to listen or keep interrupting.
- They may talk louder and faster.
- They may shed tears.
- They may storm out of your office.
- They may clam up and say nothing.

In any of the foregoing circumstances, your immediate approach should be to insist on a dialogue. Respond to loud, angry outcries with something such as "You're starting to yell, Joyce." If Joyce runs out of your office, do not chase after her. Simply wait until later in the day, or the next day, and then send for her again. Start all over. If she cries, hand her a box of tissues and wait for the tears to stop. People who suddenly clam up may be trying to decide whether to say something of a sensitive nature. If you break the silence too soon, you may never know what that was. If the silence persists, say, "Joyce, I thought we were having a conversation." Lean forward and look like you expect a response. If you repeat this without success, sigh or frown and say you will try to establish a dialogue at another time. If a second meeting also ends in failure, you must move on to take disciplinary action.

An employee might try to minimize the problem. If a person retorts sarcastically on the order of, "Okay, I haven't been the employee of the month. I'll try to do better if that'll make you happy," do not accept this. Say you are glad the person recognized there is a problem. Emphasize that this is an important issue and that something definite must be done about it.

Another scenario is that employees may challenge you. Joyce may say, "The old boss never said anything about that." If this happens, respond with, "I'm not your old boss." She may say, "If this is so important, how is it that you never said anything about it before?" In this case, respond with "I thought that you would take care of it without my direction" or admit that you should have acted sooner. If she claims that work is not affected ("I get my work done, don't I?"), respond with "Yes, but this behavior interferes with the work of others and sets a bad example for the new employees."

Sometimes employees may counterattack. They may threaten to quit or go over your head. They may accuse you of the same behavior ("You have gall, accusing me of that. I've seen you doing the very same thing."). If there is a threat to quit, to go over your head, or to expose something damaging about you, reply that the employee may do so, but that you recommend first giving serious thought to the possible consequences of those actions. Going over your immediate superior's head is a hazardous move for any employee at just about any level.

Finally, employees may try to sidetrack the discussion. They may accuse others ("Helen does the same thing. How is it you never say anything to her?"). Or they may blame a myriad of personal problems at home. If employees try to sidetrack the discussion, tell them that nothing will be accomplished by accusing others. If they blame problems at home, channel the discussion back to the work situation. If signs and symptoms suggest a serious personal problem, however, recommend professional help. Usually, an appropriate comment is, "Joyce, I'm not qualified to help you with those kinds of problems. You can confidentially access the employee assistance program, or Employee Health can recommend a professional counselor if you like, but for now let's get back to the problem at hand."

Follow-Up

The counseling process does not end with the interview. Supervisors often dismiss the subject from their minds because they are so relieved that the immediate confrontation is over and that the employee has promised to solve the problem.

Appropriate follow-up consists of monitoring performance and reinforcing desired behavior. Positive strokes motivate; negative strokes or the absence of feedback demotivate. Support improvements with smiles and compliments. Do not wait until perfection has been achieved. Reinforce each small step with something such as "I know you're making a special effort, Joyce, and I appreciate that."

Identify and address specific concerns that call for exploration or reassurance. When the problem appears to have been solved, hold a commendatory meeting. At that meeting, describe the improvement you've noted and encourage the person to relate how he or she achieved it. At this time you can offer to help with any unanticipated roadblocks. Close the follow-up meeting with expressions of appreciation and an affirmation.

If the undesired behaviors or results persist, you are faced with several choices. You can extend the deadline if there has been some progress, you can begin disciplinary action, or you can counsel again. Most often you will choose to repeat the counseling session, but now you have the initial problem plus a new one—the employee failing to deliver on his or her commitment.

A repeat counseling session has the following objectives:

- Let the employee know you are aware of the continued problem.
- Inform the employee of the risk he or she is taking by repeating the behavior.
- Offer one more chance before you take disciplinary action.

To emphasize the importance of such a meeting to the wayward employee, ask your manager or a representative of the human resources department to sit in. At this session, manifest less patience, and skip the smiles and affirmations. On the other hand, avoid accusatory expressions (which are usually the ones that start with "You didn't try very hard" or "Why did you…?").

Probe for possible obstacles that the employee cannot control. Most important, insist that the employee come up with a new solution (or resolution), and state what the consequences of another failure will be. Make certain that you set a target date for resolution.

Seven Key Points to Cover in a Repeat Counseling Session

1. Review the agreements reached at the previous session.
2. State what you have observed or learned that shows that the agreement has not been met.
3. Ask for an explanation.
4. Insist on a new solution or a renewed effort.
5. State the consequences of continued noncompliance, but avoid threats that you do not intend to carry out.
6. Agree on the new action to be taken and a new follow-up date.
7. State your reluctance to give up on the employee and your belief that he or she can correct the situation.

Common Barriers to Successful Counseling

The excuse often given by supervisors for failure to counsel is that there were so many other more important things to do that they never got around to it. Often, the supervisor is intimidated by the person or fears legal repercussions. Perhaps the supervisor is not trained in interviewing techniques or is hazy about policies or procedures.

Sometimes the supervisor is dealing with someone who is influential because of seniority, union affiliation, special expertise, or powerful friends. Sometimes one fears loss of friendship, particularly when there had been a peer relationship before one's promotion to supervisor. At other times, a supervisor may feel sympathy for a troubled person and fears making matters worse for that person.

Principles of Successful Interventions

- Initially confront as a friend, not as an antagonist.
- Be direct and honest.
- Listen more than you talk.
- Say how you feel, and ask how the other person feels.
- Select the best time and place for intervention.
- Do not nitpick.
- Expect the other person to come up with solutions.
- Strive for win–win solutions.
- Be willing to compromise.
- Work with facts, not assumptions.
- Be optimistic; expect positive results.
- Preserve the person's self-esteem.
- Do not preach or be condescending.
- Do not expect the impossible.
- Look for the good in the person.
- Monitor and reinforce.
- Be specific and consistent.
- Avoid arousing defensiveness.

WRAP-UP

Think About It

For the busy supervisor there is always the temptation to allow the signs indicating possible needs for coaching or counseling to go unaddressed, perhaps in the hope they will correct themselves or simply go away. However, a consequence of the well-known Murphy's Law suggests that "Left unto themselves, things invariably go from bad to worse." The employee who displays a need for active coaching deserves all the help that can reasonably be provided in becoming an effective producer, and an obvious counseling need is a classic case of "Pay me now, or pay me later," and the cost in time, aggravation, and stress is always greater when paying later.

Questions for Review and Discussion

1. How would you define or describe the differences between coaching and the fundamental management activity of directing?
2. Describe one significant barrier to successful counseling. Why do you believe this barrier exists, and what can be done about it?
3. How can a supervisor encourage employees to take risks without allowing them to wander into trouble?
4. What is the contingency theory of reinforcement? Provide a detailed example.
5. Why should we bother to praise performance that is not outstanding in any way but just consistently acceptable?
6. How would you relate MBWA to a supervisor's need to remain visible and available? Explain.
7. Instead of bothering to dispense praise whenever an employee does something deserving of it, why not simply save up all such instances to convey in an outstanding performance evaluation?
8. Often, when you need to counsel an employee you will already have in mind a workable solution to the developing problem. Why not simply mandate the solution and be done with it?
9. Why should the supervisor retain documentation of an employee counseling session, and why should this documentation not become part of the employee's permanent record?
10. Why do you believe some supervisors fail to counsel employees or initiate disciplinary action even when the need to do so is clearly evident?

Case: A Group Problem?

Imagine that you are the supervisor of the transcription group of the health information services department at Community Hospital. Your crew consists of several transcriptionists who handle, in addition to all medical records transcription, all the dictation from the clinical laboratories and diagnostic imaging and the word processing for several department directors. On a monthly basis you convene a brief meeting of your staff to convey current information and address issues currently affecting the department. At your February meeting you believed you had to air a problem you had seen emerging in recent months: Quality was slipping, transcription errors were increasing, and complaints about the group's work were growing more frequent. You stressed that greater care had to be taken to reduce errors. At your March meeting you said, "Transcription quality has not improved since our last meeting; in fact, it has continued to decline. I expect all of you to become more aware of errors and to begin improving immediately." When the time arrived for your April meeting, it was your best determination that transcription quality had not improved in the slightest.

Questions

1. Should you continue to deal with the entire group? Why or why not?
2. What would you suggest doing in an effort to identify the real problems?
3. How might you approach the problem of making your criticism more effective?

Case: "She Sticks Like Glue"

"Darla is really a nice girl. I like her, honestly," said housekeeping team supervisor, Wendy Smith, "but she's driving me crazy."

"What's wrong?" asked Janis Fredericks, Wendy's friend from the nursing department.

Wendy answered, "Her work is all right, but I can't get her to think for herself. She comes to me with questions about every little thing, even all the stuff she ought to be able to take care of herself. She checks with me so often that I might as well be doing her work as well as my own."

Janis said, "Maybe you should be thankful she keeps you informed. I wish some of my gang were better about bringing problems to me. I don't know if there's ever such a thing as too much communication."

"There is too much as far as Darla's concerned. Most of what she brings me is simple stuff, stuff she ought to know. And it seems like she does know it, but she won't go ahead and do it unless I say so. She's always after me to tell her what to do next. And it seems like every time I turn around, she's there. She sticks to me like glue."

Janis said, "I know you've had the job only 5 or 6 months. Any idea how Darla got along with your predecessor?"

"No idea at all. But some of the folks have told me that their last supervisor was pretty strict and not the easiest person to get along with."

"What are you going to do?" Janis asked.

"At this point I don't know. How can I get her to work more independently without just shutting her out?"

Questions

1. Why might Darla behave the way she does? Offer two or three possible reasons for her behavior.
2. How would you recommend that supervisor Wendy Smith approach the problem presented by Darla?

Case: Never to Blame

You are the administrative director of clinical laboratories at Community Hospital. One of your section supervisors has come to you with a complaint about a young man named William, one of the laboratory's messengers. The supervisor says, "I'm nearing the end of my patience with William, and I need your advice. I can't pin him down on anything. No matter what happens or how nearly certain I am that he was involved, when it comes down to assigning responsibility he was never there, he knows nothing about it, he didn't do it, or the other employees are trying to make him look bad. No matter what the situation is, he's got an excuse, sometimes a really plausible one, and I can never get him to own up to anything. Even when one of the stops on his rounds gets missed he's got a long, involved story to account for it, a story I hear only if I learned about what happened and tried to find out more. To hear William tell it, he's never made a mistake in his life. But if I could believe him for even a minute, then I'd have to believe that the whole world around him fouls up day after day and tries to lay the blame at his doorstep. Tell me—what can I do about him?"

Questions

1. What advice would you offer your section supervisor for addressing the problem of the ever-blameless William?
2. As the section supervisor's immediate superior, should you become actively involved in dealing with William? Why or why not?

References

1. Zemke R. The corporate coach. *Training.* 1996;33(12):24–28.
2. Peters T, Austin N. *A Passion for Excellence.* Random House; 1985:9.
3. Blanchard K, Johnson S. *The One-Minute Manager.* Berkeley Publishers; 1982:44.

CHAPTER 15

Motivation, Reward, and Recognition

CHAPTER OBJECTIVES

- Differentiate between the related concepts of morale and motivation and examine the interrelationship of these two critical forces.
- Identify the significant factors that have a bearing on morale in a work unit.
- Suggest how the organization can enhance employee morale, and identify strategies for enhancing the motivational climate of the organization.
- Identify the essential nature of motivation and the ultimate source of all motivation.
- Review the principal theories of motivation that provide the foundation for today's approaches to employee motivation.
- Identify the principles on which an effective reward system should be based, and describe the essential elements of a workable incentive strategy.
- Provide workable guidelines for pursuing an appropriately functioning reward strategy.
- Explore the use of financial rewards in supporting employee motivation, and examine the use and potential value of nonfinancial rewards.
- Explore the power of recognition in meeting employees' higher order needs and thus enhancing motivation, morale, and productivity.

KEY TERMS

Morale: A state of mind based largely on how individuals perceive their work, their employer, their colleagues, and their supervisors; an indicator of the degree of job satisfaction experienced.
Motivation: A cognitive drive that involves pursuit of the fulfillment of certain perceived fundamental needs; the desire for security, the desire to work, the desire to achieve or excel.

Morale and Health Care

Within the healthcare industry, the decline in job satisfaction has accelerated. Among the apparent reasons for the decline are the changes shaped by the continually intensifying nursing shortage. The recent COVID-19 pandemic has caused a chronic shortage of critical help in nursing and certain allied health occupations.[1] The pandemic has forced the adoption of reduced staffing levels and altered patterns of practice for some healthcare workers, registered nurses in particular.[2] Also, newer technologies and services require a degree of autonomy for professionals that conflicts with traditional bureaucratic hierarchies and divisions between and among departments. Long-established boundaries between functional departments and work units are rapidly being erased as workflows stream across previously untouchable borders and knock down the barriers that formerly protected various territories from intrusion. The result is stress and morale challenges for employees and supervisors alike.

Morale Versus Motivation

Morale is a state of mind based largely on the perceptions of workers toward their work, their employer, their colleagues, and their supervisors. Morale must be differentiated from motivation; morale relates to overall job satisfaction. If this is high, people are less likely to quit, complain, or become problem employees. Morale factors are represented in part by those conditions that labor unions fight for—pay, benefits, job security, and work environment; in brief, overall quality of work life.

Morale factors represent the lower three levels of Maslow's hierarchy of needs: survival needs (food, clothing, shelter), safety needs (insurance, job security, pension), and social needs (acceptance by fellow workers).[2]

Motivation, on the other hand, is a cognitive drive that occurs when Maslow's two higher order needs are involved: ego or self-esteem needs (that is, psychological needs) and self-actualization (achieving one's full potential). Unfortunately, high morale does not necessarily go hand-in-hand with strong motivation. Employees may be fully content with the circumstances of employment and yet lack the motivation needed to maximize performance. On the other hand, however, motivation dissipates when morale is low.

The work of A.H. Maslow, along with that of other significant contributors to motivational theory, will be briefly described in the section addressing motivation.

Major Factors Affecting Morale

Employee Factors

- Basic personality type can strongly influence morale. For example, the natural optimist is surely more likely to enjoy higher morale than the natural pessimist.
- Family situations and other outside factors can influence morale. It is extremely difficult for some people to keep external problems from affecting their work situations.
- The ability to adjust to the job and blend in with fellow workers often has an effect. The individual who can readily fit in is more likely to exhibit higher morale.
- Ease and safety in getting to work, finding a parking space, and getting to the job can influence morale. If the morning commute means a daily traffic jam, parking is scarce and difficult and perceived as unsafe, and long walks are involved, morale can be adversely affected.
- A mismatch of employee and job is a common morale depressor. This can consist of either being in over one's head and feeling overwhelmed or stuck in a job well below one's capability without challenge or interest. Or it can simply be the wrong person for the job.

Nature of the Job and Job Atmosphere

- Work that is stimulating and fulfilling or unrewarding and monotonous can boost morale higher or drag it down.
- Greater prestige associated with the job relates to higher morale, and the opposite is generally true regarding lack of prestige and lower morale.
- For some employees the opportunity for promotion or growth is a strong determinant of morale. Lacking such opportunity, some employees see themselves as limited, with nowhere to go.
- Job security is one of the strongest determinants of morale. One who is worried about prospects

for continued employment will not be among the happiest or most contented workers.

- The financial status of the organization, economic conditions, and threats of competitors all have their influence on morale in that they are forces beyond the employee's control that undermine feelings of job security.
- The amount of stress experienced on the job and in the organizational setting can, understandably, increase stress and relate directly to reduced morale for some employees.
- The quality, ease, and effectiveness of communication can influence morale. The better information flows up and down the chain of command, the better employee morale in general is likely to be.

Attitude and Behavior of Employer and Management

- How rewards are apportioned can have significant effects on morale. It is extremely demoralizing, for example, to hear of executives receiving generous raises or bonuses while employees are laid off, bypassed for raises, or asked to take salary cuts.
- The frequency with which promotions from within occur has morale effects. More than a few organizations have advocated a policy of development from within, but employees see most of the better opportunities filled from outside.
- The manner in which management adjusts to financial crunches and reacts to fiscal pressure affects employee morale. For example, it is demoralizing for employees to see that the first response to a financial problem is to lay off nonmanagerial employees.

Quality of Supervision

As mentioned elsewhere in this text, it should go without saying that the quality of supervision—how well and how effectively employees are led and the extent to which they are treated fairly and with respect—is a strong determinant of morale. It is not unreasonable to maintain that in many

instances the quality of supervision is the primary driver of employee morale.

Signs of a Morale Problem

Diminishing productivity frequently indicates worsening morale. When morale is low, many employees perform at the minimum level required to simply keep their jobs. When morale is low, employees complain about parking, safety, pay and benefits, the organization and its managers, and their assignments. As they become increasingly apathetic or rebellious, they are increasingly likely to voice their complaints in the presence of patients and other customers.

When morale is low, employees become more resistant to change than usual, they rarely volunteer, and they seldom pitch in to help without being required to do so. Absenteeism, tardiness, grievances, and turnover are all likely to increase significantly. Employees do not participate at meetings except to voice complaints. They avoid making suggestions or approving the ideas of others. They fall silent or walk away when managers approach. Cynicism, sarcasm, and belittling conversation flourish.

When morale is poor, conversations and energy are directed away from productive work. Supervisors hear comments like, "Thank God it's Friday," "Don't ask me, I only work here," "We need a union," or "There's no point in knocking yourself out."

Sagging morale prompts some workers to talk about retiring, changing employers, or leaving their chosen fields. They talk of how their friends and relations have better employers. As poor morale persists, the more qualified employees are likely to resign to seek better work environments while the less capable remain.

Morale improvement begins with the identification of specific morale problems. Severe morale problems are easy to spot; milder forms are more subtle and are harder to detect. Discovery of discontent at an early stage is as important as the early detection of cancer. As with cancer, the longer poor morale is allowed to continue unabated, the more difficult it is to reverse.

Methods of Obtaining Information About Morale

An organization's management can gather information about the state of employee morale by several means. Whenever a morale slippage is suspected, an alert management system will often circulate an attitude survey and share the findings with all managers. In some organizations, employee attitude surveys are undertaken periodically whether or not morale problems are evident or suspected.

Exit interviews, ordinarily conducted by human resources professionals, are also helpful. All departing employees do not need to be interviewed, but any sample used should be large enough to yield credible results.

Employee focus groups are best conducted anonymously by external facilitators to whom employees' names remain unknown. Quotes are not attributed to specific individuals. Such focus groups can be especially effective for evaluating morale during or immediately after a major organizational change.

Telephone hotlines and suggestion boxes can be effective if follow-up on complaints and suggestions is timely and visible. However, if employees do not see follow-up occurring, these processes can themselves become depressors of morale.

Finally, ombudsman programs, in which ombudsmen mediate employee concerns and report them to management, can prevent problems from getting larger or happening again. Ombudsmen can effectively advocate for employees while enhancing management credibility.

How Employers Improve Morale

Employers can sustain or improve employee morale as follows:

- Ensure timely and visible reaction to employee attitude surveys. Morale is enhanced when employees know their concerns are heard and addressed.

- Establish and maintain a problem-solving culture. Once ingrained, such a culture leads employees to believe—with justification—that emerging problems will be addressed.

- Control rumors. No organization will ever rid itself entirely of the grapevine or rumor mill, but management can go a long way in a positive direction by correcting false information that reaches employees by these informal means.

- Share financial information with employees. Being kept in the dark concerning the organization's financial condition is demoralizing for many employees.

- Insist on fair and equitable treatment of all employees. Inequitable and inconsistent treatment of employee's feeds discontent and often results in pockets of poor morale throughout the organization.

- Vigorously control harassment and discrimination, continuing to ensure that all employees are regarded with respect and that no one is singled out for unequal treatment.

- Spend more time where the work is taking place. As noted at numerous points throughout this text, a manager's visibility and availability mean much to most the employees.

- Ensure that job candidates are carefully screened. This helps new employees fit into the organization and keeps turnover to a minimum.

- Provide timely and thorough supervisory training. This applies not only to a new supervisor's training in basic supervisory skills, but also to the continuing education needed to keep each supervisor current and effective.

Compensation and Benefits Systems

Employers generally know what salaries and benefits their competitors offer, and they respond appropriately by regularly reviewing and adjusting their reward and recognition systems. Often, they introduce more flexibility into rules and regulations, modifying practices to reward teams as well as individual efforts and outcomes. Some employers offer alternative promotional ladders or parallel path progression systems to allow professionals to remain in their specialties while continuing to advance financially and professionally.

Today, more organizations promote and encourage the well-being of their employees, although their purposes are not entirely altruistic. In addition to providing a valuable service, they reduce costs by prescribing special programs that increase wellness and prevent illness. Health promotion initiatives include health education, risk assessment and screening, and special programs such as infertility care; all such employee benefits tend to function as morale boosters. Incentives offered include changes focusing on the family and lifestyles, for example, casual dress, flextime, and earlier quitting times on Fridays during summer months.

How Supervisors Influence Morale

Alert supervisors who enjoy good rapport with their employees become aware of morale problems long before these are recognized by upper management. They respond in a number of ways. Better still, they prevent the slippage in the first place by taking some of the following actions:

- Always treating people as winners or potential winners
- Rewarding and recognizing appropriately
- Ensuring social acceptance of all employees
- Instilling pride through improved orientation of new employees
- Making certain their employees know the why and how of their tasks
- Maintaining a mindset of optimism and success
- Assigning discouraged workers to teams of go-getters and upbeat individuals
- Getting rid of troublemakers and morale destroyers
- Introducing more flexible work schedules
- Keeping all staff fully informed at all times
- Becoming a change agent, proactive rather than reactive

- Involving employees in decision-making and planning
- Helping employees obtain deserved pay increases

Motivation

A Foundation in Theory

Much of today's approach to motivation in work organizations has its basis in the works of three individuals: A.H. Maslow, Frederick Herzberg, and Douglas M. McGregor. The original publication of their respective theories gives us most of what we need to know about motivation:

- A.H. Maslow, "A Theory of Human Motivation," first appearing in *Psychological Review*, Vol. 50, 1943.
- Frederick Herzberg, *The Motivation to Work*, published by Wiley in 1959.
- Douglas M. McGregor, "The Human Side of Enterprise," first appearing in *Management Review*, Vol. 46, No. 11, November 1957.

Maslow

Maslow's well-known hierarchy identifies a progression of human needs starting with the absolute basics:

- Physiological needs—the most fundamental needs; food, water, etc.; support for life
- Safety needs—shelter, protection, security, etc.
- Love needs—also referred to as sociological needs; the need to belong, the need for acceptance and inclusion
- Esteem needs—self-respect, self-esteem, the esteem of others
- Need for self-actualization—self-fulfillment; becoming what one is capable of becoming

The theory states that once one has satisfied needs at a particular level, the individual's focus then turns to seeking satisfaction of needs at the next highest level. Since many people in this country have satisfied physiological, safety, and love needs, their desires for need satisfaction have turned toward the higher-level needs. It is the quest for satisfaction of increasingly higher order needs that drive—that is, that motivates—most people.

Herzberg

The motivation–hygiene theory of Frederick Herzberg brings consideration of motivation into the workplace. Herzberg looked at factors comprising and surrounding the job and concluded that the true motivators are inherent in the work itself and that factors making up the environment are not motivators but rather are potential dissatisfiers. This suggests that managers must focus on jobs and their content as central to motivation and then look at such factors as salaries, benefits, and working conditions, which must be reinforced periodically to stave off dissatisfaction. Therefore, the factors bearing on a person's relationship with the work fall into two groups: motivating factors and environmental factors. The motivating factors can and do truly motivate a person to perform. The environmental factors, although not motivators, can influence employee satisfaction.

In this approach, the true motivators are inherent in the work and the key word describing these factors is *opportunity*. The sources of motivation are the opportunity to do the following:

- Achieve
- Acquire new knowledge
- Perform interesting and challenging work
- Do meaningful work
- Assume responsibility
- Become involved in determining how the work is done

The environmental factors exist in all aspects of the employee's relationship to the organization. Even if these are all acceptable, they do not necessarily motivate. However, if they are not acceptable, they can lead to dissatisfaction. The environmental factors fall under five general headings:

1. Communication in all of its forms, including performance feedback, knowledge of where the organization is heading, and employee confidentiality
2. Growth and advancement potential
3. Employment policies; how an employee is treated
4. Salary administration; the perceived fairness of salary and benefits
5. Working conditions

Although the environmental factors may receive regular attention, they will not by themselves move employees to greater performance. If not maintained, however, they can cause dissatisfaction that interferes with performance.

McGregor

Douglas McGregor wrote of two opposing approaches to management, which he referred to as Theory X and Theory Y. Theory X in its pure state requires autocratic leadership; pure Theory Y calls for participative leadership. Management always remains responsible for organizing the elements of all productive activity, bringing together the money, people, equipment, and supplies needed to accomplish the organization's goals. But beyond this basic assumption, the two theories proceed in opposite directions.

Theory X assumes the following:

- People must be persuaded, controlled, rewarded, or punished as necessary to accomplish the aims of the organization.
- The average person is by nature indolent, working as little as possible, lacking ambition, avoiding responsibility, and preferring to be led.
- The average person is inherently self-centered, resistant to change, and indifferent to the needs of the organization.

In contrast, the following is assumed under Theory Y:

- People are not naturally passive or resistant to organizational needs. If they seem that way, it is the result of experience in organizations.
- Motivation, development potential, willingness to assume responsibility, and readiness to work toward organizational goals are present in most people. It is up to management to make it possible for people to recognize and develop these characteristics.

- The essential task of management is to arrange conditions and methods so people can achieve their own goals by directing their efforts toward the goals of the organization.

There has been much written about employee motivation. A few who have written works concerned with management theory have even identified motivating as one of several basic management functions. However, the overwhelming proportion of published work about employee motivation either cites or is directly built upon the work of Maslow, Herzberg, and McGregor.

All True Motivation

Ultimately all true motivation is self-motivation. Managers cannot motivate employees. Rather, the most they can do is arrange the job and the work environment in ways that improve self-motivation. In other words, managers can create the climate in which employees become more likely to motivate themselves.

Efforts aimed at enhancing motivation are either proactive or reactive. Proactive or anticipative measures precede performance; reactive activities follow performance and serve to reinforce desired behavior or outcomes.

The acronym RAGWAR can help you remember Herzberg's famous list of motivating factors[3]:

R Recognition
A Achievement
G Growth (career)
W Work itself
A Advancement
R Responsibility

It has already been noted that although high morale does not motivate, true motivation cannot be achieved until morale deficiencies (what Herzberg referred to as dissatisfiers or hygiene factors) have been eliminated.[3]

Motivational Strategies for the Supervisor

That which motivates you may not necessarily motivate your employees. Supervisors and employees alike may be subject to the same set of needs, but the mix of needs and their relative strength varies from person to person. Try to view the work situation from the employees' perspective and think as they might think.

- Define expectations, set goals, delegate, train, coach, counsel, and provide performance feedback.
- Provide for the maintenance and growth of professional skills to avoid employee obsolescence.
- Relax tight supervisory controls, demonstrate trust in employees, and delegate decision-making authority.
- Alter job titles and rewrite position descriptions to make jobs more important or to appear so. This practice can of course be carried too far, but it is highly applicable to entry-level positions. For example, most workers would understandably prefer to be called "building service worker" rather than "janitor."
- Recruit and select motivated people, or at least attempt to do so. Never approach recruiting with an attitude, suggesting that "if this one doesn't work out, I can always hire another."
- Improve the job itself to the maximum possible extent. The strongest, most lasting motivation comes from the job itself or, more accurately, from one's perception of the job and its importance.
- Learn as much as you can about your people and their different personalities.
- Do not rely only on salary administration and other mechanisms for rewards and recognition; involve yourself in providing positive feedback on a continuing basis.
- Take your employees into your confidence, seek their advice, and share information. Be fair and consistent.
- Provide support for your employees. Be available to help when they need help, but do not stand in their way.
- Be a respected role model.
- Increase opportunities for education and training (see **Exhibit 15.1**).

Exhibit 15.1 How Many of These Questions About Your Educational Program Can You Answer?

1. Do you have a formal in-house education program?
2. Is this program available to each and every member of your staff?
3. Do you provide sufficient uninterrupted time for your employees to attend the in-house programs?
4. Does each employee have individualized career goals and plans? Are these discussed at annual performance review meetings?
5. Is there financial support for outside education courses? Do you modify work schedules or numbers of work hours to accommodate employees who enroll in these programs?
6. Do employees have the opportunity to cross-train or to learn new skills on the job?
7. Does each of your employees learn at least one new skill each year?
8. Are there real incentives for learning new skills?
9. When your employees attend seminars, webinars, or workshops, do you discuss the practical value to the department and to the employee before the meeting?
10. When your employees return from seminars, webinars, and workshops, do you discuss what they learned and help them put that new knowledge and skill to use?
11. When you attend professional or technical meetings, do you share what you learned with others? Do you encourage your staff to do likewise?
12. Do you include educational topics in your routine staff meetings?
13. Do all of your educational efforts focus on improved customer service?

The meaningfulness of work is based on how much it affects the worker, other people, and the organization. Jobs that require multiple skills and a variety of activities or skills are usually more satisfying. Most employees also prefer assignments that allow them to complete an entire piece of work rather than just a limited part. Interesting work and the opportunity to develop skills and abilities, to be creative, and to be challenged are powerful motivators.

A high degree of control over one's work encourages a healthy mindset. Lack of individual autonomy leads to frustration and stress, but having control translates into discretionary freedom for scheduling, prioritizing, and selecting methods.

To move up a motivational notch, switch from a directive leadership style to a participative style. To help with this, Leeds[4] recommends asking your employees these questions:

- What do you like about what you do?
- How can I help you use more of your skills?
- What do you believe you (or we) should do differently?
- How can we carry out your ideas?
- What help do you need from me or from others?

Get employees involved in decisions about their assignments. Consider differences in their motivational needs. Some people have a strong need for control or leadership, others for task achievement, and still others for socializing.

Delegate and empower. Giving ambitious people more responsibility plus the authority they need to discharge that responsibility is empowering, and it is a strong motivator. Most people like to be in charge of something, even when that something is a minor activity.

Motivating the Steady, Loyal Worker

Managers spend much time devising gimmicks for rewarding their star performers or coping with their problem people. Meanwhile, they neglect those loyal supporters who come to work every day, do not make waves, and who live up to all the specifications of their position descriptions. Most employees fall into this latter category.

Besides providing the motivators already described, meet periodically with each of these pleasing employees to tell them how much they are appreciated and that their hard work is not being overlooked. A motivated healthcare worker fulfills the organizations mission and vision.[5] Before each meeting review the employee's records and update your personal observations. Look for noteworthy behavior, such as excellent attendance or frequent volunteering to substitute for absent coworkers. Use the opportunity to ask for suggestions for improving your service or the teamwork. Ask whether there is anything you can do to make his or her job more pleasant. Most employees are more relaxed and willing to talk frankly at these informal sessions than they are at formal performance appraisal interviews.

Practical Tips for Increasing the Motivational Value of the Work Itself

- Provide a diversity of experience by giving new assignments, cross-training, or rotating workstations.
- Let people swap assignments according to their likes and dislikes.
- Assign monotonous tasks or those requiring less expertise to less-qualified employees. Doing so makes two people happy.
- Allow a little time for practical research, special projects, or service on committees, quality circles, or problem-solving groups.
- Permit a few fun tasks.
- Stimulate creativity by talking about new services, products, equipment, or procedures or by sharing publications and handouts from seminars and assigning problems for solution.
- Provide holistic tasks where employees can see the results of their efforts.

Reward and Recognition

A great many employers tend to believe they have effective reward and recognition systems in place. However, large numbers of employees disagree. One in five employees say their manager/organization is "horrible' at recognizing them.[6] The healthcare industry is ranked at the very bottom for engagement, mainly since the Covid-19 pandemic has affected the morale and motivation of many healthcare workers.

To make matters worse, in times of financial hardship many healthcare organizations cut costs by scaling down their reward and recognition systems. To compensate for losses due to fiscal belt-tightening, it is imperative for all supervisors to fine-tune their recognition and reward skills and never assume that the paycheck is all that is needed to keep each employee satisfied and productive.

An Effective Reward System
Underlying Principles

An effective reward system must be designed so that rewards are apportioned principally on the basis of performance outcomes; that is, quality of work, control of costs, customer satisfaction, or other positive contributions to the continued success of the organization. Rewards should also be based on special behavior, such as acquisition of new skills or knowledge, willingness and the ability to adjust to changes, successful cross-training, and demonstrated teamwork. Rewards must also be available for team performance as well for individual performance. And frequently of greatest importance: Rewards are often sufficient for retaining staff.

Designing an Incentive Strategy

An effective incentive strategy must provide employees with clear knowledge of what is expected of them. That is, employees must know precisely what they must do, and they must know and understand how their performance will be assessed. Incentive strategy design requires (1) ascertaining the needs and wants of customers, (2) setting performance standards or delineating expected results, and (3) measuring performance against these standards or results.

Behavior or Results to Be Rewarded

Employees often deserve to be rewarded when they delight customers. This means not simply leaving customers satisfied to have received what they expected, but rather leaving them surprised and pleased—delighted—at having in some way received more than they expected.

Reward-worthy behavior frequently involves reporting problems and customer feedback and offering suggestions for correcting problems and improving customer service. This includes actions that may go beyond what the employees would normally be expected to do.

Displays of creativity and assertiveness may also be deserving of reward. Standout employees are often those who are willing to stick their necks out, make difficult decisions, express unpopular opinions, and take actions that may risk their status.

Reward-worthy behavior is often demonstrated by employees who are regularly willing to go above and beyond the call of duty:

- Working additional hours when needed
- Willingly substituting for others
- Returning to work after hours or remaining available for advice by telephone
- Submitting results ahead of schedule
- Volunteering for unpleasant or unpopular assignments
- Rendering performance, you can always rely on; for example, backing you up when you need support, and always remaining ready to help

Reward System Guidelines

It has been suggested that the supervisor who wishes to maintain an effective and consistent reward system within a department or group do the following:

- Support and justify deserved pay raises for both the team and its star performers.
- When selecting a reward for an individual, consider that person's distinctive wants and needs. Ask people what rewards they value.

- Be consistent and fair in what is rewarded and how it is done.
- For marginal performers express appreciation for small improvements, even though outcomes are not yet up to expectations.
- Reward wanted behavior and outcomes. When people struggle against odds with less than desired results, they still deserve some credit for their efforts.
- Reward the entire team for a team success, and single out individuals who made special efforts that were recognized by the rest of the team.
- Reward what supports the values of the organization. Most organizational value statements include terms such as customer satisfaction, innovation, teamwork, career development, and cost control.[7]

Compensation: Rewards Bearing Price Tags

Wages and Salaries

Compensation that is perceived as inadequate is a dissatisfier, but generous compensation is neither a strong nor a long-lasting motivator. Although it may be true that the motivational effect of a salary increase is transient and that people are motivated more by their work than by the rewards they earn, the importance of compensation should not be undervalued. Managers can keep telling their employees what great performers they are, but if management fails to support these statements with fatter paychecks, those employees will soon realize they are being manipulated. In a very real sense, a fatter paycheck can be a scorecard indicating winning performance.

In most instances, base pay still reflects the economics of the marketplace, but there have been major changes in corporate compensation strategies in recent years. The old practice of trying to create internal job equity is becoming outdated except in strongly unionized organizations.

Compensation systems that provide merit increases have also lost much of their luster, largely because of their negative impact on those who are not selected for raises and thus feel cheated. Strident charges of favoritism and unfairness are commonplace. Even those who receive the larger slices of the pie are often left feeling uncomfortable and alienated. A more acceptable option is to reward higher performing groups as well as individuals. Whatever system is used, however, merit pay must be based on objective data that employ agreed-on and observable criteria that all concerned employees know and understand.

For a number of years compensation in some organizations was based almost entirely on meeting predetermined objectives, this approach being more or less the product of the management-by-objectives paradigm. This has given way to a different kind of outcome-based compensation system in which customer satisfaction is a principal determining factor. By incorporating customer satisfaction measures into their reward systems, employers increase their chances of pleasing their customers. Employees who fail in this effort not only miss out on the rewards, but they also put their jobs in jeopardy.

Whatever compensation system is in effect, however, the individual supervisor plays a pivotal role in explaining and implementing the system for employees.

Employee Benefits

The cost of benefits continues to increase steadily, in some instances dramatically, whereas their importance to employees continues to expand. Newer features once unheard of, such as enhanced maternity plans, adoption leaves of absence, infertility treatments, and day care for children and elders, keep appearing. Benefits have become problematic for many employers, with employee benefits packages becoming so costly the cost is shared. Employers make employees share some of the expenses. Employees are required to pay a share of the cost for the benefits they receive. Other cost-cutting strategies at large organizations have reduced the numbers of their full-time employees and increased their part-time staff because part-time employees receive fewer benefits. Another currently popular strategy is outsourcing certain operations or departments. This eliminates not only the benefits, but also the jobs.

Many organizations have been creative in tying their benefits to the specific physical, psychological, and spiritual needs of their employees. Examples include flextime and other nontraditional scheduling practices, recreational and health club facilities, wellness programs, telecommuting, and even weekly free massages. "Cafeteria plans," in which employees choose from a variety of options, are very popular.

A comprehensive program of employee benefits improves morale, reduces absenteeism and turnover, and increases productivity and customer satisfaction. Caring employers are always open to suggestions for new benefits, especially those that do not carry large price tags.

Being in a position of knowing their individual employees and at least some of their needs and wants, supervisors are in a position to propose new ways of rewarding their employees. Also, they can often pick up useful ideas at their professional meetings and from mentors and personal networks.

Other Financial Rewards

Beyond wages, salaries, and benefits, other forms of monetary reward are available:

- Promotions or alternative types of advancement, such as career ladder programs and parallel path progression systems that increase salary
- Bonuses and other cash awards
- Increased compensation for superior customer service, special competencies, and participation in special activities such as process reengineering, teaching, mentoring, or handling difficult tasks
- Financial support for education, training, or personal professional library materials
- Tickets to entertainment events
- Awards such as pins, jewelry, and mugs. (Although bonuses and salary increases possess an element of recognition, they do not have the same symbolic significance as permanent reminders of accomplishments.)

- Personal office or expanded work spaces, services of assistants, and support for educational or professional advancement
- Professional or technical publications
- Memberships in professional societies
- Funds for research or investigational projects
- Reimbursement for attendance at professional meetings, workshops, webinars, or seminars

Nonfinancial Rewards

Many rewards can have significant motivational effects at no or only nominal cost:

- Enabling employees to attend in-house educational offerings. There is the hidden cost of employee time, but there is no added out-of-pocket cost, and employee time consumed can be minimized with careful scheduling.
- Providing activities that individuals perceive as benefiting their careers or providing pleasure.
- Asking the better performing employees about serving on committees, focus groups, task forces, or cross-functional teams.
- Asking for employees' opinions and giving them credit for any advice you use.
- Rotating workstations where possible, varying the work assignments.
- Creating training opportunities for those employees who value them.
- Providing career counseling.
- Assigning the better performers to represent you at upper-level or professional meetings when possible.
- Granting additional time off for special events.
- Offering meaningful assignments, diversity of experience, or choice of responsibilities.
- Providing opportunities for employee innovation.
- Providing increased opportunities for challenging work or for the development of new skills.
- Assigning significant projects or complex tasks from beginning to end rather than in bits and pieces.

- Bringing in a treat for the group or having lunch with your group.
- Increasing the amount of information available, giving employees not just what they need to get their work done but also things about which they would like to learn.
- Asking the more advanced employees to consider serving as mentors or trainers for new employees.
- If possible, assigning certain employees more or less responsibility and authority according to their individual wishes.
- Providing more prestigious job titles, if allowed. For example, the title of dietary aide may be preferred over that of kitchen staff.
- Encouraging each employee to become a specialist in some aspect of your department's activities.
- Helping employees develop goals, objectives, and plans.
- Providing assignments that promote and enhance career development.

Implementing a Reward System

Establish the goals of your reward system. After reviewing the statements of your organization regarding vision, mission, values, and goals, decide what kind of performance output and behavior support these statements. Consider criteria such as customer satisfaction, work quality and quantity, problem-solving, achieving objectives, improving work procedures, attendance, and new skills. Benchmark by noting the systems and techniques used by other leaders who have reputations for high morale and productivity.

Determine what the team and the individual team members regard as rewards. What makes them smile or frown? What kinds of activities do they seem to like doing? What do they talk about during their free time? To avoid making poor choices, try asking people how they feel about a reward before you give it. Give them options. Avoid anything that might embarrass them. Ask their colleagues, friends, or family members for suggestions. Reward everyone who meets the established criteria. Be certain at all times to reward the right outcomes and behavior, not unwanted results.

Recognition

Recognition is our least expensive and most powerful motivational tool. To be effective it must be earned, specific, sincere, and offered as soon as possible after what the person did or said to earn it.

The principal weakness of customary institutional award ceremonies is that they are too impersonal and are delivered long after the commendatory service. Also, they usually focus on matters such as attendance or length of employment rather than on productivity or customer service. Some rituals make employees feel so demeaned or simply so bored that they do not show up at the ceremony.

The philosophical core of recognition is developing self-esteem in the individual. Employees who receive the recognition they deserve have greater self-esteem, more confidence, more willingness to take on new challenges, and more eagerness to contribute new ideas and improve productivity. We all need day-to-day recognition if we are to perform at consistently high levels. Recognition can be as simple as a smile and a sincere "good morning." When provided grudgingly or inexpertly, it is ineffective. Some people find it difficult to deliver praise, whereas others are uncomfortable receiving it. Do not, however, confuse praise with flattery.

Recognition Must Be Valued

Recognition is powerful, but the same type of recognition does not work for everyone. Different people require different approaches. If employees regard an award as having little value, or if they have little respect for its donor, that award will have little effect on the self-esteem or morale of that employee. Salary increases represent a powerful form of recognition, even if their motivational value may be brief.

Features of Effective Recognition

For recognition to be effective, it must exhibit a number of particular characteristics:

- It must be earned. If not earned, it is readily recognized as flattery or manipulation.
- It is consistent. Inconsistent recognition confuses recipients, and unequal recognition smacks of favoritism.
- It is timely. The high value of day-to-day recognition lies in its immediacy.
- It is frequent. It takes many positive strokes to neutralize the effects of one instance of criticism.
- It is ubiquitous. Most employees can be recognized for something they do well. It may also be something they do not do (for example, avoiding controversy or calmly tolerating the idiosyncrasies of fellow workers). In the case of marginal workers, little steps in the right direction can lead to still more improvement when they receive some positive feedback.
- It is valued by the recipients.
- It is sincere and specific. Telling someone that he or she is doing a good job is not specific. Telling someone that you appreciate how an irate physician was handled a short time before is both specific and timely.
- It does not embarrass. Do not praise in public when it might fluster the recipient.

To enhance the impact of praise, consider the following tactics:

- Praise in public (if not embarrassing to the recipient), and ask one of your superiors to be present.
- Address the person by name, maintain eye contact, and smile.
- State how the action or statement benefited you, the team, the department, or the organization.
- Follow up with a memo. Send a copy to human resources for the employee's file and send one to your superiors.
- Submit the honor to the institution's newsletter and to the public relations or marketing department.

Other recognition modalities include the following:

- Write a thank-you note and post it at the person's workstation.
- Brag about it to colleagues; this is sure to get back to the person.
- Display honors and pictures on bulletin boards. Place trophies and plaques at the recipient's workstation.
- Attend meetings of committees and other special work groups to thank the members.
- Select an employee of the month (the organization might be doing this overall, but there's added value in doing it within a department).

Five Cautions About Recognition

1. Avoid saying what behavior or outcomes are wanted while rewarding something else. For example, your values statement may proclaim quality, but recognition goes to people who cut corners for the sake of productivity.
2. Avoid sending mixed messages, those containing elements of both praise and criticism. The recipients are likely to become confused or angry.
3. Do not deliver praise that is not merited or is grossly exaggerated. This is not recognition; it is flattery or manipulation. When praising a problem employee, praise only what he or she has done well.
4. Do not overlook anyone. Many employees believe the only time anyone notices their work is when they do something wrong. Too often recognition is reserved for an elite few.
5. If you have an employee-of-the month program, skip those months during which no person honestly earned the recognition. But do not restrict the award to just one person per month.

WRAP-UP

Think About It

The supervisor cannot motivate employees directly; no one can truly motivate another person. Because all true motivation is self-motivation and the real motivating forces are found in the work itself, the best the supervisor can ever do is establish the correct conditions under which each employee can become self-motivated.

Questions for Review and Discussion

1. How have organizational mergers and other affiliations affected employee morale, and why do you believe they have had these effects?
2. If an employee is continually doing an acceptable job, not excelling but chugging along and producing reasonable results, why should any form of reward or recognition be considered necessary?
3. How can a system for collecting and evaluating employee suggestions become a morale depressor rather than a morale booster?
4. Why is monetary compensation not necessarily a motivator of improved performance?
5. It has been said that the time to think of conducting an employee attitude survey is not when there are obvious morale problems. Why is this so?
6. Why is it considered necessary for recognition to be delivered as soon after the deserving behavior as possible?

7. Under what circumstances could morale be high while the motivation to perform is weak or lacking?

8. It has been proven that many employees consider the opportunity for promotion and growth to be important in their organizational environment, and yet only a relative few employees take advantage of this opportunity. Why might this be so?

9. Describe the fundamental employee needs that reward and recognition processes primarily fulfill.

10. Explain your understanding of a rewards and recognition program at a healthcare organization. If you do not have an example, what would you ensure is part of the program?

Case: "When I Need Them, They're Nowhere to Be Found!"

Melissa Jones is nurse manager of a 40-bed, long-term care unit that is essentially a small nursing home contained within Community Hospital. The unit is almost always fully occupied. A number of the patients spend several hours each day in wheelchairs, but most return to their beds for a couple of hours in the afternoon.

Melissa has a constant concern that her limited staff is only marginally able to fill the needs of the elderly patients, especially given that some patients who go without visitors for prolonged periods are eager to engage staff members in conversation. Melissa has determined that a number of apparent patient needs, especially the need for socialization, could be met with volunteers, so she developed a volunteer roster consisting of persons who indicated their willingness to help, after which she developed a 30-day schedule for volunteer support.

On the initial day of the schedule, three of five scheduled volunteers failed to show up. On the following day, two did not appear. Only one appeared on each of the third and fourth days, and on the fifth day—a Friday with gorgeous summer weather beckoning all to the outdoors—no volunteers were present in the unit. Melissa gave up on her schedule.

Melissa was thoroughly discouraged by the volunteers' lack of dependability. And because she had made no secret of her new volunteer program, a number of patients were similarly discouraged, and several complained that Melissa had not delivered as promised. As Melissa complained to her friend, Carol, "I had a couple dozen supposedly willing volunteers on my list, but when I need them they're nowhere to be found!"

Questions

1. Because volunteers, as unpaid help that essentially supplement the regular staff, may often feel no compelling need to function by the clock, what might Melissa consider doing to encourage a more reliable volunteer presence?

2. How might Melissa have her regular staff assist in encouraging a continuing volunteer presence?

Case: Surprise!

When the business office employees arrived at the hospital Monday morning, they immediately noticed the apparent absence of the office manager. This was not unusual; the manager was frequently absent on Monday. However, he rarely failed to call the department when he would not be there, and on this day, he still had not called by noon.

Shortly after lunch, the two working supervisors in the business office were summoned to the administrator's office. They were told that the office manager was no longer employed by the hospital. They, the two supervisors, were told to look after things for the current week and that a new manager, already secured, would be starting the following Monday. All that the two supervisors were told about the new manager was that it was someone from outside the hospital. The supervisors were not told whether the former manager resigned or was discharged, nor were they told whether anyone within the department had been considered as a replacement.

Questions

1. What do you suppose would be the reactions and attitudes of the business office staff upon hearing about this change?
2. What circumstances will most likely prevail during this interim week without a manager? Include in your comments and consideration of both morale and productivity.
3. With what attitudes do you suppose the business office staff will receive the new manager?

References

1. Shaffer FA, Bakhshi M, Cook K, Àlvarez TD. International Nurse Recruitment beyond the COVID-19 Pandemic. *Nurse Lead.* 2022;20(2):161–167. https://doi.org/10.1016/j.mnl.2021.12.001.
2. Maslow AH. *Motivation and Personality.* Harper & Row; 1954.
3. Herzberg F. *Work and the Nature of Man.* World; 1966.
4. Leeds D. *Smart Questions.* McGraw-Hill; 1987.
5. Afolabi A, Fernando S, Bottiglieri T. The effect of organisational factors in motivating healthcare employees: a systematic review. *Br J Health Care Manag.* 2018;24(12):603–610. https://doi.org/10.12968/bjhc.2018.24.12.603
6. Wong K. The quick guide to recognition in the healthcare industry. Achievers Web site https://www.achievers.com/blog/the-quick-guide-to-recognition-in-the-healthcare-industry/. Published February 17, 2022.
7. Deeprose D. *How to Recognize and Reward Employees.* AMACOM; 1994:19, 125.

CHAPTER 16

Performance Feedback

CHAPTER OBJECTIVES

- Stress the critical nature of feedback and its importance in employee performance on a day-to-day basis.
- Establish the role of formal performance evaluations in the provision of feedback on employee performance.
- Describe the character and potential uses of multi-source feedback systems.
- Provide specific guidelines for the supervisor's conduct of a formal evaluation of employee performance.
- Furnish suggestions to guide the supervisor's conduct of an employee performance evaluation interview.
- Introduce the concept of team evaluation.
- Review the common pitfalls and shortcomings occasionally encountered in employee performance evaluations.

KEY TERMS

Feedback: In general, feedback is the crucial element of true two-way communication; relative to employee performance, it is the essential ingredient in recognizing, correcting, acknowledging, maintaining, or improving performance.

Performance Evaluation (or Performance Appraisal): The periodic review of an employee's performance for the primary purpose of maintaining or improving performance in the job the individual presently holds.

The Need for Feedback

Performance feedback has always been an important responsibility of those who manage the work of others. The rapid and tumultuous changes continuing to unfold in medical care are continually forcing employees to assume greater responsibility and learn new skills. Employees must try to keep up with new organizational initiatives such as mergers, policies, reengineering, customer satisfaction, employee empowerment, and team building. These fast-developing changes mandate more daily feedback to employees and more comprehensive evaluations of their performance.

Today's performance evaluations include new duties and new standards because health maintenance organizations and other forms of managed care demand greater customer satisfaction at a lower cost. In the past, reward systems have focused almost exclusively on individuals. However, it is now necessary to evaluate and reward the performance and competencies of teams as well as individuals.

Day-to-Day Feedback

Ideally, new employees learn on a daily basis how well performance expectations are being met, and they receive help in fine-tuning their skills until they can function independently. This coaching is in all likelihood the single most powerful form of feedback. We seek to deliver candid and constructive feedback that is both helpful and enabling, and candid feedback requires saying what we really believe. Unless it is helpful, enabling, and honest, feedback does little to help people improve.

It must be stressed at the outset of this discussion that feedback to employees concerning their performance and conduct must be provided regularly, in many instances literally every day. In the crush of business that often threatens to overwhelm the supervisor, it is easy to overlook the minor problems and digressions that occur and easier still to ignore the employee who seems to trudge along at a generally acceptable level without causing problems for the supervisor.

It pays to remain aware that the principal task of the supervisor is to make it possible for the employees to accomplish their work as accurately and efficiently as possible. This suggests that in spite of the conflicting pressures that constantly threaten to divert the supervisor's attention, it is essential that the supervisor maintain a well-working one-to-one relationship with each employee. This can be accomplished only if the supervisor remains in regular contact with each employee. If the only performance feedback an employee receives is what comes with an annual or semiannual evaluation, the relationship between supervisor and employee is seriously flawed.

Formal Performance Evaluations

A performance evaluation should involve an exchange of information and ideas and not simply be a report card. Effective interviewers help employees recognize what needs to be improved and assists them in exploring ways of capitalizing on their strengths. To instill job satisfaction and motivation, supervisors serve more as resources and enablers than as actual appraisers. In other words, although performance reviews are evaluative in comparing performance with established standards, they are also developmental in that they enhance careers. The evaluative aspect depends on documented standards and verbal reinforcement, whereas the developmental aspect requires coaching and mentoring.

Effective evaluation often combines the features of recognition, self-appraisal, joint problem-solving, and management by objectives. Evaluation emphasis is properly focused on the future rather than on the past. The past is only a starting point for a discussion of how the employee can do better in the future.

An evaluation meeting can have a positive or negative impact on employee self-esteem. To boost morale and confidence, we must strive to make our associates perceive themselves as winners. A good performance evaluation and planning session concludes with both parties believing they have accomplished something. The end product of the performance evaluation is an understanding between the employee and the supervisor that includes the employee's understanding of what is expected of him or her, how the expectations are met, and ways he or she can improve performance.[1]

Purposes of Performance Evaluation

Performance evaluations serve a number of purposes. Following are of primary interest to the supervisor:

- Ensuring understanding of performance expectations by both management and employees
- Identifying training and development needs
- Ensuring fair and equitable administration of reward systems
- Providing recognition for past service
- Assisting employees with career development

Some Special Purposes

One occasional purpose of performance evaluation dictates the need for evaluations to be thorough, honest, and as objective as possible: helping defend against discrimination charges.

Consider this scenario: The management of an organization schedules a layoff. Some of the individuals to be let go are among the higher paid but are seen as not especially productive. Say that one person who is released charges age discrimination. Although management's intent was to reduce costs, higher pay often correlates with age so the move is seen as de facto age discrimination. Management of course claims that the reason for the person's dismissal was performance, not age. The investigation turns to performance and soon settles on the employment file containing several years of "Satisfactory" performance evaluations. So "performance" as a reason for dismissal fails, and the age discrimination charge is pursued—all because of performance that was deemed "satisfactory" because it was the easy way out for a supervisor who may have been too timid or too hasty to render honest evaluations.

Simply remember that when any dismissal or disciplinary action that addresses "performance" is protested, the individual's performance evaluations will be taken at face value. Thus, evaluations must always be thorough, accurate, and honest.

Another purpose of some evaluation systems is the determination of pay increases. In such systems, the amount of an individual's pay increase is related to that person's evaluation score; the higher the score, the greater the increase. Within such systems, it is often difficult to determine how much of an increase should be attached to what level of performance score and at the same time keep the total amount of pay-raise dollars within budget limitations. To function properly, such systems require regular refresher training of evaluators and often departmental or group scoring adjustments to compensate for differences in rating practices. Systems of this kind can become difficult to administer, and they nearly always raise challenges.

Essentials of Performance Evaluation

Evaluation systems, even the more effective ones currently in use, are not all alike. (There are some ineffective or inappropriate systems still in use in some organizations, but fortunately their numbers are dwindling.) Systems may vary according to the kind of organization involved, for example, acute-care hospital versus home-health agency. They may also differ according to the population to be evaluated; for example, the system used to evaluate registered nurses is likely to be different from that used for maintenance staff. However, some broad requirements are essential to every evaluation system.

First, it is always necessary to review and clarify performance expectations based on job descriptions, work standards, rules and policies, and previously formulated objectives. All expectations, that is, all tasks, standards, and goals, should be clear and approved. It is fundamental to any fair and equitable evaluation system that the employee has clear and accurate knowledge of everything on which he or she is to be evaluated.

Second, it is necessary to evaluate past performance. The evaluation concerns what was accomplished because the true starting point of a current evaluation should be how the employee performed recently (for example, objectives met, outcomes realized) and how the employee functioned or behaved in the past (for example, teamwork, attendance, policy observance, ethics). Past performance gets the most attention because the rating process usually deals with previous outcomes and behavior. The key in using the immediate past, however, lies not in delivering praise or criticism of what occurred but in determining, in joint fashion between employee and supervisor, if at all possible, where the employee should be going in the future.

Third, the supervisor should express appreciation for what the person has accomplished. This essential step affects self-confidence, self-image, job satisfaction, and motivation, important factors that are all too often omitted or glossed over in evaluations founded largely on criticism. It is true that with some employees a certain amount of criticism cannot be avoided. Regardless of the negatives that may be present, look for the positives and give them fair hearing.

Finally, it is necessary to develop a plan. Planning moves from the past into the future and directly affects work performance. Honest, participative management demands collaboration and promises of support. An honest developmental plan will consist of much more than attempts to correct the deficiencies revealed through the examination of past performance.

Little needs to be said here about some of the inappropriate and inadequate systems that were used for many years in many organizations except to advance some precautions concerning the worst of these that might still be encountered in places. Beware of what is quite likely the oldest form of performance evaluation, appraisal based primarily on personality characteristics. These systems required the supervisor to "rate" each employee on "attitude," "cooperativeness," "adaptability," "demeanor," and such. Such assessments are totally subjective, so there is no way to "measure" how the employee rates, and subjective assessments are always open to argument. The problem, of course, is that any rating the supervisor might apply is simply that supervisor's judgment and may in no way be a true indicator of performance. Even older criteria that are not quite as "soft" as pure personality characteristics, for example "job knowledge," one that can still be found on many evaluation forms, say nothing about performance; the validity of "job knowledge" lies not with how much of it the employee possesses but in how that knowledge is applied to achieve results. Overall, the more personality judgments required or the more subjective assessments made, the weaker and less defensible the final evaluation.

Other forms of evaluation that are also inherently inaccurate and inequitable are the so-called forced-rating systems. In such systems the supervisor may be required, for example, to apportion the employees into bands under a normal distribution scheme that calls for a certain percentage to be placed in "superior," an equal percentage in "unsatisfactory," and the remaining employees into two, three, or four bands in between. This by-the-numbers approach completely ignores the reality of the work group and the differences in performance among employees. Consider just one serious flaw in this approach: If the supervisor is doing a decent job at all, "unsatisfactory" employees will have individually been helped to improve to a point where their work is acceptable or they have been weeded out, so at any given time there may be few if any "unsatisfactory" employees in the group.

We could fill considerable space describing the inappropriate evaluation systems still in existence in some organizations. Suffice it to say that to stand a chance of constituting a fair and equitable evaluation approach, a system must be job-description based and must keep required subjective assessments to an absolute minimum.

Evaluation Frequency

Some evaluation systems call for all employees to be evaluated at one time, perhaps once a year or, in some instances, once every 6 months. Other systems call for evaluation on some other basis, the most common being each person's employment anniversary date. From the individual supervisor's perspective, regardless of frequency, performance evaluation can be a great deal of work. In the all-at-once approach, the supervisor has much work to do in a limited time, but doing it this way usually means that evaluation is out of the way for nearly a full year. Using the anniversary date approach, the work is spread throughout the year, although perhaps somewhat unevenly, leaving performance evaluation as an ongoing task that is never completely caught up.

Some supervisors prefer to get all evaluations done at one time and forget about the process for a year. Other supervisors, often those with large groups of employees, prefer to spread the work out over a longer period. Either approach has its plusses and minuses for any particular supervisor, but regardless of frequency, every supervisor has the responsibility to evaluate each employee honestly and objectively.

Evaluating Leaders

In traditional organizations, all the appraising is accomplished vertically downward. Yet employees are the recipients of the leadership provided by their superiors; therefore, they are customers of the leaders and entitled to evaluate leadership performance. Although in some organizations employees provide such feedback via formal appraisal systems, most employers obtain this information indirectly via employee attitude surveys and, perhaps, other mechanisms such as exit interviews with departing employees.

Multi-Source Feedback

In the 360-degree multi-source feedback system, managers flesh out the evaluation process by obtaining input from colleagues, subordinates, and sometimes customers. This provides a 360-degree view of how people perceive others on the job. Managers may use this kind of system as a developmental tool or as a formal appraisal instrument.

Use of 360-Degree Feedback Systems as Developmental Tools

Most people are more likely to modify their self-perceptions in the face of multi-source feedback. In this kind of process, there is less likelihood that important elements of performance will be overlooked.

In systems intended to provide only employee development guidance, the recipients of the feedback are asked whom they would like included in the battery of evaluators. The data become the sole property of the recipients and are not used in the formal evaluation process. These systems have been garnering favorable comments from many employers. Most employees being evaluated find the reports helpful and sometimes surprising.

Use of 360-Degree Feedback Systems in Formal Evaluations

Multi-source feedback can make an evaluation system more comprehensive, but employees need to believe that the data are unbiased and objective. Employees must have confidence in the intentions and credibility of the evaluators. The evaluators usually remain anonymous.

Unlike those in the purely developmental approach, these evaluations become the property of management. Evaluators may or may not discuss their ratings with each other before releasing them to the person being assessed and to his or her superiors.

There are severe drawbacks to the use of these systems in the formal appraisal process. Lepsinger and Lucia[2] urge a cautious approach and suggest that management first introduce the 360-degree system to their career development program. If successful, a pilot study can then be undertaken using the system for formal appraisal.

Drawbacks to Using 360-Degree Feedback in Formal Evaluations

- Recipients may resist feedback that actually affects their salary and chances for promotion.
- When evaluators believe they may hurt others by what they report, they are less likely to be completely honest.
- The evaluators may be competitors of those being evaluated for rewards or promotions.
- The organizational culture may not support open, honest feedback.
- It makes an already time-consuming process still more demanding of time.

Preparation for Performance Evaluations of Individuals

The performance evaluation meeting consists of two major components: process and content. The process encompasses the format of the system and the skill of the interviewer. The content is what occurs during the meeting. As with any meeting, advance planning is crucial to success. Too often the interviewer's preparation consists of summarizing the employee's deficiencies while neglecting to look for the person's accomplishments and special efforts.

Review the Evaluation Form

Most organizations design their own evaluation forms, and supervisors rarely have significant input into the design process. However, this should not prevent the interviewer from introducing additional items, including those that relate to teamwork and customer service. Such items may include the following:

- Participation in team efforts
- Willingness to express opinions or assume responsibility
- Willingness to help solve problems
- Ability to adjust to major changes
- Readiness to take special actions to "delight" customers

Highlight the criteria on the form that are to receive special attention. Many all-purpose rating forms are deficient in listing the competencies of people in leadership roles. The list provided in **Exhibit 16.1** may be helpful.

Exhibit 16.1 Managerial Competencies

- Maintains contemporary professional knowledge and skills
- Keeps up-to-date in both professional and managerial fields
- Regularly attends conferences and other meetings
- Meets all continuing education standards
- Demonstrates initiative and flexibility
- Identifies needs for innovation and change and effectively implements changes
- Solves problems quickly and skillfully
- Maximizes the use of staff and material resources
- Keeps within budgetary limits
- Manages time of self and subordinates effectively
- Evaluates, selects, and maintains equipment and supplies skillfully
- Communicates effectively
- Keeps vertical and horizontal channels of communication open and active
- Enjoys good rapport with other team members
- Makes efficient use of meetings and other information systems; has mastered computer system
- Is skilled in interviewing techniques
- Possesses good writing ability
- Shows other leadership abilities
- Coaches, counsels, and evaluates performance well

- Maintains high morale, enthusiasm, and motivation
- Is skilled in selecting, orienting, and training new hires
- Deals promptly and effectively with employee problems
- Coordinates and cooperates well with other work units
- Delegates and empowers effectively
- Organizes, assigns, and schedules skillfully
- Recognized as a good team builder
- Accomplishes assignments and challenges on time and to the satisfaction of superiors

Obtain Employee Input

An employee scheduled for an evaluation conference should have the following in his or her possession before meeting with the evaluator:

- A copy of the position description, including detailed information about performance standards.
- A copy of the evaluation form used to report the evaluation. If the employee is to hand in a completed form to the interviewer, two copies are provided, and one is retained by the employee.
- A copy of this person's previous formal evaluation.
- Departmental objectives for the current year and the year to follow.
- Instructions on how to prepare for the meeting (**Exhibit 16.2**).

You may choose to ask an employee to complete a self-evaluation and bring it to the meeting. This practice has two advantages. First, it introduces a spirit of collaboration. Second, it enables the interviewer to note the areas of disagreement or sensitivity. That is, if the evaluator's rating and the employee's self-rating are far apart on any particular criteria, the two of them know at once that these criteria represent items they need to discuss in depth. But care should be exercised in attempting to get employees to perform self-evaluations; some will inevitably be uneasy about doing so, fearing (largely imaginary) consequences should they rate themselves

Exhibit 16.2 Employee Preparation Instructions

1. Review your position description. List any changes since your last review. Pencil in any changes you would recommend.
2. Scan your previous evaluation. Be prepared to discuss the objectives you achieved and those that were not achieved.
3. Prepare a new list of objectives.
4. Review your current continuing education record.
5. Be prepared to discuss the following:
   - How you feel about your performance since the last meeting
   - What do you consider your most valuable contribution to the organization since your last review and what gave you the most satisfaction
   - What changes in systems, procedures, equipment, service, cost containment, or quality improvement do you suggest we consider
   - Anything that is preventing you from reaching your full potential
   - What frustrates you most at present
   - What supervision can do to help you improve

appreciably different from the rating of the evaluator. In many situations it is best to offer self-evaluation as an option. Self-evaluation seems to be more acceptable to and generally more successful with technical and professional employees; it is not recommended for the majority of non-management staff.

A self-evaluation should be strictly voluntary; the employee should not be "asked" in such a manner as to feel compelled to comply. Some employees, regardless of level, will never be comfortable with self-evaluation; they fear that either underrating or overrating themselves will reflect poorly on them, so they try to second-guess what the evaluator is likely to say. It has been established time and again that on average those performing self-evaluations actually rate themselves somewhat lower than do the evaluators.

An employee scheduled for an evaluation meeting can be asked to prepare a list of objectives and plans relating to personal improvement needs and career development, including specific requests for assistance needed to achieve these new objectives. Encourage each employee to prepare a list of what he or she considers significant contributions to the organization, and urge each to include those activities that afforded them the most satisfaction.

Review the Employment File of the Employee Being Evaluated

Because the employment record may relate to performance evaluation, an employee's human resource file should include the following:

- The individual's current position description, complete with performance standards
- Continuing education and attendance records
- Honors and special recognitions or awards
- Incident reports
- Records of formal counseling or disciplinary actions
- Copies of previous evaluations

Schedule a Meeting

Set a date, time, and place for the evaluation meeting. Give the employee sufficient time to prepare. Allow at least an hour for the meeting.

Formulate Key Remarks

Select the exact words to use for introductory statements, to criticize, and to confront defensiveness. Anticipate problems. Be prepared to cite specific factual information to support any negative feedback or low ratings; remember to avoid generalizations and purely subjective assessments.

Four Phases of the Evaluation Interview

First, review and as necessary revise the position description and performance standards. This is often a good time to document changes relating to quality improvement, customer service, and empowerment strategies and to ensure the position description is up to date.

Second, discuss the performance ratings using the organization's evaluation form. Begin on a positive note by focusing on criteria that were rated highest by you (and also by the employee, if a self-evaluation is involved). Do not gloss over these with something like "we agree on that." Compliment the person and cite specific instances of outstanding work that led to the high rating. The individual will appreciate hearing why you thought he or she deserved a high rating, especially one that might be higher than a self-rating. Save for last the items you rated low or for which you and the employee seem far apart in your assessment of performance. These items are best left for last because they are the items likely to require the most discussion, and it also here that you may encounter defensiveness or where emotional outbursts may occur. **Exhibit 16.3** provides suggestions for discussing performance deficiencies.

A caveat: Most experienced managers will confess that the biggest mistake they made in past evaluations was to overrate marginal performers. This tendency all too often ends with an embarrassed manager trying to explain to a superior why a problem employee should be discharged.

Third, critique the person's accomplishments related to performance objectives formulated at the previous evaluation. Congratulate the person on successes in these areas. Through discussion, decide which of the objectives that were not reached should be retained and which should be abandoned. End this segment by thanking the person for his or her accomplishments since the previous review.

Finally, discuss future performance. Past performance only provides the basis for planning. Most of the interview time should deal with expectations for the future. The first goal should target activities needed to improve performance. The second should deal with career development; that is, what may be needed to reach one's full potential. Like most New Year's resolutions, goals are meaningless if there is no commitment.

Exhibit 16.3 Suggestions for Discussing Performance Deficiencies

1. Limit criticism to one or two significant issues. If there are others, discuss them at another meeting.
2. Offer the employee your support.
3. Save critical remarks for last.
4. Before you criticize, encourage self-criticism.
5. Use all your listening skills.
6. Respond supportively
   - Reinforce points of agreement
   - Handle disagreement diplomatically
   - Use joint problem-solving approaches
   - Avoid being defensive
7. Avoid nonspecific terms such as "attitude," "work ethic," "professionalism," "weakness," and "deficiency."
8. Do not use the global comment "needs more experience" when documenting improvement needs. Spell out exactly what experience is needed.

SCRAM: Characteristics of Good Objectives

Specific. Specific feedback focuses on concrete and observable behavior, not inferences about traits or personality characteristics.
Challenging. If it is not challenging, it probably is not worth very much.
Relevant. It must be related to the person's responsibilities.
Achievable. It should be challenging but feasible. Failures lead to frustration and loss of self-confidence.
Measurable. Statistics and charts are good (hard data), but sometimes behavior is not easy to quantify. Although some words, such as caring, respect, and courtesy, cannot be meaningfully measured with numbers, the key is verifiability.

Do not accept "I'll try"; the individual who says "I'll try" is simply building excuses for failure. If failure ensues, the person claims to have done what he or she said would be done—try. In this step you jointly develop a list of objectives consistent with departmental goals and objectives. When interviewees have difficulty formulating objectives, help them. Ask them what they believe should be done differently in their unit and what role they would like to play in any such change. Do not give up on this too quickly. If the person still comes up empty, suggest a few things you would like the person to do. Then ask what you could do to make the work more satisfying.

Conclude the Meeting

End the session with an affirmation, an expression of confidence in the ability of the individual to achieve the new objectives. Thank the person not only for what has been accomplished, but also for cooperation and participation during the interview. When all is said and done, the individual employee should be able to reasonably answer two questions:

- How am I doing in the eyes of my supervisor and the organization?
- Where can I go from here?

Post-Meeting Activities

Make certain the evaluation form has been filled out completely and includes documentation of new objectives and action plans. Every employee must be given an opportunity to respond both verbally and in writing to adverse comments or unfavorable performance ratings. Do not neglect the following:

- Monitor the person's progress. Provide reminders about plans and objectives if necessary.
- Congratulate the individual on reaching each objective or showing areas of improvement.
- Confirm promised support or offer more support when obstacles are perceived by the employee.
- Modify, replace, or cancel previous objectives as appropriate. Conditions change, and objectives must change with them.
- Document the employee's achievements.

Performance Evaluation of Work Teams

Different teams require different approaches to measurement and thus to evaluation of their work. Teams of floor nurses and their ancillary care providers are evaluated largely based on patient satisfaction. The performance of a laboratory team is usually judged by turnaround time, accuracy, and reliability of test results.

Appraising teams involves the "what" and "how" of team efforts. The "what" refers to the goals, objectives, and key results that the team and each individual achieves. The "how" refers to the performance behavior important in promoting teamwork and achieving the team goals collaboratively.

Teams may be evaluated by team facilitators, with or without the participation of team members. Both individual and team performance are evaluated by members of self-directed teams, except in the early phases of team building when this is still undertaken by the supervisor.

Common Pitfalls of Performance Evaluation

Performance evaluations can be a powerful mechanism for employee development when it is applied honestly and conscientiously by a manager who uses it to improve employee performance, expand employee capabilities, and enhance organizational effectiveness. However, performance evaluation is not a favorite activity of many managers because of its time-consuming nature and the shortcomings and weaknesses that are to be encountered both in system design and administration and in the attitudes of managers who may be nearly overwhelmed with work and cannot help but see evaluation as a significant imposition on their time.

Pitfalls commonly encountered relative to evaluation include the following, some of which, if cumulative, can lead to system failure:

- The process is not taken seriously by either manager or employee. This is manifested when there is inadequate preparation by the participants, when the evaluation discussion is repeatedly postponed or left until the last minute and then rushed, or when the interviewer tolerates frequent interruptions during the meeting.

- The manager has only superficial knowledge of the employee's performance. It has been truthfully said that the less a manager knows about what a subordinate does, the better chance the subordinate has to do whatever he or she wants to do and how much he or she wants to do (or feels like doing). Perhaps, with increasing spans of control, the supervisor has so many people or the people are scattered over such a broad geographic area that an employee can "get lost" for an extended time. Also, it is common in healthcare organizations, especially in hospitals where 24-hour, 7-day per week operations are the rule, that some employees seldom see their immediate supervisors. A supervisor who has direct oversight of an employee's behavior for only short periods may have to rely on only the results of behavior (did the work actually get done?) or on input from others. Reliance on secondhand information weakens the evaluation process. The first, and usually most valid, source of performance observation is your own firsthand knowledge.[3]
- Documented, up-to-date, specific work standards or objectives do not exist. This condition gives the supervisor little to measure against, and the resulting evaluation lacks concrete information.
- The evaluation consists of highly subjective assessments (usually because of a weak system or a lazy evaluator), or it lacks honesty altogether. Failure to honestly critique an employee's performance hurts both the organization and employee.

- In the evaluation meeting, the evaluator exercises excess judging and too little listening.
- There is insufficient positive feedback or respect for the employee's self-esteem. The employee who receives only negative commentary will not truly hear what is being said.
- The evaluation interview consists of generalities; the employee hears little more than "You're doing just fine." Or the evaluator hands out the written evaluation without comment or invites only questions about the report itself.
- The evaluation forms are inadequate (as a great many in active use are). Some evaluators behave as though they are required to write something significant in every space (not so—not every space may be needed for every employee), and some simply write enough to fill a given space even though more should be said. A form—almost any form—seems to establish its own constraints for some users.
- The evaluation "score" is used primarily to allocate salaries instead of to improve performance.
- Primary emphasis is on the past rather than on the future.
- New objectives are nonspecific, inappropriate, or unchallenging.
- The employee has little or no opportunity to participate in formulating objectives or adjusting or resetting standards for future performance.
- Reprimands, criticisms, or performance deficiencies had never been discussed before the evaluation meeting, catching the employee by surprise.

WRAP-UP

Think About It

If you are daunted by the process of performance evaluation or simply dislike doing evaluations, think about why you feel this way. Do you dislike evaluations because it is uncomfortable, or is it uncomfortable because you dislike it? The solution? Just do it, again and again as necessary. Why? Because it is a requirement of the organization as well as outside agencies, but mostly because you and your employees will both benefit from it in the long run. Evaluations may never become your favorite supervisory task, but it will become more tolerable as you gain experience and its value becomes apparent.

Questions for Review and Discussion

1. If we believe that it is inappropriate to evaluate an employee on a subjective characteristic such as "attitude," how then should we address employee behavior that seems to occur because of an attitude problem?

2. Some organizations evaluate all employees at the same time each year; some organizations evaluate employees throughout the year, often using the employment anniversary date. From a supervisor's perspective, explain one significant advantage and one significant disadvantage of each method.

3. Explain what is meant by the statement, "If the relationship between supervisor and employee is all that it should be, the employee's annual evaluation will be a mere formality."

4. There is often very little ongoing contact between a supervisor and those employees who go along quietly doing a passable job and causing no problems. Why can't these employees be counted on to continue working as they have been without constant feedback?

5. Why is it recommended that the initial step toward an evaluation of an employee be the review and update of the job description?

6. It is frequently claimed that an effective objective consists of three elements. One element is what is to be done and another element is how much is to be done. What do you believe is the third element, and why must all three be present?

7. Consider an acceptably performing employee who has been in the same job for many years, is at the top of the pay scale for that job, can get increases only when the scale itself moves, and has no promotion potential or other advancement possibilities. What will you accomplish by giving this employee regular performance evaluations?

8. In a few brief sentences, write a convincing argument you might use in trying to get a reluctant employee to agree to completing and submitting a self-evaluation (we are assuming that self-evaluation is optional in your evaluation system).

9. In recent years performance evaluations retained in employment files have often become determining factors in cases of age discrimination involving laid-off employees. Why might this be so?

10. Some organizations have made use of peer-group evaluations in which several members of a group of similarly situated workers provide input to each other's evaluations. Describe one significant advantage and one likely disadvantage of this process.

Case: "Let's Get This Evaluation Thing Out of the Way"

You stopped by your manager's office to relay a brief message to him. You were later to believe that this small act—which you were not obligated to perform—was a mistake on your part, because before you could get away the boss said, "Hey, while you're here, let's get this evaluation thing out of the way. Should've been done 6 weeks ago." He pulled an evaluation form from a stack on his desk and said, "Sit down—this won't take long."

The boss began by asking, "Don't suppose you did a self-evaluation?"

You answered, "No. I didn't know it was expected."

"Well, anyway, we can do without it."

"Now, to get to it. You've done some good work this past year, and I want you to know it's noticed and appreciated. Of course there are always places where some improvement could be made. Starting with the good side, your output has been great these past few months, and I'm especially pleased with the way you handled the implementation of the new billing system. You've got pretty good judgment, and this shows up in your planning. And you did a swell job with the scheduling problem—maybe I told you that at the time."

"But let me tell you where I think you can do better. I know I can speak frankly and right to the point. Your stubbornness is still a problem. I can think of three or four times when I've had to step in between you and the folks in info systems. I'm sure you agree that you haven't shown a great deal of creativity in doing your job, and that's too bad because this is an important area for us to consider when we're picking people for promotion. Another thing I've noticed is that you're too aggressive in dealings with other departments. You know we all have to pull together if this health system is to...."

Instructions

Critique the foregoing portion of the "evaluation meeting" between "you" and the manager. Indicate what you believe to be inappropriate, if anything, and what you believe to be acceptable, if anything. In mentioning something you believe was improperly done, state how it might have been done correctly. In concluding, summarize your reaction to the previous passage in a single sentence.

Case: "I'm Not Getting Any Better Than I Was?"

Supervisor Jane was not at all comfortable with the way the performance evaluation meeting with Wilma was going. Wilma was far more uncommunicative than usual; she would speak only when asked something, then answer only briefly. All of Jane's attempts to lighten up the conversation were falling flat.

Except for a brief review 3 months after Wilma's transfer to Jane's unit, this was the first opportunity Jane had had for a thorough review of Wilma's performance. Wilma had initially seemed eager for the meeting, but when they sat down and Jane laid out the completed evaluation forms, Wilma fell silent and seemed to withdraw.

Increasingly frustrated by Wilma's apparent unwillingness to participate, Jane stopped in the middle of trying to make a point and said, "Wilma, something about this evaluation is bothering you. Out with it."

"Nothing's bothering me," Wilma responded.

"I know you well enough to know that you're upset about something. Out with it, so we're not just wasting our time here."

Wilma sat silently for a moment. Then she tapped a fingernail on the evaluation form and said, "It's this—my rating."

"There's nothing wrong with it," Jane said. "It's comfortably above standard performance and very close to the average of the extremely good group of people we have on this unit."

"It's lower than any score I ever got from my last supervisor. I know I've done at least as well here as I did there, but you've given me my lowest score in 5 years."

"Wilma, this is a good evaluation score."

"I can't agree," said Wilma. "All of you who do these use the same forms and pretty much the same job descriptions, and the evaluations ought to be consistent. Compared with Sue, my last supervisor, aren't you telling me that after all my hard work I'm no better than I used to be? That I'm not getting any better than I was? Or even that my performance is slipping because I had a higher score last year?"

Questions

1. If you were in Jane's position, how would you try to explain the differences in evaluation scores to this employee?
2. What, if anything, do you believe the organization should be doing about its evaluation system?

References

1. Metzger N. Human resources management in organized delivery systems. In Wolper F. ed. *Health Care Administration*, 5th ed. Jones and Bartlett Publishers; 2010:794.

2. Lepsinger R, Lucia AD. 360 degrees feedback and performance appraisal. *Training*, 1997; 34(9):62–70.

3. Lombardi DN. *Handbook for the New Health Care Manager*, 2d ed. Jossey-Bass Publishers; 2001:294.

CHAPTER 17

Disciplining: Correction of Behavior

CHAPTER OBJECTIVES

- Establish the nature of discipline and compare and contrast disciplining and counseling.
- Introduce the concept of the reward-to-risk ratio as a sometime explanation for employee actions that require discipline.
- Introduce the concept of progressive discipline and review its essential components.
- Address possible employee responses to various forms of disciplinary action.
- Review appropriate disciplinary principles and practices available to the supervisor.

KEY TERMS

Discipline: The earliest definitions of "discipline" involve teaching; in the organizational context, the purpose of most disciplinary action is to effect *correction of behavior*.

Progressive Discipline: A process in which the disciplinary measures become increasingly severe until there is a resolution of the problem one way or the other; that is, until correction or discharge occurs.

Discharge: Involuntary termination of employment occurring for violation or violations of rules or policies; simply stated, it is being "fired."

Scenario: "Why Should I?"

You are manager of a clinical laboratory unit; you have 22 direct-reporting employees. You believe you have comfortable working relationships with all employees except one. That one employee, a laboratory technologist, continually gives you a hard time about assignments. Whenever you assign this person a task that she considers not part of her daily routine and is not specifically designated in her job description, her response is: "Why should I? That's not part of my job."

In one recent, frustrating exchange you responded angrily, "Because I said so, that's why!" This not only failed to get results, but it also generated increased hostility.

As you go through this chapter think about how you might deal with this employee.

Not Meant as "Punishment"—Usually

"Disciplining" is not the same as "punishing" as far as the supervisor's responses to most of the infractions falling under the extremely broad heading of employee misconduct are concerned. Invariably, the result of disciplinary action in some situations will have the effect of punishment, but the essential purpose of most disciplinary action is *correction of behavior*. Disciplining is largely intended as an educational process applied to correct inappropriate conduct or behavior. The intent is not to send an employee down the path toward termination of employment but rather to provide guidance with which employees can work to correct deviant behavior. When disciplining is done skillfully, employee self-esteem is preserved.

Discipline should be fair, firm, and fast. Delay increases tension, and if protracted, a delay has the effect of watering down or neutralizing discipline's effects. If all you do about a troublesome employee is complain, you probably deserve what you get: continued problems and loss of respect of your superiors and the people who report to you. Proper discipline has been likened to a red-hot stove: It provides a warning (in the forms of color or sound), it does not discriminate (everyone who touches it gets burned), and it is immediate, consistent, and effective.

When supervisors treat their employees as they would like to be treated themselves, they have fewer disciplinary problems. They spot potential trouble areas and avoid the need for discipline by using their coaching and counseling expertise. The best discipline is self-discipline, and this is achieved when employees are treated as responsible adults. Some managers treat their employees as children and are then surprised when those employees behave like children.

Supervisors who practice management by intimidation spend much of their time trying to catch people doing something wrong. Employees respond to this kind of management not so much by cleaning up their act as by learning how to avoid being caught. Many grievances come in the aftermath of disciplinary actions.

Counseling Versus Disciplining

Disciplining and counseling are closely interrelated. Counseling, addressed in detail in the section entitled "Coaching and Counseling," is often an informal first step in the disciplinary process. If initial counseling is unsuccessful, it is followed by a formal disciplinary step—the oral warning—when the employee is warned of the consequences of failure to perform up to expectations or to function according to rules and policies. Most organizations require one or more oral warnings for the more common and less serious offenses before stricter measures are administered.

Counseling sessions or oral reprimands are not appropriate for certain serious forms of misbehavior that call for immediate suspension or dismissal. Most organizations provide written guidelines for conduct and behavior that designate appropriate responses for various disciplinary infractions. A sample listing of such guidelines appears as **Exhibit 17.1**.

Exhibit 17.1 Guidelines for Disciplinary Action

Class I: Minor Infractions
Discipline

- First offense—oral warning
- Second offense—written warning
- Third offense—1-day suspension
- Fourth offense—3-day suspension

Typical Infractions

- Absenteeism
- Tardiness
- Discourtesy to patients, visitors, coworkers, etc.

Class II: More Serious Infractions
Discipline

- First offense—written warning
- Second offense—3-day suspension
- Third offense—discharge

Typical Infractions

- Failure to report when scheduled for work
- Unexcused absence
- Performance of personal business on hospital time

Exhibit 17.1 Guidelines for Disciplinary
Action   *(continued)*

- Violation of smoking, safety, fire, or
  emergency regulations

Class III: Still More Serious Infractions
Discipline

- First offense—written warning
- Second offense—discharge

Typical Infractions

- Insubordination
- Negligence
- Falsification of records, reports, or
  information
- Unauthorized release of confidential or
  privileged information
- Sexual harassment

Class IV: Most Serious Infractions
Discipline

- First offense—discharge

Typical Infractions

- Absence without notice for 3 consecutive
  days ("3 days no-call, no-show")
- Fighting on the job
- Theft
- Being under the influence of alcohol or
  drugs on premises
- Willful damage to hospital property

Reward-to-Risk Ratio

Most employees do not misbehave because they
are bad people or because they simply want to
harass their superiors. Rather, it is because they
derive some benefit, although often an unconscious benefit, from misbehaving.

When supervisors fail to detect violations
of rules, policies, or procedures or fail to take
corrective measures, employees have no incentive to change their behavior. Consider the ratio
of reward to risk. We all play the reward-to-risk
game on the highway every day. We drive a little
faster than the speed limit because we feel we
need to hurry. The reward is getting to our destination more promptly. Most of us do not drive
at a rapid speed because we know that doing
so increases the risk of arrest or accident. Once

you recognize the reward an employee derives
from inappropriate behavior and what that
person fears, you can more readily modify that
behavior by decreasing the reward or increasing
the risk.

Consider, for example, Ken, who frequently arrives late for work on the evening
shift because he knows the day crew will cover
some of his responsibilities. Ken's previous
supervisor never said anything to him about
his behavior, but his new supervisor quickly
becomes aware of the situation and tells the day
crew to stop doing Ken's work, thus reducing
the reward for this behavior. The supervisor
also warns Ken about lateness and tells him to
check in with her when he arrives, thus when
risk is increased, the individual's perceived
reward for misbehaving is diminished.

Progressive Discipline

The disciplinary process commonly used in the
majority of organizations is referred to as "progressive" in nature because in most instances the
disciplinary measures become increasingly severe
until there is a resolution of the problem one way
or the other; that is, until correction or discharge
occurs. In its traditional form, progressive discipline typically consists of four steps:

1. Oral warning or reprimand
2. Written warning or reprimand
3. Suspension or probation
4. Discharge

Oral Warning

In delivering an oral warning or reprimand,
always be conscious of the need to avoid saving up a number of complaints and then, one
frustrating day, dumping the entire load on the
individual. Deliver warnings as soon as possible after the misbehavior, although not until
you have control of your emotions. Keep it
confidential. Always reprimand in private. You
may have to borrow space for a short while
if your office is not the best location for a
private discussion.

Do not be apologetic. Describe what is wrong and how you feel about it. Do not exaggerate. Attack the problem, not the person. Avoid starting sentences with an accusatory "you," and avoid using subjective terms such as "attitude," "work ethic," and "professionalism," and avoid the absolute terms "always" and "never."

Allow the individual to respond, but cut short any litany of lame excuses that may be forthcoming. Anticipate remarks such as "You're not being fair" or "You can't say things like that to me." Say exactly what you expect the person to do or to stop doing.

If the occasion is a repeat reprimand or if the problem has previously been addressed by counseling, use the counseling technique described in the chapter entitled "Coaching and Counseling." However, be less empathetic and more formal than when first counseling. Show that your patience is running out, and warn of future action if improvement is not forthcoming. For example, "If this is not corrected immediately, it will be necessary for me to …."

If the wayward employee was hired by your superior or was recruited by someone at another higher organizational level, make certain you discuss the problem with your manager. When you discipline employees who are popular with their coworkers, you must rely on the support you have built up within your team. If team members trust you and know that you are fair, they will support your decision.

Even though you may be delivering an oral warning, document the discussion and if possible review what is written with the employee and obtain the employee's signature. Keep this in your own files, not to be placed in the employee's human resources file and never to be used unless behavior is not corrected and it is necessary to go on to the next disciplinary level. Why document an oral warning? Simple protection; when some subsequent action is legally protested, it will likely be necessary to show that all steps of the disciplinary process have been followed. (You can be sure that when a given disciplinary action is contested and there is no documentation of an oral warning, the employee is likely to say, "I was never told.")

Written Warning

The written warning or reprimand is often a significant step toward discharge with all its legal ramifications, so proceed with caution. Most likely your human resources department has a special form you must use for this purpose. Procedures vary among organizations, so it is important for you to learn whether you have the authority to issue written warnings by yourself or whether this must be done in concert with human resources or higher management or at least done with their concurrence.

Discuss the problem with your manager before generating a written warning. Craft the warning carefully; it is a document with significant legal implications, and there is always the possibility that it may end up in court. Avoid making statements that you cannot substantiate. Provide observations and facts, never opinions or hearsay. A list of written warning essentials is presented in **Exhibit 17.2**.

Exhibit 17.2 Essentials of a Written Disciplinary Report

- Description of the problem
  - State facts, never assumptions, hearsay, or opinions.
  - Whenever possible provide dates with examples.
  - Record the names of witnesses or involved persons.
- Record of previous warnings
  - Provide dates.
  - Record what was said by both you and the employee.
  - Describe resulting changes in conduct, if any.
- Record of previous written reprimands or punitive actions
  - Attach copies
  - Describe disciplinary measures taken.
  - Describe resulting changes in conduct, if any.
- Employee's documentation of explanation, denial, or rebuttal
  - If the employee chooses to provide documentation, include a copy.
  - If the employee provides nothing in writing, describe the employee's stated

Exhibit 17.2 Essentials of a Written
Disciplinary Report   *(continued)*

position as accurately as possible. Note
in writing that the employee chose not
to prepare such a document.
- Record of punitive action presently decreed
  - Note in writing that the disciplinary
    action was explained to the employee.
  - Attempt to secure the employee's
    understanding of the action to be taken.
- Description of expected performance
  - As appropriate, include a target date
    for correction.
  - Clearly indicate the conduct or behavior
    that will or will not be tolerated.
- Signatures
  - Sign the report.
  - Secure the employee's signature. If
    the employee refuses to sign, call in a
    witness (preferably another supervisor)
    and repeat the request; if the employee
    still refuses to sign, have the witness
    attest to the refusal.

When you meet with the employee, explain that a written reprimand is a formal warning and will be documented in the individual's employee file. Review any previous counseling sessions or oral reprimands that relate to the same problem.

Be specific as to your expectations and the target date for compliance. For example, "If within the next 60 days you are late for work another time without an acceptable excuse, you will be sent home on a 1-day suspension without pay." This may sound juvenile, but sometimes people who fail to act maturely must be treated that way.

As long as doing so is consistent with organizational policy, tell the person that after a specified time, for example 6 months, without further similar incidents, the record of the disciplinary action will be removed from their file. Insist that the employee read and sign the written warning. As necessary, remind the person that signing does not necessarily mean agreement but is instead a simple acknowledgment that the warning was received and discussed. Inform the person of the right to attach a rebuttal or to confer with your superior.

Suspension or Probation

Some offenses call for immediate suspension or discharge without any antecedent counseling or reprimands. In many organizations, supervisors can only recommend such severe action; the actual order has to be approved by human resources or senior management. Regardless of the severity of any particular offense, it is essential that no one ever be discharged in anger; there must always be some time available for cooling off and examining the situation rationally.

If the employee has received oral and written warnings in the past, a formal meeting may not be needed. Your human resources department will provide the necessary form or instruct you on how to prepare the report.

When an individual returns to work after a suspension, treat the person like any other employee. Be businesslike, neither solicitous nor aloof. You have already chastised the individual, so consider the matter closed.

Discharge

Today's managers are growing increasingly reluctant to fire people. Many, in fact, believe that it is all but impossible to fire anyone in some particular working environments, especially when there are protections such as certain union rules or civil service regulations in place. They cite all the roadblocks and potential legal hassles that may result from such action. However, if specific standards of conduct and behavior are in place and mandated procedures are followed, justified dismissals are not especially difficult as long as complete and accurate documentation exists.

Too often, a supervisor creates a problem by accepting substandard performance or behavior for an extended period or by evaluating performance as satisfactory when it is not. One surprising observation is that years after being fired, many people are able to admit that firing was not only justified, but was the turning point in their careers.

Employers protect themselves by providing employee handbooks that state the disciplinary policies of the organization. These handbooks avoid any mention of permanent employment and avoid statements to the effect that employees can be dismissed only "for cause." These are important precautions because it has been held in the courts time and again that an organization's employee handbook or its policy manual can be interpreted as an implied contract of employment. Employers also warn their managers about the dangers of rating people higher than they deserve; even marginally satisfactory evaluations can come back to haunt the evaluator when someone who has been dismissed for performance-related reasons protests the action.

Some cautious employers insist that their employment attorneys approve discharges before the employees are notified. This is for good reason. Many fired employees file wrongful discharge lawsuits, and these can be expensive and time consuming. Those who sue usually charge that they were fired without cause or for insufficient or discriminatory reasons. Others claim that the termination violated a written or verbal agreement they or their union had with the employer.

To sustain a discharge against legal challenges, an employer must be able to prove the following:

- Work standards and policies are specific and documented, and employees are repeatedly reminded of these.
- What was alleged did indeed take place, actually involved the employee, and warranted the discharge.
- Such behavior had not been condoned in the past or that other workers have been discharged for similar offenses.
- The sequence of discipline followed prescribed policies and procedures.
- The employee made no genuine effort to heed previous warnings even though he or she had been advised of potential consequences.
- The firing was based on behavior or results, not on any of the following:
  - Discrimination (gender, race, religion, age, disability, etc.)
  - Whistle-blowing related to safety practices, illegal acts, sexual harassment, military or jury duty, or workers' compensation claims

- Violation of implied contract (i.e., the employee was promised a permanent job)

Termination Meeting

You may choose not to hold a termination meeting, or you may be required to do so, or you may have no choice in the matter if this chore is customarily handled by the human resources department. There is no perfect time to deliver a discharge. However, if such can be arranged, a Friday afternoon after other employees have departed and shortly after the employee has been notified of the meeting could be the best of several questionable options.

Never discuss the possibility of reconsideration. All such possibilities should have been exhausted well before this final meeting. You can, of course, say you are sorry things did not work out and wish the person well. If the person gets angry or breaks into tears, remain calm. Do not get drawn into a debate, and do not agree with any charges the person makes. Say that the human resources department will discuss any additional administrative matters such as terminal pay and benefits and will make arrangements for the person's final paycheck.

Tell the person exactly what information will be released to potential employers who request the data and that it will be released only by human resources and only with the employee's signed consent. Your responsibility may include ensuring that the employee has returned keys, identification tags, and other items that belong to the organization. Security codes in computers and keys to secured areas may have to be changed.

Employee Reactions to Being Disciplined

Some employees who are disciplined simply quit. Others quit psychologically but remain on the job because of vested time, unwillingness to look for new work, or lack of opportunity elsewhere. Those who stay often become marginal performers at best. Many disciplined employees file appeals, grievances, or legal complaints, and seek redress via unions, the courts, the Equal Employment Opportunity Commission, the Occupational Safety and Health Administration, or some other governmental agency.

Other Disciplinary Measures

Other less formal disciplinary measures are available that lie outside of a formal progressive disciplinary system. Innovative supervisors can come up with almost as many punitive measures as their employees can find ways to avoid them. Any number of such measures are commonly applied in the ongoing relationship with some employees. One might, for example, withhold or delay a pay increase for an employee whose performance has been marginal compared with that of others. Surely some of these measures are recognizable as the inverse of actions the supervisor can use to reward employees; that is, that which is extended as a reward can also be withheld as a punishment. These measures include the following:

- Withholding or delaying pay increases
- Denying promotions
- Reducing performance ratings to reflect declining performance
- Placing the employee on probation
- Demoting or transferring the employee
- Denying requests for educational support or time off
- Withdrawing special privileges or authority
- Providing unpleasant assignments
- Canceling special projects
- Removing an individual from teams, committees, or other work groups

Behavior Versus Performance

Up to this point this discussion has intermingled problems of behavior or conduct with problems of job performance. These are the two principal ways an individual can lose employment, but the fundamental differences between them suggest different approaches to correction are needed. Problems of behavior involve violations of rules or policies; problems of job performance involve the apparent inability to meet the minimum requirements of the job.

Problems of behavior are addressed through the progressive disciplinary process; one must correct the offending behavior and follow the rules and observe the policies. Policies must be clearly written by the organization, and the employee must acknowledge an understanding.[1] However, problems of performance are not best addressed via warnings but rather by providing the employee with reasonable instruction and assistance intended to help the person achieve an acceptable level of performance. In other words, instead of citing rules and laying down the law as for a policy violation, it is necessary to provide the substandard performer with guidance aimed at achieving acceptable performance.

Either path can lead to termination of employment if behavior is not corrected or performance is not brought up to standard, but along the way a distinction must be made. The uncorrected rule breaker is discharged for cause and is, in everyday parlance, "fired." But the worker who is dismissed for reasons of performance—inability to meet the minimum requirements of the job—is not "fired" as such but released in a manner better described as "laid off." There is a legal distinction that immediately arises in every instance of an employee's release: One who is discharged for cause—"fired"—is technically not eligible for unemployment compensation but one who is released for reasons of performance—no policy violations involved—is ordinarily eligible for unemployment compensation.

Returning to "Why Should I?"

Certainly, "Because I said so, that's why!" is not a legitimate response, and it is not surprising that it can increase hostility in the person on the receiving end of it. Even if it prompts some action, compliance will be unwilling at best. A better response might be "Because this has to be done, and it falls within your capability."

Take a close look at the individual's job description; you may be able to point to that often used but frequently forgotten clause that in one fashion or another calls for the performance of "all other tasks as directed." If no such clause is present, revise the job description to include it. A reasonable job description for a technical or professional worker cannot possibly include everything the individual might legitimately be called upon to do. If the job description must be revised, invite the employee to participate in the revision.

If she continues to balk, politely suggest that her behavior is approaching insubordination, which it will in fact become if she directly refuses to comply.

Eight Sound Disciplinary Practices

1. Make certain your employees know the rules of employment. Periodically review all pertinent rules with all staff, and include each new employee's introduction to the rules as part of new-employee orientation.
2. Do not let misconduct or misbehavior become habitual. The more ingrained such behavior becomes, the more difficult it will be to correct.
3. Do not act before acquiring factual information; never proceed on secondhand information.
4. Always reprimand and discuss disciplinary actions in private.
5. Do not play "Do as I say, not as I do." Rather, serve as a role model for conduct and behavior.
6. Use punishment only as a last resort, mindful that the primary purpose of disciplinary action is correction of behavior.
7. Use progressive discipline according to the policies of the organization.
8. At all times remain aware of your goal in delivering disciplinary action.

Disciplinary Principles for the Supervisor

In entering any situation in which disciplinary action is a possibility, you, as the supervisor, should know exactly what the unacceptable behavior is and what policy or rule has been violated:

- Any mitigating circumstances
- The scope of your authority
- How similar offenses have been handled in the past

You should assume the following:

- Employees want to do good work.
- Employees perceive some benefit from their unacceptable behavior.
- You or others may be partly to blame.
- You ordinarily have multiple corrective options available.

You must act as follows:

- Quickly once you have the needed information
- Appropriately by consulting with your superior or the human resources department
- Consistently and fairly
- By using punishment only as a last resort
- By selecting penalties appropriate for the offenses
- By documenting, documenting, documenting
- By having the dismissed employee leave the premises as soon as possible

As a supervisor, do not make the following mistakes:

- Let inappropriate behavior develop into habits
- Act before all the facts are available
- Be apologetic
- Use imprecise terminology, such as loyalty, attitude, work ethic, professionalism, or maturity
- Hide behind "management" in taking necessary action
- Trap yourself into a series of oral warnings for the same problem with the same employee

Getting Rid of "Deadweight"

First, appreciate that in the heading to this section we have committed an act that every supervisor should never do: we are *labeling*, and labeling, which is essentially stereotyping, is rarely if ever appropriate. Consider, then, that the term "deadweight" is used here as a convenience in describing those employees who have, over time, shown themselves to be chronic substandard performers.

Dismissal may be necessary because of the inability of an employee to meet minimum work standards and the failure of retraining and other corrective efforts. Every once in a while, you will encounter an employee who makes the same mistakes or commits the same infractions over and over. He or she may even feel bad about it but yet be unable to achieve long-term correction. Bad luck seems to follow these individuals, who often admit similar problems at previous jobs. We may feel for such employees, but in health care, any number of possible mistakes can jeopardize lives. Therefore, getting such people out of the organization becomes necessary.

Before recommending the dismissal of any employee, make certain that the employee has been amply warned during performance reviews and disciplinary processes and has had abundant opportunities to shore up the deficient performance or correct the offending behavior. Make certain the unsatisfactory work record is adequately documented; even a single laudatory performance appraisal may result in a legal tangle.

If you have "carried" an inadequately performing employee by giving that person satisfactory performance evaluations that were not fully earned, or if you have inherited such a person who had regularly been given undeserved satisfactory evaluations, you may find that your hands are tied for as long as it takes to build a complete case for dismissal through repeated counseling, coaching, and honest evaluations. It is unwise to simply decide that "this nonperforming so-and-so has got to go" unless there is adequate evidence to support dismissal that can stand up to possible legal challenge. In all such instances, thorough, honest documentation is essential; never make a statement representing a step along the path to dismissal unless that statement is backed up with the appropriate documentation.

Yet for some employees there will always come a time when there is no recourse other than involuntary termination of employment. If the supervisor has not done everything reasonably possible to help an individual succeed, then the individual's failure is, at least in part, the supervisor's failure. Also, you may discover that helping to salvage a single employee who might otherwise be lost can be far more satisfying than firing the so-called deadweight you may encounter.

WRAP-UP

Think About It

Delivering disciplinary action is among the most dreaded tasks faced by supervisors and managers at all levels. Doing so honestly requires courage and emotional involvement; that is, he or she who disciplines another must feel some uneasiness about performing an unpleasant task the outcome of which can affect a person's employment or career. The supervisor who believes he or she can discipline without feeling should probably not be a supervisor.

Questions for Review and Discussion

1. Provide an example of how a supervisor might positively manipulate the reward-to-risk ratio of a problem situation so as to influence employee behavior.

2. The purpose of disciplinary action has been described as correction of behavior. How is this definition served, if at all, when an employee is dismissed for one occurrence of a serious infraction?

3. In what ways do employee counseling and the delivery of an oral warning differ from each other, if at all?

4. Under what circumstances might you go back to the first steps in the disciplinary process when you may have previously advanced to the level of written warning?

5. Most progressive disciplinary systems begin with an oral warning before a written warning but proceed to recommend that oral warnings be documented. Why document an "oral" warning?

6. Why do most disciplinary systems require the supervisor to obtain—or at least try to obtain—employee signatures on disciplinary documentation?

7. Why should we differentiate between problems of conduct or behavior and problems of substandard performance when dealing with a troublesome employee?

8. Is it appropriate to advance an employee through the disciplinary process based on multiple different offenses? For example, should a written warning for discourtesy follow an oral warning for absenteeism? Why or why not?

9. Under what circumstances might the warnings in an employee's file become legal documentation? What hazards might this present for the supervisor?

10. Why is it appropriate to purge an employee's file of disciplinary documentation after some period?

Case: The Know-It-All

Imagine yourself in the position of manager of building services at Community Hospital. One of the people reporting to you is Bill Douglas, supervisor of the maintenance crew. Douglas has come to you with a complaint about Ed Wayne, one of his half-dozen employees.

Says Douglas: "I need some help figuring out how to handle Ed Wayne. I guess his work is okay—he's not the best producer, but he certainly isn't the worst—but he's got such a know-it-all attitude that drives the rest of the crew crazy. Ed's assigned to general maintenance, but he's always trying to bust out of this and do all sorts of other things. There hasn't been a job come up in months that Ed hasn't claimed to know how to do, and he's always trying to get his hands on everything new and different that comes along. The others feel that Ed is always trying to crowd in on their territory, and to make matters worse, he's constantly criticizing the others and finding fault with what they do. And he's always quick with an 'I told you so' when someone else does something that goes wrong. The others in the crew have been referring to Ed as 'the expert,' but they no longer say it kiddingly. One of the others has even asked me to count him out when it comes to teaming him up with Wayne on jobs that take two people. I tell you, I've got to do something about this guy before his behavior destroys the whole crew's morale."

Questions

1. Do you see any specific grounds for disciplinary action in the behavior of employee Ed Wayne? If so, what are these grounds?
2. Douglas' opening description of the problem refers to Wayne's "know-it-all" attitude. Can you advise Douglas to lean on Wayne concerning attitude? Why or why not?
3. In as many briefly stated steps as necessary, outline the advice you will give Bill Douglas for addressing the problem of Ed Wayne.

Case: Pleasant Dreams

Imagine yourself as night-shift charge nurse on a medical–surgical unit. For several months you have had a problem with a staff nurse whose performance you consider unsatisfactory. She seems to continually take advantage of quiet times during her shift to doze off at the nursing station. You have orally reprimanded her several times for sleeping on the job, and you have reached the point where you believe you can no longer simply scold her for her conduct. Her position, however, is that "it's no big deal," that she's always certain to hear any call signals as long as she's at the nursing station. (Your hospital has a clear policy concerning written warnings, but policy is relatively loose concerning oral warnings; these can be unlimited and issued at your discretion, so you can deliver as many as you believe necessary.)

For a written warning to become official and be entered into an employee's human resource file, it must be agreed to and countersigned by the unit's nurse manager and the director of nursing. You issued the offending nurse two written warnings, both cleared only through the unit manager. However, you believe you can go no further without backing from the director of nursing, and there has been no follow-up from that direction. Meanwhile, the employee continues to be a problem.

Questions

1. What recourses do you have in pursuing the disciplinary policy in the manner described in the case? You know the disciplinary policy lists "sleeping on the job" as an infraction.
2. Assuming that you believe the problem to be severe enough to constitute a risk to patients under your care, what can you do about the troublesome employee?

Reference

1. Kaufmann W, Borry EL, DeHart-Davis L. Can effective organizational rules keep employees from leaving? A study of green tape and turnover intention. *Public Management Review.* 2022:1–22. https://doi.org/10.1080/14719037.20 22.2026687

Cultural Diversity: Managing the Changing Workforce

CHAPTER OBJECTIVES

- Develop an appreciation for the changing composition of the American healthcare workforce and examine the implications of an employee counterpart that is increasingly ethnically, socially, and economically diverse.
- Establish cultural diversity as a vital ongoing concern of every supervisor in the healthcare organization.
- Provide examples of cultural core values that define the kinds of differences that exist between and among groups with varying backgrounds.
- Establish the necessity for congruence of corporate values and personal core values in successfully managing a diverse workforce.
- Describe the essential elements of a diversity, equity, and inclusion program.
- Address the responsibilities of supervisors in managing an increasingly diverse work group.

KEY TERMS

Diversity Management: The ways in which managers hire, supervise, use the skills of, and promote or otherwise assign and reassign employees of varied backgrounds.

Cultural Diversity: In reference to the workforce, this is the mix of persons of racial, multicultural, ethnic, and gender-oriented backgrounds, including differences in age, education, economic level, organizational tenure, and the presence or absence of disabilities.

Core Values: Those beliefs that we hold so strongly that they affect our goals, ethical decisions, and daily behavior.

A Diverse and Changing Workforce

The management of a workforce that is increasingly ethnically, socially, and economically diverse was a topic of steadily increasing concern throughout the 1990s and into the new century. Today in the early 2020s, the concern for diversity, equity, and inclusion continues to grow in health care and all industries. The implications for anyone who manages people in work groups are likely to be increasingly diverse in their composition.

Diversity management refers to the ways in which managers hire, supervise, use the skills of, and promote or otherwise assign and reassign employees of varied backgrounds. Backgrounds encountered are primarily racial, multicultural, ethnic, and gender-oriented, but diversity concerns also include differences in age, education, economic level, organizational tenure, and the presence or absence of disabilities.

The total American workforce is steadily becoming more culturally diverse across all business and industry, but in a few settings, the increasing diversity experienced is more than in health care. Service employees, such as food service workers, aides, attendants, housekeepers, and maintenance people, are often the most multiracial and culturally diverse components of a healthcare institution. Also, diversity continues to spread in the professional, technical, and managerial ranks in health care.

The people in each separate work group value their "in-group" more positively than they do any "out-groups." Management and workers have different values and attitudes and often have different political affiliations as well. Managers and professionals usually view the world differently from the nonsupervisory employees. Professionals often bond more strongly with members of their specialty or profession than they do with other people in the same organization, and their personal networks may show little overlap with others.

Appreciation of cultural differences and appropriate bonding with employees who exhibit these differences can increase the numbers of an organization's customers and job applicants. However, failure to make the necessary adjustments creates resentment, reduces morale, inhibits efficient performance, and increases turnover. Recruitment can suffer severely, and current employees may be more prone to file appeals or grievances or create other legal problems.

Cultural Core Values

Core values are those beliefs that we hold so strongly that they affect our goals, ethical decisions, and daily behavior. Cultural core beliefs and values affect on-the-job goals and day-to-day behavior.

Different cultures place different values on privacy, courtesy, respect for elders, and the work ethic. These and other values provide the basis for attitudes and behavior. Following are some examples.

In the Philippines and in Arab countries, unequal distribution of power in institutions is highly valued, and status symbols are regarded as deserved and expected. However, in Austria and Sweden, power disparities are anathema.

Many corporations in the United States and Canada adhere to policies that limit the hiring of one's relatives, labeling the practice as favoritism or nepotism. In contrast, the cultures of South Korea, Pakistan, and Taiwan view the hiring of a relative as desirable and in some instances even obligatory.

Japan, Austria, Italy, and the United States emphasize assertiveness, competitiveness, and the acquisition of money and material things. In the Netherlands and Sweden, the opposite holds true; there, nurturing and quality of life are more highly valued. Even among American workers, there are great differences in the relative importance of money. Some people never have enough, whereas others are satisfied with just getting by.

Greeks and Japanese minimize the discomfort of risk by adhering to strict laws and rituals, whereas Jamaicans and Swedes have little aversion to risk. This list could go on at considerably greater length, but the point is made. There is simply no clear set of core values that holds across all cultures.

Corporate Values

Corporate values serve as guidelines for employee behavior. Key values are often expressed in slogans such as "The customer is always right," "Quality is number one," or "We aim to please." Some slogans, however, have been so heavily overworked, thrown around casually, and are in obvious conflict with reality ("Our employees are our greatest asset!") that they fail to pass the "snicker test." (Most employees are quick to decide whether a slogan is sincere or simply a few hollow words.)

Most corporate values and ethical considerations deal with honesty, integrity, and loyalty, the foundation of a moral organizational culture. However, what each person considers ethical or unethical depends on his or her individual value system. This is essentially why ethics, supposedly so simple in concept, can become so murky in practice.

The impact of corporate values quickly dissipates when the behavior people see around them is contrary to the expressed values. This is especially true when it is the leaders who display the inappropriate behavior. The effect of corporate values also plummets when employees who violate those values are not chastised and corrected.

Employees are most impressionable when they are first hired. Most orientation programs emphasize the values that reflect the philosophy of the organization.

Corporate decisions are often based on these values. But providing a list of corporate values to new employees has little meaning unless the behavioral aspects of each value are described. Trainees understand what you mean by integrity if you tell them that when they make a mistake they must admit it and not blame someone else. Employees know better what you mean by honesty, for example, if you clearly point out that falsifying time records and patient records is grounds for severe disciplinary action up to and including discharge.

A culture takes its tone and values from its leaders. Effective leaders hold strong values and have the courage to accomplish good works despite great obstacles. They know that improper employee behavior based on faulty value systems can be modified by using the old carrot-and-stick approach. Nevertheless, they prefer to rely on modeling the kinds of behavior they want their followers to copy. Poor role models destroy corporate and personal values. A manager can articulate the importance of integrity and honesty, but the employees may recall the many times when the manager broke a promise. Another manager may claim that quality is king, but when the work piles up, he forces his staff to hurry, knowing full well they must cut corners to do so.

Personal Core Values

When corporate and personal values are consistent with each other, a team spirit is fostered, and conflicts become less frequent and easier to resolve. Productivity increases. Teamwork demands a set of values that encourages listening and responding constructively and patiently to views expressed by others. It requires team members to provide support, share knowledge, and maintain high ethical standards.

Our primary personal values concern family, career, health, and social or recreational activities. Secondary values involve recognition, quality, political affiliation, and ethical considerations. Stress occurs when our behavior does not support our values. For example, when we value our family relationships and activities but spend most of our waking hours tending to our careers, stress results and problems are likely to arise.

Some employees value friendships; other employees are loners. The relative importance of family and career also differs widely among workers. Many people are passed over for promotion because they refuse to give up time with their families, whereas others destroy their marriages because they allow their career to take precedence over family life.

Americans are reluctant to take jobs or promotions that involve uprooting and relocating their families but would relocate for the right reasons: high salary, benefits, and relocation packages. Half[1] reports that 62% of employees would relocate for their employers. Some managers cannot understand why many professional and technical employees show no interest in becoming managers—again, a matter of values.

Value Modification

Employees who hold values that conflict with corporate values must modify their personal values to some extent. Failure to make that adjustment leads to confrontations, isolation, or rejection, and ultimately to loss of employment. Employees whose core values are markedly different from those of other members of their work and social groups find it difficult to develop personal networks.

Values, like attitudes, are difficult to alter. However, behavioral modeling by managers and coworkers can gradually influence individual values. Employees are most susceptible to change when they are first hired. Trainers and managers who earn the respect and trust of trainees have a powerful impact on value modification. The best of these leaders reinforce corporate values by sharing anecdotes of successes and failures and by providing positive feedback.

Diversity Management Programs

In an ideal workplace, complete and unconditional social acceptance is based on merit. Yet even among the most open-minded individuals, stereotypes and subtle prejudices can create difficulties. Managers can seldom change opinions, but they can see to it that all workers are treated fairly. An effective diversity program helps avoid charges of discrimination and enhances creativity.

The goal of a diversity program is to create an environment that allows employees of all backgrounds to reach their full potential and work well together. The people do not all have to be friends, but they must respect each other. Ideally, employees will go beyond tolerance to a true appreciation of differences. In such a mutual adaptation paradigm, the parties accept and understand differences and fully adapt to the entire diversity mixture.

The basic strategy is simple: Change what is not working but leave other areas alone. Be certain to abide by all laws, rules, policies, and procedures. Value modification starts with a review of current practices. This review can be accomplished using focus groups or surveys. The Allstate Insurance Company surveys all its employees quarterly on how well it is meeting its commitments. It probes how well employees believe their managers are carrying out their program. Its "diversity index" determines 25% of a manager's merit bonus.[2]

There has been widespread dissatisfaction with affirmative action for just about as long as it has existed. White males have perceived it as reverse discrimination, and highly qualified members of minority groups are also unhappy with it, pointing out that they are stigmatized as people who could not have made it on their own. Essentially, a conscientious focus on diversity management holds the most promise for the future.

The assimilation approach, in which management attempts to force minorities to become similar to the majority, seldom achieves its goal. Another unsatisfactory technique is the suppression approach in which managers admit to minorities that there is a problem but that the minorities have no choice but to put up with it.

Elements of a Diversity Program

An effective diversity management program includes the following elements:

- Training programs that provide employees at all levels with the skills needed to deal with a diverse workforce
- Monitoring, with the use of periodic attitude surveys and audits, of production and attendance records
- Holding managers accountable for reaching the organization's diversity goals within their units
- Helping employees establish networks or support groups to which minority members can turn to in times of stress
- Providing equal assistance to workers who have family problems, such as childcare and elder care needs
- Maintaining communication to reinforce the organization's commitment to diversity, equity, and inclusion and to keep the workforce aware of the need to cooperate
- Making mentors available for workers who need support and advice

Diversity Awareness Training

Health maintenance organizations and malpractice insurers recognize the importance of diversity training. One medical malpractice insurer offers discounts on premiums to physicians who attend workshops addressing cultural differences.[3]

Diversity awareness training is adapted to the culture of the organization. It can vary from a one-time session to a series of training exercises. If people have had limited contact with cultural differences in the past, they feel uncomfortable when faced with them. It is up to each employee to appreciate and value these differences and not to expect that minority customers and employees want to blend in with the mainstream culture. Most employees prefer to maintain their cultural identity while functioning effectively in the work environment.

In these programs workers learn about anti-discrimination laws, cross-cultural communication, respect, and bias. Useful techniques include role playing, videos, and discussions. The training emphasizes the importance of language or dialect, an extremely important cultural variable. For example, a Filipino patient is likely to view caregivers as authority figures and thus remain quiet and subdued in their presence. Also, people from certain Asian and other cultures are reluctant to admit they do not understand instructions; they are concerned that saying they do not understand might be taken as an insult to your teaching ability. Therefore, you must ask them questions to ensure they comprehend what you have said.

Body language is equally important. For example, Native Americans and some Asians avoid eye contact when conversing. In the United States, when you hold up your hand with thumb and forefinger together, you mean "OK." In France, it means you are a zero. In Japan it is a request for some change. In some countries it is an obscene gesture. The "V" gesture in the United States means "victory," but in Australia it is the "middle-finger salute."

Diversity training without follow-up and institutional support is incomplete. Trainers have little or no authority for follow-up or backup outside the training room.

Supervisor Responsibilities

Upper management can use surveys to detect cultural problems, but it is up to supervisors to make diversity programs work. Supervisors, those managers closest to nonsupervisory employees, are able to check for tensions that may be disrupting harmony or interfering with productivity. They implement the provisions of any diversity program.

Experienced supervisors know that corporate values mean little to employees unless they are explained in behavioral terms. New supervisors quickly learn that the things they value are not always the same things that many of their employee's value. Supervisors are more likely to enjoy challenges, interesting work, recognition, and the sense of having control. Many of their employees may only want to do their routine work and go home.

Karp[4] warns against reinforcing the role of victim of prejudice or discrimination. Victims focus on their pain and weakness. When this occurs during a training program, "suffering contests" may emerge among subgroups in which each group tries to prove that it has suffered the most. People leave these meetings feeling more vulnerable and abused than before they arrived.

Organizations must develop programs that reinforce the role of survivor of discrimination. This strengthens the individual. Ask employees how it felt and what they did to overcome discrimination. This reinforces individual responsibility for taking care of oneself.

Diversity Management Tips for Supervisors

- Remain alert to your own assumptions and those of others.
- Do not allow unfair assumptions to go unchallenged.
- Help new employees feel more comfortable by discussing any unwritten rules and practices. These may include appearance, acceptable language, how to disagree or complain, and how to ask for help from others.
- Discuss the importance of cultural diversity at orientation sessions and at staff meetings.
- Do not tell people they should not feel the way they do when they feel mistreated but do make it safe for them to have and to express those feelings.

- Challenge stereotypes and assumptions about minority groups. Avoid terms like "yuppie" (young, upwardly mobile professional), "old," "subordinate," "honey," and "girl."
- Become more knowledgeable about the religious, family, and food customs of the people with whom you work. Tactfully ask someone from that national culture after establishing appropriate rapport.
- Use humor carefully, always avoiding ethnic, sexist, or stereotypical jokes.
- Be familiar with your organization's policy on sexual harassment and observe this policy to the letter.
- Involve representatives of all minority groups in the decision-making process.
- Allow minorities to wear their ethnic clothes or hairstyles.
- Encourage all employees to get to know the people around them who are different. By embracing differences, we can all make a difference.

Generational Diversity

Often bearing little relationship to race, ethnicity, or cultures imported from other lands, diversity stemming from generational differences presents many of today's healthcare supervisors with some particular problems and challenges. A "generation" consists of people within a roughly defined age range who were born into the same period of history and culture. There are no clear dividing lines between generations; there are, however, numerous differences both real and perceived between and among generations. Some of these differences mean that some employees will be more difficult to manage than others or at least will have to be managed differently.

Once employed, workers born and educated through the 1930s and during World War II, most of whom have long since passed through the workforce, tended to remain with their employers for as long as their employers were viable and would have them. These workers tended toward organizational loyalty and held the need to work and produce in high regard. For many of them,

the job came before other concerns except perhaps family. They were dependable.

Then followed the so-named baby boomer generation, those born in the birth rate spike that followed World War II and lasted until about 1964. As teenagers and young adults many of the baby boomers went through the turbulent 1960s involved in peace movements and protests for civil rights. As a result, many of this generation display less faith in authority than their predecessors. However, idealism and unselfishness rank high with many boomers; this is especially evident in health care, where many regard their work as a moral obligation, often arriving early and staying late, loyal to employer and colleagues.

The baby boomers were followed by "Generation X," born during the second half of the 1960s and through the 1970s. Many in this generation saw their own parents working hard to succeed educationally, occupationally, and economically, and many follow their parents' examples. Many in this generation, however, are not quite as willing as their parents to offer employers their undying loyalty. Rather, they seek occupations that afford a balance between work and private life. By and large they are loyal to employers and colleagues as long as this loyalty is recognized, appreciated, and rewarded. For the most part they are willing to change employers much more readily than their parents were.

"Generation Y" (also known as the millennials) consists of those born from about 1980 through about 1996. Quite different from the previous generations, they are sometimes difficult to understand and difficult to manage. Although they may be career-minded, they do not care to sacrifice themselves to a profession or occupation. They challenge authority and are sometimes in conflict with those who manage them. They are generally less loyal to an organization than the preceding generations and will readily change employers. They consider an occupation or profession to be a relatively small part of life; private lives are more important to them.

"Generation Z" consists of those born from about 1997 through about 2012. This generation is concerned for their well-being in the workforce.

They are creative, and diversity is a cause for them. They have a desire to speak up for what is important. They are generally less loyal to an organization if they do not feel valued or heard.

"Generation Alpha" consists of those born after 2012 and who have yet to enter the workforce.

Diminishing organizational loyalty is especially evident among healthcare workers who are well educated and qualified in the allied health professions. Many healthcare professionals demonstrate stronger loyalty to profession than to organization, giving rise to the "free agent" phenomenon; when they are in demand, they are generally willing to change organizations for a "better deal." And the attraction of the opportunity to grow professionally is often a much stronger pull than loyalty to any one organization.

It is necessary to advise caution about "labeling," by mentally assigning anyone to a specific generation. Rather, the foregoing comments about generalized generational differences should serve only to remind us that the values most reflected by individual employees often vary with age and the generation that formed them and that these differences among people often dictate the supervisor's approach to managing these people. As the supervisor must be sensitive to the cultural differences accompanying race and ethnicity and such, so must the supervisor be sensitive to the generational differences to be encountered in the workforce.

The Aging Workforce

More or less a subset of generational diversity is consideration of the aging workforce. Age discrimination exists in both the employed workforce and the pool of individuals seeking employment. Because the total workforce, both the employed and the employable, is steadily aging, any consideration of generational diversity must also address the effects of age in the mix.

Unfortunately, age discrimination is alive and operating in most areas of American business. It potentially affects all mature workers. It is sometimes a problem for workers who have been steadily employed at the same jobs, those mature employees who find themselves pushed out for a variety of "other" reasons. And it is an even greater problem for those who seek to change jobs or find new employment following layoff or retirement.

Age discrimination flourishes in spite of legal prohibitions. Charges of age discrimination continue to grow as more and more baby boomers age out. Most laws dealing with employment have their weaknesses, but most of the age problem lies not with legislation. Rather, most of the problem resides in the attitudes of employers toward mature workers. Many employers automatically see mature workers as less productive and costlier than others to keep on the payroll. Yet it has been demonstrated repeatedly that mature workers are absent less frequently than younger workers, and that mature workers are less likely to contribute to rapid turnover.

Much is said these days about opportunity for mature workers, how their capabilities are not only valuable but needed. In practice, however, many see this as a good news-bad news situation, with the good news being that numbers of jobs are there, at least in some areas, but the bad news being that most of the jobs truly available to mature workers are essentially entry-level and largely part time.

The COVID-19 pandemic did not help with the shortage of healthcare professionals, specifically nurses. During the pandemic, the aging workforce was asked to come back to lend a helping hand. Today, the nursing shortage is still very much a problem, and the nurses who could not find work before the pandemic are being welcomed back with open arms in some instances.

As significantly increasing numbers of baby boomers age into their 60s, they may well discover that "ageism" is not only real but strongly entrenched as well.

Advancement for Women

We continue to hear much about the "glass ceiling" and the "old boy network" and the fact that females are still earning less than males for the same kinds of work. Although it remains true that women occupy fewer offices in the executive suites, their numbers are increasing in top management, and they fill many middle hierarchical slots as well as the majority of supervisory positions in hospitals. Take notice also of the increasing number of women in charge of nursing homes and home-care programs. Also, women are highly active in professional societies and increasingly serve as officers in these organizations. For the most part, doors of opportunity for women in healthcare institutions are wide open. Women who sincerely seek leadership roles often find the so-called glass ceiling to be less confining in health care than in many other industries.

It is interesting to note that the Equal Pay Act of 1963 accomplished little, and that this issue still remains an active concern. Women in health care are advancing in upper management position, but equal pay to men is still an issue.

More recently, men have complained that they are excluded from some informal networks in healthcare institutions. Others believe that female managers show favoritism toward female employees.

WRAP-UP

Think About It

Why value diversity? Because it is the right thing to do! Essentially, we have no choice in the face of a changing population. The demands of the marketplace and the unavoidable competition for skills and talents demand that the ability to do a particular job be the overriding criterion in employee recruitment. The supervisor has always had to deal with differences between and among employees, and the changing composition of the workforce does no more than add some additional differences to the mix.

Questions for Review and Discussion

1. What do you believe to be the strongest factors in ensuring that a diversity initiative is taken seriously throughout the organization? Why?

2. Supervisors can ensure equal treatment of employees. How can we respond to cultural differences among employees in a group without treating some differently from others?

3. What might need to be done with the organization's employment policies to accommodate workforce diversity? Provide an example.

4. Describe one of the possibly significant risks embodied in a supervisor's lack of sensitivity to diversity issues.

5. Provide at least two reasons why we can state that the total workforce in health care is more culturally diverse than other industries.

6. Describe a situation in which the stated values of an organization are in apparent conflict with the values in management behavior.

7. Explain why it is likely that personal values are difficult to alter and describe how doing so might be accomplished.

8. Describe several of the kinds of legal action that can arise from issues of workforce diversity.

9. Who is likely to be key in ensuring organizational support for a diversity initiative, and to whom will most of the implementation activity belong?

10. Provide an example or two about how assumptions about people can lead a supervisor into difficulty.

Exercise: Your Departmental Diversity Program

Assume you have spent several years as a health information management (HIM) supervisor in a relatively small hospital. Your staff of five—four people plus you—consisted of four white women and one Asian woman. Your group had been together for several years.

Your hospital recently merged with a considerably larger institution located a few miles away. The other hospital is sufficiently larger, but in spite of the frequent use of the term "merger," the prevailing opinion in both organizations is that it is more a matter of the larger absorbing the smaller.

One of the first major changes to occur was the combining of parallel departments under a single supervisor; that is, where before each hospital had a manager of HIM, the new scheme calls for one manager to supervise the HIM groups in both facilities. For perhaps 75% or more of hospital functions, the department manager in the larger institution became manager of the combined department, but in this case the expanded management role fell to you. The HIM manager in the larger institution elected to take early retirement rather than manage the combined function.

Now you have acquired, counting full-time and part-time employees, 12 more employees to manage. The composition of the acquired group is four African Americans, three Hispanics, one Asian, and one Native American. There are three whites, with one of these being the lone male in your newly constituted department. Your initial observations of the expanded department cause you to conclude that you have a great deal of work to do in bringing these groups together as an effectively functioning unit and securing your acceptance by the employees.

Instructions

Create an outline of the steps you believe you would consider taking to make your transition to your new role as smooth as possible. Your steps should include consideration of what to look for in familiarizing yourself with the department and what actions you should consider, depending on what you learn. Throughout this process, keep in mind the need to respect each person as a unique individual with unique needs and a cultural background that may differ from yours while also remaining aware of the need for equity and consistency in dealing with employees. (Hint: Based on what you learn in the early weeks of your new assignment, your response to the instruction could be anywhere from swift and simple to overwhelmingly complex.)

Case: Opposing Forces

Helen Wilson was hired from outside the hospital to be the new business office manager. She accepted the job, even after hearing that it was something of a hot seat; she would be the fifth person in the position in barely 3 years.

Although Helen did not know reasons for the short stays of her predecessors, it took her very little time to decide that the atmosphere in the department was definitely unhealthy. Her staff appeared to be split among several groups, each of which was clearly at odds with one or more of the others. The groups were divided along the lines of race and national origin, and the members of each group tended to cluster together while working, hang together during lunch and breaks, and in general behave as though each was a small subdepartment within the larger entity.

From her first day on the job, it was apparent to Helen that many of the department's problems were a result of communications barriers among groups. She tried scheduling departmental staff meetings for the purpose of improving communication, but each such gathering found her frustrated because she could barely get any of the groups to speak with her, let alone talk with the other groups.

After one particularly frustrating meeting Helen was approached by a person who appeared to be an informal leader of the department's largest group. She said to Helen, "You'll never get anything done this way. There's lots of distrust in the department, and the only way you're going to accomplish anything is to meet with each group separately."

Questions

1. Would you advise Helen to meet with each group separately, as suggested? Why or why not?
2. How do you suggest that Helen begin an effort to disband the "opposing forces"?
3. Offer a few suggestions for Helen to consider in working with her toxic, divided department over the coming weeks and months.

References

1. Half R. 62 percent of workers would relocate for a job, survey finds. Cision Web site. https://www.prnewswire.com /news-releases/62-percent-of-workers-would-relocate-for -a-job-survey-finds-300777953.html. Published January 15, 2019.
2. Wynter LE. Allstate rates managers on handling diversity. *Wall Street Journal.* 1997; October 1,B1.
3. Anders G. Doctors learn to bridge cultural gaps. *Wall Street Journal.* 1997; September 4,B1.
4. Karp BB. Choices in diversity training. *Training.* 1994;31(8):73, 74.

CHAPTER 19

Conflict and Confrontation

CHAPTER OBJECTIVES

- Identify conflict and confrontation as unavoidable dimensions of communication that can be destructive or constructive depending on how they are used or addressed.
- Identify the primary causes of conflict in the work setting.
- Establish an appreciation of the dangers inherent in escalating or suppressing conflict.
- Present several fundamental working strategies for addressing conflict in the work setting.
- Provide guidelines for the supervisor's constructive use of confrontation in managing an employee group.

KEY TERMS

Conflict: In the context of the healthcare organization, conflict is best described as the clashing or variance of opposing principles, beliefs, or ideas; that is, the presence of two or more diverging opinions on the same subject or two or more potential solutions to the same problem; a disagreement.

Confrontation: Broadly defined as the action of bringing things together for comparison; specifically, facing another person with whom one disagrees in an effort to achieve resolution or effect compromise.

Conflict and the Healthcare Organization

Beginning in the early-to-middle twentieth century and culminating with the introduction of government control over several aspects of health care, most of health care was seen as a work setting free from stress. But times changed. No longer is health care the stress-free environment it was once perceived to be. Now, the workplaces of healthcare providers are riddled with tension, and there are no signs of this changing in the foreseeable future. If anything, tension,

and conflict continue to intensify. Conflicts arise from pressure-cooker deadlines, increased workloads, escalating financial pressure, mounting fear of layoffs, and relentless pressure to increase productivity and maintain quality while consuming fewer resources. Conflicts are inevitable in today's healthcare organization, and for the individual supervisor, they are an unavoidable part of the job.

Disagreements can be healthy as long as they culminate in positive solutions that prevent serious mistakes or inappropriate actions, force second looks at questionable situations, and lead to solutions or improvement. When resolved, disputes can foster improved relationships.

Some dysfunctional work groups operate in a manner that suppresses conflict. However, suppressed conflict festers and eventually disrupts working relationships. These festering feelings can then be transferred to the home environment.[1] Some conflicts become highly adversarial, characterized by anger, hostility, humiliation, or resentment.

Principal Causes of Conflict

The etiology of any particular conflict is not always apparent. Often, there is a covert issue camouflaged by a less important overt factor; that is, a highly visible symptom obscures a true causal problem. Some conflict situations are simply murky because multiple causes are involved, rendering the central conflict difficult to identify and address.

Unclear Expectations or Guidelines

Employees sometimes do not know what they are supposed to do, how to do what is expected of them, or what outcomes they should achieve.

Policies and rules are often ambiguous. For example, a policy forbidding sexual harassment may not clearly or fully explain exactly what constitutes sexual harassment and how it is to be recognized and addressed.

Poor Communication

Conflicts attributed to ill will between and among individuals are frequently the result of communication short-circuits, especially poor listening and, often, hastily scribbled memos or unclear email messages. Faulty perceptions or assumptions cause misunderstandings. Everyone can cite personal examples of hurt feelings and damaged relationships that resulted from distortions or half-truths.

Lack of Clear Jurisdiction

When the limits of power and authority are not clearly defined, disputes erupt. Conflicts can readily arise over funds, space, time, or equipment. Disagreements involving work and vacation schedules are common.

Differences in Temperaments or Attitudes

Incompatibilities or disagreements based on differences in temperament or attitudes are often complex conflict situations that are frequently influenced by differences of race, religion, nationality, age, politics, ethics, and values. For example, nurses and physicians may disagree about how to deal with dying patients.

Individual or Group Conflicts of Interest

There can be chronic friction or long-standing differences between departments or shifts. Consider, for example, disagreements between a purchasing department charged with serving all departments with limited financial resources and a unit manager who clamors for special consideration. When the perceived objectives of such groups or individuals appear inconsistent with each other, the grounds for conflict are present.

Operational or Staffing Changes

Whenever organizational or functional changes are introduced, conflicts are bound to arise. Some of the most troublesome conflicts encountered in business are those arising because of resistance to change (see chapter entitled "Change as a Way of Life").

Dangers of Escalating or Suppressing Conflict

Conflict that is unaddressed or suppressed simply worsens. When unaddressed, conflict is essentially being allowed to escalate. No undesirable situation can be ignored in the hope that it will vanish on its own; rather, left to itself it will invariably worsen. When conflict escalates, the involved parties become impatient, angry, or frustrated, and their attention is diverted from problem-solving to attacking the other people who are involved. Blame and threats fly back and forth, and issues multiply. Old grievances come forth to compound the situation, and more often than not, relationships are damaged. Bitterness leads to thoughts of how to get even rather than how to solve the initial problem. Eventually, the parties may enlist supporters from among bystanders, resulting in the formation of opposing cliques.

When deliberate efforts are made to suppress conflict rather than deal with it, the results usually include chronic complaining, declining productivity, increased absenteeism, decreased morale and loyalty, and increased stress. In a number of worst-case scenarios, serious conflict forcibly suppressed can result in violence or sabotage.

Fundamental Strategies for Coping with Conflict

Each of the following strategies is appropriate for certain situations. Face your next conflict by selecting the most appropriate strategy.

Avoidance

Conflict avoidance may involve denying there is a problem, physically escaping the arena of the conflict, passing the buck, or procrastinating. The problem remains unresolved, and as in the suppression of conflict, the result is usually a buildup of anger that eventually explodes. Avoidance can also be an escape mechanism. For example, when you are challenged by someone in the presence of your manager, you turn to your manager and say emphatically, "I want to respond to that, but not here and now. I'll do that at the next staff meeting."

Avoidance may be appropriate under the following circumstances:

- The problem is not your problem.
- There is nothing you can do about it.
- It is inconsequential and, thus, not worth the effort to face.
- You need additional information.
- One of you is emotionally upset.
- The disruption possible from addressing the conflict outweighs the benefits of resolution.
- You can see that the situation will ameliorate if you can wait it out.

Fight

There is often the temptation to fight, but this approach has pitfalls. First, you can lose. Even if you win a disagreement, your opponents may regroup and return to the fray or wait for another opportunity to retaliate; they may become saboteurs. Fight when quick action is necessary (for example, when someone is violating an important safety regulation). Fighting is also appropriate when you observe severe ethical or legal violations.

Surrender

Nonassertive individuals often succumb to this response, thus building up internal frustration as self-esteem erodes. Nonassertive or passive individuals tend to attract conflict. However, surrender may be appropriate under the following circumstances:

- You know the other party is right.
- You have no stake in the issue; it does not matter to you.
- Your chance of winning is miniscule.
- Harmony and stability, especially important, can be achieved.
- Giving in on a minor item now can mean winning a more important one later.

Compromise

Contrary to the communications exhibited by some strong-willed but perhaps narrowly focused individuals, compromise is not a dirty word. Rarely will a person who enters a conflict situation solely dedicated to one viewpoint going to succeed in getting everything that he or she desires. Compromise is a partial-win strategy that you must settle for on occasion. Compromise allows all parties to get part of what they want, so there is some satisfaction for all. Most management disputes are settled in this manner. On the perceived negative side of compromise, neither group gets everything it wants. In addition, compromise may involve a certain amount of game playing, with each side pumping up its demands or disguising them; this is at the heart of many union contract negotiations—both sides may go in asking for more than they know they can obtain and knowing they will eventually "meet in the middle." The most frequent mistake made concerning compromise is to adopt this alternative prematurely, without first making a serious effort at collaboration. Compromise may be appropriate under the following circumstances:

- Opposing goals are incompatible, so neither side can realistically expect complete victory.
- A temporary settlement to complex issues is called for.
- Time constraints dictate the need for an expedient solution.
- Discussions have stalled.

Collaboration

The basis for collaboration is established when disputing parties attack the problems rather than each other. Problems are resolved through honest and open discussion. Collaboration builds healthy relationships. It uncovers more information, challenges false assumptions or perceptions, and promotes improved understanding. It leads to better decisions.

This true win–win approach is usually the best alternative, but it customarily requires more creative solutions. The best answer is often one that neither side had originally considered. An added benefit of this approach is that it builds positive relationships. This strategy is usually the most appropriate one, especially when the issue is too important to be settled any other way or when you must achieve a consensus.

However, the collaborative approach has negative aspects. Additional time may be required, so decisions may have to be delayed. The parties may become frustrated when no consensus is reached. Although more time is spent seeking a solution, the overall time may be much less because there is less haggling or involvement inside issues. Angry participants can prolong arguments, so it is sometimes necessary to call additional meetings to permit tempers to cool.

Confrontation and the Supervisor

Ready, Set ...

First, consider the view of many individuals of the term "confrontation." When they think of confrontation, many persons think first of an interchange that inevitably involves anger. To that extent, confrontation carries a negative connotation for some people. A confrontation can of course involve anger, especially if the confronting party has not thought through the situation, but no potentially useful confrontation is best initiated in anger. In the context of the supervisor's role, "confront" simply means to face a situation or an individual directly.

No individual can long survive in a supervisory role by avoiding confrontation. Whether with employees, peers, or others, the supervisor must confront problems, issues, or disagreements on a daily basis. Many of a supervisor's daily confrontations will not be overly dramatic, but they will nevertheless require a degree of assertiveness on the part of the supervisor.

In preparing to enter a confrontational situation, ask yourself the following questions:

- What do I want to accomplish?
- What is the most I will give up?
- What do I believe the other person wants? Does he or she have covert goals?
- What false assumptions or incorrect perceptions might the other party hold?
- Which strategy should I apply?
- What are my "hot buttons," and what should I do if they are pushed?
- If I plan to use a collaborative approach, what special precautions should I take?

Get psyched up for confrontation with the following three techniques:

1. *Practice success imagery.* Visualize a successful confrontation. Picture your body language, hear your words and vocal tone, and envision a successful outcome. Athletes and professional speakers have used this technique with great success.

2. *Adjust your self-talk.* This is a process of converting negative thoughts to positive ones when talking to yourself. All of us carry on a constant inner dialogue with ourselves. When we are in passive mode, these internal conversations are often negative and pessimistic: Our subconscious mind conjures up statements such as "I could never say that" or "She'll just blow me away." Let your positive affirmations take control. Say to yourself, "I'll be in control." Avoid weak statements such as "I'm going to try to stand up to her next time."

3. *Rehearse.* After you have selected your dialogue and its appropriate body language, rehearse the anticipated encounter. Do this over and over. Consider doing it in front of a mirror and speaking out loud. Still better, get someone to role play with you. Do not be satisfied until you have your performance down pat.

... Confront

Confrontations are seldom as bad as anticipated, especially when you go into them thoroughly prepared. Here are some practical suggestions for achieving a collaborative confrontation:

- Avoid sitting across a desk or table from the person; this invites opposition. Sit next to each other. Even better, take a stroll side by side.
- Open the discussion by saying something like "Let's see how we can solve this in a way that satisfies both of us."
- After outlining the problem, move on to areas of agreement. To do this, start with questions you are certain will be answered affirmatively. It is then easier to get a yes to more controversial questions that come later. For example, "Don't you agree that we must put team goals before our individual agendas?"
- Listen attentively, asking pertinent questions and keying in on what the other person is saying. Be empathetic. Respect the other person's feelings, but still feel free to respond forcibly.

- It often pays to ask the person what he or she wants. You may be pleasantly surprised to find that what is wanted is less than you were prepared to offer. On the other hand, do not neglect to say what it is that *you* want.
- Let the person know that you hear and understand both the content of what is said and the feelings with which it is said. Validate feelings with something like "As I understand it, you're angry because I asked one of your assistants to give me a hand with my project. Is that right?" Validating has two benefits: It clarifies the problem and lets the person know that what he or she is saying is important.
- Use the person's name frequently. Our own names are the sweetest sounds we humans hear.
- Seek a larger pie instead of dividing up the existing pie. This means finding something more for both of you, a win–win solution.
- Emphasize your inability to change the past and affirm that you want to focus on the present and future.
- Stay cool and avoid rhetorical or emotional escalation. When people become upset, they generally exaggerate. This increases anxiety and makes it more difficult to solve the problem. When forced into a corner, say, "I find myself getting upset. Let's take a 10-minute break, okay?"
- Let the other party save face. He or she should come away with something.

And to Confront More Effectively ...

- Be prepared, just as you would be for a debate.
- Choose the best time and place. Do not meet when your self-esteem is low or when either of you is upset.
- Regard the other person not as an enemy but as a partner in problem-solving.
- Clarify the other person's viewpoint as well as your own. Do not proceed further until these viewpoints and the desired outcomes are clear.
- Focus first on a point of agreement, then work from there.

- Be assertive, not aggressive. Use "I" statements (for example, "I get concerned when people approach me like this"). Use non-confrontational phrases such as "Help me understand why …."
- Attack the problem or the behavior and its results, never the other person. Disagree without being disagreeable or trying to prove that the person is wrong.
- Do not cause your opponent to lose face. Do not threaten or issue ultimatums.
- Do not be sarcastic or critical.
- Avoid using the word "you." It is frequently followed by an attack on the person's ego.
- To avoid retaliation, use the straw man technique; that is, set up hypothetical but parallel situations to address.
- Be aware of your body language. Maintain eye contact, sit or stand up straight, and appear relaxed. Do not fidget or squirm. Avoid threatening gestures such as finger pointing, fist making, crossed arms, hands on hips, or scowling. Smile when you agree; remain expressionless when you disagree.
- Control your voice. Keep its volume, pitch, and rate under control. Stop if you find it growing louder, faster, or high pitched.
- Be diplomatic and tentative when facing firm resistance. Use words such as "maybe," "perhaps," or "you may be right."
- When you are cornered or upset, escape by pleading stress.
- Do not get stuck believing your solution is the only workable one. Simply focus on the benefits of your point of view.
- Promise realistic rewards that you can deliver ("If you will …, then I will ….").
- End on a positive note.

When the Person You Are Confronting Is Angry

It goes without saying that we sometimes provoke anger in others when we criticize, pressure, threaten, deny, irritate, deride, or, in short, do anything that can be perceived as attacking self-esteem. Almost anyone can be provoked to anger if the stimulus is sufficiently intense. However, people differ from each other in terms of their anger threshold. Some associates are overly sensitive; they may exhibit explosive tempers on short fuses. Some people use anger because they have learned through personal experience that it enables them to avoid unpleasant assignments. Sensitive individuals take everything personally; they quickly and angrily charge favoritism or discrimination. Your children are probably already experts at this.

Some people use anger as a defense mechanism, exhibiting anger in defense of viewpoints or positions that they believe, perhaps unconsciously, to be weak, flawed, or incorrect. Anger often provides the shield that holds off further attack.

Guidelines for Coping with an Angry Person

- Never lose your cool. Never shout or even raise your voice. Avoid any threatening gestures or aggressive body language. Never touch the person. When you are angry, say nothing until your emotions are under control.
- Make no comments about the other person's anger or tell him or her not to be angry ("Why don't you calm down?").
- Do not patronize or lecture.
- When a person approaches you and you sense that he or she is angry, greet the individual as a friend. In most instances the person who speaks first sets the mood for the conversation to follow.
- Ask questions. The person who asks the most pertinent questions controls the agenda and the overall direction of the exchange. The key question is, "What do you want me to do?" Find out exactly what he or she wants and satisfy that want if possible. If you cannot satisfy it, offer your solution.
- Listen to the person's outbursts without interrupting. Doing so can have a powerful calming effect. The person who listens best usually comes out a winner.
- Make certain you understand the problem.
- Avoid becoming defensive or argumentative.

- Empathize by paraphrasing what you believe the person is angry about and why he or she feels that way.
- Assure the person that something will be done, if at all possible.

Negotiation, mediation, and arbitration are special forms of conflict handling discussed in the chapter entitled "Spoken Communication."

WRAP-UP

Think About It

Occasionally, a certain degree of righteous anger can be effective in resolving some difficulty, but for the most part, anger is destructive in interpersonal communication. As the level of anger in an interpersonal exchange increase, the chances of effective communication taking place decrease accordingly.

Questions for Review and Discussion

1. Why can we claim that conflict often produces growth and progress?
2. Provide two specific examples of how the interaction between departments or groups can automatically provoke conflict.
3. Describe in detail one specific instance of conflict where avoidance might be the appropriate response.
4. Explain why so many individuals in the work environment seem to go out of their way to avoid confrontation.
5. As a supervisor, how are you going to respond when an employee angrily confronts you concerning a mandate handed down by top management?
6. Describe a confrontational situation in which an individual's words seem to be conveying a message opposite from that
conveyed by the person's body language. How can you go about determining which is the real message?
7. In some areas, compromise tends to be regarded as an undesirable condition to be avoided. Why might this be so, and what is wrong with this stance?
8. Why might we say that sometimes the best immediate reaction to confrontation by an angry person is to shut down and walk away?
9. Explain in some detail the risks in continually suppressing conflict for the sake of peace and quiet.
10. Why should we want to avoid criticizing another's anger with statements such as "You shouldn't feel that way" or "You have no cause for anger"?

Case: Addressing the Squeaky Wheel

You are the supervisor of 20 people in a department of one of Central Hospital's service departments. Three of your employees are titled as working group leaders, but they are usually involved in doing the work of the department rather than overseeing others. The busiest of these, a group leader named Sally, is expected to spend 60% of her time on regular work and 40% supervising.

Several times in recent months Sally has mentioned that her group's backlog was growing and that she needed more help. She has never been more specific than saying more help was needed, and her gripes seemed to have been no more than passing remarks offered without preparation or forethought. You have been under pressure from a number of directions, and Sally's complaints seemed to represent no more than chronic grumbling, so you have not felt compelled to add her concerns to your list of worries.

But today, Monday, first thing after starting time, Sally sought you out and confronted you with "I need one more full-time person, and I need her now! I'm tired of waiting and tired of being ignored, and I'm sick of being overworked and taken for granted. If something isn't done about it by Friday, I'm out of here and you can find yourself another sucker."

Instructions
1. Describe how you will initially address Sally's outburst.
2. Propose two or three possible solutions to the problem and describe the potential advantages and disadvantages of each.
3. The situation places you in something of a trap. Describe this trap, explain why it is one, and explain how you might proceed toward a solution.

Case: The Artful Dodger

Janet had considerable difficulty developing the schedule for her nursing unit for the coming 2 weeks. The nursing department was in a marginal position overall as far as available nurses were concerned, so her flexibility was limited. To make matters worse, within an hour after Janet developed the new schedule, a part-time licensed practical nurse named Bonnie turned in a request for a personal day on one of the days she was scheduled to work.

The request caused Janet to realize that she had been seeing Bonnie's name in connection with scheduling difficulties often in recent months. Looking back over the preceding 6 months of schedules, she discovered that the current request was the fifth time in 6 months that Bonnie had requested time off on a scheduled weekend day. Even more significant was the pattern of Bonnie's use of sick time. She had called in sick four times, all of these on Saturdays or Sundays. All in all, Bonnie had worked only about half of the weekend days she was scheduled to work over a period of 6 months.

Janet was displeased with Bonnie's attendance and unhappy with herself for not discovering the problem sooner. She believed she had to confront Bonnie about the problem, but she also believed her unit could not afford to lose a nurse when replacements were so scarce. Nevertheless, she believed she could not allow Bonnie's attendance pattern to continue.

Questions
1. What are the hazards Janet faces in (a) dealing firmly with Bonnie's behavior and (b) ignoring Bonnie's absences and saying nothing?
2. Assuming Janet decides to confront Bonnie, how should she go about doing so?

Reference

1. Raja U, Javed Y, Abbas M. A time lagged study of burnout as a mediator in the relationship between workplace bullying and work–family conflict. *Int J Stress Manag.* 2018; 25(4):377–390. https://doi.org/10.1037/str0000080

CHAPTER 20

Employees with Problems

CHAPTER OBJECTIVES

- Provide the supervisor with the means of identifying employees whose performance problems could suggest underlying personal problems.
- Address the commonly experienced problem of absenteeism and suggest how the supervisor can constructively deal with chronic absenteeism among staff members.
- Explore the relationship between personal problems and particular behaviors exhibited on the job.
- Recommend procedures for the supervisor to apply in addressing performance problems that relate to employees' personal difficulties.

KEY TERMS

Marginal Performer: An employee who does enough to "just get by"; that is, one who meets but does not exceed the minimum requirements of the job.

Employee Assistant Program (EAP): An employer-sponsored program providing a confidential referral to sources of counseling or other assistance for employees experiencing problems affecting their work performance.

The Marginal Performer

The marginal performer is often one of the greatest sources of frustration for the supervisor. This is so because the supervisor may believe an employee to be capable of better performance, perhaps even outstanding performance, but there seems to be no way to get the person to perform to his or her potential. Some marginal performers are that way because they are capable of little more, but many marginal performers have the ability to perform better but for various reasons are not motivated to do so.

Among the marginal performers who could do better if they so wished are employees who are just putting in their time until retirement and those who regard their present jobs as interim employment before moving on to what they really want. Others just lack motivation for a variety of reasons. The first step in dealing with these people is to get to know them better and, if possible, find their motivational buttons and discover what would encourage them to willingly achieve.

Ask yourself these questions about your marginal performers:

- Are they simply bored with their jobs? If this is so, consider actions such as job enrichment, cross-training, special projects, committee assignments, teaching responsibilities, job rotation, or participation in research; in general, consider anything that can be done to relieve boredom and stimulate renewed interest in the job.
- Are their social needs being met? Do they prefer to work alone or as part of a group? How do they get along with their peers? Might it be possible to move these employees around so that they work with or around different people?
- If possible, consider transferring marginal performers to faster moving, more energetic groups or assigning them individual work according to their preferences.
- Are their ego needs being met? Do they seem to be getting the attention and respect they believe they deserve? And are you making a special effort to provide this attention and respect? Maybe simple status symbols would help, perhaps a change in title, a bigger desk, or a personalized nameplate. As possible, provide more recognition.

Never accept unsatisfactory performance. Do not reward poor productivity by transferring some of the work of these employees to the better performers. Do not give satisfactory performance ratings to undeserving employees. At one time or another, most experienced supervisors have made that mistake and have ultimately regretted it, especially later when "good" evaluations in their file severely complicate an attempt to discharge an employee.

Be especially careful about using marginal employees for orienting and training new employees. A poor attitude can be contagious, as can an attitude toward the work that suggests "just getting by" is enough. Use your very best producers for new-employee orientation and training.

The Mature Employee

Most experienced employees are excellent workers who can and often do run rings around their younger coworkers. However, some mature workers lose their spark, allow their expertise to become obsolete, and become unwilling to learn new skills. They may adjust poorly to organizational and procedural changes. The following may be helpful in dealing with mature employees:

- Acknowledge their experience by seeking their advice.
- Use them as mentors or involve them in orienting new employees or in providing on-the-job training (select who and what carefully).
- Explain the need for change; get them involved and give them additional training if needed.
- Encourage them to attend professional meetings.
- If they are winding down toward retirement, approve their occasional requests for time off without pay. Hire part-timers to fill the gaps, if necessary, rather than overload their coworkers while they are away.
- Listen to their plans for retirement. Be happy for them.

Goof-Offs

The goof-offs have poor attendance records. They are all great excuse makers. They always have rational-sounding excuses that invite sympathy (for example, "My wife is sick again," "My son is in trouble with the law," or "My car keeps breaking down"). They waste their time and often the time of others.

Do not allow the goof-offs to trap you into supporting their self-pity or debating the merits of their excuses. Administer sick-time or time-off policies equally for all employees regardless of "excuses," and initiate the progressive disciplinary process for all who violate the limits of policy. Whether you know for certain that a particular employee's stated reason for absence is legitimate, or that another's excuse is most likely pure fabrication, you need to treat the two equally in terms of policy application. Focus on job standards and performance objectives, and the goof-offs will eventually be weeded out as they fail to consistently perform.

Again, be conscious of labeling your staff. As a supervisor, this is never appropriate. In this textbook, labeling is used to get the point across.

Parents of School-Aged Children

Parents of children who come home from school to an empty house are understandably concerned about their welfare. This concern can result in frequent telephone calls and mental distractions that interfere with job performance. You may find these tips helpful:

- Talk with the parent about after-school childcare.
- Explain to the parent that this legitimate concern is affecting job performance and express your desire to help.
- Consider other solutions: Rearrange the parent's work schedule, if possible. For example, coffee breaks and rest periods may be scheduled to coincide with telephone calls to the child.
- Ask the parent to limit the length of calls and to restrict calls to important messages.
- Be tolerant about allowing the parent to take time off when crises develop but do so within policy limits and know where to draw the line.

You can surely appreciate some of the needs of employees who are concerned about their children during after-school hours, but you can go only so far in accommodating them. In terms of policy and such, employees with children must be treated in the same manner as employees without children. The supervisor cannot legitimately make decisions in any way based on the marital or family status of an individual; to do so is discriminatory.

The Absent Employee

Think about the following situation and how it might be approached:

Nurse manager Jane said to human resource manager Diane, "I don't know what to do with Kelly. I know she's often genuinely ill. Her sick time is always used as fast as it's earned, and she's

used a lot of vacation time to cover illness. But she's never out long enough to go on disability so I could get some reliable temporary coverage."

Diane asked, "What happened with the other absence problem you mentioned some time ago? Wilson?"

"Wilson. That one's clear cut. Sick time taken as fast as earned, patterned absences—always before or after scheduled days off. He's even been seen at the mall a couple of times when he was supposedly sick. No problem dealing with him; a file full of warnings—next time he's out.

"But Kelly—I've tried to work with her about time off. After all, I've got a unit to staff and whether somebody is truly ill or faking, the work still isn't getting done. And Kelly's pretty quick to claim that she's really sick, and she's come pretty close to threatening me with some kind of formal complaint if she gets disciplined for absenteeism. What can I do about Kelly? And can I do something different with Wilson?"

An Ongoing Concern

It has been estimated that the average American employee takes from 7 to 12 days of unscheduled time off every year. Absenteeism costs American businesses more than $30 billion annually.[1]

When we speak of absenteeism, we are ordinarily referring to what we might call external absenteeism, primarily failure to show up for work when expected but also including late arrivals and early departures. Absences may also be internal, however, occurring in the forms of extended breaks or meal periods, absence from the work area without legitimate reason, socializing, daydreaming (in place but not working), or engaging in personal business while appearing to be legitimately occupied with the organization's work.

An absentee rate may be determined by dividing total hours of absence by total paid hours and expressing the result as a percentage. An absentee rate of 3% is considered reasonable by the U.S. Department of Labor. Your organization may or may not monitor this statistic for all employees. If an absentee rate is not available for the organization as a whole, it is suggested that the individual supervisor set up a simple scheme for tracking the absentee rate for the department.

There are a number of reasons for employee absence, and legitimate illness is but one of them. In actuality the two most frequent causes of absenteeism are job dissatisfaction and the availability of paid sick leave. It has been repeatedly shown that if sick time is available, it will be used, at least up to a certain point, for reasons other than illness. Consider the experiences of two hospitals located in the same city. At one institution employees were allowed 12 paid sick days per year; on the average, employees actually used about 7.5 days each. At the other hospital employees were allowed 5 paid sick days per year; in this organization the average use was about 3.2 days per person. It has been repeatedly shown that the greater a sick-time benefit, the greater the use of the benefit.

Although individual supervisors have little control over sick leave policy, they can minimize the abuse of sick time:

- Be certain employees know that sick leave is a benefit, not an entitlement. Like certain other benefits, for example, health insurance, it is there for use when needed.
- Eliminate causes of job dissatisfaction as much as possible. The more satisfied an employee is with the working situation, the less likely the person is to abuse time off.
- Set an example. The supervisor's attendance record should be a visible, positive example for the employees.
- Maintain complete and accurate attendance records (do this yourself for your own department; do not depend on another function, for example payroll, to provide this information). Make no secret of the fact that you monitor absenteeism.
- Be conscious of patterns of absenteeism, for example, weekend stretching by being absent Friday or Monday, absence immediately before or after a holiday or vacation, absence the day after payday, and other absences that may fall into patterns.

When an employee calls in sick, try to take the call personally. If a spouse makes the call and the employee is not seriously ill, ask to speak to the employee. Ask if the person has seen a physician, whether he or she is receiving adequate treatment, if there is anything you can do, and when the person might return to work. When an individual returns from an absence of more than a single day, send the person to the employee health service for clearance to work. When absence becomes excessive and approaches limits spelled out in the policy, counsel the employee. See, for example, the counseling procedure presented in this text in the chapter titled "Coaching and Counseling."

In recent years as the financial pressures on healthcare institutions have increased and management has sought ways to reduce costs and boost productivity, straightforward sick-time benefits have begun to shrink or disappear altogether. It is becoming increasingly common to find plans that combine vacation, holidays, personal time, and a modest amount of sick time into paid-time-off (PTO) banks. Under these kinds of plans, a day taken off for "illness" reduces the PTO bank by a day and thus leaves 1 day less for other purposes. Employees tend to think twice about unnecessary absences when they cut into their total time-off benefit.

Revisiting the Scenario

Human resources manager Diane might start by reminding Jane of something she herself said: "I've got a unit to staff and whether somebody is truly ill or just faking it, the work still isn't getting done." Regardless of why an employee is absent, the fact remains that either the work is not getting done or is getting done at the added expense of replacement help or overtime. The key in applying the disciplinary process is consistency; as noted earlier, whatever action is taken with one person for a policy violation also must be applied with another for the same violation regardless of what the supervisor might believe about differing reasons behind the behavior.

Jane needs to deal with both Kelly and Wilson according to the organization's absenteeism policy. She cannot "go easier" on Kelly because of genuine health problems and implied threats. The disciplinary process should include a referral to an appropriate source of assistance, perhaps the employee health service or employee assistance program. Wilson should perhaps be subject to some serious counseling concerning motivation and attitude before resorting to dismissal. Regardless, both employees should be given the full benefit of the organization's applicable processes.

Employees with Personal Problems Affecting Performance

When it comes to dealing with employees who are experiencing personal problems, the supervisor is often in a bind. What goes on in the private life of an employee is just that: private. It is no business of the supervisor what is occurring concerning an employee when that employee is not at work. The supervisor is not permitted to ask about the nature of an employee's personal problem or to probe in any way for information about the person's private life. Although the supervisor cannot dig into the nature of an employee's personal problem, the supervisor remains responsible for the performance and output of that employee when on the job.

It is impossible, or at least extremely difficult, to separate the person on the job from the person off the job. Problems at work affect home life to some extent; problems at home and elsewhere affect work life. People vary widely in their ability to keep the two halves of their lives separated, and many people who experience personal problems find that these problems affect their work performance. When work performance is affected, the changes in performance become the supervisor's business. But the supervisor's concern must address the on-the-job *results* of the individual's behavior and not attempt to determine the off-the-job *cause* of that behavior.

Personal problems that limit an employee's ability to perform the job as expected commonly include family stress, alcohol abuse, misuse of drugs, emotional disorders, and legal or financial difficulties. Supervisors are responsible for detecting and attempting to correct deteriorating job performance, but they are not expected to diagnose or treat personal problems.

When supervisory efforts do not improve behavior or performance and a personal problem may be the cause of the difficulty, refer the employee to your employee health office, your employee assistance program, or to another source through which professional assistance may be obtained.

The presence of a personal problem that affects performance may be indicated by any of a number of changes in behavior. The more common behavioral changes are the following:

- Increased absenteeism, especially important if exhibited by an individual with a prior record of good attendance
- Frequent absences from the workstation
- Confusion or difficulty concentrating
- Decreased productivity or diminished work quality
- Friction with other employees
- Increased personal phone calls
- Unusual behavior, for example, temper tantrums or emotional outbursts
- Becoming accident prone
- Alcohol on the breath

You may also have reason to suspect drug involvement when, in addition, an employee exhibits the following:

- Receives visits from strangers or employees from other areas or meets these people outside of the building (at entrances, in parking lots, etc.)
- Is suspected of theft
- Makes secretive telephone calls
- Visits the washroom or locker room for long periods
- Wears dark glasses indoors
- Wears long-sleeved shirts in hot weather
- Has blood stains on shirt sleeves
- Perspires excessively

Company Policy Concerning Personal Problems

Every organization should have a well-documented policy and an established procedure for handling employees who have personal problems

(**Figure 20.1**). Some type of employee assistance program is usually available without charge to the worker. Employees who use the services of the program are guaranteed confidentiality because the information obtained is considered a medical record. Encourage your employees to seek assistance on their own initiative before problems affect their work. Generally, time off for counseling is treated the same as time off for any other disability.

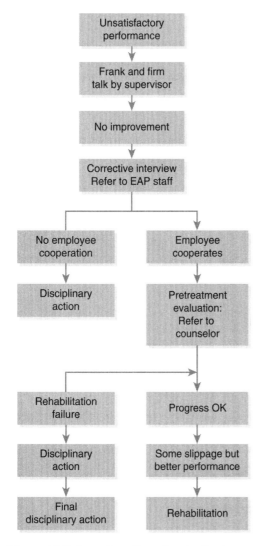

Figure 20.1 Supervisory Procedure for Employees with Personal Problems.

Recommended Procedure

Hold a performance counseling session that lets the employee know that you believe there is a problem. During this session see that you do the following:

- Make certain the employee knows what is expected and that documentation of your observations are complete.
- Describe the unacceptable behavior or results without stating what you believe the underlying problem to be. Say, for example, "Joe, your daily reports have been 1 to 2 hours late every day for the past week," rather than "Joe, you often have alcohol on your breath; you've got to get off the stuff."
- Do not accuse the employee of having a personal problem but encourage such an admission with a statement such as, "I've noticed that you seem tense recently. Is something bothering you that we can help with?"

Address the following four questions to the employee:

1. Are you aware that your performance has fallen below the standard for the job? If yes, ask when he or she first observed this.
2. Is it possible that a personal problem may be at the root of this? If yes, ask whether he or she has done something about it.
3. Are you aware of our employee assistance program?
4. Is there anything I can do to help?

If the employee's performance fails to improve, hold a second counseling session.

- If the employee still does not admit there is a personal problem, say, for example, "If you have a personal problem, I suggest counseling help. We have an excellent employee assistance program here that is completely confidential and free."
- Emphasize that the person's job may be in jeopardy if performance does not improve.

If the employee cooperates and progress is satisfactory, continue your support.

- As with many medical conditions, expect occasional backsliding or relapses.

- Make sure you acknowledge good work and noticeable improvement.
- Resist any temptation to lighten the employee's load. Treat the individual as any other employee but allow a reasonable transition period after the employee has sought help before expecting job performance to return to an acceptable level.

If the employee refuses all opportunities to seek help or if rehabilitation fails, your final recourse is to take disciplinary action.

Precautions When Addressing Employees with Problems

- Use only job performance to initiate corrective procedures. Your concern is for performance; personal reasons that may underlie flagging performance lie beyond your authority.
- Never apologize for bringing up performance deficiencies.
- Do not try to be a diagnostician. You are an "expert" only in the area of performance. Other people can better determine the nature of personal problems.
- During your counseling interview do not discuss personal problems in depth. If the employee volunteers the information, you can listen, but do not ask questions and do not attempt to offer advice. The most useless comments you can make often begin with "If I were you …."
- Do not moralize. There should be no stigma attached to personal problems.
- Be firm, but do not take punitive action until after counseling or other assistance has been suggested and declined.

A True Supervisory Challenge

Whether marginal employees, problem employees, or troubled employees, the supervisor might often believe that these people unnecessarily consume supervisory time and attention that could be put to more productive use. As one supervisor who was buried with employees' concerns was heard to say, "I could get some real work done if it wasn't for all these people problems that keep coming up." This supervisor, and a great many more supervisors, might not particularly care to hear that dealing with "all these people problems" is a legitimate and important part of the supervisory role.

It always comes down to the basic charge of every manager regardless of organizational level: getting things done through people. People are rarely if ever perfect; some of them perform well below their capabilities, some of them break rules and test the system, and some of them experience personal problems and circumstances that adversely affect their work performance. It falls to the supervisor to address these employees' apparent performance and behavior shortcomings and try to bring them to and sustain them at acceptable levels of performance.

Salvaging substandard performers may well be the single most difficult task a supervisor can face, and in light of the time and effort required, some supervisors may believe that if a token effort fails, then dismissal and replacement is the proper response. Dismissal may or may not be the answer in any given instance, but in any case, dismissal after a half-hearted effort at correction is the easy way out for the supervisor.

You surely do not want to carry an under-performer forever, but you need to be able to provide an honest answer to one question you should ask yourself: Did I do everything reasonable that I could do to help this employee succeed? Salvaging an under-performing employee can be a daunting and time-consuming task, but supervisors who have done so successfully have found that salvaging one employee is far more satisfying personally and professionally than dismissing a dozen under-performers. Also, some employees who are discharged for failure to perform to expectations will, regardless of how lax and unmotivated their on-the-job behavior had been, run straight to some advocacy agency with complaints of discrimination or unjust discharge. The supervisor who has gone the extra mile in attempting to help an under-performer improve and can demonstrate having done so has built a strong defense against such complaints.

When Employees Fail to Get Along

There are many reasons why some people may not get along with each other at work. Besides cultural, age, political, and gender differences, there may be competition for attention, promotion, recognition, turf, or resources. Personality differences seem to receive most of the blame. However, before you attribute the problem to personality clashes, look for external causes. There may be ambiguous position descriptions that do not show who does what or who has what authority. Sometimes bystanders are provoking disagreements among others.

There are three basic strategies for coping with feuding employees. First, there is avoidance. This is best, not to mention the most sensible, when it is not your problem or when you lack the authority to act. The second approach is arbitration. This consists of analyzing the situation and then taking sides or dictating a solution. This approach often fails because it usually leaves one party satisfied and the other party dissatisfied, and there can be serious side effects. Finally, there is mediation. In this approach you encourage the participants to solve their own problem, keep them from exploding, and guide them into mutually agreeable solutions. It is essential that both parties perceive you as neutral. Never take sides.

Sometimes the problem is solved simply by telling the feuding duo that they do not have to like each other to work together and that you expect them to act as adults and to treat each other civilly on the job. If that approach fails to work, talk to each person individually and look for an underlying cause of the animosity. A solution may emerge during one

of these conversations. Job redesign, clarification of limits of authority, or revising territorial boundaries may provide the remedy. If the problem is still not solved, hold a joint meeting with the intent of converting them from adversaries to problem solvers if at all possible. They must understand, however, that you will take whatever action you believe is necessary, up to and including disciplinary action, if their mutual animosity affects job performance or the morale of the department.

A recommended approach to addressing the problems presented by feuding employees consists of the following steps:

1. Caution the employees that if they do not work out a solution, you will take administrative action that may not please either party.
2. Seek some common ground or general area of agreement, for example, "You both agree that our goal is to improve customer service, right?"
3. Listen to both sides impartially. Do not tolerate interruptions, blaming, or name-calling. Make each person summarize what the other person said to clarify any flawed communication.
4. Ask each person what he or she would like to change. Review areas of agreement and disagreement.
5. Discuss the pros and cons of each alternative and get them to agree to one possible solution.
6. Clarify expected future behavior, for example, "What are we now going to do differently?" or "What are we going to do if …?"
7. Congratulate them on reaching an agreement. Express confidence in their ability to resolve their differences.
8. Follow up. Hold additional sessions if necessary.

If these employees cannot resolve their differences, you must decide whether you can live with the flawed situation. If not, you must take whatever administrative action is necessary, for example, transferring one or reassigning them so they no longer work together.

WRAP-UP

Think About It

Dealing with employees with problems is one of the hardest job responsibilities of the supervisor. It takes time and experience for the supervisor to perfect their skills. Employees will always have problems; a good supervisor will know how to handle them.

Questions for Review and Discussion

1. Why do mature employees sometimes lose their spark for their job?
2. Why do we frequently say that the supervisor should not give advice to employees concerning their personal problems?
3. Why can we not simply create a special set of conditions to apply just to single parents or parents of school-aged children?
4. Can you envision circumstances under which referral to an employee assistance program should be made a condition of continued employment? When and why?
5. How do paid-time-off programs actively discourage the abuse of sick-time benefits?
6. What do you believe is the most effective way for the supervisor to exert a positive influence on absenteeism? Why?
7. Concerning employee problems, why is it claimed that the supervisor should use only job performance to initiate the corrective process?
8. Why should the supervisor avoid inquiring into the nature of an employee's personal problem?
9. Why do we not simply address all performance problems with a disciplinary process that essentially says, "shape up or ship out?"
10. What do you do when one of your employees shows up for work showing signs of being under the influence of drugs or alcohol?

Case: When Jennifer Turned Grouchy

"I'm not trying to tell you what to do," said Mary Stone to Mark Carter, "but as your assistant I feel I've got to point out—again—that we have a problem that's generating lots of grief."

"I know," Mark responded with more than a trace of annoyance. "I'm trying to take it the way you mean it, and I've heard about it from others as well. I know we have a problem with Jennifer, but I don't know how to deal with it."

"But it has to be dealt with. As receptionist, she's in a position to make a first and lasting impression on a number of people, and she's generating a lot of complaints from patients and physicians and other staff about her blunt, rude treatment of them. It's been going on for weeks, and it's getting worse. Now she's starting to mix up appointments."

Mark said, "I'd hoped that whatever was bugging her would pass, but she's just gone from bad to worse. And it's really too bad; she's been here a long time, and this is only recent."

"One of us should talk with her and try to find out what's going on."

Mark said, "I've tried. Last week I gave her a chance to talk in private. I even asked if I could help in any way, but she told me that nothing was wrong. The way she said it, she might as well have told me to mind my own business. But she's wound up tight, and there's obviously something going on in her life that wasn't there a few weeks ago."

"Well, something is certainly wrong," said Mary, "and something's got to be done. Our receptionist has become unprofessional, and the department's starting to suffer."

Instructions

Develop a tentative approach to the problem presented by the grouchy receptionist. Be sure to provide reasonable opportunity for correction of behavior.

- Possible ways to help the employee with the problem
- The necessarily progressive nature of any disciplinary action contemplated
- The needs of the department and its customers

Reference

1. Asay GRB, Roy K, Lang JE, Payne RL, Howard DH. Absenteeism and employer costs associated with chronic diseases and health risk factors in the us workforce. *Prev Chronic Dis* 2016;13:150503.

CHAPTER 21

Ethics in the Workplace

CHAPTER OBJECTIVES

- Identify ethical behavior and how it affects ethical decision-making.
- Identify common unethical behaviors in the workplace.
- Address special problematic situations such as friction between and among employees.
- Explain how ethical principles can guide employees to make the best decisions in the workplace.
- Determine how supervisors enforce ethical behavior.

KEY TERMS

Ethical Behavior: Application of moral principles and values in a given situation. In the workplace, employees should maintain ethical standards among themselves to make certain a healthy working environment is always present.

Ethical Decisions: Legal, corporate, moral, cultural, and personal values. Personal ethics depends largely on our core beliefs and values. These are determined early in life and are based on the teachings of parents, teachers, and role models.

Organizational Ethics: Guidelines that define the boundaries of acceptable behavior within the organization, representing what we *should* do but not necessarily what we *must* do.

Ethical Behavior

Organizational ethics defines the boundaries of acceptable behavior. Ethical considerations may relate to performance appraisals, promotions, and disciplinary actions to cite but a few areas. They often involve the protection of personal privacy, discriminatory behavior, or the release of information. Nowhere is the practice of ethical behavior more important than in relationships between and among employees, superiors, and colleagues.

Ethics represent what we *should* do but not necessarily what we *must* do. Ethical standards are higher than the standards that apply in civil and criminal laws. The easiest ethical violations to recognize are those that also violate laws. For example, the pilfering of supplies is theft and is therefore both illegal and unethical. More controversial, but also well within the realm of ethics, is the "borrowing" of workplace equipment for personal use; photocopying material for personal use or for external activities is a prime example.

Ethical decisions are based on legal, corporate, moral, cultural, and personal values. What we consider ethical depends largely on our core beliefs and values. These are determined early in life and are based on the teachings of parents, teachers, and role models. Life experiences modify or enforce these beliefs about what is right and what is wrong. Complications often arise in the workplace because employees are asked to merge their values with those of the organization. Sometimes these sets of values are discordant. Value differences readily explain why people frequently disagree about what is ethical and what is not.

Unethical Behavior

Millions of people acknowledge witnessing unethical behavior in the workplace.[1] It can be something small from misusing company time to violating the internet policy. Unethical behavior in the workplace is widespread.

Here are a number of examples of unethical behavior in the workplace:

- Instructing people to do whatever is necessary to achieve results and turning a blind eye to what they actually do
- Taking credit for other people's ideas, or shifting blame for one's own failures to others
- Playing favorites among staff
- Lying or falsifying records
- Billing for work not performed
- Deliberately making false or misleading statements
- Divulging personal or confidential information
- Failing to report violations of legal requirements
- Failing to report health and safety hazards or accidents
- Theft, as it is often euphemistically referred to in policies as "unauthorized use or possession of the property of others" (This euphemism represents a necessary caution; theft is a crime defined by law and confirmed by conviction, so unless theft has been legally proven, it is best to avoid labeling someone as a thief.)

Probably the most common ethical violations are lying, falsifying records, and "unauthorized use or possession of the property of others."

Organizational Climate

Employees are more likely to make unethical decisions when management makes it difficult for them to avoid doing so. Some employees frequently feel pressured to act in ways that violate the codes of behavior of their organization. Again, the likes of, "I don't care how you do it, just get it done!" can make an employee feel forced to act unethically to stay out of trouble.

Peer Pressure

Often people fall into the behavior of their coworkers. "If they are doing it, why can't I?" People behave unethically because they tend to recognize the questionable behaviors displayed by people who are very similar to them. Bad behavior attracts bad behavior. Peer pressure and influence is a common tactic of unethical behavior in the workplace.

Code of Ethics

Employees are more likely to act out or do wrong if they have no sense of what is right. Without a code of ethics, an organization is giving employees a free-for-all to act and behave as they see fit. A code of ethics establishes values and sets boundaries. It is a proactive approach to unethical behavior.[1]

Fear of a Punishment or Blame

Employees often don't report unethical behavior they witness because they are afraid of the consequences. They do not want to place blame or be punished for something they saw but did not report. Employees don't want to ruin their career by reporting an unethical behavior, and sometimes they don't know who or how to report the incident.

Ethical Principles

The role of supervisor takes a lot of work and dedication. Leading and managing a team of people has many obstacles and challenges but is also very rewarding. A person's values and morals can have an impact on their role as supervisor. Ambition, desire, and motivation are core characteristics of those who want success but must also be guided by grounded ethical principles.[2]

Here are top ethical principles for supervisors. These are used to provide strong guidance for ethical practices in the workplace.

- Honesty. Being honest in all forms of communication and in all actions. Never telling partial truths or leaving out partial information. Honesty means sharing both good and bad information.
- Fairness. Treating all employees equally and never exercising power. Never exploiting weaknesses or mistakes for personal benefit or gain.
- Leadership. Setting positive examples of ethical behaviors. Commitment to excellence through ethical decision-making. Supervisors lead by consistently improving operational effectiveness, employee satisfaction and patient/customer approval.
- Integrity. Consistency between words and actions that lead and inspire trust and credibility. For supervisors it means keeping promises, honoring commitments, and meeting deadlines.
- Compassion. Fostering an environment that encompasses empathy and compassion for one another and the patients and customers that are served. Organization goals are designed to learn the needs of those they serve.
- Respect. Demonstrated in full capacity through human rights, dignity, autonomy, interests, and privacy of all people. It is recognizing that every person deserves equal respect and support for sharing ideas and opinions, without fear of any penalty or form of discrimination.
- Responsibility. Taking full ownership of their jobs, striving to be aware of the department and organizational environment. Taking responsibility shows maturity.
- Loyalty. Is keeping information shared in confidence. Remaining faithful to employees, coworkers, and customers. Loyal is avoiding conflicts of interest and building a solid and sustainable reputation for the organization.
- Accountability. High expectations of ethical behavior drive an organization. Total commitment to accountability to the ethical quality al all decisions, actions, and relationships.
- Transparency. Committing to being transparent in the department by sharing policies, financial decisions, and sharing criteria's for pay raises and hiring.

Supervisors can role model these behaviors to improve the ethical practices of their employees. Leading by example is a strong characteristic of an ethical leader.

Ethics Programs

Most ethics programs consist chiefly of "snitch lines" in which people are encouraged to report the perceived violations of others. Experience has shown, however, that most of the calls received concern petty complaints, such as people taking long lunch breaks.

Effective ethics programs include a code of ethical conduct, provide for employee training in the ethics of the workplace, include a monitoring system, and provide an ethics "hotline." The hotline is used less for snitching than for soliciting expert advice as to whether or not something is unethical or on how to respond to certain situations, for example, it can help determine the appropriateness of accepting a gift from a vendor or hiring a member of one's family. An additional benefit of calls for advice is that they suggest what kind of information should be presented in training programs or discussed at staff meetings. To be effective, calls for advice must be answered promptly and skillfully. Experienced advisors walk the callers through the thought process so they can reach the right decisions by themselves. The principal reasons people offer for not reporting unethical acts are (1) they doubt anything will be done, (2) they fear retaliation, or (3) they do not trust the organization to keep the information confidential.

Ethics training may consist of special courses that are given periodically and included in orientation programs. In these sessions case studies involving ethical dilemmas can be presented.

Supervisory Enforcement of Ethical Behavior

With all of the downsizing, restructuring, and reorganizing occurring in health care and with the increased workloads placed on so many employees, employees often feel pressured to cut corners. Tell your employees to come to you when they are running behind schedule so you can provide them with help or modify their schedules; it is important for them to know that getting the work done honestly and ethically is as important as getting it done at all.

Encourage employees to inform you, in confidence, of their concerns about apparent unethical acts by their coworkers. Tell them there may

be times when they must choose between betraying colleagues and being loyal to the organization.

Make your pronouncements of intolerance of unethical behavior strong and make your disciplinary reactions fast. When you observe a colleague engaging in minor unethical behavior, it may be appropriate to tell him or her that you are aware of what is going on and are obligated to report these transgressions if they continue. If the acts are illegal or represent major ethical violations, go directly to the authorities.

As necessary, discuss individual situations with your superior or a member of the human resources department. Be certain you are familiar with the organization's policies addressing unethical behavior, referring to them before making any waves. If you are a member of a professional organization to which the offending individual belongs, consult with a representative of that organization.

Finally, the supervisor must be ever conscious of the manner in which he or she is perceived by the employees. Like it or not, the supervisor is a role model for the employees. When the employees see the supervisor engaged in some practice that is questionable, many of them will believe it is acceptable for them to behave the same way. The supervisor's visible behavior can be the department's strongest encouragement toward ethical conduct.

WRAP-UP

Think About It

Ethical behavior is one of the most important areas in which a supervisor can serve as a role model for employee conduct. Those supposedly "small" ethical blunders, which some are inclined to defend with "Why not? Everybody does it," are far less likely to be considered acceptable if they are visibly avoided by the supervisor. Do not underestimate the power of a strong positive role model.

Questions for Review and Discussion

1. Do you agree that enforcement of ethical guidelines has become more difficult in most settings in recent years? Why might this be so?

2. How does your personal values and beliefs affect ethics in the workplace?

3. Explain the difference between organizational ethics and regular ethics.

4. Describe a time where you witnessed an unethical behavior at your workplace. If you've never experienced one, choose a behavior from the textbook and describe a scenario.
5. How much of an impact does the fear of punishment and blame have on reporting unethical behavior in the workplace?
6. Does your current place of employment have a code of ethics? Were they given to you during orientation and are they followed by the organization? Give examples.
7. Describe the core characteristics of a supervisor, manager, or leader that you've worked with. Is this person ethical? Do they lead by example?
8. Discuss the ethical principles presented in this chapter. Which ones hold the most weight for a supervisor and for an employee?
9. Discuss the purpose of an ethics hotline. How are they useful, and how can they significantly impact an organization?
10. Do you agree that a supervisor is a strong role model if he or she behaves ethically at work?

Case: Unethical Colleagues

Sally, Sam, and Tara work in the Admissions Department at Healthy Hospital. While working on a project near the printer and copy machine, Sally sees Sam using the laser color copy machine to make flyers for his homemade soap business. The next day, Sally decides to use the laser color copy machine to make flyers for a school fundraiser that her children are participating in. Tara saw both of them using the laser color copy machine and knows that it is against the rules to use the equipment for personal use.

A few days pass by and Tara decides to talk to Sally and Sam about it. At lunch, Tara mentions to Sally and Sam that they shouldn't be using the laser color copy machine for their own personal use. They both say, "Everyone does it." Tara was surprised by their reaction. She doesn't think they will stop using it. Tara doesn't want to tell their supervisor, but she knows what they are doing is wrong.

Questions
1. Describe what Tara should do now? What are her options?
2. What are the possible consequences for Tara if she does speak to their supervisor?
3. What happens if Tara says nothing, and the supervisor finds out that Tara knew this was happening?

Case: Is My Supervisor Unethical?

Tiffany is the supervisor of the Billing and Collections Department at Healthy Hospital. She is responsible for a large team. One of her responsibilities as the supervisor is to train the new staff when they are hired. It is the beginning of a new week, and she has a new hire to train. His name is Patrick. Patrick is very experienced in billing and coding. He has worked in a similar department at a different hospital out of state for the past 12 years. Tiffany doesn't think there will be much training to do because Patrick is very experienced in the role of billing and collections.

Patrick picked up on the job very quickly. Since he was new and had to go through the official training, he was only allowed to complete billing actions through his supervisor's online portal, but Tiffany gave him his freedom since he was very experienced. While completing training and working on active documents, he noticed something that was not adding up correctly on Tiffany's assigned forms. He began looking closer at the charges that were going to be submitted, and they did not match what was on the chart. He thought, maybe this was just a one-time mistake. He checked other patient charts, and their charges didn't match either. He realized this was not a mistake. The records had been falsified by Tiffany.

Patrick is a new employee. He is worried his supervisor is making unethical decisions and putting the entire organization in danger.

Questions

1. What immediate actions should Patrick take? What would you do if you were in his position?
2. How is Tiffany being unethical? Could this be a mistake?
3. What danger is the organization in? How bad could this be for the department and the entire organization?

References

1. Molis J. What are the causes of unethical behavior in the workplace? Bizfluent Web site. https://bizfluent.com /info-8182488-causes-unethical-behavior-workplace .html. Published October 25, 2018. Accessed November 20, 2021.

2. Marquette University. What Are the 12 Ethical Principles for Business Executives? Marquette University Business Web site. https://online.marquette.edu/business/blog/what -are-the-12-ethical-principles-for-business-executives. Published November 8, 2022.

CHAPTER 22

Managing Difficult Employees

CHAPTER OBJECTIVES

- Address the problems frequently presented by inappropriate employee attitudes, recognizing that it is necessary to always address the results of behavior rather than attempting to deal with attitude itself.
- Provide an overview of the application of coaching and counseling techniques as they relate to behavioral change.
- Identify a number of patterns of employee behavior and suggest how the supervisor might address each of these when encountered.
- Prepare the supervisor for the inevitable necessity to occasionally deal with hostile and angry people, whether employees, peers, or others.

KEY TERMS

Difficult Employee: Usually a standard or minimally acceptable performer, this is the employee who is seen as exhibiting an attitude problem: a bad attitude, a poor attitude, or a generally negative attitude.

Labeling: The tendency to apply simplistic labels to employees based on their behavior, for example, "grouch," "know-it-all," "hothead," and such. Labels will forever be used as a matter of convenience, but it must be recognized that labels tend to stigmatize, and labels, rarely if ever, are completely descriptive of individuals.

A Matter of Attitude

Most of the time incompetent employees are not those who cause supervisors their greatest frustration. There is always a chance incompetent employees can be trained. Likewise, the frustration producers are usually not the ones who violate rules. Rule breakers can be dealt with via disciplinary processes, and if they fail to change their ways, they can be discharged. Rather, the employees who give supervisors the biggest headaches are the ones who usually meet work standards but make life stressful for management with their peculiar behavior. These are the people who are usually accused of exhibiting an attitude problem: a bad attitude, a poor attitude, a negative attitude, and so on, what we may simply refer to by the all-encompassing term "negative attitude."

An employee with a negative attitude may be a chronic negativist, a goof-off, a hothead, or even a disloyal subordinate. We cannot get into the heads of these people to see what a negative attitude really is. We know that this term is universally used to excess and lacks a concise definition. What we do see are various kinds of behaviors that we find annoying. The line between negative attitude and outright disloyalty or unethical behavior, for example, can be fuzzy. We can, however, often infer the presence of a negative attitude by the presence of certain signs. Negative attitudes may be reflected in a number of ways:

- Low or diminishing productivity
- High or increasing error rate and thus diminishing quality
- Repeated minor violations of rules and procedures
- Lack of team spirit or lack of cooperation
- Public criticism of the organization and its management
- Periodic threats of resignation
- Foot-dragging and chronic resistance to change

Supervisors, when attempting to document their beliefs about negative employees, will likely use one or more of the following adjectives in their appraisals of these employees: uninterested, inflexible, complaining, indifferent, change resistant, unenthusiastic, and nonsupportive.

However, the supervisor faces a significant barrier in addressing negative attitudes: Attitude cannot be directly addressed with any of the corrective processes available to the supervisor. You cannot, for example, cite "poor attitude" as the reason for issuing a warning and have this hold up under legal scrutiny. Attitude is subjective; it is not a concrete term with a precise definition. It is always open to interpretation, and because it is subjective, it can always be argued because its presence cannot be proven. Therefore, because we are unable to cite negative attitude as a particular offense, we are left with the need to consider the behavior that the negative attitude appears to have caused. In some circumstances the supervisor might be on reasonably solid ground in discussing an apparent negative attitude and its effects with an offending employee, but it must always be the noticeable and provable results of behavior to which the corrective or disciplinary processes are applied.

Coaching and Counseling for Behavioral Change

Before taking any action stemming from an apparent attitude problem, try to determine if there really is a problem. If there is indeed a problem, how pervasive is it? A crucial question discussed in the chapter entitled "Employees with Problems" comes up whenever we face a difficult person: Does the behavior noticeably affect performance? If so, it affects the entire department and you as supervisor. If there is no apparent effect and you believe you can live with the present situation, your best move may be no move at all.

It is always best to avoid accusing a person of having a negative attitude. If you believe you must do so, provide specific behavioral examples that led you to that subjective conclusion. Failure to do so will usually elicit defensiveness or anger or, at best, confuse the person. It is not likely to achieve the desired behavioral change. If the altered behavior meets your standards, you need not be overly concerned about attitude. In the military, for example, it has been repeatedly proven that when you are able to change the behavior of trainees, it leads to pride in the service and in themselves, and the negative attitudes disappear.

Often, a negative attitude can be modified to a satisfactory extent by vigorous coaching and skillful counseling. Discuss the problem with the person candidly. Explain how the behavior in question affects you, the department, or others. Provide specific examples of how you see the person's behavior affecting services and people, especially customers and coworkers.

When it seems your coaching and counseling are having no effect, start keeping more detailed performance records. Cutting these employees loose may prove to be the best solution, but you need concrete proof of how the negative attitude plays out in behavior that has affected performance or impacted other employees. This concrete proof is best retained in the form of factual evidence of the results of behavior.

Chronically Critical Employees

Occasional criticism of the organization or its managers is to be expected from just about every employee once in a while, but when it seems that an employee is overdoing it, constantly complaining about the organization and its management, you may have to take a simple step that lets the person know you are aware of the complaining and that you find it inappropriate. A comment from you such as "I can't understand why you would stay with an organization that you seem to think is beneath you" or even "If things are so bad here, why haven't you resigned?" might help put the complaining in perspective. At the very least it may serve to let the employee know you are hearing what is said and that you disapprove.

There are two instances involving complaining in which you must take timely and definitive action before serious harm is done: (1) when the complainers badmouth the organization in the presence of patients, visitors, clinicians, or other customers, or (2) when the complaining starts to affect the attitudes and performance of other employees. These two kinds of situations often justify charges of disloyalty. In most organizations this can be grounds for serious disciplinary action, up to and including discharge (in the disciplinary processes of many organizations this kind of complaining behavior is often included in a broader category of offenses described as "misconduct").

When You Are the Focus of a Negative Attitude

At times, you may need to work with a colleague who seems to maintain a negative attitude toward you. This can result in little (and sometimes not-so-little) daily skirmishes that are not conducive to team efforts. Rapport is the key to getting along better. It begins with a genuine desire to improve the relationship.

In several places this text mentions the importance of taking risks; any situation may present a good example of a risk that is well worth taking. Grab the bull by the horns: Ask the other person what it is about you that annoys him or her. You may be in for a surprise. The irritating factor may be as simple as your sending memos or email messages that the other perceives as curt or sarcastic. It may stem from calling the person by a nickname that the individual dislikes.

If you get a frank response, thank the person, and promise to modify your behavior. Then ask the person if you can be candid about what change you would like to see on his or her part. Do not unload a stack of complaints, however. This candid approach may fail, or it may even make matters worse, but it is often worth the risk.

Negative Employees

Negative employees can often be hard workers who are competent, productive, and even loyal but who harbor a bleak outlook toward most things and people. The negativists lack excitement in life and lack enjoyment at work. If you hang around them long enough, you become infected. Negativists are often convinced that the people in power are self-serving and care for no one but themselves. In meetings when any new idea is proposed, there is usually one who can always be counted on to come up with "The trouble with that idea is …," and one who is sure to say, whenever it sounds as though the group is on the trail of a good idea, "Yeah, but what if …?" The "what-if" is, of course, followed by a litany of reasons why the idea will probably flop. And whatever negative reasons one misses, the other is sure to cover. If there are too many such people involved, nothing that entails any risk ever gets attempted.

Negative employees should not be confused with devil's advocates. Both voice concerns or ask challenging questions, but the devil's advocate does so with an open mind and is prepared to join a consensus if convinced. The negativist persists in finding reasons for opposing whatever is being proposed. Even when they lose arguments or are outvoted, they remain unconvinced.

Avoid acceptance of the contrary outlooks expressed by the negativists. Their resistive persuasion not only is depressing and self-defeating, it can be infectious as well. On the other hand, do not dismiss their comments too quickly. On occasion they could turn the group against you. And sometimes—perhaps only once in a great while, but you cannot afford to overlook the possibility—they could be right.

When a known pessimist is present at a problem-solving session, do not rush into offering suggestions. Call on others, including the pessimists. If possible, call on the pessimists first. Some pessimists are silent while a problem is being explored or when decisions are asked for, then spring into action after solutions have been proposed.

Always try to project realistic optimism. Provide examples of past successes of the action now being proposed. Concede that every action carries some element of risk. Using a worst-case scenario, show that the possible consequences are not threatening and that the chances of success are great. Explain that current conditions are not like those that were present at an earlier time when a similar project was unsuccessful.

Avoid arguing with a pessimist. Say that he or she may be right but that you still want to run with the idea. If the person persists, insist that he or she come up with a better alternative. When a person questions the wisdom of a change, assign him or her information-gathering chores relating to the change.

Keep an open mind. Occasionally, these employees are right, and sometimes you can use their negativism when you get to discussing pitfalls and contingency planning. Usually, they can tell you everything that can go wrong. If the pessimist is a colleague and the work situation does not demand that you work together, avoid him or her if you want to maintain your optimistic attitude.

Know-It-All Employees

These individuals want you to recognize them as superior. They try to maintain control by accumulating large bodies of knowledge, whether real or assumed. They are condescending if they know what they are talking about and pompous if they do not. If you object to what they say, they take it as a personal affront.

Do not pose a threat to the know-it-all and do not argue. Remain respectful, and avoid direct challenges. Resist the temptation to debate with him or her. Do your homework. Be certain you know what you are talking about. Present your ideas tentatively using phrases such as "What would happen if …" or "I wonder whether …."

The Uncooperative Silent Ones

These people are not those who fail to speak up because they have nothing to say or because they are listening intently. They are not the polite ones who fear they will say something wrong or will hurt your feelings. The silent ones discussed here are those whose silence is rooted in fear or suppressed anger.

Their silence may be preceded by a perfectly congenial conversation until you suddenly touch a sensitive area. You are highly likely to encounter this glum silence during counseling or disciplinary sessions.

For example, when it is Irene's turn to speak but she remains silent, lean forward and counter with your own silence plus eye contact and raised eyebrows. Maintain this silent, expectant stare for at least 10 seconds. If she remains silent, say, "You haven't answered my question, Irene. Is there some reason for that?" If her silence persists, say, "Irene, I'm still waiting." If there is still no response, state the consequences of her inappropriate silence, perhaps, "Irene, you may have a good reason for not talking, but I'm concerned about where this is taking us." If Irene still remains silent, terminate the interview with, "Irene, since we still must resolve this problem, I want to see you here tomorrow at the same time."

Elusive Employees

A Scenario

This involves an employee who seems determined to avoid contact with the supervisor:

Laboratory supervisor Vera was expressing her frustrations with employee Daniel to her friend Ginny, human resources representative. Said Vera, "Most of the time I have no idea what Dan's doing; I hardly ever see him. He works what I call our crazy shift, and his hours overlap the other shifts. Much of the time he's completely on his own."

Ginny asked whether the work was getting done. Vera said, "It seems to be, but it's awfully hard for me to tell because I just don't see him. A couple of times when I tried to call him from home—he was covering nights in clinical chemistry—I couldn't reach him. He claimed he was responding to stat calls, but I couldn't verify that. Twice the night nursing supervisor said it took 10 or 15 minutes to find him when she needed something."

"You're concerned about whether he's really working? Or whether his work is up to standard?"

"I've never found his work to be anything but acceptable, at least when I'm aware of what he's doing. I have two concerns: how can I adequately supervise an employee I'm able to see for only about 10% of an average shift, if that? And how can I do an honest performance evaluation of someone working like he does?"

Limiting the Elusive One

How indeed? In some healthcare activities, it is not unusual for some employees who work evenings or nights or split shifts to be off on their own for extended periods. Such employees are admittedly often more difficult to supervise, but given the nature of some healthcare organizations, particularly hospitals, different shift assignments are necessary. So the immediate supervisor has to decide how to oversee such employees.

Claiming that Dan "seems to be" getting the work done but that it is "hard to tell" may suggest that Dan is willfully elusive, and it can also suggest that Vera has not done all she could be doing as supervisor. It is not enough to try a couple phone calls from home; Vera might make a better effort to occasionally "drop in" during Dan's shift to see how he is doing. As long as Dan technically reports to Vera, Vera bears a measure of responsibility for Dan's performance. As to whether Dan is actually responding to stat calls when he says he is, the truth might be established if he was required to maintain an activity log providing a verifiable record of such calls.

There are ways that Vera can stay more closely in touch with Dan's activities. One is more direct supervision, like the unscheduled visits mentioned previously, implementation of the aforementioned activity log, and crystal-clear performance expectations communicated to Dan. Another approach is often used under such circumstances: The individual who works the off-shift without benefit of immediate supervision is required to report to whoever is in charge of the "house" at that time, in this instance perhaps the night nursing supervisor. If Vera really does see Dan for only about 10% of the shift, Dan should be required to answer to someone else during much of the other 90%. Together Vera and the night nursing supervisor may be able to keep better tracks of the "elusive" one and also collaborate on a reasonable performance evaluation.

Elusiveness and Span of Control

In circumstances like those faced by Vera in the preceding example, any supervisor can experience problems with the span of control. And when an employee is deliberately elusive, the supervisor has considerable cause for concern. It is true that some employees can be trusted completely to do what they are supposed to be doing without the constant presence of supervision. However, there are others for whom this lack of direct oversight is seen as license to do as they wish, which often involves doing as little of the real work as possible while pursuing their own interests. (In one real-life situation, a work-dodging night-shift employee devoted much creativity to finding times and places for sleeping; he had a full-time day job elsewhere.)

The principal lesson for the supervisor concerning the elusive employee resides in the need for careful selection and placement in filling any position in which the individual must work alone for prolonged periods. Independent employees need very clear performance expectations, but the real key lies in trust: the best independently functioning employees are those who have earned your complete trust.

Super-Sensitive Employees

Super-sensitive employees take offense at whatever they perceive as put-downs. They are especially sensitive to criticism, sometimes bursting into tears, shouting, or dashing off to the restroom. When this behavior is effective for them, these people find they have a potent tool for manipulating colleagues and superiors, and they make full use of it.

Handle the super-sensitive persons with care, but do not be manipulated by their reactions. Never withhold negative feedback because of previous overreactions. Do not apologize for what you said or did; avoid the likes of "Gosh, I'm very sorry that I hurt your feelings."

If, when receiving a reprimand, an employee breaks into tears, say something like, "Sue, I find it hard to discuss this when you're crying. Please take a few minutes to compose yourself." Most of the time you can simply hand Sue a tissue and go on with the discussion. But if Sue jumps up and runs out of your office, do not run after her or demand that she returns. Instead, reschedule the meeting. At the later meeting make no mention of the previous episode. Sue will have already learned that her inappropriate behavior was not effective.

If an employee loses his or her temper and starts shouting, wait silently for a minute or two while maintaining eye contact. If the employee does not calm down, leave your office.

Moody People

Most people experience some mood swings. It is the degree of the swings and the circumstances that prompt them that are important. Transient moodiness, such as that which occurs during a grieving period, seldom requires supervisory action other than offering a helping hand. A persistent or markedly depressed state, however, calls for professional help. Between these two extremes are a variety of moods manifested by sorrow, sullenness, irritability, or other personality changes.

Ignore mild transient moods. If they persist, ask questions, and listen with empathy. Do not flood these folks with sympathy. Sympathy may prolong the moods or lead to the martyr syndrome. Empathy is more effective than sympathy. If the situation does not improve, suggest professional counseling.

Jealous Coworkers

Jealousy in the workplace is relatively common when employees compete for merit pay, promotions, or recognition. Frustrated people may try to undermine your position by starting unfounded rumors, publicly berating you, becoming a bottleneck, or turning others against you. When any of these disloyal activities occurs, you must take firm action.

First, discuss the problem with your manager and get support. Then confront the envious one. Lay it on the line. Say what you have seen or heard and state that you want it stopped. Describe your future expectations; for example, "I want no arguments in front of staff, patients, or physicians. If you have a gripe, see me in my office." If the undesired behavior persists, remind the person that it is affecting future performance evaluations and can possibly affect continued employment.

Gossips

A little benign gossip is harmless, but when character is attacked or misinformation is spread that affects work or morale, something must be done. Gossips want attention, so supply it in healthy ways. Spike their misinformation by insisting on validation or by correcting false comments. Explain how their gossiping is affecting the team.

Let them know that people are withholding information from them because they fear it will be repeated in distorted forms. Do not encourage gossips by listening intently to their messages. Sometimes it is best to ignore these people.

Incessant Talkers and Socializers

These folks suffer from chronic verbal diarrhea. Monday morning finds them rehashing weekend sports or their recreational activities. They repeat their broadcasts as long as they find listeners. You must know and act when these time wasters become bottlenecks.

Break up the little group discussions in the corridors. Give the verbose one's extra assignments. When they learn that too much talk and too little work result in extra assignments, they will usually modify their abuse of time. If possible, isolate them from willing listeners. Encourage them to do their socializing during breaks. See the chapter entitled "Holding Effective Meetings" for advice on coping with the incessant talkers at meetings.

Employees of Questionable Appearance

Be careful how you deal with employees whose appearance—that is, matters of dress and grooming—you personally do not like and of which you disapprove. Before taking any action, ask yourself the following:

- Does the individual's appearance violate any policy or rule? The supervisor will find this particular issue easiest to deal with if the organization has a dress code included in the employment policy manual and the person's appearance is in clear violation of the code.
- Is there a safety hazard involved, for example wearing particular kinds of shoes that are proven hazardous in some settings?

Keep appearance in mind when interviewing potential employees. Applicants who show up for employment interviews looking like something the cat dragged in are usually exhibiting the manner in which they customarily appear. When someone appears unkempt for an employment interview, you can usually rest assured that the person's appearance will not improve upon hire and may in fact become worse. The best defense concerning employees of questionable appearance is to try to avoid hiring them in the first place.

During new-employee orientation, emphasize the importance of appearance, especially for employees who will have direct contact with customers. Review the dress code and advise them of your personal expectations. Remember that forewarning is proactive; criticizing is reactive.

Employees with Messy Work Areas

Messiness, like beauty, is in the eye of the beholder. Before you can get employees to clean up their act, you must convince them that there is a problem (parents know this is not easy). Some fastidious supervisors make a big fuss over a little disorder. The key point is to determine whether a disorderly desk or work area negatively affects performance, coworkers, or customers. For example, the condition of a receptionist's desk in full view of visitors has far more significance than a beat-up desk in the corner of the maintenance department.

There may be barriers to neatness beyond the control of the employee. For example, visiting VIPs may drop their coats on a receptionist's chair, or delivery people may place large cartons in doorways. Do what you can to help your staff eliminate such problems. Remember that conditions are always in a state of flux in a normally busy work environment, so do what can be done to keep the worst of it under control, but do not go overboard making a fuss over occasional clutter.

Coping with Hostile People

Hostile individuals are an inescapable part of daily life, whether in the work environment or elsewhere. You might be firmly convinced that people should not be that way, but you do not control their behavior and you have no control over the feelings that lead them to behave in a hostile or antagonistic fashion.

Your unspoken but assertive message to hostile people is that you respect their right to feel as they feel and to speak their minds but that you also have those rights. In addition, regardless of the rank and power of the person with whom you are in a strained situation, you do not have to listen to profane, intimidating, or obnoxious language.

To achieve and maintain personal freedom of expression, be assertive without being belligerent. If you lack assertiveness, little or no advice about dealing with hostile people will work for you; passivity will prevent you from using it. Passivity in the presence of hostile or antagonistic people only gets you walked on and pushed around. Fortunately, there are many readily available publications, and webinars/seminars on the subject of assertiveness.

The Angry Employee

Angry employees are everywhere and in every industry. Everyone probably has had the unfortunate circumstance of working with a person who shows anger as their forefront emotion on a very regular basis. This anger can stem from many things that are not even related to their job, but the anger and frustration is released at their place of employment.

Every organization will have their own policies and procedures to handle angry employees. As a supervisor it is a very fine line to tread when dealing with an employee's anger problem.[1]

Following is some long withstanding advice for supervisors on how to handle angry employees with grace:

- Acknowledge their feelings but discourage bad behavior. Some people experience their emotions more strongly and that is okay. What is not okay is cursing and shouting.
- Don't match their escalation but let them vent. Some people just need to let out their

feelings. This is acceptable as long as safety and bad behavior is not compromised.

- Try to see things from their perspective. If an angry employee is stressed and comes to you with concerns, take a step back and put yourself in their shoes. Supervisors see things differently than non-supervisors.
- Thank the employee for his or her feedback. If the feedback is bad, take it as constructive criticism. Every complaint from an employee is an opportunity to grow.
- Repeat the problem back to the employee to ensure you understand. This will ensure the angry employee is understood and that you understand the frustration of the employee. Good communication is critical when there is anger.
- Apologize only if necessary. Give the employee an apology if it is warranted. Even if it is not your fault, say something that shows the employee you are listening and that you care.
- Create actionable steps for change. Make changes, if necessary, appropriate, and allowed. Plan out the change with the employee so he or she knows you are working on it.
- Continually follow-up with the employee with one-on-one meetings. After the colleague has aired out his or her issues, make a time to meet again and in the future. This can minimize issues in the future.
- If necessary, fire or dismiss someone. Dismissing toxic or problem employees is never the go-to standard. Coaching and counseling the employee is the best, first route. Simply listening to the frustrated employee could solve a lot of issues.[2]

Passive-Aggressive Employees

Passive-aggressive employees usually believe they are getting a raw deal from their supervisors, whom they generally perceive as dictators; this causes them to feel angry and resentful. They lack sufficient confidence to challenge authority directly, so their resistance surfaces indirectly and covertly. They play many psychological games. Typical things they may do to try your patience are showing up late for meetings, submitting late reports, becoming angry with you but refusing to tell you why, or fouling up a procedure.

Passive-aggressive employees apologize superficially, give you endless excuses, or just clam up. Inwardly, they enjoy your anger or discomfort. You are not likely to change the personality of the passive-aggressive; often they are resistant even to professional psychological help. Your goal should be to insist on behavior that meets your expectations and to not let these people get you upset when they play their mean psychological games. Do not accept their excuses, and never give them the satisfaction of witnessing the anger or frustration you feel when they upset you.

Caution Is in Order

Much of what is said in this chapter is offered for the purpose of increasing understanding of the differing personalities and temperaments the supervisor is likely to encounter now and then. In doing so we have used labels for so-called types of individuals, but we have done so only as a matter of convenience in describing kinds of behavior the supervisor may encounter from time to time. Much of the time, however, real people cannot be readily or completely described with labels. Use these labels to guide your thinking concerning certain behaviors and how to react to them, but never apply a label directly to an individual in speech or writing. Labels tend to stigmatize, and rarely if ever is any label ever 100% descriptive of the person to whom it is attached.

WRAP-UP

Think About It

A supervisor must often address "attitude problems" and cope with hostility in trying to get the job done. It is best to remember, however, that attitude, whether negative, sullen, questionable, or otherwise, is not itself a problem that can be addressed via disciplinary processes. It is always necessary to look beyond the attitude and address the results of the behavior that occurs because of that attitude.

Questions for Review and Discussion

1. What, if anything, is wrong with engaging in argument with someone who is angry, upset, and whose position on the issue at hand is definitely wrong?

2. What are the differences between the power of personality and the power conferred by positional authority? Does the successful supervisor need one or the other or both?

3. What is the principal hazard of having an otherwise productive employee in the group who is constantly critical of organizational policy?

4. What do you believe could be an effective way of dealing with the know-it-all employee, and why might this work?

5. What can the individual supervisor do about employee appearance if the organization has no dress code that applies to all employees?

6. Suggest how you might deal with an employee who reacts with tears and denial to every criticism regardless of scope or importance.

7. How can you arrange your own office or work setting to minimize the chances of unintentionally intimidating others?

8. How would you attempt to stand up to a vocally intimidating individual without engaging in a fight?

9. Why is it a questionable practice to describe individuals by label or type?

10. It has been said that anger is often a shield raised in defense of a weak position. Why might this be so?

Case: The Blindsider

George did not look forward to going to the staff meetings that his middle-manager boss convened once each week. He did not always feel this way about the meetings; in fact, up until 3 months ago he rather enjoyed what he believed were productive and congenial gatherings. What made the difference was one change in the membership of this group of six supervisors: the addition of Charlie, who replaced a usually silent supervisor of one of the building services sections.

Unlike his predecessor, Charlie was anything but usually silent. In fact, it seemed as though Charlie had made it a point to become conversant with every section of their boss's territory, and he almost always had something critical to say about the weekly reports of the other supervisors.

What bothered George most was Charlie's approach to getting his issues or criticisms on the table. Charlie seemed to focus exclusively on problems and weaknesses. As if that in itself wasn't bad enough, what George resented most was Charlie's way of introducing a problem or concern in a way that ensured maximum embarrassment for whoever's area he was commenting on. It was Charlie's practice to openly drop his little bombshells in the staff meeting, where the supervisor whose area was in question first heard of a so-called problem or weakness at the same time the others learned of it.

It seemed to George that Charlie's practice of blindsiding the others in the group was coldly calculated to make himself look better by making others look worse. And George found it even more frustrating to note that their boss did not seem to recognize what Charlie was doing.

Questions

1. Do you believe there is anything George can do about Charlie's staff meeting behavior? If so, how should he proceed?

2. Do you believe George should take up his concerns directly with Charlie? Why or why not?

Case: The Sensitive Employee

Supervisor Teri Davis was dreading the coming session with clerk Anne James. As Anne entered the office, Teri went through the motions of arranging the papers on her desk for some time before looking up. Teri believed she knew exactly what was coming, and she was determined that this time she would address the continuing problem as well as the current problem.

Teri handed a warning form to Anne and said, "Anne, we have to talk about your excessive absenteeism. This is your second warning. I'm sure you knew it was coming." Anne barely glanced at the warning and dropped it back on the desk. She snapped, "I knew nothing of the kind. There's nothing excessive or unusual about my few days off because I was sick. I'm not accepting any warning."

Teri said, "Anne, you can count the days yourself. Ten sick days in the last 6 months, and 7 of them on Mondays."

"I can't help it if I'm sick a lot."

"Even if you're really ill on those days, and honestly, Anne, it's tough to accept all those Mondays as legitimate sick days, you make it tough to staff the department reliably."

"Why me? Why don't you lean on Donna for a change? She's been out as much as I have."

Teri said, "No, she hasn't, not nearly as much. Anyway, that's strictly between Donna and me. Just like this is strictly between you and me." Teri continued. "You know you've used up all of your sick time."

"I know. This place made me use vacation the last two times. And that stinks."

"You wanted to get a full paycheck, didn't you?"

Anne glared at her supervisor. "I think it's rotten to make me use vacation when I'm sick."

Teri looked at Anne. Anne's face was stony, her eyes cold, her mouth a thin line. Teri thought: *Any time now. The next thing I say will do it*. Fighting against the knot in her throat, she said, "Anne, you haven't been reliable. I just can't count on you being here when I need you. Your first warning was deserved, and this one is deserved. If you want, you can appeal through proper channels, but the warning stands."

Teri watched Anne's face. Anne's eyes grew round and suddenly filled with tears. She buried her face in her hands and began to sob. If any other employee had been involved, Teri might have felt a measure of sympathy. However, she had been through this several times—in fact every time she had occasion to be critical of Anne. The pattern was always the same: anger and defensiveness, even belligerence, followed by tears and charges of persecution and injustice. And, as always, Teri wondered what to do next.

Questions

1. Although Teri was well prepared with facts about Anne's absences, she might have considered a different opening for the disciplinary dialogue. What opening would you suggest? Why?
2. How did knowing "exactly what was coming" bias Teri in her approach to Anne?
3. What would you suggest as a possible way of dealing with this employee?

References

1. How to deal with angry employees at your workplace. AirMason Blog. https://blog.airmason.com/how-to-deal-with-angry-employees/. Published April 9, 2021.
2. Miller L. Managing problem employees: a model program and practical guide. *Int J Emerg Ment Health*. 2010; 12(4):275–285. https://doi.org/https://www.researchgate.net/publication/51598538_Managing_problem_employees_A_model_program_and_practical_guide

Complaints, Grievances, and Appeals

CHAPTER OBJECTIVES

- Describe the critical role of the supervisor in addressing complaints and provide guidelines for handling employee complaints.
- Furnish the supervisor with specific advice relative to addressing complaints about compensation (wage and salary).
- Review particular circumstances the supervisor is likely to face at times, specifically, dealing with multiple complainers simultaneously, dealing with employees who take their complaints directly to higher management, and dealing with chronic complainers.
- Establish the position of formal grievances and appeals in the handling of complaints by the supervisor.
- Address the critical issue of sexual harassment, and provide procedural guidance for reporting, investigating, and resolving complaints of sexual harassment.

KEY TERMS

Appeal: A formal employee challenge to management, for example, a questionable disciplinary action or some other perceived wrong, pursued through the application of a specific organizational procedure. An appeal usually requests that a particular decision be reversed.

Grievance: Essentially the same as "appeal" in that it also involves a formal written complaint from an employee seeking remedy or relief from management.

Sexual Harassment: Activity involving sexually oriented conduct that, in the perception of one or more persons, is offensive through either direct action or the creation of a hostile work environment. It can occur at the workplace and also at job-related activities outside the workplace. Sexual harassment is identified as a form of sex discrimination under Title VII of the Civil Rights Act of 1964.

Complaints

Complaints represent a significant source of feedback from customers of all kinds, both internal and external. Employees are among our most important internal customers, and these particular customers are usually our greatest source of complaints. Legitimate or otherwise, complaints are signs that somewhere something may be wrong and in need of attention. Most worker complaints are related to policies and rules, working conditions, compensation and benefits, leadership, and relationships with other employees.

Role of the Supervisor

The role of the supervisor is to respond effectively and promptly to both legitimate and imagined complaints. Doing so avoids formal, and often costly, grievances and legal action. Increasing numbers of lawsuits are being filed by disgruntled employees, often after disciplinary action has been taken against them.

Gripes may be articulated during staff meetings, performance appraisal discussions, exit interviews, and ordinary daily contacts. Observant supervisors suspect potential problems when they note that certain employees are unusually silent, irritable, or depressed. Managers who practice "management by wandering around" often return to their offices with a bag of assorted complaints.

Caring managers engage in "naive listening." Naive listening is nothing more than listening as though one is meeting someone for the first time, without preconceived notions. Insightful supervisors readily admit that they have a tendency to tune out long-term patients, loquacious colleagues, or boring supervisors.

Seven Essential Steps for Handling Complaints

1. Listen carefully. The initial complaint is often only a trial balloon to see how you will react. You may have to dig deeper to determine what is under the surface.
2. Investigate. Is the complaint legitimate? Are there less obvious but more serious problems behind this one? Are other people affected? Is the situation getting better, or is it getting worse?
3. Choose what, if any, action is needed. Get help if you need it. Ask the complainer what he or she wants to accomplish. Make certain your proposed solution will not make matters worse.

4. Inform the complaining employee about your findings and what you propose to do. Do this without undue delay. If your remedy is not satisfactory to the employee, seek alternatives, if appropriate.
5. Implement your decision.
6. Follow up on implementation, checking the effectiveness of your action.
7. Record what has happened, retaining sufficient documentation to be useful should the particular complaint arise again or if some new action involving the complainant must be taken.

Complaints About Compensation

Every supervisor has received complaints about pay. These surface whenever salary changes are announced or when people in other departments get larger raises than your employees. Also, employees are often well informed as to what local competitors pay their employees and are quick to point this out to their supervisors. And the greater the difference between expected and actual salary increases, the more strident are the voices. Tempers flare, especially when there is a perception of favoritism.

Many pay-for-performance strategies exacerbate salary dissatisfaction. Employees who do not receive the maximum merit increase gripe about their performance ratings. Even more disgruntled are those who were told their work has been outstanding but later found minuscule increases in their paychecks.

To avoid or address salary controversies, consider these steps:

- Do not overrate employees or make unrealistic promises.
- Know what competitors are paying; human resources can usually provide knowledge of pay rates in your area.
- Try to get more compensation for your outstanding performers by other means, such as promotions, legitimate title changes, or revision of position descriptions and job upgrading.

- Let employees blow off steam about pay. Be empathetic.
- Refuse to discuss salaries of other employees. An individual's rate of pay is personal information.
- Do not practice favoritism and try to avoid even the appearance of favoritism.
- Know exactly how salary increases are determined in your organization.
- The following is an example of how to cope with a salary complaint: "Dolores, although salary increases are based largely on performance, other things must be considered. These include market factors such as the availability of certain specialists and what competitors pay. Other considerations relate to how critical each position is to the organization, budgetary restrictions, and projected costs for other activities."

If a raise is not deserved, state the reason very clearly. The person should know exactly why he or she was passed over and how the deficiency, if indeed such exists, can be overcome.

Supervisor "On the Spot"

When Complainers Gang Up on the Supervisor

When confronted with a group of highly vocal complainers, Bernstein and Rozen[1] practice what they call "creative ignoring." The supervisor simply sits quietly and looks thoughtful. This particular response usually gets the group to quiet down and become more manageable. If it is a group of customers or colleagues, the supervisor should ask for each person's individual input before responding, calling on the least hostile person first, if possible. If the group is a crowd of angry subordinates, the supervisor should tell them to pick one spokesperson; the rest must remain quiet or leave. However, the supervisor must be extremely careful in meeting with the single spokesperson. The meeting cannot appear to be a negotiation aimed at resolving the complaint; this would put the supervisor in the position of extending recognition to a "group" through its "representative." Rather, the supervisor should use this one-on-one meeting to listen and to learn about the complaint in detail. There can always be an element of legal risk in any such one-on-one meeting with one of the group, but this risk does not exist when meeting with the entire affected group.

When Employees Go Over the Supervisor's Head

Ideally, when an employee goes over the supervisor's head, the higher manager will send the complainer back to the supervisor as soon as he or she realizes that the employee has not given the immediate supervisor an opportunity to respond. Unfortunately, some managers are all too willing to lend an ear to employees who bypass their supervisors, especially when the manager and the supervisor do not get along particularly well.

On becoming aware of one of these occurrences, the supervisor needs to confront the manager and present his or her side of the situation. Before leaving the manager's office, the supervisor needs to suggest that in the future it would be appreciated if the manager would send for the supervisor while the complainer is still in his or her office or send the complainer back to the supervisor. It is risky for anyone in the organization to bypass one's immediate superior and take a problem or issue directly to someone in a higher management position unless this is done with the knowledge and permission of the immediate superior. If it comes to that, it is best for the individual and the immediate superior to meet together with the higher management individual.

The supervisor needs to let the employee know that what the employee is doing is known and that this "end running" is not appropriate. The employee needs to hear how such activities are counterproductive and can ultimately backfire.

Chronic Complainers

A characteristic of chronic complainers is that most of their complaints lack validity. These people are more interested in registering feelings than in resolving problems. They rarely participate in finding solutions, and their daily conversations consist predominantly of negative comments. Chronic complainers constantly use absolute terms such as "never" and "always." They frequently start their negative comments with "Why doesn't someone…?"

The occasional griper can often be stopped with "Well, what are *you* going to do about that?" Unfortunately this does not stop determined chronic complainers. They bounce right back, claiming they have no influence in the organization and their suggestions are never taken seriously.

Interestingly, the typical chronic complainer is usually a conscientious and competent worker. This person's work is usually acceptable, and often it is above average. This makes it all the more difficult to deal with these annoying people.

Although you can seldom cure chronic complainers, with conscientious effort and astute informal counseling, you can often achieve the following:

- Decrease the complaining to a tolerable level.
- Limit the complaints brought to you to those about which you can do something.
- Encourage proposed solutions brought along with the problems.
- Get the complainers to spend more time working and less time griping.
- Help the complainers develop more confidence in their own abilities.
- Eliminate complaining in front of customers or higher management.

There are several practical suggestions for addressing chronic complainers:

- Apply active listening. This is essential, but it is not simple. If you ignore their complaints, you may divert the complaining to customers or competitors. If their complaints get to your superiors, your reputation as a leader suffers.
- Listen to their main points. Write down the complaints in their presence. This is good for their self-esteem. Sometimes simply listening can silence the complainer. Do not agree or

disagree with them. Maintain a noncommittal facial expression, avoiding approval nods or sympathetic grimaces.

- Direct your attention more at their feelings than at the object of their complaints. Chronic complainers are usually insecure. They are reassured when their feelings are validated; for example, "I can understand why you're upset about that." Validating feelings is different from agreeing with them; it is simply acknowledging the right to have those feelings.
- Stop them when they start repeating or if they try to move to another topic. Rein in a rambling discussion by asking, "What's your point?" Acknowledge your understanding of what was said by paraphrasing and summarizing their main points.
- Avoid arguments. Trying to argue them out of their negative stance, trying to placate them, or explaining things in detail seldom works.
- Force them to help solve the problem. After acknowledging that a problem exists, move quickly into problem-solving. Ask specific, open-ended questions: who, when, where, and how questions. Avoid the "whys" because all too often they get you into deep water. True chronic complainers are not comfortable with problem-solving questions; they just want you to agree with their complaints.
- Encourage them to research their problems. If they say that they do not have the time, respond with, "Well, if you change your mind, let me know."
- Be honest when you say what you can and will do or what you cannot do. Ask them what it is they want you to do. When they say that what you propose will not work, ask them what's the worst that can happen. Then say you are not worried about that outcome. Another ploy is to narrow the options to two and ask which they believe is the lesser of the two evils.
- When solutions are beyond your control, say so. At times you must make statements such as, "We've simply got to make the best of it."

Appeals and Grievances

A distinction must be made between the terms "grievance" and "appeal" as they are used in this text. First, they are essentially the same in that they are both formal written complaints by way of which an employee can seek remedy or relief from management. A formal appeal procedure and a formal grievance procedure may or may not differ much from each other and the intent of both is the same: to provide a channel for formal disagreement that ensures fair treatment of employees, supports healthy morale, and avoids costly court litigation. The crucial distinction lies in the common use of the two terms: Grievance is strongly associated with labor unions and when mentioned often leads to the assumption that the workplace in question is unionized. Appeal, on the other hand, although representing the same sort of process, is intended to avoid the assumption of unionization by its use in the nonunion setting. In either instance, however, there are procedures to be followed and rules for the supervisor to observe.

Employers must abide by certain requirements and limitations placed on them by collective bargaining agreements, antidiscrimination legislation, civil service regulations, and employment contracts. Grievance procedures are included in every union contract. And many nonunion organizations have formal appeal protocols that strongly resemble grievance procedures. Regardless of the name of the process and the authority for its existence, all supervisors must be familiar with its contents. Unions are not discussed in this textbook. They have many intrinsic details that can be found in other organizational textbooks.

Supervisors who are vigilant concerning conditions that can induce employee dissatisfaction and who handle gripes expeditiously and fairly seldom have appeals or grievances filed against them. When these supervisors are faced with such formal complaints, they can counter the charges effectively because they have documented all exchanges with the involved employees and can justify any measures taken leading to any particular grievance. Often, there is a direct correlation between the number of disciplinary actions taken and the number of appeals or grievances filed.

When an employee is not satisfied with the response of a supervisor to a complaint, the supervisor should make the employee aware of the process for seeking redress, even though most employees who file charges will have investigated their rights and studied the organization's policy manual before filing or going formal with a complaint.

Employers frequently lose cases that get as far as the courtroom because the involved supervisors have been guilty of inconsistent rule enforcement, unreasonable application of rules, or excessive penalties. Poor documentation is the most common cause of management loss when a dispute is brought to the stage of grievance or appeal. The importance of documentation cannot be overstated; inadequate or incomplete documentation can usually be successfully challenged, and missing documentation can be deadly: If a particular event—say a disciplinary discussion or other problem manifestation—is not documented, it is assumed, in the legal system, to have never occurred.

Sexual Harassment

Sexual harassment is one of the two biggest sources of employee legal actions (the other being age discrimination). Sexual harassment is a serious problem because of the legal costs, reduced productivity and morale, and increased absenteeism or turnover that it may cause. However, it is even more serious because its existence indicates that management has been negligent in protecting its employees or others for whom it is responsible.

Sexual harassment can occur in any organization and in any environment. It is especially prevalent in healthcare institutions because of the many power differences among members (for example, between physician and nurse) and the close customer–caregiver contacts (for example, nurse and patient). Most working nurses have experienced or witnessed multiple episodes of harassment. Also, many of the departments in a larger healthcare organization, such as a hospital, are a mix of male and female employees, making these departments fertile ground for instances of sexual harassment. There will often be employees who fail to take the notion of sexual harassment seriously, and certain actions may not necessarily strike everyone as harassment. Both men and women might willingly enter into sexual banter, but while some will feel it is harmless, others will find it offensive. To a considerable extent, the determination of whether some act is or is not sexual harassment lies in the perception of the beholder. Or some seemingly simple act might or might not be seen as harassment. For example, an individual who asks a coworker for a date is turned down; no harassment, no foul. But when the same individual continues to ask the same coworker for a date after being turned down multiple times, this can constitute sexual harassment.

Also a significant hazard is the existence of consensual relationships among coworkers or between supervisors and employees. The situation may be quiet and untroubled until there is a falling out in an intimate relationship gone sour and one party starts making charges. Some organizations have been drawn into lengthy and messy lawsuits arising from consensual relationships gone bad.

In the early 2000s, the "me too." movement was founded to help survivors of sexual violence have a place to access resources, support, and a pathway to healing.[2] In 2017 the movement went viral with the #metoo hashtag on social media platforms, bringing awareness to sexual violence in all forms. Overnight thousands of people were sharing their "me too" stories. Many of these sexual harassment events were taking place at work. Sexual harassment is a serious issue in many organizations.

Forms of Sexual Harassment

There are two major forms of sexual harassment. Quid pro quo harassment occurs when an employee is expected to give in to unwanted sexual demands to secure some benefit or advantage or to avoid suffering the loss of job or some

tangible job benefit for refusing to give in to such demands. The other form occurs in the form of a hostile work environment when an employee is exposed to sexually oriented verbal, visual, or tactile activities. Verbal abuse includes sexual language, innuendoes, and jokes. Emails are frequently mentioned, as are phone calls. Visual offenses consist of provocative gestures and sexually oriented posters, letters, notes, or graffiti. Tactile harassment can be sexually oriented touching, patting, pinching, rubbing, or pressing. The behavior that creates or defines a hostile work environment is sexually oriented and, to those exposed to it, is unwelcome, unwanted, and repeated.

Legal Issues

Under Title VII of the Civil Rights Act of 1964, sexual harassment is identified as a form of sex discrimination. The Civil Rights Act of 1991, amending the Civil Rights

Act of 1964, gave plaintiffs the right to recover compensatory and punitive damages when discrimination is found to be intentional. Cases can be tried before a jury, or plaintiffs may appeal to state human rights agencies for relief. Guidelines from the Equal Employment Opportunity Commission (EEOC), in force since 1980, state that employers are responsible for the acts of their agents, supervisors, and employees and other people on the premises (for example, patients and visitors).[3] To prove a case of sexual harassment, plaintiffs must establish that they were subjected to unwelcome sexual conduct that caused them harm.[4]

Organizational Policies and Procedures

The presence and effectiveness of policies and procedures affects the prevalence as well as the control of harassing behavior. These policies must be clear and understandable. Employers and managers must affirm that sexual harassment will not be tolerated and that violations of policy will be treated harshly. Sanctions range from verbal or written warnings to reassignments, demotions, suspensions, or dismissal.

In addition to a strong policy statement prohibiting sexual harassment in all its forms, the employer should ideally have two important procedures in place: a detailed procedure for victims of alleged harassment to follow in reporting the offending conduct and a procedure governing the investigation of sexual harassment complaints.

There must also be policy and procedure provisions officially prohibiting retaliation against anyone complaining of sexual harassment.

Human resources should provide annual training directed at all employees of the organization. This training should include explanations of policies and procedures and illustrations of the kinds of statements or actions that constitute sexual harassment. Confrontational techniques for potential victims are emphasized and role-playing is recommended. Employees should sign a confirmation they've completed the training and understand the importance and severity of the sexual harassment.

Role of the Supervisor

Insightful managers are aware of the policies and procedures relating to this form of discrimination. They enforce these vigorously and promptly and with fairness, sensitivity, and confidentiality. They do not forget the rights of the alleged harassers. They find solutions that are satisfactory to the victims. In some cases they provide security for these victims. Supervisors should ensure that the workplace environment is free of sexual humor and inappropriate behavior. Nursing supervisors should be alert to violations by patients and visitors and should, if a violation occurs, take appropriate action.

Investigation of Complaints

In some instances victims turn to their immediate superiors. However, if one's immediate superior is the alleged perpetrator, which is sometimes the case, or if a victim feels uncomfortable dealing with that person, help can be sought from the superior's manager or a specialist in the human resources department.

1. Listen carefully to the complaint. Ask the accuser to put it in writing and include dates, places, names of witnesses, and the exact statements or behavior of the alleged harasser. Note: If the complainant later decides to withdraw the charge, get that decision in writing.
2. Investigate as soon as possible. Interview witnesses and other alleged victims.
3. Confront the harasser, and inform him or her of the complaint. Listen carefully to the rebuttal. If appropriate, tell the alleged harasser that the offensive conduct must stop immediately. Often, you find they simply were not aware that what they were doing constituted sexual harassment.
4. Document what transpired at the meeting with the alleged harasser, including the exact words the person used in his or her defense.
5. Get back to the complainant and relate what happened. If no supporting evidence is found, explain this. Reaffirm your own commitment and that of the organization to the prevention of sexual harassment. Tell the complainant to report any further incidents.
6. Report the matter to your superior and to the human resources department.

When You Are the One Harassed

- Do not encourage the person, and do not remain silent.
- Clarify your position and what you expect out of the relationship (for example, "I prefer to keep our relationship on a strictly professional basis").
- If the solicitations continue, review your employment policy, and follow the recommended procedure, or seek the advice of a senior member of the human resources department.
- Warn the individual that if he or she persists, you will regard the activities as sexual harassment and will report them accordingly.

- Document each episode. Get witnesses, if possible. Remember that a single incident rarely suffices to make a case unless it constitutes blatant behavior.
- If you filed a complaint and it was not handled to your satisfaction, notify the human resources department that you intend to take the complaint to the local EEOC representative, a legal service agency, a state discrimination agency, or an attorney. When legal action is threatened, things usually start happening.
- If you remain dissatisfied, do what you threatened and file a formal complaint with the appropriate agency.

WRAP-UP

Think About It

A supervisor once said to a number of peers in great frustration, "My crew seems to get the work out—eventually—but not without enough griping to take up half of my time. I could get some real work done if it weren't for all these nagging employee problems." To this supervisor, and to others who feel the same way, it is suggested that listening to and addressing the employees' complaints is a significant and legitimate part of the supervisory role. If we had fewer employee complaints to deal with, we might legitimately need fewer supervisors.

Questions for Review and Discussion

1. What is the critical error being committed when an employee who reports to you takes a complaint directly to your manager and receives resolution?

2. Why is it claimed that sexual harassment is a serious and widespread problem? How did it become that?

3. What do you believe is the one dimension of employee compensation that triggers more complaints than any other? Why?

4. Describe a set of circumstances under which you might legitimately consider disciplinary action for a chronic complainer.

5. Under what circumstances would you consider that one employee asking another for a date could constitute sexual harassment?

6. Why should you avoid dealing with a gang of complainers at one time? Is this not more efficient than meeting with them one at a time?

7. How can you minimize the likelihood of receiving an employee complaint after a disciplinary action?

8. Provide one example of potential quid pro quo sexual harassment and one example of hostile environment sexual harassment.

9. Why might some supervisors prefer the presence of a formal grievance procedure over handling all employee complaints as they arise?

10. What is the potential hazard in a consensual intimate relationship between two employees? Between an employee and supervisor?

Case: Where Did the Complaints Go?

As a new supervisor hired from outside the hospital, it took you very little time to learn that morale in the department had been very low for quite some time. As you started getting acquainted with your employees by meeting with them individually, you were quickly inundated with complaints and various other evidence of discontent. Most of the complaints concerned perceived problems with administration and building services, but a significant number of complaints by your staff were also about other employees in the department and some thinly veiled charges suggesting that a couple of staff members have consistently been complaining about the department to your boss. (Your boss has said nothing to you about this.)

It sounded to you as though a number of common themes ran through the group's complaints, and it seemed to you that a number of differences could be cleared up by airing these issues with the entire group. You planned a meeting for that purpose, instructing all employees to be prepared to air their complaints (except for those directly involving other staff members). Your employees seemed to believe this was a reasonable idea, and several led you to believe they would be happy to speak up, but your meeting turned out to be brief. As hard as you tried to get people to air their unhappiness, nobody spoke. You tried again 2 weeks later, with the same results: No one uttered a word of complaint. Yet all the while the negative undercurrents continued to circulate through the department.

Questions
1. What can you do, if anything, to get this group to open up or otherwise get their complaints out in the open?
2. How might you go about looking into the allegations concerning the employees who are carrying complaints to your boss?

Case: We Need To Talk—Now

A month ago you assumed the role of supervisor of one section of the clinical laboratories of Community Hospital, coming from the outside and taking over leadership of what was obviously a discontented group of employees. It took you very little time to learn that your predecessor was not well liked and that this person's penchant for what a couple of employees referred to as "three Rs"—rigid, rules, and regulations—was regarded with contempt and ridicule. This was not the first time you had entered into a strained situation, and your normal approach was to spend your first 3 months getting to know the people and the procedures before making any significant changes.

On the first day of your second month on the job you were carrying your full lunch tray through the cafeteria toward what you hoped would be a quiet corner when you were approached by four of your employees, three technicians and a receptionist. All four wore scowls and frowns, although one, the receptionist, appeared uneasy to the point of being afraid. One of the technicians said to you, "Look, you've been here long enough to know what we've had to put up with, and we demand to know what you're going to do. Now!"

Standing there holding a full tray, you glanced around at the crowd. A few people were starting to take notice of your little gathering. You quietly asked, "Right this minute? Isn't this a little awkward?"

Sufficiently loud to cause more heads to turn your way, the technician acting as spokesperson said, "Now!"

Instructions
In the form of an outline of sequential steps, describe how you are going to handle this confrontation with the four employees. Be as detailed as possible.

References

1. Bernstein AJ, Rozen SC. *Dinosaur Brains*. Wiley; 1989:74.
2. Burke, T. Get to know us: history & inception. Me Too. Movement. July 16, 2020. https://metoomvmt.org/get-to-know-us/history-inception/.
3. Burns SE. Issues in workplace sexual harassment law and related social science research. *Journal of Social Issues*. 1995;51:193–207.
4. *Discrimination Because of Sex Under Title VII of the Civil Rights Act of 1964 as Amended: Adoption of Final Interpretive Guidelines*. U.S. Equal Employment Opportunity Commission Part 1604, Federal Register, November 10, 1980.

CHAPTER 24

Employee Retention

CHAPTER OBJECTIVES

- Establish the importance of employee retention in maintaining a stable, committed workforce.
- Examine the shifting role of loyalty by both employees and the organization in today's healthcare environment.
- Consider the principal reasons why employees voluntarily go elsewhere.
- Provide guidance for the supervisor to apply in determining whether a genuine retention problem exists in the department or throughout the organization.
- Identify a number of critical factors to consider in addressing an organization's apparent employee turnover problem.
- Identify the true elements of turnover, and examine the way turnover may be determined.

KEY TERMS

Retention: In the context of the healthcare organization, retention consists of conscious efforts undertaken to minimize employee turnover, especially from within the ranks of needed technical and professional workers.

Turnover: Loss of employees, for any of several reasons, usually necessitating replacement. Turnover is ordinarily measured in terms of percentage of a work group per some period (usually 1 year).

Undesirable or Controllable Turnover: Workers who leave for other employment, depart for personal or unstated reasons, or are released for failure to pass probation or failure to maintain minimum job performance.

Focus on Retention

As work processes become more complex and employees assume more responsibilities, workforce stability becomes increasingly important. A reasonably stable workforce is essential to long-term organizational success. Vulnerable to the impact of the loss of experienced workers, employers must recognize the importance of employee retention. People who remain on the job create and maintain efficiency and effectiveness by sustaining productive business relationships with customers, suppliers, and associates.

When unemployment rates are low and the talent pool from which to draw is limited, that is, when it is a "seller's market" in employment, it can be difficult to attract and retain the best people. The people who resign during such a labor market are often among the top performers who are being lured away by what they perceive as greener pastures.

Relatively high unemployment, such as that experienced during portions of this second decade of the twenty-first century, can have a somewhat stabilizing effect on some organizations' turnover rates. Many workers are not as willing to "jump ship" when the jobs are not there to lure them away. However, unemployment rates vary by geographic area and by industry, so there are always places where workforces are more or less stable than elsewhere.

The dollar cost of replacing an individual employee is considerable, often ranging, depending on the character of the position, from half the annual salary to double the annual salary of the person being replaced. This is just the dollar cost of replacement that can be reasonably determined; it is more difficult to estimate the costs resulting from losses in morale, quality, and service continuity. Each departing worker goes away with valuable knowledge, skill, and a piece of a network that may include important contacts within and outside the organization. An angry departing employee can wreak havoc. For example, a dismissed employee of an oil company erased a computer database that was worth millions of dollars.[1] Favorable employee retention translates into high productivity, fewer mistakes, less stress, greater customer satisfaction, higher employee morale, and significant direct and indirect cost savings.

Formerly, the standard response to shortages was to step up recruiting efforts. However, many managers finally realized that retaining employees is less expensive and less disruptive than replacing them. It was also discovered that the measures taken to improve retention had other beneficial effects. These effects included increased productivity, greater customer satisfaction, and reduced absenteeism. A fundamental retention strategy begins at the time of employee selection and continues through to the time an employee leaves the organization.

Loyalty and Employee Retention

Needed: A New Paradigm of Loyalty

Corporate loyalty, that traditional bond between an organization and its employees, is rapidly becoming an obsolete concept. Formerly, the loyalty of employees was measured in terms of how long they remained with the organization. When workers leave for whatever reason, some supervisors are likely to complain about the workers' lack of loyalty. When a reduction in force occurs, even one that is undeniably appropriate, employees voice the same complaint against their employers.

It is not especially difficult to understand why mutual loyalty between corporation and employee has weakened dramatically and, in some places, has essentially disappeared. In the past, say the 1940s and 1950s and much of the 1960s, many people were able to enjoy secure employment in industries that seemed rock solid: companies that had been operating for years and showed every sign of continuing to do so. Workers who were able to become employed by one of the solid companies—for example, an auto manufacturer, a steel company, or any of a number of other companies—found every reason to believe they could spend an entire career there. Given this apparent stability, it was easy for a corporation to be loyal to its workforce, and it was easy for workers to remain loyal to an employer as long as they were treated fairly. Many individuals enjoyed seemingly guaranteed job security.

But times change, and business and industry were—and in fact still are—bombarded by galloping change wrought by technological advances, foreign competition, an advancing world economy, financial pressures, outsourcing, and numerous other forces. Most people working today have seen companies come and go, technologies arise and blossom and fade out, and fewer and fewer opportunities in work environments that exhibit any degree of long-term stability.

Thus, divided loyalties thrive in our increasingly complex healthcare institutions. Employees often find it easier to remain loyal to their professional specialty groups than to their managers. Indeed, there is today a growing tendency for skilled technical and professional workers to feel greater loyalty to occupation than to organization. Prominent among professionals and other higher-level employees is the notion of the "free agent" who has skills to sell to whoever makes the best offer. For many this reflects far stronger loyalty to occupation or profession than to an organization. The indication is to be loyal to your passion, or project, and not the organization you work for.

Supervisors, especially, experience a built-in divided loyalty. They are expected to serve both their superiors and their subordinates, and if they lean too far in either direction, they are accused of being disloyal by one side or the other.

The first casualty of disloyalty is productivity. Sloppy work, mediocre quality, and poor customer service follow, and eventually apathy takes over. Disloyal employees lower work standards, withhold information, conceal problems, file grievances, and create ill will.

The causes behind loss of loyalty are principally those that destroy morale. Major factors relate to working conditions, compensation, and leadership skills. Other factors are job elimination, limited labor availability in some sectors, and an increasingly mobile workforce.

Almost everyone is loyal to something, be it an organization, a person, or a concept. Loyalty in the organization may range from resigned acceptance to fanatical commitment, and it is closely related to work ethic and duty, the unwritten contract that requires employees to be faithful to their professions, their employers, and their colleagues.

A New Employer–Employee Model

The new employer–employee model is based on two realities: (1) employers cannot guarantee permanent employment, and (2) resigning from a job is not a sign of disloyalty.

Enlightened executives realize that workers no longer accept the passivity and humility that in the past were regarded as signs of loyalty. They now know that loyalty is founded largely on trust, trust that must be earned. Corporate loyalty is providing a safe work environment and reasonable opportunities for advancement. It is offering first-class benefits, rewards for high performance, and demonstrated respect for ability.

Better organizations replace career ladders, which tend to disappear with reengineering and flattening of most organizations, with new roles, challenging assignments, and other opportunities for individual growth. They replace job security with new opportunities for their employees. Supervisors earn worker loyalty by effectively representing the interests of workers to higher management.

Supervisory Loyalty

The most important step that supervisors can take is to find a substitute for guaranteed employment. The best substitute for guaranteed employment can be described as the safety net of employability. Managers who encourage employees to learn skills and who provide the means to accomplish this reduce the spread of unemployment and increase their employees' opportunities for more rewarding careers. Other measures for strengthening loyalty include the following:

- Be honest with employees. Tell them the truth about policies and plans that may affect their jobs.
- Make your expectations clear. Position descriptions, performance standards, orientation, and training are the essential tools for conveying expectations.
- Expect the best. Look for strengths. Either eliminate weaknesses or make them irrelevant.
- Be perceived as a supporter, defender, and facilitator rather than a judge, bottleneck, or nitpicker.
- Be consistent, fair, impartial, and trustworthy. Live up to your promises and earn your coworkers' respect.
- Practice true participative management.
- Show that you value every employee.

Employee Loyalty

Some employees, primarily the mature workforce, feel guilty offering anything less than absolute loyalty. A more rational approach is to accept the proposition that if employees are reliable and can be trusted and consistently meet their employment obligations, they are loyal. Loyalty is refraining from criticizing one's organization, colleagues, or boss, in public. Loyalty is not revealing confidential information to competitors or to the press. It is behaving ethically and morally, reducing criticism, and respecting confidences.

Loyalty is making superiors look good and doing everything one can to help them meet departmental goals and deadlines. It is defending superiors against false witnesses or attacks made when those superiors are not present to defend themselves.

Communality is important from a loyalty standpoint. This is a sense of belonging to a work group. It concerns issues of interdependence, mutual respect, and a sense of responsibility for other people. The core of loyalty is genuine caring for the well-being of the others involved in a relationship.

Why Employees Seek Greener Pastures

Employees are often lured away by competitors who offer higher salaries or better benefits, or so it seems. What management often fails to realize is that many departing employees are not lured away by competitors but leave of their own volition because they cannot stand their managers; many an employee has left a job because of the treatment received from a supervisor. Other factors driving employees away are boring work, dissatisfaction with career development, or lack of appreciation for their efforts. Many overworked employees believe they are being taken advantage of, are forced to neglect their families because of work, or are experiencing burnout.

In today's culture of job insecurity, employees must be looking for the skills, information, and knowledge they can take with them in case of

another downsizing. No more can one feel secure in most employment situations; rather, a feeling of relative employment security can be found in one's *flexibility* and *adaptability*. Insightful organizations try to provide those relative security blankets, but many hesitate to provide development programs for fear their employees will leave with their newfound skills and credentials. Ultimately it falls largely to the individual to take advantage of every opportunity to learn and grow and become more valuable to employers.

Organizations that base their retention initiatives entirely on compensation find themselves in bidding wars with competitors. The more insightful corporate leaders identify morale problems and correct them. They assess the workplace environment and make needed improvements, often based on the findings of their periodic employee morale surveys.

Because supervisors have little control over salaries, they feel absolved of accountability for the departures and identify the employer as the bad guy. Managers often are misled by what they find in letters of resignation or by the information obtained from exit interviews. It is easy to challenge the validity of exit interviews. For several obvious reasons, departing employees are reluctant to reveal the real reasons they are leaving. Instead, they simply say they have been offered better jobs elsewhere. Often, the real reason for their leaving is how they were treated by their immediate supervisors.

Few employees are assertive enough to confront their superiors. Instead, they channel their feelings by directing their indignation at top management or at the ever-suspect "they." When employees say they do not receive recognition, they are usually referring to lack of recognition and praise from the person to whom they report.

Analyzing a Retention Problem

To determine whether a genuine retention problem exists, collect and study information from the following sources:

- Records of actual rates of turnover, grievances, and requests for transfer
- Exit interview documentation
- Recruiters and recruitment-retention committees
- Focus groups
- Employee attitude or morale surveys
- Performance evaluations, coaching and counseling interviews
- Personal observation

Ask yourself several questions: What attracts employees to your organization? What do they like or dislike about their jobs and the workplace? Is there really a problem? If so, when did it start? Are only certain shifts or job categories affected? (Normally, turnover rates are higher for night shifts and nonexempt workers.) How bad is the problem? Is it getting better or worse? Are there manifestations that suggest a general morale problem? What has been our response to date, and how effective have these measures been?

Consider these possible causes that directly contribute to turnover:

- Lack of competitive pay, benefits, or appealing work environment
- Location of facility, parking, and other external factors
- Weak recruiting and selection processes
- Inadequate orientation and training program
- Lack of supervisory support
- Lack of opportunity for promotion, advancement, or education
- Inability to adjust to changes, as in mothers or others who have been away from the work world for some time

Retention Incentives

Cash-Oriented Compensation Plans

The retention tools of choice for many organizations remain those based on compensation. They include (1) retention bonuses, (2) gain sharing and merit performance pay, (3) premiums for employees consistently working long hours, and (4) salary adjustments or above-market pay for key positions. These compensation plans are a favorite by employees but can fall flat when not everyone is awarded "fairly."[2]

Career Development Offerings

Ambitious employees appreciate career development programs. Many employees leave employers when such programs are lacking. The kinds of programs offered include the following:

- Career ladders
- Internal job transfers
- Job posting programs
- Tuition reimbursement
- Career planning and development center
- Formal succession planning
- Career planning training
- Outsourcing (outplacement) assistance[3]

Health-Promotion Initiatives

The initiatives becoming increasingly important to healthcare workers include (1) health education, (2) health-risk appraisals, (3) health-risk assessments or screening, (4) special programs (for example, smoking cessation, weight loss), and (5) on-site fitness facilities. Today, the focus on health and well-being is a priority for most people, not just healthcare workers. Including spouse and family to the health-promotion initiatives could increase retention.

Recruitment and Selection for Retention

Today's healthcare organizations want employees who share the values and goals of the organization and who best meet the requirements of the positions being filled. Personal referral is an excellent recruiting method; generally, candidates recommended by employees have better retention records. Mentorship is another form of retention that is popular in the healthcare industry. (See the chapter titled "Staff Development" for more on mentorship.)

You can often spot potential quitters by reviewing their past employment histories and by asking provocative questions. Also, people who have changed jobs frequently are not likely to be with you for a long time either.

Further Implications for Retention

New Employee Orientation

The skillful orientation of new hires has a powerful positive bearing on employee retention. (See the chapter titled "Orientation and Training of New Employees" for more on orientation strategies.)

Coaching

In the absence of competent and compassionate coaching, most retention efforts falter. Great coaches are out where the action is and where they are needed. (See the chapter titled "Coaching and Counseling.") Their attitude is "How can I help?" rather than "You're not doing that correctly." They know the difference between delegating, assigning, and making busywork, and they delegate often. They also know when and how to praise. They cheer loudly and publicly when a team member comes up with an innovative suggestion. Good coaches support and defend their staffs. They intercede when their coworkers are confronted by angry customers or administrators.

Effective coaching and shared governance are powerful factors in retention efforts. Coaches are able to practice situational leadership because they know the disparate motivational and educational needs of each subordinate and respond appropriately.

Team Building

Employee retention creates closely knit groups. Because loyalty locks people in place, it follows that team building can be a powerful force in any retention strategy. Two major motivational needs satisfied by team membership are affiliation (social) needs and actualization (achievement) needs. Trainees and employees with limited skills derive much of their satisfaction from team achievements.

Morale

Critical to any retention program is maintaining high morale. Morale and recognition were discussed in detail in the chapter titled "Motivation, Reward, and Recognition." Key morale factors in employee retention include the following:

- Changing management style from command and control to coach, counsel, encourage, and praise
- Treating and compensating employees as professionals
- Carefully selecting benefits and rewards
- Providing a safe and comfortable workplace
- Supporting and encouraging career development
- Keeping employees advised of what is going on in their organization
- Providing flexible and equitable work schedules
- Offering mentoring programs

Identifying and Measuring Turnover

Questions continually arise as to how turnover is defined and calculated and how the resulting information is presented and interpreted. Accurately defining turnover requires knowledge of what separations are included and what period is involved.

Turnover is generally understood to be expressed as a rate, some activity per period, usually a month or year. What does it mean if a manager reports department turnover at 6%? Without knowing the period involved, there is no way of knowing what this number means. Turnover for this group might be reasonable or not far from reasonable if it is only 6% per year, but it could be alarming if it is 6% per month because this annualizes to 72% per year. Thus any expression of turnover must be qualified with the appropriate period. It is probably best to do so with annual or annualized rates, but a reasonable annualized figure requires at least several months of data.

A working definition of turnover should initially focus on voluntary separations, excluding individuals separated because of illness, death, or retirement. It is then necessary to consider involuntary departures, especially persons who fail to pass the probationary period or who do not meet minimum standards of job performance. Such involuntary departures, "quits," suggest the possible presence of turnover-affecting problems such as lax recruiting practices, poor orientation, or weak supervision. But certain other involuntary departures, such as employees who are discharged for cause, are often considered "desirable" turnover and left out of turnover figures.

What must be measured is *undesirable* or *controllable* turnover: people who leave for other employment, those who depart for personal or unstated reasons, and employees released for failure to pass probation or failure to maintain minimum job performance.

Also to be considered is the impact of work status. Healthcare organizations, especially hospitals, use a mix of full-time, part-time, and per diem (who work only when needed) employees. A part-time or per diem employee contributes less productive capacity than a full-time employee. Two employees working half-time can leave and yet remove the capacity of just one full-time employee. So, do you count two departures and in doing so unnecessarily inflate true turnover? This feeds into the necessity to express turnover using full-time equivalents (FTEs), counting not the bodies actually departing but rather the FTEs of *productive capacity* lost (hours of capacity lost divided by the hours of a base workweek to determine FTEs).

Although the use of FTEs provides the most accurate rendering of productive capacity turning over, it is misleading in some other respects. Recruiting and training costs are essentially the same whether an employee is full-time, part-time, or per diem, so filling an open full-time position with two part-time employees' costs twice as much as filling it with a full-timer. Thus the human resources department may track some of its activities with statistics other than turnover FTEs.

It is suggested that turnover be defined in one of two ways, providing the entire organization is consistent in the use of the definition: either FTEs or the total of full-time and part-time employees (per diems not included because they work no regularly scheduled hours).

And what about internal transfers? Should these be counted as turnover? After all, a transfer going elsewhere leaves a hole to be filled. Yet a vacancy in one department becomes a position filled in another department, and total positions in the organization remain unchanged. It can be helpful to maintain transfer statistics, but these should be kept separate and not considered part of turnover.

Overall, it may make the most sense for the organization to track turnover by FTEs to provide the best picture of the ongoing loss and replacement of productive capacity, but also to track by total scheduled employees to provide the best picture of the organization's continuing recruiting load. Regardless, as an individual supervisor you should make it a point to know how turnover is reckoned and what departures are included in the calculation.

WRAP-UP

Think About It

One of the most frequently cited reasons for employees leaving their jobs is the treatment they received from their immediate supervisors. Regardless of all that can be said about the influence of pay, benefits, and working conditions on employee retention, the supervisor who manages fairly, humanely, and honestly, with respect for each individual as both a person and a creator, remains the strongest single factor in employee retention.

Questions for Review and Discussion

1. What do you believe to be the effects, if any, of technological advancement and social progress on organizational and individual loyalty?
2. How will you respond to a supervisor who says, "Just hire the first one who walks in. If that one doesn't work out, we can always get another"?
3. Why, in the present day, are you not likely to see people pursuing careers of 30 or more years with the same employer?
4. How would you structure or arrange exit interviews to maximize the chances of securing reliable information?
5. What is the importance of the opportunity for advancement in employee retention?
   Will this apply equally to all employees? Why or why not?
6. Do you believe that all turnover is undesirable and to be avoided? Why or why not?
7. What retention incentive would be most attractive to new graduates? Why?
8. Where in the healthcare organization—department, function, occupation—do you expect turnover to be greatest? Why?
9. Career development opportunities seem to mean a great deal to some employees and little or nothing to others. Why might this be so?
10. What can an individual do to ensure the maximum possible employability in today's healthcare environment?

Exercise: The Career Ladder

At one point in the chapter the concept of "career ladder" is mentioned without benefit of definition or explanation. You are to do whatever research is necessary to facilitate your understanding of the concept and explain career ladders and their application in essay form. In your write-up, provide at least two examples of multistep career ladders that might be found in a typical healthcare institution. Your choices of occupation should be appropriate to the use of career ladders; that is, professional or technical occupations rather than entry-level positions or nonspecialized occupations.

Case: "... or Else I Quit!"

You are administrative supervisor of the hospital's department of radiology. The department has been having problems with the special procedures area; you have had considerable difficulty recruiting and retaining special procedures technologists. You presently have your allotted staff of three such technologists, but these people are fully utilized, and at least two of them have recently made comments about staffing being inadequate for the workload.

The senior technologist, Carl Smithers, has been especially vocal in his comments about understaffing. Several times, and as recently as Monday, the 7th of this month, he spoke with you concerning his perception of the need for another technologist. Today, Wednesday the 9th, you received the following note from Smithers:

"As I suggested I would do in our conversation of Monday this week, I am going on record notifying you that additional technologist help must be available by Monday the 21st. If you are unwilling or unable to provide the needed help, I will be unable to continue in my present position beyond Friday the 18th."

Questions

Concerning the ultimatum delivered by your employee, what should you do?

1. Immediately request the added staff to retain Smithers. Why or why not?
2. Call his bluff; that is, wait until the 18th to see if he does indeed resign. Why or why not?
3. Take some other approach. If so, what should it be?

References

1. Farnham A. The trust gap. *Fortune Magazine.* 1989; December:66.
2. Davison B. Strategies for managing retention. *HR Focus.* 1978;74(10):S3.
3. Zemke R. Employee orientation: A process, not a program. *Training.* 1989;26:33–40.

CHAPTER 25

Privacy and Confidentiality: Employees and Customers

CHAPTER OBJECTIVES

- Review the increasing focus on matters of individual privacy, and consider how privacy issues are reshaping portions of the supervisor's role.
- Consider the manner in which this so-called information age has made an increasing number of people more sensitive to their individual right to privacy.
- Review the key items of legislation that have served to regulate the collection and use of personal information.
- Review the general requirements for present-day handling of matters of employee privacy and patient privacy and confidentiality.
- Introduce the Health Insurance Portability and Accountability Act (HIPAA) of 1996, review its expressed intent, and examine some of the diverging views concerning intent versus effects experienced upon implementation.
- Identify the principal contentious portions of HIPAA, and consider why they have generated resistance and discontent.
- Address the role and responsibilities of the individual supervisor in the ongoing implementation and observance of HIPAA.

KEY TERMS

Privacy Act of 1974: Legislation applying to agencies of the federal government widely regarded and applied as a standard for other employers, stating that an agency or employer could obtain from individuals only information relevant and necessary for the accomplishment of its official purposes.

Employee Polygraph Protection Act of 1988: Legislation that banned the practice of routinely administering lie detector tests and defined the limited instances in which such testing can be used.

Fair Credit Reporting Act: Legislation that limited the extent to which an organization can secure information about the personal finances of an individual.

Health Insurance Portability and Accountability Act (HIPAA) of 1996: Many-faceted legislation, one portion of which (Title II) has had significant and far-reaching effects on matters of privacy and confidentiality.

Privacy and Changing Times

In American society, there is a strong and continually growing belief in the right of individual privacy. There are also increasing doubts about how the government might use information that it collects about individuals. Many observers believe that the arms of government are intruding more deeply into peoples' lives as demands for information increase.

Businesses are increasingly seen as exercising their legal right to review the contents of computers and electronic documents and to monitor telephone conversations as they attempt to learn more about the people they employ. Rapidly advancing computer technology is simplifying the collection, storage, and retrieval of personal information. Since September 11, 2001, the government has been responding in a big way to a perceived need to monitor individuals and their movements, for example the Patriot Act has changed surveillance laws.[1]

As they become more aware of their rights, employees come to expect that their privacy will be protected. At the same time organizations are asking for an increasing amount of information from people when making decisions about hiring or promoting employees. When individuals seek employment, work organizations seek information about past and present employers. Depending on the nature of a particular job, the application process could include detailed security screening. Employees continue to grow more sensitive to their privacy rights as they see organizations delving continually deeper into their personal lives. Many individuals continue to believe that the organizations they work for or apply to routinely ask for more personal information than is legitimately needed. The age of social media has made it easier for employers to gather information about future employees. Social media has raised eyebrows on the level of privacy individuals have.

Consider the individual's right to privacy and present-day concerns about drug testing. Individual rights are continually giving way to perceived needs for drug testing, especially for workers who are responsible for public health and safety.

Consider AIDS and testing for the presence of HIV; this represents a constant collision of individual rights with the need to have information about people seeking treatment and providing care. This controversy was largely responsible for the adoption of universal precautions under which all bodily fluids are regarded as potentially hazardous.

Overall, issues of employee privacy and confidentiality are pervasive in contemporary organizations. This is especially true in health care. The supervisor must be familiar with the debate between employee privacy on one hand and the right to know on the other hand. Putting the controversy into other terms, the conflict usually boils down to a matter of individual rights versus business needs.

Privacy and the Law

Once upon a time large amounts of personal information were requested on job applications and demanded in employment interviews. Such practices ended (although not completely, as violations are still encountered) when antidiscrimination laws began to limit the kinds of personal information employers could request.

Title VII of the Civil Rights Act of 1964 was the first major legislation to significantly address individual privacy. One decade later came the Privacy Act of 1974. Officially, the Privacy Act applied only to agencies of the federal government, but it became widely regarded as a standard for other employers. This law stated that an agency could obtain only information relevant and necessary in the accomplishment of its official purposes. It also required that as much essential information as possible should be obtained directly from individual rather than from secondary sources. Still in effect, the Privacy Act ensures record confidentiality, guarantees employees the right to examine their employee files, and requires that no information be disclosed without the consent of affected employees. These latter two points—employees' right to examine their own files and no disclosure of information without employee consent—continue to figure strongly in employee relations matters. Many organizations have policies governing both practices, although concerning employees examining their own files, an organization can require the presence of a human resources person to ensure that no material is removed.

In addition to serving as a helpful model for many employers, the Privacy Act has provided the pattern for privacy laws in many states. In most states, privacy laws allow employees to know that an employee file is maintained and to examine it when desired. Many state statutes also permit employees to enter information in their files to clarify perceived inaccuracies.

Years ago many organizations routinely used polygraph (lie detector) tests to screen potential employees and to make random checks of employees. Adverse reactions to these practices led to passage of the Employee Polygraph Protection Act of 1988, which banned the practice of routinely administering lie detector tests, considering such to be an invasion of privacy in most instances. The Act prohibits the use of lie detectors in most screening situations, states that employees cannot be randomly tested, and allows polygraph use only if there is a reasonable suspicion of involvement in workplace incidents resulting in economic loss or injury. However, the Polygraph Protection Act does allow testing of certain employees in positions of responsibility of significant dollar value, including armored car employees, employees of alarm and security-guard firms, and current and prospective employees of firms dealing in controlled substances.

The Fair Credit Reporting Act limits the extent to which an organization can look into the personal finances of an individual. This law regulates the conduct of consumer reporting agencies and users of consumer credit reports, prevents unjust damage from inaccurate or arbitrary information in credit reports, and prohibits employers from obtaining reports about employees except for specifically defined purposes related to work.

Employee Files and Employee Privacy

An employee file is considered the property of the employer. However, any organization having a privacy policy in place strictly limits access to those having a legitimate need for the information. For instance, a manager considering an employee of another department as a transfer candidate may be given temporary access to that particular employee's human resources file. However, one's status as a manager does not confer the right to browse files; there must be a specific, legitimate need to have certain information. The privacy policy will usually also state that employee information will be released outside of the organization only upon employee authorization or to satisfy legitimate legal requirements, such as court orders or subpoenas.

Legal Orders

It is a common practice for agencies to serve subpoenas, summonses, and warrants to employees in the workplace. Many such orders are served at employees' homes, but servers often try to serve them at job sites because often no one can be found at an employee's last known address. If process servers enter via the administrative office, they are most likely referred to the human resources department. Although practices vary from one employer to another, many organizations prefer to have human resources arrange for such orders to be served in private to avoid unnecessary employee embarrassment. Sometimes human resources may be able to accept an order on behalf of the individual, for example, for an employee being summoned as a witness in a legal proceeding.

Employee Searches

It can sometimes be necessary to conduct searches of areas such as desks and lockers that legitimately contain the personal property of employees. Every organization should have an official policy governing such searches, publicized so that employees know that searches can occur and the basis for the searches, specifically whether they can occur at random, for reasonable cause, or both. It is necessary to ensure that a search policy is justified and that there are good reasons for random searches, and the policy must be applied uniformly and consistently to avoid any possible perception of discrimination. No employees should be exempt from a search. Employee consent should be requested before a search. Consent may not be legally required, but it can often help avoid charges that might arise after the fact.

Access to Employee Information

Employee confidentiality always involves questions of access to information; once information is collected, who is entitled to see it? Arguments can always be made about the need to know, but legitimate needs can usually be determined by answering the following question: What will be the result if this information is not made available?

Employee Health Records

Many organizations formerly kept records related to workers' compensation, disability, and the like in employee files. Because they address employee health or physical condition, these records are now considered legitimate medical records and thus subject to stricter rules of accessibility. Employee health records are now usually filed separately from human resources information, often in a different office, such as the employee health service where they are subject to the same rules of access that govern patient records in a physician's office.

Patient Privacy and Confidentiality

Brief Scenario

A man arrived at the hospital to visit his mother, a patient on an upper floor. He stepped into an elevator which was holding two or three people bunched in the rear of the car and was immediately joined by two white-coated individuals who might have been young resident physicians or other direct caregivers. The two spoke with each other in hushed tones but still loud enough to be overheard, one asking the other whether he was checking in with his "least

favorite patient." The other responded with, "Selfish and demanding and she says some crazy things. I am wondering if I should order a psych consult." The elevator stopped and the visitor and the two people in white coats stepped out. Then the visitor saw the individual who spoke of a "psych consult" step into his mother's room. Instead of following, the visitor returned to the ground floor and sought out the administrative offices.

What might follow the foregoing incident?

Patient records, including results of tests, diagnoses, treatments, and any other information pertaining to persons for whom the organization is providing or has provided service, should always be held in the strictest confidence. It is considered a violation of ethical principles to reveal patient information to anyone outside of the organization without the express written authorization of the patient or the patient's guardian, administrator, or executor. The only legal means other than the previously mentioned permission is a court order or other appropriate legal instrument.

Internal to the organization, patient information is to be retained in complete confidence, revealed on a need-to-know basis only. Generally, the need to know is used in reference to anyone who needs specific patient information for the furtherance of that patient's care or for legal reporting or reimbursement purposes. At any given time this can exclude most of the organization's employees and outsiders; patient information should always be restricted to those who have a direct interest in serving the particular patient.

No information about a patient's condition— in fact, not even acknowledgment that a specific individual *is* a patient—should be given out without the express permission of the patient (or individual empowered to act for the patient). And even in the presence of permission, information should be dispensed according to the requester's need to know.

One of the most common violations of patient confidentiality occurs—often quite innocently—when two or more caregivers discuss a "case" in the presence of others. Many an uninvolved person has received an earful concerning a patient's situation by overhearing a medical conversation carried on in an elevator, corridor, cafeteria, or other public space. After a scenario like that noted earlier, perhaps nothing would happen, or perhaps the visitor might vent some anger about what occurred. Or perhaps the visitor might insist on seeing "the big boss" or registering a formal complaint. Nevertheless, one caregiver's brief indiscretion violated an individual's privacy (because three or four people heard the remark) and gave at least one person cause for complaint.

Needless to say, patient information passing between caregivers should be exchanged in private. In many healthcare provider organizations, especially those of sufficient size and employee numbers to have employee policy manuals and formal disciplinary processes, violation of patient confidentiality is cause for disciplinary action.

Information Security Considerations

Services should always be provided so that confidentiality, privacy, and data security are continually observed. The following steps are recommended:

1. Health information management (HIM) employees must be fully orientated and properly trained and should actively participate in the orientation of all new employees of the facility.
2. All HIM employees should be required to complete a confidentiality statement to be placed in each employee's file and reviewed and updated annually or whenever the employee's job duties change significantly.
3. Students, researchers, and others having access to healthcare data should also receive the orientation and execute the confidentiality statement.
4. Provisions for data security should be included in any contract for external services.
5. All requests for the release of information should be processed centrally in HIM according to the release-of-information policy.
6. Detailed rules should be developed and enforced to limit the use of healthcare data and to specify the conditions under which such data may be used.

7. There should be appropriate safeguards for computerized processing and storage of healthcare information.
8. Only persons with a legitimate and verifiable need to know should be permitted access to areas in which confidential healthcare information is processed or stored.

Health Insurance Portability and Accountability Act

When it became law in 1996, as far as the duties of most persons working in health care were concerned, HIPAA had little effect. At the time the most visible portion of HIPAA addressed "portability and accountability" in reference to employee health insurance. The intent was to enable workers to change jobs without losing coverage. This enabled workers to move from one employer's plan to another without gaps or waiting periods and without restrictions based on preexisting conditions. A worker could move from plan to plan without interruption of coverage.

Many managers in health care did not concern themselves with HIPAA in 1996. Human resource (HR) managers were the ones who became most aware of this legislation because it affected their benefit plans. However, during this time, even many HR managers had little involvement with HIPAA; in most instances the required notifications were handled by the employers' health insurance carriers, so there was little for HR to do other than answer employee questions. At that time nothing about HIPAA affected the role of the individual non-HR manager. In the minds of many who did not look beyond the simple implications of the law's title, the organization had little more to do than ensuring the portability of health insurance. However, the real impact of HIPAA was yet to come, and its arrival was a surprise to many.

This legislation consists of five sections or "titles." Four of these sections, Titles I, III, IV, and V, deal with the continuity and renewability of employee health insurance, promote the use of medical savings accounts, and set standards for the coverage of long-term care. Title II, devoid of any significant reference to health insurance, addresses privacy and confidentiality.

HIPAA's Title II

The portion of HIPAA having the most far-reaching effects is Title II. The formal name of the section is "Preventing Health Care Fraud and Abuse, Administrative Simplification, and Medical Liability Reform," but it is generally referred to as just "Administrative Simplification." The purpose of this portion of the HIPAA rule was to encourage development of health information systems through the establishment of standards and requirements for the electronic transmission of certain health information.[2]

Managers within health care, some to a greater or lesser extent than others, have found or are finding or are yet to find their jobs affected by portions of HIPAA. Eleven separate "Rules" have been designated. Even though HIPAA became law in 1996, not all of the 11 rules have yet been fully released for implementation, so for some healthcare managers, HIPAA implementation will be a continuing process for some time to come. Fortunately, the majority of healthcare supervisors will find their roles are not affected by most of HIPAA's rules (HIM is affected by more of the rules than other departments). However, all supervisors, and in fact potentially all employees, are affected by the Privacy Rule.

The controversy over the intent versus the reality of HIPAA primarily concerns the requirements of the Privacy Rule. The intent was to strike a balance between ensuring that personal health information is accessible only to those who truly need it and permitting the healthcare industry to pursue medical research and improve the overall quality of care. Essentially, patient privacy is at the center of most current interest in HIPAA.

Because of privacy concerns, HIPAA has affected very nearly all departments and divisions of all healthcare organizations from the largest of medical centers and hospitals down to individual practitioners' offices. Although there may be future modifications in some of its rules and mandated procedures, the heightened emphasis on personal privacy and the confidentiality of patient information is here to stay.

Implementation

The implementation of HIPAA is overseen by the U.S. Department of Health and Human Services. In December 2000, the Department of Health and Human Services released the "final" health information Privacy Rule, the requirements of which were met with mixed reactions throughout the healthcare system. Much of the healthcare industry, and particularly health maintenance organizations and other managed care plans, greeted this collection of new rules and requirements as a hindrance to the fulfillment of their objectives of service. On the other hand, patient advocates believed that the new rules did not go far enough in protecting patients' medical information. Compliance with the nearly 1,500 pages of the Privacy Rule, causing the most frustration with HIPAA, was ordered for April 2003. Most healthcare organizations were in reasonable compliance by that date or well on their way to being so.

The first version of the Transactions and Code Sets (TCS) Rule was published in August 2000 with a compliance deadline of October 2002, later extended to October 16, 2003. Affected organizations were to file TCS compliance plans with the Centers for Medicare and Medicaid Services by October 16, 2002, to qualify for the extension.

The Security Rule was published in its final form on February 20, 2003. Two dates were set for its implementation: April 21, 2005, for larger organizations like hospitals and April 21, 2006, for smaller organizations such as physician practices. Specifically, a "small" organization is a provider of services having fewer than 25 full-time equivalent employees or an involved supplier (other than a provider of health services) having fewer than 10 full-time equivalent employees. The Security Rule addresses the confidentiality, integrity, and availability of electronic patient data. The Privacy Rule covers paper-based, oral, and electronic patient health information, whereas the Security Rule applies only to electronic health data stored or transmitted electronically.

The Privacy Controversy

Reactions to the Privacy Rule were many and varied. Patients and patient advocates claimed that these new requirements were forcing people to choose between access to medical care and control of their personal medical information. Federal officials, however, were claiming that the rules would effectively balance patient privacy against the needs of the healthcare industry to provide everyone with effective access to health care. Therefore the Privacy Rule would ensure that personal health information was available only to those who needed it while allowing the healthcare industry to pursue research, promote public health objectives, and work to improve the quality of care.

When many of HIPAA's regulations first received widespread exposure, hospitals, insurers, and others claimed that the Privacy Rule would impose costly new burdens on the industry. They lobbied to have the proposed regulations killed, while at the same time Congress was claiming that HIPAA's proposed protections were immensely popular with consumers. Consumer advocates praised the proposed rules as an important step toward comprehensive federal standards for medical privacy, while at the same time suggesting that they did not go far enough.

To comply with the Privacy Rule, affected organizations were required to do the following:

- Revise, or develop as necessary, policies and procedures for handling patient medical information.
- Train employees in the handling of protected health information, including the orientation of new employees to all confidentiality requirements.
- Provide for the active management of administrative issues arising from or associated with the handling of protected health information.
- Monitor compliance with all requirements for handling protected health information.
- Maintain documentation as proof that all pertinent information-handling requirements were being fulfilled.

Privacy and the Individual

It would be difficult to deny that patient privacy is at the heart of most interest in HIPAA. For a provider's compliance with the Privacy Rule, all patients who begin a relationship with the provider are asked to sign a statement acknowledging receipt of a privacy notice. A typical privacy notice is a lengthy document; one might reasonably wonder whether very many patients who have signed for and received one have taken the time to actually read it all. The form and format of the privacy notice may vary from one organization to another, but it must provide all of the information required by HIPAA.

The following summarizes the rights of patients under HIPAA:

- Patients are entitled to know how their personal medical information will be used or disclosed.
- Patients may request and receive copies of their health records (a significant change from past practice, when a patient record was considered the provider's property).
- Patients may ask for corrections, amendments, or restrictions to their personal medical information.
- Patients may request a full accounting of disclosures of their personal medical information; all persons are entitled to know who is in receipt of their information.
- Patients may file complaints if they believe their privacy rights have been violated by improper or unauthorized disclosure.
- Employers and marketers are prevented from obtaining patient medical information without the patient's express written authorization.
- A hospital inpatient may forbid the facility to release information on his or her medical condition to anyone, whether relatives or the public, and may even forbid the facility to even acknowledge one's presence as a patient.

In many instances these privacy requirements are causing frustration for patients and others. Consider, for example, a spouse or other family member who is expected to help obtain a referral or follow up on a test result, or a benefits representative trying to resolve a simple billing problem. In brief, nothing related in any manner to a patient's medical condition can be addressed by anyone other than the patient unless the designated party has the signed authorization of the patient (except when the patient is a minor or legally incapacitated). There are, however, instances in which personal medical information can be used without patient consent:

- Information can be provided for certain purposes of research or study when no patient is directly identified and there is no way to infer a patient's identity.
- Information can be given to someone else in the provider's practice who has a legitimate need for it, for example, a billing service.
- Personal medical information can be given to a legal representative of a patient (parent or guardian of a minor, a designated healthcare proxy, a medical power-of-attorney agent, a person with a patient's written permission, or such).
- Medical information can be gathered by a legal public health authority to be used to prevent or control disease, injury, or disability.
- Information can be supplied to the U.S. Food and Drug Administration in the form of reports of adverse events, for product recalls, or to track healthcare product problems.

Effects on the Organization

All healthcare plans and providers are required to comply with HIPAA. Provider organizations include physicians' and dentists' offices; hospitals, nursing homes, and hospices; home health providers; clinical laboratories, imaging services; pharmacies, clinics, and free-standing surgical centers and urgent care centers; and any other providers of health-related services to individuals. Also required to comply are other organizations that serve the direct providers of health care, such as billing services and medical equipment dealers. All affected entities must do the following:

- Safeguard patient information in all forms from unauthorized use or distribution.

- Protect patient information from malfeasance and misuse.
- Implement specific data formats and code sets for consistency of information processing and preservation.
- Establish audit mechanisms to safeguard against fraud and abuse.

All subcontractors, suppliers, or others coming into contact with protected patient information must also comply with the Privacy Rule. In addition, all arrangements with such entities must define the acceptable uses of patient information. Overall, contracts with involved organizations must comply with the following:

- Define the proper uses of all patient data.
- Specify necessary audit mechanisms and other safeguards.
- Require disclosure when patient information is improperly used or disclosed.
- Call for the destruction or return of all remnants of protected patient information once it is no longer needed.

Depending on organization size and structure, compliance with the HIPAA Privacy Rule could involve several departments as in a large hospital, a few people as in a small hospital or nursing home, or a single person as in a small medical office. Whether accomplished by separate departments, a person or two, or an office manager, compliance involves several activities:

- Information technology
- Health information management
- Social services
- Finance
- Administration
- Various ancillary or supporting services

There was little doubt from initial exposure to the new regulations that every provider organization would have to make some changes and adopt some practices that would add to their workload. The most visible new requirement was the "notice of privacy practices" to be provided to each individual beginning a relationship with the provider.

Providers must now obtain written consent from patients or their legal representatives for the use or disclosure of information in their personal health records; this permission is granted by signing an acknowledgment indicating receipt of the privacy notice. The privacy notice must define the acceptable use of patient information and forbid its use for all other purposes. Providers are also legally required to disclose when patient information has been improperly accessed or disclosed.

The HIPAA Privacy Rule created a widespread need for healthcare providers to reengineer their systems to protect their patient information infrastructures and combat misuse and abuse. Providers now must comply with the following:

- Guarantee protection of patient information in both paper and electronic forms.
- Protect their information systems from unauthorized access.
- Implement specific data formats and code sets as specified in the law.
- Monitor systems to safeguard sensitive information against fraud and abuse.
- Monitor compliance by conducting periodic formal audits, investigating complaints and incidents, and generally overseeing internal compliance with the rules.
- Establish and maintain policies and procedures for the use and disclosure of protected information.
- Ensure that all employees are trained in HIPAA's privacy requirements.
- Compel the organization's business partners such as contractors, suppliers, consultants, and business services to return or destroy protected health information once it is no longer needed.

Also, a provider organization's remote employees or home-based software program must also be HIPAA compliant, so specific privacy guidelines for remote working employees must be created and implemented.

In addition, the HIPAA Privacy Rule has necessitated changes in physical arrangements to ensure that no one other than the patient and involved caregiver or other legitimately involved person knows the nature of the patient's problem. For example, at one time a physician's office

nurse might have given a patient specific care instruction at a front desk where other persons could hear what was said. This can no longer happen; any information about a patient's medical condition must be conveyed with a guarantee of privacy. This applies in any instance in which information of a personal medical nature must pass between patient or representative and a legitimately concerned party.

Every healthcare provider organization must designate an individual to oversee HIPAA compliance. In a large organization, this could be a full-time coordinator; in a small organization, the task is likely an additional responsibility for whoever manages the office. In addition to monitoring all aspects of compliance on an ongoing basis, this individual must also ensure that appropriate policies and procedures are in place and kept current.

HIPAA and the Supervisor

Depending on the kind of activity you supervise, the requirements of HIPAA can significantly affect your role. For example, in addition to being concerned with the Privacy Rule, as are all supervisors to some extent, someone supervising within health information management must also be concerned with implementation of the TCS Rule. Also, a supervisor involved with information technology or information systems will be significantly concerned with the Security Rule because of its applicability to health data stored or transmitted electronically.

Like other laws affecting the workplace, compliance with HIPAA is more than just putting policies and procedures and systems in place and mandating their use. Some HIPAA regulations are relatively complex, and in the areas of an organization that are most affected, a significant amount of training can be required. Also, HIPAA necessitates some training for most staff regardless of department; anyone who comes into contact with protected patient information must receive privacy training. This suggests that supervisors need to be both trainers and learners.

As a supervisor you need to be aware of HIPAA's requirements, especially as they affect your particular work activity. You need also to know and understand the contents of your organization's privacy notice and all applicable policies and procedures. And beyond this familiarity, your behavior should reflect obvious respect for every person's right to privacy. As far as all personal health information of all persons is concerned, never has the phrase "need to know" been so completely applicable as it is today. An individual's health information must never be communicated to anyone who does not have a legitimate need for the information in the fulfillment of the individual's needs, and then only with agreement of the individual or that person's legal representative. Also, the supervisor has an obligation to safeguard all personal health information against accidental disclosure.

Not About to Go Away

A number of HIPAA requirements continue to be shaken out, but it is nevertheless clear that the law's essential privacy requirements are here to stay in one form or another. Although there may be changes in how some dimensions of privacy are addressed, it remains likely that the privacy rules will continue to affect every healthcare provider and all other entities having contact with patient medical information in any form. HIPAA and all its entities will likely remain for some time to come.

WRAP-UP

Think About It

Respect for one's privacy and for the confidentiality of the individual's personal information is essentially synonymous with respect for the person. In these days of concerns about privacy, never has there been so much relevance to the meaning of "need to know" and never has there been so much truth in the admonition to do unto others as you would have them do unto you.

Questions for Review and Discussion

1. In your own words explain the HIPAA Privacy rule. Use outside resources as necessary.
2. Provide a couple of examples, other than those listed in this chapter, of jobs for which random drug testing might be allowable. Why might these be legitimate uses of random testing?
3. Title II of HIPAA is often referred to as "Administrative Simplification." What, if anything, has really been simplified?
4. What would be your response to an attorney representing an employee who demands access to the employee's human resource file?
5. How might HIPAA affect the practice of some hospitals in small communities that publish hospital discharges and births in the local newspaper?
6. How do concerns for public health and safety fare when considered against individuals' right to and desire for privacy?
7. Cite at least two facts about HIPAA that might lead some to express the belief that HIPAA does not go far enough on the patient's behalf.
8. Why do you believe HIPAA makes it necessary for even one's spouse to have written permission to learn one's condition when hospitalized?

9. What do you suppose is the ultimate test for whether someone's supposed "need to know" is truly legitimate?

10. Why should workers' compensation records be maintained separate from employees' human resource files?

Exercise: Writing a Department Privacy Policy

In your capacity as a supervisor in a mid-size community hospital, you oversee a group of some 12 people who are about equally divided between technicians and support staff. Most of these employees are mobile throughout the institution; most of them have regular contact with patients and visitors and are continually asked questions about patient status. Outline a policy for your department that provides guidance for your employees in responding to questions. Keep in mind the need to be as genuinely helpful as possible while observing patient privacy and confidentiality.

Case: Do You Really "Need to Know"?

Kathy Winslow worked as an employment representative in the human resource department of Community Hospital. One day she received a visit from Ed Smith, business office manager, who was actively recruiting to fill an open administrative assistant position. Ed had already interviewed three candidates who all happened to be current employees seeking transfer. Ed preferred someone with at least a small amount of office experience. One of the transfer applicants, a young woman named June, appeared to Ed to be the only real possibility available. The pertinent part of the conversation between Kathy and Ed proceeded as follows:

Ed: "The only strong possibility you've given me is this young woman, June. I really don't want to go with someone completely inexperienced. Got anyone else for me? Someone from outside?"

Kathy: "We haven't had any outside applicants, and you've seen all three transfer candidates."

Ed: "I was afraid of that, so I pulled June's HR file to check her out."

Kathy: "Oh? Who got the file for you? Elaine?"

Ed: "I pulled it myself."

Kathy: "You know you're not supposed to do that. You needed to ask Elaine."

Ed: "I didn't see her, so I helped myself. Anyway, this tells me almost nothing."

Kathy: "Everything's there, evaluations, attendance records, everything."

Ed: "I've heard that June's had a stretch of disability time off and that she was once a workers' comp case. I need the *complete* file so I can judge whether she's what I want for the job."

Kathy: "You *have* the whole file. Disability reports and other health-related stuff are in a separate file in the employee health office."

Ed: "That all used to be in one file."

Kathy: "Not anymore."

Ed (impatiently): "Then get me the file from employee health."

Kathy: "Can't do it."

Ed: "Part of that HIPAA nonsense?"

Kathy: "Yes and no. The files were separated before HIPAA, but HIPAA rules apply to the files in employee health."

Ed: "It makes no sense to have parts of the same file kept in two different places. And I need to know whether this June is likely to be reliable."

Kathy: "You're not entitled to the other file. In fact, neither am I. You'll have to go ahead based on your interview and the file you can review here."

Questions

1. Why do HIPAA rules apply to the file maintained in the employee health office?
2. Why would Ed be forbidden to see the record kept in employee health?
3. Because he is not allowed to see June's employee health file, how can Ed judge whether June might or might not be reliable?
4. In just a few words, describe the fundamental distinction between the file kept in human resources and the one maintained in employee health.

References

1. ACLU. Surveillance under the Patriot Act. American Civil Liberties Union. https://www.aclu.org/issues/national-security/privacy-and-surveillance/surveillance-under-patriot-act

2. U.S. Department of Health and Human Services. Health Insurance Portability and Accountability Act of 1996. ASPE. https://aspe.hhs.gov/reports/health-insurance-portability-accountability-act-1996

Healthcare Cost Control

CHAPTER 26

Managed Care

CHAPTER OBJECTIVES

- Define managed care as an innovating force that has significantly altered the organization and delivery of healthcare services throughout the United States.
- Highlight the principal features of managed care, and briefly describe how they function.
- Review the primary strategies of both healthcare providers and managed care agencies operating in the managed care environment.
- Introduce the concept of outcomes management.
- Review the common reactions of professional and supervisory employees to managed care initiatives.
- Review the employment opportunities that have been created or expanded concurrent with the advent of managed care.

KEY TERMS

HMO Act of 1973: Federal legislation passed as a cost containment initiative intended to favor competition in healthcare delivery and preempting existing state regulations that posed barriers to HMO formation.

Managed Care: A system of care delivery involving complex organizational arrangements between institutions and clinicians, explicit financial incentives, defined access to services, controls on the use of services, and coordination and integration of services.

Balanced Budget Act of 1997: Legislation adopted in part as an effort to relieve fiscal pressure caused by the growth of Medicare costs and overall to attempt to achieve a balanced federal budget.

Patient Protection and Affordable Care Act of 2010: Legislation intended to increase health insurance coverage and affordability for more people, requires insurers to cover all applicants regardless of preexisting conditions, and reduces costs and improve healthcare outcomes.

Capitation Reimbursement: A prospectively determined payment system based on the number of persons in the population to be served, transferring financial risk from the insurer to the provider based on some anticipated level of activity.

Outcomes Management: An approach to care delivery intended to reduce medical costs while preserving or improving quality.

Benchmarking: The comparison of quantitative indicators from one healthcare entity with others. Comparisons may be between hospitals or medical staffs, comparing physician practice patterns (clinical benchmarking) and financial and administrative data (operational benchmarking).

Value-Based Care: A healthcare delivery model where providers are paid on the outcomes of their patients and the quality of services provided.

The Arrival of Managed Care

During the late 1960s and early 1970s, the nation's healthcare system constantly reinvented itself and continually refined the changes that were made. Alarmed at the continuing high rate of growth of healthcare costs and the resulting impact on health insurance premiums—to this day still subject to double-digit annual increases in many parts of the country—employers and consumer groups mounted major efforts to evaluate how well health insurance plans, hospitals, and physicians provide care. The pervasive growth of managed care has forever altered the lives of consumers and providers alike. However, even with today's maximum penetration of managed care organizations, the increasing rise of healthcare costs is alarming, even more so after the COVID-19 pandemic.

The first approach to healthcare delivery under managed care came in the form of the health maintenance organization (HMO). HMOs were created as a result of the HMO Act of 1973, part of a cost-containment initiative intended to favor competition in healthcare delivery and preempting existing state regulations that posed barriers to HMO formation. This act established Title VIII of the Public Health Service Act and, along with subsequent amendments and implementing regulations, established the conditions for becoming a federally qualified HMO.

Since its inception, managed care has been focused significantly on cost control. The continuing question has been whether costs can be reduced without adversely affecting the quality and availability of services. Over the years not a great deal has been heard in the way of answers from the primary accrediting organization for HMOs, the National Committee for Quality Assurance. However, it is known that a great many patients express unhappiness with the availability of care, the lack of choice of providers, restrictions on services, and various other inconveniences. Some of these complaints may simply be those that inevitably follow change, but it is becoming increasingly clear that some do

represent a curtailment of benefits as the healthcare cost picture continues to worsen.

Even today, HMOs frequently boast about their preventive care initiatives aimed at keeping people healthy. This is potentially a real plus for managed care if it can be established that illnesses can be minimized and life prolonged without incurring large medical expenses. However, these preventive measures must consist of more than measures to prevent infections and make maternity care more available, two obvious areas of concentration.

Chronically ill people provide the most crucial test for managed care. It is the chronically ill and those who need the costlier diagnostic procedures or therapies who have been turning to lawyers to help them with everything from interpreting contracts to taking insurers to court when they are denied care. Many patients feel vulnerable and perceive that such advocacy can help them.

Features of Managed Care Plans

Managed care is a system of care delivery in which care providers receive predetermined compensation for delivery of services. According to Lohr, managed care plans exhibit some or all of the following features:

- Complex organizational arrangements between institutions and clinicians
- Explicit financial incentives for providers and enrollees
- Defined access to the physician panels and other services
- Strong controls on the use of services, especially the services of healthcare specialists
- Coordination and integration of services
- Accountability for an enrolled population and for quality of care[1]

Providers strive to reduce utilization rates by offering health promotion programs that target the most costly diseases, such as diabetes, cardiovascular disease, and cancer. They work to limit the use of hospitals in favor of outpatient care and home visits. One result is that nurses and other health professionals who worked in hospitals now find themselves working in other healthcare specialties and organizations other than hospitals.

Capitation Reimbursement

One special feature of managed care is capitation reimbursement, a predetermined payment system (with capitation meaning "per head" or per person). This approach transfers financial risk from the insurer to the provider based on some anticipated level of activity. The set amount of monthly reimbursement fluctuates only as the size of the enrolled population changes.

Managed Care Variations

Managed care is found under several different labels for plans or approaches that all essentially have the same meaning and intent: to control healthcare costs by emphasizing preventive care and by controlling access to various services. A significant feature of all managed care plans is the use of the primary care physician as "gatekeeper" to the healthcare system. That is, a patient accesses specialists or obtains other healthcare services only upon referral by his or her primary care physician. A person can, of course, elect to individually obtain any services desired if willing to pay the full cost personally, but the insurers reimburse providers only if proper referrals have been obtained through the primary care physician.

In addition to the HMOs, which were the first form of managed care, managed care variations encountered in various areas include the following:

- Independent practice associations (IPAs)
- Preferred provider organizations (PPOs)
- Point-of-service (POS) plans
- Physician–hospital organizations
- Physician management companies

Significant Challenges

The overriding challenge is to ensure that every managed care plan delivers high-quality service at an affordable price to all enrollees. The organizations that survive are those whose leaders are able to continually respond to changing needs. These organizations always know how they are positioned in relationship to competitors; they are knowledgeable about who the customer is and what the customer expects.[2] As rival organizations become more aware of and more responsive to the needs of their enrollees, competition between and among them becomes more intense.

Providers must be skilled administrators of resources while still delivering quality care. To provide quality services within the parameters of fixed budgets, extensive restructuring and reengineering of the delivery systems of care are unavoidable. Simply limiting diagnostic and therapeutic services is not enough.

Many services traditionally delivered by physicians are now delivered by clinicians other than physicians. There is active delegation from professional to technical. Technical employees turn over many of their functions to employees who are less qualified or have less education. The challenge here is to select these representatives carefully and provide them with the necessary training. Employers seek workers who are proactive, autonomous, creative, and possess interpersonal skills.

Since the introduction of managed care there has been a decrease in certain services and an increase in other services. Benge and his associates[5] reported a sharp fall in the number of laboratory tests per inpatient. There has been a marked increase in the number of hospitalized patients who are sent home to recover. Although early discharges require more nursing care than they did in the past, insurance agencies are allocating fewer funds for home services. There are additional challenging factors:

- Today's patients on average show less trust and less respect for care providers than did patients of an earlier generation.
- Care providers are more stressed; understaffing is common, often leading to increased turnover and decreased morale.
- Work units and departments are forced to adjust to frequent organizational changes.
- "Reengineering," "downsizing," and other such reorganizing activities have reduced job security.

- Increased errors have become a problem by the perceived shift from quality improvement to cost cutting.
- Reductions of space and budgets may restrict services.
- Rapidly growing regulatory agencies add to the confusion and frustration.

The true value and impact of managed care are widely debated. Many of managed care's critics claim that for-profit managed care has increased costs overall. Criticism of HMOs and other forms of managed care has led many of the states to pass legislation mandating managed care standards. Nevertheless, it is presently estimated that the majority of insured Americans are enrolled in plans utilizing some form of managed care.

The Balanced Budget Act of 1997

By the early 1990s, Medicare had become the largest single source of reimbursement for the majority of healthcare provider organizations. In 1997, the Balanced Budget Act (BBA) was passed in large part to address the increasing fiscal pressure caused by the growth of Medicare payments. By mandating that federal revenues and federal expenditures be balanced each fiscal year, the BBA fundamentally altered the rules of fiscal policymaking in the United States. A balanced budget would surely be sensible, but it was the manner of implementing balancing that forced disproportionate reductions in healthcare reimbursement.

The reductions required to balance the budget were not taken equally from all parts of the budget. More than one-half of the federal budget—including Department of Defense spending, Social Security, and interest on the federal debt—was insulated from cuts, so the balancing reduction would have to come from the remaining less-than-half of the budget. Medicare had already become the nation's largest third-party payer for healthcare services. So as a direct result of the BBA, drastic cuts occurred in Medicare reimbursement, affecting the income of healthcare providers. The BBA required $122 billion in spending cuts over a 5-year period beginning with 1998, with the overwhelming majority of reductions—95% or $116 billion—coming from one single source: Medicare. And most of the reductions were attained by eliminating or reducing payments to providers of health care.

The elements of the healthcare system most affected by the BBA were a matter of opinion, but it was clear that the provider population was significantly affected. According to some sources, the BBA reductions targeted post-acute care services such as skilled nursing facilities and home health agencies. A number of healthcare professionals were affected by the BBA, including physical therapists, occupational therapists, and speech pathologists whose reimbursement was severely capped. The BBA cap on combined rehabilitation services had the effect of dramatically reducing the number of rehabilitation professionals employed in long-term care facilities and also resulted in the closing of some facilities.

Those in post-acute care who felt targeted were not alone; operators of many hospitals likewise felt singled out for significant reductions. For most hospitals, Medicare had become a significant source of income; for some it had become their largest third-party payer. For years Medicare had been the single major payer that essentially contributed the full cost of care and helped many institutions remain financially viable. However, the BBA's reimbursement reductions forced many acute care institutions into the red, increased pressures for cost reductions, brought about closures, and prompted an increased number of mergers and other affiliations.

Some relief from the BBA arrived in the form of the Balanced Budget Refinement Act (BBRA) of 1999, seemingly recognizing the BBA went too far in reducing reimbursements. The BBRA suspended the cap that had been placed on outpatient rehabilitation services and paved the way for the design of a new payment mechanism. Also providing some relief for providers was a December 2000 infusion of cash provided in recognition of many managed care plans' abandonment of Medicare participation.

Strategies of Care Providers

Healthcare institutions have an obligation to redefine and clarify their missions and values. They must then put in place the kinds of people who can and will carry out those missions and support those values. Their missions should include vigorous efforts to prevent as well as to treat disease.

Successfully surviving the transition to managed care requires a blend of well-timed and coordinated strategies. Chief executive officers reengineer many of their systems and processes. Initiatives such as bedside testing, expanded computer systems, outsourcing, and modifying locations and hours of service help to ensure economic survival.

Providers display many innovative and diverse modalities for meeting these new challenges. Clinical enterprises are restructured to compete for the managed care dollars and to develop strategies to recapture lost clinical revenue. Sometimes these initiatives are controversial. For example, the practice of using nurse practitioners in place of primary care physicians has come under fire from both patients and physicians.

Providers must overhaul costs and procedures without alienating staff or allowing quality to suffer. This involves reducing numbers of nurses, adding aides, revising treatment procedures to achieve faster discharges from the hospital, and employing more outpatient treatment. Even a simple mechanical change such as pneumatic tubes to shoot laboratory specimens around the hospital saves time.

Hospitals that have purchased physicians' office practices must align the financial incentives of their physicians with their own. They may appoint incentive compensation committees to achieve these alignments.

Clinical Pathways

Clinical pathways are written templates of expected interventions and outcomes for selected groups of patients. Clinical pathways allow health systems to standardize care and to improve the processes and outcomes of care where possible. These pathways provide multidisciplinary healthcare strategies that optimize patient care by streamlining and coordinating care delivery. Clinical pathways involve collecting patient-treatment data from physicians to compare the cost of service and to devise the best methods for standard treatments. This provides standardized service for specific illnesses or procedures such as pneumonia, hip replacement, and coronary artery bypass surgery.

Patient-Focus Care Model

The patient-focus care model is a healthcare delivery structure that seeks to streamline care by restructuring hospitals into delivery units that are more self-sufficient. A premise of this type of system is to provide care to each patient by using fewer providers with a greater number of skills and responsibilities.

Integrated delivery systems put more care into the hands of interdisciplinary teams and coordinate care across many workstations. Computerized clinical assessment systems and automated performance appraisal systems can increase efficiency.

The study of critical patient care paths is essential for managed care environments. Supervisors must know how to develop clinical paths that create excellence in outcomes. There must be emphasis on avoiding all errors. Errors result not only in increased costs because of repeated diagnostic tests and delayed patient discharges, but also in less satisfactory medical outcomes. Some of these mistakes can be life threatening.

Strategies of Managed Care Agencies

Managed care agencies and their providers spend considerable time trying to determine what their enrollees want. Responses to what is wanted and what will be paid for result in termination of some services and addition of others.

Insurers resist reimbursement for treatments they deem investigational. Sophisticated drugs and improved disease-monitoring techniques will remain no more than medical journal jargon as long as health insurance fails to pay for these advances under the cost-cutting ethic that dominates much of today's health care.

Although the coupling between managed care organizations and their affiliated healthcare facilities is a loose one and little face-to-face communication occurs between these two groups, both parties are now attempting to get to know each other better and to meet each other's expectations. Managed care has exacerbated the reimbursement wars between insurers and hospitals, physicians, and other care providers.

According to Kongstvedt, managed care has imposed quality management principles of measurement, customer focus, and statistically based decision-making. He describes three sets of criteria:

1. *Structure criteria*: including certification of employees, licensure of facilities, compliance with safety codes, record keeping, and physician network appointments.
2. *Process criteria*: used to evaluate the way care is provided. Clinical algorithms, health screening rates, and evaluations against national criteria (benchmarks) are essential.
3. *Outcomes criteria*: such as infection rates, morbidity, and mortality.[3]

Outcomes Management

Advocates of outcomes management seek to reduce medical costs while preserving or improving quality. Outcomes managers develop appropriate descriptors to identify points within the healthcare system at which resources are under- or over-utilized and where professional skills need to be upgraded. Outcomes management depends on quantitative indicators that compare one healthcare entity against another in the process known as *benchmarking*. The comparisons may be between hospitals or medical staffs. For benchmark comparisons, practitioners of outcomes

management usually use financial and administrative data.

There are two types of benchmarking. The first is clinical benchmarking, in which physician practice patterns are matched. The second is operational benchmarking, which compares organizations from the standpoint of staff productivity, staffing mix, and the use of space and resources. Clinical benchmarking systems indicate how well one group of physicians performs against other groups. Process indicators such as length of stay, variability in practice patterns, and the impact of clinical pathways are assessed. Quality indicators such as mortality, complications, functional status, and patient satisfaction are tracked.[4]

Operational benchmarking programs are critical tools in reengineering processes in institutions. These programs allow administrators to evaluate the productivity of staff and to determine where the areas of greatest opportunity lie. There are two types of operational comparisons. The first is an internal comparison that follows trends of key indicators over time, for example, cost per billable test. The other operational programs allow for external comparisons, for example, against peer facilities or best-in-class organizations.[5]

Education

Utilization experts provide practical advice. Physicians and administrators are broadening their focus to include patient education, disease prevention, and health maintenance. Medical staff leaders help management reorient physicians to practice more conservative, cost-effective medicine.

Existing educational efforts must be bolstered, and orientation programs upgraded. Education and training programs should be based on needs assessments in which management determines what supervisors need to know. Appropriate topics include meeting the expectations of enrollees/patients/consumers, cost-effectiveness, time management, and personal empowerment.

For employees to feel empowered, they must have access to the kinds of information that in the past were available only to upper management and leadership. Computerized information systems and software make it a simple matter to summarize and disseminate appropriate information. Supervisors and team leaders should have, at the very least, access to the financial data of their own departments. All employees should be kept informed of the financial status of their organizations. Transparency is necessary for success.

At a time when many organizations necessarily focus on economic survival, patients and employees are all too frequently lost in the shuffle. Management must promulgate a value system of patient service, articulate clear standards of care, and provide practical guidelines. Managers must motivate care providers at all levels to put the patient first and to be personally responsible for maintaining appropriate ethical standards of care.

Managers and supervisors should insist on educational programs on the subject of managed care. Management should provide supervisors with training in developing budgets that reflect clinical realities, cost accounting, and strategic planning.

Provider Reactions to Managed Care

Organizational and personal survival in these turbulent times is more likely when every employee thinks in terms of what is best for the patients and the payers. It also helps when there are collegial relationships between and among various care providers, payers, and suppliers.

Employees and their leaders who understand the implications and make the necessary changes are well positioned in this era of managed care. Insightful supervisors develop partnerships. Their partners are in finance, utilization review, human resources, and departments that control the resources needed to manage job performance outcomes.

Health professionals must stay abreast of the dynamic knowledge base within their specialties. They must take responsibility for explaining to their patients the processes and expected outcomes of care. Management must insist on maintaining high standards for licensure, certification, and recertification for all individuals and units.

The challenge for the individual supervisor is to develop a responsive work group that can change quickly to meet the ever-changing requirements of the healthcare workplace. Stucky and Waltrip list four competencies that can help providers survive in managed care settings:

1. *Clinical management*: resource allocation, productivity measurement, disease management
2. *Financial management*: budgeting, management of variance, cost analysis, statistics
3. *Information management*: communication flow, medical records, quality improvement
4. *Leadership*: employee management, communication skills, team building, time management[6]

Employment Opportunities in the Managed Care Industry

With focus on the provisions of managed care programs, there is room for growth. Like all rapidly growing industries, especially healthcare, there are new buildings, multiple hierarchical levels, internal politics, and the usual growing pains associated with change. Many opportunities exist if professional and management staff look for them and are willing to adjust to new roles and responsibilities.

New opportunities are also available in hospitals and other provider institutions. Attractive positions are available for health professionals and supervisors who are multi-skilled and willing to master new competencies. Many employers are looking for multidisciplinary professionals, managers, and supervisors to replace highly specialized staff in certain settings.

Case Managers

Case managers are found both in healthcare institutions and in payer organizations. They function through third-party administrators or self-administered programs. They may also work for patients or family members. Case managers deal with managed care patients who have extensive medical problems or are expected to receive care over an extended period. These managers determine whether the care being received is appropriate for both fiscal and quality assurance purposes.[7] Kongstvedt lists the following activities performed by case managers:

- They coordinate, facilitate, and educate.
- They collaborate with physicians, medical equipment providers, home care agencies, therapists, and other providers.
- They ensure that patients follow prescribed treatment plans and that the equipment delivered to the home is what was ordered.
- Along with benefits administrators, they pursue alternatives to the plan package in the best interest of the patient and the payer.[8, p. 274]

Utilization Reviewers

Utilization reviewers are healthcare administrators and other professionals who conduct evaluations to determine resource usage patterns of patient care. The objective of utilization review is to provide cost control, promote quality of care, and guarantee enrollee satisfaction. These reviewers submit their findings to the appropriate authorities for remedial action.[9]

Advice Nurses

Many plans operate 24-hour nurse advice telephone lines. Nurse advice lines provide members with access regarding medical conditions, the need for medical care, health promotion and preventive care, and many other advice-related activities. These nurses are also called triage nurses.[10, p. 250]

Enrollees are encouraged—and, under some plans, required—to call nurse advice lines before going to emergency departments. The nurse uses a clinical protocol to evaluate the member's complaints and then renders advice about what the member should do.[11, p. 336]

Authorizing Authorities

In some PPOs hospital treatment authorization may require the approval of a primary care physician, the so-called gatekeeper. In other PPOs and in managed indemnity plans, elective hospitalization and various procedures may be authorized by staff rather than physicians. These authorizing employees are usually nurses.[12]

Claims and Benefits Administration Employees

These employees do not ordinarily require any special medical training, although one who is new to such employment may have an advantage by possessing some familiarity with the healthcare environment.

Here to Stay

As noted earlier, in the four decades since its inception, managed care in its various program forms has grown to involve the overwhelming majority of provider organizations and most insured Americans. Although managed care likely has as many critics as proponents among both providers and patients, it is not about to go away. One can argue forever about whether managed care is controlling costs or adding cost to the healthcare system, but managed care will prevail. The COVID-19 pandemic made it very clear that the healthcare system continues to evolve and still faces many challenges that include how to provide quality healthcare services. *Value-based care* is a healthcare model where providers are paid on the outcomes of their patients and the quality of services provided. This managed care model is considered to be the new model of healthcare.

Regardless of the forms or models it may assume in the future, we can rest assured that the provision of health care will always be "managed" in some way.

The Patient Protection and Affordable Care Act of 2010[13]

The major legislation known as the Patient Protection and Affordable Care Act of 2010 (the ACA, "health care reform," or "Obamacare") is affecting the healthcare system at all levels. Since its implementation in 2010, the legislation's passage initially sparked efforts aimed at repeal, but such efforts have diminished. The federal mandates of the ACA have been generating companion state-level legislation, though not uniformly throughout the country. More than 100 regulatory agencies, boards, and councils have been empowered to issue guidelines and regulations.

It is not possible in the limited space of a few paragraphs to convey the implications of the ACA. The text of the Act itself runs to more than 1,000 pages, not counting the implementing regulations that follow the passage of the law (and in most cases, the regulations implementing a new law are more voluminous than the law itself). However, implications of the ACA suggest that the healthcare system may experience the following:

- *In healthcare organizational settings:* Increase in community health centers; development of independence-at-home programs; creation of community-based transition programs for Medicare patients at high risk for readmission to acute care; and phasing out of physician-owned specialty hospitals
- *In patterns of care:* More wellness programs and preventive care; wellness care incentives; increased emphasis on coordination of care for all stages of care; and creation of medical homes or health homes programs for chronic illness care (Note: "Home" in this context is not a place to live; it means the primary caregiver who coordinates various aspects of care including referrals to specialists.)
- *For healthcare practitioners:* Increased funding for training; increased utilization of physician assistants and nurse practitioners; and increased roles for pharmacists in direct counseling concerning medication management
- *For customers:* Increased numbers as more people come under new health insurance coverage; a surge in demand for specific services as coverage for these services unfolds (e.g., free annual physical exam); increased need for client education about the details of coverage; increased need to capture eligibility data; and increased sensitivity to patients' concerns about their coverage and their continued access to care

Following is a greatly abbreviated sampling of perceived problems and issues that have arisen out of the implementation of the ACA:

- A mandate requires all employers having at least 50 full-time employees to offer affordable health coverage to at least 95% of their full-time employees or be subject to fines. The reaction of some employers has been to convert positions to part time.
- The government dictates plan requirements, telling those who provide or purchase plans what must be covered.
- It has been reported that some insurers are reducing agents' commissions to discourage the sale of the ACA plans on which they are losing the most money.
- Most upsetting to some individuals has been the imposition of a monetary penalty for failure to secure health insurance, a "tax" to be collected at income tax time from individuals not covered under an employer's plan or a welfare plan such as Medicaid.

After the 2016 election, a new presidential administration tried to repeal the ACA with no success. The ACA will continue to shake out for some time to come and depending on what follows political elections throughout the years, we may also continue to see renewed efforts to repeal or at least alter it significantly.

WRAP-UP

Think About It

Managed care has become the predominant approach to healthcare delivery in the country. Although it continues to change in a number of ways, the changes are directed toward improving and strengthening managed care, not replacing it with something else. Chances are that managed care is not simply a phase, it is certain to continue its movement away from fee-for-service reimbursement in favor of some form of reimbursement by positive outcomes. For all practical purposes, the old way of purchasing medical care is gone forever.

Questions for Review and Discussion

1. What is utilization review? In your own words explain the function and purpose.
2. Will managed care ever go away? What is the outlook for the future?
3. What perceived risks are present when all patients are free to select their own specialist providers?
4. What appears to be the primary advantage of using clinical pathways?
5. What can managed care plans potentially do, or what do they actually do, to encourage preventive health care?
6. How can a case manager position pay for itself in savings to the healthcare system?
7. What is the principal advantage of benchmarking? Provide an example.
8. Explain why value-based care is better for patients.
9. Will straight fee-for-service health care continue to exist at all? Why or why not?
10. What is likely the strongest cost-saving feature of every managed care plan? Why is this so?

Exercise: Operational Benchmarking

According to this text, operational benchmarking "compares organizations from the standpoint of staff productivity, staffing mix, and the use of space and resources." You are to select one particular health facility department or function, preferably one with which you have some knowledge or familiarity, and develop a benchmarking profile for that department or function; that is, develop a detailed listing of the features or characteristics of the operation that can have a bearing on cost, and indicate what benchmarking data you perceive as necessary or helpful. (You are looking for indicators such as output in units per period, items processed per person per hour, etc.) As indicated previously, consider staff productivity, staffing mix, and the use of space and resources. Use outside resources if necessary.

References

1. Lohr KN. Measuring and improving quality and performance in an evolving health-care sector. *Clinical Laboratory Management Review.* 1997;11(4):265–272.
2. Kerfoot K. Today's patient care unit manager. *Nursing Economics.* 1994;12(6):340–341.
3. Benge H et al. Impact of managed care on the economics of laboratory operation in an academic medical center. *Archives of Pathology and Laboratory Medicine.* 1997; 121:689–694.
4. Kongstvedt PR. *The Managed Health Care Handbook*, 3rd ed. Aspen Publishers; 1996:402, 577, 659.
5. Vance RP. Resource utilization and outcomes management: Opportunities for the entrepreneurial pathologist. *Clinical Laboratory Management Review.* 1997;11(5):318–321.

6. Vance RP. Resource utilization and outcomes management: Opportunities for the entrepreneurial pathologist. *Clinical Laboratory Management Review.* 1997;11(5):318–321.

7. Stucky S, Waltrip L. Managed care: Are your middle managers ready? *Caring Magazine.* 1995;14(10):94–98.

8. Kongstvedt, *supra* note 7, at 274.

9. Landry & Knox, *supra* note 1.

10. Kongstvedt, *supra* note 7, at 250.

11. *Id.* at 336.

12. *Id.* at 470.

13. Portions of the section adapted from: Liebler JG, McConnell CR. The challenge of change. Chapter 2 in *in Management Principles for Health Professionals,* 7th ed. Burlington, MA: Jones & Bartlett Learning; 2017.

CHAPTER 27

Budgets and Cost Control

CHAPTER OBJECTIVES

- Introduce the concepts of budgets and budgeting, and establish their essential role in the operation of an organization or organizational unit.
- Identify the significant functions and elements of budgets, and enumerate the principles and rules of budgeting as they apply to the supervisor.
- Introduce the controlling process as related to budgets.
- Identify overtime as a sometimes-significant cost element, and suggest steps for keeping overtime under control.
- Describe a number of significant cost-reducing measures, including rightsizing and reengineering, that the supervisor may encounter.
- Identify the role of benchmarking in cost control.

KEY TERMS

Budget: A financial plan for the conduct of business for some period in the near future, usually 1 year. As such, the budget provides a financial map of coming activities.

Variance (or Budget Variance): The amount by which the actual outlay for a particular expense category is less than the budgeted amount (usually a favorable condition) or more than the budgeted amount (usually an unfavorable condition).

Rightsizing: The process of matching staffing to workloads to become more efficient.

A Key Supervisory Activity

The cost-containment measures imposed on healthcare providers have greatly increased the importance of cost control. Supervisors are key people in the control and reduction of expenses. Essential parts of the supervisory role are participating in the preparation of departmental budgets, suggesting cost-cutting measures, and directing the application of control measures.

Budgets and Their Functions

Planning

The preparation of a budget is part of the planning function. A budget is itself a plan, a financial plan for the conduct of business in the near future. A budget provides a financial map of coming activities. It also contains information vital to the potential determination of new charges and adjustments to various costs of doing business. Budget planning normally starts at executive levels and trickles down to first-line managers. It should coincide with the review of major policies and the reassessment of plans and goals.

Controlling

The administration of a budget is part of the controlling function, and the budget itself is the most powerful tool available for controlling. A budget creates a greater awareness of costs on the part of employees, and it also helps them achieve goals within stated cost expenditures.

The finance department usually provides supervisors with weekly or monthly cost reports of expenditures against the budget. These reports highlight variances that serve as red flags for remedial action.

Evaluating

Performance appraisals of supervisors usually include the assessment of how accurately they forecast their expenses and how well their expenditures match the monies allocated. Variances can reflect poorly on a supervisor's financial skills unless the deviations result from factors not under his or her control. Staying under budget is not always a cause for celebration. Having funds left over at the end of the year might sometimes indicate efficient management of resources, but it can just as readily result from careless budgeting.

Principles and Rules of Budgeting

- Expenses must always be charged to the department or cost center that incurs the expenditures.
- Every item of expense must be under the control of someone in the organization.
- Supervisors and managers responsible for complying with expense budgets must participate in budget preparation.
- Supervisors must not be held responsible for expenditures over which they have no control.

- Unused budgeted funds may not be carried over from one annual budget to the next.
- Unused funds for capital expenditures may not be transferred to operating expenses or vice versa.
- Requisitions for individual expenditures require approval by some authority.
- "Slush funds" or contingency funds not specifically identified are not permitted, but supervisors should try to allocate some monies for unexpected needs.

Revenue

Depending on the budgeting approach of a particular organization, revenue figures may come from finance or from the information services department. Computerized billing makes it possible to calculate revenue for each department or section and to use these figures to project anticipated future revenue.

Most supervisors are usually not directly accountable for revenues, but revenues can be helpful in determining charges for the services their departments render. Without the supervisors' cost data, finance departments have no legitimate basis for determining charges or for forecasting profit or loss. In predicting revenue and costs, it is necessary to consider not only historical growth trends but also changes in the anticipated workload because of the introduction of new services, procedures, or equipment.

Preparation of Budgets

A breakdown of expenses charged to a department by categories, such as salaries, benefits, and supplies, is essential (**Table 27.1**). Expenses should be recorded on an ongoing basis. A budget cannot be adequately prepared the week before it is due. To prepare an itemization of expenses, collect expense figures for several months. Annualize the figures by dividing the year-to-date expenses by the number of months recorded, then multiply by 12.

During the year, suggestions or proposals may turn up that involve additional expense or cost-cutting opportunities. Record all of these.

Table 27.1 Example of a Forecast Budget: Chemistry Section

Item	Annual Expense ($)
Medical/surgical supplies	300
Employee welfare	20,640
Pension	2,112
Postage, freight, express	408
Salaries and wages	281,572
Departmental supplies	367,800
Quality control	28,667
Travel	672
Publications	100
Education	336
Repairs and maintenance	12,000
Total Direct Expense	714,607

Take into account increases in supply expenses, service contracts, and continuing education expenses when planning a forecast budget.

Capital Equipment

Usually a separate budget or a section of the overall budget is set aside for capital equipment. Many organizations project their capital equipment budgets out for 2, 3, 4, or 5 years into the future. This extended capital budget may change from year to year as priorities change and unforeseen circumstances arise, but more often than not, capital funds are strictly limited organization-wide, and what one department might want in the short run may have to defer to something another department critically needs. Supervisors, who must be knowledgeable of rates of obsolescence of major pieces of equipment, often seek this kind of information from manufacturers or suppliers.

Replacement items and new equipment are among the most expensive budgetary items for some cost centers (for example, laboratory or radiology services, where single pieces of equipment can run into the hundreds of thousands of dollars). The capital equipment budget should reflect the costs of these items.

Wages, Benefits, and Overhead

The figures for salaries, benefits, and overhead are not budgeted by the operating departments. These numbers come from elsewhere, primarily from the finance department. However, other areas may be involved; for example, budgeted benefit costs may come from the human resources department. This is appropriate because supervisors have no control over these items and cannot be held responsible for them.

Salaries represent more than 60% of operating expenses for most cost centers in the typical healthcare organization. Therefore, when administrators feel the need to cut costs, the first area they scrutinize is usually employee expenses. It is essential to keep detailed records to justify work hours and overtime and make certain that the figures going into the budget are as accurate as possible.

Management is ordinarily unwilling to approve requests for additional staff, even when there is a projected increase in the workload, unless the need can be proven on paper. Reports of crises that have occurred because of employee shortages can help in the justification process. This also holds true for equipment problems and requests for new apparatus.

Controlling Process

Always be prepared to defend the budget figures you submit. With or without modifications by higher management, the budget revisits supervisors at least monthly in the form of a responsibility summary (**Table 27.2**). This simplified report shows actual expenditures compared with budgeted amounts for the month. The full report received by the supervisor also shows cumulative actual and budget figures for the year to date, so it is possible to track performance against budget in cumulative fashion throughout the year. Variances are shown for each budget category. When variances exceed a certain amount, supervisors are usually required to submit an explanation.

Table 27.2 Responsibility Summary

Current Month	Actual ($)	Budget ($)	Variance ($)
Inpatient revenue	160,414	167,081	6,667*
Outpatient revenue	106,591	78,129	28,462
Total patient revenue	267,005	245,210	21,795
Medical/surgical supplies	207	25	182*
Employee welfare	2,299	1,663	636*
Pension	1,059	1,059	0
Postage, freight, express	31	34	3
Salaries and wages	25,166	23,263	1,903*
Departmental supplies	43,788	30,650	13,138*
Quality control	211	211*	0
Travel	118	118	0
Publications	59	59	0
Education	49	1,000	951
Repairs and maintenance	72,810	57,871	14,939*
Total direct expense	267,005	245,210	21,795
Total patient revenue	72,810	57,871	14,939*
Operating gain or loss	194,195	187,339	6,856

*Unfavorable variances (i.e., low revenue or high expenditures)

Review these reports soon after receiving them. If an item is not clear or may be in error, seek clarification from finance or information services, whichever division issues the report. Be prepared to discuss the variances with your immediate superior.

Continuing Control of Overtime

One area in which supervisors can have a significant effect on a department's cost picture is the control of overtime. Overtime is an organizational necessity that is misused or abused as often as it is applied correctly. As an element of labor cost, it is sometimes seen as an extra expense to be avoided by all means, yet there are times when overtime is the best response to a particular need. The determination and payment of overtime are dictated by provisions of the Fair Labor Standards Act, the federal wage and hour legislation that governs a number of aspects of employment. Overtime is often taken for granted, and it can readily get out of control. It is the task of the department supervisor to maintain control of overtime, adhering to a budget and taking active steps to ensure that only essential overtime is approved and worked.

- Overtime is viewed and applied in a number of ways. As suggested, it is often used to correct mistakes, and as certainly implied previously, it is used to compensate for inefficiencies and time wasted. However, it is used primarily, at least in intent, to accomplish necessary, or perhaps unanticipated, work when there is more work to be accomplished within a given period and too little regularly scheduled staff available to get it done.

- Overtime is a constant concern for a great many working healthcare supervisors. There are almost always needs arising, and the nature of a healthcare operation dictates that coverage be present. In some healthcare organizations, functions that cannot be accomplished today can be left until tomorrow, but a great many necessary tasks cannot wait until the next day.
- Some overtime is essential and absolutely unavoidable. Some, however, is questionable and perhaps optional, and some is unnecessary and completely avoidable. All overtime, even to some extent that which is essential, is controllable. And the strongest point of control is the first-line supervisor, the immediate supervisor of the people who work the overtime.
- The continuing emphasis on the need for cost containment undoubtedly increases the pressure on supervisors to control overtime and to economically justify all overtime used. Certainly, the department that uses too much overtime—and "too much" can be difficult to define—will have cost problems. However, there may also be a problem in a department that seems never to use overtime; it is highly probable that such a department is overstaffed.

Causes of Overtime

The causes of overtime are many and varied, but within the organization that may be experiencing excessive overtime, these causes often include all or most of the following:

- Variations in workload: unexpected changes in demand, unanticipated changes, deadlines, and genuine emergency situations
- Absenteeism: there is usually a demonstrable, direct relationship between employee absenteeism and the need for overtime
- Tolerance of substandard performance
- General acceptance of overtime as a normal practice rather than an exception

- Lack of supervisory accountability (for example, if the supervisor does not have to answer for overtime use, it becomes accepted as normal and less likely seen as a recourse for handling true exceptions)
- Rigid scheduling practices
- Bargaining unit work rules stating that only certain classifications of employees can perform certain kinds of work
- Inappropriate or insufficient equipment and inefficient physical work area

At its worst, continuing overtime is costly, disruptive, and counterproductive. Even at its best, continuing overtime becomes part of the employee's supposedly "normal" time available for doing work, and the work tends to spread over that available time.

Toward Control of Overtime

Several general approaches are available for controlling overtime.

- *Regulate demand.* In some departments it is possible to take actions that regulate the demand on the department's services. The approaches available for the regulation of demand include working on a reservation or appointment basis, promoting low-demand periods, and using complementary scheduling. In general, any steps that can be taken to regulate demand serve to decrease the need for overtime.
- *Analyze and improve staffing practices.* Possibilities include cross-training employees; using floats as appropriate; using per diem, casual, or optional staff; increasing hours of some of the department's part-time employees; and constantly reevaluating scheduling practices.
- *Analyze and improve work methods.* Ineffective work methods and procedures and inappropriate equipment and workplace layout all tend to depress productivity and increase the pressure for overtime.
- *Control absenteeism.* To address absenteeism directly is to directly address the problem of excess overtime as well.

- *Manage responsibly*. Consider yourself accountable for the level of overtime usage in the department.

Cutting Costs

When there is a severe financial crunch, organizations take multiple remedial measures. When drastic action is not imperative, managers usually introduce changes one at a time to observe the effects of each change before undertaking the next measure.

Cost control involves more than cutting staff and working more efficiently. It can also involve improving inventory control and seeking price relief from suppliers. Reductions of salary, overtime expenses, and benefits may be necessary but are often counterproductive if made prematurely or without examining their full implications.

Typical hospital responses are the laboratory responses.[2] These include freezing or limiting expenditures for filling vacancies, capital spending, salary increases, and cutbacks in continuing education. If these are not sufficiently effective, layoffs follow.

Rightsizing

Rightsizing is matching staffing to workloads to become more efficient. It differs from downsizing, which is simply laying off people in response to declining business or to save money, although more often than not the terms are used interchangeably, along with several other labels for adjusting the size of the workforce. Restructuring, acquisitions, mergers, and financial reverses all frequently result in reductions in force. Employers can accomplish reductions in force through early retirements, attrition, hiring freezes, voluntary separations, or reduced work hours. These measures are often insufficient, however; thus, involuntary separations—layoffs—are exercised as the last resort.

The best time to begin this process is before financial constraints demand major staff reductions. The first step for executives is to analyze the workload and find out what can be done to reduce it without decreasing services or turnaround times. The second step is process reengineering or restructuring.[3]

Chief executive officers must decide whether to base furloughing on seniority or on a person's value to the organization. If the latter, supervisors play an important—and often painful—role in the selection process. Also, it is extremely important that whatever scheme is used for determining staff reductions is applied consistently throughout the organization and in a completely nondiscriminatory manner and that documentation exists to support the rationale for selecting those who are to be laid off. Ideally the organization should have a published policy and procedure that describes in detail the basis on which individuals are identified for layoff, and this must be faithfully followed and consistently applied.

Responses to the Call for Reduced Employee Costs

Initially you should try to determine whether you can increase efficiency or reduce costs by transferring or merging activities within your organizational unit. If you must transfer tasks from professional or highly trained technical employees to less educated workers, insist that the latter be trained first or that they are closely supervised until they have the work fully under control. Tap into the observations and recommendations of the people who do the work. They have practical ideas on how workflows can be streamlined. When workers participate in the planning, they are less likely to object to changes, even when the changes involve staff reductions.

If the mandate calls for reduction of payroll to a certain level, hold brainstorming sessions with your employees. Get their ideas for reducing salary costs without laying people off. Some senior people may decide that this is a good time for them to end their careers. Some full-time employees may opt for part-time employment, and part-timers may be willing to reduce their hours, especially if they have more schedule options.

Handling Those Who Leave

Supervisors must face the anger of those who leave and the apprehension of those who remain. The reaction of some people who are laid off is often much like that of patients when they are told they have cancer. First, there is disbelief, then anger or depression, and finally acceptance. Be tolerant of their anger, bitterness, and hostility, and be empathetic when the tears flow. Console yourself with the knowledge that most of these people will recover and find new and sometimes more satisfying positions. Answer their questions honestly, and make sure they get the information they need about benefits and eligibility for unemployment benefits. If you know your employees reasonably well, you may be able in limited instances to predict how someone may take the news, but do not count on this. Some may shrug it off and calmly accept their fate; some may be highly emotional and react with anguish and tears or extreme anger or even threats. There is no sure-fire way of knowing in advance how any particular employee will react to a layoff notice.

Outplacement services, often made available in response to a layoff of significant numbers of employees, can serve as a small ray of hope for some in the midst of a highly negative experience. If such services are available, encourage employees to take full advantage of them. These may include placement services, help with job applications and interview techniques, psychological testing, and training for new vocations. Use your personal network to try to find new jobs for them or at least to steer them in the right direction. Do not hold out false hopes for recalls. If the likelihood of rehire is high, keep in touch with them.

Handling Those Who Remain

Layoff survivors often feel guilty and depressed after losing friends and colleagues. They may experience a drop in self-esteem and morale. In the back of their minds is the fear of future layoffs. Remain visible. Do not hide in meetings or bury yourself in paperwork. Share their concern about their friends who are laid off.

One mistake made at times by well-meaning managers is trying to provide the survivors—many of whom will naturally wonder, "Am I next?"—with assurances that there will be no more layoffs. Regardless of how solid the organization may appear, no one can guarantee the future, and if one tries and is proved wrong, the reaction can be devastating.

Distance yourself from idle gossip but keep yourself informed. Share all the information you have or can acquire. Explain the rationale for the changes. Answer questions honestly and listen to expressions of frustration and fear. Do not wait for staff meetings or newsletters to keep your team informed. Call special meetings whenever you acquire new information.

You and your staff must pick up the slack. Ask for the participation and cooperation of your staff in closing ranks and getting the job done with fewer people. Point out the increased need for teamwork and for everyone to make a special effort. Prepare a list of duties and responsibilities that others must assume. Announce assignment changes and provide any additional training that may be needed. Use your reward and recognition system to reward your team or individuals who make special efforts.

Process Reengineering

Reengineering may prove to be the most cost-effective mechanism in healthcare institutions. Without reengineering, cost-reduction initiatives achieve only modest results. The major savings will not come from departmental reengineering but from those initiatives that address interdepartmental functions and that break down compartmentalization. These initiatives include abandoning obsolete systems, forming cross-functional, self-directed teams, amalgamating jobs, discarding old rules and assumptions, introducing new technologies, and creating new principles for task orientation. For more concerning reengineering, refer to the information presented in the chapter titled "Reengineering, Mergers, and the Supervisor."

Benchmarking

Benchmarking is the search for best or preferred practices and is accomplished by comparing current systems or processes with highly successful ones. Your goal is to increase efficiency, cut costs, or improve service. The comparisons may be with standards reported in the literature or with observations at the facilities of recognized leaders. Benchmarking usually leads to some form of process, system, or structural reengineering. It is an essential tool in cost control and quality improvement with improved patient and fiscal outcomes at stake.

A benchmarking strategy usually requires data searches, networking, and creation of cross-functional teams. When national standards are unavailable, your external networks can be crucial to establishing standards. Questionnaires and other survey tools are often used to locate the best benchmark sources.

The usual approach consists of (1) a data-collection phase that may include literature searches or site visits, (2) an analysis phase, and (3) an action plan. The planning process may involve use of flowcharts and other problem-solving tools; it is frequently necessary to dissect workflows to find problems or weaknesses.

Kreider and Walsh[4] reported a highly successful benchmarking project that ensured decreased ventilator-associated pneumonia and intensive care unit costs. With a cost-restructuring plan based on benchmark information, one hospital reduced its operating budget by $33 million.[5] Rotondi et al.[6] benchmarked their preoperative patient-routing system. After they identified causes for variation, they created multidisciplinary improvement teams to improve the pinpointed areas. Mitchell[7] found that the national benchmark for turnaround time between surgical cases was 13.5 minutes, whereas his hospital's time was 19.9 minutes. A quality improvement team carried out solutions that produced an 18% improvement. The cost–benefit analysis showed a potential revenue enhancement of about $300,000.

WRAP-UP

Think About It

The best defense against having to make painful reductions at crunch time is to have your unit's costs under control at all times. Control consists of more than just monthly budget reports to review. The information comparing budgets with actual expenditures is important, but it is only part of the equation. True cost control is information plus action.

Questions for Review and Discussion

1. Often, the productivity of a work group decreases after a layoff, even though there is more work to be done overall. Why might this be so?

2. In budgeting, why are funds for operating expenses and funds for capital expenditures always kept separated?

3. Describe one set of circumstances under which a supervisor may be largely powerless to affect a particular expense charged to the department.

4. Is overtime expense fully controllable, partially controllable, or not at all controllable by the supervisor? Explain.

5. If the numbers say the organization has to reduce 20 positions, and 20 employees leave via resignation and retirement, why might it still be necessary to reduce positions further and even engage in some hiring?

6. How can benchmarking assist the supervisor in determining whether a staff reduction may be necessary?

7. What conditions or circumstances in your own department should you consider before deciding to reduce staff?

8. The term "reengineering" literally means "engineering again." Why is so much so-called reengineering not true reengineering?

9. As a department supervisor, why might you often not get what you have asked for in the capital budget?

10. What information can the department supervisor often supply to finance or information services that can help in developing revenue projections?

Case: Let's Cut the Deadweight

Two supervisors, Robert and Janet, were in charge of sections of the building services department of Central Hospital. They had a fairly close working relationship; they were in a position to cover for each other on occasion and usually did so successfully. Overall, however, they had quite different styles of dealing with their employees.

The long-anticipated word came down that declining admissions and sharp cuts in reimbursement rates necessitated staff reductions. Robert's staff would have to be reduced by three people; Janet's staff was projected to lose two people. On Monday they learned officially of the impending cuts; they had to have names turned in by Wednesday, and layoffs would actually occur Friday. Monday afternoon they found themselves discussing the layoffs.

Robert said, "How is this supposed to be done? I missed the meeting with the boss this morning thanks to a toxic material spill. I got the information secondhand, and all I know is that I've got to dump three people."

"Right," Janet replied. "And I have to lose two. These are the times when I'm almost sorry I took a supervisory job."

"Why? Employees come and go. This just means a few have to go unwillingly. I figure on taking advantage of this to cut some deadweight."

"How can you do that? You weren't there this morning—it was pretty strongly indicated we should go by seniority. You know, last in, first out. Unless there's some compelling reason to the contrary."

"Compelling reasons I've got lots of," Robert responded. "One of mine who's going is the last in, no trouble there. But the other two are major pains I've wanted to get rid of for a long time."

"Got lots of documentation?"

"Who needs it?" Robert tapped the side of his head. "It's here. Overall, I'll be getting rid of the three worst producers in the group. Nobody will have any idea how people are picked for layoff, and anyway, at least two of these bozos should already figure they're on the way out."

Questions

1. Is Robert justified in wanting to get rid of "the three worst producers in the group"? Under what circumstances might he be able to do this without creating another kind of problem?

2. What is the possible exposure to the organization and to Robert if he were to go ahead and "cut the deadweight" as planned?

3. What can you infer from the case about the supervisory styles of both Robert and Janet?

References

1. Sattler J. *Financial Management of the Clinical Laboratory*. *Medical Economics*; 1980:124.
2. Jahn M. Laboratorians speak out on benefits, managed care, and the bottom line. *Medical Laboratory Observer*. 1995;27(5):29–33.
3. Medvescek P. Rightsizing the right way. *Medical Laboratory Observer*. 1997;29(7):102–106.
4. Kreider C, Walsh BA. Benchmarking for a competitive edge. *Medical Laboratory Observer Supplement. September* 1997:S26–S29.
5. Cohen E, Anderson-Miles E. Benchmarking: A management tool for academic medical centers. *Best Practical Benchmarking in Healthcare*. 1997;1(2):57–61.
6. Rotondi AJ et al. Benchmarking the perioperative process. 1. Patient routing systems: A method for continual improvement of patient flow and resource utilization. *Journal of Clinical Anesthesia*. 1997;9(3):159–169.
7. Mitchell L. Benchmarking, benchmarks, or best practices? Applying quality improvement principles to decrease surgical turnaround time. *Best Practical Benchmarking in Healthcare*. 1997;1(2):70–74.

Developing Employees

CHAPTER 28

Staff Development

CHAPTER OBJECTIVES

- Specify the benefits of and the necessity for an employment development program.
- Identify the accountability for planning staff education and for creating and promoting the opportunity for career development.
- Introduce the essentials of staff education needs assessment, and highlight the elements of an effective staff development program.
- Address mentoring as an especially valuable approach to job-specific staff development.
- Stress the need to encourage creativity and innovation in employees.
- Define the creative process in everyday terms and highlight the behavioral characteristics of creative people.
- Review the commonly encountered barriers to creativity and suggest how the supervisor can overcome these and stimulate and reward creativity in employees.

KEY TERMS

Skills Inventory: A skills inventory is a comprehensive listing of all employees in the group matched with the jobs or major job components they are capable of handling.

Career Development: Consisting of both education and experience, career development is essentially lifelong learning aimed at keeping employees abreast of rapidly changing skill needs so they can maintain their employability and marketability.

Mentoring: Mentoring consists of an arrangement in which an experienced or influential person can guide and nurture an individual or a small group of employees, teaching them how to survive, thrive, and progress within an organization or profession.

Education and Experience

Throughout this chapter the terms "staff development" and "career development" are essentially used interchangeably. They can, of course, be differentiated by purpose, with one oriented primarily toward supporting and improving skills related to a person's present employment (staff development) and the other encompassing not just one's present employment but one's lifelong work (career development). Even differentiated, however, it is necessary to accept that at any given time staff development is often a component of career development.

Career development must always consist of both education and experience. Employees may have to reinvent their careers numerous times and must continuously update their technical, soft, and hard skills to remain employable. Unfortunately, most employers are unable to tell their workers what skills will be needed in the future. Therefore, a paradigm of lifelong education and training must replace short-term consideration of an education completed at the end of college.

Benefits of a Career Development Program

Development programs for employees benefit the employees by making them more versatile and thus more eligible for promotion, increasing their self-esteem, and injecting more interest into their jobs. Such programs keep employees informed of fast-changing skill needs so they can maintain their employability and marketability.

Employers benefit from staff development because it fosters a more knowledgeable and flexible workforce. To remain competitive, organizations must help their employees adapt to today's rapid cycle of change. Career development enhances morale and motivation and increases employee retention, productivity, and service quality. Recruitment is stimulated when candidates learn about the educational advantages offered by the institution.

Some executives express concern over the effort and expense expended in developing promising employees who then leave for better jobs. This disadvantage, however, is balanced by the enhanced expertise of those who do not leave. There is also the goodwill of the people who have resigned; this often benefits the organization indirectly.

As employees become more highly qualified, supervisors can delegate more to them and therefore have more time to spend on higher priority responsibilities.

Educational Planning

Educational planning is most effective when it is tailored to fit individual needs. Some healthcare workers seek promotions to managerial positions; others avoid supervisory responsibilities, preferring to climb a professional career ladder if it is available. The overwhelming majority of employees want some growth within their current positions; it adds spice to work and prevents boredom.

A review of the position descriptions of your employees to ensure compliance with various laws (for example, the Americans with Disabilities Act) presents a good opportunity to consider revisions to establish the criteria necessary for employee advancement. Such revisions usually address titles, responsibilities, and the amount of supervision that the incumbents require.

When you interview job candidates, offer them a brief explanation of your career development program. This can be a strong incentive for the more ambitious candidates.

Discuss goal changes or modifications at performance review meetings. Action plans to help employees work toward these goals should be a major agenda item at these meetings. Affirm your confidence in the ability of each employee to achieve these goals. Employees are motivated more strongly when their desire to move up in the organization is accompanied by an expectation of success.

Accountability for Career Development

Top management is accountable for the educational facilities, staff, and resources. Supervisors are partly responsible for developing and implementing the programs for their own departments. They share this responsibility with the staff education departments or human resources departments of their institutions.

In the long run, career development is primarily self-development, just as ultimately all lasting motivation is self-motivation. Many healthcare professionals complain about not being trained for supervisory jobs before they assume those roles. Most of these people knew for a long time that this opportunity would be available. They often had years to get the necessary training but failed to do so, perhaps assuming that management was responsible for this. This is learned from our public education system, in which the programs and schedules are prepared for the students, who quickly learn that if they pass a few tests, they will be promoted—and sometimes advanced without even passing the tests.

After accepting supervisory roles, some professionals continue to focus their educational efforts on the clinical aspects of their jobs. They often limit their managerial training to the mandatory programs provided by their organization.

In organizations in which promotions have stalled, supervisors can encourage employees to consider lateral moves or to take advantage of cross-training opportunities. These moves have motivational value and increase the marketability of employees.

Educational Needs Assessment

Any training program worthy of the name should be preceded by a needs assessment. This assessment should consider the following questions:

- What expertise is needed by the department now, and what will be needed in the future? This involves obtaining product- or service-forecasting information from top management. Skills inventory charts list the employees who are qualified to handle each major job component. These charts are invaluable for planning skills enhancement, cross-training, and workstation rotation.
- What is needed by individual employees to meet or exceed the requirements of their jobs or to be ready to assume greater responsibilities?
- What is needed to bring long-time employees up to date? Job obsolescence occurs at an ever-increasing rate, and because women play a major role in healthcare institutions, many positions are filled by employees who have interrupted their careers to start or raise families.
- What is needed to energize stalled or marginal workers whose interest in work needs rekindling?

- What is needed to make you dispensable? The highest order career development program is succession planning. Supervisors who make themselves dispensable by training capable successors are more eligible for, and worthy of, promotion.
- How does the knowledge of the employees compare with the skills demanded in their field?

Bartsch[1] offers the following tips for determining training needs:

- Ask your human resources department to give you a list of performance deficiencies frequently documented in performance appraisal reports.
- Review your department's performance appraisals, looking for specific problems or training needs.
- Observe the behavior of people at work, especially their interactions with customers and coworkers.
- Study patient and employee satisfaction surveys.
- Keep abreast of legal and legislative issues that could lead to performance problems (for example, the Americans with Disabilities Act, which is constantly being affected by court decisions).
- Review your organization's mission statement and values to find out what kinds of training can contribute to realization of long-term goals.

To assist you in deciding how well your current training program meets basic needs, answer the questions in **Exhibit 28.1**.

Exhibit 28.1 Questions Related to Staff Skills Enhancement

- Do you have an in-house educational program for each staff member? Does it include a minimum number of hours of participation or some evaluation method for results? Are records kept? Are you satisfied with the results?
- Are training materials (books, journals, tapes, and other teaching tools) easily available? Do you know how frequently these are used? Are they regularly updated?

(continues)

Exhibit 28.1 Questions Related to Staff
Skills Enhancement *(continued)*

- Is there an ongoing professional or management training program readily available?
- Do your employees have the time to make use of the training materials? Do they have time to attend lectures, demonstrations, or other educational sessions?
- Is there financial support for continuing education? Are schedules flexible enough to permit employees to attend programs at educational institutions?
- Do your employees get intellectual stimulation through problem-solving sessions?
- Do your employees have the opportunity to cross-train? To rotate work-stations? To assume greater responsibilities? To serve on committees, quality circles, task forces, and other work groups?
- Do you delegate tasks that provide valued educational experiences for your employees? Do they assume greater responsibilities? Do you empower them sufficiently to carry out these responsibilities?
- Are educational topics presented at routine staff meetings?
- Are there real opportunities for promotion? Do you have dual career tracks? Can your employees be promoted within their current roles?
- Does each employee have an individualized career growth plan that is jointly formulated?
- When employees plan to attend outside seminars or workshops, do you jointly establish practical goals for that experience? Are these discussed when the employee returns? Do you provide opportunities to put those new skills to work?

Development Program

The major goal of any program is self-reliance. Employees are introduced to a lifelong process dedicated to learning and development. Trainers make available a variety of self-assessment instruments such as the Myers-Briggs Type Indicator.

With the guidance of career counselors, employees use benchmarking techniques with which they learn how to identify the best and the brightest in their organization and field and how to determine what makes them successful. They then compare their preferences and skills with those of the top performers. The skills gaps are used to identify development goals when the employees put together action plans for continuous learning. Other available modalities include the following:

- Orientation and on-the-job training of new employees
- In-service education, including the use of guest speakers and consultants
- Workshops, seminars, and webinars
- Formal programs at educational institutions
- Job rotation and cross-training
- Self-education
- Books, journals, online videos
- Participation in any educational endeavor
- Special assignments
- Committees and other special work groups
- Assignments as trainers, instructors, or lecturers
- Duties as coordinators or facilitators (for example, quality assurance, safety, or data processing)
- "Horizontal promotions"
- Temporary assignments at satellite facilities or elsewhere
- Substituting for absent employees

Exhibit 28.2 displays some practical tips for career building.

Exhibit 28.2 Practical Career-Building
Tips

- Work on easier skills first to ensure early success.
- Ask others to help.
- Maintain a high ratio of praise to criticism.
- Correct errors before they become habits.
- Be patient. Expect plateaus in progress.
- Serve as coach, facilitator, advisor, and cheerleader, not taskmaster.
- Use adult training methods. Employees are not schoolchildren.
- Encourage mentorship.

Mentoring

In mentoring, an experienced person guides and nurtures an individual or a small group of employees. Mentors teach protégés how to survive, thrive, and progress within an organization or a profession to attain their full potential.

Mentoring may begin shortly after a new employee comes on board. During orientation, new hires have an excellent opportunity to spot managers or senior team members they would like to have as a mentor.

Corporate Mentoring

Some organizations provide formal mentoring programs. They assign mentors to new employees and provide training to mentors and protégés. In the past, employers crafted special programs for women and minorities as part of affirmative action. However, today this practice may expose employers to charges of reverse discrimination, so, for the present, most programs are made available to all employees.

Mentor

A mentor can be someone on the same team, in another department, a retiree, or an outsider. He or she may be a senior manager or an expert in the same field. An employee's immediate supervisor is not the ideal choice because protégés are more reluctant to ask questions for fear of appearing ignorant or irritating the supervisor.

A mentor is one who

- helps protégés make career decisions,
- introduces them to the intricacies of political savvy,
- enhances their sensitivity to organizational culture, and
- helps them enlarge their personal network.

A mentor is an experienced professional or technical expert who shares knowledge and skills that help protégés fine-tune their expertise.

Mentors teach their protégés how to be successful in a particular organization or profession. They suggest ways to (1) cut bureaucratic red tape and (2) avoid troublesome people, policies, or practices. They point out cultural sand traps, identify rituals that must be followed, identify who has the clout, and describe how decisions are made. They highlight pitfalls, obstacles, and hazards.

Mentors share visions of the futures of their protégés, perceive their potential, and challenge them when they are not living up to this potential. They detect real and potential hindrances and recommend ways to eliminate or reduce these.

Mentors take an active interest in the continuing education of the employees. They recommend literature and seminars or workshops. They are readily available for questions and are open, authentic, and receptive. They provide appropriate affirmation and offer opinions in a way that promotes feelings of self-worth and competence.

Mentors help individuals enhance their careers by removing obstacles, teaching team skills, advising on career development strategy, and serving as role models. In brief, they may teach, sponsor, advise, coach, counsel, guide, motivate, or critique.

Great mentors are empathetic and inquisitive and enthusiastic about the organization and its mission. They listen more than they talk and avoid excessive direct advice. They avoid remarks such as "Let me give you a piece of advice" or "You ought to …." Instead, they relate their experience (for example, "What I've found helpful in that situation is …").

Mentor–Protégé Relationships

Protégés must respect their mentors and must not disclose confidential information. A little deference is appropriate. Most mentor–protégé affiliations are similar to doctor–patient or attorney–client relationships. Protégés must have a sincere desire to assimilate information and reconceptualize ideas. They should keep their mentors informed of their progress but not make pests of themselves. Associations may end quickly or gradually. Some change into collegial relationships or social friendships.

Recent Developments in Mentoring

With managed care programs and various organizational changes, mentoring programs are showing up with innovative twists. One of these is reciprocal mentorship, in which peers exchange expertise. For example, a laboratory supervisor who has a master's in business administration but lacks laboratory experience may help a lead technologist prepare for a supervisory role. The technologist, in turn, helps the manager understand the intricacies of laboratory procedures. Another form is team or big-brother mentorship. Here, senior team members offer assistance to struggling junior colleagues. Group mentorship, where a mentor serves a group of protégés, can save time and elicit broader discussions. The protégés develop the agenda, and the mentor responds to their needs. Online mentoring is another form of mentorship. It can be much easier to meet online than in-person today with busy schedules and the risk of spreading illnesses. The online mentoring relationship is essentially the same—help make career decisions, open conversations—but the meetings are held online through web-based platforms.

Creativity in Employee Development

Employers who have tunnel vision seem to believe that all worthwhile ideas are generated in executive suites or research departments, but all employees have the best opportunity to see how any particular job can be improved. Employee input results in better cost control, higher quality, greater productivity, and improved customer service.

Organizational infrastructures are shifting to make room for people who are innovative. Those with innovative potential now outrank those with graduate degrees in some progressive organizations. The fundamental driver of continuous quality improvement and cost reduction is innovation. Failure to promote innovation leads to lower quality or more rationing of care, equally undesirable results.

Downsizing, with its adverse impact on morale, has greatly affected employee creativity in many organizations. However, it has also stimulated creativity where economic survival is at stake or competition is keen.

Although workers at all levels have ideas about how to improve things, some are blessed with greater innovativeness, intuition, or entrepreneurship. These creative employees can be among the most valuable members of an organization if their supervisors treat them well. Your goal as supervisor is to keep these people flooding you with ideas—without letting them get out of control.

Creative Process

Innovative creativity is the ability to come up with truly new ideas. Inventors use innovative creativity. Just as a kaleidoscope forms new patterns from many disconnected pieces, the creative person forms new patterns from many seemingly unrelated ideas. The process usually starts with a problem. Problems are opportunities in disguise.

Adaptive creativity is displayed when people find better ways to do their work. This may be putting old ideas together in new ways or simply putting the creative ideas of others into practice. Entrepreneurs exhibit adaptive creativity. Because creative people are often unable to work out the details of their ideas, we need both types of creative people, the inventors and the entrepreneurs.

When you challenge employees to think creatively about their work, they seek to learn more about their jobs. In the process they become more competent and more efficient. It is creativity that leads to new services and products.

When supervisors suppress creativity in favor of conformity, the creativity resurfaces outside the workplace in hobbies, recreational activities, and artistic endeavors. Back on the job, stifled operational creativity may be expressed in unique ways to annoy bosses or to bypass policies and rules.

Intuition

Intuition has long been regarded as a mystical power that originates below the conscious level.

We refer to it euphemistically as flashes of insight, hunches, and gut reactions. Intuition is knowledge gained without rational thought or logic. Think of intuition as experience stored in the unconscious mind.

Intuition is a sixth sense. Everyone is born with it, but it deteriorates with disuse. The more attention we pay to our intuition, the more useful it becomes. For example, before you sign a contract, make a checklist of pertinent questions, then take time to completely identify feelings about each of those questions. This combination of rational and intuitive decision-making is more effective than either process alone. The same holds true for selecting new employees.

Characteristics of Creative People

People who are creative possess a sort of restlessness. Confident that there is always a better way of doing things, they challenge systems, processes, procedures, tradition, practices, policies, and rules. Most creative people share many of the following characteristics:

- They possess innumerable bits of information (the pieces in the kaleidoscope) that relate to the focal point of their interest.
- They blot out what to them seems irrelevant or unimportant, sometimes to the annoyance of their supervisors and colleagues.
- They are curious, open, and sensitive to problems. They may bombard their supervisors and others with questions, many starting with "why," "why not," or "what if."
- They are optimistic risk takers who like challenges and rarely talk about failure.
- They often appear preoccupied. At times they work furiously. Their ideas usually come in spurts.
- They dislike rigid routines, monotonous tasks, restrictive policies, and bureaucratic interference.
- They tolerate isolation and ambiguity.
- They value independence and autonomy.
- They often enjoy the innovative process more than the results of the innovation.

- They sense when things are right and when they are not right.
- They bounce ideas off others and build on the suggestions of their associates.
- They are voracious readers.
- They are often nonconformists, regarded by their peers as different. At meetings they are likely to play the role of devil's advocate.
- They may like to hang out with other creative people, although many are loners.

Innovative Supervisors

Innovative supervisors are characterized by a combination of most of the following characteristics:

- They believe there is always a better way and are always on the lookout for that better way.
- They overcome the egotism of thinking that one's own idea is unique.
- They view problems as challenges rather than annoyances.
- They chalk up failures as learning experiences.
- They use brainstorming techniques for making decisions and solving problems.
- They are tolerant of ambiguity and the idiosyncrasies of teammates.
- They cut red tape when they encounter it.
- They set aside some time each day for reflective thinking.
- They inject humor into situations (some of the best ideas originate as jokes).
- They are willing to stick their necks out in support of their ideas.

Barriers to Creativity

The following attitudes, conditions, or circumstances can restrict creativity:

- Prejudgment of ideas. We tend to accept ideas more readily from authority figures or people we respect and reject those from marginal performers or individuals below us in the hierarchy.
- Fear of failure. This is a significant inhibitor of creativity.
- Restrictive policies, rules, rituals, and procedures.

- Strict controls and limited budgets.
- Complex or slow approval procedure for suggestions and projects.
- Demands for a consensus.
- Understaffing and excessive work group assignments.
- A lengthy chain of command.
- Group norms.
- Disparaging or discouraging remarks.

Stimulating Creativity in Your Staff

Creativity flourishes only when employees feel secure and free of the fear of failure. Insightful employers establish corporate cultures that support new ideas. To switch from a culture that endorses conformity and compliance to one that fosters innovation is not easy. Here are some suggestions for stimulating creativity in your department or unit:

- Identify your innovative people and strive to know them better. Focus on the unique expertise of each person.
- Emphasize creativity during the orientation and training of new employees. Present problems as challenging opportunities. Be alert for and encourage employee statements that begin with "Maybe we could ..." or "What if ...?" These flash the message that a creative idea may soon be born.
- Give people the opportunity to pursue and develop new ideas. Tolerate some daydreaming. They need this to fire up their creativity or to retrieve information stuck in the catacombs of their unconscious minds. Use idea traps, such as quality circles, brainstorming sessions, incentive awards, and suggestion boxes.
- Do not nitpick or demand perfection. When employees start to neglect their routine duties in favor of pet projects, you may have to tighten the reins but do not say, "You can't do that." Instead, say, "You can get back to your project when ...."
- Let them take some risks and make mistakes without risking their jobs. Tolerate failure and mistakes as the cost of innovation and progress.

- Provide the necessary resources and psychological boosts. Give them some discretionary time for nondirected research. The ones who are already spending weekends so engaged are the most deserving.
- Expose employees to in-house and outside learning:
  - Seminars, webinars, and professional meetings
  - Consultants and guest speakers
  - Publications, simulations, and online videos
  - Customer input
  - Vendors and sales representatives

Expect some creative ideas from everyone and tell them that. Those supervisors who complain that their people never come up with creative ideas should consider this question: If you walked around your department with a roll of $100 bills and offered one for each idea, would you get any suggestions? You bet you would! Also, dispense lots of praise and rewards. When responding to new ideas, keep in mind the "PIC" response (**Exhibit 28.3**).

Communication Precautions

Do not say yes or no too quickly. A quick "no" leaves the employee feeling you have not given his or her idea serious consideration. When you say yes too quickly, you may find yourself in hot

---

Exhibit 28.3 Use the PIC Response to All Ideas

P = Positive: If you find an idea worthwhile, say "Great idea, let's try it" or "What can I do to help?"

I = Interesting: If there may be merit, say "That sounds interesting. Tell m e more."

C = Concern: If you cannot find anything of value in the idea, say that you have some concerns and express them. Avoid killing the suggestion directly.

water or forced to renege on your promises. Avoid idea-killing statements:

- "You've got to be kidding."
- "That would never work here."
- "The trouble with that idea is …."
- "I'm paid to do the thinking."

And substitute the following:

- "Keep talking, you may be on to something."
- "How can I help?"
- "Let's give it a try."
- "Can you get me the figures for that?"

Rewards for Creativity

Because creativity is usually expressed in bursts, rewards of all kinds are best delivered in bursts.

Bonuses that follow specific accomplishments are more motivating than end-of-year bonuses. Do not save recognition for the next performance appraisal.

Base recognition and rewards on outcomes and their value to the organization. These values may relate to teamwork, quality, new services, and customer satisfaction. These systems demand factual and fair performance appraisals.

Give rewards not only for suggestions, but also for criticisms that lead to improvements. Creative people are likely to hold reward values that differ from those of their colleagues. For example, they usually value financial support of their projects more than they value salary increases.

Shower them with recognition. Encourage them to publish. Let them attend meetings where they meet other creative people.

WRAP-UP

Think About It

Education is lifelong, and the person who becomes educated is the person who knows how to find out what he or she wants to learn and how to go on learning it throughout a lifetime. In other words, this is the person who has mastered certain methods of dealing with subject matter; this is the person who has learned how to proceed, who has, in effect, learned how to learn.

Questions for Review and Discussion

1. Why is it stated that career development must largely be self-development?
2. Do you believe that everyone is potentially creative to some degree? Why or why not?
3. Why is mentoring so important for career and self-development?
4. Should all employees in an organization have a mentor?
5. Why is significant emphasis placed on career development? Wouldn't it be more sensible to advise each employee to carefully select a job or occupation or employer and stick with it?
6. Why is it claimed that employees need to be allowed the freedom to fail?
7. Why would any department supervisor deliberately wish to make him or herself "dispensable" through self-development?
8. Why is it said that all employees are well positioned to find creative ways of improving work methods?
9. What is a significant advantage of a career development program other than the obvious one of stimulating the development of present employees?
10. Why should acknowledgment or reward occur as close in time as possible after a creative accomplishment?

Exercise: Your Career Development Plan

This is an especially personal exercise in that it asks you to plot out a likely career path for the remainder of your working years, subject to the following guidelines:

- Begin with your present working (or student) status, briefly described, stating why you are where you are.
- State where you intend to go next, and where after that, and after that, etc., as necessary.
- For each move you propose to make, indicate what you need to do to make that move (for example, how much education of what kind, experience of what kind).
- Provide estimates of how much time each step may require (something of a variation on "where would you like to be in 5 years? 10 years?").

Finally, for each major milestone in your career plan, indicate what you would plan on doing—that is, how your overall plan might change—should any of your critical career milestones prove impossible to attain.

Reference

1. Bartsch M. Go beyond surveys to assess needs. *Training*. 1996;33(5):15.

CHAPTER 29

Change as a Way of Life

CHAPTER OBJECTIVES

- Identify the kinds of change affecting organizational functioning, the essential elements of change in the organization, and the most commonly encountered barriers to successful change.
- Highlight the general concerns of employees concerning change.
- Identify the essentials of the successful implementation of change.
- Describe how the supervisor can help employees through the most stressful stages of change.
- Deliver workable advice concerning means of addressing and overcoming employee resistance to change.
- Establish the concept of job enrichment, and identify its relationship to employee job satisfaction.
- Identify the guiding principles of job redesign and continuing methods of improvement.

KEY TERMS

Competencies: The technologies, capabilities, and expertise that enable organizations to satisfy customers and meet new standards of care delivery. Competencies are affected most by hiring and training systems.

Job Enrichment: Job enrichment is the continuous process of encouraging employee participation in multiple activities, thus expanding each employee's capabilities and building a more flexible staff.

Cross-Training: The process of training employees of comparable skill level and pay grade in the performance of each other's jobs.

Job Redesign: Job redesign involves improving the manner in which a job is performed to serve the task—that is, to save time or money or material or improve quality—and to meet the needs of the workers—that is, to make the task more interesting or appealing.

Job Sharing: Job sharing is an arrangement in which multiple (usually just two) employees divide the hours and duties of a single full-time position between them.

Telecommuting: Also known as remote work and "work from home." An arrangement under which a person works a regularly scheduled amount of time each week at home or some other external location with the support of the appropriate equipment and services.

A New Broom Does What?

Shari, new nurse manager for the emergency department, was frustrated; just one month on the new job and already she felt like walking away. The problem, she decided, was staff resistance to change. She knew that some resistance to a new manager's ways was inevitable, but it seemed like employees resisted everything she said or did merely because it came from her. So much was needed in this department, but it had coasted for so many years under indifferent management that she hardly known where to begin, so she had jumped in and began fixing everything that needed fixing as rapidly as possible. Among her numerous changes: updating the dress code and insisting on professional appearance; putting a stop to personal telephone calls and the use of food and drink within view of the public; and enforcing policies on attendance and tardiness.

What would you suggest might be causing most of the resistance Shari is encountering? How should she proceed from there?

Constant and Inevitable

Nothing in life is as constant or inevitable as change. Almost weekly we hear about a technological advance or another medical breakthrough. New areas of specialization spring up and older ones phase out. Acquisitions, reductions in workforce, mergers, reorganizations, and changes to managed care and reimbursement systems stir tremors throughout the healthcare industry. In addition, every few years another "revolutionary" management concept surfaces, only to run its course and sputter and die within a few years. Consider, if you will, management by objectives (MBO), guest relations, quality circles, and the various variations of quality improvement such as total quality management (TQM) and continuous quality improvement (CQI).

There are significant differences between the ways that successful and not-so-successful organizations cope with change. A change-oriented culture requires flexibility, rapid responsiveness, and adaptation. Employees must master new technologies and adjust to new systems and procedures as a matter of course.

Effective supervisors are change specialists who know what their clients want and how well these wants are being met. Too many managers at all levels make changes based on their own perceptions of what is best for the customers without finding out what those customers really want or need. Three general kinds of change are encountered in organizational functioning:

1. Organizational changes in which departments are altered, interdepartmental relationships or reporting relationships are changed, or new management takes over.
2. New systems, structures, procedures, or equipment are introduced.
3. Jobs are restructured.

Essentials of Change

For change to successfully occur, a number of essential elements must be present and appropriately aligned:

- *Motivation.* Motivating people to change is a major challenge of leadership. Managers must understand why people resist change and must work to overcome that resistance. The presence of appropriate motivation is a significant part of what is required for successful change.
- *Competencies.* These are the technologies, capabilities, and expertise that enable organizations to satisfy customers and meet new standards. Competencies are affected most by hiring and training systems.
- *Creativity.* New, untried, and innovative ideas are required. Brainstorming is often needed to open up new ways of thinking. Change also requires the skills that turn ideas into entrepreneurship.
- *Employee commitment.* Employees must "buy in" for any change to fully succeed.
- *Adaptability.* Retraining and new learning are the orders of the day. Some employees must be completely "recycled."

- *Stability of workforce.* Stability requires low employee turnover, and the lower the turnover, the greater the chances of successful change implementation.
- *Patience.* Whereas everything seems to be rush and more rush, supervisors must show a small amount of patience with those people who learn or adjust a little more slowly than others. They must couple patience with persistence.
- *Reward and recognition.* People who must adjust to change expect some kind of a payoff for their cooperation and assistance.

Barriers to Change

Positive change may sometimes be forestalled because of the absence of appropriate technology or a lack of financial resources. However, the most numerous and significant barriers to change are the barriers presented by human attitudes and behaviors. The following may frequently work against change:

- Dysfunctional teamwork, typified by individuals pulling in separate directions instead of acting together
- Satisfaction with the status quo, the absolutely progress-killing attitude that things are just fine as they are
- Unjustified pessimism about the ability to change; that is, the feeling that "we can't do this, so why try?"
- Ego or personality problems, as evidenced by those who are "always right" and must have their way or be the ones in charge
- Territorial imperatives, which cause much energy to be directed at defending one's boundaries or seeking to annex the territory of others
- Lack of vision or support by upper management
- Inflexible systems, policies, or procedures
- Work overload, causing those who recognize the need for change to be unable to take the time necessary to improve their circumstances
- Lack of confidence in leaders

Employee Concerns

Change experts know what may be felt and experienced by employees who are affected by change, and they anticipate a spectrum of emotional responses. Even changes that some individuals hope for can be upsetting when they become reality. For example, a promotion elicits mixed feelings: The pride and the increased paycheck are gratifying, but the altered relationships with former coworkers may be upsetting, and new responsibilities may be intimidating.

The more a change affects established habits and relationships, the greater the stress produced. Fear is the strongest stressor. Many kinds of fear are likely to come into play: fear of the unknown; fear of failure or reduction in one's influence; and fear of job loss, demotion, transfer, or reassignment. It is likely that the most common personal fear stems from doubts about one's own ability to cope with new tasks or different responsibilities.

Loss of control is another factor. Reactions are more intense when changes reduce employees' control over their daily tasks. People who worked hard to achieve influence are likely to oppose, overtly or covertly, any threat to this status.

Mindsets are significant. People can perceive changes as threats or as opportunities. There may be a pervasive perception that a given change is either impossible or not practical. This is most likely to occur with employees who have experienced or witnessed failures in the past.

People with low self-esteem and a great need for basic security are reluctant to commit to change. Others balk because they receive too little information or may not have been given the opportunity to participate in the planning process.

Preparing for Change
Role of Supervisors

Supervisors are frequently called on to carry out changes mandated by upper management or regulatory agencies, but they also have occasion to introduce some changes of their own. Through networking, they find out as much as they can about current and rumored changes. Then they provide training and support, and they monitor results. If supervisors drag their feet, stonewall, or complain about what they have all been told to do, they cannot expect exemplary behavior by their employees or expect to win points with upper management.

Goals and Plans

A well-defined goal is a prerequisite for productive action and arches over four critical objectives:

1. Selecting the right people
2. Preparing and motivating people to change
3. Obtaining the other necessary resources
4. Carrying out the change

Every successful initiative requires a workable, clearly defined master plan, a written plan to which the supervisor must be fully committed. The plan must address the following crucial "W" questions:

- *What is the proposed change?* Is it customer-oriented, quality conscious, and cost-effective? What do we hope to achieve? What are the risks, constraints, and barriers? What additional data do we need? What resources are essential? What did we do wrong last time? What additional training will be necessary? What will be the impact on existing power and status relationships?
- *Will the change fit the existing organizational culture?* Will the people affected see a payoff or a setback? Will the change increase or decrease revenue, morale, quality, and productivity? Will the change provide an opportunity to better utilize available skills? Will people have more autonomy over how they do their work? Will the changes make employees' jobs (and mine) easier or harder?
- *Who wants the change?* And for what reasons? Who will benefit, and who will be affected adversely? Who will resist? Who will be supportive?

- *When should serious planning begin?* Will there be sufficient time? When will the work start and when must it be completed?
- *Where will we find the space, funds, and people?*

Assess the compatibility of the proposed change in light of the current organizational culture and goals. The change should not violate cultural norms.

Gather information about previous successes and failures. Experience is still the best teacher. Focus on activities that strongly influenced success and those that presented barriers.

Set a timetable complete with checkpoints and completion dates. Install a feedback system so people know how they are doing. Be flexible. Successful plans are usually revised often over the course of implementation.

Test your plan by asking these questions:

- Is it concise and clearly written? Does it include action steps?
- Was it distributed to the right people?
- Has there been sufficient input from others?
- Are there formal and informal networks that can lend support?

Communication

Alert your employees to upcoming changes as soon as possible. Outline the challenges and the opportunities they present. Involve them early while evaluating new technology or new procedures. This also gives them time to adjust to the idea of a major change.

Explain the need for change in practical terms, then patiently listen to them blow off steam. Reassure them about things that are not going to change; usually, what will not change is more extensive than what will change.

When employees report rumors, tell them as much as you are able. Once they are comfortable that they know as much as you do, they will gain confidence. The very act of talking about the change reduces fear and resistance, especially if you acknowledge their concerns and anxieties as legitimate. Tell them that what they feel is perfectly normal and that those feelings will pass.

When you must champion a change that you believe is inappropriate, avoid making remarks such as, "The people upstairs issued these orders." This serves only to increase resentment, reduce morale, and delay implementation. Also, this attitude gains you no points with employees.

Name of the Game Is Commitment

Obedience is good, but commitment is better. We succeed only when we get commitment from the people who carry out the change or who are affected by it. Ideally, you invite this participation when a change is first contemplated. We all support what we create and may even be ecstatic over our own ideas, but it takes considerably more effort to get enthusiastic over another person's brainchild. When a team lacks ownership of a plan, getting commitment is more difficult. If you demand it, all you get is lip service.

If it is not possible for employees to participate in the planning sessions, it is even more important for them to be involved in designing or scheduling the implementation process. Follow through on as many of each person's suggestions as possible.

Explain the rationale behind the change. Articulate in detail the reasoning in terms that make sense to the workers. Does it improve customer service, profits, or competitiveness? Detail the shortcomings of the old way. Show them how the change will affect them. What is in it for them if they do well? What happens if they do not?

If the history of change is one of failure, explain the new change fully, and point out how this change is different. Provide examples of how plans succeeded elsewhere.

Upgrade Your Employee Selection Process

The chapters titled "Employee Recruitment" and "Interviewing and Employee Selection" have much to say about selecting job applicants. When recruiting, choose people who have displayed their ability to adjust to change. You want the

ones who have the willingness and ability to participate in planning.

Train, Train, and Keep Training

Because fear of the unknown is the source of the most anxiety, strive to eliminate the unknown. The dual approach is to hold enough discussions before the change occurs and to provide sufficient training to ensure confidence.

Clarify training objectives using a thorough needs analysis. Ask the learners what they want and incorporate as many of their suggestions as possible into the program. Design training that provides the needed job-related skills.

Enlist the highly motivated and influential end users first. Provide the training just before it is needed and to those who are going to use it first to ensure that it is fresh in their minds.

Carrying Out the Plans

It is important to avoid early failure or disappointment at the start. To increase the likelihood of quick and favorable results, introduce changes by using pilot projects and highly motivated teams.

Take change one step at a time. Resist the urge to carry out every aspect of a change at once. Empower employees to make changes happen. Build in incentives for using the change. Stay in touch with workers' daily efforts. **Exhibit 29.1** lists seven keys for successfully implementing plans.

Exhibit 29.1 Seven Keys to Successful Implementation

- Clarify strategies and plans.
- Mobilize resources. (Choosing the right people is especially critical.)
- Introduce new practices slowly.
- Provide all needed education.
- Provide and solicit feedback continuously.
- Run interference for team members.
- Do not be too critical or overbearing.

Monitor Progress

Major change efforts require constant monitoring. Things do go wrong. Unexpected situations develop. Unanticipated changes may have occurred in the environment since the plan was set in motion. Some resistance may occur because of certain aspects of the plan that were wrong to begin with or that were improperly implemented. As people are forced to break familiar routines and patterns, performance lags, confusion follows, and job stress increases. People see and hear things that disturb them. They are often disappointed and frustrated by all the problems or bottlenecks that develop.

Some people will hastily conclude that the plan is not working. The grumbling will grow louder unless leaders have made it clear that the change will not be trouble free. When employees complain, showcase the benefits accruing or the progress that has been achieved to date. Make it easy and safe for them to express new concerns.

Talk to people. Track results. Look for symptoms like slippage in timetables, productivity downturns, and increased customer complaints. Be aware of signs of uncooperativeness, complaining, or criticizing the folks in charge. Also remain aware that workers may start regressing to the old way of doing things if follow-up on implementation is lax and inconsistent. It cannot be too strongly stressed that incomplete or nonexistent follow-up is behind many implementation failures. If you pay attention, you can address problems before they get out of hand.

Use weekly meetings to discuss modifications and problems. Continue the group meetings throughout the implementation process. Interactions include give-and-take exchanges. Accept, even welcome, appropriate critical comments. For the first 15 minutes of each meeting, let the complaints and frustrations be aired. Then switch to a brag session where individuals can talk about their little victories. Pay close attention to what is said out in the corridors after the meetings break up; on occasion, this is when the most honest reactions occur.

Monitoring performance and tracking results also enable you to identify the role models who are contributing most to the change effort. Honor them and celebrate their achievements.

Reward

Hanging on to established habits makes sense to employees when their former reward system remains in place. Therefore, try to restructure the way people are compensated. Money is a limited and transient motivational force, but the lack of a fair compensation system is a strong demotivator.

Autonomy is a powerful reward for some people, so delegate authority to those who show the interest and display the ability to use power judiciously. For achievers who relish challenges, the strongest reward may be to get involved in another change, perhaps a bigger or more challenging one. Most employees feel rewarded to some extent if they perceive the change will enable them to get their work done faster, more easily, or more enjoyably. See the chapter titled "Motivation, Reward, and Recognition" for more about rewards and recognition.

Helping People Through the Stressful Phase

Employees are usually relieved when told that their concerns are normal and will pass. The principles of stress management apply here. The earlier you take remedial measures, the better results you will get. Workers appreciate reassurance that their jobs or their teams will not be altered. You may be able to reassure employees whose positions are in jeopardy by doing the following:

- Promising new positions if this is indeed possible (Do not make promises you cannot keep.)
- Offering retraining opportunities
- Recommending early retirement packages

Vital elements of the coping process should be applied as needed by the supervisor:

- Use active listening skills, isolation avoidance, and empathy.

- Legitimize employees' feelings and expressions.
- Ensure that training measures meet the needs of employees.
- Show understanding but hold firm on the need for the change.
- Search for specific needs and problems and bring them into the open.
- Explore ways of achieving desired changes through conflict management skills and win–win negotiation.
- Display technical and managerial expertise pertinent to the situation.
- Be patient.
- Never promise what you cannot deliver.

Employee Responses to Change

Sweeps Clean but Incrementally

Resistance to change is highly likely in a group that has been self-reliant with little or no management for a long period. It seems that Shari has attempted a number of important changes in a short time. But the problems took a long while to develop; they cannot be resolved quickly and certainly not all at once; her steamroller tactics can easily be perceived as insulting. After years of coasting, employees are now in effect being told that they have done little or nothing right, breeding resentment, which in turn leads to resistance. Shari has much work ahead of her, and it will get done only if she involves the staff in deciding what the problems really are and which one major problem to tackle first. Trying to do too much too quickly and doing so by edict will only serve to strengthen resistance,

People and Change

Individuals vary significantly in their openness to change. Few thrive on change, but the majority of people do not. Some employees sense that they will be affected; others convince themselves that they will not be involved.

Employees often go through the stages of anticipation, denial, anger, bargaining, depression, and, finally, acceptance. The first opposition to change may take place when news of possible change surfaces.

Although most employees show some degree of support, others take a wait-and-see attitude, and some actively reject the process. The two undesirable responses are resistance and the development of stress. Absenteeism, turnover and grievance filing may increase. Hostility, moodiness, and slowed output may result.

Fortunately, most employees eventually settle down and accept the change. Later, many fight to prevent any return to the old system. For example, a computer breakdown that requires a temporary return to the old manual system can cause great disappointment for the team.

Happy Campers

A few members of any work group, clearly a minority of employees, embrace new marching orders enthusiastically. The better the preparation for change, the larger this percentage of people will be. Alert managers make full use of these eager beavers by assigning them to pilot programs and having them report on successes during the early phases of a new initiative.

Fence Sitters

Most employees are fence sitters. Fence sitters are not obstinate or uncooperative, but they do fret about how a change may affect them. Although not hostile to change as such, neither are they enthusiastic. They want proof or at least strong evidence that the change will work. They ask where the change was tried before and what the outcome was. Most will join in the endeavor when they see colleagues commit themselves and when they witness early successes.

When people believe they will be unaffected by a change, some of them become amused bystanders. They show little sympathy for the people who are involved. Sometimes they taunt those who are struggling with the new initiative. Do not tolerate snide remarks from supposedly "disinterested" parties.

Cynics

One highly vocal cynic can infect an entire department. Cynics often have some measure of truth to support their pessimism. There may have been failures in the past, or there may be formidable barriers ahead.

When you hear grumbling, investigate the problem, and address it without delay. It helps to have some team members relate successes during the early phases of the change.

Rational arguments, such as pointing out that this change is unlike other failed initiatives, may not achieve the desired effect. In that situation the best strategy may be to admit that you also have concerns but decided to risk going ahead with the change. Add that you hope the cynic will also make the same choice. When this does not work, you may have to spend your efforts trying to limit the influence of the cynic on other employees. Occasionally, you can convert cynics by giving them more of the action or getting their ideas for expediting the process.

Resisters

Resistance can be overt or covert, active or passive, well intentioned or subversive. People fight change in ways that best fit their individual personalities, so expect a wide range of tactics at work when resistance emerges.

Managers often mistake the lack of overt opposition for support. Covert resisters disguise their resistance to make it safer or more politically correct. People in this category are cunning. These saboteurs operate undercover, resisting on the sly, fighting change carefully to reduce their chances of being caught. They may claim that they did everything in their power to support the change. Subtle sabotage can be expressed in a number of ways:

- Intentionally "forgetting" to do things
- Inciting the resistance of others

- Doing exactly what the supervisor requests when they know that such action will be detrimental
- Setting up roadblocks

Your job is to blow the cover of these saboteurs. Look for signs of passive resistance, such as foot dragging, quiet uncooperativeness, or malicious compliance. When you spot people behaving this way, corner them and give them an earful. If counseling is not effective, consider appropriate disciplinary measures (especially if an employee's resistance goes to the extreme of insubordination, which should always be addressed regardless of how it arises).

Among the resisters there may be a few firebrands who are loud and outspoken in their opposition to change. One or two highly vocal critics can rock the boat, so it is hazardous to ignore them. Often, you may find it necessary to get rid of such obstructionists. Pritchett expresses the opinion of many of us when he writes, "Make an example of someone who resists. If this sounds ruthless, remember that it is their choice to resist. Something has to suffer, either them or the change effort."[1]

How to Overcome Resistance

Resistance to change is not all bad. It can be valuable, sometimes keeping leaders from making critical mistakes. In fact, it can be extremely fortunate for the supervisor to have a couple of loyal employees who will speak up when they see the leader heading for trouble. However, for the most part, resistance is a roadblock that you must remove.

When employees do not accept change, it may be because they do not understand it. They may believe it will be bad for them. Some employees lack confidence in the ability of their leaders or their teams to make it work.

Chances for success decrease when change occurs without proactive analysis, planning, or direction. The likelihood of success increases when you understand how your people react to change and use that awareness to help navigate them through the process.

Participation by Stakeholders

The importance of getting employees involved in the planning and implementation processes has already been discussed. By involving people before specific changes become reality, a leader confronts deep-seated negative attitudes before they become barriers.

Education

Do not overlook the knowledge gap that a change can create. There is usually much to be learned. Make certain that people have the necessary understanding. They may need to handle new kinds of equipment and face unfamiliar methods. Once workers realize that they will be retrained, their resistance often plummets. When they receive instruction manuals, hands-on training, and the time to use new equipment, they quickly develop self-confidence.

Communication

Earlier we discussed the importance of communication when laying the groundwork for change and when anticipating employee concerns. In the implementation phase, bring developing resistance out into the open. Make it safe and easy for people to express their feelings. Be patient enough to get beyond superficial answers so you can reach the true issues. Try to understand their positions. Evaluate the legitimacy of their resistance. You might discover that some of their reluctance keeps you from making a mistake. At the very least, they can educate you about why they are resisting and how you can elicit their support.

When people say that things were better before a particular change, remind them of the problems that existed then. We tend to forget many of the negative aspects of "the good old days." For example, although people may gripe about the new computer system, few would elect to go back to the old system.

Supervisory Commitment

Your actions speak far louder than your words in this regard, so "walk the talk." Be obvious and passionate in your determination to follow through. Do not try to reduce resistance by softening your position; doing so will only stiffen the resistance. Employees will fully commit only when they trust their superiors, and it is up to every supervisor to earn this trust.

Job Enrichment

For a number of years health care has been experiencing a paradigm shift from a technical model to a socio-technical model. Thus, today, advances in equipment and instrumentation and automation are no longer enough. To please our most important external customers, our patients, more high touch is required. To satisfy our major internal customers, our employees, job enrichment is required. And to appease the third-party payers, controlled costs are required.

The term "job enrichment" does not refer to undertaking one single specific project at a time. Rather, it is a continuous process of encouraging employee participation in multiple activities. Job enrichment capitalizes on and makes full use of all available professional abilities and individual skills and doing so requires taking a closer look at how people are assigned and how jobs are designed. Each employee perceives job satisfaction and enrichment a bit differently. It is necessary to know the motivational needs of individual team members. For employees who desire more control, we provide delegation and empowerment (see chapter titled "Delegation and Empowerment"). For those who want greater task satisfaction, we provide training, challenge, and job enhancement. For those who have a strong affiliation (social) need, we provide increased opportunities for team efforts (see chapter titled "Team Leadership").

Job Fit

Before embarking on cross-training or other job-enrichment measures, first concentrate on placing the right people in the right jobs. If the individual and the job are appropriately matched at the start, short-term changes are far less likely to be required. Begin with accurate position descriptions (see the chapter titled "Policies and Policy Making") and comprehensive recruiting and selection of new hires (see chapters titled "Employee Recruitment" and "Interviewing and Employee Selection"). Assign employees tasks that take advantage of their strengths and make their weaknesses irrelevant (see the chapter titled "Reengineering, Mergers, and the Supervisor"). Ensure that employees are not handicapped by oppressive or restrictive policies and rules (see chapter titled "The Supervisor's Legal Environment").

Quality of Work Life

The physical work environment, social relationships, style of supervision, and other morale factors determine the quality of work life. For the most part, employees now take these circumstances for granted, and they—and their unions, should they be organized—will fight to maintain them. These essentially generic factors must be favorable before significant socio-technical breakthroughs can be achieved.

Job Redesign

To be effective, any job design must both serve the task and meet the needs of the workers. Many common job redesign measures are available to supervisors:

- Cross-training
- Rotation of workstations, departments, or shifts
- Job transfer
- Changed work hours (flextime)
- Status changes from full time to part time or vice versa

- Deletion or addition of specific duties
- New locations for workstations
- Improved instrumentation, flow patterns, communication, and methods
- Altered team membership or roles
- Encouragement of creativity and entrepreneurship
- Delegation of more challenging assignments
- Appointments to committees, quality circles, or other work groups
- Involvement in research or development
- Assignments to teaching or training roles

When Should Job Design Changes Be Considered?

Anytime! The considerations may be formal or informal, planned in advance, or undertaken on the spur of the moment. A number of more opportune times may be available:

- During the latter phases of probationary employment
- At performance appraisal time
- When salary discussions are initiated by employees
- When new services are contemplated
- When reductions-in-force (layoffs) are necessary
- When organizational expansion, merger, acquisition, or other restructuring happens, altering the basic organizational configuration

Key Questions Affecting Job Redesign

- Does the individual employee want more authority or autonomy?
- Does this employee prefer to work alone or on a team?
- Will the organization and the employee benefit from a particular change?
- What can be achieved without an immediate change in job classification?
- Will the budget and current staffing configuration permit changes?
- How will the changes affect workflow and other people?

- Will the results improve customer service, costs or charges, or employee morale?
- Will the changes enhance TQM (CQI) measures?

Guidelines or Cautions for Job Redesign

- Never attempt to use job redesign or job enrichment as a cure-all.
- Tailor the changes to the needs and wants of both the employees and the organization.
- Know the motivational drives of each employee.
- Consider the effects of any change on other people.
- Ensure that the employee endorses the new redesign.
- Be certain the employee has a reasonably good chance of succeeding.
- Make the goals and plans flexible and reversible.
- Update position descriptions as appropriate.
- Provide feedback and support.
- Do not promise what you cannot deliver.

Special Considerations

Job Sharing

Sometimes it is beneficial to both the department and some of its employees to alter the way a job is covered by having it shared, changing hours and people rather than work procedures. Job sharing is the name commonly given to the practice of having one full-time position shared by two workers, each working part time and dividing the job's responsibilities between them. Along with flextime, job sharing is one of the so-called nontraditional scheduling schemes that have seen increasing use in recent years. The most common job-sharing arrangements involve two employees evenly dividing a single full-time position. Arrangements might consist, for example, of one person working mornings and the other working afternoons, or both working

full days with each working 2 days one week and 3 days in alternate weeks.

In judging whether job sharing is appropriate for your situation, it is necessary to look closely at three dimensions of the practice: the benefits available to the organization, alternatives that might be considered, and the attitudes that the job-sharing employees bring to the arrangement.

Recognize right away that most of the advantages of job sharing accrue to employees and most of the disadvantages attach to the employer. A major disadvantage for the employer is that a job share potentially doubles the supervisory attention necessary to oversee the position; when a job is shared, the supervisor then has two people to supervise, two possible sources of problems, and two evaluations to do. Depending on the kind of position shared, there can also be some loss of productivity as two people go through start-up and shut-down each time they work. And if a shared job involves customer contact, customers need to relate to two people rather than one.

What benefits are available to the organization? The status of any employee is subject to change. Consider a key employee whose personal circumstances suggest the need for reduced work hours. An important employee can be lost altogether if continuing full time is the only option, but this person can perhaps be retained as an active contributor at half time if the job can be shared with another employee. Doing so prevents the loss of critical talent, protects against productivity lost while a position stands vacant, and avoids needless recruiting expenses. Thus, job sharing can also help reduce employee turnover. In addition, the organization may realize some savings in benefits costs because part-time employees ordinarily do not receive certain benefits available to full-time employees.

What are the alternatives to job sharing? Most of these are implicit in the advantages described previously. A common alternative to job sharing is covering the needs of the position with overtime or temporary or contract help while attempting to recruit to fill the position on a full-time basis. It may also be possible to apportion the major duties of the job among a number of other employees, but realistic opportunities to do so are not common.

The key to the success of any job-sharing arrangement lies in the attitude and behavior of the job-sharing employees. Two employees who are completely on the same page, who are both committed to making the arrangement work, and who treat each other fairly and equitably can make a job-sharing situation work to everyone's benefit. Conversely, what causes the failure of more job shares than any other circumstance is a condition of unequal sharing arising because one employee continually tries to gain the advantage over the other in terms of favorable hours, duties, and such. In other words, when one employee attempts to gain something at the expense of the other, the job share is headed for failure, and increased supervisory headaches are coming.

Also, the employees involved in any job-sharing situation should be advised up front that the arrangement is not to be considered permanent. Should either one or the other of the employees leave, it's back to the drawing board to determine whether continued sharing is appropriate.

Telecommuting

Telecommuting, remote work or "work from home," is an arrangement in which a person works a regularly scheduled amount of time each week at home or some other external location with the support of the appropriate equipment and services. "Work from home" and remote work became extremely popular in early 2020 when the COVID-19 pandemic took the world by surprise. People could no longer share the same working environment anymore but had to continue with their daily job responsibilities. Many industries kept their employees home and monitored their daily production through software and advanced technology. Even today, 25%–30% of the workforce are working from home 1 day per week.[2]

Sometimes existing informally by arrangement between manager and employee, remote work is not a radically new idea. Many outside salespersons as well as consultants of various kinds have done it for years, working out of offices in their homes and visiting "headquarters" just occasionally. However, remote work possibilities have been significantly expanded and enhanced by advances in computers and telecommunications technology.

Whether full time or part time, telecommuters are regular employees of the business. They are decidedly not "independent contractors" or "freelancers" who are paid per piece or per job and excluded from employee benefits. They are regular employees on the employer's payroll. It may be tempting to treat such workers as independent contractors, but this can be accomplished only if the arrangement can pass several tests that legally define independent contractor— tests that all normal telecommuting arrangements will not pass.

We tend at times to think of "work from home" as simple—just having an employee work at home rather than the office—but effective remote work is considerably more involved. Many employees might wish to work in remote situations, but it is the organization and not the employee that sets the criteria. Remote work is never appropriate for employees whose primary duties involve direct interaction with customers, and it is sometimes inappropriate for people who work on team projects that require face-to-face, hands-on interaction. Advancements in technology have allowed teams and groups to "meet" online. Remote work should never be considered for employees who have yet to prove themselves as reliable self-starters.

Telecommuting cannot be a hit-or-miss proposition. It requires a consistent policy delineating the rules for its use, specifying the following:

- *Where* the telecommuter can work, whether just home or other sites
- *Work status*, whether full time or part time
- *When* one can work, whether the employee sets the hours, the employer sets the hours, or the employee is allowed to flex about required "core" hours
- *Technology* required, whether what is needed is determined by the telecommuter or designated by the organization

In developing a telecommuting policy, it is best to secure the input of not only managers, but some of the likely telecommuters as well. The telecommuting policy should require that any such arrangement be described by specific objectives, detailed results expected, and how accomplishments are measured.

For certain kinds of activities, remote work has been practiced for years. For example, traditional telecommuting has included data entry, customer billing, and medical transcription. However, many jobs that are independent of other people and that do not require high-cost specialized equipment are possibilities for remote work. Many jobs can lend themselves to telecommuting as long as the arrangement can satisfactorily serve the needs of customer, employee, and employer.

The individual in a telecommuting situation stands to benefit from reduced travel time and fewer transportation concerns, comfort of work environment and dress, freedom from interruptions, possibly flexible hours, and in some instances relief from child-care concerns. Some professional and technical employees find that on "work from home" days they are more available for telephone consultation than when in a busy office. The department frequently gains productive efficiency and is often able to reduce office expenses and save energy and in general reduce the strain on facilities and services. Remote work can also aid in recruiting and retaining employees.

Remote work is not likely to succeed with the occasional employee who is unable to cope well with isolation from coworkers and the absence of traditional supervision. And the supervisor who is constantly—or, at the other extreme, never—checking up on the unseen employee will not do well with "work from home" employees. Supervisors inexperienced with telecommuting often fear they will not be able to monitor employee activities sufficiently, perhaps feeling they cannot effectively manage people not under their full-time direct supervision. Thus, the supervisor of telecommuters must necessarily manage by results, using goals, objectives, and quotas.

Only you can decide if telecommuting is appropriate for your department/organization. But do the following before going forward:

- Check with other places of comparable size and complexity about their experiences with telecommuting.
- Be certain what you want to do is consistent with your business systems (time reporting, payroll, etc.).
- For unionized employees, sound out the union about their stand on telecommuting and bring them into the process early.

Never adopt telecommuting simply because some employees want to do it. As with any other significant decision you make, go forward only if it seems to make good sense for the department and its customers.

WRAP-UP

Think About It

In the final analysis there are but three ways to get employees to adopt change: you can tell them what to do, you can convince them of what must be done, or you can involve them in addressing the need for change. The best way, involvement, should be the first one considered, but it may not always be possible. The second-best way, convince them (or "sell them," if you will), is always an option; many will cooperate if they understand why the change must be made. The first way, tell them, is to be avoided; simply ordering compliance might get some grudging cooperation, but usually it creates resentment and fosters resistance.

Questions for Review and Discussion

1. Why is it that even a successful change implementation plan will probably have to be revised over the course of implementation?

2. As a supervisor, how are you going to approach the implementation of a none-too-popular change being mandated by your state's Department of Health?

3. It is frequently said that the weakest part of the change implementation process is follow-up. Why?

4. If a particular change that reaches you is of such an urgent nature that you have no time to explain in detail to employees or sell them on what must be done, how would you proceed?

5. Who exercises the ultimate control over whether or not a particular change is successful? Why is this so?

6. What do you consider to be potentially the most upsetting change that can affect a department or team or other specific work group? Why?

7. Are there any times when job redesign might not be especially appropriate? Why or why not?

8. How would you go about ensuring that the right person is matched with the right job as early in employment as possible?

9. Describe two characteristics you would look for if you were considering employees who might fit well into a telecommuting or "work from home" situation.

10. What would you consider to be at least three advantages of successful job redesign? Why?

Case: 'Round and 'Round Again

The position of business office manager at Central Hospital has been a "hot seat," frequently changing officeholders. When the position was vacated last June, the four most senior employees in the department were interviewed. All were told that because they were at the top of grade and the salary structure for new supervisors "had not yet caught up with that of other jobs," the position would involve only a miniscule increase in pay. All four declined to interview for the position, but in the process, all four were given the impression that they were not really considered qualified anyway. They might, however, be considered at a later date.

That same month a new manager was hired from outside, and the four senior employees were instructed to "show the new boss everything she needs to know." Over the next few months, the finance director, to whom the business office reported, told the four senior employees that they had "come along very nicely" and that they would be considered candidates if the position should open up again.

Barely 8 months after being hired, the manager resigned. However, none of the four senior employees got the job; the process described previously was repeated, and again a new manager was hired from outside.

Questions

1. How are the four senior employees going to feel, having been through this frustrating process twice?
2. What are likely to be the attitudes of the business office staff toward the organization?
3. How are the four senior employees likely to regard their boss's boss, the finance director?
4. What would be your recommendation for attempting to correct (over time) the damage done in the business office?

References

1. Pritchett P. *Resistance: Moving Beyond the Barriers to Change.* Pritchett & Associates; 1996:21.
2. Lister K. "Work-at-home after COVID-19—our forecast. Global Workplace Analytics. April 17, 2022. globalworkplaceanalytics.com/work-at-home-after-covid-19-our-forecast

CHAPTER 30

Delegation and Empowerment

CHAPTER OBJECTIVES

- Define the differences between delegating and assigning.
- Review the principal reasons why some supervisors are reluctant to delegate.
- Differentiate between proper delegation and "dumping."
- Present an approach to delegation that includes consideration of what to delegate, to whom to delegate, and how to properly implement delegation and monitor progress.
- Briefly introduce the concepts of horizontal delegation, reverse delegation, and hopscotch delegation.
- Address the numerous similarities and parallels between proper delegation and the practice of empowerment as it is understood in today's organizations.

KEY TERMS

Delegation: Delegation is the assignment of a task to an employee with full instructions and preparation, including the transfer to the employee of authority for task completion along with full responsibility.

Horizontal Delegation: Horizontal delegation is delegation to an individual over whom you have no authority; it is essentially getting someone else to do something for you when there is no official requirement for the other party to do so.

Reverse Delegation: Reverse (or upward) delegation is the art of passing a task up the chain of command, usually to one's immediate superior.

Hopscotch Delegation: This occurs when your manager bypasses you and gives an assignment directly to your subordinate without including you in the process; this is a dangerous practice that tends to undercut your authority.

Empowerment: Empowerment might be best described as total, proper delegation, giving people the authority to do what they are capable of handling and encouraging them to make judgments, form conclusions, reach decisions, and then act.

Why Does It Not Always Work?

Imagine yourself in the position of administrative manager of a diagnostic imaging department. You have found your workload increasing to the extent that you definitely need assistance with some of your nonmanagerial duties. One of the first tasks you see as available for delegation is your monthly statistical report. The report itself is easy to create, but gathering the data is time-consuming.

You select an employee to do the report, and you provide instructions. You are careful to choose an employee who seems capable of doing a decent job and who has sufficient time available. The person you select expresses no opinion for or against taking on the report.

Two days after assigning the task you find that the report has not yet been started. You remind the employee; you are told that completion of other work has delayed the data gathering. You emphasize the need to get the report done on time, but the employee seems in no particular hurry to get into the task.

One day later you accidentally overhear a portion of a conversation in which the employee to whom you have assigned the report says to another employee, "… her lousy statistics, and I think she should do it herself. It's her job, not mine."

What might have been done incorrectly in delegating the report to this particular employee? And what, if anything, can you do to try to correct the employee's attitude as revealed by the comments to the other employee?

Assigning Versus Delegating

Assigning is telling a person what to do, how to do it, and when the task must be completed. The tasks are usually of a nonsupervisory nature and for the most part is found in the position descriptions for particular jobs. There may or may not be an assignment of authority. Delegation, on the other hand, is the transfer of authority, responsibility, and accountability. The tasks are activities that the delegator was previously doing or is expected to do should they arise. Delegation is usually negotiable or optional and requires a commitment by the delegate; concerning assignment, the employee need only do what he or she is told to do, usually without question.

Why Some Supervisors Are Reluctant to Delegate

Some supervisors hesitate to delegate or avoid doing so altogether for a number of reasons:

- They are workaholics or perfectionists.
- They are insecure because they are afraid that (1) the individual will fail, (2) the employee will do it better than the supervisor could do it, or (3) they will be accused of dumping.
- They do not like to turn over tasks they enjoy doing.
- They do not believe their employees are ready or willing.
- They have had unpleasant experiences with delegation.
- They do not know how to delegate properly and effectively.

Supervisors who are reluctant to delegate make statements such as the following:

- "I don't have the time."
- "The last time I tried that it didn't work."
- "If you want things done right, you've got to do them yourself."
- "Why delegate it? I can do it faster and better."
- "When I try to delegate, the employees say that it's not in their position descriptions, or they ask what's in it for them."

Willingness of Employees to Accept Delegated Activities

The willingness of employees to accept delegated tasks is usually determined by whether the following are true or not:

- They believe themselves to be qualified.
- Their previous efforts have succeeded.
- They are concerned about what their teammates may say or think.
- They believe they have sufficient time available.
- They like the delegated activity or see some reward in it.
- They believe they will have enough authority to get the job done.
- They believe the delegator will support them.
- They believe they are being manipulated or dumped on.

Dumping

Delegation is a double-edged sword. It can be the key to increased productivity, better time management, and improved motivation, or it can be a wet blanket that squelches initiative and reduces morale. The latter outcome occurs usually because the supervisor has been "dumping" rather than delegating.

Dumping occurs when employees are loaded with repetitive, mundane work that has little value to the organization or to their careers.[1] Because dumping is often done on the spur of the moment, the recipient feels like an errand runner, the proverbial "gofer."

The most common responses to dumping are resentment and anger. The perception of being dumped on is just that: a perception. Delegation is more likely to be perceived as dumping by the involved employees under the following circumstances:

- Have poor working relationships with their superiors
- Have been dumped on in the past
- Know that others have resisted undertaking the same task
- Fail to see any personal advantage in carrying out the assignment
- Have not been told that occasionally they will be asked to do things not in their position descriptions
- See the delegator wasting time while they do all the work

If you enjoy good rapport with a subordinate and rarely take advantage of your authority, the subordinate will not mind some of the less pleasant or less challenging assignments.

When you assign a task to an employee and another employee asks, "How come you never ask me to do that?" what you have accomplished is most likely delegation. When an employee says, "How come you always stick me with this?" you are most likely dumping.

It Does Not Always Work Because...

The opening example involved assignment, not genuine delegation, and the employee felt burdened rather than flattered by the new responsibility. Clues were there in the initial lack of enthusiasm as well as the later procrastination. If the supervisor endeavors to *influence* rather than simply assign, employees are more likely to be committed to invest time and energy in performance.

To influence this employee, various "perks" might be assigned to the job. If this employee is interested in moving into management, letting the employee present the report might be of value. Perhaps if the report's cover sheet clearly lists the employee as author, this individual will be motivated by recognition. Giving the employee a stretch of uninterrupted time to prepare the report is another strategy.

This employee may simply be unmotivated; however, if the supervisor practices honest participative management, some employees may then display an interest in furthering the goals of the department as well as bettering themselves. An employee must be able to see some personal advantage to taking on a delegated task; the employee must always be able to satisfactorily answer one important question: What's in it for me?

How to Delegate
Four Simple Ways to Pick What to Delegate

1. As you go about your daily routine, just before you tackle a task, ask yourself whether

this is something that someone else in your group could do.

2. When you return from a vacation, list your duties that subordinates took care of while you were away. Some of these temporary assignments could become permanent.

3. At performance reviews, when you discuss future career plans for your associates, ask them whether they would like to take over any of your responsibilities.

4. Select tasks from those listed in your position description (see text that follows).

Delegating Using Your Position Description

• List 10 or more of your tasks, excluding any that cannot or should not be delegated (see list that follows).

• Select those that someone could assume now and those that a member of your group could learn to do.

• Prioritize each task according to how much time you would save by delegating the task, how significantly it would benefit or be acceptable to the delegate, and the degree of difficulty.

What May Not Be Delegated

• Accountability: Delegators remain accountable to higher authorities for delegated work; you can delegate the task, but you remain accountable for the results.

• Powers other than task performance authority: Only formal power, or authority, can be delegated (see **Exhibit 30.1** for distinctions among kinds of power).

• Activities forbidden by law, regulation, or policy (licensure, certification, special training, qualification, or education is required for some duties).

• Activities that involve too great a career risk for the supervisor or the delegate relate directly to the delegate's current assignments or ones that are discrete segments of a complex task.)

Exhibit 30.1 Kinds of Power

■ Authority—Delegated power: "You all report to me because the organization chart says so."

■ Competency—The power of expertise: "See Louise; she's the only one who really knows this stuff."

■ Knowledge—The power of information: "Ask Joe; he's on the committee, and he has all the figures."

■ Physical—The power of brute force: "If you want to stay healthy, you'll do as you're told."

■ Connections—The power of who they know: "His mother is on the board."

■ Fiscal—The power of who has the bucks: "He who gets grant money gets promoted."

■ Union— Power conferred by one's peers: "Nora will get action; she's the union rep."

■ Charisma—Persuasiveness: "He can talk you into anything."

What Should Be Delegated Only Partially and Always with Caution

Be cautious with sensitive or high-leverage activities dealing with people:

• Interviewing, selecting, and orienting new employees (a delegate's role here is that of making recommendations, never actually deciding)

• Approving new hires (again, the delegate should be limited to making recommendations to the supervisor)

• Coaching and counseling (a constructive use of senior employees who can also serve as mentors)

The Supervisor's Two Kinds of Tasks

In almost all instances, the job of a supervisor can be divided into two kinds of tasks: technical tasks and management tasks. These two kinds of tasks are differentiated by the kinds of authority associated with their performance. The technical tasks require what may be referred to as task-performance authority conferred through a job description or other designation of duties but not requiring the exercise of any management authority. Any of these technical tasks are reasonable candidates for delegation.

The majority of the true management tasks, those that cannot be reasonably delegated, involve human resource matters, such as hiring (although you can secure recommendations, as noted previously); disciplining, up to and including discharge; promoting; demoting; transferring; rewarding; and such. The supervisor will also retain approval of the department's budget submission, although staff may provide input, just as staff may also provide input to the development of policies and procedures.

Select the Delegates and Get Their Acceptance

Select delegates who have the necessary competence and display the willingness to take on the task. The most qualified person for a particular activity may not be the one who benefits from it most. A less experienced employee may try harder and do a better job in the long run.

Seek cooperation. Avoid petulant or grudging compliance. Consciously or unconsciously, delegates ask you or themselves, "What's in this for me?" If their perception is negative, the delegation is in trouble. Be wary if you hear the following:

- "Is that an order?"
- "Do I have to?"
- "That's not in my position description."
- "Nobody told me I have to do all that."

People are more willing to take risks if they know for certain what is involved. Perhaps in the past someone took a small step, and Pandora's Box opened. Tell them exactly what they are getting into and give them possible outs. Start by telling them the following:

- Why you decided on the change
- Why you picked them
- Whether or not they have a choice
- What you expect

- What resources and authority are available to them
- What you are going to tell other members of the group if they are affected
- What, if any, modifications will be made to their current assignments
- The checkpoints and, when appropriate, a target date or timetable

When employees object because they do not have the time, agree to share some of the work or apportion some among others. At other times you can relieve them of other responsibilities. Usually, you can promise them that the delegation is reversible (for example, you will relieve them of the responsibility with no loss of their prestige). This is seldom necessary if you picked the right task, selected the right person, and prepared the delegate sufficiently.

How to Implement the Delegated Action

- Select the right task and the right person.
- If it represents a major change, get permission from your superiors.
- If you are operating in a team mode, discuss the change with your team.
- Provide essential training, resources, and authority.
- Agree on an action plan. Listen carefully to delegates' ideas about how to get it done.
- Set up checkpoints. Checkpoints enable you to monitor progress and to give some pats on the back.

Monitor Progress

Be patient and persuasive, not demanding. Avoid statements such as "Don't worry," "You should have …" or "I wish you had …." Help delegates when they get stuck.

Periodically stop by and ask how things are going. Avoid constantly looking over their shoulders or asking too many questions. Questions should reflect your interest in their approach rather than exhibit nervousness that you may have about their ability to finish the job.

When Delegation Falters

Avoid the temptation to abandon ship when there are problems. Allowing people to make some mistakes is the best way to encourage meaningful growth. Although a delegator accepts responsibility for a failure, confidence in the delegate is not readily restored. When employees have done their best but failed, have them prepare a balance sheet in which they identify what went well and what did not. Always let them criticize themselves first. Ask how you could have helped more, because when your delegate fails, you too have failed.

Delegation Variations

Horizontal Delegation

Truly skilled delegators can delegate (or "hand off") to people over whom they have no authority. These individuals may be colleagues or volunteers. Horizontal delegation increases in importance as healthcare institutions feature more cross-functional activities and make greater use of volunteers. Success depends largely on factors such as the following:

- Persuasiveness
- Influence
- Interpersonal skills
- Rapport
- Degree of teamwork
- Past favors done for the other person
- Strength of one's network
- Rewards and recognition for past cooperation

Reverse (Upward) Delegation

Upward delegation is the art of passing along to superiors what employees do not want to do. Employees are often successful in this because their bosses just cannot say no. Managers who seldom delegate are especially susceptible to upward delegation. Drucker and Flower write: "Every subordinate is good at delegating upstairs. It's hard to resist because it's very flattering. You must learn to say 'no.'"[2]

Reverse delegation often follows attempts by a manager to delegate. The delegate reluctantly accepts a task. At the first obstacle, he throws up his hands and tries to pass the buck back to the manager. The manager thus becomes the reluctant delegate.

Sometimes upward delegation is necessary. For example, a supervisor may delegate so much work to an assistant that the assistant cannot complete his or her routine work. It is then up to the delegator to consider various options: take back some work, establish new priorities, or transfer some tasks to another employee.

Hopscotch Delegation

Hopscotch delegation occurs when your manager bypasses you and gives assignments directly to your subordinates. To correct this, it helps to have good rapport with your superior. If you confront your superior when he or she is in a belligerent mood, you may get a response such as "Well, you're never around when something has to be done." If this shunting of authority rarely happens, it is probably best to ignore it. However, if you believe that a confrontation is necessary, take a positive approach by playing down the issue of authority. As you negotiate with your manager, focus on the advantages of you knowing what he or she wants done or of how your people get confused when they get conflicting orders from different managers.

If you cannot get action through your boss or if you want to avoid a confrontation, try acting through your staff. Instruct them to hold up action on nonurgent orders from other people until they have checked with you. Another tactic is to have your associates ask your boss in a polite way to please make the request directly to you because they are working on a priority item of yours.

If it continues unchecked, hopscotch delegation can be deadly. Every time your superior bypasses you and goes directly to your employees, your boss is violating the chain of command and is thereby undermining your supervisory authority. If this hopscotch delegation becomes a chronic problem, it is then likely to be followed by another condition that will further undermine your supervisory authority: your employees may begin bypassing you and taking their questions and problems directly to your superior.

Empowerment

Empowerment is one of the "in" terms to arise in management in recent decades, prominent in the terminology of the total quality management movement. Yet as often as it is used, there remains some confusion as to its real meaning and its actual appearance in practice. In fact, in any good dictionary or thesaurus, "empowerment" and "delegation" are offered as synonyms for each other. However, it seems that in practice empowerment has taken on the connotation of an activity that is somehow more appropriate and more complete than delegation.

Empowerment is a frequently misunderstood word. It decidedly does not mean that employees may do as they please without orders, monitoring, or control. In practice, empowerment means providing an environment and affording opportunities for employees to enhance their competencies and accept more responsibility.

External empowerment is giving people the authority to do what they are capable of handling. It encourages people to make judgments, form conclusions, reach decisions, and then act. It liberates workers from rigid oversight and direction.

Internal empowerment, or self-empowerment, is what individuals generate intrinsically, like they generate enthusiasm or optimism. It reflects competence, experience, assertiveness, character, personality, and charisma.

Benefits of Empowerment

Empowerment enhances feelings of self-efficacy, a state of mind that causes people to believe they can cope effectively with situations and people. Empowerment reduces or eliminates feelings of helplessness. The more that people feel they are in control of their work and their lives, the greater their enthusiasm, optimism, self-confidence, and energy.

With empowered staff, leaders can mobilize stronger forces when responding to crises and with less risk of chaos. The leaders can also set higher performance goals and standards.

Excellent healthcare service requires empowered care providers, especially when they interact directly with customers. Patients and other customers want providers who respond with confident empathy, not with calloused indifference, apathy, or plastic smiles.

Empowering Actions

Employees must know more than how to perform their daily tasks if they are to maximize their contributions. They feel more empowered when they learn about organizational financial matters and their role in providing excellent services.

Ten Steps That Empower

1. Know what each of your employees does and how well the tasks are done. Review position descriptions, performance standards, and previous performance appraisal reports.
2. Decide what additional authority they can handle right now. In their performance reports, look for notes regarding competencies, experience, and training needs.
3. Establish what preparation each of your employees needs to achieve the competencies and mental toughness that empower them. Such preparation may involve training, coaching, psychological support, and incremental delegation.
4. Conceptualize a new supervisory role that reduces micromanaging and matches the level of supervision with the ability, maturity, and motivation of each employee.
5. Ensure that workers know the purpose (mission) of their jobs. Is this stated in their position descriptions and stressed during their orientation? If necessary, clarify each job and your expectations of what outcomes should be.
6. Delegate activities that involve decision-making and problem-solving.
7. Review your education and training program. Empowered organizations are learning institutions. Design a cross-training and

job rotation program so that people become more flexible and more aware of customer problems and their solutions.

8. Make tasks more challenging. Assign complete rather than fragmented tasks. Assign progressively more difficult tasks, starting with ones that ensure success, an essential aspect of situational leadership.
9. Provide sufficient resources, time, and psychological support.
10. Emphasize commitment rather than conformity.

Potential Problems with Empowerment

It was previously noted that delegation involves risk. With universal empowerment, this risk is even greater. It is also greater than forming autonomous teams because you do not have teammates exerting a tempering effect on other members.

Some empowered employees do silly things; a few abuse their new authority. When employees are ill-prepared or when they believe you have not adequately rewarded them, they may rebel actively or passively.

Many workers are uncomfortable with more power, especially if they are passive or have victim mindsets. They prefer conformity and safety to entrepreneurship and risk. An often-heard comment from these folks is, "I just want to do my work and go home."

Employees may lack confidence in their leaders. Those who have been jerked around during a series of failed management initiatives are not likely to join in the celebration of still another program *du jour*. Instead, they hunker down and wait for it to pass as most of the previous ones have.

Some managers simply do not want to share power. They believe they worked hard to earn the power they have and are reluctant to give up any of it.

WRAP-UP

Think About It

Failure to delegate regularly, honestly, and properly is a major cause of supervisory failure, and if not failure, then it is often the reason why a supervisor may go no higher in the organization. The supervisor who fails at delegation is doing considerable self-damage by limiting his or her chances for growth and is hurting employees by denying them the opportunity to learn and grow. Some employees thus stifled seek their futures elsewhere, and it is often the ones you want most to keep who are the first to leave.

Questions for Review and Discussion

1. What do you believe would be the result if your boss consistently practiced hopscotch delegation?
2. What do you consider to be the best way to get a dull, repetitive task accomplished? Why?
3. When is it appropriate for the supervisor to go ahead and do a given task himself or herself rather than delegate it?
4. Why is it said that accountability or ultimate responsibility cannot be delegated?
5. One reason often given for the failure of a supervisor to delegate is fear of competition from subordinates. Instead of fearing competition, why should the supervisor welcome it?
6. What will be your principal response to the employee who says to you, "I don't have to do this—it's not in my job description"?
7. If delegation and empowerment are synonymous in so many contexts, why

do they seem to be differentiated so often today?

8. Why is it important for employees who are given a delegated task to know what is in it for them?

9. What does the supervisor need to be most careful of in following up on delegation? Why?

10. What is over-delegation, and what is its principal hazard? Explain.

Case: If You Want Things Done Well...

John Miller, manager of laundry and linen for City Medical Center, dreaded the one day each month he had to spend doing the statistical report for his department. Miller was responsible for all laundry and linen activities in the 800-bed hospital, two smaller satellite facilities, and several municipal agencies whose linen needs were filled by the hospital. At one time the report had been relatively simple, but as Miller's scope of responsibility grew and administration requested increasingly more detailed information each month, the report had become more complicated. Miller had simply modified his method of preparing the report each time a new requirement was placed upon him, so there was no written procedure for the report's preparation.

Faced once again with the time-consuming report—and confronted, as usual, with several problems demanding his immediate attention—John Miller decided it was time to delegate the preparation of the report to his assistant, Bill Curtis. He called Curtis to his office, gave him a copy of the previous month's report and a set of forms, and said, "I'm sure you've seen this. I want you to take care of it from now on. I've been doing it for a long time, but it's getting to be a real pain, and I've got more important things to do than to allow myself to be tied up with routine clerical work."

Curtis spent perhaps a half minute skimming the report before he said, "I'm sure I can do it if I start on the right foot. How about walking me through it—doing just this one with me so I can get the hang of it?"

Miller said, "Look, my objective in giving you this is to save me some time. If I have to hold your hand, I may as well do it myself." He grinned as he added, "Besides, if I can do it, then anyone with half a brain ought to be able to do it."

Without further comment Curtis left the office with the report and the forms. Miller went to work on other matters.

Later that day Curtis stopped Miller in the corridor—they met while going in opposite directions—and said, "John, I'm glad I caught you. I've got three or four questions about the activity report, mostly concerning how you come up with the count and percentages for the satellites." He started to pull a folded sheet of paper from his back pocket.

Miller barely slowed. "Sorry, Bill, but I can't take the time. I'm late for a meeting." As he hurried past Curtis, he called back over his shoulder, "You'll just have to puzzle it out for yourself. After all, I had to do the same thing."

The following day when the report was due, Miller found Curtis's work on his desk when he returned from lunch. He flipped through it to assure himself that all the blanks had been filled in, then scrawled his signature in the usual place. However, something caught his eye—a number that appeared to be far out of line with anything he had encountered in previous reports. He took out two earlier reports and began a line-by-line comparison. He quickly discovered that Curtis had made a crucial error near the beginning and carried it through successive calculations.

Miller was angry with Curtis. The day was more than half gone, and he would have to drop everything else and spend the rest of the afternoon reworking the figures so the report could be submitted on time. Miller was still working at 4:30 p.m. when Pete Anderson, the engineering manager, appeared in the doorway and said, "I thought we were going to rework your preventive schedule this afternoon. What are you up to, anyway?"

Miller threw down his pencil and snapped, "I'm proving an old saying."

"Meaning what?"

"Meaning, if you want something done right, do it yourself."

Instructions

1. Miller committed several significant errors in "delegating" the activity report to Curtis. Identify at least three such errors in the case description.
2. Using as many steps as you believe necessary, describe how this instance of delegation might have been properly accomplished.

Case: Some Delegated Research

You are manager of biomedical engineering at Central Hospital. You are discussing an information need with your superior, General Services Vice President Peter Gideon. You both agree that your equipment maintenance and repair records are not revealing the kind of information they need to reveal—the nature of breakdowns and failures, maintenance problems, and unique situations encountered—to design an effective preventive maintenance program.

Gideon asks, "Since we started the department year before last, haven't we kept records of all the work done by you and the technicians?"

You respond, "Sure we have, but they won't tell us anything useful without lots of digging. We have nearly 24 months' worth of completed work orders filed in chronological order."

"Could someone sort through the work orders and separate them by kind of work required?"

"I suppose so," you reply, "but I don't have time to do it myself, and both techs are swamped with open work orders. I guess I could always get my secretary, Sharon, to do it. Just tell her what I want and let her go about collecting it in her own way."

Gideon asks, "Does Sharon know the language? All the work order codes? You might want to provide her with some detailed instructions and maybe even give her a deadline for completion or a schedule for finishing various steps of the project."

You answer, "I don't see much point in delegating the job if I'm going to have to do all that work just to get it ready. It ought to be enough for me to give her my objectives, suggest an approach, let her add her own ideas to it, and turn her loose."

"Could this become a regular part of her job?"

"It should," you state. "Hers or somebody's. Then we could monitor the kinds of information we need rather than having to dig for it like we do now."

Gideon states, "Between us we seem to have tossed out three ways of using Sharon on this project." He proceeded to outline the three possibilities as (1) tell her what is wanted and let her do it in her own way; (2) provide her with expected results, a procedure or other instructions, and a schedule or deadline; and (3) tell her what is wanted, recommend an approach, and turn her loose.

Questions

1. Assuming Sharon is qualified for the project, what should determine whether you do indeed assign the task to her rather than doing it yourself or looking for another way?
2. Identify the advantages and disadvantages of the three possibilities outlined previously.
3. Which of the three approaches should you most seriously consider following? Why?

References

1. Werther, Jr. WB. *Dear Boss*. Meadowbrook; 1989:162.
2. Drucker P, Flower J. *Being effective. Health Care Forum Journal.* 1991;34:52.

Special Supervisory Skills

CHAPTER 31

Spoken Communication

CHAPTER OBJECTIVES

- Identify the common barriers to effective spoken communication.
- Emphasize the importance of listening skills, and suggest how the supervisor can become a better listener.
- Review the uses of the telephone and its aides.
- Introduce negotiation, provide guidelines for preparing for negotiation, and outline the major steps involved in effective negotiation.
- Identify the common barriers to successful negotiation, and suggest how these may be avoided.
- Provide the supervisor with suggestions on how to negotiate with his or her superior.

KEY TERMS

Communication: Communication is a word that has a number of dictionary definitions, some of which are fairly complex; however, within the context of work, organizational communication can be simply defined as *the transfer of meaning*.

Grapevine: The grapevine is most accurately described as *the communications system of the informal organization*. On many occasions it is appropriately described as the *rumor mill*.

The Most Important Managerial Skill

As technical experts, supervisors provide scientific information and technical advice, usually by way of speech. As leaders, supervisors use communication skills to discharge their management responsibilities. Communication is by far the most important managerial skill. Without it, all other skills are inoperative or ineffective. The importance of oral communication in daily work becomes painfully apparent when one experiences acute laryngitis.

Communication systems form the cornerstone of cultural shaping and participative management. To improve quality, customer service, and productivity it is necessary to take a close look at these systems and how they are used.

Most workers believe that bosses hold back things that employees should hear. Subordinates may withhold important information from their superiors if they dislike or mistrust them or if they fear the information will adversely affect their relationship.

Effective information sharing has the following characteristics:

- Multidirectional, moving up, down, laterally, and diagonally with equal facility
- Objective, factual, and true
- Comprehensive but not excessive
- Credible
- Timely

The Informal Communication System

There are serious limitations to formal communication systems. Such systems depend largely on written messages, formal meetings, and orders or instructions issued orally by higher management. Supervisors who depend entirely on formal sources are soon out of touch with what is going on in the organization. Watered-down newsletters or notices on bulletin boards are not enough and do not reach the masses anymore. Electronic bulletin boards, voice mail, email, and one-on-one contact are more effective.[1]

Every organization has a grapevine, and when managers tune in to the grapevine, they come to realize that the information they receive via some formal systems is often late or incomplete.

The informal communication network, or grapevine, flourishes especially when official information is scarce or delayed or when organizational changes take place. The grapevine is usually rapid, up to date, and pervasive and distributes information quickly. Network senders translate complex directives into understandable language. Like other communicators, the senders add their personal spins to these messages. Managers who tap into the informal communication systems learn what is bothering their employees and how their leadership is perceived by the workers.

On the negative side, much of what is transmitted via the grapevine is rumor and gossip. Rumor mills are subject to distortions and omissions. Many reputations and careers have suffered as the result of misuse of this channel. The grapevine is sometimes a major time waster and often sends shock waves through organizations that, later, turn out to be unsubstantiated.

Supervisors must know who the grapevine's principal receivers are and keep tuned in to them.

When you hear distorted or false news, put out corrections promptly via both formal and informal channels. Use the grapevine to counter misinformation and to distribute good news.

Sending More Powerful Messages

Effective care providers command respect by displaying self-confidence and poise. Their unspoken message to customers and subordinates is, "I can help you because I know what's going on and can make things happen."

This unspoken message is transmitted through words, vocal tone, facial expressions, and body language. Mehrabian, in his studies at the University of California, Los Angeles, found that words convey only 7% of the feeling in spoken messages.[2] Voice characteristics supply 38%, and 55% comes from facial expressions and body language. Every message consists of two parts, the content and the emotional component. When the words do not jibe with the emotional message, the words lose their power. Picture a clearly distraught supervisor yelling at a subordinate, "I'm in control here." The subordinate inwardly grins, knowing that the supervisor has lost control and thus the encounter.

Avoid the assumption that your message has been received and understood. Do not rely on a positive response to your "Do you hear me?" or "Do you understand what I said?" Do not believe that because no one asks a question everyone knows what you said. Although you cannot give a quiz after each communication, you can ask people to paraphrase important things you say or ask for comments on specific points. Watch their body language as they respond. The knitted brow or the blank stare speaks louder than the words.

Practical Tips for Better Messages

- Speak with conviction. Remember the power of voice quality and body language.
- Substitute strong responses for weak ones. Instead of "I wonder if you would send ..." say "Please send me ...."
- Call a difference between people a misunderstanding rather than a disagreement.
- Say what you can do, not what you cannot do.
- Shake hands with enthusiasm and smile.
- Be assertive. Maintain your right to be recognized and to state what you believe.
- Use people's names often and pronounce them correctly. People feel validated when we do that. It says, "You are important to me."

Barriers to Verbal Communication

Electronic Barriers

Now that we have had them for a number of years, we could not possibly get along without our computers, email, voice mail, and such, or our cell phones with their ever-expanding capabilities. However, these can all adversely affect relationships with customers and collegiality with colleagues. Because managers can get masses of data instantly, they often believe they have a complete handle on things. Unfortunately, not all significant information gets into the computer or comes through it.

Semantic Barriers

Every day we speak in as many as five languages:

1. English
2. Body language
3. Professional and technical jargon
4. Organizational and bureaucratic talk
5. "Computerese"

We often fail to consider the educational, cultural, and mental status of each of our customers and employees. A nurse who uses the same phraseology when conversing with a mentally challenged patient as she does when she talks to a physician confuses the patient or angers the doctor. Garbled messages, jargon, acronyms, and computer language may baffle even our fellow professionals. Mixed messages, those occurring when words do not match body language, confuse everyone.

Psychological Barriers

Psychological barriers are the most damaging barriers:

- Interrupting, arguing, blaming, talking down to, kidding, or being sarcastic
- Offering inflammatory utterances (e.g., name calling or threatening)
- Using patronizing words or sexist terms such as "you girls"
- Making statements indicative of indifference or apathy:
  - "You have to realize that we're understaffed."
  - "I don't know" (without offering to find out or refer).
  - "We can't do that."
  - "You'll have to ...."
  - "That's not my responsibility."
  - "That's not our policy."
  - "It must be a computer error."

Body Language

Listening is visual as well as auditory. Make certain that your facial expressions, posture, and movements match your words. You can learn much about a person's thoughts by observing behavior.

Signs of attentiveness or interest often include rubbing the chin, maintaining eye contact, leaning forward, and smiling. Signs of disinterest or disagreement can include touching or rubbing the nose, rolling the eyes straight up, leaning backward, tugging on the ear, folding the arms across the chest, frowning, shaking the head, drumming the fingers, avoiding eye contact, or rearranging papers.

Concealment or deception can sometimes be discerned when someone puts the hand partially over the mouth, avoids eye contact, exhibits nervous fingers, blinks quickly, squirms, blushes, or acts like a shirt collar is too tight. When you hear many expressions such as "to tell the truth" or "honestly," be suspicious.

Phonetics Count Heavily

How you say something is just as important as what you say. Vocal tone, volume, and rate vary with emotional state. For example, a subordinate may say the words "I'm okay" but actually convey "I feel miserable." Verbal patterns that can reduce your power in an interpersonal exchange include the following:

- Posing questions to make requests or demands: "Would you like to get me a cup of coffee?"
- Using disclaimers: "I know this sounds silly, but …."
- Using weak qualifiers such as "sort of" and "maybe"
- Tolerating interruptions

Listening Skills

There are some fundamental problems with listening. The other communication processes—reading, writing, and speaking—are active processes; one must take a deliberate step to engage in any of these. Listening, however, although it *should* be active, is entered into passively; that is, we can hear without conscious effort. Many people do not go beyond simple hearing, perhaps not realizing that to listen—*really* listen—requires concentration and conscious effort. Most people are not effective listeners; our spouses and children usually affirm this. If your training program accomplishes nothing more than improving the listening skills of your staff, it will have been well worthwhile.

Three Keys to Successful Listening

1. *Look as though you are listening.* Face the person and, if sitting, lean forward. Establish eye contact. Good eye contact is not staring down the other person; it is shifting your

gaze from the person's eyes to other parts of his or her face or occasionally glancing away entirely. Nod, smile, or frown at the appropriate times. Avoid a poker face. Let your facial expressions show your feelings. Your body language must be congruent with your verbal messages.
2. *Sound as though you are listening.* Use conversational continuers such as "please go on," "I see," or "um-hum."
3. *Provide feedback.* This is the most effective of the three. Only when feedback is involved does the speaker know that he or she has sent the right message. Paraphrase what you heard and saw, translating the message content and the associated feelings. The objective of most interpersonal contacts is to transfer the desired information from the mind of the speaker to the mind of the listener, and the way to ensure this has happened is to require feedback even if the speaker has to be as blunt as: "In your own words, please tell me what I just told you."

Skilled listeners make frequent use of empathetic, that is, supportive, responses, and they avoid defensive, judgmental, and advisory ones. Questioning is appropriate unless it sounds like cross-examination. Skilled listeners also listen carefully for underlying feelings.

Avoid the following:

- Criticizing
- Diagnosing
- Falsely praising
- Ordering
- Name calling
- Advising
- Moralizing
- Threatening
- Cross-examining
- Diverting
- Feigned listening
- Insincerely reassuring

Naive Listening

We often tend to tune out mentally confused patients, aides, members of the housekeeping service, and even some colleagues, friends, and family members. To overcome this, stop occasionally and listen as you did the first time you had any contact with that person. This is naive listening, proceeding as though this individual has just entered your life for the first time.

Telephone etiquette often appears to be a low-priority item in some healthcare organizations and physicians' offices. That is unfortunate because it affects client satisfaction and time management. Managers should be choosy when hiring receptionists; they should insist that receptionists and others who handle many incoming calls attend a training session on telephone technique, especially matters of courtesy.

How your telephone is answered says much about you and your department. An answering voice may express an affirmative, helpful attitude or convey an I-don't-really-care attitude. Callers mirror how they are treated. If we sound friendly, our callers respond in kind.

A Test for Telephone Etiquette and Helpfulness

Anonymously call your department after regular hours and ask a complex question about an aspect of your service. Be prepared for a shock.

Tying up telephone lines with personal calls angers callers. So does transferring callers through a series of departments.

Everyone assumes they know how to use the telephone. When you suggest that an employee attend a workshop on telephone courtesy, that employee may become upset. A somewhat manipulative trick is to tell the person that you want someone to attend the training session and then come back and teach what was learned to the rest of the staff. This sensitive issue can be avoided if the organization mandates periodic training programs for the entire staff or includes this training in its orientation program. An added benefit is that such group education promotes uniform telephone etiquette, which, in turn, has a reinforcing effect.

What All Telephone Users Should Know
Answering the Phone

Answer within three rings or apologize for the delay. Sit up straight. Project helpfulness. A smiling face helps; smiles do indeed travel over telephone lines. To remind employees how important customers are, put stickers next to each phone that read, "The CEO is calling."

Identify self and unit, then offer to help. Sound enthusiastic and helpful. If the person states his or her name, use it at least once. If the name is not offered, ask for it.

Take messages when appropriate. The message should include the person's full name, organization, phone number, any information they would like to leave, time and date of message, and your initials. (Note: A special phone log is helpful.)

Placing Someone on Hold

Being put on hold is a frequent complaint, especially when a person believes the length of the hold is excessive. Apologize when you cannot connect the person at once. Avoid saying, "Just a second, I'll be right back." This is rarely true and is annoying. Offer a choice of waiting or being called back. When on hold, check every 30 seconds and repeat the offer. If the caller states a preference for calling back, make sure this is done. Also, avoid use of call waiting. Call waiting forces a choice between which caller is the more important. One or the other is offended.

Screening Calls

If it is necessary to screen calls, do it politely and tactfully. An effective screener helps callers by trying to answer their questions or by directing them to someone who can answer them. To avoid transfers to wrong parties, the screener must be knowledgeable about departmental matters. People who screen calls should know which callers are always to be put through immediately and those who should not be put through at all. They should also know the questions or problems they should handle and the ones they should refer to other people.

The phraseology used is important. Here are some examples of overused or rude phrases:

- "Alice hasn't come in yet."
- "Joe just stepped out."
- "She's in a meeting." (This is used so often that few callers believe it.)
- "I never heard of her."
- "You'll have to call back."
- "What's your name, and what do you want?"

By contrast, this is what should be heard:

- "Dr. Jones is out of her office right now. May I ask her to call you?"
- "He's not available at the moment. May I tell him who called?"
- "Doctor, Miss Smith is meeting with our supervisors. The meeting usually ends by 9:00 a.m. May I have her call you then?"
- "That name doesn't sound familiar. Can you give me more information?"
- "He's not in right now. I expect him back about 2:00 p.m. Will you be available then?"
- "Yes, she's in. May I tell her who is calling?" (Do not ask for callers' names before telling them that their party is not in.)

Some consultants recommend that special customers be given the unlisted phone numbers of key employees, always with the permission of the latter, of course.

Transferring Calls

Before you transfer a call, ask if you can help or if the caller would like to be called when the person becomes available. Being transferred from one extension to another is a frequent source of irritation. A courteous transfer requires a brief explanation of why the caller is being transferred. The caller is reassured that his or her questions will be answered. To avoid the consequences of a disconnection, give callers the name, title, and extension number of the person to whom they are being transferred. Do not hang up until the connection has been made.

Taking Messages for Another Person

Detailed forms that have enough space for the following information are recommended instead of the "little pink slips":

- Name of caller (phonetic version if the name is difficult to pronounce)
- Caller's organization or department and phone number
- Time, date, and purpose of call
- Impression of caller's mood (for example, angry, unhappy, stressed)
- Any promises made to the caller
- Callers' unwillingness to talk to anyone else
- Any known previous important contacts with caller (if so, it may be appropriate to attach copies of that prior correspondence)[3]

Telephone Recommendations for All Employees

- Use the caller's name frequently.
- Say what you can do, not what you cannot do.
- Mitigate anger by answering empathetically.
- For outbound calls, state your business first and save the small talk for last.
- Answer promptly and identify yourself.
- Sound enthusiastic and cooperative.
- Keep the person focused on the reason for the call.
- Keep personal calls short and infrequent.
- End conversations on a positive note, and thank the person for calling.
- Make sure that the callers know what you are going to do, and do it promptly.

Forbidden Phrases

"I don't know."	"Why didn't you...?"
"That's not done in this department."	"I'll try."
"There's nothing I can do about that."	"You can't have ...."
"You have to ...."	"Our policy is ...."
"You should have ...."	

Conversation Ending

In telephone conversations, as in interviews or written correspondence, the beginnings and the endings make the strongest impressions. Conclude calls with a verification of key points covered. You want to be remembered as a pleasant, efficient person to deal with. Therefore, take the time to thank the person for calling. Say you were glad to be of service (or sorry that you could not help). End the conversation on a pleasant upbeat note, but refrain from using that tiresome cliché, "Have a nice day" or, even worse, "bye-bye." Instead, say "goodbye" in a pleasant voice or with an appropriate comment such as "It was nice hearing from you again" or "Thank you for filling me in; I appreciate it." Let the caller hang up first.

Telephone Tag

We all know the frustration of calling people when they are out and when you are not available when the calls are returned. This can go on for hours, even days. There are effective ways to avoid phone tag.

- Pick the best time to call. People are most likely to be in their offices just before lunch and late in the afternoon. Ask when it is a good time to call. You can say when you will call again and ask that this information be placed on the person's desk.
- Ask the person to page your party or ask if there is another number at which you can reach the person.
- Ask if there is someone else who can answer your question.
- Leave a message.
- Use voicemail or email.

Tips for Outbound Calls

- Have an up-to-date telephone directory nearby. Keep a list of frequently called persons and their phone numbers. Add the best time to call and any other helpful information.
- Set aside a period each day during which to make outbound calls. If it can be helped, avoid calling before 9:00 a.m., after 5:00 p.m., or between noon and 1:30 p.m.
- Most people do not like to be called at home when the subject is one that can be handled during the workday.
- Keep in mind any time differences when you make long-distance calls.
- Plan what you are going to say. Have available any documents you might need.
- Let the phone ring at least five or six times before hanging up. If a secretary initiates the calls, make certain you remain close by. It is irritating to the person being contacted and embarrassing to a secretary who has to hunt for you.
- Start conversations by stating your name. Do not wait to be asked.

Voice Mail

Make certain employees are trained in the languages of email, voice mail, and cell phone technology. After all, management has held classes for telephone use for years, so why not teach about these technological variations as well?

Many callers are annoyed by voice mail. Some refuse to leave messages. When used properly, however, voice mail can eliminate frustrations for both caller and recipient. Following is some excellent advice for using voice mail effectively:

- Change your greeting regularly to let callers know your situation (for example, "I'm on another call right now," "I'll be back in my office at noon," or "I'll be out of my office until Monday, February 12th").
- In addition to your name, organization, and phone number, state the time and date, the nature of your call, when it is convenient for you to be called, or when you will call back.
- Substitute a message for a request to be called back.
- Suggest an email response if a response is needed; provide your email address.
- Let your callers know when you make call-backs (if you screen calls as a time management technique).[3]

Negotiating Skills

Whether we realize it or not we all engage in negotiations at work and at home on a daily basis. Many of us start the day negotiating with offspring over what they will wear to school. Supervisors negotiate with vendors; workers negotiate over vacation schedules. When we hold a performance review, a counseling session, or moderate a problem-solving meeting, we often wish we were better negotiators. A characteristic of effective leaders is that they are persuasive negotiators who obtain commitment rather than obedience from their people.

Basic Forms of Negotiation

The *power play* or *"gotcha" approach* is authoritarian and is based on marshaling enough power to overwhelm opponents. People who play this game may have prestigious titles, powerful friends, or weighty professional expertise. Many such people consider it naive to believe that cooperation works; they believe their way is best. However, their attempts at dominance often meet counter-dominance and become less effective as others learn how to cope with them.

There are several ways to cope with power plays:

- Develop a thick skin. Do not take the nasty things you hear personally.
- Do not be intimidated. Be assertive without being aggressive.
- If someone tries to intimidate you with technical jargon, do not hesitate to speak up (for example, "I need you to put that in one-syllable words").
- Request a third-party mediator.
- Respond to threats with "Why would you want to do that?"
- Taking fixed positions is a "take-it-or-leave-it" approach in which both sides adopt rigid positions and are reluctant to compromise. They become locked into defending those positions to save face, and negotiations become contests of will rather than problem-solving exercises.

In the *haggling approach,* experienced hagglers ask for more than they expect to get. They offer options that are favorable only to them. They try to create an obligation by giving the other party a little something or make them feel guilty (for example, "I take that remark personally"). They promise more than they know they will deliver.

The *high–low-dollar approach* is a game in which sellers quote figures much higher than they expect to get. Buyers respond with figures much lower than they expect to pay. The expectation is that the agreed-on amount will be somewhere in the middle. Although this game may be appropriate in some instances, the outcome depends too heavily on the persuasiveness of one party or on how badly the buyer wants the product or service. If you are the buyer and you have done your homework, avoid the high–low-dollar game and make one honest offer and stick to it. You always have the option of turning around and walking away.

Collaboration or value adding is more likely to result in win–win outcomes. You achieve your goals while helping others achieve theirs. Collaboration is based on the premise that you make the pie bigger rather than fighting over the size of each party's slice. The negotiators add value to the package rather than seeking concessions from each other. The more creative they are, the better the results. For example, an employee seeks permission to leave work early each day so she can pick up her child at school. Her supervisor balks. When the employee proposes to make up the time by accepting more weekend assignments, the supervisor readily agrees. They both win.

Preparing for Negotiation

Assemble Your Wish List

Each person has different interests and being well-prepared helps you understand what these interests are. At the very least you must know what you want and what you are willing to concede. Sometimes it helps to have thought out not only a specific goal, but also several fallback positions or alternative goals. For important negotiations, put these goals in writing.

Before the meeting, try to find out what the other side wants and how badly they want it. What are they likely to propose? What advantages do they have?

Collect Data

The information you take into a negotiation may be copies of laws, policies, protocols, guidelines, or other backup material. Get up-to-date information through your formal and informal communication channels. Organize information so it is concise and understandable. Include handouts, graphs, charts, and other visual displays.

Organize Your Approach

- Sketch out the options you can offer.
- Prepare your opening remarks.
- Ready the arguments you can make to maximize the positive aspects of your interests and to counter the other person's arguments.
- Role-play what you plan to say or offer with a friend or mentor.
- Choose the best time and place for the meeting.

Major Steps in Negotiation

1. *Clarify interests.* Ask people how they view the situation and what is important to them. Paraphrase their message and ask if you have interpreted their view correctly. Then state your position. Do not continue on until these viewpoints and desired outcomes are clear.
2. *Focus initially on points of agreement.* Center on what you perceive as areas of agreement. Work from there. Get into the problem areas later.
3. *Formulate possible options.* Usually, the more options you can identify, the better prepared you are. Articulate the benefits of each option to the other person. Do not get stuck believing that your solution is the only good one. Be gracious. If the person has a valid argument, say so. A common mistake that novice negotiators make is to think that something is not negotiable. This may be based on past experience or what you have been told by others. But these assumed constraints are often just that: assumed. You may later regret not exploring such possibilities. Instead of presenting your idea as a proposal, test the waters by stating your case as a question (for example, "I wonder what would happen if we …?"). If it gets a cool reception, you can easily drop the subject with a simple, "Yeah, that's right." It you believe your idea has great merit and has a good chance of being accepted, the previous approach may lead to others taking it over by adding an additional twist. To prevent that, have a written outline of your proposal and introduce it into the discussion.
4. *Agree on the best option.* If you cannot reach complete agreement, be willing to compromise, but not until you have explored all possible win–win solutions. Contrary to what some people seem to believe, "compromise" is not a dirty word; it does not signify weakness. Unwillingness to compromise contributes to inflexibility and can destroy any chance of achieving a win–win outcome. Be willing to give ground on some issues to get what you want on others. No negotiation is successful unless both parties believe they have gained something.
5. *Be prepared to encounter an impasse.* Keep the meeting going even though your initial efforts are unsuccessful. The longer the discussion continues, the more likely the other party is to give in. He or she may be reluctant to invest a lot of time in a negotiation without achieving any result. If things continue to stall, call for a break or a postponement. Each of you may need more information or to consult with other individuals.

6. *Perfect the deal.* Refine the selected solution to ensure that each of you is comfortable with it.

7. *Wrap it up.* Review what is agreed and document that fact. If it was a long or rigorous negotiation, compliment the other party on being a tough negotiator. This helps you to end on a positive note.

Barriers to Successful Negotiation

Fear

Negotiation may give rise to fear of loss of friendship or future cooperation. Some people cave in quickly because they do not have the stomach for any kind of disagreement. Others are inflexible or demanding because they fear that people will take advantage of them.

When you are negotiating a salary increase and you believe the organization or your manager is taking advantage of you, there may be times when you must consider threatening to resign. Never do this, however, unless you are willing to follow through. Still better, wait until you have a bona fide offer elsewhere.

Secrecy

Some negotiators mistakenly believe that they will win more often if they withhold information.

Ultimatums and Deadlines

Avoid making threats unless they are absolutely necessary; once in a while the threat to walk out of a bargaining session will get results. Once you make such a threat, be willing to do it. If you do not follow through, your bluff will be called in future negotiations.

Anger, Induction of Guilt, Ridicule, or Tears

These emotional responses or attempts to manipulate are seldom useful. Experienced negotiators are not moved by these gimmicks, but some novice negotiators are.

Team Approach

Although team efforts have some advantages, such as augmented expertise and mutual support, there are potential problems with the team approach. Showing up with a team of supporters may suggest that you lack the ability to handle the process by yourself. Sometimes one member of your group may make a remark that hurts your case or reveals disunity among the group's members. The team approach also takes longer and is more likely to end without a consensus being reached.

Reliance on Data

Statistics are useful if valid and not redundant. However, too much reliance on them backfires when the other party finds flaws in your data or comes up with data more impressive than yours. You do not often convince people with facts and figures. Search for something in your proposal that appeals to them, and then keep pushing that hot button. Say, for example, that during bargaining the other person frequently mentions paperwork. When negotiation stalls, repeatedly come back to your offer to help with the documentation and reports.

Delaying Tactics

Repeated and unnecessary delays often postpone needed action. They also erode the spirit of cooperation and can be very frustrating to both parties.

Negotiating with Your Boss

Unless you are a clone of your manager, the two of you will sometimes experience disagreements. Most of the time, you reach amicable solutions. On rare occasions your boss may reject something you feel very strongly about (for example, an ethical problem or a raise for you or one of your employees). After the first rebuff, try a second verbal approach at a more convenient time or place, and bring more ammunition with you. If that attempt stalls, put your request in writing. Emphasize your strong feelings about the request. If that does not work, you must decide whether the matter is important enough to challenge your boss and possibly to risk your career.

If you believe the matter is worth pursuing, tell your manager that you would like the two of you to discuss the problem with his superior. If he declines to accompany you but tells you to go ahead, do so after telling him exactly what you plan to say to his boss. If his response is to threaten you in some way, you must be prepared to react appropriately.

WRAP-UP

Think About It

We frequently complain about "no communication" in the workplace, especially when something goes wrong. When we do so, it is not likely that we are talking about ourselves, so we are blaming others for leaving us out of the flow of information. However, we will never improve communication until we recognize that each of us is part of the problem. It pays to remember at all times that each of us is not nearly as effective at communication as we assume we are.

Questions for Review and Discussion

1. What is the greatest shortcoming of the informal communication system, that is, the grapevine? Why is this so?
2. If we are generally aware that face-to-face is the most effective form of interpersonal communication, why do we use this approach today considerably less than it was formerly used?
3. It has been said that effective listening is difficult because we can hear without listening. What is meant by this statement?
4. Why do many employees tend to believe that management is usually holding back important information from them?
5. Which seems to work more readily as far as information flow is concerned: upward communication or downward communication? Why?
6. Why might an employee not ask for clarification, even if he or she has no understanding of what the supervisor has said?
7. What advantages of face-to-face communication are not available in various other means of interpersonal communication?
8. What do you believe the individual supervisor can do to influence the contents of the grapevine and its relative accuracy?
9. What forbidden phrases have you ever experienced at work or as the customer? How did this make you feel? Why?
10. Reference has been made regarding negotiations with employees. In what ways, if any, might negotiation enter into a performance appraisal discussion?

Case: Why Are They Noisy Alone and Quiet Together?

As a new supervisor hired from outside the hospital, it took you very little time to learn that morale in the department had been low for quite some time. As you started getting acquainted with your employees by meeting with them individually, you quickly became inundated with complaints and various other evidence of discontent. Most of the gripes concerned perceived problems with administration and building services, but there were also a significant number of complaints by your staff about other employees in the department and some thinly veiled charges suggesting that a couple of staff members have consistently been complaining about the department to your boss. (Your boss has said nothing to you about this.)

It sounded to you as though a number of common themes ran through the group's complaints, and it seemed to you that a number of differences could be cleared up by airing these issues with the entire group. You planned a meeting for that purpose, instructing all employees to be prepared to air their complaints (except for those directly involving other staff members). Your employees seemed to believe this was a reasonable idea, and several led you to believe they would be happy to speak up.

However, your meeting turned out to be brief. Hard as you tried to get people to air their gripes, nobody spoke. You tried again 2 weeks later, with the same results: No one uttered a word of complaint. Yet all the while the negative undercurrents continued to circulate through the department.

Questions

1. Why do you suppose you get only silence from these employees when you attempt to deal with them as a group?
2. Why might the complaints that several of your employees raised involving administration and building services be a reasonable place to start working on this group's communication problems?
3. How long do you believe it will take to bring this group around to where you need them to be? Why?
4. Is this the best way to deal with problem? What other alternatives can used instead of a group meeting?

Case: Will You Argue with the Boss?

You are at a meeting with your manager, another middle manager, and four other supervisors. The subject of the meeting is the manner in which the supervisors of the organization are to conduct themselves during the present union-organizing campaign.

Your manager makes a statement concerning one way in which supervisors should conduct themselves. You are surprised to hear this statement because earlier that day you read a legal opinion describing this particular action as probably illegal. You interrupt your manager with, "Pardon me, but I don't believe it can really be done that way. I'm certain it would leave us open to an unfair labor practice charge."

Obviously annoyed at the interruption, your manager says sharply, "This isn't open to discussion. You're wrong."

You open your mouth to speak again but are cut short by an angry glance. You are absolutely certain your boss is wrong; he had inadvertently turned around a couple of words and described a "cannot do" as a "can do." Unfortunately, you are in a conference room surrounded by other people, and the document that could prove your point is in your office.

Question

1. What can you do to straighten out this communication problem without distorting yourself with your manager any more than necessary?

Case: An Ultimatum

You are an administrative supervisor of the hospital's department of diagnostic imaging (radiology). The department has been having problems with the special procedures area; you have had considerable difficulty recruiting and retaining special procedures technologists. You presently have your allotted staff of three such technologists, but these people are fully utilized, and at least two of them have recently made comments about staffing being inadequate for the workload.

The senior technologist, Carl Smithers, has been especially vocal in his comments about understaffing. Several times, and as recently as Monday of this week, he spoke with you concerning his perception of the need for another technologist. Today, Wednesday the 9th, you received the following note from Smithers:

"As I suggested I would do in our conversation of Monday this week, I am going on record notifying you that additional technologist help must be available by Monday the 21st. If you are unwilling or unable to provide the needed help, I will be unable to continue in my present position beyond Friday the 18th."

You immediately called Smithers and said, "Come to my office right now, Carl. We need to talk." Your intent is to come up with some course of action that will take care of the department's needs and keep your senior technologist in place.

Questions
1. What has Carl Smithers done to his own negotiating position by delivering an ultimatum?
2. Granted, you want to address the problem as soon as possible, but what, if anything, should you have done before sending for Smithers? Why?
3. What are you going to do or suggest doing if available resources continue to forbid adding any new staff?
4. Is there anything positive to immediately come of Smithers' ultimatum? If so, what?

References

1. Sonnenberg F. The essentials of on-the-job information. *Supervisory Management*. 1992;37:8.
2. Smith D, Sutton H. *Powerful Proofreading Skills*. Crisp Publishers; 1994:29.
3. Deeprose D. Making voice mail customer friendly. *Supervisory Management*. 1992;37:7, 8.

CHAPTER 32

Written Communication

CHAPTER OBJECTIVES

- Provide guidance for selecting the appropriate channels for written communication.
- Outline the general steps involved in preparing a document.
- Provide step-by-step guidelines for preparing a document of any nature.
- Suggest how the supervisor should approach the editing of an employee's written communication.
- Provide a brief introduction to the subject of grant writing.

KEY TERMS

Grant Writing: Grant writing is the process of preparing a document to serve as an application—or part of an application—for grant funding; that is, for funds made available for certain purposes by organizations such as departments of government, various corporations, and foundations and trusts.

A Widespread Need

A significant number of employers are not pleased with the writing ability of today's graduates. Ricks, for example, states, "The secondary schools have disgorged a generation of workers who cannot write a three-sentence memo."[1]

Educators at healthcare institutions recognize the importance of helping employees upgrade their writing skills. However, they lack the time to focus on grammatical errors or to search for spelling mistakes. They must limit the little time they have to bare-bones writing competencies.

Educators depend on supervisors to define the writing skills their employees need on the job, for example in writing memos, emails, and preparing reports.

Customer satisfaction often depends on employees' writing skills. Customers want simple and clear messages they can understand.

Writers of memos and letters must consider the level of education of their readers. The writer displays a significant measure of courtesy by making it as easy as possible for people to respond. For example, it is often appropriate to invite readers to return your letter with their responses noted on the letter, thus eliminating the need to compose and print a new letter (in the instance a letter is the intended form of written communication).

Selecting an Appropriate Communication Channel

We find it necessary to select the most appropriate channel of communication on a daily basis. These selections affect efficiency, expense, and client satisfaction. Spoken communication is usually the fastest means because it allows complex exchanges and transmits feelings better than other forms of communication. Use it when you want immediate responses or reactions or when discussion or lengthy questioning is needed.

Written messages can mute hostility or emotion. For all practical purposes, they are permanent, and usually—but not always—are less susceptible to misinterpretation. A significant advantage is that they do not interrupt the recipient's work as face-to-face exchanges and phone calls do. Some of the writing choices include memorandum, letter, email, and instant message/text message.

It is important to know the preferences of one's superiors and clients. Some prefer spoken messages; others like everything in writing. We all know people who refuse to leave messages on voice mail; commercial recordings can be irritating, not to mention the oft-encountered music guaranteed to annoy some callers. And how often does a recorded voice tell us that our message is very important and then place us on hold for interminable periods?

Letters are for external, private, or formal purposes. Memos are more suitable for in-house, less formal messages. A great many of these are now transmitted via email. Use a letter when transmitting extensive data or information that will be retained as a permanent record. One simple rule in deciding between memo and letter is that any message that requires a stamp to reach its intended recipient should be a letter.

Steps in Preparing a Document

Before preparing a written communication of any kind, define your target audience. You will usually have a primary audience consisting of the person or persons who most need the information, who must perhaps act upon it or use it in a decision-making process. You may also have a secondary audience consisting of people who have an interest in the subject but need not act upon it. Your communication must be targeted toward your primary audience, and thus your language must be the language of that audience. Always write with your primary audience in mind; do not attempt to write so broadly as to be fully understandable by anyone else who may read it.

Anatomy of a Memo

To: Often it is best to send a memo to a position rather than to an individual. If the person is on extended leave, the memo may reside in an in-basket for weeks. Use the person's name only if assured the person is available.
From: This is the originator of the message, not the person who types it or an assistant who prepares it for an executive.
Date: The date the memo leaves the department, not the date dictated or typed.
Subject: Keep it brief but make it clear, for example "Third Quarter Results."
Message:
Action: What are you going to do or what do you expect the receiver to do?
Copies: Send copies to everyone you want to take action or be informed.
Attachments: These may be references, copies of previous reports, or special precautions.
Other: Name or initials of the typist may be appropriate.

Keep your language consistent with the likely level of understanding of the target audience. For example, in writing from professional to professional in the same field, you generally might be free to use the language of that field with all of its "inside" terms and jargon. However, in writing to someone of a different educational level or occupational field, match your language to the likely level of understanding of the person or persons comprising your target audience.

Define the purpose of the message. What do you hope to accomplish? Is the message really needed? Do you expect the receiver to take some kind of action, or do you merely want to inform? What is the best sending channel to use? Must it be typed? Should it be a memo or a letter? Do you have all the information you need?

Write a rough draft, initially not being overly concerned with rules and structure. Picture the reader sitting across from you. Start with the person's name or with "you." Front-load the opening paragraph with the core of the message; the first paragraph gets the most attention and is what readers remember best so deliver a positive message or conclusion up front. Use a hook to stimulate the reader's interest (for example, "You're going to like what we're doing about your recent suggestion"). Prepare a strong closing statement; the last paragraph gets the next most attention. Do not waste time correcting grammatical errors or spelling in the first draft. Concern yourself only with content and clarity.

Rewrite. Many writers of business correspondence fail to give rewriting and editing the attention they deserve; doing so takes time. However, this step provides assurance of clarity, and time spent up front often pays itself back in avoiding misunderstanding and other problems. Check your draft for conciseness, clarity, and personal touch. Does it answer what, who, when, where, why, and how? Improve readability by using stroking words (for example, the reader's name, "you" and "we," compliments, or expressions of appreciation) and converting negative or impolite statements into positive, tactful, and courteous ones.

Strengthen vague or abstract wording. Do not use "We're going to try to decrease the turnaround time"; it is imprecise. Use "We're going to decrease the turnaround time by an hour." Use gender-inclusive language. The simplest way to neuter sentences is to use "he or she," but this gets cumbersome. Substitute titles, such as "the employee," or refer to groups in the plural and use "they."

Edit carefully. Observe the following rules:

- Keep the message simple and specific.
- Check the paragraphs. Keep them short, with one major thought for each.
- Use lists, columns, headings, and alphanumerics.
- Highlight key words or phrases by using bold-face or underlined type.
- Allow plenty of white space by using wide margins, generous spacing, and a limited number of lines per page.
- Check the sentences. Vary their lengths to avoid telegraphic sound; break up the long ones.
- Convert passive to active voice. "Our monthly meeting has been discontinued" is passive. "We elected to discontinue monthly meetings" is active.
- Convert some active to passive voice for diplomatic reasons. It softens statements and avoids finger pointing. "Dr. Jones objected to your appointment" puts Dr. Jones on the spot. "An objection to your appointment was raised" diffuses responsibility.
- Convert "-ion" nouns to verbs: "It is my intention" becomes "I intend."
- Check punctuation, spelling, and grammar.
- Eliminate overused phrases: "Upon receipt of your reply …"(say "When we hear from you).
- Eliminate unnecessary words, phrases, or modifiers: "The consensus of opinion" (use "The consensus").
- Substitute strong words for weak ones. Not "We think that we give good service," but "We strive for outstanding service."
- Drop excess pronouns and prepositions: "The decrease in profit is of great concern to us" is better expressed as "We're concerned about decreased profit."
- Stay away from slang, jargon, acronyms, buzzwords phrases: "down the tubes," "out of this world," "belly up," "bottom line," etc.

Editing an Employee's Writing

Do not return an employee's document marked up like it was a school paper, with corrections all over and lacking only a grade to look like a real school assignment. Never use red for your comments on an employee's writing; in addition to making errors painfully obvious, this is another practice that marks you as more schoolteacher or critic than supervisor.

Review the document with the person who wrote it. Focus on major defects. Is the piece organized logically and supported by data? Does it clearly state its purpose? Provide specific examples of what you want to see conveyed. If you find too many minor flaws, the employee will believe you are nitpicking or will become discouraged. End with an encouraging comment about how the person's reports have improved in content, readability, or promptness.

Of course, you do not want to see glaring language errors in a document that might go outside the department, but your first concern in serving as editor should be clarity of thought and presentation rather than observance of all so-called "rules" of writing.

Email

In many respects, email is a marvelous technological advance, but significant risks come with it. Stored messages can become evidence against an organization if it is sued. There have been suits charging sexual harassment, race or age discrimination, and other violations in which email messages have figured. On the other hand, trying to police email can conceivably expose employers to charges of invasion of privacy.

Email enables all employees to access just about anyone in the organization; they do not even need to knock on the door. On the one hand, executives are sometimes more receptive to email messages because they can read them when convenient. On the other hand, when they return to their offices and find hundreds of messages, they may be less responsive.

No modern business technology is more misused and abused than email. Email not only carries a high volume of nonbusiness material, it also carries business information that is communicated carelessly and frequently does more to raise questions than convey information.

If you have to spend one-third to one-half of your email time sorting through unimportant communications and personal information before getting to pertinent messages, many of which you must then interpret or question before passing along or acting upon, your email is out of control. To bring it under control, consider the following suggestions for regulating the flow of messages:

- Emphasize deleting rather than reading. In most instances a quick look at the subject line along with your knowledge of the sender indicate whether a message should be read in full.
- Get to know your frequent senders and what they are likely to send.
- Similar to the age-old advice about handling each incoming piece of paper only once, try to deal with each email message once and only once. When you open and read a message, reply to it, forward it, delete it, or put it away in an electronic folder whenever possible.
- When sending a message, use a clear, understandable subject line that tells the addressee in a few words what to expect of the communication. However, when replying to or forwarding a message, it is usually best to keep the original subject line intact.
- Inform your employees of the proper business use of email and train them in handling incoming mail as suggested previously. You might also remind them that email is not as private as they might believe; messages are regularly misdirected accidentally, and it's easy for some computer users to tap into others' email.
- When sending a message, consider carefully who should receive it and whether others should be copied (cc or bcc).
- When attaching files to a message take care to avoid overloading the message with numerous files. When sending a number of related files for the sake of efficiency bundle them in a compressed (ZIP) file for transmission.

Concerning the seemingly prevalent careless use of email, at times it seems that email brings out the worst in many writers of business communications. Email is such a readily available and easily usable means of interpersonal communication that its relatively severe shortcomings are easy to overlook. When you speak with someone face-to-face, in addition to words you also have facial expression, vocal tone, and immediacy of feedback and, thus, interchange. Even in a telephone conversation, in addition to words you have vocal tone and immediacy of feedback. But an email message is like a letter or memo—all you have to convey the message are words for someone to read.

Misunderstandings abound because so many users simply "dash off" messages minus the care they might apply to letters or memos. Some who would never allow a letter to go out containing obvious errors think nothing of emailing unedited ramblings devoid of capitalization and normal punctuation, overflowing with misspellings and incorrect terms.

Editing a letter takes time, but we usually do so. What is different about an email message that makes a person forget to edit and clarify? Perhaps it is the seeming immediacy of email, the feeling it provides of talking directly to someone via the computer screen. It is always far better to edit and rewrite—and certainly spell-check—before sending each message. Clarity of content is most likely to accompany clarity of presentation.

Think of email as one of a subset of tools in that versatile tool kit. Like any good tool, to retain its usefulness keep it in good order and use it for its intended purposes only. Your employees need to know that they must restrict email usage to business purposes, and they must further know what should or should not be transmitted via email. It is advisable to express what email should and should not be used for in a formal policy.

Instant Messaging/Text Messaging

Instant messaging, consisting of text-based exchanges that occur in real time, is becoming increasingly popular in organization as communications technology advances. Messages travel between two or more participants over the internet or over other types of networks. Many organizations use instant messaging applications and software to allow quick communication at the employees' fingertips. Its strength resides in its capacity to permit immediate feedback to messages in the form of acknowledgement or direct reply.

Text messaging, another form of instant messaging but mostly used on an employee's personal cell phone is becoming the preferred alternative to communication by telephone or email when an immediate response is required. Organizational policies will dictate the rules of text messaging and personal cell phones at the workstation/desk area.

Grant Writing

Grant writing is the label used to describe the process of applying for funding—for "grants"—made available by organizations such as certain government departments, various corporations, and foundations and trusts. This is written communication of an extremely important kind. Grant writing involves developing and submitting proposals that convey to the prospective grantors the reasons for the request and the specific intended uses of the desired funding.

Inexperienced applicants need to do some serious study and research before writing and submitting grant requests; "grantsmanship" has essentially become a specialized field in its own right. The competition for grant money is strong, especially among nonprofit healthcare and human service organizations, many of which are looking to expand or launch new programs or secure funds for research. Before plunging into grant writing, engage the assistance of someone experienced in writing successful grant requests, or study grant writing and exhaustively research the requirements of the potential grantor. A careless or incomplete submission can create a poor impression with the grantor, affecting chances of future success.

WRAP-UP

Think About It

Written communication is one of the several subjects addressed in this text that could readily fill one or more books of its own. Learning to write clearly is an ongoing process that requires practice; one learns to write better by writing and rewriting, as well as reading well-written materials. It can be said that the most important part of business writing is rewriting—never let a document go out after just an initial pass to get the words on paper. Rather, edit and rewrite, aiming for clarity.

Questions for Review and Discussion

1. It has been said that most business documents contain from 25%–100% more words than needed to properly convey their messages. Granted, this makes for longer documents, but is there harm in this?

2. What means would you likely use to communicate your observation of a serious ethical breach committed by a licensed professional? Why?

3. When you happen to be upset about a particular issue, what are the advantages of responding in writing rather than speaking face-to-face with the other party?

4. What are the primary advantages of communication in writing over face-to-face communication?

5. What are the primary advantages of face-to-face communication over communication in writing?

6. Has technology advancements of instant messaging helped or hindered communication in the healthcare setting? Explain.

7. What are the risks of email communication?

8. Does a memo convey the same message as a letter or email communication? What should be written in a memo rather than a letter?

9. What rules of email communication do you currently observe? And which rules do you not currently follow? How will you change your current email practices to observe email etiquette?

10. What is your experience with grant writing? If you do not have any experience, is this something you could see yourself doing in the future?

Exercise: The Smith Letter

Rework the following letter, your objective being to clarify and convey the intended message while reducing the total number of words as much as needed and practical.

Gentlemen:

In reference to the above collection item, which you instructed us to hold at the disposal of the beneficiary, we wish to advise that Mr. Smith has not called on us, nor have we received any inquiries on his behalf.

The above information is provided to you in the event you wish to give us any further instructions in the matter.

Sincerely,

Exercise: What Did He Say?

This is the text of a letter provided by a health-care facility's pension-servicing organization to a question asked by a benefits specialist. See if you can understand the true message and express it with clarity.

Dear (Benefits Manager):

Re: Date of Termination for Retirement Plan Purposes in the Payroll/HR System

In connection with your payroll/HR system, you asked us whether we thought it would be a good idea to have as an additional data item in the payroll system, beyond an employee's traditional last day worked (i.e., the last day the employee is physically at the Company), the date of termination/retirement for Retirement Plan Purposes (i.e., the date that a terminating or retiring employee's vacation payments are exhausted). For consistency and for administrative ease in having the last day worked and day of termination/retirement needed to determine Retirement Plan benefits all in the same information source, we think it would be a good idea to have both dates for an employee in the payroll system.

Sincerely yours,

(Hint: The message can be clearly conveyed in one relatively brief sentence. Think about it.)

Reference

1. Ricks DM. Why your business-writing courses don't work. *Training.* 1994;31:49–52.

CHAPTER 33

Holding Effective Meetings

CHAPTER OBJECTIVES

- Review the primary purposes of meetings.
- Identify the principal components of a properly structured meeting.
- Review the necessary preparations to be made in advance by the individual who is to chair the meeting.
- Provide tips for meeting attendees to operate as active participants.
- Review the various kinds of problem attendees whose behavior threatens to disrupt the meeting and suggest how the chairperson may cope with nonconstructive behavior.

KEY TERMS

Abilene Paradox: The inability to manage agreement, occurring when members approve an action contrary to what they really want because they fail to express their true opinions and vote for something to which they object but believe the group favors.

Online Meetings: A meeting that is held virtually through the internet, computer software, or an organization's secured network. Attendees are not physically in the same place while attending the meeting together.

Getting Together to Solve a Problem

A scenario: A problem developed within the hospital's finance department in the report receiving processing, from the receipt of incoming material to the completion of payment. The purchasing manager, Mr. Sampson, recognized the problem and pointed it out to his immediate supervisor. Sampson said he understood the situation and knew how it should be corrected, but to do it

right would involve five different departments. Sampson was directed to "get together with the other four supervisors and work out a solution."

On short notice Sampson called a meeting of the affected supervisors. Only two of the other four were able to attend; of the other two, one was ill, and the other was on vacation. So, the three persons who were available went to work on the problem. They developed a workable solution that required little implementation effort on their part but called upon the two missing supervisors to take nearly all the required action. Sampson put the results of their decision in a memo to the two supervisors who were expected to implement the decision.

Assuming that what Sampson and his companions arrived at was the most reasonable solution possible, could there be any legitimate reasons for resistance from the two supervisors who were expected to carry it out? If you were one of the two supervisors left out of the meeting, how would you react to the "directive" from Sampson and what would you do about it? Think about this while going through the next few pages.

A Necessity

Despite their tainted reputation, meetings remain one of our most valuable communication tools. We use them for team building and coordination, cross-functional activities, dissemination of information, training, problem-solving, and decision-making. Committees, task forces, and focus groups could not function without meetings. Ad hoc problem-solving meetings conducted in a brainstorming mode are often among the most valuable of meetings.

We must, of course, not forget departmental and staff meetings. Essentially every department or departmental subgroup holds regular staff meetings. Indeed, there may be few if any healthcare institutions that do not encounter a shortage of places to meet. It seems that only vehicle parking space is in greater demand than meeting space. The amount of information flowing out of computers has made meetings even more important because there is an ever-increasing amount of information to be shared and discussed.

Many managers believe they spend too much time in meetings and that a great many meetings are a waste of time. They are correct on both points. Nevertheless, the higher people rise in the organization, the more time they spend in meetings. Insecure managers call meetings for the sole purpose of getting moral support or sharing responsibility. Perhaps the biggest time waster is the regularly scheduled meeting, often held even when there is nothing important to discuss.

Major Purposes of Meetings

Meetings as we know them in organizational life are held to share, exchange, or disseminate information. Specific purposes for holding meetings are as follows:

- To explain new policies, laws, services, protocols, systems, or restructuring activities; in general, anything that involves change
- To accept reports or recommendations
- To make decisions, solve problems, allocate resources, prepare plans, establish priorities, generate ideas, or assign tasks
- To persuade or obtain commitment for an idea, program, or proposal
- To teach, train, demonstrate, or explain tasks and procedures
- To congratulate or reward

Components of a Meeting

All properly structured and conducted meetings include the following essential components:

- *Purpose*: the reason for the meeting
- *Input and content*: leader, attendees, agendas, visual aids, handouts, meeting room facilities, objectives, facts, and opinions
- *Process*: presentation, discussion, consensus, voting, negotiation, information exchange, expression of feelings, planning, problem-solving, and decision-making
- *Product*: problems solved, decisions made, compromises reached, commitments obtained, schedules, assignments, priorities, resources allocated, and action plans
- *Responses and follow-up*: actions taken, information provided to meeting constituents and other people affected by the decisions

Advance Preparations by the Chairperson

In addition to preparing an agenda and ensuring that meeting space and resources are available, chairpersons improve their effectiveness by soliciting ideas, opinions, and information before the session. They encourage attendees to submit suggestions for topics. Talking to attendees before a meeting often eliminates the need for that meeting. This is also a technique for getting opinions from passive individuals who may be reluctant to speak up at the meeting. Let the participants know what you expect of them. Designate whom you will call on to discuss certain points.

Morning meetings when everyone is awake and fresh are ideal. After lunch, some people get sleepy. Many people find it productive to hold meetings at 4 p.m. By that hour they have ideally taken care of most of their major daily problems and still have a little time to return to their offices for last-minute details after the session.

The selection of attendees is important. You can reduce costs and avoid displeasure if you limit attendance to those you absolutely need and who are willing to serve. The attendees should collectively have the necessary knowledge and experience. They should be the kind of people you can depend on to show up and participate.

The larger the number of attendees, the slower the meeting progress and the more difficult it is to stick to the agenda. A group of five to eight people is ideal for most action meetings. To help reduce meeting size, consider part-time attendance; that is, ask people to be present only when you need them. Encourage them to leave when they have made their contributions (busy people are grateful for this).

Select a Competent and Conscientious Record Keeper

Meeting records are important, so you want a recorder or note-taker who takes clear and concise notes throughout the entire meeting. The note-taker summarizes and condenses the information into the minutes and submits them to the chairperson for review and approval.

Agenda

The agenda is to a chairperson what a recipe is to a cook. Condense the topics in action- or goal-oriented statements. Avoid the word "discuss" when the purpose of the meeting is to recommend action. Discussions that do not lead to actions are usually little more than hot air. After each item on the agenda, show the expected kind of result (for example, "to prepare the final draft of our mission statement").

Indicate the time allocated for each topic and the names of the people you expect to report. Use a computer to prepare your personal copy of the agenda. List everything you want to cover and then cut the agenda in half, either combining items or eliminating those of lesser importance. Always include a start and end time for each topic. Use action phrases like "to recommend" or "to make a final decision" rather than "to discuss" or "to consider."

Distribute the agenda several days before the meeting. If you issue the agenda too long before the meeting, some people may lose their copies and forget the contents. But if you do not give them enough time to read and digest the content, they lack time to prepare for the session.

Reviewing the Sampson Scenario

Even if the solution developed by Sampson and his two colleagues was the most reasonable available, there remains legitimate reason for resistance from the two supervisors who were expected to carry it out. These two are not in a position to feel any sense of ownership in the solution, and since they did not participate in the process, they are not guaranteed to see the result as "the most reasonable answer available."

No one is likely to react completely favorably to the "directive" from Sampson. If we were the absentees, we may well see the result as piling the work onto those who weren't at the meeting. The perception of anyone outside of the decision-making threesome is likely to be that Sampson and company railroaded the decision through to their own advantage. Anyone who had been left out of the process might well ask for another meeting at which the five can work toward a solution that all can accept—even though it may still look much like the Sampson-and-company solution.

It is absolutely fundamental to problem-solving and decision-making meetings that those who will in any way be affected by the results have a voice in developing a solution.

The Meeting

Get Started

Regardless of the setting—online setting or face-to-face meeting—the chairperson should arrive early to ensure that everything is ready and set-up. For an online meeting, the computer software settings should be checked to ensure they are working properly and audio and video are formatted correctly.

Consider memorizing your opening statement, making it clear, concise, and to the point. The opening statement establishes the direction for the meeting.

If this is the first meeting of a particular group, establish some ground rules before any discussions start. Here are some usable guidelines:

- We will begin and end the meetings on time.
- We will listen to others without interrupting.
- We will not allow sarcasm, ridicule, or intimidation.
- Everyone gets a chance to talk and is expected to do so.
- We will seek consensus rather than a majority vote.

Sound and look enthusiastic as you review the highlights of the previous meeting and ask for any comments or corrections. Note any progress made since that meeting.

How to Encourage Participation

- Call each member by name.
- Respond enthusiastically to all suggestions.
- Split into breakaway groups.
- Let others lead some questioning or chair the session.
- Reinforce participation from reserved members, for example: "Thanks, Erica, for speaking so candidly."
- Use nonthreatening, open-ended questions, such as, "How do you think someone opposed to that idea will respond?"
- Withhold your opinion until everyone else has spoken.
- If a person's suggestion cannot be accepted in full, try using part of it.
- Encourage members to build on the ideas of others.
- Preserve the egos of all members.

Avoid the Abilene Paradox

The Abilene paradox is the inability to manage agreement.[1] It occurs when members approve an action contrary to what they really want. This occurs because they fail to express their true opinions and vote for something to which they object but believe the group favors. This scenario is common when chairpersons are domineering. When the result turns out unfavorably, members either accuse each other or make lame excuses for not speaking up. This paradox can be avoided when participants have the courage to speak their minds honestly or when a devil's advocate is present.

Maintain Control

Keep people from going off on tangents. When they stray, say something like, "Jessica, that's interesting. We'll consider that at another time. Now about …." Summarize progress periodically. Call for a break when things stall.

Force Decisions

Ask if anyone needs more data before a decision can be made. Ask a proponent to sum up his or her opinion or perspective. Do the same for an opponent. Go around the table and ask each person for his or her position and then try to achieve a unanimous decision. Call for a vote only when a serious effort for a consensus has failed or you need a record of how each member has voted.

Ensure that recommendations are phrased in specific terminology. For example, "to improve emergency room service" is too general. "Decrease average waiting time in the pediatric clinic to less than 15 minutes" is more specific.

Close the Meeting

To avoid confusion, summarize the discussion and decisions. Indicate the areas still requiring consideration. Review assignments and select the date for the next meeting.

Important "Do Nots" for Chairpersons

- Do not try to dominate the meeting.
- Do not state your opinion before others have given theirs.
- Do not tell a participant that he or she is wrong.
- Do not instruct or lecture unless that is the purpose of the meeting.
- Do not argue (disagreeing is acceptable).
- Do not ridicule, kid, or use sarcasm.
- Do not take sides early in the discussion.
- Do not fail to control problem members.
- Do not allow the meeting to run overtime.
- Do not try to accomplish too much at one meeting.

After the Meeting

Notify the appropriate people of decisions, if appropriate. Send thank-you notes or a group email to all individuals who attended the meeting.

Prepare meeting minutes without delay. Have meeting minutes prepared and ready for distribution within 24 to 48 hours. The minutes should include the following:

- Time started; time adjourned
- Who was present and who was absent
- Statement that previous minutes were read and approved
- Brief discussion or presentation of each item on agenda
- Record of agreement or disagreement, record of vote, or decisions made
- Follow-up actions to be taken
- Date, place, and time of next meeting

Tips for Meeting Attendees

- Ask yourself why you have been invited and come prepared to actively participate.
- Arrive on time.
- Listen thoughtfully to others and try to understand their points of view.
- Ask for clarifications.
- Respect the opinions of those with whom you disagree.
- Offer honest opinions, even when these are unpopular.
- Try to separate facts from perceptions, assumptions, or opinions.
- Disagree without being disagreeable.
- Seek win–win solutions, and be willing to compromise.
- Accept special assignments such as searching the literature or serving as the note-taker.
- Avoid being a problem attendee.

For Nonassertive Attendees

Some individuals hesitate to speak up at meetings, thus depriving the group of their knowledge and opinions. One of the best approaches is to come fully prepared. Another is to use escalating dialogue. Here, you break your silence by asking questions, starting with benign requests for information or clarification, followed by more challenging queries. Finally, you start to express your opinion.

Another technique is to maintain a state of interest and active neutrality during controversies. Opposing members try to convince fence sitters, who then become centers of attention. Simply listening to both sides and asking appropriate questions provides the neutral observer with clout.

Use power language by avoiding discounters like "I know this sounds silly, but …." Do not use clichés like "It goes without saying …." Eliminate those dreadful fillers such as "Ya know" or "Uhhhhhh."

Sound enthusiastic, speaking clearly and forcefully. Do not tolerate interruptions. Say, for example, "I wasn't finished, Lou." Then go on without waiting for an apology.

Support your vocal expressions with appropriate body language. When a speaker looks at you, give a head signal that shows your reaction. If you nod agreement or shake your head, the person will give you more attention.

Problem Attendees

There are all kinds of participants: incisive thinkers, impatient doers, chronic objectors, speechmakers, shoot-from-the-hip decision-makers, and ultraconservatives; you can probably name others. Following are descriptions of several who tend to give chairpersons the most difficulty.

Latecomers

Encourage chronically tardy members to arrive on time. Do not reward their tardiness by reviewing what transpired before they appeared; this only encourages more tardiness. If all of your meetings start at the stated time even though all attendees are not present, most of the chronic latecomers will get the message and begin arriving on time. In some online meeting formats, latecomers will need "approval" from the host to be allowed in the meeting. Reminding participants that latecomers will not be allowed in will encourage prompt attendance.

Attendees Who Offend Others

No attendee has the right to mock or insult others. The leader should immediately interrupt the wayward behavior and apologize to the person who has been ridiculed. Admonish the offender (for example, "Jack, that is uncalled for, and I'm sure the rest here agree. Let's keep this on a professional level").

Intimidators

Intimidation is a common method used to force opinions. The three primary intimidation tactics are appearing to be angry, assuming a superior attitude, or using ridicule. The chair must stop this quickly.

Hostile or Angry Attendees

If you know who these people are, plan what you will say to them if necessary. Practice by saying it aloud several times before the meeting; visualize a successful confrontation. At the meeting, encourage venting in a respectful manner. The more anger that pours out, the less there is left.

Nonparticipants

Nonparticipants' thoughts are elsewhere. Bring their minds back on track by posing questions directly to them or asking for their opinions.

Side Conversationalists

Some private conversation is natural. Timid members may be afraid to speak up, so they whisper to each other. These attendees may be bored or may just be discourteous. Ask them to share their conversation with the group.

Comics

We all enjoy a little humor, but individuals who overdo this can be disruptive. Stop them in their tracks by not laughing, giving a wry smile as you shake your head, and say that you want to get on with the business. The most appropriate humor arises from the material and the discussion; forced humor more often than not falls flat with some attendees.

Motor Mouths

These people are enthralled by their own voices and never seem to run out of gas. Their comments are endless, and their questions are really just more comments. Jump in when they pause for breath. Say, for example, "Just a minute, Rita, let's hear what others have to say."

Some try to engage you in repeated one-on-one conversations, usually by asking many questions. Ask them to stay after the meeting to discuss these; they rarely do.

Destroyers

Some participants become emotionally rather than rationally involved. They play psychological war games and demand attention by criticizing, interrupting, or taking offense at innocent remarks.

Committee Meetings

Committee meetings are subject to the same rules and conduct as other meetings. Standing committees are permanent and meet regularly. The Joint Commission (TJC) [formerly the Joint Commission on Accreditation of Healthcare Organizations (JCAHO)] requires a number of such committees. Standing committees deal with matters such as quality, safety, infections, ethics, and credentials. Bylaws, union contracts, and operational procedures or protocols list the functions and responsibilities of standing committees.

Ad hoc committees are temporary, created to deal with a single or a one-time problem. A task force is a special kind of ad hoc committee created for a specific purpose. It is unfortunate that so many healthcare workers dislike committee assignments because committees are constantly growing in number and importance.

Managers at any level can appoint ad hoc committees. When you appoint a committee, be specific about what you expect. Answer the following questions:

- Who is to chair the meetings, and does that person have the power to appoint members, schedule meetings, and prepare agendas? Select the chairperson carefully.
- Is membership voluntary?
- What is the goal or mission of the committee?
- When is a report due? Are there to be interim reports? If so, at what intervals?
- If it is a decision-making committee, what are the alternatives to be considered?
- If it is a problem-solving committee, do you want only what is deemed to be the best solution or do you want a list of all the alternatives?
- Will you carry out whatever the committee recommends, or only the parts you like?
- What facilities and fiscal support are available?
- If the committee is to serve permanently, have terms of tenure and plans for rotation of membership been provided?

Telephone Conference Calls

The telephone conference call is still being used today when a quick opinion or feedback is needed by people of varying departments and geographic locations, but the use and ease of online meetings has increased significantly over the past few years and has taken over the common need of the conference call.

WRAP-UP

Think About It

The most important single point about convening and conducting meetings is this one thing: Is this meeting really necessary? Any time a meeting can be avoided with no harm to organizational communication, problem-solving, or decision-making, it should not be held. What gives meetings their generally bad reputation is the number of them that are unnecessary.

Questions for Review and Discussion

1. Why should there be a separate recorder/note-taker appointed for a meeting? Why not have the chairperson fulfill this function and thus keep down the number of essential attendees?

2. Can online meetings be successful? Why or why not?

3. Why and how can the active presence of a devil's advocate help avoid falling prey to the "Abilene paradox"?

4. What is one form of meeting for which it is appropriate to expect everyone present to actively participate? And one form of meeting where little or no attendee participation is expected?

5. Have you ever been on an online meeting? Compare and contrast the face-to-face meeting with the online meeting.

6. When you are convening a meeting, why not make your position, opinion, or recommendation clear at the outset to let attendees know where you stand?

7. Why are so many regularly scheduled meetings wasteful and inefficient?

8. What is the best time for a meeting? Why?

9. How would you handle a meeting participant who behaves as though he or she knows considerably more about the subject of the meeting than you, the chairperson?

10. Do you believe that meetings in general have a tainted reputation as claimed in the chapter? Why or why not?

Case: Is the Meeting the Problem?

You are supervisor of the central transcription service at City Hospital. Your group includes several transcriptionists who handle all the dictation from laboratory and radiology and all medical record transcription.

You are in the habit of holding a brief online informational meeting with your staff early each month. The entire staff work from home. At your June meeting you felt obliged to point out that quality was slipping, errors were on the increase, and more care had to be taken with transcription.

At your July meeting you made the following statement: "The overall quality of transcription has not improved at all over the past month; if anything, it has gotten even worse. I expect all of you to begin improving your work quality immediately."

It is now almost time for your August meeting. In your estimation transcription quality has not improved. It is your belief that as many as half of your employees are contributing to the problem, but you have yet to identify all the offenders by name.

Questions

1. Should you address this continuing problem with the group at large at your August meeting? Why or why not?
2. Should you do some research aimed at identifying the more troublesome employees and address their quality problems at the August meeting? Why or why not?
3. How would you suggest mobilizing your transcription group to address the quality problem and recommend solutions? Is the online meeting format the issue?

Case: Your Department's Staff Meeting

There are 15 people in your department at City Hospital. It has been your practice to hold a weekly staff meeting at 3:00 p.m. each Wednesday. Rather, we should say that you attempt to hold it at 3:00 p.m. because about half of your people are more than 5 minutes late, and a couple of them are usually late by 15 minutes or more. And one of these latecomers can always be counted on to ask, "What have I missed?"

You have made repeated announcements about being there on time, but to no avail. Come Wednesday at 3:00 p.m. you usually find yourself and the same six or seven punctual attendees present and waiting for the latecomers.

Question

1. What can you do to improve punctuality in attending your staff meetings? List all the options for improvement.

Reference

1. Harvey JB. The Abilene paradox. *Organizational Dynamics.* 1988;17:35–80.

CHAPTER 34

Decision-Making and Problem-Solving

CHAPTER OBJECTIVES

- Establish the importance of decision-making in today's work organizations, and outline its implications for the role of the supervisor.
- Present a generalized process for logically approaching and solving large or complex problems.
- Introduce various tools useful in problem-solving activities.
- Explore the intuitive process and its key role in problem-solving.
- Briefly explore the role and potential usefulness of group problem-solving.

KEY TERMS

Dual Cognitive Functions: These are the two cognitive approaches to decision-making and problem-solving: analytical and intuitive. Analytical, or left-brain function, provides rational, logical, scientific thinking. Intuitive cognition, or right-brain function, provides creativity and inspiration.

Brainstorming: Brainstorming is the generation of ideas in group fashion in which participants essentially "play off" each other to capture as many ideas as possible related to the problem at hand; no idea is rejected out of hand no matter how foolish it seems, recognizing that the foolish idea can sometimes guide thought processes in productive directions.

Problems Are a Given

Problems are inevitable when people work together. The hallmark of a well-managed team is not the absence of problems but whether the team resolves problems effectively. Many managers continue to blame their employees for most of the problems that occur, but all too often the real villains are faulty management decisions.

Decision-Making Today

The rate of organizational, technical, legal, and operational change constantly increases. Many of the decisions related to these changes have great impact on financial stability or job security, role alterations, assignments, and customer satisfaction.

Today's supervisors are forced to make decisions that were less common previously, decisions related, for example, to downsizing, reassigning, cross-training, and replacing professional employees with less qualified staff. Also, critical shortages of certain specialists demand quick hiring decisions before competitors snap up these scarce resources.

Flawed decisions lead to legal nightmares, for example harassment and discrimination complaints. Employee safety, satisfaction, and ethical issues are becoming more numerous and complex.

People-related decisions are by far the most important to the individual supervisor. The processes of hiring, training, disciplining, promoting, and dismissing employees demand careful consideration.

Decision-Making and Leadership

Autocratic leaders make decisions without soliciting input from others. Consultative leaders get input from others before deciding. Participative leaders involve their staffs in making decisions, and delegative leaders turn the process over to others.

Higher management deals chiefly with decisions that relate to major outcomes or long-range strategies, the *"what"* of running the organization. Supervisors deal principally with operational processes, *"how"* day-to-day-operations are conducted.

When to Avoid Making Decisions

Every situation needs to be considered in light of one simple question: is a decision really necessary? Avoid making a decision under the following circumstances:

- The apparent difficulty is not your problem (others will take care of their own problems).
- The problem is likely to correct itself, or interfering is likely to make matters worse.
- You or others are emotionally upset or there are serious attention distractions (see discussion below of stress and emotion).
- More information or advice is needed before an informed decision can be made.

- The problem is one that should be delegated. Most decisions should be made at the lowest possible organizational level—as close to the scene of action as possible—as long as those delegated to do so are capable and willing.

The Effects of Stress and Emotion

Stress and emotion, closely interrelated and usually overlapping, affect decision-making to some degree ranging from nearly negligible to severe, depending on surrounding circumstances and the mindset of the decision-maker.

Consider stress. A great many circumstances in the world of work create stress for some supervisors. People are of course different from each other when it comes to handling stress; a few seem to thrive amid stress, but some are hampered by it to the extent of reacting physically (anxiety, nervousness, and such) and feeling pressured to rush and do less than their best. Often stress is created by time constraints or a demanding manager or perhaps a combination of these and other factors. Many supervisors would be capable of handling many decision situations quite capably if they had plenty of time and no one pushing them for answers. Unfortunately, however, there is rarely enough time to thoroughly address all aspects of a given situation, so decision-makers are forced to proceed in the face of the risk and uncertainty that seem magnified by the presence of stress.

Emotion, either positive or negative, can affect one's decision-making. Maybe Employee A is a slightly better fit for a particular assignment than Employee B, but the supervisor likes B better than A so B gets the nod. Likes and dislikes and wants and needs regularly sway some supervisors' decision-making, and much of this is reflected—often largely unconsciously—in the choices the supervisors make. And emotion in its more extreme forms, such as fear or intense dislike or seemingly intolerable anxiety, can push decision-makers into choices made not to provide rational solutions but rather to escape their discomfort.

Life can be difficult for a supervisor who may be overworked and always pressed for time, especially if the supervisor's immediate superior is overly demanding and unsympathetic. However, knowledge of the possible effects of stress and emotion on decision processes can help the supervisor cope with such effects when they occur. And the truly enlightened supervisor will learn enough from a stressful relationship with a superior to avoid communicating similar stresses downward to the employees.

Risk, Uncertainty, and "Perfect Information"

Because you do not know everything potentially affecting the decision, you remain uncertain as to whether your choice is the right one. And because you are uncertain, you face a certain amount of risk—the risk that something may be lost if your decision is wrong. Depending on the magnitude of the decision, risk may range from negligible to deadly serious.

It is the presence of risk and uncertainty that makes some supervisors uneasy with decision-making; you never know for sure if your decisions are the right ones when you make them. Therefore, we offer advice such as this chapter presents to enable an orderly approach to decision-making that reduces risk and uncertainty to the lowest practical extent. Thoughtful, systematic analysis of any problem or decision situation will usually reduce risk and uncertainty to a tolerable level.

Essential Three for Effective Decisions

An effective decision must be

- the most logical decision;
- timely as to when it is made and when it is implemented; and
- acceptable to the people affected.

Dual Cognitive Functions

There are two cognitive approaches to decision-making and problem-solving: analytical and intuitive. Analytical, or left-brain function, provides rational, logical, scientific thinking. Intuitive cognition, or right-brain function, provides creativity and inspiration.

Left-brain thinking is essentially a flowchart process. Analytical people rely on algorithmic processes, plans, reports, hard data, and step-by-step procedures. They exercise judgment at each step and exclude anything that is irrelevant. Managers and investigators who treat problem-solving as a science often fail to come up with creative ideas because they depend entirely on this rational approach. In an earlier chapter it was stated that managers tend to use more left-brain thinking and that more effective leaders rely to a great extent on their intuition.

Intuitive thinking depends on data buried in our unconscious minds, which are like computers with almost unlimited memory storage capability. Unfortunately, what we file in these cerebral banks may be difficult to recall; it can be like trying to access a computer file for which we have lost the password. Unlike computer-stored data, brain information is constantly and unconsciously analyzed, synthesized, and reformatted.

Innovative people possess deeper insight or experience stronger gut reactions. They visualize more than their rational counterparts. They prefer diagrams to printouts. They often throw logic out the window. An intuitive thought process can seldom be flowcharted; rather, it is hop, skip, and jump.

Common sense is a combination of logic and intuition, the left and right brain working in tandem.

Coping with Many Minor Problems

Supervisors face countless little problems and decisions every day. Much of the time, solving problems is the most important responsibility of the supervisor. If there were no problems, we might need no supervisors or at least fewer supervisors. Their subordinates bring problems into their offices by the carload. Better training, planning, coaching, delegating, and policy making work wonders in cutting down on the number of these daily interruptions.

The Stop-Look-Listen Approach

Approach these daily questions or problems like you approach a railroad crossing:

- Stop what you are doing.
- ·Look interested.
- Listen carefully.

If the problem remains unclear, ask pertinent questions. Then ask those who bring you the problems what they believe should be done. Much of the time they will have thought through their problems and may have better solutions than you can offer on the spur of the moment. If you agree, approve their suggestions and congratulate them. If they keep bringing in the same problem, tell them that they do not need your decision every time.

Tell your people that you expect them to practice completed staff work. Explain to them that completed staff work means that a staff member who comes in with a problem must also bring in ideas on how best to solve the problem and perhaps also a recommendation as to which possible solution may be best. Participative management requires much completed staff work.

If the problem is one that only you can solve, provide your answer on the spot or get back to them without undue delay. Follow up when appropriate.

The Logical Process: Key Steps in Solving Large Problems

Step 1. Prepare a problem statement. Diagnosis is often the most important part of problem-solving, but it is often the most neglected part. Too often, people offer solutions before they really understand the problem. Poor problem statements can lead people astray. For example, the problem statement "Lack of clear policy relating to sick leave" is not likely to lead to solving a problem of excessive absenteeism that exists because of poor enforcement by the supervisor. Also, do sufficient digging to ensure that you are looking at the actual problem and not simply a visible symptom.

Step 2. Obtain and interpret the facts or data by asking the following questions:

- When was the problem first noted?
- How serious is it?
- Is it getting better or worse?
- Is it more complicated than it first appeared? In what way?
- What is the cause? (This is the most important question.)
- How was this handled in the past? What were the results?

Step 3. Generate alternatives (as many as possible).

Step 4. Formulate criteria to evaluate the alternatives. There are two types of criteria. Absolute criteria must be satisfied by an acceptable solution (for example, "No increase in costs"). Differential criteria are used to compare and contrast the various alternatives (for example, turnaround time, schedule convenience, availability of supplies, and degree of expertise required).

Step 5. Evaluate the alternatives and select the best one.

Step 6. Look for flaws in the choice. Ask many "what ifs." Avoid the jigsaw puzzle fallacy. The jigsaw fallacy is based on the false assumption that there is only one good solution (for example, a jigsaw puzzle must have four straight edges). Often there are several equally satisfactory solutions: The edges of life's puzzles are seldom straight lines.

Step 7. Develop an action plan.

Step 8. Carry out the plan. If there is hesitation about implementing the plan, ask what would be the worst possible thing that could happen if the plan was carried out. Also ask what the worst possible thing would be if you do not take the risk.

Step 9. Follow up. If what you are doing is not working well, make the needed changes.

Useful Tools for Problem-Solving

Bar graphs (**Figure 34.1A**) display a series of numbers (for example, the number of patient visits on each day of the month). When a bar graph shows the distribution of a variance, it is called a histogram (**Figure 34.1B**). *Pareto diagrams* (**Figure 34.1C**) display the frequency of occurrences listed in order of importance or frequency. A *scattergram* (**Figure 34.1D**) shows the correlation between two variables. *Run charts* (**Figure 34.1E**) plot data over time. They Exhibit trends, cycles, or other patterns in a process (for example, attendance records, turnover, or customer complaints).

Control charts (**Figure 34.1F**) illustrate values that are either in control or out of control. In Figure 34.1F, the solid horizontal line represents an average or normal value. The spaces between the solid line and the dotted lines are acceptable values, usually plus or minus two or three standard deviations. Any value outside the dotted lines is an out-of-control value.

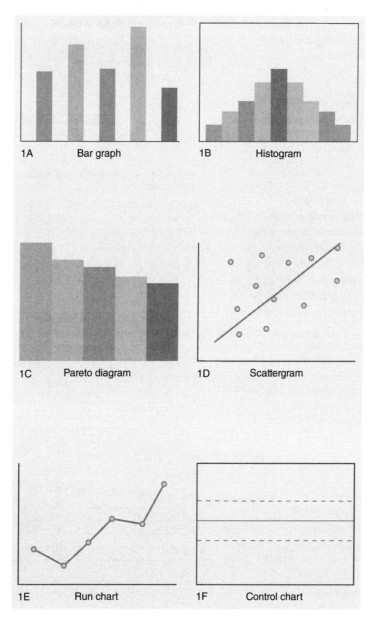

Figure 34.1 Useful Tools for Problem-Solving.

A *flow chart* (**Figure 34.2A**) represents a series of steps or events arranged chronologically. *Cause and effect diagrams*, also known as fishbone diagrams, are useful in an early stage of problem-solving or when one is considering potential problems (**Figure 34.2B**). A cause and effect diagram forces a focus on potential causes. On each leg (each bone), possible factors are recorded and grouped according to different categories (e.g., process, human, equipment, or policies). *Pie charts* (**Figure 34.2C**) illustrate relative numbers or percentages. *Gaussian curve charts* have bell-shaped curves that show frequency distributions. These are among the most common quality control charts (**Figure 34.2D**). *Force field charts* are useful when considering the advantages and disadvantages of a new service, process, procedure, or piece of equipment. The opposing considerations can be illustrated and quantified by a force field chart (**Figure 34.2E**).[1] *Checklists* (**Figure 34.2F**) are used as reminders or for documentation of activities. Shopping lists,

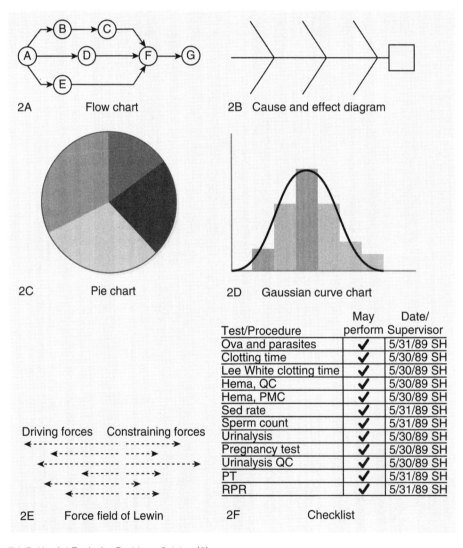

Figure 34.2 Useful Tools for Problem-Solving (2).

daily "to-do" schedules, and validation of records are just a few uses for this ubiquitous tool. Figure 34.2F is a partial list of tests that a new laboratory technician must be qualified to do.

The *Gantt chart* (**Figure 34.3**) is a graph with activities listed on the vertical axis and time units on the horizontal axis.[2] It is used to find the shortest total time required to reach a goal by showing how much time each activity requires and which activities can and cannot be done simultaneously. In Figure 34.3, note the overlapping of several activities.

Program evaluation and review technique (PERT) charts (**Figure 34.4**) were developed to reduce and control the time required for large projects. The PERT chart is composed of activities and events. On the chart, events are represented by circles. Arrows show the time necessary to complete events. When there are steps carried out simultaneously, different times are needed for each of these parallel steps. In Figure 34.4, the lines could represent the following steps:

A–B = time for a request to reach a workstation
B–C = time for blood collection and delivery to a laboratory

C–D = time for serological testing
D–E = time for immunohematological testing
E–F = time for delivery of blood product to patient

The critical path represents the sum of the times for individual steps in the path that require the most time. In Figure 34.4, the critical path is A-B-C-D-F because it takes longer to do the serological tests than to do the routine compatibility tests.

The *break-even chart* is a scatter diagram (or scattergram) in which the procedures and the expenses—variable and fixed—are plotted with diagonal lines representing total revenues and total costs (**Figure 34.5**). The point at which the diagonal lines cross represents the financial break-even point. The number of procedures performed below that crossing shows a loss; those above that crossing show a profit.

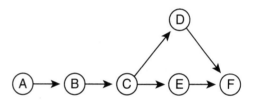

Figure 34.4 PERT Chart with Critical Path.

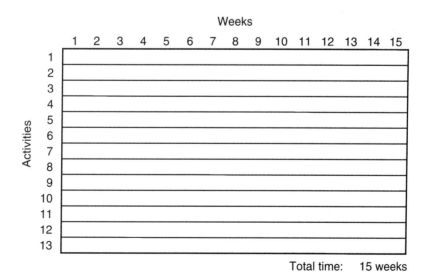

Figure 34.3 Gantt Chart.

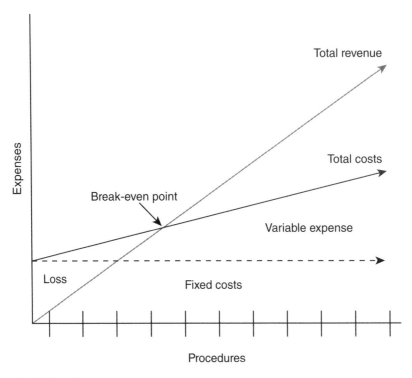

Figure 34.5 Break-Even Chart.

Likert charts (**Figure 34.6**) are useful when one is comparing and contrasting multiple factors of performance at two different times (e.g., before and after a change).[3]

Computer Applications

For as long as they have been in practical business use, computers have been used to file data, reassemble information and data into new formats, and perform logical operations and calculations. An exciting trend evident in computer problem-solving is in the growth and applicability of expert systems. These rely on stored facts and rules of thumb to mimic the decision-making of human experts.

Your Intuitive Process: Key to Creative Problem-Solving

Give your intuitive process time to act. Set aside some think time each day. Capture thoughts as

they occur, like the ringing of a muted telephone. These are most likely to pop up when your logical thought process is on hold. Turn off conscious cerebration to let your cerebral energy flow into your unconscious mind. Daydreaming, relaxation, and meditation help. Walking, jogging, and other kinds of exercise increase cerebral blood flow, and this improves the thought generation process. Solitude can be effective, particularly when it is enhanced by listening to ocean sounds (real or recorded) or background music.

Pay attention to the nagging doubts you feel when you are trying to make a decision. They may represent experience stored in your unconscious mind. A strategy espoused by Dr. Joyce Brothers, the well-known television psychologist, is to think about a problem just before dropping off to sleep.[4]

Simple Way to Stimulate Your Intuitive Process

Document your problem at the top of a sheet of paper. Under this heading, number the lines

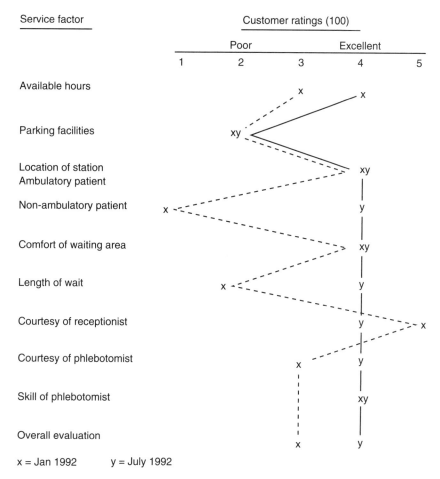

Figure 34.6 Likert Chart.

1 through 20. Now force yourself to write down 20 solutions. The first few will come easily (these are usually the ones that you have already considered and discarded). Do not automatically discard an idea because it seems foolish or unworkable. Subsequent alternatives surface with increasing difficulty and are more likely to have originated in your unconscious mind and are more inspirational.[5]

Group Problem-Solving

A problem of any appreciable scope is like a world globe. From any one spot you cannot see the entire globe. Neither does any one person have an all-encompassing view. In group problem-solving, more ideas are generated. An added bonus is that a group is more likely to support the choice it made.

Group discussions increase the likelihood of serendipity, the fortuitous result of two or more elements or events accidentally coming together to create an opportunity. When people put their heads together, they come up with more solutions than when they work individually.

Importance of Consensus

A group often makes decisions before all the opinions of the members have been explored. Participants who are not heard from may leave a meeting angry. They may not support the

Exhibit 34.1 Basics of Consensus Decision-Making

- Ensure that each person expresses his or her viewpoint fully.
- Avoid hasty conclusions or agreements.
- Explore the positive features of each alternative.
- Expose and analyze the negative features of each alternative.
- Resolve disagreements.
- Avoid techniques of voting, averaging, or bargaining.
- Insist that each member agree that he or she can live with the solution.

If any member balks, you do not have a consensus.

implementation of the decisions. A few may even sabotage the initiative. A consensus prevents such occurrences (**Exhibit 34.1**).

A consensus is a genuine meeting of the minds. It is not reached by voting. Even a unanimous vote does not represent a consensus if some members are denied an opportunity to speak up. With a consensus, some members may prefer different solutions, but after full and fair discussion they agree that they can live with what the group decided. Be wary of the possibility of the Abilene paradox described in the chapter titled "Holding Effective Meetings."

Creative Problem-Solving Groups

Brainstorming Groups

Unstructured brainstorming meetings are typically lots of talk, lots of wandering off the topic, and not much action. All too many committee meetings degenerate into these kinds of sessions. There are exceptions, of course, especially when entrepreneurs or creative people get together. Talking about specific topics can lead to many great ideas to solve problems.

Structured brainstorming groups generate ideas guided by certain rules. The meetings usually have an agenda and a problem or issue to be addressed. The group knows of the problem before the scheduled meeting, so ideas are already generated before the meeting begins.

To get the maximum benefit of unstructured or structured brainstorming groups, make certain that participants know beforehand what is going to be discussed and encourage them to come loaded with ideas. Set a good example by bringing a large collection of your own suggestions, including some really wild ones. And when brainstorming, never reject an idea out of hand because it sounds ridiculous, highly impractical, or downright stupid; you never know when a dumb idea will lead someone's thought processes to a workable solution.

WRAP-UP

Think About It

In making any but the simplest of decisions or addressing any problem, it is always necessary to accept some risk and uncertainty. The uncertainty is that you cannot be completely sure that the decision is absolutely the correct one, and risk is that there are consequences to making the wrong decision. Accept the risk and the consequences.

Questions for Review and Discussion

1. What is the true difference between consultative leadership and participative leadership in decision-making?

2. What is the difference between an analytical brain and an intuitive brain?

3. No matter how simple a decision situation seems to be, why can it be said that there are always at least two alternative choices available?

4. Isn't it the responsibility of the boss to make decisions and solve problems? Why push these activities down to employee level?

5. What is the primary drawback likely to be encountered in making a decision when the problem is not your problem?

6. In creative idea-generating situations, why should wild or foolish ideas not be rejected as soon as they arise?

7. What us your experience with group problem-solving? Explain.

8. Why might we say that ignoring or even forgetting a problem can itself be considered a decision?

9. What should be the ultimate determinant of how much time and effort is put into any particular decision situation?

10. What are the essential differences between decision by vote and decision by true consensus?

Case: More Pleasant Dreams

Imagine yourself as nightshift charge nurse on a medical-surgical unit. For several months you have had a problem with a staff nurse whose performance you consider unsatisfactory. She seems to continually take advantage of quiet times during her shift to doze off at the nursing station. You have reprimanded her several times for sleeping on the job, and you have reached the point where you believe you can no longer simply scold her for her conduct. Her position, however, is that "it's no big deal," that she's always certain to hear any call signals as long as she's at the nursing station. (Your hospital has a clear policy concerning written warnings, but policy is relatively loose concerning oral warnings; these can be unlimited and issued at your discretion, so you can deliver as many as you believe necessary.)

For a written warning to become official and entered into an employee's human resource file, it must be agreed to and countersigned by the unit's nurse manager and the director of nursing. You issued the offending nurse two written warnings; both warnings cleared through the unit manager. However, you believe you can go no further without backing from the office of the director of nursing, and there has been no follow-up from that direction. Meanwhile, the employee continues to be a problem.

Questions

1. What would your decision be concerning the sleeping employee if it were not necessary to discuss with the director of nursing?

2. Assuming you have indeed "hit a wall" as described in the final paragraph of the case, what would you consider doing to try to get some action or support?

3. If you feel stuck with the reality of having your decisions approved—or essentially made—by higher management, what information would you assemble and how would you prepare yourself to try getting a decision favorable to you from your chain of command?

4. What is the director of nursing actually doing by reserving the right to approve or veto your decisions?

Case: The Long-Time Employee

Assume you have been head nurse of the same medical-surgical unit for nearly 20 years. One of your employees, a licensed practical nurse named Hilda, has been part of the unit's day shift for even longer than you have been head nurse. In fact, Hilda is the only original member remaining of the crew that existed when you first took over the unit.

About 6 months ago Hilda returned to work after an extensive illness that left her noticeably changed in a number of ways. Where once she was energetic and seemed to possess considerable stamina, now the hustle and bustle of the day shift and always being on her feet and on the move seem to wear her down rapidly. You have felt a growing concern for Hilda, and for the rest of the team as well, because it has become obvious to you that Hilda is not bearing her share of the load. Other members of your already overworked crew are working extra hard to make up the difference.

Your concern reached a peak this week when three of your staff nurses came to talk to you about Hilda. Although they came with apparent reluctance—Hilda had always been well liked by both staff and patients—they were quite convinced that something had to be done for both Hilda's sake and the sake of the department. It seems that Hilda has barely been able to accomplish half of what she should be expected to do in an 8-hour shift.

Hilda knows only nursing; she has been an LPN for all of her working life. She will not be eligible for retirement for 5 more years.

It is evident that you need to make a decision concerning Hilda and her apparent inability to keep up with the work.

Questions
1. Identify at least three alternatives that you believe might be possible solutions.
2. Which alternative appears most workable in this situation? And what information do you need to assemble in preparing to justify your decision?
3. If your initial decision is found unworkable or unacceptable, which alternative would be your second choice? Why?

References

1. Lewin K. *Field Theory in Social Science.* Harper & Row; 1951.
2. Gantt H. *Industrial Leadership.* Hive; 1973.
3. Likert R. *New Patterns of Management.* McGraw-Hill; 1961.
4. Sullivan D. *Work Smart,* Not Hard. Facts on File; 1987.
5. DeBono E. *Lateral Thinking: Creativity Step by Step.* Harper & Row; 1970.

CHAPTER 35

Time Management

CHAPTER OBJECTIVES

- Explore the implications of various factors bearing on the use and management of time by the individual supervisor.
- Identify the more commonly encountered time wasters and suggest how the supervisor can counter these when they arise.
- Offer some practical tips for saving time.
- Suggest how the supervisor can effectively address the abuses of time perpetrated by others.
- Review some additional elements of personal effectiveness that can affect the supervisor's use of time.

KEY TERMS

Management by Crisis: This is the process of addressing problems as they arise, with no thought given to advance planning or the establishment of priorities; this mode of operation is probably the greatest waster of a supervisor's time. Also known as "fire-fighting management."

The 3-D Technique: As applied to the handling of all forms of written communication—letters, memos, email messages, printed material, etc.—endeavor to handle each item once and only once: Do, Delegate, or Discard.

Delegation: As it applies to time management for the individual supervisor, delegation is the greatest supervisory time saver of all.

Ten Minutes to Spare?

A scenario: This morning you returned to work after a 3-day absence to find your in-basket overloaded and your desk littered with message slips. You were greeted by your assistant, Ellen, who informed you that you were expected to substitute for your boss at an outside meeting. You will have to leave no later than 9:30 a.m., and you will be gone for the remainder of the day.

You have 1 hour to start making order of the chaos on your desk. True to your usual pattern, you review the items on your desk and from the in-basket and create separate stacks according to apparent importance. You feel that you can perhaps get sufficiently organized to begin the following day with emphasis on the most important tasks.

Halfway through your hour Ellen enters to say, "The finance director is here. He wants

10 minutes of your time to discuss a minor question about last month's operating expense report. Shall I tell him you'll call him? Or that he should send you an email?"

The last thing you need at this time is an interruption, especially for something nonurgent. It occurs to you that Ellen has described two possible choices for you, to which you have quickly added another, so that you have three options:

1. Say you cannot get involved at the moment but that you will call the following morning.
2. Ask for him to send you an email about the problem so you can take care of it when time is available.
3. Meet with the finance director then and there and try to limit the discussion to 10 minutes or less.

What are the advantages and disadvantages of each of the three choices? Which one might you choose, and why?

Time and the Supervisor

Most supervisors are well aware of the value of their time. Deadlines, turnaround times, emergencies, and interruptions constantly challenge them. Seldom are there enough hours to complete all their tasks. A great many members of management put in long hours on the job and often take unfinished work home. Then there are the hours that conscientious supervisors spend at home worrying about problems back at work.

Time management programs, like weight reduction programs, succeed only if one commits to reaching a goal and sticks to that commitment. Experts can tell you how to save time, but you must supply the necessary discipline. To lose weight, people sacrifice things they like to eat. To gain time, people give up some activities they enjoy doing, especially when they perform those tasks so well. Practical time management strategies are twofold: managing your own time and eliminating the time-wasting practices of the people who report to you.

Time Problems of Supervisors

Supervisors who practice management by crisis have major time problems. They react rather than anticipate and plan. They spend large chunks of time running around trying to resolve crises instead of preventing them.

Then there are the perfectionists. These people are not satisfied with excellence; they strive for perfection. Perfectionists check and double-check everything. They invariably obtain more data and opinions than they need.

Leaders who cannot or will not delegate are always running out of time because they try to do things that others could do for them in addition to the things that only they can do.

Passive individuals have the same kinds of time problems as those who fail to delegate. Because they cannot turn down requests that consume their time, they too are constantly struggling to keep up with their own work while serving on numerous committees, doing favors for colleagues, and listening to people problems that should be addressed by others.

Your Office or Workstation

The best place to start a time management program is in your personal work area. There you can see results quickly. To avoid distractions, if possible, move your desk so that it does not face the door, or keep your door closed. Arrange filing cabinets and other furnishings to provide ready access to documents.

A messy desk does not necessarily mean a messy mind or a haphazard way of operating. If you can quickly find what you are looking for and other folks, such as secretaries, do not need access to items strewn about in your office, there is no harm in retaining your organized clutter.

Instruct your secretary and others on how you want papers, manuals, office supplies, and other items stored. Revise your filing system. Use a desk drawer file for papers you refer to often. Put other papers in cabinets. Sort and batch your documents, using folders that you label appropriately. Set aside a drawer as a slush file for documents that you are not likely to need but are reluctant to discard right away. Clean out that drawer each month.

Paper Flow

Supervisors often feel overwhelmed by the volume of information they face. It once was thought that the computer would alleviate the paper overload, but this is not the case for all industries, unfortunately.

Filing begins when you sort your incoming mail. Try to handle each item only once. Practice the 3D idea: Do, Delegate, or Discard. When you hesitate to discard, ask yourself "What is the worst thing that could happen if I do not have this?"

Do not let your in basket or folder get out of control. Review the items there daily, and act on as many as you can. Jot down a throw-out date on major filed items. Clear off your desk every night to avoid chaos when you arrive the next day.

Additional Ways to Cope with Information Overload

- Be ruthless about what to read and what not to read. Reduce your "to read" pile after screening for relevant information.
  - Check the messages you are sending out. Do they improve customer service or provide essential information? If not, rethink their contents.
  - Answer memos by writing your responses on the memos rather than preparing additional memos.
  - Purge your email of nonessentials.
  - Let your computer replace your address or telephone book.
- Maximize the value of your reading time.
  - Scan articles, memos, journals, newspapers, and other documents.
  - Read the introductions and closing paragraphs to decide if you need to read the rest.
  - Highlight or underline key passages. Use a scanner to transfer needed information into your computer.
  - Prepare and file summaries of important books or lengthy documents.

- Take reading material with you when you have appointments or find it necessary to travel.
- Set aside blocks of time for reading.

Planning and Scheduling

When you fail to plan, you are planning to fail. Establish goals, priorities, schedules, and deadlines for all major undertakings. The more time you spend preparing for meetings, the less time is wasted at those meetings.

Most supervisors have little slack time these days. Make good use of what you have to catch up on, email, inventory, files, and low-priority items. Get your administrative tasks out of the way early or late in the day when there are fewer people around to take up your time. Leave some time for unexpected occurrences. Differentiate between real deadlines, such as for payroll input data, and less urgent ones, such as for the minutes of meetings.

Our physiological clocks are all different. We each have hours of the day when our productivity and ability to concentrate are greater than during the rest of the day. Use those hours to work on major items (for example, presenting ideas to your manager, high-priority discussions, and important correspondence). During periods of low productivity, undertake tasks that are less challenging mentally, such as reading mail, making routine telephone calls, filing, and other routine chores.

Be sure that projects have priorities, due dates, and time estimates. Set realistic time frames. Review long-range goals frequently with superiors.

Use "To Do" Lists

Group similar tasks together on a "to do" list. Number the actions in order of importance and urgency. Label each item as must, should, or maybe. Do not expect to accomplish everything on your list every day. Remake or update the list daily. At the end of your workday, the items you did not get to should be low priority ones that you can transfer to the next day's list. Doing this faithfully every day will help ensure that you are always at work on your most important priority at any given time.

Delegating

The greatest supervisory time saver of all is delegation. Every hour that someone else does something that you previously did is an hour of your time saved that can be constructively utilized elsewhere. The art of delegation takes time and practice to perfect; with time, it becomes a skill of great sipervisors.[1] See the chapter titled "Delegation and Empowerment" for a discussion of delegation. It is absolutely fundamental to any supervisor's long-term success that he or she can delegate properly, wisely, and effectively.

Procrastination

At the very least, procrastination results in spending your time doing tasks that have a lower priority than the one you should be working on. This is compounded when you are immobilized because you have placed an important or difficult task on hold.

To minimize procrastination, consider the following practical suggestions:

- Use prioritized task lists. At the end of each day, rework your priority list for the next day.
- Start the day with the high-priority or unpleasant tasks. Once the dreaded or difficult is out of the way, all that follows seems easier.
- Avoid the temptation to stall.
- Do not get involved by something nonessential that appeals to you as fun or interesting.
- Block out enough time to complete time-consuming tasks.
- Subdivide a large task into smaller, discrete pieces more easily completed.
- Convince yourself that what you are facing truly needs doing.
- Challenge your excuses.
- Do not reward procrastination. Do not allow yourself to engage in pleasant activities while you delay action. Sit in a straight chair, perhaps without coffee and certainly without conversation.
- Set a timer for 5 minutes and force yourself to start when it goes off.

Time Wasters and What to Do About Them

Use a time log to determine how you spend your time. This enables you to ferret out your wasted time and alter your time schedules. We are told that it takes 21 days to establish a habit; although this process may take more or perhaps even less time for some individuals, 21 days remains appropriate for most people. Select your top five time wasters, and work on them for 3 weeks. Here are the principal offenders:

- Doing things you do not need to do personally or do not need to do at all, including tasks that could be delegated.
- Inefficient planning, organizing, and scheduling.
- Unnecessary or poorly run meetings.
- Interruptions, particularly drop-in visitors, emergencies and other unanticipated situations, and telephone calls.

Do Not Let People Take Advantage of You

To avoid over-commitment of your time and other resources, learn to say "no" diplomatically but emphatically. With subordinates, this often means not allowing them to delegate their work upward to you. Caution is advised; avoiding upward delegation may not be easy for the supervisor who is readily flattered or manipulated.

Offer alternatives to colleagues. When a superior makes a request that creates a serious time problem for you, nail down priorities (for example, "Should I stop working on the …?" or "Will someone else handle …?").

Visitor Control

Do not refer directly to visitors as annoyances or time wasters, even though many are just that. Most visitors are external or internal customers, and you should treat them as such. Efficient managers save time elsewhere so that they can spend more time with their customers.

Unfortunately, we all have to deal with people who are excessively verbose or have lots of time to kill. Certain sales representatives and casual acquaintances may be high on your list of pests. The worst of the lot are those who cannot take hints that you are very busy and would like to end the conversation. Here are a few suggestions for handling visitors who abuse your time:

- Train and empower your staff so they have less need to consult with you or to get your permission on routine matters.
- Train your staff to help visitors when you are not immediately available.
- Meet people in their territory rather than in yours. That way you can better control the time of the meeting.
- Shut your door when you really need privacy.
- Intercept visitors outside your office. Once people get into your office, transaction time increases.
- Remain standing and do not invite the visitor to be seated.
- Use verbal and nonverbal language to signal that you wish to end the meeting:
  - Reduce eye contact.
  - Glance at the clock or your watch.
  - Start shuffling papers, tapping a pencil, or drumming your fingers.
  - Put your hand on your telephone.
  - Say "Could we continue this later when I'm not so swamped?" or "I won't take any more of your time."
  - Stand up and extend your hand.
  - Come out from behind your desk and walk toward the door.

Group Meetings

Try to limit group meetings to 45 minutes if at all possible. People start becoming restless after that, especially those who are concerned about the work or problems piling up while they are away from the job. If you must go on for a longer time, call a short break. If you are not the chairperson and the meetings usually begin late, bring work with you so as to productively fill the waiting time.

Send members of your staff to represent you as long as your specific decision-making authority is not likely to be required. For more on meetings, see the chapter titled "Holding Effective Meetings."

One-on-One Communication

Apply all of the communication skills discussed earlier. Communication competency prevents misunderstandings, mistakes, and the need for repeats, all of which are major time wasters.

If you tend to be verbose on the telephone, put an egg timer next to the phone. When excessive talkers trap you in a corridor, wait until they pause for breath, then summarize what was said and start edging away. If they continue to talk, ask them to excuse you and leave. Say that you have an appointment (you can always have an appointment with yourself for some quiet, uninterrupted time).

Significant Time-Consuming Errors

The following are representations of time poorly spent by supervisors:

1. Tolerating abuses of your open-door policy. You should want to be available and helpful, but do not let others waste your time.
2. Overuse of memos, reports, and email.
3. Unnecessary or poorly run meetings, often a major concern because they waste the time of a number of people.
4. Lack of assigning and delegating, which not only wastes the supervisor's time, but also fails to use employees' time efficiently.
5. Excessive socializing. A bit of social conversation is to be expected, but it is far too easy for this to get out of hand.
6. Doing other people's work and solving their problems instead of expecting them to take care of their own tasks and problems.
7. Accepting too many unimportant assignments.
8. Lack of planning, usually resulting in a management-by-crisis approach.

9. Inadequate paper flow and storage, too often resulting in excess time spent looking for needed items.
10. Procrastination, always a thief of time and leaves important matters unaddressed.

Tips for Saving Time

The following were already suggested as time savers:

- Avoiding procrastination or perfectionism
- Delegating what others can do or can be trained to do
- Planning, scheduling, and setting priorities
- Improving your communication skills
- Learning to say "no"
- Reducing wasted time at meetings
- Using margin replies for informal written correspondence
- Keeping your desk ready for action
- Selecting the most appropriate channel for every communication

Here are some additional time savers:

- Expressing as much appreciation to people for saving your time as you do to people who help you save money
- Reducing interruptions by coming to work early or staying late, by finding a good hiding place, or by using a "Thank You for Not Disturbing" sign
- Monitoring your time usage; keeping a log
- Using waiting times to read or to do short tasks
- Making phone calls in batches
- Referring calls and visitors to others
- Decreasing your socializing time
- Studying and streamlining your workflow patterns
- Asking for help when you need it

Time Theft by Others

The first step in eliminating or decreasing time waste is to be aware of it. The strategy of managing by wandering around pays off handsomely; merely appearing on the scene flattens idle conversations and lets people know you are aware of their inappropriate absences from the work area.

Changes in workstations can often help. Some employees accomplish more when they work alone; certain others get more done when working in a group. Study workflow patterns and other systems to find out whether you can achieve more efficiency.

The following are significant forms of time theft most often encountered:

- Taking unjustified sick days, always a problem where paid sick time is available
- Arriving late or leaving early, thus shortening productive time
- Taking long breaks or extended meal periods, again reducing productive time
- Leaving one's office for personal trips (shopping, banking, etc.)
- Performing personal tasks on the job
- Socializing excessively, a chronic problem almost everywhere
- Interrupting others needlessly
- Wandering about the facility when supposedly working
- Making excessive personal phone calls and texting, another universal chronic problem
- Spending excessive time on social media
- Allowing personal or family visitors
- Daydreaming

What About Those 10 Minutes?

Regarding the opening scenario: In putting off your visitor and promising to call in the morning, you avoid an unwelcome intrusion at a busy time. But this might annoy the finance director (who is higher than you on the organization chart though not in your chain of command), who may see this as unnecessarily delaying a matter that could easily be disposed of in only a few minutes.

Asking for an email also delays the intrusion, but this choice creates work for both parties and again may be seen as delaying something that also could be taken care of in only a few minutes.

The third choice, giving in to the request and addressing the issue immediately, is clearly the most efficient for all concerned: It can dispose of the issue quickly without causing more work for either party. The risk, of course, is that once he has his "foot in the door" the finance director will attempt to consume more of your time. You cannot let this happen; you need to make it clear that you are leaving very soon and even, if possible,

continue with your preparations to leave while talking with the finance director.

If the supposedly minor issue was important enough for the finance director to bring it to you personally, it probably deserves your attention. If it can be resolved in a few minutes, it is finished; if not, then it has to become part of the next day's workload as would be the result with either of the other options.

WRAP-UP

Think About It

Always keep in mind that time is the ultimate nonrenewable resource. Most other resources required in operating the organization can be renewed, recovered, or replaced, but a moment of time, once gone, is gone forever.

Questions for Review and Discussion

1. Why is delegation clearly identified as the greatest supervisory time saver?
2. What is the strongest force acting to prevent us from improving our use of time? Why is this, and what can be done about it?
3. Why do some individuals spend time focusing on low-priority tasks even when they know there are more important tasks waiting?
4. How might some supervisors feel trapped into overcommitting their time?
5. Why is it often suggested to begin the workday by first tackling the unpleasant tasks?
6. Share a tip for saving time that has worked for you. Explain how this was accomplished.
7. What particular characteristics might be exhibited by a supervisor who continually seems to become caught up in people problems that should actually be addressed by others?
8. What is wrong with the process of gathering more data and opinions than may be needed? Is this not a sound means of ensuring accuracy?
9. How can you learn to say no when the overload comes via demands from your immediate superior?
10. What time theft are you guilty of in the workplace? Explain.

Case: Where Does the Time Go?

Kay Thatcher, director of staff education, decided she had to get organized. Recently, her workdays had been running well beyond quitting time, cutting noticeably into the time required by family responsibilities. And all the while her backlog of work was growing.

Inspired by an article about planning and setting priorities, Kay decided to try planning each day's activities at the end of the previous day. This Monday Kay came to the office with her day planned out to the last minute. During the morning she had to complete a report on a recent learning-needs analysis, write the performance appraisals of two part-time instructors, and assemble the balance of the materials for a 2-hour class she was scheduled to conduct that afternoon. After lunch she had to conduct the class, complete the schedule for the next 3 months' training activities (now 10 days overdue), and prepare notices—which should be posted this very day—for two upcoming classes.

Kay got off to a good start; she finished her report before 10 a.m. and turned her attention to the two performance evaluations. However, at that time the interruptions began. In the next 2 hours she was interrupted six times—three telephone calls and three visitors. The calls were all appropriate business calls. Two of the visitors had legitimate problems, one of them taking 30 minutes to resolve. The other visitor was a fellow supervisor simply passing the time of day. Neither performance evaluation was completed, and the training materials were assembled in time only because Kay put them together during lunch while she juggled a sandwich at her desk.

Kay's afternoon class ran 20 minutes over time because of legitimate questions and discussion. When she returned to her office she discovered she had a visitor, a good-humored, talkative sales representative from whom Kay occasionally bought audiovisual materials. The sales rep, who "happened to be in the area" and just dropped in, stayed for an hour and a half.

After the sales rep departed Kay spent several minutes simply wondering what to do next. The performance appraisals, the 3-month class schedules, the class notices—all were overdue. Deciding on the class notices because they were the briefest task before her, she dashed off both notices in longhand and asked the nursing office secretary to type them, copy them, and post them immediately. Then she tackled the training schedule.

When Kay looked up again from her work it was nearly an hour past quitting time. She still had a long way to go on the schedule and had not yet started on the two performance appraisals. As she swept her work aside for the day, she sadly reflected that in spite of all her planning she had not accomplished two-thirds of what she intended to do that day. She decided, however, to try again; when she could get a few minutes of quiet time late in the evening, she would plan her next day's activity.

On her way out of the hospital she happened to glance at the main bulletin board. The small satisfaction she felt when she saw the posted class notices vanished instantly when she discovered that both were incorrect—the dates and times of the two classes had been interchanged.

Questions

1. What mistakes did Kay make in attempting to improve her use of time by planning and establishing priorities?
2. How should Kay plan her Tuesday?

Reference

1. Bergman C, Shubert L. Interactive strategies. *Nurse Educator.* 2013:38(4);137–138. https://doi.org/10.1097/nne.0b013e318296dcb6

The Supervisor's Continuing Development

CHAPTER 36

Coping with Stress and Burnout

CHAPTER OBJECTIVES

- Identify the various causes of stress, both internal to the individual and in the environment in which the individual functions.
- Provide the supervisor with guidelines for reducing stress within the department, including the use of departmental stress reduction programs.
- Address the subject of burnout, including identification of the signs of burnout and its usual stages.
- Suggest what the supervisor can do to minimize personally experienced stress caused and aggravated by conditions and experiences in the workplace.

KEY TERMS

Burnout: Burnout is a condition of emotional and physical collapse caused by the unchecked escalation of stress; as such, it is considerably more than just accumulated boredom or unrest or the feeling of lack of control of one's environment.

More Prominent Today Than Ever

American workers across the nation have reported an astounding level of stress and burnout. In 2021, 79% of adult workers reported they had experienced work-related stress.[1] The estimated cost of stress-related illness is in the billions, and everything that has been experienced in business and health care in particular over the recent years, mostly due to the COVID-19 pandemic, suggests that the cost of stress-related illness continues to escalate.[2] Transitioning from the pandemic back to "business as usual" has caused stress and burnout to increase dramatically. Other stress-related problems in the healthcare system as marked by rapidly advancing technology, dramatic organizational changes, and especially by staffing shortages in critical areas such as nursing also lends itself to the rise in overly stressed healthcare workers.

In this country four of the most used kinds of drugs—headache remedies, tranquilizers, antihypertensive agents, and ulcer medications—are used primarily for treating stress-related conditions.

© antishock/Shutterstock

407

External Causes of Stress

Most working individuals have limited control over factors external to themselves that contribute to stress. External stressors related to work include the following:

- *Work environment*: parking difficulties, uncomfortable or noisy surroundings, equipment failures, and safety concerns (infection and safety concerns are especially prevalent in healthcare institutions)
- *The job itself*: too much work, time pressures, organizational and procedural changes, and job insecurity
- *Work relationships*: harassment, threats, personality incompatibilities, difficult patients or patient families, competition between and among departments and workers
- *Hierarchical factors*: nonexistent or uncertain goals, mission or objectives; confusing or difficult policies; lack of support from management
- *Poor leadership*: flawed communication, favoritism, discrimination, insufficient authority to fulfill responsibilities, nitpicking, and unclear responsibilities
- *Outside factors*: family, financial, legal, or health concerns

Internal Factors Aggravating Stress

The following causes of stress dwell within ourselves, and they act as multipliers of the external factors that surround us:

- Lack of confidence or self-esteem due to lack of expertise or experience.
- Health problems resulting in decreased immunity and frequent illnesses.
- Irrational thinking. False perceptions of powerlessness and flawed assumptions may be rampant. Some people set unrealistic goals and aspirations.
- Clash of actions with values. Stress occurs when our actions are not congruent with our values. For example, when we spend long hours at work (action) and neglect our family responsibilities (value).
- Emotions. Being struck by a negative emotion such as fear, guilt, anger, or resentment is like trying to drive a car with the emergency brake on; movement is limited, and the strain on the parts is great.
- Fear. We are overwhelmed with all kinds of fear, with or without basis in reality: fear of job loss, fear of failure or rejection. These fears are compounded by the ever-increasing rate of technological and organizational changes and lack of job security.
- Guilt. Guilt is characterized by feelings of inadequacy and inferiority. It makes us indulge in self-criticism and in the criticism of others. People who feel guilt use "victim language" such as "I should," "I have to," or "It wasn't my fault."
- Anger. The stress produced by daily contact with difficult people is often associated with anger. When anger is not resolved, frustration sets in. There is usually an underlying hurt or fear, especially the fear that you cannot cope with the situation or that you are regarded as unimportant.
- Resentment. Resentment is a subtle, continuous, seething anger that is seldom expressed directly to the person or persons who are resented.

Management Style and the Responsibilities of Supervisors

One of the most common reasons for employees voluntarily leaving their jobs, sometimes but not always cited during exit interviews, is the style of the employee's immediate supervisor. The supervisor who continually pushes employees, who is quick to dispense criticism but rarely if ever offers praise, who assigns and delegates task after task heedless of overloading employees, and who insists on setting impossibly tight deadlines, is invariably creating stress among the employees. The occasional supervisor—thankfully there are not a great many of these—treats employees as tools to be used until they wear out or break, after which they are replaced.

Hard-nosed authoritarian supervisors are an inexcusable source of employee stress. The fundamentals of the supervisory role include the belief that the supervisor is there to ensure that the employees accomplish the work of the group. In doing so, it is the supervisor's job to see that the employees have everything they need to do the job, to remove obstacles for them, and to generally support them in the accomplishment of their work. The supervisor who pushes, who treats workers as just another category of expendable supplies, creates stress that causes physical and psychological problems for some employees and encourages the voluntary departure of others.

Because leadership plays such an important role in the amount of stress prevalent within a group, supervisors have considerable accountability for stress control. Supervisors have four major stress-related responsibilities:

1. Reducing the stress that they may personally cause
2. Protecting their employees from stress induced by other people
3. Empowering their employees and raising their self-esteem
4. Recognizing the signs and symptoms of burnout and taking remedial steps

How to Reduce Stress in Your Department

Hire Stress-Resistant People

Endeavor to select employees whose needs and abilities correspond with the demands of the job. See the chapter titled "Interviewing and Employee Selection" for the kinds of questions that can help in spotting people susceptible to stress during employment interviews.

Train Thoroughly

Well-designed orientation and training programs reduce anxiety, create realistic job expectations, and provide the skills needed to work effectively. Clear, unmistakable policies and procedures, when enforced uniformly and fairly, reduce hierarchical pressures. Active mentoring provides additional stress resistance.

Empower Employees

Individuals who believe they are in control of their work and their future are better equipped to handle stress. When they are competent and their skills are marketable, they become more burnout resistant. Self-empowerment and empowerment by management are essential to the development of this mindset. (See the chapter titled "Delegation and Empowerment.")

Advise Stressed Workers

Support your employees by word and action, especially when performance drops off. Get them to express their concerns and frustrations. Help them to reinforce the good things about themselves by reviewing their past successes. Encourage them to adopt realistic goals. Refer them to professional counselors if this seems indicated and appropriate. Eliminate specific stressors when possible, without interfering with the workflow or imposing on other workers.

Ensure Time for Breaks

Make certain your people get their breaks. Encourage them to use the time in a healthy way (for example, socializing, exercising, relaxing, and meditating). If possible, provide healthy alternatives to the regular offer of doughnuts and coffee.

Modify Assignments, Team Compositions, and Management Style

Rotating assignments or shifts may be appropriate in specific instances. Transfers or changes in work schedules may also be therapeutic.

Departmental Stress Programs

Support groups are most effective when they function under their own leadership. Participants can talk openly about their personal responses to the demands of their work. They find common problems and search for remedial measures. At their meetings, they may use guest speakers, live streaming webinars, reading materials, and brainstorming.

Interest in wellness and disease prevention is increasing. Exercise, healthy diet, and supplemental vitamins and minerals appear to increase immunity and counter the harmful physiological effects of stress. Health stores feature many herbs and nutraceutical combinations that are alleged to help cope with stress. Also, employees generally appreciate talks from dietitians and health experts.

Coping methods commonly used in departmental stress management programs include the following:

- Relaxation or meditation techniques
- Exercise
- Diet adjustment
- Review of job designs, policies, and procedures
- Solution of communication, ethical, and workflow problems
- Resolution of conflicts

Burnout

Burnout is the condition of emotional and physical collapse caused by the unchecked escalation of stress. It is perhaps cited too often in describing boredom or unrest or the feeling of lack of control of one's environment, but in its true form, burnout is a very real condition that afflicts many individuals who have existed "too close to the edge" for too long. Everyone has a breaking point, but some emotionally stable people protect themselves intuitively by focusing on current tasks while shutting out most past or future problems. This is a desirable skill.

The employees most vulnerable to burnout are the perfectionists, workaholics, overachievers, insecure job holders, and people with low self-esteem. Also highly susceptible are internally focused caregivers who become so emotionally involved with patients that they constantly experience the pain of others. A career in health care is very rewarding but can hold a certain level of stress.

Signs and Symptoms of Burnout

The signs and symptoms of burnout experienced by individuals ordinarily include one or more of the following:

- Anxiety or depression
- Waking up tired
- Chronic fatigue
- High blood pressure
- Insomnia and nightmares
- Cardiac irregularities
- Headaches, backaches, premenstrual syndrome
- Elevated cholesterol
- Stomach ulcers
- Loss of appetite
- Compulsive eating

Employees, colleagues, and families may notice the following:

- Emotional outbursts; displays of short temper
- High-pitched, nervous laughter
- Increased use of sick leave
- Increased resistance to change
- Avoidance of decision-making
- Increased use of alcohol or drugs
- Frequent talk about escaping
- Increased irritability and complaints
- Decline in work performance

Typical Stages of Coping with Burnout

1. Doing nothing, more or less hoping it will go away
2. Self-medicating, seeking fast relief through alcohol, drugs, or pharmaceuticals

3. Taking out accumulated stress on others
4. Seeking professional help

When an employee is ravaged by full-blown burnout, continued employment is impossible, and the person must receive extended professional counseling. In its early stages, remedial measures can reverse the condition.

It is the responsibility of supervisors to be alert for the signs and symptoms of burnout and to persuade those so afflicted to get professional help. Supervisors can also modify or eliminate major stressors and provide psychological support during the employee's therapy.

Managing Your Personal Stress

Self-empowerment is the key to immunizing yourself against stress and preventing burnout. You have more power than you realize. You have some degree of control over every one of your major stressors:

- You can reduce or eliminate your job insecurity by making your services more marketable.
- You can fire (for cause and with proper documentation) an employee who makes life miserable for you.
- You can exercise your power to make most of the daily decisions you face.
- You can make people smile, laugh, frown, and even cry.
- You do not need permission to do most of the things you do (for example, thank someone, hold a meeting, ask for help, say "no," or pack up and leave).

You can enhance your competencies and generally decrease stressful feelings of insecurity that can come upon you:

- Keep up to date technically and professionally.
- Fine-tune your interpersonal skills.
- Concentrate on making yourself more marketable.
- Request more educational support.
- Train for alternative jobs.

Improve Your Self-Talk

Shower your subconscious with positive affirmations. Affirmations are simple statements that proclaim positive facts about yourself or someone else. Articulate them plainly and emphatically. They are clear, brief, strong, and positive, and they grow more effective with repetition. Some examples are "I will" (instead of "I should" or "I will try"), "I am in control here," "I am a worthy person," "I feel good about that," or "I earned that." Affirmations have a way of becoming reality. Practice these daily.

Kick the habit of putting yourself down. Instead of criticizing yourself and telling yourself what you cannot do, congratulate yourself for the things you can do. Do not compare yourself unfavorably with others. When criticized unfairly by a superior, say to yourself, "That's only one person's opinion."

Surround Yourself with Optimistic and Enthusiastic People

The people you associate with affect the way you feel and how you ultimately behave. Examine your friendships and relationships at work and during your leisure hours. If you have been lunching with negative and critical people, find more upbeat folks. Eat with a different group each day. Put some limits on the time you spend with negative friends and relatives.

Join social and community organizations. Most such organizations feature optimistic, energetic people. Become a leader or member in one of these organizations. Spend your time around positive people.

Practice Success Imagery

There are two kinds of success imagery. In results imagery, you visualize a highly successful outcome of a future event. For example, when preparing to give a talk, you picture your audience giving you a standing ovation. In process imagery, you visualize every step of the activity and feel each emotion. For example, in the previous scenario you visualize the moderator introducing you. You feel your heart pounding. You see yourself taking a deep breath and forcing a smile. You hear your introductory remarks.

Laugh More

The simple act of laughter increases our body's endorphins, the stress fighters. People who watch a comedy video have higher levels of endorphins and lower levels of adrenaline and cortisol, the stress producers. Chuckle when you make a little mistake. Enjoy a hearty laugh, and actively seek humor. When you visit a worksite, notice the differences in the amount of joking and smiles. You can sense the deflection of stress. There are other ways to relieve stress as well:

- Escape, literally or mentally.
- Take a walk on your breaks.
- Find a quiet place to relax and daydream.
- Learn relaxation or meditation techniques.
- Expand your supportive network.
- Keep a log of your successes.

WRAP-UP

Think About It

Supervisors tend to manage their employees the way they were managed, and their behavior often includes the residual influences of autocratic, authoritarian, stress-inducing management behavior. Today, however, it is necessary to recognize that the supervisor who bosses, pushes, or intimidates creates stresses in the work group that actually hinder effective performance and undermine working relationships. More focus is being put on the overall well-being of a person. The more time we care for our complete selves, the better we can care and supervise those around us.

Questions for Review and Discussion

1. How does the COVID-19 pandemic continue to affect stress and burnout of American workers even today?
2. How can circumstances in one's private life outside of work contribute to stress on the job?
3. How can ethical considerations affect the level of a supervisor's job-related stress? Provide an example.
4. Describe one way in which a supervisor can at least partially control the level of stress experienced by his or her employees.
5. What should you look for in recruiting new employees to improve your chances of hiring a stress-resistant staff?
6. Why are appropriately empowered employees less likely than others to experience excessive stress or burnout?
7. Have you expressed stress and burnout in the workplace? How did you cope?
8. What can a supervisor do to protect the department's employees from stress coming from sources outside the department?
9. How can the goals of an individual employee contribute to stress or help to control or avoid stress?
10. What is one present stressful situation affecting health care in general?

Case: Surprise!

On Monday morning when the business office employees arrived at the hospital, they immediately noticed the absence of the office manager. This was not unusual; the manager was frequently absent on Monday. However, he rarely failed to call his department when he would not be there, and on this day he still had not called by noon.

Shortly after lunch, the two working supervisors in the business office were summoned to the administrator's office. There they were told that the office manager was no longer employed by the hospital. They, the two supervisors, were told to look after things for the current week and that a new manager, already secured, would be starting the following Monday. All the supervisors were told about the new manager was that it was somebody from outside of the hospital.

The supervisors were not told whether the manager resigned or was discharged, nor were they told whether anyone from within the department had been considered as a replacement.

Questions

1. What was right or wrong about the manner in which the change in business office manager was made?
2. What do you suppose would be the attitudes of the business office staff upon hearing of the change?
3. What do you believe would have been the level of stress among the department's staff before the change was announced and immediately after the change was announced? Why the difference, if any?
4. What can the two working supervisors do to help control the stress level in the group during the week spent waiting for the new manager?

References

1. Abramson A. Burnout and stress are everywhere. *American Psychological Association.* 2022:53(1);72. https://www.apa.org/monitor/2022/01/special-burnout-stress

2. Youn S. America's workers are exhausted and burned out—and some employers are taking notice. *Washington Post.* June 29, 2021. https://www.washingtonpost.com/business/2021/06/28/employee-burnout-corporate-america/

CHAPTER 37

The Supervisor's Future

CHAPTER OBJECTIVES

- Review the generally accepted criteria for success and suggest how to enhance your career development by increasing your promotability and marketability.
- Review steps to success that can enable a person to succeed to the full extent of his or her determination and ability.
- Establish the value of succession planning process from the department supervisor's perspective.
- Examine the phenomenon of politics in the workplace and suggest how the supervisor could effectively cope with job-related politics.
- Examine the benefits of networking and their likely composition from the supervisor's perspective.
- Provide the supervisor with advice for relating to and coping with his or her immediate organizational superior.
- Discuss the need for a balanced approach in fulfilling the responsibilities of supervision while also preparing for career advancement.

KEY TERMS

Career Development: Career development is a process consisting of continuing education and development in one's present position while adapting to continuing change and preparing for ongoing growth and advancement beyond today's job.

Networking: Networking is the utilization of acquaintances and other contacts to share advice, facts, techniques, job leads, plans and dreams, and moral support.

Split-Reporting Relationship: An organizational relationship is one in which an individual, whether supervisor or non-managerial employee, must officially answer to two superiors.

Criteria for Success

Success is not defined in the same way by everyone; among individuals there are differences, often vast, in how they would describe success in terms of their own wants and needs. Most people would be reasonably content with their lot in life if they could obtain peace of mind, enjoy good health, maintain a loving relationship, enjoy freedom from financial hardship, and feel personally fulfilled. But the strength of some of these criteria—perhaps all except peace of mind and good health—can vary greatly from person to person. Some people seem satisfied with the status quo and do not strive for more; however, some will continually strive for more and better. Those who strive are the achievers, and it is the achievers who succeed as outstanding employees and supervisors.

Characteristics of Achievers

Achievers will exhibit most if not all of a number of positive characteristics:

- Exhibit a winning attitude
- Be enthusiastic about their work
- Possess flexibility, adjusting quickly to change
- Accept ambiguity and uncertainty
- Be rapid learners and invest in lifelong education
- Hold themselves accountable for outcomes
- Manage their own morale and empowerment
- Be problem solvers, not complainers
- Set goals for themselves
- Manage their time wisely
- Be known for innovativeness
- Be technically or professionally competent
- Be assertive and stress resistant
- Be effective communicators
- Always be customer oriented

Worthwhile Careers Involve Taking Risks

Excellence requires deviation from accepted norms, and deviation involves risk. You achieve excellence by not backing away from unpopular or risky decisions that are avoided by others. Doing so requires courage.

Risk taking is essential to personal advancement. Preparing for the future requires making decisions, some of which involve considerable time, expense, and sacrifice. Risk takers exhibit the flexibility that today's employers appreciate. Self-confident, enthusiastic, and optimistic, risk takers regard mistakes as learning experiences.

We are not recommending taking foolish risks or neglecting to gather sufficient information for making sound decisions. Risk taking can be overdone. Avoid making the same mistake twice. Do not disregard your intuitive warnings and past experience. Reduce risks by adding safety measures. For example, find a new job before putting your present employment on the line.

Eliminate Your Fears

Two of our most powerful fears are fear of failure and fear of the unknown. You must be willing to take career risks and regard failures as learning experiences; anyone who has never failed has never attempted anything of significance. Be prudent, however, and carefully assess apparent risks against your particular situation and needs. Before taking a major risk, consider the following questions:

- What is my goal or objective?
- What are the best and worst possible outcomes?
- What additional information do I need? From what sources?
- What are the alternative measures?
- What are the relative rewards and risks of each alternative?
- What barriers must I overcome?
- What support is available?
- What contingency plan is available?
- How can I reduce the amount of risk?
- How will delay affect the benefit and the risk?

Look for Opportunities in Your Workplace

Healthcare delivery is constantly changing, and new services invariably present new challenges. Recommend projects or new assignments that solve problems for your employer or your manager.

Be mindful of all the emerging roles needed to carry out organizational changes. We see the loss of jobs at various institutions, but as employers are eliminating some positions, they are also creating new ones. Reengineering, alliances, new services, and the mandates of state and federal regulations create needs that require new positions.

The best new jobs in your organization are not found in the want ads of the local newspaper. More often than not they reach you via the grapevine or your personal network. Some recruiters claim that more of the better positions are filled through networking than through any other means. It is always time to expand your network and latch onto mentors who are at the forefront of your organization's initiatives.

What initiatives are your superiors contemplating? Reflect on how you can benefit from these changes. Still better, suggest some changes of your own; perhaps you can create a new and better job for yourself. Consider possible new services or customers, marketing strategies, satellite operations, or restructuring. Look, sound, and act as someone who is already qualified to assume a new role.

Be Alert for Outside Opportunities

Do your own personal market research. What are trends in the industry or in other areas where you may have career interests? What skills do you need now and in the future? Consider the advantages and disadvantages of each type of position or employer.

Consider a change. Consider obtaining a certification or licensure. Many nurses and other healthcare supervisors are finding their niches in managed care organizations. Many people use career changes to do things they never had time for or to develop previously latent talents.

Increase Your Promotability and Marketability

Hard work alone rarely earns promotions or brings substantial raises. Employers applaud and reward excellent performance, but they have an even greater incentive to promote people who have the potential for doing more for them in the future. The manager who considers promoting someone usually thinks, "How will promoting this person help me?"

Employers look for people who can make sound decisions quickly, who can solve problems, and who exhibit enthusiasm and initiative. They want leaders who can coordinate new teams, integrate new technology across departmental lines, and accept altered supervisory roles created by workforce reductions. Employers want leaders who are observant, proactive, and innovative. They value flexibility and adaptability more than ever.

Look at your career as it now stands by asking yourself if you are really doing what you want to do and if you are presently enjoying most of what you do. Are there any aspects of your present situation you are reluctant to change? Are your actions consistent with your personal values? Are you willing to make the sacrifices necessary to reach your new goals, and how might your family members feel about your changing? Should you look within your present organization or elsewhere? Do you value challenge, interesting assignments, recognition, involvement, control, or innovation? Is the absence of stress important? Do you prefer independence to teamwork? Is increased income a high priority, or can you postpone monetary rewards while preparing for a new career? Honest answers to these several questions will help you chart your career path.

Expand Your Competencies and Promote Your Capabilities

You must make up your own mind about whether to specialize or generalize. Some employers are constantly looking for people with hard-to-find skills, yet still more employers want people who can broaden their competencies when occupational needs change. Remaining attentive to what is happening in your occupation and your organization will help you decide which direction to take.

All healthcare supervisors must continue to balance their educational efforts between those professionally or technically oriented and those that are management related. However, in today's organizational environment, supervisors' performance evaluations depend more on their leadership ability than on their professional expertise.

Also, develop a reputation for innovativeness, flexibility, and customer service. Directly or indirectly, service evaluations by both internal and external customers greatly influence the success of care providers.

Make yourself more visible. Be assertive, but not pushy. Come to meetings prepared and participate actively. Ask questions and make suggestions. Look and sound like someone who is on the way up; appearances still count. Acquire personal business cards and use them. Keep a file of your accomplishments and bring them up at your performance reviews.

Steps to Success

1. Begin with a vision. Be sure that you know what you want to accomplish. Fame and fortune? Running a large department or an entire organization? Being highly respected for your technical expertise? Imagine what you would like a speaker to say about you upon your retirement.
2. Select your mission statement and major goals. A mission statement is the "why," the reason for your goals, a declaration of direction that has the power to guide your activities for the rest of your life. Mission statements provide the motivation to accomplish goals. A goal is the "what." Once you have settled upon a goal, you will find that the workings of your unconscious help you to reach it. Because of limitations of time and money, you may have to sacrifice some goals to serve others. Before you finalize goals, discuss them with family, close friends, mentors, and your manager. Document your mission statement and goals.
3. Prepare a list of objectives for each major goal. A sound objective should be specific, challenging, realistic, achievable, and measurable.
4. Inventory your strengths and weaknesses. Be honest and forthright about weaknesses; you will not correct them if you refuse to admit they exist.
5. Prepare a needs analysis. Catalog your development needs using your list of weaknesses, breaking them down into smaller categories if necessary. The acquisition of new education, skills, and experience is imperative.
6. Document potential barriers and how you plan to cope with them. Common barriers are time, finances, and resistance from family.
7. Chart your action steps and add target dates.
8. Implement the process. Transfer your action plans to daily to-do lists.
9. Monitor, evaluate, and reward. Your motivation is strongest if you enjoy the process as well as reaching your goal. Reward yourself for what you accomplish; self-evaluation and self-reward decrease your need for the approval of others.

Beware the Career Killers

Many people who fail, tend to blame other people, society, or fate. However, in most cases such failures represent self-destruction.

A major career killer is *lack of appropriate goals, objectives, or priorities*. Without such guidance, a "career" may be no more than a random series of pinball bounces among unrelated milestones. It cannot be too strongly stressed that the unfocused or undirected "career" is likely to be no career at all.

Many career killers are found within the individual; thus, it is up to the individual to avoid falling victim to *fear and self-doubt, lack of motivation or enthusiasm, lack of self-control, unwillingness or inability to adjust to change, weak interpersonal skills, ineffective leadership*, and the *inability to be an effective team player*.

On the practical side, careers have been hampered or derailed by *too many diversions or outside interests, poor time management*, and *failure to stay current with technology*. The latter point about failing to stay current looms large in this present age of rapid change. A significant amount of new learning is necessary to simply "stay even"; thus the individual who fails to continue learning is not just standing still; he or she is falling behind.

Negotiating for More Compensation

There is a myth that if you work hard you will automatically be rewarded. In a typical healthcare organization, a person whose performance is rated as outstanding may receive a salary increase of little more than the average worker. This pertains to supervisors as well; in most instances, they receive the same token percent increases as the general workforce.

Are you—truly, honestly—worth more than you are receiving? If you never ask, you are not likely to receive what you may be worth. To receive a substantial salary increase, you must earn it *and* usually negotiate for it. If you are as good as they have said you are via performance evaluations, your leaders should take your request seriously. Your manager probably has the power to get you more money despite what he or she says. Employees who resign when told that funds were not available often learn that their replacements started at higher salaries than they were being paid.

As in all negotiations, preparation, confidence, and sales ability are critical. Your first requirement is knowing your market value and using that value to decide on the figure you will aim for. Research the pay scale for your kind of work; know what competitors are paying for comparable jobs. Numerous online sources can help you can find your market value. You can also check with your mentors and other members of your personal network.

Do not be passive in your approach. However, it is equally bad to barge into your manager's office and demand more money. You must use a little finesse. Despite that squeamish feeling about a confrontation over salary, you must be assertive. If you are a worthy recipient, your manager will feel just as uncomfortable about your request as you do.

The timing of your pitch is critical. When your employer is in financial difficulty or your manager is experiencing problems, do not expect a favorable response. Never approach a boss who is extremely busy, upset, or in the middle of an important project or a crisis. Sometimes a good opportunity is right after you have received a glowing performance appraisal.

If you are turned down, ask what you must do or achieve to earn a raise. Use the response to make appropriate modifications to your career development program (or to start looking for another job). Check back periodically with your manager to find out how you are doing.

But do not derail your pitch by doing any of the following:

- Telling your manager you deserve a raise because of the length of time you have been with the organization. It is value and potential that count, not seniority.
- Telling your manager that you should get a raise because you need more money.
- Threatening to resign, at least not early in the process, unless you have a solid offer of another job in hand.

Succession Planning

In today's uncertain times, the need for succession planning is more important than ever. Organizations are becoming increasingly unstable. Mergers and acquisitions and other affiliations are causing the movement of supervisors like never before as jobs are changed, upgraded, downgraded, created, and eliminated. Therefore, everyone who is in charge of a work unit should answer these questions:

1. If my services suddenly become unavailable, how would my job get done?
2. How long would it take to find and train my replacement?
3. Who is on board right now who could take over?
4. What have I done to prepare a successor?

Benefits of Succession Planning

The strength and adaptability of an organization are linked to how fully it has developed its workers. This development depends largely on the willingness and capability of supervisors to share their expertise with potential successors.

When you have mastered your job and are looking for advancement, you need to make yourself dispensable. To fail to do so freezes you into your present job because your superiors will come to regard you as indispensable in that position, not because you are so good but rather because it would be a time-consuming process to replace you and bring your replacement up to speed. The more successful supervisors are clearly dispensable; they can readily be plucked from their positions and moved up, especially if *their* superiors have also conscientiously developed potential successors.

Also, when you have a trained backup, you can do things you did not have time for previously. This increases your value to the organization and enhances your career. You can be absent with the assurance that your unit will function smoothly in your absence.

Risks in Picking and Training a Successor

There is always the possibility that you pick a lemon, but remember that the only people who never fall down are those who always remain seated. All leaders worthy of the title have made poor decisions, but they regard such mistakes as learning experiences and move on. Careful planning and preparation minimize this risk. Also, it is better to learn early that a particular individual is unsuited for supervision than to have this surface only after the person has moved up.

A more frequent risk is that your protégé gets promoted out from under you or is enticed away by a competitor. Although this elicits disappointment proportional to the effort you made in developing the individual, you still get important benefits: a reputation as a career builder, the gratitude of the person you trained, supporters (your former protégés) in other units or organizations, and the ability to repeat the process with greater competency.

Some supervisors fear competition from subordinates, worrying that a protégé may prove to be a more effective leader than the supervisor. They believe they may be putting their jobs in jeopardy. These supervisors usually have already displayed this fear through their reluctance to delegate. However, such concerns are based on false assumptions. It is rare for a supervisor to lose a job because a protégé outperforms the supervisor. Having one or two sharp, ambitious subordinates coming up behind you with their eyes on your job or a similar position should serve as a positive incentive for you to continue to grow as a manager and remain in full control of your job.

Selection and Training Plan

Finding the appropriate understudy can be simple or complicated. You do not have far to look if you already have an assistant and are satisfied with that person's potential. In that situation you have probably already trained that person to handle supervisory tasks and to demonstrate leadership ability. You already know his or her strengths and where additional training or experience is needed.

If you do not have an assistant and must choose from several employees who have the same potential, do not simply assume that all these people are interested in your job. Do not waste your time preparing reluctant successors, and do not be in a hurry to designate a single candidate as the anointed one. The moment such a move becomes apparent, others stop striving for the job.

When you have identified several prospects, treat them as equal contenders. Delegate supervisory and administrative activities to each and document how they handle them. Let them take turns moderating staff meetings or representing you at interdepartmental meetings. When you are going to be absent, appoint different substitutes. Pay close attention to how they handle these situations. Does the work get done? Do they try to do everything themselves, or do they get the cooperation of other team members? How did their fellow workers perceive their performance? The fairness of these delegated responsibilities and the documentation of performance may later save you the embarrassment of being charged with discrimination or favoritism.

Grooming Your Successor

How you prepare the chosen one is extremely important. The process consists largely, but not exclusively, of a series of delegations and special assignments. Ensure that the person does each of these tasks often enough to become competent and comfortable. Make certain that he or she has enough time to handle daily responsibilities.

Besides these delegations and assignments, take your protégés to some of your meetings. Let them sit in on interviews you hold and accompany you as you "manage by walking around." Work jointly on things like budgets or plans.

Developing a successor involves much mentoring. Provide opportunities for meeting senior managers and important customers. The latter include internal customers, those units that serve or are served by your department. Provide visibility by letting your successor present reports and chair meetings.

A worthy protégé will do most of the planning and energizing independently, deciding what seminars to attend, what courses and workshops to take, what books to study, and what periodicals and established blogs to read. The person will also set goals and develop action plans and make the extra effort needed to work on career development while still discharging daily responsibilities.

Workplace Politics

Politics, as commonly used and generally understood, is seen primarily as the pursuit of power. However, the original meaning of the word was "to act in the service of society." Therefore it once meant a relatively high form of public service. But politics has been reinterpreted to often mean primarily service to self, self-empowerment with what is usually a negative connotation. Career failures can result from political as well as professional incompetence; unwillingness to address the political components of a job has halted many a promising career.

Corporate politics is gamesmanship, using forces other than good performance—and at times in addition to good performance—to improve one's stance in an organization. This includes trying to influence superiors and gain a competitive edge over one's peers. If your political script is a positive one, you play the game fairly and ethically.

At one end of the scale politics is selfish, unethical, or illegal. At the other end, political behavior can supplement professional competence; it is often beneficial not only for the political person, but also for his or her subordinates, superiors, teammates, and employer.

Negative Politics

Negative politics may be dysfunctional, unethical, or even illegal, receiving the blame for almost everything: poor communication, inappropriate behavior, unpopular promotions, discrimination, and favoritism. Organizational politics is partly based on the time-honored bureaucratic wish to be blameless and safe. Negative politics can surface in the presence of a lack of clear organizational goals or of communication of goals; autocratic or bureaucratic leadership; multiple layers of management (the more layers, the more politics); stifled upward communication; frequent organizational changes; controversial management power shifts; and poor relationships between workers and managers.

Political Games That Subordinates or Colleagues Play

- Taking advantage of being indispensable
- Abusing friendships
- Probing for weaknesses of others and revealing those weaknesses
- Undermining operations or new services
- Starting rumors or providing misleading information
- Creating crises or discord
- Displaying undue emotional distress to achieve selfish gains
- Discrediting teammates in public or undermining them in private
- Intimidating new employees and provoking sensitive people

Political Games That Managers Play

- Stealing ideas or credit from others
- Excluding others from meetings or information to gain personal advantage by keeping certain people uninformed
- Eliminating or downgrading the jobs of employees whom they dislike or distrust
- Assigning unpleasant tasks
- Delegating work that places delegates at risk or that prevents them from handling their regular work
- Pitting one employee against another
- Giving unfair or false performance appraisals
- Not hiring employees who could be threatening to them

Manipulation

Manipulators invoke the names of high-level people to get their way. They take advantage of friends and colleagues. Threats or even bribes may be part of their strategy. They usually "forget" their promises. Political savvy to these folks means passing the buck, procrastinating, and saying what they do not mean.

You know others are attempting to manipulate you when they lead off with "You don't value my service anymore, do you?" or "You owe me one," or "The boss will back me on this."

Positive Political Scripts and Tactics

Assertiveness

Assertiveness consists of standing up for one's own rights and expressing those feelings and beliefs in direct, honest ways that do not violate the rights of others. The theme of the assertive person is "You're okay, I'm okay." Lack of assertiveness is detrimental to one's self-image and self-respect. Ask yourself the following:

- Do I often say yes when I should say no?
- Do I allow people to interrupt me?
- Do I use self-deprecating comments like "I know this sounds stupid, but …"?

- At meetings, do I want to speak up but seldom do?
- Do I avoid controversial issues?
- Am I doing work that others should do?
- Am I the one who always gives in?
- Do others take advantage of me?
- Do I find it difficult to negotiate?

If you answered yes to several of the foregoing questions, consider the following for increasing your assertiveness:

- Attend a workshop or read a book on assertiveness and apply what you learn.
- When others say something negative about you, reply, "Are you trying to make me feel guilty?" Watch for a surprising reaction.
- Appreciate the fact that you have more power than you realize.
- Set boundaries or limits. Learn to say "no."
- Rehearse expressing yourself or engage in role-playing with a close friend.

Rapport with People Who Report to You

One thing employees notice quickly is whether "the score" is being kept equitably. The score refers to how you evaluate performance, how you treat each employee, and how you enforce the rules.

Political power is short circuited when employees believe they are being manipulated. Negative political statements and unfulfilled promises lead to resentment, anger, and loss of trust. On the other hand, if mutual trust and respect exist and if your people perceive you as their champion, your personal power will skyrocket.

Networking

Developing relationships with individuals beyond your department and outside of the organization is largely a matter of networking. Networking has become one of the many ways to advance your career.[1] We still hear the old (and generally true) cliché, "It's not what you know, but who you know that counts."

Fortunately, there is abundant opportunity to get to know people who can help us if we are willing to make the effort. Networking is largely a matter of knowing how to be helpful to your contacts and how to ask them for help.

Benefits of Networks

Networking is invaluable to teams for improving daily productivity, efficiency, and achievement. It also enhances personal growth. People who build connections within and outside organizations are much more likely to succeed. Prominent among the benefits of active networking are the following:

- Technical, professional, legal, or financial advice
- Advance information about trends, new projects, or organizational changes
- Opinions on proposals, ideas, speeches, or reports
- Moral support
- Mentoring or counseling help
- Information about job opportunities
- Awareness of the availability of job candidates
- Sharing experiences, both successes and failures

Potential Network Participants

All *customers*, both external and internal, are potential network participants. Externally, patients, physicians, and others can be a constant source of suggestions for improving service; satisfy these clients, and you gain enthusiastic supporters. Internally, all persons within the organization with whom you have any dealings at all are a potential part of your network.

Other potential participants in your network are *coworkers*, who precede or follow you in workflows; *colleagues*, who work with you on committees or in other groups; former *teachers* under whom you studied; *vendors* with whom you do business; *community associates*, fellow members of your various organizations; and "gatekeepers," those who can provide access to important people, services, or knowledge.

Also, do not overlook *competitors* as potential network participants. Your counterparts at other organizations in the community can be valuable contacts. And finally, never forget *family members*, some of whom can have numerous contacts in their own personal networks.

Making and Maintaining Contacts

At the heart of making and maintaining contacts is your willingness to reach out and make yourself visible to others. Do not wait for opportunities to present themselves; rather, take the initiative to reach out. Among the best means available today are business or professional computer-based networks such as LinkedIn and social networks such as Instagram, Facebook, and Twitter. Make use of these, but do not overlook the traditional networking opportunities that remain available. Establish contacts at professional gatherings, conferences, workshops, social functions, and through exposure to others at schools, clubs, churches and synagogues, hobby groups, and among your neighbors. Keep your mind open by refusing to bypass a potential contact because it may seem to hold no value for your network; you never know when a seemingly unintentional contact will be a steppingstone to a valuable connection.

Increase your visibility by giving presentations, holding office in organizations you belong to, or volunteering as a spokesperson when the opportunity arises. If you are able to earn a reputation as a recognized expert in some aspect of health care, this will cause others to reach out to you. Constantly expand your network. Concentrate on doing favors for others rather than asking favors of them; those who feel obligated to you will remember you when they have something potentially helpful to communicate.

Do not overlook contacts available within your sphere of daily activity: other supervisors and managers, employees of other departments, and persons in other healthcare institutions and agencies you may have to deal with from time to time. Overall, appreciate the fact that everyone whose path you cross at any time is a potential contact.

Characteristics of Successful Networkers

- They know how to interact with people; they ask good questions and listen attentively.
- They keep in touch with their contacts.
- They are active joiners.
- They circulate at parties and meetings and introduce themselves rather than waiting for someone else to do the honors.
- They are cordial and courteous to all but selective about the people with whom they develop special rapport.
- They use coffee breaks and lunch times to chat with different people.
- They volunteer for committees and other group functions.
- They teach, coach, and mentor.
- They serve as officers in social and professional organizations.
- They go out of their way to establish relationships with newcomers.
- They share clippings, reports, articles, and other information.
- They send out many thank-you notes, and they remember birthdays and other special occasions.
- They express their appreciation for favors in special ways.

Relating to the Person to Whom You Report

In taking your present position you essentially had no choice as to who your immediate superior will be, so you may or may not approve of your manager. However, if you are job hunting or transferring within your organization, one of your important considerations should be your assessment of the person to whom you will report. You want someone with whom you can get along. You also want to know as much as you can about the leadership style of this manager and about morale and turnover in the new unit. This information is not found in any handout; however, you can learn much with some probing. Question some of the employees who work in the unit.

Get to Know Your Manager's Expectations, Likes, and Dislikes

Managers are sometimes insecure because they do not know a great deal about what you do on the job. Clarify this by reviewing your goals and priorities with your manager and by asking the manager if he or she agrees with your goals. In this way, the manager will also be in a better position to offer more specific support.

Leadership styles are important, as are communication preferences. Learn how the manager wants to receive messages. Some like to read them; others prefer to listen to them. Keep your manager informed. Never hide problems, and when you report them, offer solutions. Do not waste your manager's time with gossip. Learn when to speak up and when to remain silent.

Avoid disagreements in public, and never embarrass the boss in front of others. Pick the right time and place for presenting your ideas. Some managers like input first thing in the morning so they can get a handle on operations. Others do not want to hear or see anyone until they complete their morning chores.

Other considerations are the manager's likes and dislikes, decision-making style, tendency to stereotype, or other hang-ups. Most importantly, what are his or her expectations and priorities concerning your performance? Ask the manager to review your position description and work standards with you.

If you are able to discern problems that your manager has with his or her superiors, provide whatever support you can. Do everything you can to make your manager look good to upper management.

Accept delegated tasks with enthusiasm. When you step-in for your manager, consider this as a chance to try out the job. Remember that promotions are based not so much on what you have done as on what your superiors believe you can do for them in the future.

Direct Your Manager's Behavior

You can influence your manager's behavior verbally or by means of thank-you notes or emails. When one of your requests is granted, a thank-you message is appropriate. Do you respond enthusiastically and gratefully when your manager approves your request to attend a professional meeting or to take a long weekend? Expressions of appreciation are always appropriate, and they are much more effective in channeling behavior than using complaints, ultimatums, or threats.

Be Loyal and Show Respect

Being loyal and respectful includes making your boss look good. You can display loyalty by defending your manager when he or she is criticized, arriving on time at meetings, making extra effort, and expressing enthusiasm.

Most important is a respectful tone in daily communications. Know when and how to dissent. Most managers accept disagreement if it is offered tactfully. Learn how direct you can be and be diplomatic. Remember that what you believe is a bad decision by your manager may be one that was imposed from above. Share credit for your accomplishments with your manager.

To Relate Successfully with Your Manager

- Make honest complimentary comments about your manager to other people—your boss will get the message.
- Act as a devil's advocate occasionally, then yield gracefully (bosses like to persuade people).
- Develop a reputation as a problem solver. Be willing to risk your reputation by offering innovative suggestions or introducing new techniques in your unit.
- Have the courage to stand up for what you believe is right.
- Deliver on your promises.
- Protect and defend the reputation of your organization and your boss.

- Keep your frustrations and negative thoughts to yourself.
- Know when and how to resign or ask for a transfer.

Behavior to Avoid

A number of important prohibitions should be observed in relations with your immediate superior:

- Do not do anything that would lead your boss to regard you as a threat.
- Do not say "That's not my job" or "I wasn't hired to do that."
- Do not let pessimism or negativism creep into your attitude.
- Do not steal credit.
- Do not criticize your boss, coworkers, or organization in public.
- Do not distort the truth.
- Do not threaten to resign when you do not get your way.
- Do not sacrifice your professional and ethical values.

And an additional extremely important prohibition: Never go to your manager's superiors with problems or complaints before discussing them with your boss. If you are frustrated over not getting satisfaction from your superior and want to talk to a higher authority, disclose your intention to your manager first and suggest that you both make the visit. If the manager refuses, tell him or her exactly what you are going to say to the higher up. Always follow the chain of command.

When You Have More Than One Immediate Superior

Today, many healthcare employees report to two or more superiors. This can lead to conflicts of time sharing or priorities or even of conflicting orders. When you get competing assignments, inform both of your managers of the conflict and ask for their direction or advice.

The success of split-reporting relationships depends largely on the attitude and conduct of the two managers. Such relationships can be extremely stressful if the two superiors are not on the same wavelength. If they are not in constant agreement with each other, such relationships are doomed to failure when one or the other presumes to put his or her demands on the subordinate always first or consistently tries to consume more than a fair share of the subordinate's time.

If you are subject to a split-reporting relationship, it is generally up to you to keep both superiors advised of your overall workload and to keep each aware of the assignments you are receiving from the other. It is also up to you to avoid clearly favoring one superior over the other; this behavior may work for a while, but eventually it causes trouble. When problems with the arrangement seem to be developing, consider it your responsibility to ask for a joint meeting with both superiors to try to work things out. Split-reporting relationships can work satisfactorily, but only with the whole-hearted cooperation of all three participants.

Difficult Bosses

At one time or another in a lifetime of work, most people will have to deal with an unpleasant or incompetent superior. When you encounter one of these early in your career, you have an excellent opportunity to fine-tune your skills for getting along with someone who has power over you. Often you can learn a great deal about management from the negative examples offered by a tyrannical or incompetent superior.

Before you blame your manager, examine your own behavior. Are you doing anything that evidently irritates him or her? Is your work area a mess while the boss's office is orderly? Do you show up at meetings late and without excuses? Are you occasionally careless about your appearance while your manager always dresses impeccably? Do you get frequent personal phone calls or visits or sometimes have to drop everything and run home? Do you routinely get to work after your manager does and consistently leave earlier? Have you been insensitive to things you say or do that you know annoy the boss? Make certain you are not guilty

of any of the foregoing transgressions before assigning blame for your apparent problems on your manager.

Procrastinators

The procrastinators, whether they are managers or others, are usually agreeable, well-intentioned people with perfectionist tendencies. They avoid or postpone decisions for fear of making mistakes or offending others. Try to find and eliminate the reasons for their hesitancy. Praise them when they do make decisions or take action promptly, for example, "We really appreciate it when you're so proactive. It helps us meet our schedules and get home on time."

Be reassuring of and optimistic toward procrastinators. When you need to get something approved, have all the supporting data ready. Tell them that you have checked out all proposals carefully. Instead of asking permission, send a memo stating what you intend to do unless you hear to the contrary. Make sure that you give them sufficient time to get back to you.

Unfair Bosses

If you are getting more than your share of unpleasant assignments, instead of accusing your manager of sticking it to you, state exactly what is bothering you. You will usually find that the manager is not aware of the situation or that you are upset about it. If the boss is dumping excessive busywork on you or is delegating too much, ask him or her to help you to set your work priorities or provide additional help.

If you believe your manager is discriminating against you, point this out diplomatically and in behavioral terms ("It seems to me that perhaps I was bypassed because …"). If the discrimination gets out of hand, blow the whistle after you are certain that your evidence is firm and specific. Be prepared to provide examples and have corroborating evidence. Check with your mentors and local governmental agencies as necessary. Be extremely careful and absolutely sure of your position before acting; in most such instances, calling out your boss for an act of discrimination will forever alter the relationship between you two.

Bosses Who Bypass You

These managers frequently give orders to your subordinates without your knowledge, usually when you are not present at the moment. You can eliminate most of these intrusions if you are able to discuss the problem with them. Point out how this undermines your authority and confuses your staff, always providing specific examples.

Tell your staff that they are to keep you informed about instructions or requests from others. Except in emergencies, they are not to carry out such orders until they have consulted you. If you believe your employees can diplomatically tell certain of these order givers that they must get your approval first, try that approach. You may want to authorize your team members to decide when they should honor extrinsic orders. You can provide a discretionary task list.

You must have the courage to protest when a superior repeatedly issues orders to your people in your presence. Try diplomacy first. Tell him or her that results will be better if requests are made of you. If this practice continues, point out that your employees are confused about some of his or her orders and that they are afraid to ask for clarification. If this behavior continues and results in genuine problems for you and your people, you may be justified in going over the superior's head with your complaint.

Laissez-Faire Leaders

These "managers" are not really leaders; they just hold managerial titles. They have abandoned their responsibilities. They are never around when you need them, and when they are on site, they provide no help.

Know what your authority is and use it. Revise your position description to include more control over your areas of responsibility. Seek broad approval for your objectives, plans, and schedules and then go ahead with them. Pin the boss down when vague directives are issued. Gradually assume more responsibility and control.

Doing Today's Job While Preparing for Tomorrow

A successful, satisfying, and fulfilling career usually does not just happen. One does not ordinarily step into a job and follow a path of least resistance through a series of advancements that constitute a rewarding career. Rarely if ever does "going with the flow" carry you to where you are best suited or potentially most fulfilled. Rather, those who go farthest in the direction that is best for them usually have a clear vision of their intended direction; they know where they are going.

The growth-oriented supervisor cannot help possessing a split focus as far as employment is concerned. Although every supervisor should of course be largely attentive to the job at hand, the growth-oriented person can be expected to experience two important concerns—doing the present job and preparing for the next job.

Present Employer or Elsewhere?

Is it best to seek your next upward move within your present organization or elsewhere? Some extend their loyalty to a particular organization and seek to advance within that organization. Others envision themselves readily going to another employer while still others remain open to either possibility. Whether one's present organization or another organization receives the growth-oriented supervisor's attention depends on the supervisor's perception of where the greater opportunity exists and where the opportunity is perceived as greater or more immediate.

Upward Versus Downward

At any given time the supervisor may tend to "face upward" toward higher management or "face downward" toward the work group.

There are needs causing one to do either at any particular time, and tendencies in the individual favor facing either upward or downward. The pressures to face upward or downward are rarely equal.

Downward-facing pressures consist of the needs of your direct-reporting employees; the needs of your clients, patients, or customers; and generally, all the responsibilities of your present position. Downward is in fact the direction in which most managers of people should face most of the time; this is especially true of first-line supervisors. It is necessary to face toward the staff, to in fact be a functioning part of the staff, to best fulfill the responsibilities of the position in the most basic sense of management: getting things done through people. But downward facing also runs counter to a number of tendencies that result from pressures that encourage many supervisors to face upward.

Facing upward is a natural inclination of many supervisors. Reward and recognition come from above; to enhance your chances of advancing it is necessary to be known and appreciated at higher levels. Some upward facing is appropriate, even essential. But it must be accomplished in ways that do not detract from the supervisor's basic job responsibilities. Excessive upward facing detracts from the supervisor's visibility and availability where these count most: within the supervisor's direct-reporting work group.

A Matter of Motivation

It becomes a matter of individual motivation when a person responds to what are essentially psychological needs. People are dramatically different from each other in terms of what they respond to most readily. In planning out a supposedly desired career path it is not simply *where you (believe you) want to go* that is important. Rather, it is necessary with each move you make to reassess where you are and where you want to go. Your ultimate objective is only what you *believe* you want; you will never know for certain until you get there if it is what you really wanted. Also, what some individuals *believe* they want can

carry them too far too rapidly, setting them up for eventual failure.

Dedication and the Balancing Act

Total dedication to self over all else is of course an inappropriate strategy. The individual who is fully focused on growing and advancing to the extent of subordinating all other considerations is making a number of crucial errors. The person who behaves so is cheating the employer by performing what may be a minimum of useful work while occupying a position that could otherwise be filled more productively by someone else. However, because so many people ascribe to the perceived need to "look out for number one," some people have a tendency to place themselves ahead of other considerations at all times. The individual who behaves in this manner is concentrating more on making the next upward move than on mastering his or her present role.

Some degree of dedication to both self and employer is necessary, but this must be achieved with a healthy balance. This must also be achieved amid changing perceptions of loyalty of both employer to employee and employee to organization.

Balancing your own needs with the needs of the organization can be a difficult task. Most supervisory, managerial, and professional jobs are by nature open-ended; there is always something to be done, whether urgent, essential, marginally important, or just desirable. Therefore, a genuine balance of service to the job and to yourself is a necessity for personal health and survival.

The Supervisor's Obligations

You owe it to your employer to do the best you can at your present job. However, if you wish to advance, you also owe it to yourself to see that you are prepared to advance and take on greater responsibilities. These obligations must be balanced for both purposes to be served. It is too easy to be diverted into one of the extreme paths, focusing solely on yourself and thus doing a lesser job than you are capable of doing or becoming totally consumed by your present job.

Your essential task is to seek ways to meet your obligations to your employer and yourself at the same time. Luckily, one of the most effective ways of preparing for your next job is to improve your mastery of your present job.

Some Unchanging Fundamentals

Goal Alignment

Examine your goals to determine how consistent they are with your employer's goals. If some of your goals align with the organization's goals, working toward these mutual goals benefits both. And if goals do align, a career focus on your current organization might be appropriate for you at least in the short run because the goal consistency means that you can benefit personally while benefiting the organization.

If your goals do not line up at all with your employer's goals, you are faced with other necessary choices. For example, if you are an environmental services supervisor but you would like to eventually work in finance and you are studying accounting part time, pursuing the organizational goal of keeping the facility clean gains you nothing toward your personal goal. Therefore, much of your focus will be largely external because that is where your personal goal support will be found.

Supporting Skills

Whether your focus is internal or external, certain skills noted throughout this text are always valuable in helping you perform your present job while making you more suitable for advancement. These include all the basic management skills and the essential communication skills. To rise in management, you must master management fundamentals and should also expect to have to develop competence in *writing, public speaking*, and *interpersonal communication*.

Improvement in dealing with people is a dimension of job performance often overlooked. Individually, we all tend to believe we are better communicators than we actually are. But we constantly deal with people—employees, peers, superiors, clients, customers, whomever—and should do so in ways that allow all of our interpersonal contacts to feel respected and important.

Make Yourself Valuable

In pursuing goals of career advancement, it helps a great deal if you report to a manager who delegates well, truly empowers, and practices employee development. An effective manager with strong feelings for employee development, confident and unafraid of sharp, strong, subordinates, is one of the greatest advantages you can have in your job.

One way you can be valuable is to know enough about your manager's job to make it easy for your manager to delegate to you. And one of the most valuable functions you can perform, preventing your boss from making an obvious mistake or stepping unknowingly into a dangerous situation, is always appreciated by a confident manager.

Pursuing your desire to advance may be more or less difficult depending on your manager's attitude toward employee development and on your relationship with that manager. But although advancement is your goal, first get your present job responsibilities well under control. When that control is achieved, however, you can then carefully select and pursue opportunities that seem to hold the most potential to do good for you. In the long run, however, the surest way to advance is through a track record of demonstrated success in fulfilling your job responsibilities and meeting the expectations of your employers.

The Supervisor's Future

Mergers and acquisitions and changes in patterns of healthcare delivery continue to result in staff reductions in many healthcare facilities. There remain, however, worker shortages in certain key professional occupations, such as registered pharmacists, registered nurses, and other allied health professions.

There will continue to be jobs in health care, and therefore healthcare supervisors will always be needed. However, the task of the healthcare supervisor is likely to become increasingly more challenging. Pulling together a few points that have been made throughout this text and adding some future perspective, healthcare supervisors of the near future can most likely expect the following:

- To experience continued pressure to do more with less, as financial resources continue to tighten while the government and the public demand more and better-quality care
- To see new modes of treatment and new technologies arise, improving the health of many but intensifying the financial pressures on the system
- To see more movement away from hospitals and into other modes of care delivery (free-standing surgical centers, free-standing emergency rooms, imaging centers, group practices, community health centers, etc.), creating new and different job opportunities
- To witness more hospital mergers, more affiliations, and the continued creation of large healthcare systems
- To experience horizontal job expansion as major organizational changes, broaden supervisors' areas of responsibility and increase the numbers of people supervised
- To learn to supervise a workforce that is becoming increasingly more culturally diverse and educated.
- To be able to bridge a substantial generation gap in supervising a group of any size, including dramatically differing values and work ethics within the same department
- To be able to continue emphasizing high-quality customer service in the face of significant pressure to cut corners in the name of efficiency

We should certainly add: to expect to obtain great satisfaction from meeting numerous difficult challenges while delivering an essential, critical service to individuals in need.

WRAP-UP

Think About It

Career development should be a concern and priority throughout your entire working lifetime. In each managerial job you hold, your career development should be bolstered by your development of one or more potential successors. And considering the continued acceleration of technological and social change, remember that most working individuals—and especially those supervising and managing in rapidly evolving fields such as health care—may experience two, three, or even four different "careers" in a single working lifetime. Lifelong learning is essential for a successful career.

Questions for Review and Discussion

1. What are the advantages and disadvantages of focusing your self-development on achieving excellence in a specific technical or professional specialty?

2. Why is it claimed that the acceptance of risk is essential in career development?

3. In making yourself increasingly visible to higher management, could you experience

any risks relative to your department? Explain.

4. What is the difference between an objective and a goal? Provide an example related to career development.

5. Why might a person in health care have to look forward to experiencing multiple careers? Why not simply pick one line of work and stick with it?

6. What would you do if it becomes clear that the potential successor you were training is not going to make the grade as a supervisor?

7. How can your external customers be of value to you in networking?

8. Why do you suppose networking is frequently a more successful means of finding a new position than other means such as submitting job applications?

9. How might effective internal networking be of assistance to you during a period of personal reengineering or reorganizing?

10. The future of health care is evolving. What can supervisors expect in their future careers?

Case: Tough Politics: Coping with the Blindsider

George did not look forward to going to the staff meetings that his middle-manager boss convened once each week. He did not always feel this way about the meetings; in fact, up until 3 months earlier, he rather enjoyed what he believed were productive and congenial gatherings. What made the difference was one change in the membership of this group of six supervisors: the addition of Charlie, who replaced a usually silent supervisor.

Unlike his predecessor, Charlie was anything but usually silent. In fact, it seemed as though Charlie had made it a point to become conversant with every section of their boss's territory, and he almost always had something critical to say about the other supervisors' weekly reports.

What bothered George most was Charlie's approach to getting his issues or criticisms on the table. Charlie seemed to focus exclusively on problems and weaknesses. As if that in itself wasn't bad enough, what George resented most was Charlie's way of introducing a problem or concern in a way that ensured maximum embarrassment for whoever's area he was commenting on. It was Charlie's practice to openly drop his little bombshells in the staff meeting, where the supervisor whose area was in question first heard of a so-called problem or weakness at the same time the others learned of it.

It seemed to George that Charlie's practice of blindsiding the others in the group was coldly calculated to make himself look better by making others look worse. And George found it even more frustrating to note that their boss did not seem to recognize what Charlie was doing.

Questions

1. What do you recommend that George do about Charlie's staff meeting behavior?

2. Should George take up his concerns directly with Charlie? And if so, should he do it one-on-one or in the context of the staff meeting?

Reference

1. Francisco G, Kouchaki M, Casciaro T. Learn to love networking. *Harvard Business Review.* May 2016. https://hbr.org/2016/05/learn-to-love-networking

Index

A

Abilene Paradox, 375, 378
Absent employee, the, 231
Achievers, characteristics of, 416
Action plans, 26–27
Address complaints, 17–18
Affiliations(s), 37, 41–43, 41–44
Affirmative action, 85, 87
Affordable Care Act of 2010. *See* Patient Protection and Affordable Care Act (PPACA) (2010)
Age discrimination, 217
Age Discrimination in Employment Act (ADEA) (1967), 74, 88
    effects on retirement, 74
Aging workforce, 89, 217
Americans with Disabilities Act (ADA) (1990), 49, 77–79, 87, 88–89
    effects on position descriptions, 53–54
    interview questions illegal under, 88
Appeal(s)
    defined, 257
    and grievances, 261
Applications, employment, 91–92
Assertiveness, 422
Assigning, 29–30
    versus delegation, 342
Attitude, employee, 245–246
Authoritarian leadership, 141, 144
Authority, 27–28
    authorizing, 298
    limits of, 34
    scope of on position description, 51–52

B

Baby boomers, 216–217
Balanced Budget Act (BBA) (1997), 291, 294
Balanced Budget Refinement Act (BBRA) of 1999, 294
Balancing Act, 428

Bar graph, 388
Barriers to communication, 355–356
    body language as, 355–356
    phonetics count, 356
    psychological, 355
    semantic, 355
Basic management functions, 32
Behavior
    correction of, discipline as, 200
    versus performance, 205
Behaviorally anchored performance standards, 59–60
Benchmarking, 60, 291, 296, 310
Benefits
    compensation and, 172–173
    employee, as reward, 179
    of empowerment, 347
    of networks, 423
    of succession planning, 419–420
    of team(s), 121
Body language, 355–356
Bomb threats, 136
Bona fide occupational qualification (BFOQ), 74, 88
    age as, 74
Brainstorming, 385, 394
Break-even chart, 391, 392
Budget(s)(ing)
    for capital equipment, 305
    controlling process, 304, 305–308
    defined, 303
    forecast for, 305
    functions of, 303–305
    preparation of, 304–305
    principles and rules, 304
    revenue, 304
Budget variance, 303
Bureaucratic leadership, 141, 145
Burnout
    defined, 407
    signs and symptoms of, 410
    stages of coping with, 410–411
Business process re-engineering (BPR), 37

C

Capital equipment budget, 305
Capitation reimbursement, 291, 293
Career development
    accountability for, 316–317
    avoiding career killers, 418
    benefits of program, 316
    defined, 315
    expanding competencies, 417–418
    increasing promotability and marketability, 417
    opportunities in present workplace, 416–417
    outside opportunities, 417
    for personnel retention, 271
Career killers, 418
Career planning
    goal alignment, 429
    supporting skills and, 429
Case managers, 297–298
Cash-oriented compensation plans, 271
Cause-and-effect diagram, 390
Change
    assisting employees with, 330
    barriers to, 327
    behavioral, coaching and counseling for, 246–247
    commitment and, 329
    communication for, 328–329
    continuing, health care and, 41–42
    cynics, 332
    employee concerns about, 327
    employee responses to, 331–332
    essentials of, 326–327
    implementing, 329
    inevitability, 326
    overcoming resistance to, 332–333
    participation by stakeholders, 333
    people and, 331
    planning for, 328
    resisters, 332
    supervisor's role in, 327–328
    training for, 329

Checklists, 390
Civil Rights Act of 1964, 72, 73–74, 87, 88, 278
Civil Rights Act of 1991, 79
Classic reengineering error, 40–41
Clinical pathways, 295
Coach(es)
    characteristics of effective, 154
    as facilitator, 156
    role of in performance improvement, 154
Coaching, 272
    and counseling for behavioral change, 246–247
    defined, 153
    feedback on, 156–159
    pitfalls of, 159–160
Code of ethics, 240
Collaborative negotiation, 360
Committee meetings, 381
Committees, 31
Communication
    for change, 328–329
    channel for, electing, 368
    defined, 353
    as important management skill, 353–354
    one-on-one, 401
    written, 367–371
Compensation
    and benefits, 172–173
    cash-oriented retention plans, 271
    negotiating for more, 418–419
    as reward, 178–182
Competencies, 325
Complaints
    about compensation, 258–259
    bypassing supervisor, 259
    sources of, 257–258
    steps for handling, 258
    supervisor's role and, 258
Completed staff work, 153
Computer-assisted interviews, 96
Conflict
    avoidance of, 223
    collaboration and, 224
    compromise in settling, 223–224
    dangers of escalating or suppressing, 222–223
    defined, 221
    and the healthcare organization, 221–222
    principal causes of, 222
    strategies for coping with, 223–224
    surrender, 223
Confrontation
    achieving collaborative, 225

with angry person, 226–227
defined, 221
preparing for, 224–225
the supervisor and, 224–225
Consensus decision making, 393–394
Consolidated Omnibus Budget Reconciliation Act (COBRA) (1986), 76
Constructive feedback, 159
Consultative leadership, 141, 144–145
Control charts, 389
Controlling, 21, 31–32
    process, budget, 305–308
Control of overtime, 306–307
Coordinating, 21, 30–31
Coordination, interdepartmental, 31
Core values, 211
Corporate values, 27, 212–213
Cost(s)
    cutting, 308
    of poor hiring choice, 86
    reduced employee, 308
    right-sizing, 308
Counseling, 153
    barriers to successful, 166
    common reasons for, 160
    determining need for, 160
    employee reactions to, 164–165
    follow up to, 165–166
    interview, 161–164
    kinds of, 160
    repeat sessions, points to cover in, 166
Counseling versus disciplining, 200–201
Creative people, characteristics of, 321
Creativity, 320–323
    barriers to, 321–322
    in employee development, 320
    intuition in, 320–321
    process of, 320
    rewards for, 323
    stimulating in staff, 322
Credentialing, 92
Criticism, preserving self-esteem during, 158–159
Cross-training, 325
Cultural change, 43
Cultural core values, 212
Cultural diversity, 211
Customer(s)
    external, 13
    internal, 13
    satisfaction system, designing, 17–18
Customer-oriented culture, 16
Customer-oriented performance standards, 56

Customer service
    concepts, 18
    employees and, 16
    essentials, 15
    expectancy-disconfirmation model, 18
    expectancy-value theory, 18
    inservice education in, 17
    and orientation and training, 16–17
    orientation and training in, 16–17
    position descriptions, 16
    recruiting process, 16
    selection process, 16
    strategies, 16
    systems supporting, 15
    techniques for improving, 16–17
Cynics, 332

D

"Deadweight," 207
Decision, effective, 387
Decision making
    consensus, 393–394
    and leadership, 386–388
    risk and uncertainty in, 387
    stress and emotion, effects of in, 386–387
    when to avoid, 386
Dedication, 428
Defamation, 95
Delegat(e)(ion), 29
    assigning versus, 342
    defined, 341
    dumping versus, 343
    how to, 343–344
    implementing, 345
    partial, 344
    research, 350
    supervisors' reluctance to, 342
    and time management, 400
    using position description in, 344
    variations of, 346–347
    what not to, 344
Departmental diversity program, 219
Departmental orientation, 109
Departmental team, 120
Difficult employee, 245
Difficult superior, 426–427
Disability, pregnancy defined as, 76
Discharge
    basis for, 203–204
    defined, 199
Discipline
    action guidelines for, 200–201
    versus counseling, 200–201
    definition, 199

employee reactions to, 204–205
practices, sound, 206
principles for supervisors, 206
progressive, 199, 201–204
Diversity
awareness training, 214–215
departmental, 219
generational, 216–217
management, 211, 214–216
Division of Human Rights (DHR), 85
Document, preparing a, 368–369
"Do, Delegate, and Discard," 397, 399
Drug-Free Workplace Act (1988), 77
Dual cognitive functions, 385, 387

E

Education, 296–297
Educational needs assessment, 317–318
Educational planning, 316
Electronic barriers, 355
Elusive employees, 249–250
Email, 370–371
abuse of, 370
editing and clarifying, 371
regulating messages with, 371
Employee(s), 93–94
absent, 231
administration, 298
with appearance problems, 251
attitude, 245–246
benefits as reward, 179
caution in dealing with, 253
chronically critical, 247
development, creativity in, 320–323
difficult, 245
elusive employees, 249–250
exempt and nonexempt, 49
failure to get along, 236
gossips, 250–251
incessant talkers and socializers, 251
inherited, 117
jealous coworkers and, 250
know-it-alls, 248
labeling, 245
leaving job, reasons for, 270
loyalty, 270
and messy work areas, 251
moody, 250
negativists, 247–248
passive-aggressive, 252–253
personal problems affecting
performance, 233
reactions to counseling, 164–165
reactions to discipline, 204–205
recognition, 181
reduce costs, 308

retention, 17
selection, 16, 85–86, 91–92
self-sufficiency of, 155–156
sensitive, 254–255
super-sensitive, 250
supervisors by, 7
team, 120–121
uncooperative, 248–250
unethical behavior, addressing, 240
Employee assistance program (EAP), 229
Employee Polygraph Protection Act
(EPPA) (1988), 77, 277, 279
Employee problems
precautions for addressing, 235
procedure for, 234–235
as supervisory challenge, 235–236
Employee Retirement Income Security
Act (ERISA) (1974), 75
Employee selection interview, 95
Employment
application, 91–92
opportunities in managed care,
297–298
references, 105–106
referral programs, 91
résumés, 91–92
Employment legislation, 71
list by decades, 82
Empowerment
benefits of, 347
defined, 341
versus delegation, 347
potential problems with, 348
steps for, 347–348
Equal Employment Opportunity
Commission (EEOC), 85
Equal Pay Act (1963), 73
Ethical behavior, 239–240
Ethical decisions, 239
Ethics
organizational, 239
principles, 241
programs, 241–242
Executive Order 11246, 87
Exempt employee, 49, 50, 54
Expectancy-disconfirmation model,
13, 18
Expectancy-value theory, 13, 18
External customers, 13

F

Fair Credit Reporting Act, 277, 279
Fair Labor Standards Act (FLSA)
(1938), 49, 50, 72, 73
Family and Medical Leave Act (FMLA)
(1993), 76, 79–80

Feedback
complaints as, 257
day-to-day, 186
defined, 185
multi-source, 189
need for, 185
negative, employee reaction to, 158
providing constructive, 159
Fights, breaking up, 136
Financial plans, 23
First-line supervisor, 3
Flattening, 44
Flattening, organizational, 37
Flow chart, 390
Force field charts, 390
Full-time equivalent (FTE), 273
Functional plans, 23

G

Games, political, 421–422
Gantt chart, 391
Gatekeeper, 298
Gaussian curve charts, 390
General orientation, 109
Generational diversity, 216–217
Generations X and Y, 216
Goal alignment, supervisor's, 429
Goals and objectives, 25
Gossips, employees, 250–251
Grant writing
defined, 367
process of, 371
Grapevine, 30, 353
as informal communication system,
354
Grievance(s)
appeals and, 261
defined, 257
Group norms, 123

H

Haggling negotiation, 360
Health and safety policies, 67
Health care reform, 299
"The healthcare team," 119, 120
Healthcare violence
causes of, 130–131
primary perpetrators of, 130
Health Insurance Portability and
Accountability Act (HIPAA)
(1996), 80–81, 277, 281–286
effects on organization, 284–285
human resources and, 280
implementation of, 282
patient rights under, 283
Privacy Rule, 282, 283, 284

Health Insurance Portability and
Accountability Act (HIPAA)
(1996), 80–81, 277, 281–286
(*continued*)
Security Rule, 282
the supervisor and, 285–286
Title II, 282
Health maintenance organization
(HMO), 292
Health Maintenance Organization Act
of 1973, 291, 292
Herzberg, Frederick, motivation-
hygiene theory of, 173–175
High–low-dollar negotiation, 360
Hiring, legal constraints on, 86
Histogram, 389
Hopscotch delegation, 341, 346
Horizontal delegation, 341, 346
Hostile people, dealing with, 251–252
Human resources, HIPAA and, 280

I

I-9 Forms, 76
Immediate superior, 425–426
Immigration Reform and Control Act
(IRCA) (1986), 76
Informal organization, the, 30
Information overload, coping
with, 399
Information security, 281
Inherited employee, 117
In-service educational programs, 17
Instant messaging, 371
Interdepartmental coordination, 31
Internal customers, 13
Internship programs, 90
Interventions, successful, 166
Interview(s)
candidate untruthfulness in, 102
computer assisted, 96
concluding, 104
counseling, preparing for and
conducting, 161–164
employee selection, 95
evaluating candidate, 103
follow up on, 105
legally valid, 95
performance evaluation, 191–193
post-interview activities, 104–106
preparing for, 96–97
questions from candidates, 103
questions to ask, 97–100
questions to avoid, 98–100
reporting on, 104
starting, 97
team approach to, 96

Interviewer
experienced, 96
primary, 96
Intimidation, 380
Intuitive process, stimulating, 392–393

J

Jealous coworkers, 250
Job
enrichment, 325, 333
fit, 334
offers, extending, 103–104
redesign, 325, 334–335
sharing, 325, 335–336
Job description. *See* Position
description(s)

L

Labeling, employee, 245
Labor-Management Relations Act (Taft-
Hartley) (1947), 73
Labor-Management Reporting and
Disclosure Act (1959), 73
Laissez-faire leadership, 141,
145–146, 427
Leader(s)
authoritarian, 141
bureaucratic, 141
characteristics of effective, 147–149
commandments of, 147
consultative, 141
foundations of, 147
laissez-faire, 141
paternalistic, 141
situational, 141
Leadership, 38–39
contemporary activities of, 146–147
decision making and, 386–388
versus management, 142–143
manipulation and, 146
and organizational culture, 141
situational, 10
style(s), 126, 144–146
team, 124–125, 126
Legal environment, 71–72
Legally valid interview, 95
Likert charts, 392
Listening, keys to successful, 356–357
Loyalty
employee, 270
supervisory, 269

M

Managed care, 13, 14–15, 41
agencies, strategies of, 295–296

arrival of, 292
challenge of, 293–294
defined, 291
employment opportunities in,
297–298
features of plans, 292–293
influence of, 14–15
provider reactions to, 297
variations of, 293
Management
by crisis, 146, 397
defined, 3, 5–6
definition, 31
by exception, 146
by objectives, 146
of time, 397–403
by wandering around, 146, 154, 155
Manager
defined, 3
first-line, 3
middle, 3
relationship with, 9–10
as title, 5
Managing personal stress, 411
Marginal performer, 229–230
Maslow, A. H., need hierarchy of,
173–174
McGregor, Douglas, Theory X and
Theory Y, 174–175
Meeting(s), 214
agenda for, 377
attendees, guidance for, 379
chairperson, advance preparation
by, 377
chairperson, behavior of, 379
closing, 379
comics, 380
committee, 381
components of, 376
destroyers, 381
force decisions, 379
guidelines for starting, 378
latecomers, 380
motor mouths, 381
necessity of, 376
nonassertive attendees, 379
participation, encouraging, 378
problem attendees, 380–381
purposes of, 376
recorder for, 377
and time management, 401
Memo, anatomy of, 368
Mentor, 115, 319
Mentoring
corporate, 319
defined, 315, 319
developments in, 320

Mentor–protégé relationships, 319
Merger(s), 37
  and affiliations, 41–44
  cultural differences in, 46
  cultural effects, 43
  human values, 46
  staff reductions and, 42
  supervisor's role, effects on, 43–45
Messages
  powerful, 354
  tips for better, 355
Micromanagement, 141
"Middle management," 44
Middle manager, defined, 3
Mission, 24–25
Morale
  defined, 169
  factors affecting, 170
  and health care, 169–170
  improving, 172
  information about, obtaining, 172
  versus motivation, 170
  problem, signs of, 171
  supervisor's influence on, 173
Motivation(al)
  defined, 169
  matter of, 428
  strategies for supervisor, 175–176
  theoretical foundations of, 173–177
  true, self-motivation as, 175
  value of work, increasing, 177
Multi-institutional arrangements, 42
Multi-source feedback, 189
Myers-Briggs Type Indicator, 318

N

Naive listening, 356–357
National Labor Relations Act (NLRA)
  (1935), 72–73, 120
Needs assessment, educational,
  317–318
Negativists, 247–248
Negligent hiring, 95
Negotiation
  barriers to successful, 362
  basic forms of, 360
  with boss, 362–363
  major steps in, 361–362
  preparing for, 360–361
Networking, 415, 422–424
Networks
  benefits of, 423
  characteristics of successful
    networkers, 424
  contacts in, 423
  potential participants in, 423

Nonassertive attendees, 379
Nonexempt employee, 49, 50
Nonfinancial rewards, 180
Norris–LaGuardia Act (1932), 72

O

Obamacare, 299
Objectives, goals and, 25
Occupational Safety and Health Act
  (OSHA) (1970), 74–75
Older Workers Benefit Protection Act
  (OWBPA) (1990), 79
One-on-one communication, 401
Operational plans, 23
Oral warning, 201–202
Organization(al)
  climate, 240
  culture, 141, 142
  employment legislation effects on,
    81–82
  ethics, 239
  flattening, 37
  informal, 30
  plans, 23
Organizing, 21, 27–30
Orientation
  assumptions about, 111
  checklist, 116
  departmental values and, 114
  first day of, 113
  general, topics included in, 111–112
  meeting coworkers during, 114
  objectives, 110–111
  preparation for, 112
  timing, 109–110
  tour, facility, 114
Orientation and training, customer
  service and, 16–17
OSHA and workplace violence, 132
Outcomes management, 291, 296
Outsourcing, 37
Overtime
  causes of, 307
  controlling, methods for, 306–307

P

Paper flow, coping with, 399
Pareto diagrams, 389
Participative leadership, 141, 144
Passive-aggressive employees, 252–253
Paternalistic leadership, 141
Patient-focus care model, 295
Patient Protection and Affordable Care
  Act (PPACA) (2010), 81, 291, 299
Patients' rights, HIPAA, 283
Peer pressure, 240

Pension Benefit Guarantee Corporation
  (PBGC), 76, 80
Pension Protection Act (1987), 76–77
"Perfect information," decision making
  and, 387
Performance
  behavior versus, 205
  deficiencies, discussing, 192
  personal problems affecting, 233
Performance evaluation
  common pitfalls of, 193–194
  defined, 185
  employee input to, 190–191
  essentials of, 187–188
  formal, 186–189
  frequency of, 188
  individuals, preparing for, 189–191
  interview, phases of, 191–193
  of leaders, 188–189
  purposes of, 186
  of work teams, 193
Performance review, customer service
  and, 17
Performance standards, 54–55
  characteristics of appropriate, 55–56
  compliance standards, 55
  customer-oriented, 56
  examples of, 58
  importance, 55
  levels designated for, 54–55
  for phlebotomists, 59
  pitfalls in formulating, 57–58
  preparing, approach to, 56
  sources of, 58
  task standards as, 55
  temperament and interrelationship
    standards, 55
  tips for formulating, 57
  uses of, 54
Performer, marginal, 229–230
Personal core values, 213
Personal values, 27
Physical plans, 23
Pie charts, 390
Placement interview, 95
Plan(s)
  action, 26–27
  classifications of, 23
Planning, 21, 22–27
  for change, 328
  educational, 316
  key elements of, 23–24
Polic(y)(ies)
  and Americans with Disabilities Act,
    67–68
  defined, 63
  employee behavior and, 65–66

Polic(y)(ies) *(continued)*
   introduction to, 63–64
   new or change, need for, 65–66
   problems with, potential, 66–67
   procedure for formulating, 65–66
   safety and health and, 67
   schedules, 67
   uses of, 64–65
Political games, 421–422
Politics, workplace, 421
Position description(s), 49, 61
   authority, scope of, 51–52
   competencies, required, 51
   as contract, 50
   customer service and, 16
   effects of ADA on, 53–54
   independence, degree of, 52
   job duties, 52–53
   nature of, 50–51
   performance standards and, 54–55
   relationships and, 51
   summary statement of, 50–51
   uses of, 54
   working conditions, 52
Power play negotiation, 360
Praise, 156–158
   actions to, 156
   how to, 157–158
   specific nature of, 157
   what to, 156–157
   when not to, 157
Pre-employment testing, 92
Pregnancy Discrimination Act (1978),
      75–76
Primary interviewer, 96
Privacy
   changing times and, 278
   and confidentiality, patient,
      280–281
   employee files and, 279
   employee health records and, 280
   employee searches and, 279–280
   and the individual, 283–284
   and law, 278–279
   legal orders and, 279
Privacy Act of 1974, 277, 278
Privacy Rule, HIPAA, 282, 283, 284
Probation, suspension or, 203
Problems
   large, steps for solving, 388
   minor, coping with, 387
Problem solving
   group, 394
   tools for, 388–392
Procedure(s), 63

Procrastination, 400, 426
Program evaluation and review
      technique (PERT) charts, 391
Progressive discipline, 199, 201–204
Prohibited question, 95
Project team, 120–121
Promotability and marketability,
      increasing, 417

Q

Quality improvement coordinator, 115
Quality of work life, 334
Questionnaires, 92
Questions, interview, 97–101

R

Reasonable accommodation, 67, 68, 88
Recognition
   cautions about, 182
   effective features, 181–182
   employee(s), 181
   reward and, 177
Recruit(ing)(ment)
   customer service and, 16
   mature workers, 89–90
   during shortage periods, 90–91
   sources, 89
   supervisor's role in process of, 91
Reengineering, 28, 37–41
   classic error in, 40–41
   consultants and, 40
   definition, 37
   interdepartmental collaboration
      and, 39
   and leadership, 38–39
   need for, signs of, 39
   process, 309
References, employment, 105–106
Rehabilitation Act (1973), 75, 88–89
Relating to superior, 424–427
Resistance to change, 331–332
   overcoming, 332–333
Resisters, 332
Résumés, employment, 91–92
Retention
   analyzing problems of, 270–271
   defined, 267
   focus on, 267–268
   further implications for, 272
   incentives for, 271
   loyalty and, 268–269
   morale and, 272
   orientation and, 272

   recruitment and selection for,
      271–272
Retirement Equity Act of 1984, 75
Retirement plans, government
      requirements for, 75
Retirement Protection Act (1994), 80
Revenue, budgeting, 304
Reverse delegation, 341, 346
Reward(s)
   customer service and, 17
   financial, 179–180
   guidelines, 178
   non-financial, 180
   and recognition, 177
   system, effective, 177
   system, implementing, 180–181
   for team performance, 127
   wages and salaries, 178–179
Reward-to-risk ratio, 201
Rightsizing, 303
Risks in career development, 416
Rules, reasons for violations of,
      160–161
Run charts, 389

S

Safety coordinator, 115
Scattergram, 389
School-aged children, 231
Security Rule, HIPAA, 282
Self-confidence, 7
Self-evaluation, 191
Self-perpetuating team, 125
Semantic barriers, 355
Sensitive employee, 254–255
Sexual harassment
   defined, 257
   as form of sex discrimination,
      261, 262
   forms of, 262
   investigation of, 263
   policies and procedures governing,
      262–263
   role of supervisor concerning, 263
   as source of legal actions, 262
   victim conduct, 263
Shared services, 41
Situational leadership, 10, 126, 141,
      145
Skills inventory, 315
Small Business Job Protection Act
      (1996), 80
Social Security Act (1935), 72, 73
Span of control, 21, 28, 44, 249–250

Split-reporting relationship, 415, 425–426
Staff development
    versus career development, 315–316
    education and experience, 315–316
    program for, 318
Staffing, 28–29, 222
Staffing reductions, 42
Standards, compliance, 55
Steps to success, 418
Stop-look-listen approach, 388
Strategic plans, 23
Strategy, 25
Stress
    external causes of, 408
    internal aggravating factors, 408
    management style and, 408–409
    personal, managing, 411
    reducing in department, 409
Subordinates, relationships with, 8
Success, criteria for, 415
    steps to, 418
Succession planning, 419–420
    benefits of, 419–420
    selection and training successor, 420–421
Superior
    difficult, 426–427
    immediate, 425–426
    relating to, 424–427
Super-sensitive employees, 250
Supervision
    adjusting to, 10
    behavioral pitfalls of, 10
    transition to, 7–8
Supervisor(y), 413
    career, successful, 10–11
    common mistakes, 149–150
    defined, 3
    disciplinary principles for, 206
    diversity management, 215–216
    effective, traits of, 7
    by employees, 7
    essential skills of, 6
    ethical behavior, enforcement of, 242
    ethical principles for, 241
    first-line, 3
    as focus of negative attitude, 247
    influence on employee morale, 173
    innovative, 321
    legal definition of, 5
    loyalty, 269
    management functions of, 6
    motivational strategies for, 175–176
    obligations, 428–429

performance appraisals of, 304
and policies, 65
relationships of, 9
reluctance to delegate, 342
responsibilities, 5–6, 9, 215
tasks of, types, 344–345
time problems of, 398
training of, 133–134
Supervisor's future, the, 429–430
Suspension or probation, 203

T

Tactical plans, 23
Team(s), 119
    benefits of, 121
    constant risk, 120
    departmental, 120
    disadvantages, 121
    dynamics of, 122–123
    effective, characteristics of, 121–122
    failure of, reasons for, 122
    formation and development of, 123
    group norms and, 123
    health care, 120
    inherited, taking on the, 126
    kinds, 120
    leadership, 124–125
    need for, 119–120
    project/employee, 120–121
    rewarding performance of, 127
    rituals and status symbols, 123–124
    self-perpetuating, the, 125
    types of, 120
Telecommuting, 325, 336–337
Telephone communication, 357–359
    for all calls, 358
    answering, 357
    conference calls, 381
    hold, using, 357
    messages, taking, 358
    outbound calls, 359
    screening, 357–358
    transferring, 358
    voice mail, 359
Telephone tag, 359
Termination meeting, 204
Testing, pre-employment, 92
Text messaging, 371
Theory X and Theory Y, 174–175
3-D technique, 397
Time management
    and abuses by others, 401
    delegation and, 400
    and errors, time-consuming, 401–402

meetings and, 401
one-on-one communication, 401
paper flow and, 399
planning and scheduling and, 399
procrastination, effects of, 400
reading and, 399
time savers, using, 402
time wasters, coping with, 400
"to do" lists and, 399
visitor control and, 400–401
at work station, 398–399
Trainer/educational coordinator, 115
Training, orientation and, 109–116
True leadership, 145
Turnover
    defined, 267
    measuring, 272–273
    undesirable/controllable, 267, 273

U

Undesirable/controllable turnover, 267, 273
Unethical behavior, 240, 243
Unity of command, 21, 28, 44
Upward delegation, 346
Utilization reviewers, 298

V

Value adding negotiation, 360
Value-based care, 291, 298
Value modification, 213–214
Values
    core, 27, 211
    corporate, 27, 212–213
    cultural, 212
    personal, 27, 213
Variance
    budget, 303
    delegation, 346–347
Verbal communication, 355
Violence
    characteristics of individuals prone to, 131
    communication for control of, 134
    control programs, 132–134
    education for control of, 133–134
    effects on victims of, 131–132
    environmental factors affecting control, 134
    factors predisposing to, 130
    in healthcare, 129–130
    laws and standards relating to, 132
    policies for control of, 132–133

Violence (*continued*)
  principles for reducing, 134–136
Violence-prone individual, 129
  characteristics, 131
Virtual meeting platforms, 126
Visibility and availability, supervisor's, 44
Vision, 23–24
  example, 24
Visitor control, 400–401
Voice mail, 359

W

Warning
  oral, 201–202
  written, 202–203, 209
Women, advancement for, 217–218
Worker Adjustment and Retraining
    Notification Act (WARN) (1988),
    77
Workflow coordination, 30

Workforce
  aging, 89, 217
  diverse and changing, 211–212
  supervisor responsibilities and, 215
Workplace, opportunities in present,
    416–417
Workplace politics, 421
Workplace violence, 129–136
Written communication, 367–371
Written warning, 202–203, 209